THE BABYLONIAN WORLD

———— •◆• ————

As the layers of the foundations of modern science and mathematics and the builders of a towering, monumental urban city, the Babylonians were by far the most insistent people of the ancient world in addressing an audience beyond their time. This lavishly illustrated volume reflects the modernity of this advanced and prescient civilization with thirty-eight brand new essays from leading international scholars who view this world power of the Ancient Near East with a fresh and contemporary lens.

Drawing from the growing database of cuneiform tablets, epigraphic research, and the most recent archaeological advances in the field, Gwendolyn Leick's collection serves as the definitive reference resource as well as an introductory text for university students.

By bringing into focus areas of concern typical for our own time – such as ecology, urbanism, power relations, plurality and complexity – this essential volume offers a variety of perspectives on certain key topics to reflect the current academic approaches and focus. These shifting viewpoints and diverse angles onto the 'Babylonian World' result in a truly kaleidoscopic view which reveals patterns and bright fragments of this 'lost world' in unexpected ways.

From discussions of agriculture and rural life to the astonishing walled city of Babylon with its massive ramparts and towering ziggurats, from Babylonian fashion and material culture to its spiritual world, indivisible from that of the everyday, *The Babylonian World* is a sweeping and ambitious survey for students and specialists of this great civilization.

Gwendolyn Leick is presently senior lecturer at Chelsea College of Art and Design. A specialist in the Ancient Near East, she has published extensively on the topic, including *The Dictionary of Ancient Near Eastern Architecture* and *Who's Who in the Ancient Near East*.

THE ROUTLEDGE WORLDS

THE GREEK WORLD
Edited by Anton Powell

THE ROMAN WORLD
Edited by John Wacher

THE BIBLICAL WORLD
Edited by John Barton

THE EARLY CHRISTIAN WORLD
Edited by Philip F. Esler

THE CELTIC WORLD
Edited by Miranda Green

THE MEDIEVAL WORLD
Edited by Peter Linehan and Janet L. Nelson

THE REFORMATION WORLD
Edited by Andrew Pettegree

THE ENLIGHTENMENT WORLD
Edited by Martin Fitzpatrick, Peter Jones,
Christa Knellwolf and Iain McCalman

THE HINDU WORLD
Edited by Sushil Mittal and Gene Thursby

THE BABYLONIAN WORLD
Edited by Gwendolyn Leick

Forthcoming:

THE EGYPTIAN WORLD
Edited by Toby Wilkinson

THE VIKING WORLD
Edited by Stefan Brink and Neil Price

THE RENAISSANCE WORLD
Edited by John Jeffries Martin

THE ELIZABETHAN WORLD
Edited by Susan Doran and Norman Jones

THE OTTOMAN WORLD
Edited by Christine Woodhead

THE BYZANTINE WORLD
Edited by Paul Stephenson

THE BABYLONIAN WORLD

Edited by

Gwendolyn Leick

Routledge
Taylor & Francis Group

NEW YORK AND LONDON

First published 2007
by Routledge
2 Park Square, Milton Park, Abingdon, Oxon OX14 4RN

Simultaneously published in the USA and Canada
by Routledge
711 Third Avenue, New York, NY 10017

Reprinted 2008

First published in paperback 2009

Routledge is an imprint of the Taylor & Francis Group, an informa business

Typeset in Garamond 3 by
Florence Production Ltd, Stoodleigh, Devon

British Library Cataloguing in Publication Data
A catalogue record for this book is available from the British Library

Library of Congress Cataloging in Publication Data
The Babylonian world/edited by Gwendolyn Leick. – 1st ed.
p. cm.
Includes bibliographical references and index.
1. Babylonia.   I. Leick, Gwendolyn, 1951–
DS69.5.B23 2007
935′.02 – dc22   2006102809

ISBN13: 978–0–415–35346–5 (hbk)
ISBN13: 978–0–415–49783–1 (pbk)
ISBN13: 978–0–203–94623–7 (ebk)

*Lebensalter**

Ihr Städte des Euphrats!
Ihr Gassen von Palmyra!
Ihr Säulenwälder in der Eb'ne der Wüste,
Was seid ihr?
Euch hat die Kronen,
Dieweil ihr über die Gränze
Der Othmenden seid gegangen,
Von Himmlischen der Rauchdampf und
Hinweg das Feuer genommen;
Jezt aber siz' ich unter Wolken, darin
Ein jedes eine Ruh' hat eigen, unter
Wohleingerichteten Eichen, auf
Der Heide des Rehs, und fremd
Erscheinen und gestorben mir
Der Seeligen Geister.

Friedrich Hölderlin

* Translation is on p. 591.

This book is dedicated to the memory
of Blahoslav Hruska (1945–2008)

CONTENTS

———•◆•———

List of illustrations   x
List of contributors   xiv

1   Introduction   1
    Gwendolyn Leick

PART I: LAND AND LAND USE

2   The world of Babylonian countrysides   13
    Seth Richardson

3   Land and land use: the middle Euphrates valley   39
    Lucia Mori

4   Agricultural techniques   54
    Blahoslav Hruška

5   Urban form in the first millennium BC   66
    Heather D. Baker

PART II: MATERIAL CULTURE

6   Architecture in the Old Babylonian period   81
    Harriet Crawford

7   Babylonian seals   95
    Dominique Collon

8   Babylonian sources of exotic raw materials   124
    D. T. Potts

9   Cloth in the Babylonian world   141
    Irene Good

10 The Babylonian visual image   155
    Zainab Bahrani

11 Food and drink in Babylonia   171
    Frances Reynolds

PART III: ECONOMIC LIFE

12 Economy of ancient Mesopotamia: a general outline   187
    Johannes Renger

13 The Old Babylonian economy   198
    Anne Goddeeris

14 Aspects of society and economy in the later Old Babylonian Period   210
    Frans van Koppen

15 The Babylonian economy in the first millennium BC   224
    Michael Jursa

16 The Egibi family   236
    Cornelia Wunsch (translated from German by Gwendolyn Leick)

PART IV: SOCIETY AND POLITICS

17 Social configurations in Early Dynastic Babylonia (c.2500–2334 BC)   251
    Petr Charvát

18 The palace and the temple in Babylonia   265
    Walther Sallaberger

19 Power, economy and social organisation in Babylonia   276
    Gebhard J. Selz

20 Arameans and Chaldeans: environment and society   288
    Frederick Mario Fales

21 Women and gender in Babylonia   299
    Laura D. Steele

PART V: RELIGION

22 The role and function of goddesses in Mesopotamia   319
    Brigitte Groneberg

23 Inanna and Ishtar – the dimorphic Venus goddesses   332
    Joan Goodnick Westenholz

24 The Babylonian god Marduk   348
    Takayoshi Oshima

25 Divination culture and the handling of the future   361
    Stefan M. Maul (translated from German by Gwendolyn Leick)

26 Witchcraft literature in Mesopotamia   373
    Tzvi Abusch

— Contents —

PART VI: INTELLECTUAL LIFE: CUNEIFORM WRITING AND LEARNING

27 Incantations within Akkadian medical texts   389
   M. J. Geller

28 The writing, sending, and reading of letters in the Amorite world   400
   Dominique Charpin (translated from French by Dafydd Roberts)

29 Mathematics, metrology, and professional numeracy   418
   Eleanor Robson

30 Babylonian lists of words and signs   432
   Jon Taylor

31 Gilgamesh and the literary traditions of ancient Mesopotamia   447
   A. R. George

32 Mesopotamian astral science   460
   David Brown

33 Late Babylonian intellectual life   473
   Paul-Alain Beaulieu

PART VII: INTERNATIONAL RELATIONS: BABYLONIA AND THE ANCIENT NEAR EASTERN WORLD

34 Egypt and Mesopotamia   487
   David A. Warburton

35 A view from Hattusa   503
   Trevor Bryce

36 Relations between Babylonia and the Levant during the Kassite period   515
   P. S. Vermaak

37 Looking down the Tigris: the interrelations between Assyria and Babylonia   527
   Hannes D. Galter

38 The view from Jerusalem: biblical responses to the Babylonian presence   541
   Baruch A. Levine

39 The Persian empire   562
   Amélie Kuhrt

Index   577

ILLUSTRATIONS

———•◆•———

FIGURES

2.1	Sustaining areas of Babylonian settlements	21
3.1	The middle Euphrates valley today, from the ruins of Doura Europos	40
3.2	A map of the middle Euphrates valley showing the different cultivated zones	43
4.1	Archaic sign for 'ard', 'farmer' and 'to plough'	55
4.2	Soil preparation with hoes	57
4.3	Seal impression showing animal traction, working team and seeding plough	61
5.1	Plan of Nippur, *c.* 1500 BC	75
6.1	A hypothetical reconstruction of the temple at Tell Rimah	85
6.2	Plan of the temple at Tell Rimah	86
6.3	'Barley sugar' pillars at Tell Rimah	88
7.1	Warrior king, Lama and small naked woman	96
7.2	Lama, the warrior king and the goddess Ishtar	96
7.3	Representations of the Lama goddess	97
7.4	Presentation scene before seated king	98
7.5	Impressions of seals, probably of the seventeenth century BC, showing the use of cutting wheel and drill	98
7.6	Envelope fragment from Sippar with impressions of a Babylonian presentation scene, and a seal combining Babylonian and Syrian motifs	99
7.7	Impression of *purkullu* seal	100
7.8	Nude hero fighting bull-man; nude hero fighting lion; naked woman; Ishtar; filling motifs	101
7.9	Four winds; small storm god on lion-dragon; small priest; filling motifs	102
7.10	Presentation scene before seated goddess	102
7.11	Lama; king with offering; the sun god Shamash; lightning fork of the storm god Adad	103

7.12 Warrior god; priest on dais with cup and bucket; warrior god; warrior god brandishing sword, whirling mace and treading on fallen enemy 104

7.13 The gods Amurru (with crooks) and Adad; robed king with offering; robed god 105

7.14 Lama; warrior king; god with ladder-patterned robe; filling motifs 106

7.15 Lion-griffins attacking goat; lion attacking one of two nude heroes fighting lion 106

7.16 Two figures; filling motifs 107

7.17 Seated god; filling motifs 108

7.18 Worshipper with fan before seated figure with cup; filling motifs 109

7.19 Scene based on Egyptian depictions of Levantines 109

7.20 Water god, with flowing vases, between mountains and flowers 110

7.21 Animal; tree; border of triangles 111

7.22 Robed figure holding staff 112

7.23 Votive seal carved in relief (NB). The storm god Adad on a dais 112

7.24 Bird-griffin and winged gazelle 113

7.25 Hero fighting lion 114

7.26 Hero and ostrich 114

7.27 Hero fighting lion 115

7.28 A god and mythical beasts 115

7.29 Winged heroes with bird and sphinx; filling motif 116

7.30 Winged hero between ibex-horned, winged sphinxes; filling motifs 117

7.31 Winged hero fighting inverted lions; filling motifs 117

7.32 Winged hero between bird-griffins 118

7.33 Tree flanked by winged heroes with cone and bucket 118

7.34 Priest with cup and bucket before offering table and altars with symbols 119

7.35 Pyramidal seal. Priest before altar with symbols 119

7.36 Enlarged ancient impressions, made by two Babylonian seals 120

8.1 The 'Loftus Hoard' 125

9.1 Seal of a presentation scene of a figure being led by a goddess to a seated male deity 142

9.2 Scene from a wall painting found at the palace of Mari, showing multi-colored wrap garments 144

9.3 Relief sculpture from Khorsabad showing fringed skirt 148

9.4 Seal depicting a hero fighting wild animals 149

9.5 Assyrian palace relief sculpture of a threshold with fringe outer border, from Khorsabad 149

9.6 Close-up of textile pseudomorph from Abu Salabikh 152

10.1 Stele of Ashurbanipal, 668–652 BC 156

10.2 Stele of Hammurabi, 1760 BC 159

10.3 Lu-Nanna votive portrait, 1792–1750 BC 161

10.4 Kudurru of Nebuchadnezzar I, 1125–1104 BC 164

10.5 Kudurru of Marduk Nadin Ahhe, 1099–1082 BC 165

10.6 Throne room wall of Nebuchadnezzar II, 604–562 BC 166

10.7	Portrait of a woman, third–second centuries BC	167
11.1	Assyrian palace relief showing a fisherman	181
14.1	Map showing changes in the main inter-regional trade routes of the early second millennium BC	213
14.2	Two impressions of the same seal on a tablet from Hursagkalama dating to the eighteenth year of Ammisaduqa	214
16.1	Tablet from the Egibi archive showing a field plan	242
16.2	Schematic interpretation of the field plan	243
17.1	Seal impression of king Mesannepada of Ur, 2563–2524 BCE	252
17.2	A Sumerian temple of early third millennium BCE	255
17.3	Fragment of a storage jar from Tepe Gawra, layer VI, twenty-fourth century BCE	258
18.1	Reconstructed map of Babylon in the first millennium	266
18.2	Model of the Marduk sanctuaries in Babylon; the Processional Way and the Ishtar Gate	267
19.1	Detail of the Code of Ur-Nammu, showing the measuring rope	278
20.1	Kudurru of Marduk-apla-iddina II	294
20.2	Assyrian palace relief showing Chaldean captives in a date palm grove	295
21.1	Babylonian terracotta relief of couple making love, while the woman is drinking beer through a long straw	304
21.2	Old Babylonian terracotta bust of a woman	306
23.1	Green calcite cylinder seal and impression depicting a cultic scene	334
23.2	Drawing of the top two registers of the cultic vase from Uruk	334
23.3	Impression of Old Babylonian cylinder seal	337
24.1	Drawing based on a cylinder seal of Marduk dedicated by the Babylonian king, Marduk-zakir-shumi	350
25.1	Old Babylonian clay model of a sheep's liver, *c.*1700 BC	370
27.1	Seal impression showing an incantation priest at work on a patient	391
28.1	Example of a memorandum which shows signs of carelessness	402
28.2	Passage of a letter which shows a change of mind by the scribe	404
28.3	Envelope of a letter by Zimri-Lim Tiš-ulme	405
28.4	Label of a tablet-basket in the shape of an olive	406
28.5	Example of a copy of a letter within a letter	410
28.6	A short letter of accreditation	412
29.1	The obverse of a mathematical tablet	420
29.2	The geometrical manipulations implicit in YBC 6967	423
30.1	A fragment of the first tablet of Erimhush from Nineveh	439
30.2	An example of the first tablet of Ea, from Assur	441
30.3	An example of the second tablet of Aa, from Sippar	441
31.1	Ashur-ra'im-napishti's copy of Tablet VI of the Babylonian Epic of Gilgamesh	454
32.1	Copy of part of a Babylonian treatise on astronomy and astrology	466
33.1	Kudurru of the Babylonian king Marduk-zakir-shumi	482
34.1	Letter from Burnaburiash, king of Babylon, to Amenophis IV, king of Egypt	489

35.1   The restored ramparts of the Hittite capital Hattusa   504
37.1   Tablet containing the so-called 'Synchronistic History'   529
37.2   Central panel of the throne base of Shalmaneser III from Nimrud   531
37.3   Assyro-Babylonian treaty, written in 821 BCE   532
37.4   Assyrian relief depicting the deportation of the Babylonians   534
39.1   Drawing of part of a panel from Persepolis, showing Babylonians
       bringing gifts   564
39.2   Seal inscribed with the name Darius in Persian, Elamite
       and Babylonian   572

TABLES

2.1   Number of villages (≤ 2 ha.) in selected middle/lower Babylonian
       areas   16
2.2   Distribution of settlements as percentage of total occupational
       area   17
2.3   Old Babylonian Sumero-Akkadian varietal terms for
       countryside places   19
8.1   Sources of Mesopotamian copper through the millennia   126
34.1   Middle Babylonian period, c. 1600–900   492

CONTRIBUTORS

Tzvi Abusch is Rose B. and Joseph Cohen Professor of Assyriology and Ancient Near Eastern Religion at Brandeis University. He received his Ph.D. in Assyriology from Harvard University. He has taught at the Jewish Theological Seminary of America and The Hebrew University of Jerusalem and has held a number of awards and fellowships. Most recently, he was a member of the Institutes for Advanced Study in Princeton (2003–4) and in Jerusalem (2006). His primary fields of research and publication are Mesopotamian religion, magic, literature and thought, as well as biblical and Babylonian interconnections. A number of his studies on magic and mythology are to be found in his *Mesopotamian Witchcraft: Towards a History and Understanding of Babylonian Witchcraft Beliefs and Literature* (Leiden: Brill/Styx, 2002) and *The Epic of Gilgamesh: Male and Female Encounters and Other Issues* (Winona Lake, IN: Eisenbrauns, in press).

Zainab Bahrani is the Edith Porada Associate Professor of Ancient Near Eastern Art History and Archaeology at Columbia University. She is the author of, among other publications, *Women of Babylon: Gender and Representation in Mesopotamia* (London: Routledge, 2001), and *The Graven Image: Representation in Babylonia and Assyria* (Philadelphia: University of Pennsylvania Press, 2003). Prior to her appointment at Columbia University, Professor Bahrani taught at the University of Vienna in Austria, and The State University of New York, at Stony Brook, and was a curator at the Metropolitan Museum of Art's Near Eastern Antiquities Department from 1989–1992.

Heather D. Baker, after graduating in Archaeology from the University of Cambridge, participated in numerous excavations in Britain, Cyprus, Jordan, Turkey and especially in Iraq. At the University of Oxford she gained an M.Phil. in Cuneiform Studies and a D.Phil. in Assyriology. Since January 2003 she has been working as a Researcher with the START Project on 'The Economic History of Babylonia in the 1st millennium BC' at the University of Vienna. Her publications include a monograph, *The Archive of the Nappahu Family* (2004), and (as editor) *The Prosopography of the Neo-Assyrian Empire*, Part 2/I (2000), Part 2/II (2001), Part 3/I (2002), and *Approaching the Babylonian Economy* (2005, with M. Jursa). Her research interests are in the social and economic history and material culture of Babylonia and Assyria in the first millennium BC. She is currently working on a monograph on The Urban Landscape in First Millennium BC Babylonia.

Paul-Alain Beaulieu is Visiting Associate Professor of Near Eastern Languages and Civilizations in the University of Notre Dame, Notre Dame, Indiana, USA. His main research interest is the history, culture, religion and intellectual life of Ancient Mesopotamia in the first millennium BC. His publications include *The Reign of Nabonidus, King of Babylon (556–539 BC)* (Yale University Press, 1989), and *The Pantheon of Uruk During the Neo-Babylonian Period* (Brill-Styx, 2003). He is currently preparing two monographs on Neo-Babylonian archives, one documenting a family of entrepreneurs from Larsa in the sixth century, the other one detailing the contribution of the city of Uruk to the construction of king Nebuchadnezzar's North Palace in Babylon.

David Brown is currently researching the transmission of astral science in the pre-Muslim period at the Free University of Berlin, funded by the German Research Council. He was previously an Alexander von Humboldt fellow, a Lecturer in ancient Near Eastern history at University College London for two years, and has taught Assyriology at Oxford, Cambridge, and SOAS. His first degree was in physics.

Trevor Bryce is presently Honorary Research Consultant at the University of Queensland, Australia. He has conducted research on the History and Civilization of the Near East in the second and first millennia BC, with particular emphasis on Anatolia. Recent publications include *Life and Society in the Hittite World* (Oxford University Press, 2002), *Letters of the Great Kings of the Ancient Near East* (Routledge, 2003), *The Kingdom of the Hittites* (Oxford University Press, new edition, 2005). Forthcoming are *The Trojans and their Neighbours* (Routledge), *Hittite Warrior* (Osprey) and *Dictionary of the Cities and Kingdoms of the Ancient Near East* (Routledge).

Dominique Charpin has taught at the Sorbonne since 1975, then also at the École Pratique des Hautes Etudes. He specializes in the Old Babylonian period and works on archives from Iraq and Syria, especially Mari. He has recently published *Mari et le Proche-Orient à l'époque amorrite: essai d'histoire politique, Florilegium marianum V* (Paris, 2003) (with N. Ziegler). His more popular book, *Hammurabi de Babylone* (Paris, 2003) has been translated into English and Italian. He has just edited a work called *Lire et écrire en Babylonie ancienne. Écriture, acheminement et lecture des lettres d'après les archives royales de Mari* and is about to publish *Writing, Law and Kingship in Ancient Babylonia*.

Petr Charvát was born in 1949. He studied Assyriology and Archaeology at Charles University, Prague, and has spent all his active research career in two Institutes of the Czechoslovak Academy of Sciences and Academy of Sciences of the Czech Republic (after 1993): Archaeological (1975–1990) and Oriental. His main interest is the study of the emergence of statehood and literate societies in prehistoric and ancient Western Asia, based on archaeological and textual sources. His publications include *On People, Signs and States: Spotlights on Sumerian Society, c.3500–2500 B. C.* (Prague: The Oriental Institute, 1997) and *Mesopotamia Before History* (London and New York: Routledge, 2002).

Dominique Collon has recently retired from the British Museum where she was a curator in the Department of the Ancient Near East with particular responsibility for Seals, Anatolia and Mesopotamia. Her numerous publications include three volumes of the catalogue of the Museum's seals (she is working on a fourth), *First Impressions – Cylinder Seals in the Ancient Near East* (London, 1987; new edition 2005), and *Ancient Near Eastern Art* (London, 1995) based on the Museum's collections. She has travelled extensively throughout the Near East, led many tours and excavated in Iraq, Syria and Turkey.

Harriet Crawford specializes in the later prehistory of Mesopotamia and is an honorary Visiting Professor at the Institute of Archaeology, University College London. She is also a Research Fellow at the McDonald Institute Cambridge and the author of *Sumer and the Sumerians* (Cambridge: Cambridge University Press, 2004), as well as a number of books on the archaeology of the Arabo/Persian Gulf.

Frederick Mario Fales is Full Professor of Ancient Near Eastern History at the University of Udine (Italy). His main scholarly interests concern the Neo-Assyrian period, and range from historical studies to the edition of Assyrian and Aramaic texts of this age. He is on the editorial board of two international projects on Neo-Assyrian texts, *State Archives of Assyria* (Helsinki), and *Studien zu den Assur-Texten* (Berlin), to which he has also contributed three co-authored monographs. He has founded an international journal on Neo-Assyrian studies, the *State Archives of Assyria Bulletin* (Padua), which has now reached its thirteenth annual volume. His most recent book, *Saccheggio in Mesopotamia* (Udine [Forum], 2004) is an analysis of the 2003 pillage of the Iraq Museum in Baghdad, framed within a history of the museum and of its rich archaeological heritage, from Gertrude Bell to Saddam Hussein.

Hannes D. Galter is Universitätsdozent for Assyriology at the University of Graz. He teaches Assyriology and Ancient Near Eastern History at the University of Graz and is co-editor of the 'Grazer Morgenländische Studien'. He published several books on Ancient Near Eastern topics such as *Der mesopotamische Gott Enki/Ea* (1983), *Die Rolle der Astronomie in den Kulturen Mesopotamiens* (1993) and *Kopftuch und Schleier* (2001). His main interests and working areas are Mesopotamian history, historiography and literature and especially Assyrian royal inscriptions.

M. J. Geller is Professor of Semitic Languages at UCL, in the Department of Hebrew and Jewish Studies. He spent the 2005–2006 academic year in Paris as Visiting Professor at the École Pratique des Hautes Études, with a grant from the Wellcome Trust. He has published 'Renal and rectal disease', *Babylonisch-Assyrische Medizin*, Vol. 7 (2005).

A. R. George is Professor of Babylonian at the School of Oriental and African Studies, the University of London. His chief research focus is on Babylonian civilization, especially literature, religion, mythology and intellectual achievement and his most recent book is *The Babylonian Gilgamesh Epic: Introduction, Critical Edition and Cuneiform Texts* (OUP, 2003). His new translation of Gilgamesh for Penguin Classics won the 2000 Kuwait-British Fellowship Society prize for Middle Eastern Studies.

Anne Goddeeris is based at the University of Leuven and is a specialist in economic texts from the Old Babylonian period. Her book *Economy and Society in Northern Babylonia in the Early Old Babylonian Period (ca. 2000–1600 BC)* appeared in 2002.

Irene Good is an archaeologist of Central and Western Asia and the Indo-Iranian borderlands. She received her doctorate from the University of Pennsylvania in 1999 and since 2001 has been an Associate of the Peabody Museum at Harvard University. Her specific research interests concern cloth in all its aspects, from labour, technology and materials, to social uses, semiotics, iconography and the symbolic uses of cloth as a major component of material culture. As a Guggenheim Fellow, Dr Good embarked on a major study entitled *A Social Archaeology of Textiles*, and is now completing a book entitled *Cloth and Carpet in Early Inner Asia*, to be published through Brill's Inner Asia series. She has curated important textile collections as Hardy Visiting Curator at the Peabody Museum, and has developed a novel application of biochemical techniques to the study of severely degraded archaeological fibres. Dr Good's current research is focused on the later Bronze period of Western China, Afghanistan and the Indo-Iranian borderlands. She is currently directing a new archaeological survey in southern Tajikistan.

Brigitte Groneberg is Professor for Assyriology at the University of Göttingen, Germany. Her research interests are Akkadian grammar, Mesopotamian literature and the Cultural History of the Ancient Near East. Her most recent book *Die Götter des Zweistromlandes; Kulte, Mythen, Epen*, (Artemis & Winkler, Düsseldorf/Zurich: 2004) provides an overview of religious concepts and cosmology in the Ancient Near East.

Anthony Howell was born in 1945. By 1995 he was a dancer in the Royal Ballet. Soon after, he left the ballet to concentrate on writing. In 1973, he was invited to join the programme for International Writers at the University of Iowa. Since then his output has included many collections of poetry, mainly published by Anvil, the most recent being his *Selected Poems* and *Dancers in Daylight*. His versions of Statius and those of W. G. Shepherd were published by Anvil in 2007.

Blahoslav Hruška studied Assyriology and Archaeology at the Philosophical Faculty of Charles University, Prague, and Sumerian at Munich. Since 1982, he has been studying the theme of traditional Mesopotamian agriculture throughout several research projects (Berlin: Free University and Max Planck Institute for the History of Science; Oxford, UK: Sumerian Agriculture Group). He works as a researcher at the Oriental Institute of the Czechoslovak and the Czech Academy of Sciences, and he also teaches History, Culture and Religion of the Ancient Near East at the Hussite Theological Faculty of Charles University, Prague.

Michael Jursa is Associate Professor at the University of Vienna. His main research interests are Babylonian social and economic history and material culture. Currently he is director of a project funded by the Fonds zur Förderung der Wissenschaftlichen Forschung (Vienna) which aims at writing a comprehensive economic history of Babylonia in the first millennium BC.

Frans van Koppen is a Ph.D. candidate at the University of Leiden. His main interest is the second millennium BC.

Amélie Kuhrt is Professor for Ancient Near Eastern History at University College London, and a Fellow of the British Academy. Her research areas are: Mesopotamia in the first millennium BC; the Achaemenid Empire; Seleucid rule in Mesopotamia and Iran. She is the author of *The Ancient Near East, c.3000–330 BC* (2 vols; London: Routledge, 1995) and of the forthcoming volume *The Achaemenid Persian Empire: a corpus of sources* (London: Routledge, 2007).

Gwendolyn Leick is Senior Lecturer at Chelsea College of Art and Design in London. Her last books were *The Babylonians. An Introduction* (Routledge, 2003) and *Historical Dictionary of Mesopotamia* (Scarecrow Press, 2003).

Baruch A. Levine is Skirball Professor Emeritus of Bible and Ancient Near East Studies, New York University. He is the author of commentaries on Leviticus and Numbers, and his main research interests are religion and institutions of biblical Israel. He is a student of the West-Semitic languages with publications on epigraphy and recently published *Assyrian Ideology and Israelite Monotheism* (2005).

Stefan M. Maul is Professor of Assyriology at the University of Heidelberg and is a recipient of the Leibniz prize. He specializes in the study of Babylonian incantations and divination literature. His translation of the Gilgamesh epic into German was published in 2005.

Lucia Mori teaches History of the Ancient Near East at the University of Tuscia, Viterbo, Italy. She is involved in a long-term historical project aiming to reconstruct the rural landscape in the ancient Near East, which has been promoted and directed by Mario Liverani since the 1970s. In this broad project, her main interest has been the study of the Middle Euphrates valley, and in 2003 she published a volume, *Reconstructing the Emar Landscape*, for the series 'Quaderni di Geografia storica' published by the Università 'La Sapienza', Rome. Since 1987 she has been working in Fezzan, Libyan desert, in an archaeological investigation carried out by the Università 'La Sapienza' aimed at the study of the Saharan caravan trade routes in proto-historical times. A first volume, *Aghram Nadharif, the Barkat Oasis in Garamantian Times*, was published in 2006, edited by Mario Liverani. A second volume on the archaeological investigation in the oasis of Fewet is in preparation. In addition, she is a member of the archaeological mission of Yale University in Tell Leilan, Syria, directed by Harvey Weiss, and she collaborates in the study of the Akkadian occupation of the site, which has been investigated during the past decade.

Takayoshi Oshima was born in Japan in 1967 and studied at the Hebrew University of Jerusalem. He now teaches Jewish Studies at the University of Bucharest. His research interests include the study of Mesopotamian religion and his Ph.D. dissertation was entitled *Hymns and Prayers to Marduk and his Divine Elements in the Texts*. A book, *Cuneiform in Canaan: Cuneiform Sources from the Land of Isarel in Ancient Times*, with Wayne Horowitz, is in press.

D. T. Potts was educated at Harvard and the Free University of Berlin and is Edwin Cuthbert Hall Professor of Middle Eastern Archaeology at the University of Sydney. He has conducted fieldwork in Iran, Saudi Arabia and the United Arab Emirates, and is editor-in-chief of the journal *Arabian Archaeology & Epigraphy*. He is the author of numerous books and articles on the archaeology of Iran, Mesopotamia, the Persian Gulf and the Arabian peninsula, including *Mesopotamian Civilization: the material foundations* (1997), *The Archaeology of Elam* (1999), *Ancient Magan* (2000) and *Excavations at Tepe Yahya 1967–1975: the third millennium* (2001).

Johannes Renger is Professor Emeritus of Ancient Near Eastern Studies, Freie Universität Berlin. He studied Theology (i.a. Old Testament Studies), Assyriology, Egyptology and Semitic Languages at the Universities of Leipzig and Heidelberg (gaining his Ph.D. in Assyriology from the University of Heidelberg 1965). He was a research associate and taught at the Oriental Institute, University of Chicago. From 1976 to 2002 he was Professor of Ancient Near Eastern Studies at Freie Universität Berlin. Special interests are economic and social history of the Ancient Near East Mesopotamia, comparative economic history, history of Assyriology, and literary criticism.

Frances Reynolds is a Shillito Fellow in Assyriology and Senior Research Fellow of St Benet's Hall at the University of Oxford. She is also a Sessional Lecturer at Birkbeck College, University of London, and an Honorary Research Fellow of the University of Birmingham. From September 2007, she will be contributing to a project on cuneiform libraries at the University of Cambridge. Dr Reynolds' research interests include Mesopotamian intellectual life and religion, and she is working on her forthcoming book, *Scholars and Invaders: Babylon under Threat in Astrology, Ritual, Myth and Prophecy*. Other forthcoming publications include 'A divine body: new joins in the Sippar Collection', in *Your Praise is Sweet: A Memorial Volume Presented to Jeremy Allen Black by Colleagues, Students, and Friends* (eds H.D. Baker, E. Robson and G. Zólyomi, Oxford: Griffith Institute, in press). Her first book was published in 2003: *The Babylonian Correspondence of Esarhaddon and Letters to Assurbanipal and Sin-šarru-iškun from Northern and Central Babylonia: State Archives of Assyria Volume XVIII* (Helsinki University Press).

Seth Richardson has been Assistant Professor of Ancient Near Eastern History at the University of Chicago's Oriental Institute since 2003. He received his Ph.D. from Columbia University in 2002, writing his dissertation on the collapse of the First Dynasty of Babylon. He is now conducting research work on Old Babylonian economic and administrative texts, Assyrian political history, an intellectual history of early Babylonian liver divination, and problems in Ancient Near East labour history, state collapse and chronology.

Dafydd Roberts studied social sciences and philosophy. As a freelance translator from French and German, he has translated a number of scholarly works in these fields. Interested, too, in art and cultural history, he has also worked for the Louvre, the Centre Georges Pompidou, the Tate Gallery, the Pergamon Museum and a number of other such institutions.

Eleanor Robson's work focuses on questions of numeracy and literacy in ancient Iraq. Her publications include *Mesopotamian Mathematics, 2100–1600 BC* (Oxford, 1999) and, with Jeremy Black, Graham Cunningham and Gábor Zólyomi, *The Literature of Ancient Sumer* (Oxford, 2004). She is a university lecturer in the Department of History and Philosophy of Science, University of Cambridge, and a Fellow of All Souls College, Oxford.

Walther Sallaberger is Professor of Assyriology at the University of Munich. His research interests include: Mesopotamian history, society, culture and religion, based on Sumerian and Akkadian texts; Sumerian administrative texts; Sumerian lexicography; text linguistics. He is the author of *Sumerer und Akkader – Geschichte – Gesellschaft – Kultur* (C.H. Beck Verlag, Munich 2005) and the forthcoming (2006) *Glossary of Neo-Sumerian Royal inscriptions.*

Gebhard J. Selz is Chair of Ancient Oriental Languages and Oriental Archaeology at the University of Vienna. He is the editor of several academic journals, such as *Archiv für Orientforschung*, *Wiener Zeitschrift für die Kunde des Morgenlandes*, and *Wiener Offene Orientalistik.* His research centres on religions and economics of third millennium BC Mesopotamia, early classification systems and early empiricism.

Laura D. Steele is completing her doctoral dissertation on Mesopotamian slave women in the Graduate Group in Ancient History and Mediterranean Archaeology at the University of California, Berkeley. Her other research interests include Anatolian archaeology, digital-assisted analyses of ancient architecture, and connections between Greece and the Near East; she also has worked with excavation teams at Çatal Höyük (Turkey) and at Tel Dor (Israel). Among her most recent publications are papers on Herodotus and Urartu in the *American Journal of Ancient History* 3/1 (2004) and on Parmenides and Shamash in the *Classical Quarterly* 52/1 (2002).

Jon Taylor is curator of the cuneiform collections in the Department of the Ancient Near East at the British Museum. London. His research interests include literacy and education in the ancient world.

P. S. Vermaak is Associate Professor in Ancient Near Eastern Studies at the University of South Africa. Trained initially as a theologian he specialized in the Semitic Languages and currently teaches Ancient Near Eastern Culture, Classical Hebrew, Ugaritic, Sumerian, Akkadian and Egyptian. He gained his Ph.D. in 1989 on the temple officials in the Ur III period. The focus of his current research is the cultural background of the Ancient Near East with special reference to the cultural exchange in the Ancient Near East during the second millennium BC.

David A. Warburton (D.Phil. University of Berne, Switzerland) teaches Near Eastern Archaeology and Egyptology at universities in Denmark, Switzerland and France. A former director of the American Institute for Yemeni Studies in Sana'a, he has participated in archaeological field work in France, Switzerland, Egypt, Syria, Iraq and Yemen. His research interests centre on economics and politics in the ancient world, but also include religion, architecture, colour terminology, chronology and stratigraphy. The most recent books are *Macroeconomics from the Beginning* and *Archaeological Stratigraphy: A Near Eastern Approach* (both 2003); he is currently working on another volume on ancient economics, as well as collaborative efforts on religion and chronology.

Joan Goodnick Westenholz holds the posts of Chief Curator of the Bible Lands Museum Jerusalem and Senior Visiting Associate on the Chicago Assyrian Dictionary Project of the Oriental Institute of the University of Chicago. She has published extensively on various topics in Babylonian religion and literature as well as on issues of gender, women and goddesses. Her books include *Legends of the Kings of Akkade, Cuneiform Texts in the Bible Lands Museum Jerusalem: The Emar Texts* and *Cuneiform Texts in the Bible Lands Museum Jerusalem: The Old Babylonian Texts*. Her present research is focused on the most archaic lexicographical series and the earliest anatomical lexicon.

Cornelia Wunsch is Research Associate at the Department of Languages and Cultures of the Near and Middle East at the School of Oriental and African Studies, University of London. She is a specialist in Neo- and Late Babylonian documents and the author of various works on Neo-Babylonian economy, especially the archives of the Egibi family.

CHAPTER ONE

INTRODUCTION

——— .◆. ———

Gwendolyn Leick

In the book of Genesis (XI, 9) the etymology of 'Babel' is given as 'confusion', the result of divine intervention in order to punish a people for their wish 'to make a name for themselves' by building 'a city and a tower whose top may reach unto heaven'. Language or indeed the proliferation of languages, urbanism (it is the first mention of a city in the Bible), monumental architecture and historical memory, are thus all associated with the toponym 'Babel'. In the later Biblical books a great deal more will be said about Babylon and its kings who waged war against Judah. While in these accounts, the Babylonians, just like other powerful and repressive nations of the Ancient Near East, were to be doomed to destruction and annihilation, the Biblical writings did keep their memory alive until the post-Enlightenment explorers brought back tangible evidence of ancient writings, monuments and cities.

For the last century and a half, the Babylonians have once more become part of our modernity. Cuneiform documents are relatively robust and they survived the sacking of cities; having been buried in the sand for millennia they now constitute an ever growing data bank comprising many thousands of tablets. The current state of affairs in Iraq, however, has a serious impact on scholarship; witness the destruction of sites by looters and military activities, the dispersal of material without established context and the loss of unpublished artefacts from Iraqi museum collections. Scientifically conducted archaeological excavations have almost ceased. Academic life in Iraqi departments has suffered from the destruction of libraries and facilities. The trauma of displacement will echo across the Assyriological world for some time but it is also affected by developments in the academic world in general. Considerable economic pressure on universities to follow the 'market' jeopardizes 'minority subjects' such as Assyriology and this has led to the closure of several departments and has restricted research funding. On the other hand Assyriology has spread around the world, with institutes in China, Japan, Latin America and South Africa, and the current volume documents the continuing vitality of the subject and the commitment of scholars from all continents to keep connected to the Babylonian world.

BABYLONIA: PART OF MESOPOTAMIA

Babylonia can be defined geographically as the southern half of Mesopotamia, beginning where the rivers Tigris and Euphrates approach each other, forming a strip of land like a pinched waist. At the very south lie the marshes and, beyond, the waters of the Persian Gulf. The northern half of Mesopotamia was known as Assyria. Most of the Assyrian cities were situated along the Tigris, those of Babylonia along the Euphrates, a major trade route in itself, or on the intermediary canals. The Zagros mountains form a natural border to the east, as does the great Arabian desert to the west. The climate is hotter and drier in southern Mesopotamia; agriculture is only possible through irrigation and the landscape is marked by a dense network of canals, levees and dams. The date palm flourishes only south of Baghdad and their graceful fronds marked the Babylonian skyline for millennia.

Babylonian history is embedded within the *longue durée* of Mesopotamian history but closely associated with the eponymous city of Babylon. Lying on the Euphrates, some ninety kilometres south of Baghdad, the city was founded sometime in the third millennium: the Akkadian king Shar-kali-sharri provides the first historical mention, a reference to its temples. Babylon was thus perhaps always a holy city; the etymology of a possibly non-Semitic original name was interpreted by cuneiform scholars as *bab-il*, 'gate of the god'. During the time of the Third Dynasty of Ur, around 2000 BC, it was a provincial capital and some hundred years later, after the disintegration of the Ur empire, it became the seat of a small kingdom founded by the Amorite chief, Sumu-abum. His grandson Hammurabi managed to unite all of southern Mesopotamia, as well as much of the middle Euphrates region. Although this First Dynasty of Babylon could not hold all these lands together for long, its rulers brought a degree of cultural and administrative uniformity to Babylonia which is documented by abundant textual sources. The city of Babylon, as the seat of king-ship, was lavishly endowed with temples and palaces. So splendid did the city become that it attracted the cupidity of a far distant ruler, the Hittite king Mursili, who swept down the Euphrates to attack the city and plunder its riches.

The Amorite chiefs who had founded the First Dynasty were part of a Semitic people who had migrated into Mesopotamia from the west in search of pasture and new strategies for survival. Those who adopted the settled and urban way of life became acculturated to the 'Babylonian' ways, which can be seen clearly in personal names which reflect an acceptance of the established religious practices. Their language ('Old Babylonian') replaced the previously spoken Sumerian, and only the most learned of scholars were familiar with written Sumerian.

The assimilative powers of Babylonian culture became again apparent when another group of immigrants, this time arriving from the east, and known as the Kassites, took political control. Their first kings still bore outlandish Kassite names, the later ones adopted 'good Babylonian' names and titles. They continued to exercise their duties towards Babylonian gods and their temples and though they built a new capital, Babylon remained the ceremonial and religious centre of the country which came to be known as 'Karduniash'. The Kassite kings established the first properly unified state system in Babylonia and during their long reign (almost 500 years) Babylonian civilization crystallized: it was a relatively stable period in which much wealth was generated through trade in luxury goods and a strong rural agricultural base. In the mid-second millennium, Babylonian became the international language of diplomacy, utilized by the court scribes of all major powers: the Egyptians, Hittites, Mitanni, as well in various Levantine states. Unlike most of the major players at the time, Babylonia avoided getting drawn into military conflicts. However, the wave of disruption and violence that affected especially the western part of the Ancient Near East in the thirteenth century eventually triggered massive displacements of populations which destabilized Babylonia too. The end of the second millennium is poorly documented, one short-lived dynasty followed another, as various tribal groupings fought for control of the main cities.

Babylonia's fate in the first millennium was initially determined by the rise of Assyria as the most powerful state in the region. While Assyrian monarchs acknowledged the religious and scholarly status of Babylonia, it did not stop them from imposing direct rule which was to last for nearly two centuries and which was fiercely resisted. A coalition with the neighbours in the east, first Elam and then the Medes, strengthened Babylonian efforts to end Assyrian domination which succeeded in 612 with the fall of Nineveh. Under the rule of military leaders, such as Nebukadrezzar II, Babylonia claimed a good portion of Assyria's wealth, boosted by the conquest of the old enemy's dependencies. The money was ploughed into making Babylon the most fabulous of cities, with its massive ramparts, dazzling ceremonial streets, the towering ziggurat and vast temple complexes. Babylonian learning reached its zenith at this period, especially in astronomy and mathematics. The end of Babylonian political independence, caused by the integration of the country into the Persian empire brought little change to Babylonian society and business. Though no longer a centre of political power, Babylon, as well as many other of the ancient Mesopotamian cities, retained its religious and cultural importance. It was only when the balance of influence decidedly shifted to the west in the long Hellenistic aftermath of Alexander's conquests that Mesopotamia became marginal, a march between the east, dominated by Persian kings, and the west, under the rule of Rome.

THE PRESENT VOLUME

We can only experience the remote past in a tentative and fragmentary way and through the lens of our contemporary patterns of thought. How we think about history always reflects our current preoccupations. The Babylonian world seen through the eyes of the leading specialists in the field at the beginning of the third millennium AD brings into focus areas of concern typical for our time: ecology, productivity, power relations, economics, epistemology, scientific paradigms, complexity. The general division of the volume proceeds from the general 'hard facts' – geography, ecology, material culture, to the 'software' provided primarily by cuneiform tablets, our richest source of information and, at a time when archaeological research in Iraq continues to be practically impossible, the only current opportunity for new insights. The majority of the articles are based on primary epigraphic research.

Some subjects invite a longer perspective of time and more of an overview than others where the focus is more narrowly defined. I did not wish to enforce a common approach and manner of writing, in order to allow for variation of voices and accents and attitudes. There are overlaps and occasionally the same subject is treated several times but with different perspectives; this helps to give a flavour of the contemporary debates and issues. Some authors interpreted their topic in a manner that conveyed their 'take' on the subject within an academic discourse, others were more interested in providing an account of facts and data. The 'Babylonian' framework was also interpreted in different ways. Some scholars have participated who normally are more at home in the pre-Babylonian era; their contributions are justified on the grounds that Babylonian technology or administrative practices followed traditions that were established at an earlier phase of Mesopotamian history. There are also chapters by specialists in other areas of the Ancient Near East who were invited to reflect on the relationship between 'their' cultures and the Babylonians. Such shifting viewpoints, from far and near, from below and beyond, from the periphery to the centre, provide a greater diversity of angles onto the 'Babylonian World', a kaleidoscopic rather than panoramic show, which might make us see patterns and bright fragments and so reveal aspects of the 'lost world' in unexpected ways, without the inherent delusion of the magisterial omniscience of an encyclopedia.

Part I introduces the land and techniques of working the land, the preconditions for the emergence of Mesopotamian civilization. The understanding that this civilization was a primarily urban one is based on the fact that the surviving written documents inevitably came from urban centres, the product of an urban literary culture, and that archaeological excavations generally targeted conspicuous and promisingly large mounds, remains of ancient cities. In the last twenty years, due to various factors, not least the absence of funding for long-term excavation projects and the political instability in the country, new archaeological techniques have developed. When the results of aerial and other surveys are calibrated with the textual records, especially the administrative documents that record a great variety of place names, we get a very different understanding of settlement patterns. Seth Richardson's chapter explicitly refers to the plurality of 'countrysides' in the title of his contribution to emphasize the constantly shifting configuration of Mesopotamia's rural areas. He not only corrects the outdated view of Babylonia's primarily urban configuration but traces patterns of state involvement in rural areas and the ideological claims made by rulers in connection with the countryside across the main phases of Mesopotamian history. Lucia Mori draws on her research in a much more localized environment, the upper Euphrates valley which, though not within the 'Babylonian heartland', was for centuries closely connected politically and culturally with the Mesopotamian south, especially during the Old Babylonian period. The most important and richest archive of this era comes from the palace of Mari, situated in the Middle Euphrates region. The letters and documents of this collection provide detailed information on how the arable and pasture land was managed in order to make optimal use of this particular eco-sphere. Blahoslav Hruška concentrates on the alluvial plains of Babylonia, known as 'Akkad and Sumer' in the third millennium. He provides a survey of the agricultural techniques that were perfected during this time, to remain almost unchanged for millennia. Sumerian compositions, such as the 'Farmer's Almanac' – instructions for a ploughman – as well as economic texts from large estates and temples, contain invaluable references to the vital tasks of husbandry and agriculture, on which the whole economy was reliant. A Babylonian city was always a compound of its extramural, agricultural land and pastures, with the residential and public spaces, gardens, orchards, and waterways enclosed by the city walls. The 'countryside', as pointed out by Richardson, for which there was no emic terminology, was the area beyond those that 'belonged', in one way or another, to a particular city. Heather Baker's chapter concentrates on Babylonian cities during the first millennium BC. She discusses the infrastructure, street systems, canals, city walls, gates, temples and other monumental buildings, paying particular attention to the often neglected domain of residential quarters. She also raises the question of whether one could detect any design or planning strategy in the urban lay-out and how tradition, inheritance patterns and topography determined the use of private and public space.

Material culture is an almost inexhaustible subject; in Mesopotamia it had been the subject of scholarly scrutiny from the earliest period of writing, when the first word lists were devised which eventually classified both man-made objects (from tools to medicines) and natural phenomena (from birds and fishes to the planets).

In Part II, Harriet Crawford, when discussing the built environment of the Old Babylonian period (roughly, the first half of the second millennium BC), stresses how the configuration of buildings and streets reflects and determines social behaviour. She also takes a close look at new architectural techniques that were introduced at this time, especially in the middle Euphrates region, where ambitious projects, such as the palace of Mari, attracted attention throughout the Ancient Near East for their innovative designs. Following on from Heather Baker's chapter, it gives an opportunity to compare to what extent the Babylonian urban environment changed and remained the same across the span of some 1,000 years.

Cylinder seals were a unique invention of Mesopotamian culture, closely associated with the emergence of a complex bureaucracy and urbanism in the late fourth millennium BC. Dominique Collon, for many years in charge of the seal collections of the British Museum, presents an overview of the Babylonian seals, their usage, materials, iconography and design. Seals not only reveal much about managerial processes and accountability in all kinds of transaction, but also about religious beliefs, notions of kingship, modes of clothing, links of trade and beliefs in the magic properties of certain minerals. Mesopotamia's alluvial soils were famously fertile but poor in metals and minerals. Dan Potts describes how coveted exotic materials, both organic and inorganic, were imported to Babylonia, focusing primarily on the east and south-east, a main source for Mesopotamian trade across the ages. Given that, in archaeological terms, most of the Babylonian periods belong to the Bronze Age, the procurement of copper was of vital importance. Many other substances, known primarily from cuneiform texts, such as precious stones, aromatics, cloths, resins, were an integral part of the rich material culture which relied on long-distance imports by sea and land to satisfy the increasingly demanding consumers of luxury goods. Textiles, on the other hand, were a famous and highly prized export commodity. Irene Good examines the evidence, epigraphic and archaeological, for the materials, techniques and design of cloth in Mesopotamia. Though 'fashions' in the cut and draping of clothes seem to have changed little over the centuries, this may be an impression conveyed by conservatism in modes of visual representation. Zainab Bahrani takes key examples of public and private monuments that have encoded culturally specific messages. Bahrani evokes the notion of 'image magic' which endows visual representations with agency to make things happen rather than passive 'reflection' of reality. It shows that the Babylonian world was one in which human beings experienced themselves as part of a continuum that enmeshes the 'supernatural' with the mundane. Even food and drink were more than just nourishment for the body. Frances Reynold shows the huge range of cuneiform writing devoted to the subject, which ranges from ration allocations, over lexical lists of food items, to collections of highly sophisticated recipes. The important social role of 'civilized' food and drink is illustrated in literary compositions, such as the Epic of Gilgamesh. Babylonian fields and orchards produced a variety of cereals and vegetables, most importantly, the salt-tolerant barleys and protein rich pulses, while domestic and wild animals, from sheep to turtles, provided meat which benefited mainly the elite strata of society. Babylonians were beer drinkers; nutritious, made from clean water, it was a safe option in the unsanitary conditions of the cities.

Agricultural productivity was the basis of the Babylonian economy, the subject of Part III. Johannes Renger delivers a general introduction to theoretical issues raised and presents an overview of the main forms of economic organization, from the *oikos* economy of the forth and third millennia to the emergence of a tributary economy at the beginning of the second millennium. He shows the reciprocity and redistribution operated side by side throughout the entire history of Mesopotamia, with the first operating primarily in the 'countryside', while redistribution was the preferred form of operation for the large institutional establishments in the cities. Anne Goddeeris concentrates on developments during the Old Babylonian period which saw the integration of existing self-sufficient household into a patrimonial economy. Of particular consequence was the move towards privatization, as the large institutions, especially the palace, began to rely increasingly on managerial and risk-accepting input from 'the private sector'. While these developments helped to foster entrepreneurship and diversify the economy, they also led to unprecedented insolvency and indebtedness which the many royal decrees sought to alleviate. Frans von Koppen's chapter follows with a closer look at some of the consequences of policies instigated by the First Dynasty of Babylon and shows how the unification of the north and south laid the basis for socio-economic conditions in Babylonia that were to endure for centuries. Michael Jursa, addressing conditions during the first millennium, shows how trends towards monetization of the economy increased, how growing urbanization and population growth intensified agricultural production. The export trade, notably of textiles, continued to bring in revenue in the form of silver. The institutional households, especially temples, were struggling to keep up with diverse and vibrant private firms. Cornelia Wunsch draws on the abundant archive material of one such family firm, the Egibi, who were active in sixth and fifth centuries BC, during a time that saw the end of Babylonian political independence and the beginning of Persian rule. The documents allow a reconstruction of the strategies and opportunities of such companies in their dealings with investors, the state and temples. The archives also document family quarrels, legal challenges and the varying fortunes of subsequent generations and thus allow an unusually detailed view into the world of the late Babylonian business elite.

Part IV assembles contributions about the Babylonian socio-political world. The Czech scholar Petr Charvát shows how Mesopotamian society was configured in the mid-third millennium BC, during the Sumerian (Early Dynastic) period. The hierarchical division structured with a ruler (king) at the top, an elite engaged in the administrative and executive tasks of government, as well as private enterprise, commoners dependent on large institutions and responsible for the provision of services and labour, and the most exploited and underprivileged – enslaved prisoners of war at that time – also persisted in the Babylonian world. Walther Sallaberger explains the workings of the two most important Babylonian institutions, the palace and the temple. Both functioned as centres of economic activities, owning and exploiting large tracts of agricultural land, and significant sectors of the population depended on them for their survival. They competed for resources but played complementary roles in society. Gebhard Selz focuses on the mechanisms that underpinned the exercise of power in Babylonia. He underlines the ideological remit of royal inscriptions that are all too often taken as 'straight' historical data, and the importance of the economic as well as social equilibrium that a successful ruler had to maintain. Mario Fales takes a close look at two of the most prominent ethnic groups, the Arameans and Chaldeans, during the first millennium BC and sets their social history within their particular environmental frameworks. Both joined in the efforts to eliminate Assyrian control of Babylonia, with the Chaldeans in particular bearing the brunt of Assyrian retaliation as well as reaping the rewards by assuming control of the country themselves. The Arameans seemed to have been less united and culturally defined but made a lasting impact on the whole of the Ancient Near East since their language and writing system became the most important vehicle of communication for centuries after the demise of Assyria and Babylonia. Laura Steele's chapter concerns the role of women and gender. It draws particularly on law codes, letters and legal documents. Steele discusses the possibilities and constraints of different classes of women: of free married and eligible upper-class women, of unmarried but free women (such as widows, priestesses and 'prostitutes'), and those who served as slaves.

The conservatism of Mesopotamian culture applies in particular to religion, which is the subject of Part V. Temples lasted for millennia, permanent landmarks of the cities. Lexical tablets from the beginning of writing testify to the antiquity of divine names. However, some deities figure more prominently in myths and rituals than others, some have therefore more personality than others. Brigitte Groneberg, following Laura Steele's chapter with a discussion of the role of goddesses in Mesopotamia, examines how the divine world was not exempt from issues of gender. Her case-study is the city of Nippur during the time of the Third Dynasty of Ur, which is particularly rich in cuneiform sources. She shows not only how the various female deities display different functions, such as healing and protection, but that their cult and personnel were subject to political developments, as well as changes in preference. Joan Goodnick Westenholz concentrates on one particular deity, Inanna/Ishtar, the most colourful divine personalities of the Mesopotamian pantheon. She combines contradictory aspects of character: warlike and compassionate, the seductive embodiment of sexual desire and the regal queen of heaven. Westenholz argues that such mutability was a consequence of the astral dimorphism of the planet Venus, Inanna/Ishtar's celestial embodiment. The prime god of the Babylonians, Marduk, later simply known as Bel, was closely associated with the city of Babylon. Takayoshi Oshima traces his rise, as well as the various kidnappings of the god's statue; Marduk's eventual triumph, elaborated in the famous Epic of Creation, was perhaps the more resounding. His cult endured well into the Hellenistic period. The Babylonians did not just rely on placating the mighty gods with prayers and sacrifices. They attempted nothing less than a coherent early warning system that would decode the hidden messages sent by the gods about their intentions. Stefan M. Maul takes on the arcane and thorny subject of Babylonian divination. Babylonians were acutely conscious of the porosity of human life to supernatural interference. They were also long used to detailed observation of the world, from the movement of the stars to the sometimes bizarre behaviour of human beings and animals. Convinced that all observable phenomena can encode divine messages they set about to systematize procedures and the collection of data. Diviners were the most highly skilled and respected practitioners of cuneiform learning, giving advice to kings and, thus, indirectly influencing the course of history.

Their only rivals were the exorcists engaged in anti-witchcraft rituals. Tzvi Abusch presents an overview of the voluminous cuneiform literature on the subject. This reveals again to what extent fear and anxiety were both fostered and alleviated by a highly complex and prestigious system of neutralizing 'evil'. While in many cultures the suspected 'witch' is socially close, a co-wife or younger brother, whose jealousy or resentment activates an inner force, the Babylonian witch constructed by the texts and rituals, became a pervasive and cosmic power that could only be neutralized by summoning all the divine forces and binding them together in lengthy and elaborate ritual performances.

The separation of religious and intellectual life would not have made much sense for a Babylonian. Here, it serves only to distinguish chapters that are primarily concerned with cuneiform traditions from those that also consider cult and ritual behaviour. Even so, the one would not have functioned without the other. In Part VI, Mark Geller shows that incantations formed an essential part of the healing practice and process, combating the source of the affliction and eliminating obstacles for the patient's recovery, but they were not understood to constitute treatment because this relied on the use of diagnosis and the prescription of medicines. While writing was always restricted to a literate elite throughout Mesopotamian history, there were periods when more people had access to written information. One such time was the Old Babylonian period which saw a proliferation of cuneiform writing. Drawing on the famous palace archive of the Middle Babylonian city of Mari, Dominique Charpin shows that letter writing and sending was widespread and not restricted to the 'large institutions'. A rudimentary but efficient postal system, with relay stations, linked the major centres of the kingdom. It was a vital tool of intelligence at a time when political alliances were formed and reformed continuously. In addition to their historical importance, the letters allow us precious glimpses into people's private affairs. Mathematical skills were indispensable to Babylonian scribes and many school tablets have been preserved showing problems and exercises. Eleanor Robson gives a general account of the various numerical systems, from the sexagesimal to the decimal, methods of computation, arithmetic and the numerical tasks that were performed by Babylonian professional specialists and she explores to what extent these systems allow us insights into the peculiarities of the Babylonian mind. This is also a theme explored by Jon Taylor in his chapter about lexical lists. They were much more than a reference tool, which incidentally have also been invaluable for our contemporary dictionaries of Sumerian and Akkadian. Lists were highly valued as an index of wisdom and cultural continuity reaching back to origins of cuneiform writing. While the appreciation of lexical lists is generally the preserve of specialists, stories provide a much more vivid and accessible entry to the Babylonian world and none better than the story of Gilgamesh. Andrew George, who has recently completed the mammoth task of providing a new edition of all available texts, as well as a modern English translation, himself takes up the guise of a story teller to introduce the scribes who, at different periods of history, were committing the narrative to writing. David Brown's account of Babylonian astronomy charts the development of this 'very Babylonian' discipline from the second millennium onwards. The careful observation of stellar phenomena and the meticulous record keeping over centuries, together with advances in mathematical computation, resulted in astonishingly exact predictions. Brown argues that this shows the methodology and intellectual aim of a true science whose real scope and significance is only beginning to be understood.

Many of the astrologers and astronomers are known to us by name and they formed the apex of Babylonian intelligentsia, the subject of Paul-Alain Beaulieu's article. He looks at the late periods of Mesopotamian civilization, a time when all the powerful empires had long ceased to exist. Some of the temples of the ancient gods continued to operate and they provided a base for scholarly activity which, as Beaulieu shows, always had a theological grounding.

Finally, Part VII sets the Babylonian world within the historical context of the Ancient Near East. David Warburton takes on the other great civilization of antiquity, Egypt, and charts the interconnections between the two, practically non-existent in the beginning, to direct military confrontation in the first millennium. He also provides a detailed account of the complex rivalries between the major and minor states in the mid-second millennium, which is so vividly illuminated by the cuneiform tablets found at Amarna in Egypt. Trevor Bryce, metaphorically speaking from the Hittite capital Hattusa, covers some similar historical ground, but both writers also consider the relationship in terms of ideas, technologies and mutual influence. Petrus Vermaak introduces the notion of 'gateways' to understand the complicated and shifting politics in the Levant and Syria which impacted on Kassite Babylonia despite the policies of containment deployed by Kassite rulers. Assyria was always much closer and Babylonia's fate was, for centuries, directly affected by Assyria's ambition to be the most powerful state in the Near East, as Hannes Galter documents. Israel, by contrast, was never a major adversary as far as the Babylonians were concerned but the Hebrew writers conveyed their situation most memorably, as demonstrated by Baruch Levine. Amélie Kuhrt straddles the camp between Assyriology and Achaemenid studies and draws on sources from both cultures, as well as classical authors to provide an account of how Babylonian fared under Persian rule.

We have seen how scholars of today respond with diligence and acumen to the efforts of their colleagues in antiquity to keep their memory alive. Of all the peoples of the ancient world, the Babylonians were by far the most insistent on addressing an audience beyond their time. The future king, coming across their tablets in the sand, is told to read them carefully and treat them with respect lest their gods avenge neglect with dreadful curses. This desire finds an echo in our time, however foolishly our 'kings' declare the end of history and wreak havoc among 'the cities of the Euphrates'.

PART I
LAND AND LAND USE

CHAPTER TWO

THE WORLD OF
BABYLONIAN COUNTRYSIDES[1]

———•◆•———

Seth Richardson

> The existence of an area of free land, its continuous recession, and the advance of American
> settlement westward explain American development.
>
> Frederick Jackson Turner, *The Significance of the Frontier in American*
> *History*, Columbian Exposition, Chicago, July 12, 1893

INTRODUCTION:
A CIVILIZATION OF VILLAGES

Turner's famous thesis – revolutionary in 1893 – is by now long out of fashion in telling American history, useful only as a talking point for revisions and reappraisals. The original thesis was about a pericentric process: the western frontier, through its cornucopia of resources and refuges, shaped the society of the metropole (the urban East). Frontier history has now become a discipline concerned with the diversity of places (emphasis on the plural) that accommodated a variety of societies, politics, and economies.[2] At the same time, critiques from the fields of geography and comparative politics are reviving attention to spatial relations as an irreducible political element of the state.[3] These critiques are both long-anticipated (especially following the influence of Robert McC. Adams)[4] and newly received by the archaeological arm of Ancient Near Eastern studies.[5]

Historical studies of the Babylonian countryside are only recently looking at place and not process.[6] Whether the countryside was a landscape accommodating Orientalist narratives about the-desert-and-the-sown, the symbiotic thesis of dimorphism, or the passive actor to the expansionist state, the countryside has appeared as an undifferentiated foil to state narratives, rather than a subject in and of itself. One of the results has been to relegate rural political history to the most remote end of antiquity, because histories typically require that urban dominance of their hinterlands be a finished process by the end of the proto-historic period (twenty-fourth century BC) so they can get on with the business of telling stories about territorial states, empires, and international relations.

In material studies of settlement pattern and economy, the Babylonian countryside is commonly avowed to be the major catchbasin for population and production – this society was ninety percent non-urban. The duty of reporting on this thing, "the countryside," is normally considered to be thereby discharged: ex-urban communities seem historically irretrievable, insufficiently represented in documentary sources, and only contingently appearing when intersecting with the particular interests of cuneiform-writing urbanites.[7] Thus has an overwhelmingly rural and agricultural landscape of villages and villagers been upstaged by what we call the world's "first urban civilization."

These constructs sound patently false when stated so baldly, but are difficult to re-orient without the presentation of a counter-narrative. Counter-narrative is, indeed, the conceit of this chapter, but it essays upon territory which is doubly anachronistic: not only was there no native expression for "Babylonia,"[8] but also no single, stable, and emic term for "countryside," either (see Table 2.3). And so what is meant here by "Babylonian countrysides"? I mean to use a geopolitical definition, to refer to those settled zones, no further north than the latitude of Sippar, which looked to second-tier settlements as their central places, rather than to cities, and which were not always securely fastened to the political order of any urban state. It would be a mistake to insist that this refers to only a few places: about half of all known Old Babylonian place names, for instance, are only known from a single attestation,[9] and their political affiliation is then obscure. Excluding the areas that were only environmentally conducive to semi-nomadic pastoralism, "countrysides" here means those settlements and lands that lay beyond the cities' immediate areas of cultivation.

Such divisions are more easily proposed than mapped out. First, "countryside" does not have the typological validity that the designation "city" does (urban variation notwithstanding):[10] it includes rural villages, fishing towns, merchant posts, military fortresses, bandit hideaways, seasonal pastoralist villages, purpose-built new foundations, tribal outfits, private landed manors, kin-based collectives, work camps, and émigré outposts, in a variety of built and natural environments – too much heterogeneity to argue for group consciousness or cognitive unity (hence the plural "countrysides"). A second problem is diachronic: areas sometimes in the "countryside" were not always so: productive fields lying just outside Uruk and Nippur in the thirteenth century BC, for instance, were, by the late eighth century BC, the territories of Aramaean pastoralists, Chaldaean tribesmen, and even Arabian camel-herders.[11]

Third, a functionalist problematic: not everything rural was necessarily "countryside." For instance, Āl-Iškun-Ea was an Old Babylonian village with its own fields; yet it fell within the farmland of the city of Larsa, under its direct and daily administrative control. Under this definition, Āl-Iškun-Ea was not in the countryside, though its character was certainly that of a rural village. Rather, we will focus as much as possible on areas beyond the administrative and legal reach of urban states. This brings us to the *raison d'être* of our definition: "countrysides," well-studied for demography and agricultural production,[12] are here treated as political subjects in order to emphasize their active and agentive roles in political ideology and economic security.

First we will examine demographic characteristics of this rural landscape, its heterogeneous character, and divergences from patterns and periods of state history; next, a look at how countrysides were deployed in urban literatures, to detect this interstitial and non-literate world in the very discourses that hoped to elide it.

A SURVEY OF VILLAGE SETTLEMENT

Early foundations and areas

The earliest settlements in Lower Mesopotamia (*c*.6000 BC) already post-dated a ±3,000-year sequence of farming cultures in the rainfed north, and thus already benefited from a well-developed toolkit of technologies. In hand were all the major domestic herd animals, a long menu of cereal strains, and stable control over ceramics production; the signature adaption for this new alluvial environment was irrigation. Yet although irrigation was the *sine qua non* for farming in Babylonia, irrigation did not require state control (the "hydraulic civilization" model), but was also managed at the level of independent small communities in all periods.[13] The Mesopotamian alluvium could boast some of the most productive agricultural lands of antiquity, but with so many braided, natural channels, irrigation did not so much permit cultivation, as extend and intensify it.

Village settlement gradually extended into the alluvium from the rainfed Zagros foothills, but also by deliberate origin or transplant[14] into wetland ecosystems in southernmost Babylonia, where people had originally subsisted by hunting and fishing, and only later by farming. The intensive agricultural regime of Babylonia helped to create a local specialization of labor between irrigated and non-irrigated areas. The north Mesopotamian mode of mixed farming (single producers with both herds and fields) was never a practical option in the south, where semi-nomadic pastoralism and sedentary farming were particularized in adjacent micro-climates, undertaken by neighboring and economically complementary communities. With the productive cells of pasture and marshland never far away from farming, Babylonia formed a more chambered and differentiated economic landscape than the north.

There were, nevertheless, identifiable sub-regions of Babylonia: a river-plain in the north from Sippar as far south as Nippur, with constantly shifting, meandering channels; a flatter delta plain from Isin to Ur, in which irrigation regimes were more stable; marshlands spreading out to the southeast of Ur; and an estuarial zone beyond that. Regional variation also ran east–west: the Euphrates channels shifted more frequently (with greater consequences for all settlements) than the deeper, lower Tigris.[15] Along the northwestern edge, Uruk, Kiš, and Sippar sat next to a well-defined desert frontier, a steppeland with few permanent settlements, supporting only nomadic herders bringing wool and caprids to market. Along the eastern flank across the Tigris, from the Diyala plain down to the marshlands, cities such as Umma, Girsu, and Lagaš lay along a less severe ecological border, some 15,000 square kilometers of meadowland running up to the Zagros foothills, supporting cattle pasturage and even limited agriculture. In the very south, one might further distinguish a "Lagaš triangle" and an "Uruk triangle." The former, delimited by Lagaš, Larsa and Ur, was continuously settled and cultivated, with its individual fields closely contested and administered; the latter, around Uruk, Larsa, and Ur, featured more open space and free-standing villages, with a looser degree of central control.[16]

How many villages?

Some typologies rank settlements according to function or adjacency, but it seems most useful for present purposes to look at only the smallest sites (hereafter, "villages"),

Table 2.1   Number of villages (≤2 ha.) in selected middle/lower Babylonian areas[a]

Period	Area			
	Uruk	Nippur	Eridu	Total
All sites (in all periods)	466	1,139	190	1,795
Early-Mid Uruk (4000–3500 BC)	53–94[T7]	92[F15]	—	145–186[b]
Late Uruk (3500–3100 BC)	56[F15]–82[T7]	20[F15]	—	76–102
Jemdet Nasr (3100–2900 BC)	63[T7]	23[F18]	—	86
ED I (2900–2750 BC)	38[T7]	22[F19]	—	60
ED II/III (2750–2350 BC)	6[T7]	10[T14,c]	8	24
Akkadian (2334–2193 BC)	7[T14]	8[T14]	—	15
Ur III-Larsa (2112–1800 BC)	27[T14]	43[T14]	12	82
Old Babylonian (1800–1595 BC)	19[T14]	43[T14]	37	99
Kassite (1475–1155 BC)	19[T14]	79[T14]	20	118
post-Kassite MB (1155–626 BC)	10[T14]	48[T14]	18	76

Notes

a   Figures for the Uruk and Nippur areas derive from Adams and Nissen 1972, Table 7 and Figures 15, 18, 19 (F 15, 18, 19), and Adams, 1981, Table 14 (superscripted T7, T14, respectively); figures for Eridu are from Wright's survey (Wright 1981) Fig. 25.

b   This total refers to the range of possible sites whose datation is less secure within the Uruk sequence.

c   Adams 1981: site 1175 is a larger mound, but was probably ≤2 ha. in this period.

those ≤2 hectares (160 meters diameter), with about fifty dwellings and a ±250-person population.[17] These places are difficult to find, not only less identifiable than larger ones by survey, but have also been disproportionately reported where they are closer to large sites. Thus, there were more small villages than survey figures suggest, and especially sites away from cities have been underrepresented, yet still the fluctuations in number tell us something about these early periods.

These survey areas cover only a portion of Babylonia – the north is not represented at all[18] – and the historical periods are not of comparable length.[19] One aspect that stands out clearly in this 3,000-year survey, however, is just how anomalous were the ±500 years of "rural abandonment" in the mid-third millennium; otherwise, Babylonia had always been home to hundreds of small settlements arrayed around a finite number of cities. Most villages at most times could point back to centuries of stable occupation, reinforced by kinship, property, or administrative mandate. Despite this stability, only rarely did these tiny places ever become larger; conversely, villages were almost never the result of the dwindled occupation of a previously larger place.[20] Villages were typologically adapted to environmental niches, purpose-built (like cities) into the landscape to serve particular needs.

More important than aggregate numbers, village settlement did not always move in lock-step with the fortunes of urban states. Two sequences of small-site longevity (i.e., sites which survived across period-lines) can be discerned, one in the Early–Middle–Late Uruk, another from Ur III to Kassite times. These were both long stretches of time during which the number and size of major cities fluctuated drastically, but many villages maintained continuous occupation sequences which must be understood on their own terms, not as responses to urban expansion and collapse.[21]

Table 2.2   Distribution of settlements as percentage of total occupational area (Adams 1981)

	ca. 2ha	*ca. 7ha*	*ca. 15ha*	*ca. 30ha*	*ca. 100ha*	*ca. 200ha*
Late ED	3.1	6.8	4.5	7.2	66.3	12.1
Akkadian	6.1	12.4	9.5	8.5	63.6	—
Ur III-Larsa	10.5	14.6	8.8	11.0	40.4	14.7
OB	12.1	17.6	8.4	11.7	39.1	11.2
Kassite	25.2	31.6	8.0	4.6	30.6	—
MB	32.5	31.8	4.9	14.6	16.2	—

In the Uruk region, thirty-five of fifty-three villages identifiable in the Early Uruk were still occupied in the Late Uruk (±500 years), but no more than 200 years later, only seven of those original villages were still there, and no Uruk village appears to have survived into the ED II/III. Meanwhile, the number of villages with single-period-only occupation was much higher during the transitional Jemdet Nasr and ED I than in preceding or succeeding phases.[22] The period 3100–2750 BC was, then, a time of wholesale abandonment of older villages, with only a few new ones replacing them; this subtle change would be hidden if one only looked at overall numbers of village sites.

The Ur III-Kassite longevity sequence presents something of the opposite picture: it crosses the OB collapse, characterized by massive deurbanization in all areas. Indeed, viewed as a snapshot by period, there was a sudden doubling of villages, but it must be stressed that this was accomplished by the survival of existing villages with the addition (rather than substitution) of new foundations.

Table 2.2 shows an emphatic growth in village (and a dramatic decrease in city) occupational space. Around Nippur, the number of villages crested in the Kassite period (Ur III: 43, OB: 43, Kassite: 79, MB: 48), but many of these replaced the existing inventory. A majority (61 per cent[n=48]) of Kassite-period villages were new, but the majority (70 per cent[n=30]) of OB villages had also survived. In the following Middle Babylonian period, the majority (77 per cent[n=37]) of villages were precisely these new Kassite towns, and only three of the OB villages (6.9 per cent) now remained. A ruralizing transition had taken place, but it occurred *within* the Kassite period, not *between* OB and Kassite times.[23] Where the Uruk sequence had terminated with few villages of any kind (and massive urbanization), the second millennium sequence involved not only growth in village populations, but also their gradual relocation to different sites, a complex outcome to a *longue durée* ruralization trend.[24] Down to the Parthian period, cities and towns indeed continued to strongly re-emerge, but the number of tiny villages never stopped growing by leaps and bounds.[25]

Varietals: environment, typology, and adaptation

Most villages were socially and economically organized around primary agricultural production, yet these regimes always displayed heterogeneity and specialization. Settlement layout of even the smallest villages displayed a great range of form, including: multiple, paired, or composite pattern-clusters; tiny sites laid out in ring-shape;

with canals radiant in all directions; with enclosing walls, large institutional buildings, or fortresses.[26] Layout patterns show differential community access to irrigation water and, thus, different relationships both between rural neighbors, and with urban authorities. Some villages in linear-array along riverbanks needed no communal organization for water access;[27] others, supplied with water via take-offs directly from major watercourses, required only modest interdependence; still others, employing the lowest dendritic levels of large managed canal systems, coordinated their activities closely with state authorities (e.g., in *ugāru*-districts).

Other primary and secondary subsistence modes flourished in the micro-environments which permitted specialized[28] orchard and reed cultivation, fresh- and saltwater fishing, and water buffalo husbandry; yet others provided secondary services of trade and transport when they were located on important waterways. Archaeological survey has indicated specialized production at even the smallest sites, with some villages exhibiting high concentrations of brick- or pottery-kiln slag, luxury goods (e.g., copper finds), or even status objects such as maceheads, wall cones, obsidian, and stone bowls.[29] Other occupational communities – millers, brewers, ox-drovers, soldiers – were stationed in non-urban places, leaving traces only in the textual record. These varieties of layout and function reveal a textured landscape amidst the verities of primary production, stable across time and space. Compare these against the range of toponymic terminologies in use: Table 2.3 illustrates the wide variety of terms from a single historical period alone, each with its own administrative,[30] social, or geographic particularity. While none of these terms was exclusive of all others, the proliferate terminology reveals a spectrum of differentiation: permutations of character were as numerous as permutations of terms and forms.[31]

THE COUNTRYSIDE IN URBAN LITERATURES

Belles-lettres and law

From earliest times, the *mise-en-scène* of Mesopotamian literary narrative was firmly rooted in the urban landscape.[32] Deserts, steppes, and wastelands were employed in Sumerian stories and poetry as loci of disorder, danger, and backwardness. In proverb collections, Dumuzi songs,[33] and etiologies such as the "Marriage of MAR.TU" (featuring the notorious raw-flesh-eating nomad), the countryside acted as literary counterpoise to the organized safety of the cities. Rural village life was rarely depicted for its own sake, though pastoral images were not uncommon: in the "Debate between Winter and Summer," Summer claims credit for the abundance of rural households (é), farmsteads (é.meš), and villages (é.duru₅); a Lagaš hymn praises the countryside for its wine; the prosperous fields and villages of Zabalam are the place to which the uncouth Gudam, unfit for city life, is remanded by the goddess Inanna.[34] Few pieces, however, chose rural life as a subject for celebration. Even the late "Farmer's Instructions," though set entirely in the fields, never suggests that its "farmers" are countryfolk – the piece is no Theokritan *Idyll*. The "Debate between the Hoe and the Plow" is a rare exception, not only celebrating the Hoe's superiority, but also asserting a note of disdain for the urban, elite Plow. The home of the Hoe is with the laborers, in their reed-huts out in the plains and along the riverbanks – Hoe tells Plow, in a nearly unique expression of "country pride" and separatism:

Table 2.3   Old Babylonian Sumero-Akkadian varietal terms for countryside places

CIVIL SETTLEMENTS

āl pāṭi	"border town"
āl-PN	"village of PN"
dadmū	"settlements (and inhabitants)"
du₆-GN	"ruin-mound of GN"
é / é-PN / é-DN	"house (of PN/DN)"
é.duru₅ (*adurû / edurû*)	"hamlet"
é.duru₅-PN (*kaprum*-PN)	"village/outfit of PN"
é.há / é.há *Kaššî*	"encampments"
kar-GN / ᵘʳᵘkar-GN / ᵘʳᵘkar.há	"harbor(s)"
kuštāru ᶜᴬᴰ ᴷ ⁶⁰¹ ᵈ	"tent (encampment)"
maškan-GN / *maškan*-RN	"farmstead (of GN/RN)" (lit. "threshing floor")
*nammaššû*ᵈ (~ á.dam) ᶜᴬᴰ ᴺ¹²³⁴	"settlement, habitation"
ᵘʳᵘGN / ᵘʳᵘGN₁ ša ᵘʳᵘGN₂	"town, town₁ of (larger) town₂"
uru.ki(-PN) (*kaprum*(-PN))	"farms (of PN)"
uru.meš / uru.didli.didli / uru.didli.ma.da / *ālī ṣiḫruti* ᶜᴬᴰ §¹⁸¹ᵃ	~ "little towns"

ROYAL/MILITARY INSTALLATIONS

*āl ḫalṣi / ḫalṣu*ᶜ	"fortress (town), district"	é kaskal	"caravanserai"
*birtum*ᶜ	"fortress, fortified district"	é-RN / uru.ki-RN	"royal household"
dimtu / dimat-PNᶜ	"tower, (fortified) district"	Iškun-DN/-RN	"emplacement (of DN/RN)"
*dunnum*ᶜ	"fort, fortified area"	(uru.)izi.gar	"watch-tower"
dūr-GN / *dūr*-RN	"fortress (of GN/RN)"		(lit. "torch-place")

DISTRICTS/AREAL UNITS

a.gàr / a.gàr-PN	"irrigation district (of PN)"	*lētu*	"nearby region"
*abunnatu*ᵈ	"center of the country"	*libbu mātim*	"countryside, heartland"
aburru	"pasture by the city wall"	*limītu*ᶜ	"adjacent region"
aḫāt āli	"side of the city"	*mātu / māt* GN	"land/territory (of GN)"
bal.ri / gú íd.[FN]	"bank of the river FN"	*mērештu ša* GN	"cultivated land of GN"
ḫamātu	"open country, plain"	*namû* (é/a.ri.a)	"pasture, steppe"
erṣet GNᵇ	"land (lit. earth) of GN"	*pan ṣēri*	"before-the-steppe"
išru / išrātu	"rural district(s)"	*pilkātu (ša* PN)	"district (of PN)"
kīdū / kīdātu	"outskirts, countryside	*ṣēru* (edin)	"steppeland"

DELIMITATIONS

*itû*ᶜ	"boundary, territory"
kisurrû (ki.sur.ra)	"boundary"
*pāṭu*ᶜ	"border (district)"
pilku (in.dub)	"boundary"

a   This list is illustrative, not exhaustive. Excluded here are terms in use only at Mari (e.g., *ḫaṣāru, ḫamqum ša* GN, *namlaktu*) and those which only later had one of the substantial meanings above (e.g., *miṣru* in the OB is only used in the sense of the edge of a field, not a territory).

b   Attested at multiple, overlapping levels of administrative geography; i.e., an *erṣet*-GN may include dozens of *ugārū*, but individual plots of land within those *uguaru* may also be called *erṣet (ša* a.gàr).

c   Denotes areal and local units in context.

d   Use limited to literary contexts.

(The laborer and his family) can rest because of me in a cool, well-built
  dwelling.
And when the fire-side makes the hoe gleam, and they lie on their side,
You are not to go to their feast![35]

Little in Akkadian literature contradicts the premise of this urban bias. City and
land often appear as word pairs, as in *ludlul bēl nēmeqi*: "My city frowns on me as an
enemy; indeed my land is savage and hostile."[36] In isolated instances, the countryside
is served up in pastorales as an image of purity[37] or stolidity,[38] and some ambitious
poetics extended the sun god's protection over even "he whose family is remote, whose
city is distant . . . so far as human habitations stretch, you (Šamaš) grant revelations
to them all."[39] Rural locales could even play host to divine chapels or other small
religious establishments.[40] Most often, however, rural lands were social voids, home
only to the brigand and the fox, places from which gods were simply absent; only
cities were the true seats of the civilization ordered by divinities and kings.

The countryside is also missing from early law. Since even the political relations
of urban rulers and subjects had not been legally clarified, it is unsurprising that no
constitutional system of state and land was articulated. Kingship only resided, strictly
speaking, within cities, and state and personal status[41] were legally defined by city
and class – not territory.[42] One notes the disparity between the insistent demarcation
of boundaries in royal inscriptions, and their utter absence in the law codes; there is
also a mutual exclusion in the codes between the term "dumu GN" (also in common-
use) and the relative class structure of *awīlum-muškēnum-wardum*. "Jurisdiction," as
such, was an absent feature. We are presented with the seeming conundrum of states
that had sovereignty externally, but were internally segmentary; consequently any
discussion of constituted, Westphalian states is anachronistic.[43] The ambiguated
internal political relations of the state were mirrored in its legal structures, which
persisted in a multiplicity of executive, precedentary, and traditional laws. The rare
mention of the countryside in the law codes (2100–1750 BC), however, leaves little
doubt that the state's legal power did not extend continuously into the hinterlands.
If a slave ran away to the countryside,[44] or an ox was killed by a lion *ina ṣērim*,[45] no
legal remedy was offered by the state, only a regulation for compensation between
private individuals. The palace household simply did not have the ability (though
certainly the ambition) to assert power everywhere.[46] Rather, royal legal authority
was fully vested in rural areas only where the crown acted as founder and owner, e.g.,
fortresses and garrison towns.[47]

Politics and rhetoric: the third millennium

Turning to historiographic inscriptions, it becomes rapidly apparent that the state
had deeper interests in the countryside. The earliest royal narratives were not only
largely concerned with conflicts over rural borders (especially the Gu'edenna fields
between Lagaš and Umma), but the cause, action, and even the physical texts themselves
were set in the countryside. The "Stele of the Vultures" monument of Eanatum, ruler
of Lagaš, was erected on the boundary line of the irrigated farmland, and the text
mentions at least two fields (Dana-in-Kiḫara and Badag) by name. His subsequent
inscriptions document many other fields: Usurda'u, Sumbubu, Eluḫa, Kinari, Du'ašri,

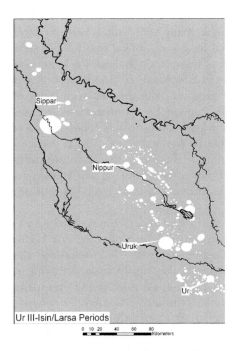

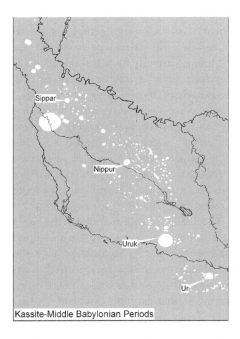

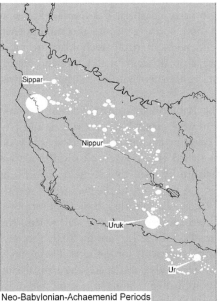

WHITE AREAS represent productive zones based on site size, population estimate, and minimal sustenance requirements, as follows:

Populations were estimated according to site size (see n.49) at a constant residential density of 75 persons per hectare.

Assuming minimal caloric needs of 250 kg barley per person per annum, and an annual production rate of 881 kg barley / hectare, every hectare of occupied settlement required roughly 21 hectares of sustaining area.

These figures are closely adapted from the working standards of the Oriental Institute's Modeling Ancient Settlement Systems (MASS) Project, developed by Tony Wilkinson.

© Carrie Hritz, Oriental Institute MASS Project

Figure 2.1   Sustaining areas of Babylonian settlements, including sites of all sizes.

Du'Urgiga, and Lumagirnunta-šakugepada.[48] This detailed knowledge of specific fields at the edge of the state illustrates (as much as the conflict itself) how crucial these productive areas were to the state. Yet claims were not control: a mid-twentieth-century AD "Sumerian temple state" model took many such state claims of total control over hinterlands at face value, but it has long been shown that neither state nor temple directly owned more than a fraction of these lands. Indeed, the Lagaš case may have been anomalous: only in this area was Babylonia so densely settled and cultivated. In most places and periods, open space was available on many sides of almost every major city, and the modest production catchment-areas of these cities do not suggest that either daily administration or political control of hinterlands was "naturally" consequent. Figure 2.1,[49] which models the actual production zones of all identified Babylonian sites in three different periods, shows that non-contiguity of production was the norm in most periods. Borders were political and ideological constructs, not the natural result of material conditions, and border-conflict thus not necessarily a paradigm for early states.

The Lagaš-Umma texts describe constantly shifting boundary lines, revealing the vital interest of the central authority to establish a spatial basis of power. At Lagaš, the border was first marked by a "no-man's land" between the Nun-canal and the Gu'edenna; then at a levee called Namnundakigara; then again from Antasura to Edimgalabzu; yet again to a place called Mubikura; the last ruler would eventually claim the boundary of Lagaš had historically run "to the sea."[50] Contemporaneously, King Lugalzagesi of Uruk meticulously detailed an eleven-sided point-to-point boundary demarcated by canals, fortresses, and villages.[51] The political and legal relations of persons collected within these Sumerian city-state boundaries is elusive, but royal interest in borders is not in doubt. In early northern Babylonia, extension of state control over the countryside was even more contingent and incomplete than the comprehensive system of the south, and independent rural freeholds were more common in hinterlands surrounding Kiš, Sippar, and Akšak.[52] In all times and places, however, it was in the state's interest to tell its constituent audiences that its power across space was unlimited.

And then, all of the physical features of the Babylonian countryside disappeared in Sargonic royal inscriptions; the concerns here were city walls, city rulers, and city dwellers. The conceptual map of the Akkadian state incorporated no landscapes beyond the city walls.[53] Sargon claimed to have demolished three dozen city-walls in wars throughout Sumer; Rimuš expanded this campaign by also "expelling" (>*wāṣû*) tens of thousands of city people into the countryside.[54] A typology of the conquered reveals that exile meant non-existence: those killed and taken prisoner, the physically destroyed, were at the bottom; at the top were those granted subject status and still within the political realm; those "expelled," however, were also said to be "annihilated," because those discorporated from urban communes were political non-beings. There never was any reckoning of victory in terms of land – only in body counts, and the capitulation of specific, named elite persons. Instead of geographic expressions of control, we must read clues such as temple-hymn lists to discern the extent of Akkadian control – a pointillist state, elite by elite, household by household, city by city.[55]

Yet Sargonic rule could never afford to neglect rural borderlands: letters between administrators show that villages still acted as boundary-markers, that persons who were "citizens" (dumu GN) should not reside in or flee to other city-states, and that local elites continued to compete for territory even within the bounds of the larger kingdom.[56] It was an Akkadian administrative practice to create new agricultural estates by uniting lands formerly belonging to two city-states, but this did not so much alter some (chimeric) fixity of city-state boundaries as it weaned the allegiance of elites away from specific cities. The dynasty was chiefly content to control urban nodes of power by retaining city rulers (ensí's) as provincial governors, and govern the countryside via a manorial system of clientage (in the south) and royal estates (in the north), with a few "intercity" administrative outposts providing further control of interstitial areas in the south.[57] When the Akkadian state fell, there was a resurgence of interest in local borders: Gudea, ruler of Lagaš, was the first to proclaim legal protections for persons within the city-state borders (ki.sur.ra GN), and gave to the goddess Nanše the epithet "lady of the boundary" (nin.in.dub.ba).[58] Utu-ḫegal of Uruk, who soon after conquered Lagaš, was also concerned with restoring its boundaries – not against foreign encroachment, but against "the man of Ur."[59]

City-state borders simply never became superannuated within larger states until the first millennium;[60] internal, rural hinterlands remained contested places that required the exercise of political control. After the recovery of territories from Elam, Ur-Namma of Ur "determined" (KA . . . gi) boundaries of the city-gods of a half-dozen city-provinces in his famous "cadastre" text,[61] and ki.sur.ra's are known for five more Ur III cities.[62] Borders were not uniformly demarcated: some provincial borders were simply lines connecting four points, others connecting more than twenty-seven,[63] and neither the ordering (i.e., N-S-E-W)[64] nor the terminology (both ki.sur.ra and á are used) of boundaries was fixed. Multiple features acted as border-markers: towers, villages, canals, riverbanks, hills, shrines, households, and tells (no inscribed monuments are mentioned). Only the vaguest expressions ever suggest a "national" boundary: Ur-Namma mentions a "border of the land of Sumer" (in.dub.ki.en.gi), and Ibbi-Sin's seventeenth year celebrated the submission of the Amorites of the "southern border" (á-IM.ùlu).[65] The "core" provinces were administered by a dual system of provincial rulers (city ensí's) and generals (šagina's) whose zones of authority did not always coincide geographically. To say that šagina's controlled the countrysides would be simplistic, but they indeed tended to be *novi homini* remunerated with rural estates; meanwhile, the growing number of villages demanded closer rural governance.

The Old Babylonian period (2004–1595 BC)

By the turn of the millennium, countryside boundaries formed a patchwork of private, city-state, temple, and manorial lands. The second millennium would see not only the expansion of palatial regimes, but also a recalibration of royal authority within and without city walls. During these four critical centuries, states became increasingly shaped by rural populations. Before the Old Babylonian period was over, in fact, cities and temples would have to begin a long struggle to preserve their holdings from the state by protectionist measures.[66] The designations "Amorite" and "Akkadian," once perceived by scholars to be ethnic designations, likely acquired geographical meanings in this time, i.e., non-urban and urban peoples. Twentieth- and nineteenth-century rulers asserted chieftaincy of Amorites – but later OB rulers claimed kingship over Amorite *lands*.[67] Early kings in these dynasties were slow to adopt urban royal titles: not until Iddin-Dagan did a First Isin dynasty ruler claim to be a "king of

Isin"; no "king of Larsa" until Gungunum (fifth dynast); no "king of Babylon" until Hammurabi (sixth dynast).[68] The twin ideologies reflected urban and non-urban power bases, pointed up by the continued use of both old, established titles such as "king of the land of Sumer and Akkad," but also epithets addressing new, national audiences: "true supreme authority/god of his nation" and "lord who extended the land."[69]

Only in the southernmost Babylonian kingdom of Larsa did local borders remain an important topic in royal rhetoric – and here only prior to 1800 BC, and limited to those areas of the old Lagaš[70]and Ur states. Warad-Sîn paid some deference to Nanna's ki.sur.ra at Ur, and Nūr-Adad also to Utu's at Larsa (both probably concessions following their usurpations); Sîn-iddinam connected the Tigris River to "the [eastern] border, the boundary of *my choice* (ki.sur.ra in.dub.pà.mu.še)."[71] Much more pronounced across all four centuries of the period were claims to have resettled "scattered people" (unság.du$_{11}$.ga). Šu-ilišu of Isin (fl. 1980 BC) boasted of regathering people of Ur from as far as the border of Anšan and "the upper and lower lands" in the land around Isin (GN ma.da.sig.nim); Nūr-Adad settled possibly "captive people" (un dab$_5$.dab$_5$) around Larsa and Ur (latterly, within "Nanna's boundary"); Rīm-Sîn gathered Jamutbal people at Keš; Hammurabi gathered the scattered of Sumer and Akkad (in his thirty-third year-name) and of Isin (in his law code); Samsuiluna, those of Idamaraṣ, Ešnunna, and Warûm.[72] Towards the latter half of the OB, the former "scatteredness" of people was de-emphasized in favor of their "settledness" in pastoral quietude, perhaps reflecting some demographic change.[73] The extent and nature of these "resettlements" is unlikely ever to become clear (in part, the claim is antiphonic to poetic motifs of "scattered" people in city-laments), but what is certainly new in the OB is the expression of royal responsibility for the residence of non-urban people in official rhetoric.

The management of non-urban populations by OB kings went hand-in-hand with the progressive ruralization of Babylonia.[74] There was a fundamental shift not only in the socio-economic makeup of the state, but also in the ideological content of "the land" in royal titulary. Individual royal titles were never synecdochic to some super-category of kingship; when Abi-sare, for instance, is described as "King of Ur, King of Larsa," these were not attributes of some overall kingliness, they were two distinct and separate titles. Accordingly, two observations about the countryside: first, kingship over the "land" (of "the l. of Sumer and Akkad," of "his l.," of "all the Amorite l.," etc.) was parallel, not paramount, to these segementary kingships;[75] second, the deferential epithets of stewardship often used to politely indicate city rule (e.g., "provider/protector for GN"[76]) were rarely used for the *mātum*. There was a newfound concern for popular politics, that the royal works ("the wonder of the nation") and person ("resplendent to remote places") would be seen by publics near and far. "I let the nation," Warad-Sîn wrote, "see the greatness of my kingship" (he even inquired of Nanna *how* to "make the people know [it]"). His construction of the Nergal temple at Ur was to evoke the "wonder of numerous people *like a distant mountain*," explicitly targeting non-urbanites as the audiences for monumental architecture.[77] Royal rhetoric was now specifically concerned with the happiness of the land, part of a new political discourse binding up space, distance, and nationhood.[78]

Politicization of the countryside was a double-edged sword for the state. On the one hand, the countryside was a source of power. OB kings appealed directly to rural constituencies by regulating market prices (even if notionally),[79] and declarations of "justice" (nì.si.sá)[80] and debt relief[81] which all specified "the land" and its inhabitants as specific beneficiaries. OB kings were also energetic in their detailed administration of productive lands, the source of institutional wealth and political entitlements.[82] Administrators called *šapir mātim* (and *šapir nārim, ḫalṣim*), *bēl dimti*, and *rabiānum* held authority over lands undefined by any city.[83] A term for rural citizenship (*mār(at) mātim*) begins to be attested,[84] and also rural assemblies (villages which gather and "speak with one voice")[85] and councils of elders *šībūt* GN/*māti*). Among these sons-of-the-soil were people settled in ex-urban fortresses, on whom kings increasingly relied as their military base.[86] On the other hand, the countryside was politically volatile. The "rebellious land" is alluded to in many royal inscriptions which make clear that the enemies they discuss were abroad in the state's own countrysides: Larsa's wars against Pī-nārātim, Ammiditana's against Araḫab, "man of the lands," Ammiṣaduqa's letters about enemies *ina libbi mātim*, the emergent ḫāpiru, etc.[87] The state's engagement of the *mātum* and exposure to its dangers were closely related aspects of a single dynamic which changed the nature of the state itself.[88] Comparing the archaeological and textual records, one observes that although palatial dynasties did not survive the "Dark Age" of the sixteenth/fifteenth centuries, rural corporations endured as the foundations of state power in the second half of Mesopotamian history.

National states (1475–985 BC)

In the next epoch, a succession of national, dynastic states arose, replacing city-state confabulations with genuine territoriality; this territory finally had a name, *māt Karduniaš* (lit. "land of the quay of the god Duniaš").[89] Though a unified Babylonia was now the rule, there were periodic and areal exceptions. Political unification of the Kassite state was not accomplished until *c.*1475 BC with the overthrow of the long-lived "Sealand Dynasty" of the marshy south.[90] The "Sealand" was kept as a province and perhaps tacitly honored in early Kassite titulary, preserving the kingship of Ur. This area periodically reasserted its autonomy: a second[91] dynasty (1025–1005 BC) extended as far north as Nippur, and repeated provincial uprisings came during later Assyrian domination. A short-lived Bazi Dynasty (originally Bīt-Bazi, 1004–985 BC) was based in the northeast reaches across the Tigris in the old "Jamutbal" region.[92] The most important post-Kassite state, however, was the earlier second Isin Dynasty (1157–1026 BC), which brought back the cult image of Marduk from Elam to Babylon, and thereby expounded a rhetoric of proto-nationalist unity.

The early Kassite administrative system developed around *pīḫatū* ("districts"); at least twenty are known, with most provincial designations still in use six centuries later.[93] Ten were governed by officials called *šakin māti* ("governor of the land"), others by a *šakkanak ša* (or *bēl*) *pīḫāti* or *šaknu* GN, but the scope of powers of these governors is unclear. Still other Babylonian rural provinces were under the residual tenancies of autarkic Kassite "households" (*Bīt-PN/DN/GN*). Headmen of these areas (especially east of the Tigris) indeed operated as governors, but their title was *bēl bīti* ("lord of the household") rather than *bēl pīḫāti*. The administrative geography is difficult to clarify: of twenty *pīḫātū*, five were called Bīt-GN – but more than 90 other places called Bīt-GN were either villages within provinces, or large territories outside the provincial system altogether. These territorial "households" were often substantial in size (containing several settlements, e.g. the twelve towns of Bīt-Enlil), with defined borders (im.si.sá, im.mar.tu, etc.), their own lands (*māt* GN),[94] their own officials (e.g. *ḫazannu*'s). A *bēl bīti* who controlled such an area was, nevertheless, no independent tribal ruler, but still a *de jure* administrator who had to be "installed" (> *šakānu*) by the king.[95]

Rural lands were also classified by watering district (*ugār* GN) and source of irrigation water (*kišād nār* GN); other fields were called *ḫarbu*, cultivated under institutional plow-teams.[96] Another important form of tenancy was the royal grant of land, known from *narû*-monuments, given to (usually noble) individuals for service. These grant-lands typically provided a sustaining area for about 200 persons, but they were not normally politically autonomous or tax exempt, as temple lands sometimes were.[97] It cannot be said that feuds were a dominant mode of rural land-holding; what can be said, however, is that rural fiefs were a normal feature of securing elites to the Crown.[98] There were, in short, feuds without feudalism, and the effect was to distribute political capital across the rural landscape,[99] amidst tribal territories and administrative districts that were overwhelmingly village-based. Most cities were now enclaves isolated within open productive land that stretched out to the steppe (*ṣēru*), an area now distinguished as "open country" (*pān ṣēri*).[100] One feels keenly the increasing insularity of cities in post-Kassite chronicles and royal inscriptions detailing the despoliation of "cult cities" by Aramaean invaders abroad in Babylonia.

Intrastate boundaries persisted, now more often denoted by province than by city or city-god.[101] Most terms for internal borders went out of use by the end of the period,[102] but many *narû*-texts (despite curse-warnings) either altered or "re-established" boundaries, a redistricting which seemingly accelerated in the immediate post-Kassite period.[103] Rural *pīḫātū* were not bedrock social communities, but administrative units subject to revision. Unfortunately, we have a poverty of data regarding the legal status of rural persons in relation to larger communities beyond knowing that independent freeholds and freeholders did exist alongside a growing class of dependent *ikkaru*-farmers.[104] Virtually no information about the sale or lease of rural fields exists outside of the *narû*'s (already exceptional cases), except insofar as they show that the king's right to dispose of tracts of land was not unlimited. In sum, the post-Kassite sources present a paradox: an overwhelmingly rural society with little textual comment devoted to countrysides.

From hetarchy to core to borderland (985–129 BC)

With the advent of the Aramaean irruptions into the Babylonian countryside, yet another articulation of land and society came into force. Tribes took advantage of the divided dynastic situation to occupy fields even at the very outskirts of Babylon and Borsippa, but chronicles also report the deliberate "scattering" of some urbanites into the countryside by invading Elamites.[105] The extent to which ruralization was a reversion to rural subsistence, and how much a result of occupation by new peoples is an open question. Evidence is sparse: Nippur, the largest source of Middle Babylonian documentation, produced little about the countryside between the eleventh and eighth centuries except patchy reports about brigands and hostile tribes throughout the lands.[106] Several large Chaldaean (Bīt-Dakkūru, -Amukanu, -Jakīn) and Aramaean (Gambūlu, Puqūdu) tribes became more politically prominent in later centuries, but in this time no single group dominated the countrysides: chronicle refers to the incursion of "105 kings of the lands of the Aḫlamu" and the "(numerous) houses of the land of the Aramaeans."[107]

These tribes did not form any essential state-level unity, and the insistence of inscriptions and chronicles on their hostility to "cult-cities" does not indicate any organized control of the countryside. Throughout the first millennium BC, there were resident in Babylonia more than 175 (mostly Chaldaean) groupings called *Bīt-*(PN/DN/GN) and twenty-nine distinct Aramaean tribes that did not all "belong" to the five larger groups. Toponymic variants point to fifty-plus settlements simply called *ḫuṣṣēti* ("the reed huts"), others simply named *bītāti* ("the houses"), *kaprini* ("the villages"), *bīrāti* ("the forts"). Urban documents show little interaction with most of these tribes: 119 (68 percent) of Chaldaean "households" and 18 (62 percent) of Aramaean tribes are attested only once or twice. The further away groups were located from cities, the less specific geographic knowledge is attested: thirty-nine settlements of Bīt-Amukanu, around Nippur, Uruk, and Isin, are known by name (twenty-seven close to Uruk); sixteen settlements of Bīt-Dakkūru, on the western fringes between Borsippa and Uruk; and only eleven of Bīt-Jakīn, in the deep Sealand south, most named only in Assyrian sources.[108] Babylonian texts documented primarily *ḫaṭru-*lands parcelled out to state clients (*bīt-qašti, -narkabti, -sīsê, -kussê*), dependent farm-steads, and the vast estates of banker-families such as the Murašûs,[109] but the toponymy and population of Babylonian villages were now overwhelmingly West Semitic.[110] Many Aramaean tribes practiced seasonal transhumance (ranging as far as Syria), but Chaldaean settlements were sedentary at an earlier point, and often fortified. By 700 BC, Chaldaeans were also resident in the Babylonian cities, and Arab settlements had moved into Bīt-Dakkūru and Bīt-Amukanu in "walled towns, each surrounded by numerous unwalled hamlets."[111]

The political structures of rural groups are obscured by the etic, statist terms used to describe them. The Assyrian kings Šalmaneser III (850 BC) and Adad-nerāri III (c.800 BC) would refer to Chaldaean "kings" as tributary, but gifts inscribed by Bīt-Dakkūru and Bīt-Jakīn leaders use instead titles such as *šaknu ša* GN or simply "son/descendant of GN," even when referring to their "palaces." Our best information about political power in the countryside derives from the accusations against the Dakkūrian Nabû-šuma-iškun, who expelled Babylonian citizens to the steppe and "directed his attention (away) from Babylon to his own land," which he mobilized by "treaty and oath" (*adê u māmīt*). The formalities of "lords" and "servants" were employed in letters between headmen, but the basis of tribal politics was "brotherhood," and rule possible only when there was a *primus inter pares*.[112] Yet within a generation, some of these ambitious chieftains (with tribal backing) would seize Babylonian kingship: a certain Baba-aḫa-iddina, called a *paqid mātāti* ("caretaker of the lands") was probably the same man elevated to kingship c.812 BC; around 770 BC, the first certifiably Chaldaean king, Erība-Marduk of Bīt-Jakīn, would take the throne of Babylon.[113] This hardly initiated a "Chaldaean" dynasty, however: within the next forty years the throne would be usurped by leaders of Bīt-Dakkūru and Bīt-Amukanu before returning to a Jakīnite, Marduk-apla-iddina II.

By the mid-eighth century BC, a twin system of authority held sway where lands were either royal or loyal: the *bēl pīḫatu* and *šakin ṭēmi* emerged as important officers, with powers even over the disposition of land grants. Aramean, Chaldaean, and Kassite tribal territories were under the authority of powerful sheikhs (*nasīku*, *ra'su*, and *bēl bīti*, respectively).[114] Their jurisdictions were only local, but with powers close to kingship within their own lands. Urban officials now needed active alliances with rural chieftains for their cities to survive. Nippur's *šandabakku*, for instance, was semi-independent from the Crown at Babylon, but this was due to (rather than resulting in) his alliances with tribal chiefs. Multi-centered, hetarchic political authority now prevailed in Babylonian lands,[115] balanced precariously throughout the coming sixth to fourth centuries when Babylon was simultaneously an imperial world capital and satrapal seat. The term (*māt*) Karduniaš had fallen into complete desuetude (except in Assyrian parlance); kings of Babylon might proclaim themselves "King of (the land of) Sumer and Akkad," but only *māt Akkadî* was still in independent use outside of this phrase. In the south, little land remained attached to urban corporations, and Bīt-Jakīn and the Sealand (*māt Tâmti*) occupied a vast swath of territory. The distribution that pertained prior to 2000 BC (i.e., a rural/tribal north, and a densely urbanized south) was almost fully reversed after 1000 BC. Babylonian cities, once the nuclei of bordered, cellular territories, now sat on frontiers between tribal countrysides. In the millennium prior to the eighth century AD founding of Baghdad, this transformation was amplified at the superregional level, too: where Babylonia had for 3,000 years been the urbanized center of the Ancient Near East, it was, for the next 1,000 years, a borderland between other empires – first Rome and Parthia, then Byzantium and Sassania.

CONCLUSION

The state is first of all a claim; it carries a constant and urgent burden to present and re-present itself as natural, to achieve an elusive coextensivity with its landscape.[116] Every day the state must wake up and cajole, propagandize, persuade, and coerce its constituencies and clientele, using powers only made real when exercised. The identity of the Mesopotamian state with the land was asserted (as most propaganda is) through a deliberate disambiguation of social relations and political unity, a discourse created from the elision of affinities which never ceased to be multiple, overlapping, or hermetic (e.g., groups based on law, ethnicity, household relations). Nor did "unity" always require poetic sleight-of-hand: it was inscribed at the most fundamental levels of signification. The Sumerian sign UN (Akk. *nišū*) "people" and kalam (Akk. *mātu*) "land," for instance, is one and the same.[117] This imbrication of meaning is common to most languages, and implicit within translation issues – when is *mātu* "land," when is it "country," "kingdom," "nation," "countryside"? – but the symbolism is no less arbitrary and constructed.[118] What the state wished most to obscure was that it was not natural, but a network of urban elites resting atop irreducibly local hierarchies; the image it wished to assert was that the state was cellular and uninterrupted in space. Yet sub-state constituencies – competing, coexisting, collaborating – never ceased *to act politically*, even when they had no political ambition of achieving state identity.

Two specific episodes illustrate this rhetorical foreshortening, and the implacable specificity of place. Gudea, a ruler of Lagaš in the twenty-second century BC, presented the analogue of the land to be the (natural) family: "the land of Lagaš (ki.lagaš^ki) is of one accord as the children of one mother." The loyalty ethic was quickly cemented with this pointed proverb: "No mother would have words with her child, and no child would disobey its mother."[119] Yet Gudea's expressions of unity are betrayed by his own description of the segmentary constituencies he called on to do the work of the "land of Lagaš." Gudea had to solicit eleven work-parties, one each from his "Land" (kalam), his "realm" (ma.da), the "built-up city" (iri.dù.a), the "rural settlements" (á.dam), five separate "clans" (im.ru.a) under standards of three different gods, and the areas of the Gu'edenna of Ningirsu and Gu-gišbarra of Nanše.[120] Politics required the simultaneous elision *and* solicitation of local identities.

A second "scene from the land": Sumu-el of Larsa's eighth year-name (*c.*1886 BC) celebrated a military victory over a place called Pī-nārātim ("Mouth-of-Rivers"). The place is virtually unknown[121] – and certainly out of company with Sumu-el's victories over Kazallu, Uruk, and Kiš– but this campaign was important enough to provide mu.ús.sa names for his next three year-names. Although Sumu-el "destroyed" Pī-nārātim, the Larsa king Sin-iqīšam had to "destroy" it again forty-six years later (before warring with Uruk, Kazallu, Elam, and Isin). Finally, in 1808 BC, Rīm-Sîn of Larsa had to fight it again in the year after he defeated "Uruk, Isin, Babylon, Sutu, and Rapiqum." Only in year-names is Pī-nārātim ever dignified with the determinative [uru], and in other writings is denied [ki]. It was hardly even a place – how could it have been a major enemy? Yet the Larsa kings celebrated year-names recording defeats of a dozen such little places, sometimes not even bothering with names (e.g., "Euphrates villages").

That kings warred against hinterland villages at the same time as they contended against international superpowers is truly arresting. Yet it reminds us of the military role of rural areas in other Babylonian "scenes from the land": the Umma-Lagaš border conflict; the collapse of the Akkadian,[122] Ur III,[123] and First Dynasty of Babylon states;[124] the isolation of Babylonian cities in the post-Kassite.[125] Rural space continued to play a critical role in the political life of historic states: in times of stability, safe passage across open space required political negotiation, outreach, and maintenance; in times of change, the interruption of networks by non-urbanites realigned the balance of urban states.[126] These facts dispel easy assumptions that rural lives and places were undifferentiated or unchanging (either synchronically and diachronically), some substrate culture from which states were secondarily assembled, disassembled, re-assembled. State–countryside competitions were dynamic processes under way at the same time as (and in connection with) state–state competitions. To restore telicity and historical change for the countryside is to give better recognition, in the end, to the nature of the urban state, and its daily struggle to animate itself.

NOTES

1 The titles of several standard works used herein will be abbreviated as follows: the series *Répertoire Géographique des Textes Cunéiformes* (Wiesbaden: Reichert Verlag) as *RGTC*; vol. 2, Edzard and G. Farber 1974; vol. 3, Groneberg 1980; vol. 5, Nashef 1982; vol. 8, Zadok 1985. The series *Royal Inscriptions of Mesopotamia. Early, Babylonian*, and *Assyrian Periods* (Toronto: University of Toronto) as *RIME, RIMB*, and *RIMA*, respectively: *RIME* vol. 2, Frayne 1993; vol. 3/1, Edzard 1997; vol. 3/2, Frayne 1997; vol. 4, Frayne 1990; *RIMB* vol. 2, Frame 1995; and *RIMA* vol. 3, Grayson 1996. *CAD = Chicago Assyrian Dictionary* (Chicago, IL: The Oriental Institute).
2 Limerick 1987; Kearns 1998.
3 Tilly 1985; Bufon, 1998.

4 E.g., Schwartz and Falconer 1994, especially essays by G. Stein (Ch. 2) and C. Kramer (Ch. 14).

5 Smith 2003; Algaze 2001.

6 Notably, Fleming 2004, Steinkeller 2007, pp. 37–48; the defensibility of even the largest geographical term in our field was already brilliantly interrogated by J.J. Finkelstein in his article of 1962. Other Assyriological literature has sometimes assumed too much a total state power over hinterlands, e.g., Bailkey 1967 and Leemans 1982, pp. 245–8.

7 A welcome exception is G. van Driel's "On Villages" (2001); E. Stone's fourteen-page study (though promisingly entitled "Mesopotamian Cities and Countryside"), in Snell 2005, devotes only the last page to the countryside as a subject of social and political interest.

8 Rather, (*māt*) Karduniash, restricted in emic use to the fifteenth to tenth centuries BC (*RGTC* 5; cf. *RGTC* 8). A few references to a "land of Babylon" (kur *Babilunê* / ká.dingir.ra^[ki]), either derive from outside Mesopotamia, or have a strictly local meaning, i.e., the land around the city of Babylon, not "Babylonia" (PBS 1/2 43 32: *ṭuppi tēlīti ša* igi.eden *ù* kur ká.dingir.ra^[ki]).

9 Of 1,225 whole place-name entries in *RGTC* 3, 604 (49.3 percent) are known only from a single text or year-name formula. Methodological problems in accounting for these "lonely onlys" abound (e.g., GNs may not be in rural zones, they may not be in Babylonia, there has been much new evidence since the publication, etc.), but the estimate nevertheless suggests a certain distribution of evidence. Of even later times, Sancisi-Weerdenburg 1990: "The Persian empire may well have included many villages or niches inhabited by Asterixes and Obelixes, besides those whose existence is known."

10 Cf. Hallo 1971.

11 Cole 1996, Ch. 2.

12 On agricultural production, e.g., Hruška (this volume), Renger 2004, Eyre 1995, esp. his bibliography. On demography and settlement, see Stone 2005.

13 Indeed, large-scale cultivation required such management, but not all production was large scale: Butzer 1995.

14 Wright 1981.

15 Butzer 1995, p. 323; on historical patterns of riverine regime change, see also Gasche and M. Tanret 1998.

16 Only for the conquest of Uruk did Sargon specify the submission of multiple (i.e., fifty) governors (*RIME* 2 1.1; Irdanene of Uruk (Year "ba") claimed to have given freedom for the "surrounding villages" of the region; Rīm-Sîn's defeat of Irdanene's state specifically included uru.didli.ma.da.nun^[ki].ga, the "various cities of the land of Uruk" (*RIME* 4 2.14.9).

17 These definitions generally prefer Steinkeller 2007 ('City and Countryside'), who distinguishes six grades of sites as small as 2 ha. (in the Ur III province of Umma alone, he already estimates around 110 of these smallest communities) to Adams 1981 and Adams and Nissen 1972, who accounted for "villages" as occupying up to 10 ha. and 6 ha., respectively. Differential rank-sizes are observable even within the modest frame of ⩽2 ha: most sites cluster around modal sizes of 0.1, 0.5 and 1.0 hectares; cf. Stone 2005, pp. 153–4.

18 The village-heavy territories around Kiš, Dilbat, Babylon, Sippar, etc., are not represented.

19 In terms of area: the Uruk survey covered about 2,800 square kilometers; the Nippur-Adab survey was approximately four times this size. In terms of time: the shortest period here is the Akkadian state (ca. 140 years), which cannot be directly compared to the ±500-year Early–Middle Uruk or Middle Babylonian periods.

20 Alone among the sites Adams 1981 surveyed at 2.0 ha. or below in this respect is Site 99, with a very small Akkadian occupation, grown larger in Ur III-OB times (slightly larger sites between 2.0 and 4.0 ha. seem to have had some greater chance of becoming larger). Isin is another rare example, a major urban center which appears to have had modest beginnings (i.e., below 10 ha. in Early Dynastic occupation).

21 The fourth to third millennia boasted many small sites whose number indeed gradually declined all the way into the Akkadian period. In the north, this decline harmonized with shrinking urban occupations, but in the south the number and size of cities crested as village occupation fell. The better-surveyed south presents a coherent picture of urbanization, but the northern area does not seem to have undergone the same transformation.

22 Of twenty-six middle Babylonian villages identified as occupied for a single-period only within the timespan of 4000–2350 BC, twenty-three were identified within these three centuries (i.e., 3100–2800 BC), Adams 1981. In the fourth and third millennia, single-period occupancy was uncommon and longevity the rule, when compared to the post-Ur III period.

23 A similar pattern can be evinced in the southern survey data (Adams 1981: 9 of 19 Kassite villages (47.3 percent) were new in that period, but 10 of 19 OB villages (52.6 percent) survived into that time as well; 9 of 10 MB villages (90 percent) had prior Kassite occupation, but only 1 of 19 OB sites (5.3 percent) survived through all three periods.

24 There was also a major increase in villages between 2.1 and 4.0 ha. in the Ur III-OB periods.

25 Adams 1981, Table 15.

26 Adams and Nissen 1972, Fig. 11: Ring-shape: site 156 (Ur III/Larsa); radiant canals: site 403 (Kassite); enclosing walls: 336, possibly 385, and Ur-Eridu site 72; large institutional buildings: 336, 443; Ur-Eridu site 166; fortresses: 11, 1075, and possibly 1230, 1341, and 1503. While these forms are not in and of themselves so noteworthy, that they are attested at even the smallest sites is of interest here. Stone 2005, p. 153 also points out that sites below 2 ha. such as Tell Harmal had economic and cultural features that were distinctly urban.

27 Though there are many examples of this type of settlement layout, a particularly interesting string of these is evident in the OB-Kassite levees at sites 1584, 1589, 1590, 1592, 1600, and 1601 (Adams 1981).

28 Rather than secondary (what the Ammiṣaduqa Edict calls *ṣiḫḫirtu*, the "minor crop" beside cereal) crops.

29 Adams 1981, sites with: brick-kiln slag: site 827; pottery-kilns: 175, 428, 443; maceheads: 274, 680, 1312, 1432, 1448; copper: 247, 272, 274, 285, 314, 406, 573, 574, 940, 1432, 1448; Ur-Eridu site 24.

30 One might, via an "archaeology of knowledge," add those communities which were tied together by administrative land grants and cadasters, i.e., ideated "communities of the tablet."

31 See especially C. Kramer in Schwartz and Falconer 1994, on variability of scale and specialization in otherwise "ideologically egalitarian rural settlements."

32 For a discussion of this urban bias, see Van De Mieroop 1997, esp. Ch. 3.

33 Though Dumuzi himself is called in one version "brother of the countryside" by Inanna, šes úru bar.ra.

34 Several proverbs suggest that the village was a dwelling-place of Inanna (Electronic Text Corpus of Sumerian Literature (hereafter, ETCSL: http://www-etcsl.orient.ox.ac.uk), 6.1.21, 6.2.3, 6.2.5).

35 Vanstiphout 1997, Text I.181, ll. 135–7, pp. 578–81.

36 Lambert 1960: 35, ll. 82–3.

37 Foster 1993, "The Sacrificial Gazelle," III.51d, cf. his comment vol. I, p. 30, and n. 79 below (re: *RIME* 4 1.4.6).

38 E.g., the "Babylonian Theodicy's" aphoristic "You are as stable as the earth, but the plan of the gods is remote," (Lambert 1960: 75 l. 58).

39 Lambert 1960, l. 135f., and pp. 122–3, on the passage's material common with Šurpu.

40 Examples of these are too dispersed and numerous to receive full treatment here, but can be found from the Early Dynastic period onwards. Rural temples and temple personnel are known as having been located at boundaries, fields, riverbanks, and even in open country; the importance of rural shrines in early state formation in ancient Greece has been argued by de Polignac 1995.

41 dumu GN was, of course, a longstanding term for a citizen of an urban corporation, but the extensibility of the term to non-urbanites is doubtful (cf. below, re: *mār mātim*).

42 This absent *mentalité* is also reflected in the slow development of cartography within the scribal curriculum. Geography was mostly documented in the textual list-form of cadasters and point-to-point itineraries; not until post-1500 BC are even a few regional maps attested (Röllig, *Reallexikon der Assyriologie* "Landkarten," pp. 464–7).

43 Wilcke 2003: 0.1.2, 2.0 (especially 2.1.1 and 2.1.3.2), 4.1; Westbrook, "Introduction: The Character of Ancient Near Eastern Law," pp. 1–90, esp. pp. 25–6 (the state was not an

"autonomous entity nor the king merely its representative," and his ownership of (the) land was politically, not legally, constituted), and "Mesopotamia: The Old Babylonian Period," pp. 361–430, esp. pp. 363–4, both in Westbrook 2003; cf. Bailkey's 1967 essay on Mesopotamian constitutionalism.

44 Abbreviations follow Roth 1997: LU ¶17 and LH ¶17: slave re-capture beyond city border (ki.sur.ra uru.na.ka) or open country (*ina ṣerim*), respectively, requires private compensation on return; cf. LL ¶12 (treats flight within city only), LE ¶¶29–30, 50–1. Snell 2001, has convincingly argued that both the low incidence of documentation about slave flight to rural villages (rather than to other urban households – but see, e.g., P. Michalowski 1993, no. 119), as well as the legal sanctions related to slave return/harboring, reflect the state's limited legal powers to actually control flight; the emphasis is, rather, on the protection of the property rights of urbanites. In this connection, one might note the absence of "flight romances" in Mesopotamian literature analogous to the stories of Sinuhe, Idrimi, or David (1 Samuel).

45 Roth 1997, LH ¶244, SLEx ¶9′, SLHF vi 16–22, 32–36.

46 Compare the delegation of legal sanction/remedy in territorial cases (e.g., Roth 1997, LH ¶¶23, 54, 103, 136) against those in which royal property is specified (e.g., LH ¶¶27, 32 (grudgingly)).

47 E.g., *RIME* 3/2 1.4.1 iv 34f.; cf. *RGTC* 8, 75, sub. Bīrānāti and Bīrāti, and the Achaemenid-period *uzbarra*.

48 Specific names are rendered here in order to illustrate the level of detail specified by these early inscriptions, increasingly absent in later periods.

49 Figure 2.1 combines the data of the Akkad, Kiš, Uruk, and "Heartland" surveys and augments them with data derived from Corona and other satellite-imaging technologies to produce the fullest possible settlement survey: Adams 1981, Gibson 1972, including R McC. Adams' Akkad Survey data therein; and Hritz 2005. NB the Akkad Survey area documented by Adams in Gibson 1972, did not specifically take note of Middle Babylonian sites; thus a small northerly portion of the Kassite-Middle Babylonian map in Figure 2.1 is incomplete.

50 This claim was, it seems, subsequently confirmed by Sargon of Akkad (*RIME* 2 1.1.2).

51 Cooper 1986: La 9.1 and Um 7.2.

52 Steinkeller 1993, pp. 107–29, esp. p. 118f.; ki.sur.ra's are not attested for northern cities until Ur III times, when Kiš and Sippar are said to have them (*RGTC* 2 309).

53 Only for foreign lands was there any expression of interest in geographic extents – in lands attached to cities along the Ḫabur, or in the territories of Syrian cities comprising Dagan's "Upper Land": *RIME* 2 1.1.12, 1.4.21, and 1.4.30.

54 *RIME* 2 1.2 (*passim*), but note especially 1.1.11 (34 cities) and 1.2.4, in which Rimuš gives a running total of 14,100 men expelled "from the cities of Sumer"; no episodes of exile are recorded in non-Babylonian campaigns. Presumably the tropic pairing of "expelled and annihilated" in this context is parallel in meaning.

55 *RIME* 2, p. 7; B.R. Foster ("Management and Administration in the Sargonic Period," in Liverani 1999, p. 31, in arguing for an "archaeology of knowledge," catalogs nine areas of economic management undertaken by the governors of the Akkadian state – which can be further summarized as commodities, labor, and markets – but land is not among them.

56 Michalowski 1993, nos. 4, 5, 19.

57 Foster, "Management," in Liverani 1999, pp. 30–1; Sallaberger and Westenholz 1999, p. 50.

58 *RIME* 3/1 1.1.7.StB and .29; Nanše is also described as "living in the land" and "queen of lands" in Cyl. A iii 1–2, iv 13. Other texts of Gudea's show interest in describing specific agricultural plots (StI ii 1–2, StR ii 9–10; cf. paeans to the fields, Cyl. A xi 12–15, Cyl. B xv 1f.).

59 *RIME* 2 13.6.1–.3.

60 Michalowski 1993 no. 148: Gu'edenna, for instance, was still an identifiable district in Ur III times; B. Gandulla's dismissal of Mesopotamian terms for "borders" as an anachronistic "far-off reality" fails to explain their political importance (Gandulla 2000).

61 For Kiritab, Apiak, Marad, and at least one other broken place-name; the adjacent city-state borders of Kiš and Kazallu are also mentioned. *RIME* 3/2 1.1.21: The territory de-lineated in ex. 1 ii 24 – iv 24 includes Puš, later the seat of a governorship, Ḫiritum, and

Šarrum-laba, all places close to Sippar; the indicated city-god, however, is Sîn, not Šamaš. The passage in ex. 2 from i 1 – iv 32 otherwise clearly refers to Marad, but twice refers to sides totalled as á-IM.mar-dú-bi, "its western side" (ii 16 and iv 28). This confusion is exacerbated by the broken passages between i 16 and iii 1, where at least twenty-seven lines are missing.

62 Adab, Nippur, Sippar, and (unsurprisingly) Kisurra; the "side" (da) of Umma is also attested (*RGTC* 2 306, 309).

63 Kiritab's boundaries were simply delineated by four features on four sides; Marad's border, by contrast, included at least twenty-seven sides with only the western side listed in full, and an unknown portion of the southern side. Apiak's eastern border is drawn by connecting only two points, while its northern border connects six. The single most detailed border is Marad's western one (abutting Kazallu and Kiš), with seventeen loci.

64 Kiritab: S-E-N-W; Apiak: N-E-S-W; [name lost]: N-W-S-E; Marad: (x-W?-x-x?-S-W).

65 *RIME* 3/2 1.1.1. l. 11′ and p. 364; cf. the hymn Ur-Namma C (ETCSL, op. cit., 2.4.1.3, l. 82), in which the boundary (kir.sur.ra) of Ur and Sumer are seemingly identified as one and the same, and A.K. Grayson, "Grenze," in D.O. Edzard (ed.), *Reallexikon der Assyriologie* Bd. 3, Berlin: de Gruyter, 1957, pp. 639–40, on the Assyro-Babylonian border.

66 The articulation of these privileges and holdings were not abstractly formulated as rights by law attached to city or temple (i.e., *kidinnūtu*) until the first millennium; this was preceded by a long period during which the assertion of privileges, protections, and exemptions were derived by charter or precedent.

67 *RIME* 4 2.4.1 and 2.6.1: Zabāia and Abī-sarē of Larsa as "Amorite chiefs"; 4.1.2, Sîn-kāšid as "king of the Amnānum"; later: 2.13.3 Kudur-mabug as ad.da.kur.már.du, "father of the Amorite land" and 3.6.10 and 3.9.1, lugal.da.ga.an.kur.már.du.ki, "king of all the Amorite land."

68 *RIME* 4 1.3.2: *contra* Charpin 2004, p. 61 who lists the first as Išme-Dagan, the king following; previous dynastic titles included, rather: "lord/king of (t)his land," and "god of his nation"; 2.5.3 and 3.6.1, respectively. The sparse contemporary inscriptions of early Babylonian kings testify only to their position by sealings identifying them as lugal (once), and ìr PN (in servant-sealings); their year-name formulae refer not to royal succession, but an "entering of his father's house."

69 *RIME* 4 2.6.1, 3.6.10, 3.7.8.

70 Warad-Sîn and Rīm-Sîn were last to distinguish the "land of Lagaš" in city lists (*RIME* 4 2.13.13, 2.14.8); the ma.da Kutalla is also specified by Sin-iddinam and Warad-Sîn (2.12.1, 2.13.1).

71 Both ki.sur.ra and in.dub: *RIME* 4 2.8.3 and .7 (in which the "boundary of Utu" is said to be fixed *at* the city-wall), 2.9.2, 2.9.11, 2.13.21. Iddin-Dagan ("Hymn B"): "You have marked the borders(?) and fixed the boundaries, you have made Sumer and Akkad raise their necks" (ETCSL website, op. cit., 2.5.3.2). Mesalim, Ur-Namma, and Sîn-iddinam are the kings (rather than gods) said to have established borders.

72 Isin: Šu-ilišu: *RIME* 4 1.2.2 and .3; Iddin-Dagan: 1.2.3; Larsa: Gungunum ("Gungunum A," ETCSL website, op. cit., 2.6.2.1); Nur-Adad: *RIME* 4 2.8.1, .3, and .6–.7; Sin-iddinam: 2.9.14; Warad-Sîn: 2.13.6 and .27; Rīm-Sîn: W.H. van Soldt, *Letters in the British Museum* vol. 2 (=*AbB* 13), Leiden: Brill, 1994, no. 53; Babylon: Hammurabi: *RIME* 4 3.6.2, .7 and Roth, op. cit., p. 78 ii 48–54; Samsuiluna: *RIME* 4 3.7.2 and .8; Ammiditana: 3.9.2; Ammiṣaduqa: 3.10.2. Hammurabi's thirty-third year-name, crowning his serial conquests of Elam, Larsa, Ešnunna, and Mari, boasted of "restoring Sumer and Akkad which had been scattered"; this invites some question as to whether these resettlements were specific single events.

73 Kings employing language of settlement in rich pasturage, etc. (see prior note for citations): Sin-iddinam, to settle "his land," Warad-Sîn for Larsa, Ur, and "the broad land," Hammurabi for Sippar and Babylon, Samsuiluna for Sumer and Akkad, Ammiditana and Ammiṣaduqa both for "the widespread people."

74 *Contra* Leemans 1982 who neglected such terms denoting farmsteads as é PN, é.ḫá, and é.duru₅-PN.

75 See below nn. 78–80 about the legal distinguishment of "the land"; *RIME* 4 2.9.15, in which Sin-iddinam calls himself "the one whom his numerous people truly chose."

76 Royal rule of countryside domains, this implies, did not require negotiated political authority. Conditional (urban) epithets, meanwhile conspicuously replace titles of kingship for Larsa kings Ṣilli-Adad and Warad-Sîn (*RIME* 4 2.12.1, 2.13.13); the lengthiest list of epithets appears in the prologue to the Code of Hammurabi, in which he never claims to be king *of* anywhere, per se – just "king"; cf. LL i 38–55 (Roth, op. cit.). See also van Soldt 1990, no. 166, for an intriguing (but sadly broken) allusion to differential royal control.

77 u$_6$.di.kalam.ma.ka: *RIME* 4 2.13.6, .12, .16; sù.rá . . . pa.gal mi.ni.in.è: 2.9.12; 2.13.21; 2.13.26: nam.gal.nam.lugal.la.gá kalam.ma igi ḫé.bí.in.du$_8$; 2.13.23: ḫur.sag.sù.rá.gin$_7$; cf. 3.7.2. Note as well the insistence on civic corvée-labor as participatory and profitable, e.g. 2.8.7, 2.9.6, 2.13.20–21; note especially the idealized statements of abundant wages, and the consequent rhetoric of worker happiness.

78 Lengthy paeans to the contentedness of the land, kings' familiarity with the open countryside, and refulgent pastorales were propagated by Išme-Dagan (*RIME* 4 1.4.8) and Enlil-bani of Isin (1.10.1001), Warad-Sîn (2.13.24) and Rīm-Sîn (2.14.15) of Larsa, among others. On "the land," see also Postgate 1994, esp. pp. 4–5.

79 E.g., *RIME* 4 2.8.7 (ganba šà.ma.da.gá.ka), 2.9.6 (note the serial phrase ganba šà.uri^{ki} larsa^{ki} ù ma.da.gá.ka, "the markets of Ur, Larsa and my land" – three distinct markets), 4.1.10–11 (ganba ma.da.na.ka/.gá.ka).

80 Nowhere is this more evident than at Babylon: the year-names of this dynasty specify equity and freedom for šà.ga ma.da.na (Hammurabi 02); šà ma.da du$_{10}$, (Samsuiluna 02), kalam.ma (Abi-ešuḫ 02 and 13(?)), (ur$_5$.ra) ma.da (Ammiditana 21 cf. year 03, conscription of un kalam.ma) and Ammiṣaduqa 10); Horsnell 1999. *RIME* 4 1.4.6, Išme-Dagan of Isin's removal of service obligations is extended to three types of corporations: temples, cities, and the "land of Sumer and Akkad;" cf. Enlil-bani of Isin (1.10.1001 vi 1–23), who established justice for Isin and Nippur, but only made the "heart of the land (šà.kalam) content." See also year-names for Lipit-Ištar (a) and Irdanene (ba); Ur-Namma, however, was the first to specify kalam as the direct object of his justice.

81 I have discussed elsewhere the most famous such edict, that of Ammiṣaduqa (Richardson 2005).

82 Hammurabi's numerous letters to his Larsa administrators are the best known case, adjudicating private holdings, and balancing them with administrative distributions of *ṣibtu, ilkum* and šuku-allotments.

83 E.g., *šāpir mātim Jamutbalum^{ki}*. One might note also the absence of OB state administrators with the wide-ranging powers of city-based ensí's of the Akkadian and Ur III state.

84 A term for rural persons is anticipated from Old Sumerian sources as kalam.ma.ka ("of (our) country"), Wilcke 2003, 4.1.2. A parallel construction of urban and rural citizenships appears in LL ii 1–15 (Roth 1997: 25) for the liberation of citizens of Nippur, Ur, Isin, and the "lands of Sumer and Akkad" (dumu.níta dumu.munus ki.en.gi ki.uri). cf. OB sources for *mār mātim*, a "citizen (lit. "son") of the land," including R. Westbrook 2003, "Introduction," pp. 36–44, sub. 4.1.1 (cf. LH); CAD M$_1$ 5b-c (also *mār mātim elîtim, mār ugārim*) verus *ṭeḫḫûtu*, "position of clientage").

85 E.g., TCL 17 10:42 (CAD K 189b sub. *kapru*), and M. Stol, "Die altbabylonische Stadt Ḫalḫalla," in Dietrich and Loretz 1998, p. 433.

86 *RIME* 4 2.9.6 and .15, 2.13.13 and .27, 4.6.3; note also the specific connection between kingship and fortresses evident in 1.4.10 (Durum was Išme-Dagan's "military governorship" and "city of his princeship"), 3.7.5 (Samsuiluna's fortresses are the "foundation" of his land), and 4.1.13 (Sin-kašid, not content to be king of Uruk, is also military governor of Durum). On the Late OB trend towards a militarization of the countryside, see also Richardson, op. cit., esp. pp. 282–4 and Appendix: the reign of (and revolt against) Samsuiluna was certainly a critical moment of change for Babylonia in this respect: if the construction of city walls was the hallmark of early OB kingship, the emphasis later shifted squarely to the construction of fortifications in the countryside. This, together with the massive deurbanization

of south and central Babylonia following 1720 BC, produced the conditions for the rural character of the Kassite national state emergent later around 1500 BC.

87 *RIME* 4 2.9.13 (cf. 2.5.3, Larsa wall name ᵈUtu.ki.bal.e.sá.di), 2.13.13 (the gú ma.da made peaceful, and enemies as the "snare of the land"), 2.14.10, 3.7.3 (esp. ll. 47–54); Richardson, 2005, on the unstable north-Babylonian countryside in the late seventeenth century BC.

88 See, for instance, Maeda 1992.

89 Cf. n. 8, above.

90 This dynasty was also not rooted in any urban kingship, and the putative and unlocated capital uru.kù^ki was probably notional.

91 The Dynastic Chronicle accorded to Simbar-Šipak (fl. 1025 BC) a direct link to "a soldier of the dynasty of Damiq-ilišu" (fl. 1650 BC); Grayson 2000, Chron 18. ll. v. 1–4, p. 142.

92 Note the prior extensive land grant by Nebuchadnezzar I in this area, Brinkman 1968, pp. 113–15.

93 Sassmanshausen 2001, pp. 22–3, listing one additional *pīḫatu elītu* and *pīḫāt šarri*; Brinkman, 1968, pp. 296f.

94 In general, however, these cases seem to be restricted to those places on the state's northern fringes, along the Assyrian border.

95 *Contra* CAD B 295, the passage *lu en é ša* GN *arkû ša iššakkinu* is MB, not NB, in date.

96 J.A. Brinkman, "Kudurru," in *Reallexikon der Assyriologie* Bd. 6, Berlin: de Gruyter, 1980, p. 272.

97 Sommerfeld 1995; cf. Slanski 2003, esp. p. 488, regarding exemptions on royal estates.

98 Perhaps the elites/officers that Chronicle P refers to as the lú.*rabûti*.meš *šá* kur.*Akkadî*^ki (Grayson 2000, pp. 170–7, Chron. 22 iv 8 and *passim*.

99 Cf. van Driel's, 2001, interpretations, p. 117.

100 Nashef 1992, pp. 151–9; the *pīḫatu* known by this name near Nippur likely included at least ten villages.

101 Cf. CAD M₂ 113 for BE 1 83, which refers to a lone *miṣru* of Nanše.

102 *kisurrû, kudurru, miṣru*; rarely, *pulukku*; *taḫūmu* was never a Babylonian term for an intrastate border. Areal terms like *mātu* and *qaqqaru* were still in use, but with little sense of territorial fixity; cf. Cole, op. cit., Letter 27, which may indicate someone as expelled from Nippur (*ina qaqqar* en.líl^ki). Cameron (1973) demonstrated conclusively that Persian *daḫḫya* meant "people," not "district."

103 Brinkman, "Kudurru," p. 274; Slanski 2003, p. 314, sub. "Royal adjudications."

104 Edens 1994, pp. 209–24, esp. p. 212.

105 Grayson 2000, Chrons. 22 (iv 15), 176, on people "scattered" (*sapāḫu*) from Nippur, and 24 (rev. 11), 182, on seized fields.

106 Cole 1996, pp. 13–16.

107 Brinkman 1968: 132; Grayson 2000, Assyrian Chronicle Fragment 4, p. 189, l. 11.

108 RGTC 8, *passim*.

109 By M. Stolper's count, the texts of this family entailed business (if not actual holdings) in "about 180 villages" ("Murašû," in D.O. Edzard *et al.* (eds), *Reallexikon der Assyriologie* Bd. 8, Berlin: de Gruyter, 1995, pp. 427–9.

110 *RGTC* 8, "Introduction," ix–xxx; the intervening twenty years of prodigious publication of first millennium texts (especially the energetic *Zadokliteratur* on geography) cannot be incorporated here; one expects the net effect would be an increase in both the number of new groups and attestations.

111 Cole 1996, Ch. 2; one notes how little can be said about "genuine" Babylonians by this time!

112 *RIMB* 2 6.14.1 iii 48′–49′, 54′–55′; on treaties and "brotherhoods" both between tribal leaders, and between urban officials and tribal leaders, see Cole 1996, pp. 25, 27–8, 31–2, 50, and Letters 7, 13, and 19.

113 *RIMA* 3 102.29 and 104.8; Chaldaeans: *RIMB* 2 6.7.2001, 10.2001–2; Baba-aḫe-iddina *RIMB* 2 6.9.

114 J. Oelsner, *et al.*, "Neo-Babylonian Period," in Westbrook 2003, p. 917, sub. 2.1.3.2.

115 Cole 1996, p. 50; LaBianca 1999, pp. 19–29, defines a hetarchic state as comprising "several political centers of gravity within each kingdom."

116 Smith 2003, pp. 45–54.

117 A related case is KUR (*mātu*), most often referring to foreign lands, but by implication also their peoples.

118 See especially Westbrook 1999, pp. 101–6, for a concise exposition of this problem, and Smith 2003, Ch. 1, *passim*, and pp. 77, 100–9, on state pretensions to geographic universalism; cf. Morris 1991, pp. 25–58, who takes up the ambiguous, multivalent meanings lying behind the Greek term *polis*.

119 *RIME* 3/1 1.1.7.Cyl. A xii 21–27 and xiii 3–5 (here and elsewhere (e.g., Cyl. A xix 1, Cyl. B iv 13–14), the "land of Lagaš" is distinguished from the city of Lagaš; the term would survive into the Old Babylonian period, see above, n. 69); state segments: xiv 7–27.

120 State segments: *RIME* 3/1 1.1.7.Cyl. A xiv 7–27; these social units are then paralleled by geographic constituencies in the songs of Cylinder B (xi 15–xii 23), in which the composite state is constituted by units of fields, marshes, steppes, and cities; cf. *RIMB* 2.4.9 (Nebuchadnezzar I) ll. 3–4.

121 See my short study on Pī-nārātim, "Brush Wars and Bull Wages" (forthcoming).

122 Michalowski 1993, the "Gutian letters," nos. 22 and 51.

123 ETCSL letters 3.1.07., .08, .11, and, famously, .17–18.

124 See Richardson 2005.

125 See, e.g., *RIMB* 2 6.1.

126 Frayne 1983, pp. 739–48.

BIBLIOGRAPHY

Adams, R. Mc. 1981 *Heartland of Cities*, Chicago, IL: University of Chicago Press.

——— and H. Nissen 1972 *The Uruk Countryside*, Chicago, IL: University of Chicago Press.

Algaze, G. 2001 "The Prehistory of Imperialism," *Uruk Mesopotamia and its Neighbors*, Santa Fe, NM: School of American Research: 27–83.

Bailkey, N. 1967 "Early Mesopotamian Constitutional Development," *American Historical Review*, 72 (4): 1211–36.

Brinkman, J.A. 1968 *A Political History of post-Kassite Babylonia*, Rome: Pontifical Biblical Institut.

Bufon, M. 1998 "Borders and Border Landscapes: A Theoretical Assessment," in M. Koter and K. Heffner (eds) *Borderlands or Transborder Regions*, Opole/Lódz: 7–14.

Butzer, K.1995 "Environmental Change in the Near East and Human Impact on the Land," in J. Sasson (ed.) *Civilizations of the Ancient Near East*, vol. I, New York: Scribner's: 123–5.

Cameron, G. 1973 "Persian Satrapies and Related Matters," *Journal of Near Eastern Studies* 32: 47–5.

Charpin, D.D, O. Edzard, and M. Stol 2004 *Mesopotamien: Die althabylonische Zeit*, Freiburg: Universitätsverlag Freiburg.

Cole, S.W. 1996 *Nippur in Late Assyrian Times* (=*SAAS* IV), Helsinki: Neo-Assyrian Text Corpus Project.

Cooper, J. 1986 *Presargonic Inscriptions*, New Haven, CT: American Oriental Society.

de Polignac, F. 1995 *Cults, Territory and the Origins of the Greek City-State*, Chicago, IL: University of Chicago Press.

Dietrich, M. and O. Loretz 1998 *Studien zur Altorientalistik* (FS Römer), Munster: Ugarit-Verlag.

Edens, C. 1994 "On the Complexity of Complex Societies," in G. Stein and M. Rothman (eds) *Chiefdoms and Early States in the Near East*, Madison, WI: Prehistory Press: 209–24.

Edzard, D.O. 1997 *Royal Inscriptions of Mesopotamia Early, Babylonian*, and *Assyrian Periods*, Vol. 3/2, Toronto: University of Toronto.

——— and G. Farber (eds) 1974 *Répertoire Géographique des Textes Cunéiformes*, Vol. 2, Wiesbaden: Reichert Verlag.

Eyre, C. 1995 "The Agricultural Cycle, Farming, and Water Management in the Ancient Near East," in J. Sasson (ed.) *Civilizations of the Ancient Near East*, Vol. I, New York: Scribner's: 175–90.

Finkelstein, J.J. 1962 "Mesopotamia," *Journal of Near Eastern Studies* 21 (2): 73–92.

Fleming, D. 2004 *Democracy's Ancient Ancestors*, Cambridge University Press.

Foster, B. 1993 *Before the Muses*, Bethesda, MD.

Frame, G. 1995 *Royal Inscriptions of Mesopotamia Early, Babylonian Assyrian Periods*, Vol. 3, Toronto: University of Toronto.

Frayne, D. 1983 "Šulgi, the Runner," *Journal of the American Oriental Society* 103: 4.

—— 1993 *Royal Inscriptions of Mesopotamia Early, Babylonian Periods*, Vol. 2, Toronto: University of Toronto.

—— 1990 *Royal Inscriptions of Mesopotamia Early, Babylonian Periods*, Vol. 4, Toronto: University of Toronto.

Gandulla, P. 2000 "The Concept of Frontier in the Historical Processes of Ancient Mesopotamia," in L. Milano *et al.* (eds) *Landscapes* (= *HANE* Monographs III/2), Padua: Sargon srl: 39–44.

Gasche, H. and M. Tanret (eds) 1998 *Changing Watercourses in Babylonia*, Ghent: University of Ghent.

Gibson, M. 1972 *The City and Area of Kish*, Coconut Grove, FL: Field Research Projects.

Grayson, A.K. 1996 *Royal Inscriptions of Mesopotamia, Assyrian Periods*, Vol. 3, Toronto: University of Toronto.

—— 2000 *Assyrian and Babylonian Chronicles*, Winona Lake, IN: Eisenbrauns.

Groneberg, B. (ed.) 1980 *Répertoire Géographique des Textes Cunéiformes*, Vol. 3, Wiesbaden: Reichert Verlag.

Hallo, W.W. 1971 "Antediluvian Cities," *Journal of Cuneiform Studies* 23: 57–67.

Horsnell, M. 1999 *The Year-Names of the First Dynasty of Babylon*, Hamilton, Ontario: McMaster University Press.

Hritz, C. 2005 "Landscape and Settlement in Southern Mesopotamia," Ph.D. dissertation, University of Chicago.

Kearns, G. 1998 "The Virtuous Circle of Facts and Values in the New Western History," *Annals of the Association of American Geographers* 88 (3): 377–409.

LaBianca, O.S. 1999 "Excursus: Salient Features of Iron Age Tribal Kingdoms," in B. MacDonald and R. Younker (eds) *Ancient Ammon*, Leiden: Brill: 19–29.

Lambert, W.G. 1960 *Babylonian Wisdom Literature*, Oxford: Clarendon.

Leemans, W.F. 1982 "The Pattern of Settlement in the Babylonian Countryside," in W.F. Leemans and M. Dandamaev (eds) *Societies and Languages of the Ancient Near East*, Warminster: Aris & Philipps: 245–8.

Limerick, P. 1987 *The Legacy of Conquest*, New York: Norton & Co.

Liverani, M. 1999 "The Role of the Village in Shaping the Ancient Near Eastern Rural Landscape," in L. Milano *et al.* (eds) *Landscapes* (= *HANE* Monographs III/1), Padua: Sargon srl: 37–48.

Maeda, T. 1992 "The Defense Zone during the Rule of the Ur III Dynasty," *Acta Sumerologica (Japan)* 14: 135–72.

Michalowski, P. 1993 *Letters from early Mesopotamia*, Atlanta, GA: Scholars Press.

Milano, M. *et al.* (eds) 1999 *Landscapes* (= *HANE* Monographs III/1), Padua: Sargon srl.

Morris, I. 1991 "The Early Polis as City and State," in J. Rich and A. Wallace-Hadrill (eds) *City and Country in the Ancient World*, London: Routledge: 25–58.

Nashef, Kh. 1982 *Répertoire Géographique des Textes Cunéiformes*, Vol. 5, Wiesbaden: Reichert Verlag.

—— 1992 "The Nippur Countryside in the Kassite Period," in M. deJong Ellis (ed.) *Nippur at the Centennial*, Philadelphia, PA: University Museum.

Postgate, N. 1994 "In Search of the First Empires," *Bulletin of the American Schools of Oriental Research* 293: 1–13.

Renger, J. 2004 "Die naturräumlichen Bedingungen im Alten Orient im 4. und frühen 3. Jt. v. Chr.," in S. Burmeister (ed.) *Rad und Wagen*, Mainz: Verlag Zabern: 41–8.

Richardson, S. 2005 "Trouble in the Countryside *ana tarṣi* Samsuditana," in W.H. van Soldt *et al.* (eds) *Ethnicity in Ancient Mesopotamia*, Leiden: PIHANS: 273–89.

Roth, M. 1997 *Law Collections from Mesopotamia and Asia Minor*, Atlanta, GA: Scholars Press.

Sallaberger, W. and Å. Westenholz 1999 *Mesopotamien: Akkade-Zeit und Ur III-Zeit* .(=*OBO* 160/3) Freiburg: Universitätsverlag Freiburg.

Sancisi-Weerdenburg, H. 1990 "The Quest for an Elusive Empire," in A. Kuhrt and H. Sancisi-Weerdenburg (eds) *Centre and Periphery*, Leiden: Nederlands Institut voor Het Nabije Oosten: 263–7.

Sassmanshausen, L. 2001 *Beiträge zur Verwaltung und Gesellschaft Babyloniens in der Kassitenzeit* (=*BaF* Bd. 21), Mainz: von Zabern.

Schwartz, G. and S. Falconer 1994 *Archaeological Views from the Countryside*, Washington, DC: Smithsonian Institution.

Slanski, K. 2003 "Middle Babylonian Period," in R. Westbrook (ed.) *A History of Ancient Near Eastern Law*, Leiden: Brill.

—— 2003b *The Babylonian Entitlement narû's (kudurrus)*, Boston, MA: ASOR.

Smith, A.T. 2003 *The Political Landscape*, Berkeley, CA: University of California Press.

Snell, D. 2001 *Flight and Freedom in the Ancient Near East*, Boston, MA: Brill.

Sommerfeld, W. 1995 "The Kassites of Ancient Mesopotamia," in J. Sasson (ed.) *Civilizations of the Ancient Near East*, Vol. I, New York: Scribner's. Vol. II: 917–30.

Steinkeller, P. 1993 "Early Political Development in Mesopotamia and the Origins of the Sargonic Empire," in M. Liverani (ed.) *Akkad: The First World Empire*, Padua: Sargon: 107–29.

—— 2007 "City and Countryside in Third Millennium Southern Babylonia," in E. Stone (ed.) *Settlement and Society*, Princeton, NJ: Cotsen Press.

Stol, M. 1998 "Die altbabylonische Stadt Ḫalḫalla," in M. Dietrich and O. Loretz, *Studien zur Altorientalistik* (*FS* Römer), Munster: Ugarit-Verlag.

Stone, E. 2005 "Mesopotamian Cities and Countryside," in D. Snell (ed.) *A Companion to the Ancient Near East*, Malden, MA: Blackwell: 141–5.

Tilly, C.H. 1985 "War Making and State Making as Organized Crime," in P. Evans *et al.* (eds) *Bringing the State Back In*, Cambridge University Press: 169–91.

Van De Mieroop, M. 1997 *The Ancient Mesopotamian City*, Oxford University Press.

van Driel, G. 2001 "On Villages," in W.H. van Soldt (ed.) *Veenhof Anniversary Volume*, Leiden: Nederlands Instituut voor het Nabije Oosten: 103–18.

Van Soldt, W.H. 1990 *Letters in the British Museum*, vol. 1 (=*AbB* XII), Leiden: Brill.

Vanstiphout, H. 1997 "The Disputation between the Hoe and the Plow," in W.W. Hallo (ed.) *Context of Scripture*, Vol. I, Leiden: Brill.

Westbrook, R. 1999 "Codex Ḫammurabi and the Ends of the Earth," in L. Milano *et al.* (eds) *Landscapes* (= *HANE* Monographs III/3), Padua: Sargon srl: 101–6.

—— (ed.) 2003 *A History of Ancient Near Eastern Law*, Leiden: Brill.

Wilcke, C. 2003 *Early Ancient Near Eastern Law*, Munich: Verlag der Bayerischen Akademie der Wissenschaften.

Wright, H. 1981 "The Southern Margins of Sumer: Archaeological Survey of the Area of Eridu and Ur'," in R. McC. Adams, *Heartland of Cities*, Chicago, IL: University of Chicago Press.

Zadok, R. 1985 *Répertoire Géographique des Textes Cunéiformes*, Vol. 8, Wiesbaden: Reichert Verlag.

CHAPTER THREE

LAND AND LAND USE
The middle Euphrates valley

——— .◆. ———

Lucia Mori

THE ENVIRONMENT

Unlike Mesopotamia's lower alluvial plain where, if suitably irrigated and managed, the land allows for the exploitation of substantial rural areas, a large part of the middle Euphrates valley winds though an arid plateau, where the potential for settlement and agriculture is dependent on the waters of the river and its tributaries, the Balikh and Khabur (Sanlaville 1985: 20), the only perennial watercourses in the area alongside the Euphrates itself. The landscape is characterized by a clear distinction between the steppe plateau, with its limestone and especially marly and gypsum soils, unsuited to agriculture (Geyer 1985: 296), and the river valleys with their silty soils, fertile and productive if suitably irrigated and drained. These two contexts offer very diverse potential for the exploitation of natural resources.

The middle stretch of the Euphrates, from the Turkish–Syrian border in the north to the Iraqi towns of Hit and Ramad in the south, cuts into the arid plateau to a depth ranging from a few tens of metres to over a hundred metres. Its valley is relatively narrow, from five to eight kilometres, increasing in width to the south from Deir ez-Zor. Floodplains open up in some sections of the valley, forming a series of more or less independent 'cells' (Sanlaville 1985: 21–22). The main floodplains are found, from north to south, near Raqqa, at the confluence of the Euphrates and Balikh at Abu Leil, near the confluence with the Khabur, and then further downstream at Ashara and Hariri (Geyer 1990: 68). Alternating with these are narrower sections where the valley takes the form of a gorge (Qara Qozak, Tabqa, unsurprisingly selected in recent years for the construction of dams, and Halabiya) (Sanlaville 2000: 101).

A series of alluvial terraces make up the complex geomorphology of this area (Geyer and Monchambert 1987: 293; Margueron 1988: 49): in proximity to the plateau, Pleistocene terraces develop from eight to ten metres above the waters of the Euphrates. These are covered mainly by the grassy steppe also present on the plateau; cultivation is scarce, due on the one hand to the distance from the river and on the other to the presence of gypsum crusts covering large areas (Geyer and Monchambert 1987: 297). Descending towards the valley bottom are two levels of terracing dating to the early Holocene, bounding the lower alluvial terrace at a height of up to two metres. The

Figure 3.1   The middle Euphrates valley today, from the ruins of Doura Europos
(photo: Lucia Mori).

latter dates to historical times and closely follows the path taken by the river bed. These areas are generally suitable for agriculture, with the exception of the lowest-lying zones (such as water basins or niches near ancient meanders of the river), where water tends to stagnate and, due to evaporation, salinize the soil (Geyer and Monchambert 1987: 298). The terrace belonging to the historical period, however, is subject to flooding when the Euphrates is in spate, and is therefore a hazardous zone for both agriculture and settlement. The Holocene terrace, on the other hand, only marginally affected by river floods (Sanlaville 1985: 22), is the area most suited for settlement and agricultural exploitation as long as the problem of water supply is resolved; this area is, in fact, that with the highest concentration of ancient settlements (Geyer and Monchambert 1987: 304–305) (Figure 3.1).

Climate conditions are characterized by the arid continental climate of the plateau. As the distance from the Mediterranean increases, there is a transition from a Mediterranean climate to a continental desert climate (Wirth 1971: 104). This region is located south of the isohyet of 200 mm of annual rainfall, the minimum amount that allows for dry farming. The annual variability of precipitation, another important factor determining the potential for agriculture without irrigation (Wilkinson 1990: 88–89), is extremely high, and the number of rainy days per year is fairly low. All this entails the need in modern times – and in ancient times – to exploit the waters of the river using irrigation systems to cultivate the fertile valley lands. The river valley represented the main pole of attraction for the communities, both sedentary and semi-sedentary, who lived in the region; however, also the plateau areas, in the past considered marginal in terms of their potential for settlement and agriculture, were used for complex long-term exploitation (Bernbeck 1993).

THE EVIDENCE FROM THE ANCIENT TEXTS

Direct evidence on the ancient territory of the middle Euphrates valley and its exploitation for agriculture comes from cuneiform documentary sources. Among these, the most important for their relevance, textual typology, wealth of information and number of documents are the tablets found in the archives of Zimri-Lim's Royal Palace at Mari, dating to the eighteenth century BC. The ancient site, near the modern Tell Hariri, was an important urban centre already during the third millennium BC, as a commercial junction between Lower Mesopotamia and Western Syria. Mari became the ruling capital of the middle Euphrates region at the beginning of the second millennium BC, and was eventually defeated and destroyed by Hammurabi of Babylon.

The tablets found in the archives here, over 20,000, mainly consist of letters and correspondence between the city's rulers and the governors of the districts into which the kingdom was divided, and other members of the royal family. These represent a substantial source of information on the environment of the middle Euphrates valley and on how the land was exploited by the mixed population that inhabited this area at the beginning of the second millennium BC.

Unlike Babylon, the cradle of the urban revolution in which the city with its temple and palace 'organizations' remained from the outset the main poles of the socio-political and territorial organization of Mesopotamia's lower alluvial plains, settlement patterns in the Euphrates valley were characterized by the coexistence of different communities: an urban one, which detained political power only in some historical periods, and a tribal community. The latter settled in villages, exploited the land differently, had greater mobility linked to pastoralism and made more intense use of the steppes and, over the long term, proved to be better suited to life in an area with constraining geographical conditions, surviving far longer than the former. The texts indicate a profound interrelationship between the semi-nomadic and sedentary populations which, together, formed the social system of the kingdom of Mari. These were defined according to the general categories of 'beduins of the steppe' (LÚ *ḫa-na* MEŠ *ša na-wi-i-im*) and 'men of the towns' (LÚ. MEŠ *ša a-la-ni*).[1] The former closely linked geographically to the 'high country', in other words the steppeland plateau, whereas the latter related to the only region where stable settlement could be sustained, 'the banks of the Euphrates' (*aḫ Purattim*).[2]

THE RURAL LANDSCAPE

The *aḫ nārim*, the river bank, is the area where settlement and the agricultural exploitation of land is made possible by irrigation. The *nawûm* is the plateau, and especially its areas of pasture, and is conceived as a territory external to the urban sphere, whose control is less stable, though essential for pastoralism, the paths followed by which are determined by the presence of wells.

The valley (*ḫamqum*) is the vital territory for the sedentary population and for the palace. This is the only area where planned agriculture is possible. The primary interest in this area is reflected in the greater specificity of the terminology used to describe the various geographical contexts. The texts indicate that it was subdivided into different cultivated zones, defined terminologically according to the geographical context in which they were located (Figure 3.2). The historical terraces ('low' area, *šupālûm* in Akkadian) along the river were exploited for pasture and, in suitable areas, for cultivation (*usallum* fields). These could be characterized by abandoned meanders of the river with their stagnant waters (*balītum*) that were sometimes used for fish farming, and arable areas could be cultivated in their vicinity.

The Holocene terraces were characterized by the presence of irrigation channels and most of the cultivated fields, organized into irrigation districts (*eqlum ugārum*). This was also the most densely populated zone, where, in the areas close to towns, there were fruit orchards and vegetable gardens, watered by hand (*salḫum* area).

Climbing towards the edge of the plateau, crops could be sown in the areas crossed by wadis (*nib'um* fields, watered intermittently by seasonal rivers), especially in those areas where the less salty groundwater allowed this to be exploited by digging wells (*daluwātum* lands) (Durand 1990).

THE IRRIGATION SYSTEM

The irrigation network played a vital role in making stable agricultural exploitation possible in the kingdom of Mari. This represented one of the main sources of care and concern for the rulers, whose agricultural production depended essentially on the ability to exploit as successfully as possible the low, and above all variable, availability of water in the area. In the middle Euphrates valley, periods of intense drought, especially in the summer, are followed by periods in which the rains (late autumn–winter and spring) and the melting of the snows in the Taurus mountains (spring), cause an increase in the amount of water in rivers and wadis in this area. These are sometimes sufficient to cause violent flash floods which, if not adequately controlled, damage crops on the lower terraces of the river valleys. This periodic flooding is unsuited to the farming cycle since water is needed at the beginning of autumn to prepare fields for cultivation, whereas at this time the rivers still suffer the effects of summer drought; in spring, by contrast, when the crops have germinated, flooding becomes dangerous.

Water management, therefore, involved designing and constructing hydraulic structures to make up for the shortage of rainfall (channels and collection basins through which to transport water to fields, or store it as much as possible), and which were able to contain, channel or mitigate the impact of spates and floods on these structures and on the fields (dykes, sluices, barrages).

The irrigation network documented in the Mari texts consisted of channels of different types. The first level consisted of the main channels running parallel to the Euphrates, into which part of the waters of the Euphrates and the Khabur were channelled. These were indicated by the Sumerogram ÍD = *nārum*, and by the Akkadian term *rākibum*, literally 'rider', probably referring to their physical aspect, raised with respect to the valley, with banks constructed by heaping up large quantities of earth, allowing water to flow to the agricultural districts by gravity (Durand 1998: 580–581). Secondary channels (PA5 *atappum*)[3] led off the large channels, taking water directly to the fields.

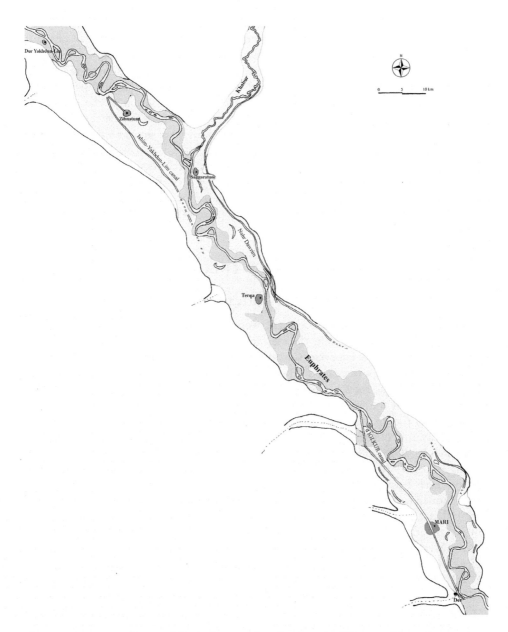

Figure 3.2 A map of the middle Euphrates valley showing the different cultivated zones: along the river the dark grey region is the river meadow and pastureland area; the light grey region is the area of the irrigation districts, while, around the ancient town, orchards were cultivated (redrawn from an original published in *Florilegium Marianum* III: 538).

The water flow was controlled and managed, both to ensure that the correct amount of water reached the fields and to withstand any natural calamities that might undermine these structures. Seasonal floods caused breaches in the channels' banks, and carried large amounts of sediment which might obstruct the channels. Constant maintenance was therefore needed, together with developed hydraulic technology. The pressure exerted by floods on the banks was lowered with a system of sluices (*erretum*) (Klengel 1980: 82, fn. 32; Durand 1990: 132), which allowed part of the water to drain away, lowering its level. The technical supervision of the irrigation network was carried out by a particular officer, named *sēkerum* in the texts, lit. 'he who closes', a sort of specialized technician whose skills were sought after and prized (Kupper 1988: 98; Finet 1990: 147–150).

Among the most frequent maintenance operations is the seasonal clearance of the beds of the channels (described in the texts with the verb *ḫaṭaṭum*) to ensure that the water flowed properly. This could involve a large number of workers, and usually took place during the summer, after the winter crop had been harvested and transported to threshing grounds.

AGRICULTURAL EXPLOITATION

Cereal cultivation

The fields in irrigation districts, *ugārum*, were cereal cultivation lands *par excellence*; within the royal administration, the execution of agricultural labour was organized around the cereal cultivation cycle. Cereal production was fundamental for the subsistence of a centralized power based on an economy of redistributive type. The official calendar began in the month of *urāḫum*, March–April, coinciding with the ripening of the harvest, but the most important farming cycle, that of barley, began with the preparation of the fields to be sown at the beginning of autumn.

The cultivation of royal lands was managed by farming teams designated with the term 'ploughs' (GIŠ.APIN); these were made up of individuals defined as *ālik eqlim* (lit. 'he who goes to the field'), each of whom had a specific role,[4] and of working animals. Each team had oxen to pull the plough; these animals were assigned food rations just like other members of the team. The farming teams carried out the more technical tasks, linked to the various types of ploughing and sowing with the seeder-plough. A catalogue of rations specifying the function of the members of a plough (*ARM* IX 26) lists four leaders of oxen (LÚ.MEŠ *kullizū*); two waterers of oxen (LÚ *mušaqqû*); five weeders (LÚ *kāsimū*); one overseer, lit. 'carrier of the throne' (LÚ GU.ZA.LÁ *guzalûm*); two millers (MÍ *te'inātum*); the latter probably had the task of milling food rations for the farming team itself. These numbers correspond roughly to the indications given in a letter (*ARM* XXVII 1), which mentions fifteen workers as a suitable number for each 'plough', however, in this same text, and in a series of other letters, the lack of manpower is frequently lamented, and the number of individuals making up each farming team may therefore have been lower.

The palace administration assigned quantities of land to be sown and seed to the overseers of the 'ploughs' at the beginning of the sowing season (ARM XXVII 2); receipts dated the seventh, eighth and ninth month of the local calendar have been found, corresponding roughly to the period between mid-September and mid-

December.[5] Alongside barley, these also document the cultivation of smaller amounts of different types of cereal, emmer-wheat and *šaḫlātum* (*ARM* XXIII 123).

Particular circumstances, such as abundant rainfall, could allow for cultivation later than the normal sowing season (*ARM* XXVII 2). After germination, the crop had to be protected from potential threats until it could be harvested; these hazards mainly included river floods, forays by wild animals (*ARM* XXVII 6 and 44 mention the need to protect crops from wild donkeys, gazelles and buffalo) and, above all, locusts. The danger represented by locusts (defined in the texts with the terms *erbum* and *ṣarṣar*) is mentioned frequently in the letters, in particular for the Qattunan[6] district on the Khabur, but also for Dur-Yahdun-Lim, Terqa and Der (the southern Der, south of Mari), basically along the entire course of the middle Euphrates.[7] Among the expedients adopted in an attempt to stop their spread, the texts document the raising of water levels in secondary channels in the hope of creating a barrier, and the beating of the ground by the population and any available livestock to frighten them.

The task of harvesting was heavy, and had to be carried out fairly promptly in order to avoid the problems described above. The manpower employed was of varying origins, depending on availability and requirements. Certainly, alongside palace staff, the population contributed to harvesting the royal fields. The amount of land to be reaped by each individual labourer depended on the ratio of land worked by the 'ploughs' to available manpower. However, according to evidence from *ARM* XXVII 37, the surface area of one *ikû* seems to represent a conventional reference point for the administration. Taking as a reference point the figure calculated for Iraq in the first half of the past century, according to which a labourer reaping with the help of a sickle could harvest an area equivalent to 0.05 ha (200 m^2) per day (Charles 1990: 54), and assuming the *ikû* to be equivalent to the Babylonian *ikû* of 3,600 m^2, each labourer would have needed about eighteen days to complete his part of the harvest in the palace land. To this we should add the time needed for the subsequent tasks of transporting the harvest to threshing floors, and for threshing.

Once the harvest had been accumulated on the threshing floors, the debts contracted in previous months were settled. The cultivation of sesame began at the same time as threshing.[8]

The cultivation of sesame

Although winter cereals represented the agricultural staple for the palace administration, the cultivation of sesame (ŠE.GIŠ.Ì = *šamaššammū*) was also extremely important. This took place in the hot season, since the plant requires a soil temperature of at least 20°C in order to germinate (Powell 1991: 162). Sesame was grown to produce a stable vegetable oil, suitable for storage and redistribution, as the middle Euphrates valley, like lower Mesopotamia, is unsuitable for the cultivation of olive trees, in contrast to the Mediterranean area where this cultivation is well attested.[9] We do not know when sesame was introduced to Mari, but its cultivation was certainly well-established and documented in the texts by the eighteenth century BC. However, the cultivation of valley lands during the summer months interfered with the opportunity of semi-nomadic populations to use these lands for pasture and ad hoc cultivation.

For the populations of villages in the middle Euphrates, dependent on a mixed agricultural and pastoral economy, the possibility of using these fields filled with the stubble of winter cereals, as summer pasture had an economic importance. The establishment of this type of cultivation by a centralized power involved the occupation of the valley lands even during the summer, and thus came into conflict with the transhumance of the flocks.[10]

The cultivation of sesame ended with its harvest, by uprooting the plant (*nasahum*) in autumn, before the fields were prepared for the sowing of barley, thus marking the beginning of a new agricultural cycle.

Vegetable gardens, vineyards, fruit orchards and woods

The areas around larger settlements, defined as *salhum* in the texts, were in part destined for growing vegetables; the areas devoted to arboriculture were described with the term *kirûm* (GIŠ.KIRI$_6$) (Durand 1990: 128). The technical tasks relating to the plants grown in these plots were carried out by 'gardeners' (NU.GIŠ.KIRI$_6$ *nukaribbum*). These did not belong to the palace farming team responsible for cereal cultivation, and were counted independently of the members of farming teams and included in the generic category of 'specialists' LÚ.MEŠ *ummênu* (*ARM* IX 27). The areas destined for horticulture were separate from cereal growing areas, and located near settlements, in a similar way to that documented in later texts from Emar, the current Meskene (Guichard 1997: 181, for Emar: Mori 2003: 134–146). We have information on the vegetables grown in gardens principally from the lists of foods arriving at the palace, and which were accounted for as 'the king's meal'. Various species of legumes are present: GÚ.GAL (*hallūrum*), GÚ.TUR (*kakkū*) and *appānu*, which can probably be identified with broad beans, lentils and chick-peas (Stol 1987b).

We also have evidence for the cultivation of garlic (*hazannum*) in different texts which mention sowing and harvesting by uprooting and drying (*ARM* XXVI 446; *ARM* X 16 (= *DEPM* 1158). Onions (SUM.KI.SIKIL *šamaškillum*) were also grown, and these two plants are often listed together (*ARM* IX 238; XII 241, 729, 731, 733, 734, 728; XXI 103,104; XXIII 367, 368, 465 and 370) (Stol 1987a). Leeks (*karšum*) are mentioned alongside a series of typical herbs used at the palace, including saffron (*azupīrum*), white cumin (*kamūnum*) and black cumin (*zībum*), coriander (ŠE.LÚ.SAR = *kisibirrum*) and thyme (*satarum*) (*ARM* XXIII 368 and 371). A letter from the time of Zimri-Lim lists the vegetables, herbs and spices to be sent to him, and gives an idea of what was used for cooking: '15 litres of garlic with their skins [?], 7 litres of leeks, 120 litres of onions, 120 litres of mustard (*kasū*), 60 litres of coriander, 60 litres of "beer bread" (*happirum*), 10 litres of white cumin, 3 litres of black cumin, 7 litres of *samīdum* plant, 5 litres of *ninûm* plant, 5 litres of juniper seeds (*kikkirēnu*) and *ballukkum* plant' (FM II 4).

'Desert truffles' (*kam'atum*) were not cultivated, but collected in the steppe in the Saggaratum[11] and Qattunan district (*ARM* XXVII 54 and *FM* II 62), following the Euphrates and Khabur upstream; these are a sort of whitish tubers, still found in the area, often presented to the ruler as gifts.

As far as fruit trees are concerned, fruit orchards are differentiated in the texts from the small groves of trees, especially poplars, further away from towns near the irrigation districts (Durand 1990: 128). In the woods (GIŠ.TIR.RA *qištum*), trees could be planted for building timber (Postgate 1987: 115), whereas fruit trees were grown by the palace administration in genuine 'nurseries', probably located near the banks of the river (Lafont 1997: 266–267). In a sort of inventory mainly concerning fruit trees under the care of single individuals, probably palace 'gardeners' (*ARM* XXII 329), areas of land used as fruit orchards are listed, naming the number and types of trees present. The most common plant is the fig (GIŠ.PÈŠ *tittum*), planted together with other fruit trees, especially apple trees (GIŠ.HAŠUR) (Postgate 1987: 117–118); the association between fig and apple trees is also documented in Lower Mesopotamia at the time of Ur III (Postgate 1987: 122 fn. 31). Also documented are pear trees (*kamaššarum*) (Postgate 1987: 138 fn. 4), pomegranates (GIŠ.NU.ÚR.MA *nurmûm*), poplars (GIŠ.A.AM *adārum/ildakkum*) (Postgate 1992: 179), tamarisks (GIŠ.ŠINIG *bīnum*) and an unidentified type of tree, the *baštum*, whose wood was used to make furniture (Soubeyran *ARM* XXIII: 442).

Vines (GIŠ.GEŠTIN *karānum*) are accounted for separately, and planted in special plots; sensibly, these are accounted for according to the surface area of land cultivated, and not the number of plants. The only plant mentioned alongside the vine is the poplar. The cultivation of vines in the middle Euphrates valley was a recent introduction at the time of the kingdom of Mari; vines and the production of wine are typical of Mediterranean Syria (Yamkhad), the upper Euphrates (Carchemish) and the southern slopes of the Jebel Sinjar (Finet 1974–77: 122), and Mari imported the alcoholic drink from these areas. However, one text (*ARM* XXI 99) mentions jars of wine from various *kirûm* at Hishamta, in the Terqa district, for a total of 212 jars produced by local vineyards, and a letter provides information on the working of vineyards in that district (Lion 1992).

The tamarisk, mentioned in the context of fruit orchards in *ARM* XXII 329, is present in the Zurubban area, south of the Terqa floodplain, according to (*ARM* XIII 122 = *DEPM* 153).[12] The presence of cornel trees is documented on the banks of the Khabur; turpentine trees or pistachios, on the other hand, are frequently mentioned as coming from the north-eastern area and mount Murdi, probably the western part of the Jebel Sinjar where these nuts are still produced today.

SHAPE AND SIZE OF FIELDS

The absence of legal and administrative texts from Mari referring to the management of agricultural lands makes it impossible to describe the organization of farming zones in detail.[13] However, some sporadic evidence allows us to assimilate the terminology used to describe the sides of fields – and thus the tendency of plots of cultivated land to adopt an identifiable shape and layout – to a middle-Euphrates tradition which continues in time, and is well documented in later texts from Terqa and especially Emar. The names given to the sides of fields inside the ugārum are basically identical, and presumably result from a way of organizing land dictated by the need to optimize access to water from the irrigation network. The terminology used for field sides, in texts from all three archives, characteristically makes a distinction between pairs of opposite sides, two long sides, upper and lower (*itûm elûm, itûm saplûm*)[14] and two short sides (SAG 1 and SAG 2) (*ARM* VIII 3), indicating that the basic shape was rectangular. The identification of these sides remains identical for 'long' sides, always defined as 'upper' and 'lower' at Mari, Terqa and Emar; the short sides are identified at Mari and Emar by a cardinal number (first side and second side), whereas at Terqa they are specified as for long sides. The fact that the way of referring to the long sides remains linked to a fixed terminology is evidence that, for these sides, geographical orientation was of primary significance, since this was linked to the flow of the river. The main directional concepts used, *elûm* and *saplûm*, indicate both the higher and lower part of the valley, and the ideas of 'upstream' and 'downstream' with reference to the Euphrates. The direction followed by the river was the fundamental factor in the organization of farming areas. It is thus plausible to imagine an irrigation district made up of plots of rectangular fields, adjacent to one another and with access to water on one of the short sides, parallel to the irrigation channel and probably the Euphrates, and with the long sides upstream and downstream with respect to the flow of the river.

For the size of fields, too, given the small number of legal texts found, information must mainly be extrapolated from letters. The state of the valley lands appears to be fairly complex and difficult to determine (Durand 1998: 513–535); however, a large portion of the agricultural land was managed – and probably owned – by the palace (defined in the texts as A.ŠÀ *e-kál-lim*). In part, this land was exploited directly by farming teams, and in part allocated on a usufructuary basis, usually in exchange for services of administrative or military nature. Private property must have existed, as is documented by sporadic deeds of sale or purchase for fields, but its precise impact on the territory is impossible to determine. Alongside 'individual' property, property of 'collective' type seems to persist (cfr. *ARM* VIII 11). The small number of legal documents from Tell Hariri use formulaic expressions which imply that the purchaser was acknowledged as a clan member, through 'false' adoptions (*ahhūtu*), aimed at making the alienation of lands from the family 'acceptable' on a formal and ideological level (Liverani 1983: 158–159). These legal formulas find counterparts in later texts from Emar in the practice of describing an outside purchaser as a 'brother', and of declaring formally alien a member of the family who acquires clan lands in order to safeguard the purchase (Zaccagnini 1992: 36); these are evidence for the persistence in the middle Euphrates valley of community institutions extraneous to the large royal administration, and which play an important role in land management.

To return to the size of fields, some texts tell us of expanses of farming land belonging to the palace, since they are assigned to his farming teams. Each 'plough' was assigned a 'task' (ÉŠ.GÀR/ÁŠ.GÀR GIŠ.APIN), quantified both in terms of the amount of land to be worked and of the production quota of 'finished products' to be delivered (Talon 1983: 48). The teams generally belong to 'rural domains' (*bītum*) destined to support the royal family and palace officials (Joannès 1984: 113–115). This fact implies that royal lands were divided into plots managed by the latter. However, the frequent mentions in the letters of problems relating to the allocation of work quotas to the teams suggest a more complex situation, which was far from being planned in a stable and lasting manner. Unexpected problems force governors to diminish or increase the work quotas of the 'ploughs', and thus the actual surface area of land cultivated directly by the palace administration.

Evidence for the amount of land allocated to each team provides different figures;

however, the surface area considered a reasonable amount of work for a farming team was between 70 and 100 *ikû* (*ARM*XXVI/1 76),[15] between 25.2 and 36 ha if we consider one *ikû* equivalent to 3,600 m². Although this was the surface area corresponding to the rulers' expectations, in practice the areas documented in the letters differ significantly. However, these generally refer to extreme cases which are reported precisely because there is an untenable situation to be resolved, either by excess or deficit.[16]

Governors and high officials, like members of the royal family, could own great properties and large areas of land, probably exploited using farming teams provided by the palace administration.[17] District governors received fields upon their nomination; though the size of the areas allotted may vary, these seem to coincide roughly with the work quota of a royal farming team, more or less numerous depending on the land to be worked (from 50 to 100 *ikû*).[18] The allocation of fields by the palace administration was often problematic and a cause for complaints: there are frequent cases when a functionary is assigned a piece of land already given to a member of the royal family or a notable of the kingdom (cfr. *ARM* XIV 81 = *DEPM* 752). Alternatively the allocation conflicts with the needs of local governors to use palace farming teams; they therefore appeal to the king to stop these concessions (see, for example, *ARM* XIII 39 = *DEPM* 781). Nor should collaboration between royal farming teams and local populations be taken for granted.

In addition to notables, some categories of palace 'staff' were also allotted fields for sustenance; these however were significantly smaller in area. A letter tells us that five *ikû* of land were allotted to some categories of soldiers, and three *ikû* to the 'inhabitants of the village' (*ARM* XXVII 107). The texts document the tendency of the rulers to allocate fields for growing food to those able to cultivate them, whereas those without the means to exploit the land (tools and working animals) are described as dependents to be allocated rations (*ARM* IV 86 = *DEPM* 772).

Little information is available on the size of fields not belonging to royal lands. Among the rare deeds of sale and purchase for fields between private individuals, the sizes documented generally concern small surface areas in the order of a few *ikû*, similar to the subsistence fields assigned by the rulers. These are plots bought and sold which do not provide information on the actual extent of the land actually owned by the rural families.

The text richest in information from the point of view of reconstructing individual field plots within agricultural areas (*ARM* XXII 328) lists small plots bought by a single individual, Warad-Sin, for a total of 16 *ikû* (ŠU.NIGIN 2 ÉŠE 4 GÁN A.ŠÀ). These were probably located along the Khabur, since the sellers are defined collectively as 'sons of the Khabur' (Villard 2001: 99–100). The total of 16 *ikû* is made up of smaller plots, generally measuring one *ikû* each, and mainly located in a single irrigation district, 'the *ugārum* of Il-aba'. Within the irrigation district the size of individual plots seems to be more or less identical; presumably they also had the same orientation. It is significant that, whereas for plots of one *ikû* a single individual is named as the vendor, for the one larger plot of five *ikû* there are eight sellers (although also four sellers for a plot smaller than half an *ikû*). It therefore seems that the larger of the plots belonged to a 'family group' and was divided, and that the *ikû* represents a sort of basic unit, the 'minimum' cultivable plot.

NOTES

1 Cf. *DEPM*, 297.

2 In the political terminology, the Euphrates bank *aḫ Purattim*, represents the territory of the four main districts of the Mari reign: Mari, Terqa, Saggaratum and Qattunan, (Lafont 2001: 218–219).

3 'Aus dem *atappum* wird Wasser zur bewasserung der Felder (*ana šiqītim*) abgeleitet' (Stol 1980: 346).

4 Rations to *ālik eqlim* are listed in text *ARM* IX 25, and in a series of administrative texts referring to the same 'rural domain': *ARM* XXIII 106, 107, 108, 109, 110, 111, 112, 113, 114, 115, 117, 119, 120; *ARM* XXIV 14, 15, 16. In texts *ARM* XXII 285 and XXIV 20 quantities of grain defined as ŠE.BA É ('barley rations for the rural domain') list rations both for men and working animals.

5 *ARM* XXIII 121, 122, 123, 124, 460, 461, *ARM* XXIV 2.

6 Birot in *ARM* XXVII, pp. 10–11, comments on the six letters entirely devoted to the subject of a locust invasion in the district of Qattunan (*ARM* XXVII 26–31) and the shorter mentions (*ARM* XXVII 32–35, 38). See also Lion and Michelle 1997.

7 See texts *ARM* II 107 = *DEPM* 354; *ARM* III 62 = *DEPM* 178 and A.3872+ (Durand 1990: 109).

8 Cf. *ARM* XXVII 38.

9 For the cultivation of olive trees at Ebla, see Archi 1991; for the region of Alakhtum, probably Alalakh, see Durand 2002: 82–84 and texts *FM* VII 28, 35, 36.

10 Cfr. *ARM* XIII 39 = *DEPM* 781, and Luke 1972.

11 *ARM* II 104 = *DEPM* 179, *ARM* XIV 35 = *DEPM* 181, *ARM* XIV 36 = *DEPM* 393, *FM* II 34

12 It was present also along the Khabur banks (Morandi Bonacossi 1996: 47).

13 A sporadic case is *ARM* XXII 328.

14 *ARM* VIII 6, similarly to what is attested in a text dating to the *šakkanakku* period, M.10556 (Durand 1982: 81).

15 100 *ikû* seems to be the surface of a 'standard field' given to a 'farmer' responsible for one 'plough' also in lower Mesopotamia in neo-Sumerian times (Liverani 1988–89: 299 and fn. 17; Liverani 1998: 47).

16 The following texts mention a surface of land assigned to the Mari ploughs: *FM* 11, 32, 5 *ikû*; *ARM* XIII 39, 50 *ikû*; *ARM* XXVI/I 76, 70–100 *ikû*; *ARM* XXIII 37, 80 *ikû*; *ARM* XXVII 36, 166.66 *ikû* (for six ploughs) or 142.85 *ikû* (for seven ploughs); *ARM* XXVIII 36 + *ARM* XXVII 100, 150 *ikû*.

17 See text *DEPM* 6 and *ARM* XXVI.

18 Cf. *ARM* I 56 = *DEPM* 756; *ARM* XIV 81 = *DEPM* 752 and A.450 (Durand 1998: 533–534).

ABBREVIATIONS RELATED TO THE MAIN EDITIONS OF THE MARI TEXTS

ARM – *Archives Royales de Mari* (28 vols).

DEPM – J.M. Durand, *Les documénts épistolaires du palais de Mari*, Littératures Anciennes du Proche-Orient, 16–18 (3 vols – Tome I 1997; Tome II 1998; Tome III 2000).

FM – *Florilegium Marianum* (7 vols: I – 1992 J.M. Durand (ed.) *Recueil d'études en l'honneur de Michel Fleury*; II – 1994 D. Charpin and J.M. Durand (eds) *Recueil d'études à la memoire de Maurice Birot*; III – 1997 D. Charpin and J.M. Durand (eds) *Recueil d'études à la memoire de Marie-Thérèse Barrélet*; IV – 1999 N. Ziegler, *La population feminine des palais d'après les archives royales de Mari: le Harem de Zimri-Lim*; V – 2003 D. Charpin and N. Ziegler, *Mari et le Proche-Orient à l'époque amorrite: éssai d'histoire politique*; VI – 2002 D. Charpin and J.M. Durand (eds) *Receuil d'études à la mémoire d'André Parrot*; VII – 2002 J.M. Durand, *Le culte d'Addu d'Alep et l'affaire d'Alahtum*).

BIBLIOGRAPHY

Archi, A. 1991 'Culture de l'olivier et production de l'huile à Ebla', in *Mélanges P. Garelli*, pp. 211–222.

Besançon, J. and P. Sanlaville 1981 'Aperçu géomorphologique sur la vallée de l'Euphrate syrien', *Paléorient* 7: 5–18.

Bernbeck, R. 1991 *Steppe als Kulturlandschaft*, Berlin.

Buccellati, G. 1990a 'The Rural Landscape of the Ancient Zor: the Terqa Evidence', in B. Geyer (ed.) *Techniques et pratiques hydro-agricoles traditionnelles en domain irrigué*, Paris, pp. 155–170.

—— 1990b 'River Bank, High Country, and Pasture Land: the Growth of Nomadism on the Middle Euphrates and the Khabur', in S.Eichler, M. Wäfler and P. Warburton (eds) *Tall al-Hamidiya* 2, Orbis Biblicus et Orientalis. Serie Archeologica, pp. 67–83.

Cadelli, D. 1994 'Lieux boisés et bois coupés', *FM* II, pp. 159–173.

Charles, M.P. 1985 'The Husbandry of Pulses and Oil Crops in Modern Iraq', *BSAg* 2, pp. 39–62.

—— 1990 'Traditional Crop Husbandry in Southern Iraq (1900–1960 AD)', *BSAg* 5, pp. 47–64.

Charpin, D. and J.M. Durand 1986 'Fils de Sim'al. Les origines tribales des rois de Mari', *Revue d'Assyriologie* 80: 141–191.

Chavalas, M.W. and J.L. Hayes (eds) 1992 *New Horizons in the Study of Ancient Syria*, Bib. Mes. 25, Malibu.

D'Hont, O. 1990 'Evolution récente dans l'utilisation des espaces de la moyenne vallée de l'Euphrate', in B. Geyer (ed.) *Techniques et pratiques hydro-agricoles traditionnelles en domain irrigué*, Paris, pp. 239–247.

Durand, J.M. 1982 'Sumerien et Akkadien en pays amorite, I. Un document juridique archaique de Mari', *MARI* 1, pp. 79–89.

—— 1990 'Problèmes d'eau et d'irrigation au royaume de Mari: l'apport des textes anciennes', in B. Geyer (ed.) *Techniques et pratiques hydro-agricoles traditionnelles en domain irrigué*, Paris, pp. 101–142.

—— 1998 'Propriété du sol et l'attribution des terres; Irrigation et travaux des champs', *DEPM* vol. II, pp. 513–676.

Finet, A. 1974/77 'Le vin à Mari', *Archiv für Orientforschung* 25: 22–131.

—— 1990 'Les pratiques de l'irrigation au XVIIIe siècle avant notre ère en Mésopotamie d'après le textes de Mari et le Code de Hammurabi', in B. Geyer (ed.) *Techniques et pratiques hydro-agricoles traditionnelles en domain irrigué*,Paris, pp. 143–154.

Fortin, M. and O. Aurenche 1998 *Espace naturel, espace habité en Syrie du nord (10e–2e millénaire av. J.-C.), Actes du colloque tenu à l'Université Laval (Qébec) du 5 au 7 mai 1997*, Québec – Lyon.

Geyer, B. 1984 'Mari dans son cadre: Environement et cadre naturel', *Histoire et Archéologie* 80: 13–16.

—— 1985 'Géomorphologie et occupation du sol de la moyenne vallée de l'Euphrate dans la région de Mari', *MARI* 4: 27–39.

—— 1990 'Aménagements hydrauliques et territoir agricole dans la moyenne vallée de l'Euphrate', in B. Geyer (ed.) *Techniques et pratiques hydro-agricoles traditionnelles en domain irrigué*, Paris, pp. 63–86.

—— 1998 'Géographie et peuplement des steppes arides de la Syrie du Nord', in M. Fortin and O. Aurenche (eds) *Espace naturel, espace habité en Syrie du nord (10e–2e millénaire av. J.-C.), Actes du colloque tenu à l'Université Laval (Qébec) du 5 au 7 mai 1997*, Québec – Lyon, pp. 1–8.

Geyer, B. and J.Y. Monchambert 1983 'Prospection dans la basse vallée de l'Euphrate Syrien', *AAAS* 33: 261–265.

—— 1987 'Prospection de la moyenne vallée de l'Euphrate: rapport préliminaire', *MARI* 5293–344.

Guichard, M. 1997 'Le sel à Mari (III). Les lieux du sel', *FM* III: 167–200.

Joannès, F. 1984 'Un domaine agricole', *ARM* XXIII, pp. 105–126.

—— 1994 'L'eau et la glace', *FM* II, pp. 135–141.

—— 1996 'Routes et voies de comunications dans les archives de Mari', *Amurru*, pp. 323–362.

—— 1997 'Palmyre et les routes du désert au début du deuxième millenaire', *MARI* 8, pp. 393–415.

Klengel, H. 1980 'Zum Bewässerung Bodenbau am Mitteleren Euphrat nach den Texten aus Mari', *Archiv für Orientforschung* 7: 77–87.

Kupper, J.R. 1957 *Les nomades en Mésopotamie au temp de rois de Mari*, Paris.

—— 1959 'Le rôle des nomades dans l'histoire de la Mésopotamie ancienne', *Journal of the Economic and Social History of the Orient* 2: 113–127.

—— 1988 'L'irrigation à Mari', *BSAg* 4: 93–103.

—— 1992 'Le bois à Mari', *BSAg* 6: 163–170.

Lafont, B. 1990 'Une nuit drammatique à Mari', *FM* I: 93–103.

—— 1997 'Techniques arboricoles à l'epoque amorrite. Transport et acclimatation de figuiers à Mari', *FM* III: 263–268.

—— 2001 'Relations internationales, alliances et diplomatie au temps des royaumes amorrites', *Amurru* 2: 213–328.

Lion, B. 1992 'Vignes au royaume de Mari', *FM* I: 107–113.

—— 2001 'Les gouverneurs du Royaume de Mari à l'époque de Zimri-Lim', *Amurru* 2: 141–209.

—— and C.Michelle 1997 'Criquets et autres insectes à Mari', *MARI* 8: 707–724.

Liverani, M. 1983 'Communautés rurales dans la Syrie du IIe millénaire a.C.', in *Les communautés rurales – Rural Communities II': Antiquité – Antiquity, Recueils de la Societé Jean Bodin pour l'histoire comparative des institutions* 41, Paris, pp. 147–185.

—— 1984 'Land Tenure and Inheritance in the Ancient Near East: The Interaction between "Palace" and "Family" Sectors', in T. Khalidi (ed.) *Land Tenure and Social Transformation in the Middle East*, Beirut, pp. 33–44.

—— 1988–89 'La forma dei campi neo-sumerici', *Origini* XIV: 289–327.

—— 1990–91 'Il rendimento dei cereali durante la III dinastia di Ur. Contributo ad un approccio realistico', *Origini* XV: 359–368.

—— 1991 'Recenti ricerche sull'agricoltura sumerica', *Studi Storici* 32: 220–226.

—— 1996 'Reconstructing the Rural Landscape of the Ancient Near East', *Journal of the Economic and Social History of the Orient* 39: 1–41.

—— 1997 '"Half-nomads" on the Middle Euphrates and the Concept of Dimorphic Society', *Archiv für Orientforschung* 24: 44–48.

—— 1999 'The Role of the Village in Shaping the Ancient Near Eastern Rural Landscape', in L. Milano, S. de Martino, F.M. Fales and G.B. Lanfranchi (eds) *Landscapes, Territories, Frontiers and Horizons in the Ancient Near East. Papers Presented to the XLIV Rencontre Assyriologique Internationale Venezia, 7–11 July, 1997*, vol. I, pp. 37–47.

—— 2001 'Agricoltura e irrigazione', in S. Petruccioli (ed.) *Storia della Scienza, vol. I La scienza nel mondo antico*, pp. 447–456.

Luke, J.T. 1972 'Observations on ARMT XIII 139', *Journal of Cuneiform Studies* 24: 20–23.

Margueron, J. Cl. 1988 'Espace agricole et aménagement régional à Mari au début du IIIe millénaire', *BSAg* 4: 49–60.

—— 1990 'Aménagement de la région de Mari: quelques considérations historiques', in B. Geyer (ed.) *Techniques et pratiques hydro-agricoles traditionnelles en domain irrigué*, Paris, pp. 171–192.

—— 1998 'Aménagement du territoire et organisation de l'espace en Syrie du Nord à l'âge du Bronze: limites et possibilités d'une recherche', in M. Fortin and O. Aurenche (eds) *Espace naturel, espace habité en Syrie du nord (10e–2e millénaire av. J.-C.), Actes du colloque tenu à l'Université Laval (Qébec) du 5 au 7 mai 1997*, Québec – Lyon, pp.167–178.

Masetti-Rouault, M.G. 2000 'Aspects du paysage social et politique du Moyen Euphrate syrien à l'âge du Fer', in L. Milano, S. de Martino, F.M. Fales and G.B. Lanfranchi (eds) *Landscapes, Territories, Frontiers and Horizons in the Ancient Near East. Papers Presented to the XLIV Rencontre Assyriologique Internationale Venezia, 7–11 July, 1997*, vol. II: 129–138.

—— 2001 *Cultures locales du Moyen Euphrate. Modèles et événements*, Subartu VIII.

Morandi Bonacossi, D. 1996 *Tra il fiume e la steppa*, Padua.

Mori, L. 2003 *Reconstructing the Emar Landscape*, Quaderni di geografia storica 6, Rome.

Postgate, N. 1983 'The "Oil-plant" in Assyria', *BSAg* 2: 145–152.

—— 1987 'Notes on Fruit in the Cuneiform Sources', *BSAg* 3: 115–144.

—— 1992 'Trees and Timber in the Assyrian Texts', *BSAg* 6: 177–192.

Powell, M.A. 1987/90 'Masse und Gewichte', *Reallexikon der Assyriologie* 7.

—— 1991 'Epistemology and Sumerian Agriculture. The Strange Case of Sesame and Linseed', *Aula Orientalis* 9: 155–164.

Rouault, O. 1998 'Villes, villages, campagnes et steppe dans la région de Terqa: données nouvelles', in M. Fortin and O. Aurenche (eds) *Espace naturel, espace habité en Syrie du nord (10e–2e millénaire av. J.-C.), Actes du colloque tenu à l'Université Laval (Qébec) du 5 au 7 mai 1997*, Québec – Lyon, pp. 91–198.

—— 2000 'Quelques remarques sur la societé de Terqa', in O. Rouault and M. Wafler (eds) *La Djeziré et l'Euphrate syriens de la protohistoire à la fin du II millenaire av. J.-C.*, Subartu VII, pp. 265–269.

—— and M. Wafler (eds) 2000 *La Djeziré et l'Euphrate syriens de la protohistoire à la fin du II millenaire av. J.-C.*, Subartu VII.

Sanlaville, P. 1985 'L'espace géographique de Mari', *MARI* 4: 15–25.

—— 1990 'Pays et paysage du Tigre et de l'Euphrate. Reflextions sur la Mesopotamie antique', *Akkadica* 66: 1–12.

—— 2000 *Le moyen Orient arabe. Le milieu et l'homme*, Paris.

Stol, M. 1985 'Remarks on the Cultivation of Sesame and the Extraction of its Oil', *BSAg* 2: 119–126.

—— 1987a 'Garlic, Onion, Leek', *BSAg* 3: 57–80.

—— 1987b 'Beans, Peas and Vetches in Akkadian Texts', *BSAg* 3: 127–139.

—— 1995 'Old Babylonian Cattle', *BSAg* 8: 173–223.

Talon, P. 1983 'A propos du personnel agricole à Mari', *Iraq* 45: 46–55.

Villard, P. 2001 'Les administrateurs de l'époque de Yasmah-Addu', in *Amurru* 2: 9–140.

Wagstaff, J.M. (ed.) 1987 *Landscape and Culture. Geographical and Archaeological Perspectives*, Padstow, Cornwall.

Weulersse, J. 1946 *Paysans de Syrie et du Proche Orient*, Paris.

Wilkinson, T.J. 1990 'Soil Development and Early Land Use in the Jazira Region', *World Archaeology* 22: 87–103.

Wirth, E. 1971 *Syrien: eine geographiche Landeskunde*, Darmstadt.

Zaccagnini, C. 1992 'Ceremonial Transfers of Real Estate at Emar and Elsewhere', *VO* 8/2, pp. 33–48.

—— 1999 'Economic Aspect of Land Ownership and Land Use in Northern Mesopotamia and Syria from the Late Third Millennium to the neo-Assyrian Period', in M. Hudson and B.A. Levine, *Urbanisation and Land Ownership in the Ancient Near East*, Cambridge.

CHAPTER FOUR

AGRICULTURAL TECHNIQUES

———·◆·———

Blahoslav Hruška

INTRODUCTION

Domesticated plants and animals became an important food source for the populations of the Ancient Near East in the Neolithic age. They became ever more widely used during the periods which may be dated approximately from the eighth to the fourth millenium BC, and throughout all subsequent phases of Mesopotamian history. Both in the alluvial plains and in semi-arid steppes, Mesopotamian agriculture yielded surprisingly good results, and was capable of sustaining the large populations of the first city-states and the later territorial states. On this agricultural base, developed in the third millenium BC, the later, well-known Assyrian and Babylonian empires emerged.

This study focuses on agricultural production during the third millennium BC, when the chief language written in Mesopotamia was Sumerian. Our knowledge of plant cultivation in the flood plain between the Euphrates and the Tigris is gained less from direct archaeological evidence than from cuneiform texts.[1] Sumerian decorative art also offers only a limited amount of relevant iconographic evidence pertaining to cereal growing and animal husbandry, quite unlike the richly informative visual sources from ancient Egypt. Fortunately, a great number of the early texts deal specifically with agricultural activities. These 'economic' texts originate mainly from the archives of temple and palace estates and furnish information about the management of food production. Of great interest is the Sumerian composition known as 'Farmer's Instructions', also referred to as 'Georgica Sumerica' or 'Farmer's Almanac' (Civil 1994: 1–6). An experienced 'ploughman' gives detailed instruction on various agricultural matters, such as the labouring of grain fields prior to sowing, how to sow grain, on the maintenance of ards (including seed ards), on irrigation, on harvesting and, finally, on the winnowing and transport of grain. The text refers to accompanying religious rituals, as its doxology identifies it as 'instructions of the god Ninurta, son of Enlil, Ninurta, faithful farmer of Enlil'. The composition survives in 33 mostly broken examples from Nippur, other fragments have turned up at Ur, Sippar and Babylon, or come from unidentified sites. I believe that the 'Farmer's Instructions' might have been transmitted orally throughout the third millennium, to be written down in the eighteenth–seventeenth centuries BC.

33 APIN, ENGAR, URU$_4$

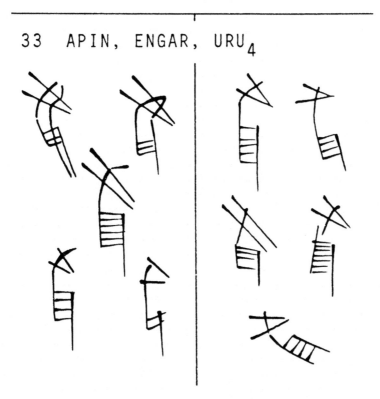

Figure 4.1 Archaic sign for 'ard', 'farmer' and 'to plough'
(Green and Nissen 1987: 176: 33).

Also significant are the somewhat later Sumerian literary compositions, dating after 2000 BC. Since agricultural technology was fairly conservative and did not change much over time, these early records are important for the understanding of the fundamental techniques of Mesopotamian farming.[2]

Although Mesopotamians obviously were in close contact with their natural environment, it is surprising that in cuneiform texts[3] there are few assessments of the relation between humans and water, soil and nature in general. The Sumerians and Babylonians visualized Earth as a flat body floating on a 'Sweet-water Sea', the source of rivers, wells and springs, as well as of groundwater. Like the Earth, the Sky had also its 'interior', 'height', horizon, border and cardinal directions. The heavenly bodies (Sun, Moon, stars) and all atmospheric phenomena such as heat, cold, rain, wind and storm, were perceived as deities coming from Heaven and proceeding from horizon to horizon, from the east to the west or from the north to the south.

There was no word for the overall designation of 'soil'. The lexemes ki (place, spot) and saḫar (clay, dust) both refer to the inhabited and exploited segments of the landscape in contrast to the untilled 'steppe' in which sheep, goats and cattle grazed seasonally. Landscapes were animated by 'living' people, animals and plants. All human beings and the whole of humanity bowed to the will of gods and tilled their land. The Sumerian and Akkadian language also lacks a word for the overall designation of 'plants'. The realms of vegetation are represented by particular kinds of green undergrowth (u_2-šim), of herbs (u_2) grazed upon by livestock. Higher green plants are represented by reeds (gi), the stalks of which acquire a wood-like structure in the autumn (giš-gi). Denizens of the animal world were the 'quadrupeds' (nig_2-ur_2-$limmu_2$), especially 'small livestock' (udu, $maš_2$ 'sheep, goat'), 'cattle' (gu_4) and 'donkey' (anše) in the stock phrase $maš_2$-anše ('domesticated animals').

ARTIFICIAL IRRIGATION

At the end of the prehistoric age, water and soil conditions of Mesopotamia underwent a series of changes not exactly favourable for the development of traditional hoe agriculture. The average annual temperatures increased while precipitation figures fell from the optimum of 600 mm per annum down to the tricky isohyet 250 mm per annum, all of which resulted in the emergence of extensive steppe areas. The Euphrates, Tigris, and other watercourses relocated their riverbeds. The Persian Gulf coastal seascape changed as well. In the age of the Ubaid- and Uruk cultures, agricultural production shifted southwards into the alluvial sector of the Mesopotamian basin (Nützel 2004: 85–124). Even there, however, natural precipitation was insufficient (Nissen 1988: 43, 141–145) and this triggered the development of artificial irrigation systems. The South Mesopotamian arable consisted of artificially irrigated field systems complemented by garden areas for growing onion-type plants (ki-sum, 'onion fields'), pulses and oil plants (LaPlaca and Powell 1990: 84–104). To maintain productivity it was necessary to put into operation complex and sophisticated water-management facilities, such as systems of channels, retention tanks and reservoirs, as well as the conveying of water towards individual cereal-field tracts, divided into 'ridge-and-furrow' (the furrows were water trenches).[4] The building and maintenance of artificial water-supply lines, sluices, reservoirs and water-conveying facilities (Pemberton *et al.* 1988), were all a protracted and demanding affair (Hruška 1995: 46–57). Beyond the capacities of individual families and clans, it evolved into collective ventures of major communities (Adams 1982: 131–135). The construction of complex water-management systems (Steinkeller 1988; Renger 1990) could last for generations. A new type of work organization was needed to deal with the planning, direction and the employment of a labour force *en masse*, as well as the formation of both seasonal and permanent work gangs with foremen and labour hands, the logistics of their food and drink supplies, etc. Economic texts contain data on labour expenditure during excavation work and during the sinking and building of channels and conduit trenches by means of simple manual tools such as hoes, spades and shovels (Renger 1990: 35–36). In minor channels and trenches the calculated 'daily norm' could rise to 6 m^3 (Powell 1988: 163, 165–166). A literary text, known as the Lagash King List, illustrates the crucial importance of irrigation. It tells us that after a 'deluge', which swept off entire landscapes, the gods An and Enlil restored the 'seed of mankind', as well as principalities and kingdoms. But since human beings did not manage to bring water toward their fields, Girsu of Lagash was stricken with a famine (Selz 2002: 27–29).

The water carried by the rivers decreases steadily from July to November. They rise between January and March, and reach peak flow between April and June when the maxima per day differ as much as 6 m from the minima. The irrigation season

Figure 4.2 Soil preparation with hoes (Butz 1980–83: 478).

lasts from the end of November until May (from sowing to growing of ears of wheat and barley) and water thus had to be stored and distributed gradually. The process of carrying water from retention tanks to the fields and cereal ridges was dominated by the effort to minimalize losses by selection of the appropriate widths, gradients and sections for canals and conduit trenches (Hruška 1988a: 64–69). M. P. Charles (1988: 11) believes that minor canals conveying water from the tanks to the fields could have had flat bottoms and vertical banks. Such sections could minimize water erosion and eliminate the sedimentation danger in cases of gradients lower than three per cent.

The essential first irrigation procedure consisted of so-called leaching.[5] The future production area was flooded prior to sowing, up to 10 cm above the soil level, which caused a soaking of water to the depth of 60 cm. If water was plentiful the soil could be leached between 15 and 20 cm deep, to provide the future root system with sufficient moisture (Charles 1988: 32–33).The term ki-duru$_5$ (wet place) probably designated a field irrigated with water after short-term fallow in order to facilitate ploughing (tugur-si-ga). No known text can be used to identify the month of the year in which leaching was done. LaPlaca and Powell (1990: 80) believe that basic ploughing went on after the harvest at the end of summer. This would nevertheless entail two separate ploughing campaigns while the animal teams, ploughing implements, such as ploughs and seeder ploughs, seed and fodder were distributed only once (Maekawa 1990: 127–129). Leaching consumes some 35–40 per cent of the entire water volume necessary for the whole period between sowing and harvest, since annual precipitation does not surpass the critical minimum value of 200 mm. One half of the remaining irrigation water was used in the time of sprouting, rooting, and the initial stalk growing of the cereals. The other half provided for further growing phases, including the flowering and putting on ears of the grain (Charles 1988: 14–15). Water from leaching and from soakage could have been used for the regulation of groundwater. The danger was that if drainage was insufficient and the groundwater level unstable, artificial irrigation could increase salinization which ultimately ruined the fertility of the soil. In extreme cases, a field can be ruined for cultivation after seven years of continuous irrigation. Field agriculture thus could never do without regular and frequent episodes of fallow.

The 'Farmer's Instructions'[6] recommended three irrigation campaigns at various stages of the development of the cereal plants to follow after the first leaching: (1) 'When the plants are higher than the furrow tops' (after stalk development?); (2) 'When the plants are as high as reed for mats' (before putting on ears of corn?); (3) 'When the grain hulls get thicker' (putting on the ears of corn).

From the Old Babylonian period onwards, the calculation of water volume in tanks in relation to the area of irrigated fields was a standard mathematical problem in 'school exercises'. The only aspect of reality in such exercises may have been the indication of the water level in one single leaching application (for instance, to the depth of one digit (1 šu-si = 1.66 cm). The essential key to rapid conversions was the 'level of water 1 šu-si deep on an area of 1 *iku*', that is, 1.66 cm over 3,600 m^2, or 166 litres per square metre (Powell 1988: 162–163).

THE AGRICULTURAL LANDSCAPE

The inhabited landscapes were characterized by fields and field systems, garden plots, pastures,[7] by greenery of grassland, reeds and woods.[8] The cultivated 'earth' stood in opposition to the wild and untamed land, the place of 'foreign realms'. The familiar landscape was, in fact, enclosed from all cardinal points by 'all the foreign lands', on the north and east by mountains.

In the third and second millenia BC, the intensive agricultural activities (Salonen 1968; Butz 1980–1983) took place in three zones:

1   Strips along natural and artificial water-courses and water reservoirs such as rivers, channels, lakes, buffering 'ponds', with gardens, vegetable fields and with minor grain fields. Given the need to walk to the fields and to use animal teams for ploughing, the extent of such strip zones would not have been much wider than 4 km.
2   Artificially irrigated fields with cereal (Maekawa 1984; Renfrew 1984), oil-plant (Waetzoldt 1985), pulse (Stol 1985; Van Zeist 1985; Renfrew 1985) and onion-like monocultures (Stol 1987; Waetzoldt 1987).
3   Pastures adjacent to fields and water sources. This zone included land lying fallow and parts of cultivable steppe, both representing the only reserve of the soil fund.

The division of arable land, either freshly brought under cultivation or lying fallow, was determined by the quality of the soil. The most fertile tracts fell under the management and control of the sovereign while lower-quality fields were leased out for cultivation. The palace and the temple administrations enabled the leaseholders to till the leased fields by means of animal-traction ploughs (ards) and also supplied traction animals, fodder, and seed at the onset of the autumn tilling season. The leasing fees might have included as much as 50 per cent of the harvest. The compulsory deliveries, as well as the 'irrigation taxes', were controlled by collectors (Steinkeller 1981).

Other plots[9] were held by various agents and dignitaries, perhaps on a temporal basis. The 'Sovereign' fields belonging to the palace and temples provided for the needs of non-agricultural workers, such as builders or craft workers.

Considerable efforts were made to preserve soil quality. Measures include the division of field systems into fields and plots, the practice of long- and short-term fallow, soil leaching, as well as the probable crop rotation. Fields were separated by wider zones of overgrowth, which protected the soil from wind erosion. The actual situation of fields and plots was described in survey texts. The upper and lower margins of the field system close to water sources were employed for cultivation of vegetables and spices. Tamarisks grew along the sides of the field system and perhaps also in some inner orchards. Although the general situation of individual fields must have had a considerable agrotechnical significance – access roads, irrigation, direction of the 'ridges' and furrows – these purely practical questions of tillage did not concern the palace or temple administration because they were the responsibility of the 'farmer' (Sum. engar).

ARABLE SOIL AND THE PREPARATION OF FIELDS

According to the records on cultivation and overgrowth control,[10] the palace and temple administrations dedicated most attention to the land assigned to cereal cultivation.[11] Texts focusing on the overgrowth can in some cases be interpreted as rough harvest estimates but the term could also be used in references to full grown cereals[12] before harvest which would have made it possible to determine the appropriate lease fee. Texts that set the lease fee after the harvest remain problematic.

Such fields must have been in an excellent state in order to calculate the expected harvest. Analyses of soil probes taken in Mesopotamia have shown critically low proportions of humus and nitrates even for ancient strata. Improvement of soil quality by compost and manuring are, nonetheless, attested in the texts. Animal dung was spread over the fields either during movement of herds or during carefully monitored grazing on young grain stalks which supported stalk emergence and growth. Unfortunately, ancient soil improvement practices are difficult to document archaeologically (Nützel 1981).

The soil preparation was connected with the adoption of plough agriculture (Hruška 1985, 1988). The development of plough agriculture, which took place in Southern Mesopotamia in the fourth millenium BC at the very latest, relied on the traction of cattle, donkeys and other hooved animals of the *Equidae* family. Attempts at the zoological identification of hybrids[13] have resulted in a debate that has not produced unequivocal conclusions (Zarins 1986: 185–188). Since the harnessing of bulls is impossible, young animals must have been castrated, except for those kept aside for breeding purposes. Donkeys and hybrids first bore the yoke when they were four years old. Both young, yoked, and 'reserved or replacement' animals were regularly controlled by an 'inspector' (nu-banda$_3$). The young animals were put together with mature ones during the month named for this practice 'house of the herds'.[14] 'Draught donkeys' for wagons (anše-mar) were calculated singly not in teams. The 'animal-team administrators' were obviously superior to draught-animal herdsmen, much as the farmers (engar) were to the ploughmen (sag-apin).

The new soil-preparation technology (Hruška 1984), employing traction implements such as ards, harrows and sleighs, brought a four- to five-fold rise in productivity as against hoe agriculture. Ploughing and subsequent harrowing resulted in a much more thorough removal of clods and homogenization of arable soil than could be achieved by manual implements such as hoes, shovels or wooden mallets. On the other hand, it did not lower labour intensity. The direction of an animal team before the plough, as well as production and maintenance of such implements, required cooperation of a number of workers and a different organization of labour. Plough work was irregularly timed in the course of the agricultural year and was apparently divided into two periods. In the case of primary soil preparation on hitherto untilled areas or after long-term fallow, the ploughing with a ploughshare took place in the late spring when the water tanks were emptied, before the annual floods and arable soil could have been leached. In the case of soil preparation after long-term fallow, the ploughing preceded seeding and one single ploughing season finished in November-December when traction animals were unharnessed (Hruška 1990: 105).

This was the reason why soil preparation techniques made but slow progress, and were perhaps used systematically only on palace and temple estates. In a somewhat ironic literary 'Dispute between Hoe and Plough' (Vanstiphout 1984: 239–251), the god Enlil finally decides that 'the hoe surpasses the plough', since the hoe helps to dig and clean water conduits, enabling work even in wet fields.[15] The plough needs too many working hands and animals: '(Plough), yours are six oxen, yours are four people – yourself is the eleventh of the unit'. Finally, the plough is vulnerable since frames and poles break in operation, wedges and bindings fall out and tear apart. The ploughman, unable to repair the implements himself, has to call upon specialists.[16] The personified hoe asserts that, though the plough leaves 'splendid traces' in the field (furrows), it otherwise accomplishes 'little work'. A farmer wields his hoe for the entire year, a ploughman can use his machine for only four months (verses 107–108). The plough lies idle for eight months and thus it is out of work for twice as long as it works (verses 109–110).

The pictograph for plough (apin, *epinnu*) or simply 'wood' (giš) turns up frequently in all groups of archaic texts and in many sealings. It represents a stylized depiction of a simple wooden ard with a double handle and curved shaft (see Figure 4.1). The APIN sign emphasizes by dashed lines the link beween the shaft and pole, sometimes also the pole carries a transversal neck yoke. The analysis of other expressions in economic, literary and in lexical texts gives us a fairly detailed idea of the construction components of the ards ('tongue', replaceable ploughshare; 'tooth', replaceable plough-share tip; frame behind ploughshare; shaft, pole; handle, the steering apparatus).[17]

Thus the Sumerians and Babylonians employed, as early as the third millenium BC, much more sophisticated ploughing implements than simple hook ards (Hruška 1985). An oblique ploughshare without the supporting frame could cut the soil to maximum depths of 15 cm while, in some 40–50 per cent of arable land, clods larger than 5 cm remained in the furrow. Clods had to be broken by repeated transversal and sometimes even diagonal ploughing or by harrowing.[18] The final adjustment of the arable land before the manual preparation of cereal ridges took the form of driving sledges, consisting of transversal beams with spikes, over the field. The sledge spikes could have been substituted by branches of thorny shrubs. The author of the 'Farmer's Instructions' recommends a triple harrowing with manual levelling of the irregularities with a broad furrow-sinker or hoe.[19] Soil preparation by means of ploughing and harrowing ended by manual levelling of the areas where the animal teams wheeled around (Civil 1976: 89, verses 122–132). As well as serving as access, such areas[20] along the field edges might have been sown with supplementary crops.[21]

According to the 'Farmer's Instructions', cereal ridges ('closed furrows') were shaped manually,[22] with a recommended count of eight furrows per 1 nindan (= 6 m). The text also contains detailed advice for the preparation of the plough[23] and records the distribution of supplies to ploughmen (sag-apin). A team of four and more paired oxen (Selz 1993) harnessed to a wooden ard need 120 hours for the preparation of one hectare of arable land, including the preparation of the ridges. The same team will sow this area with a seeder plough in 60 hours. The work of the team must be interrupted by frequent pauses. The author of 'Farmer's Instructions' says that in the ploughing season a quota of one plough amounted 18 iku (6.35 ha); in order to make the recommended eight furrows per 1 nindan, the ploughman would have to plough more than 83 km.[24] M. Powell (1984: 48, 53, 56) estimates that a simple breaking into straight furrows would have taken at least eight days. If we add transversal ploughing and several harrowing shifts, the ploughing season could well have extended over one month and perhaps even longer. The dated texts of Ur III times indicate that seed and fodder were usually issued from the stores for two to three months (Yamamoto 1979: 85–86). Verses 54–63 and 67–68 of the 'Farmer's Instructions' give a full description of the procedures of ploughing and shaping the field furrows. The final adjustments of cereal ridges, as well as of the direct-irrigation trenches, were undoubtedly carried out manually with the aid of hoes (al) with broad trapezoidal blades, and shovels (mar), used both for digging and shovelling (Hruška 1995: 34–36).

Figure 4.3   Seal impression showing animal traction, working team and seeding plough
(Hruška 1988: 143).

A NEW MANNER OF SOWING

According to iconographic (see Figure 4.3), literary and lexical sources[25] the plough was used not only for soil preparation but also for sowing (Maeda 1995). For such purposes the ploughs received funnel-shaped seeders fastened on the shaft or at the side of the frame, behind the ploughshare. Seeder ploughs used special (obviously lighter) ploughshares. The mechanization of sowing is one of the most significant technological innovations of Mesopotamian agriculture (Pettinato and Waetzoldt 1975). Sowing by means of a seeder on a moving plough allowed the deposition of grain into the soil at a regular depth and at regular intervals. This encouraged the growth and stalk-building of the plants and ensured more efficient harvesting. The use of the seeder plough also brought a 30 per cent saving of seed compared with manual broadcasting out of a basket. The sowing itself was a demanding procedure, requiring cooperation between ploughman and the 'seeder man', who had to take care in measuring out the seed.[26] In 'The Farmer's Instructions' the ploughman instructs his son to sow into eight furrows per 1 nindan,[27] which means into furrows spaced at an interval of 0.75 m (1 nindan = approximately 6 m).

HIGH YIELDS?

Herodotus (*Hist. I*, 193) and Pliny the Elder (*Hist. Nat.* 18.21, 94–95) cite yield figures with a seed–yield ratio 1 : 200–300, the famous 'hundredfold harvest', for Near Eastern agricultural systems. They refer to the Ancient Near East as a 'blessed land', where yields much surpassed those usual for Greece. Both authors are likely to have cited the seed–yield ratio in accordance with the agriculture cycle from fertilization to the following long-term fallow period. They might also have added yields for the entire tenancy period, which might have extended over three, five, or even ten years. The Old Testament (Exodus 23: 10–11) prescribed at least one annual fallow period after a six-year cerealicultural cycle. It seems that the data from the New Testament (Mark 5: 8, Luke 8: 8), giving the seed–yield ratios of 1 : 100, 1 : 60 and 1 : 30), must be divided by the year count of such a cycle. This results in real harvest estimates of 1 : 16.6, 1 : 10 and 1 : 5.[28]

The situation in the dry-farming area above the 300 mm isohyet is illuminated by sources from the fifteenth–thirteenth centuries BC. After thorough soil preparation and relying on normal precipitation, farmers around Nuzi managed to attain seed–yield ratios of 1 : 4 and 1 : 7 and the same figures are valid for arid and semi-arid steppes of both North Africa and the Sahel belt, as well as for Afghanistan, West Pakistan and India. The seed–yield ratios beween 1 : 3 and 1 : 7 are thus not exceptional. The higher yields (1 : 16 and more) over short time periods could have been achieved only in South Mesopotamia, on fertile fluvial sediments, where cereal ridges were properly leached prior to sowing and irrigated several times during the growth period. The relatively wide spacing of the furrows may imply that the plants were hoed manually, a significant expenditure of labour. The economic texts do not give any figures as to how many seeds actually sprouted. The grain counts for 'Sumerian' seeder ploughs resulted in the seed loss of some 20 per cent, but still more than 100 stalks with fertile ears grew out of 100 seeds after putting up shoots. Well-watered and well-drained fields in semi-arid steppes can give yields of 800–1,000 kg per hectare, with seed quantities between 35 and 50 kg per hectare.

There is no evidence on the number and positions of field threshing floors, halfway storage facilities and transport areas. The 'Farmer's Instructions' emphasize the need to trace out access space for the storage of grain and to clean the threshing-floor bottom thoroughly prior to the beginning of the harvest in areas lying fallow over shorter annual period.[29] The threshing floor, prepared beforehand by levelling using heavy timber, was to remain untouched for five days, perhaps with the intention of letting the threshing surface dry sufficiently.

NOTES

1 Archaeological finds relating directly to field systems – agricultural implements, remains of cultural plants or bones of domesticated animals – are very rare.
2 The agricultural production of pastoral nomads, active in the dry-farming zone remains outside the scope of this study.
3 Eyre (1995: 176); Hruška (1990: 31–33, 401–403); Hopkins (1997: 22–25).
4 Pettinato (1967: I/1 16–37; 1969: 32–38).
5 a-de$_2$ 'pouring out of water', ki-duru$_5$ 'wet place'; Civil (1994: 1–2, 28–29, 67–70; verses 2–7).
6 Civil (1994: 30–31, 88–89; verses 67–73).
7 eden, meaning also 'steppe'.
8 tir 'orchard, wood'.
9 aša$_5$-šuku(KUR$_6$).
10 (aša$_5$-še-mu$_2$-a).
11 (aša$_5$-še).
12 Main individual cereal types: še, gig, ziz$_2$; see Powell 1984.
13 Common expression anše, kunga = BAR.AN, perhaps for *E. asinus*, *E. caballus* and *E. hemionus*.
14 itu-amar-a-a-si-ga
15 Verses 83–86, in contrast to 'Farmer's Instructions', verses 3–12; Civil (1994: 28–29, 68–72).
16 Verses 95–101, Hruška (1985, 57–59).
17 Hruška 1985, 1988; 1990, I 110–115, II 443–445, 456–465.
18 'Farmer's Instructions', verses 30–34, 54–59; Hruška (1990: 453–455); Civil (1994: 28–31, 76–78, 84–86).
19 Verses 32–37; Civil (1994: 77–79).
20 lu-gu$_2$; 'Farmer's Instructions', verses 12, 58; Civil (1976: 89; 1994: 28–31, 86).
21 Hruška (1990: I 117–118, II 313, 471–472).
22 Verses 46–47, 60–62; Civil (1994: 30–31, 81–82, 86–87).
23 In verses 13–21.
24 Verses 26–27.
25 Hruška (1988: 142–144; 1990: 112–114, 449–452).
26 'Farmer's Instructions': verses 41–45; Civil (1994: 30–31, 79–8).
27 Verses 46, 50–51; see Powell (1984a: 53–54, 57, 62).
28 Butz and Schröder (1985: 172–174); Postgate (1984).
29 Verses 90–95: Civil (1994: 32–33, 93–94).

REFERENCES

Adams, R. McC. 1982 'Die Rolle des Bewässerungsbodenbau bei der Entwicklung von Institutionen in der altmesopotamischen Gesellschaft'. In: *Produktivkräfte und Gesellschaftsformationen in vorkapitalistischer Zeit.* Joachim Hermann, ed., pp. 131–148. Berlin: Akademie–Verlag.
Butz, K. 1980–1983 'Landwirtschaft'. *Reallexikon der Assyriologie*, Vol. 6, pp. 470–486. Berlin and New York: W. de Gruyter.
—— and Schröder, P. 1985 'Zu den Getreideerträgen in Mesopotamien und in dem Mittelmeergebiet'. *Baghdader Mitteilungen* 16: 165–209.

Calmeyer, P. and Wilcke, Cl. 1972–1975 'Hacke'. *Reallexikon der Assyriologie*, Vol. 4, pp. 31–38. Berlin and New York: Walter de Gruyter.

Charles, M. P. 1988 'Irrigation in Lowland Mesopotamia'. *Bulletin on Sumerian Agriculture* 4, Part 1: 1–39.

Civil, M. 1976 *The Song of Plowing Oxen*. Alter Orient und Altes Testament 25. Neukirchen-Vluyn: Verlag Butzon and Bercker Kevelaer, Neukirchener Verlag, 83–96.

—— 1994 *The Farmer's Instructions. A Sumerian Agricultural Manual*. Aula orientalis, Supplementa 5. Barcelona: Sabadell, Editorial AUSA.

Eyre, Chr. J. 1995 'The Agricultural Cycle, Farming, and Water Management in the Ancient Near East'. In: *Civilizations of The Ancient Near East*. J. M. Sasson *et al.*, eds, New York: Simon and Schuster Macmillan, Vol. I, pp. 175–190.

Green, M. and Nissen, H. J. 1987 'Zeichenliste der Archaischen Texte aus Uruk'. In: *Archaische Texte aus Uruk*. H. J. Nissen, ed., Berlin: Gebr. Mann Verlag.

Hopkins, D. C. 1997 'Agriculture'. In: *The Oxford Encyclopedia of Archaeology in The Near East*. E. M. Meyers, ed., New York and Oxford: Oxford University Press, pp. 22–30.

Hruška, B. 1984 'Die Bodenbearbeitung und Feldbestellung im altsumerischen Lagaš'. *Archiv orientální* 52: 150–157.

—— 1985 'Der Umbruchpflug in den archaischen und altsumerischen Texten'. *Archiv orientální* 53: 46–65.

—— 1986 'Die wichtigsten Faktoren der altmesopotamischen Agrarwirtschaft.' *Economic History* 15. Prague: Institute of Czechoslovak and World History of the Czechoslovak Academy of Sciences, pp. 7–25.

—— 1988 'Überlegungen zum Pflug und Ackerbau in der altsumerischen Zeit.' *Archiv orientální* 56: 134–158.

—— 1988a 'Die Bewässerunganlagen in den altsumerischen Königsinschriften von Lagas'. *Bulletin on Sumerian Agriculture*, Vol. 4, Part 1: 61–72.

—— 1990 *Tradiční obilnářství staré Metopotámie* (Der traditionelle Ackerbau im alten Mesopotamien). Vol. I–II. Praha: Orientální ústav ČSAV.

—— 1990a 'Das landwirtschaftliche Jahr im alten Sumer'. *Bulletin on Sumerian Agriculture*, Vol. 5, Part 2: 105–114.

—— 1995 'Sumerian Agriculture: New Findings'. Preprint 26. Berlin: Max Planck Institute for the History of Science.

Jacobsen, Th. and Adams, R. McC. 1958 'Salt and Silt in Ancient Mesopotamian Agruculture'. *Science* 138: 1251–1258.

Landsberger, B. 1949 'Jahreszeiten im Sumerisch-Akkadischen'. *Journal of the Near Eastern Studies* 8: 248–297.

LaPlaca, P. J. and Powell, M. 1990 'The Agricultural Cycle and the Calendar at Pre-Sargonic Girsu'. *Bulletin on Sumerian Agriculture* Vol. 5, Part 2: 65–104.

Maeda, T. 1995 'Three Men of a Gang for Plowing and Four Men for Sowing'. *Acta Sumerologica Japanica* 17: 333–337.

Maekawa, K. 1984 'Cereal Cultivation in the Ur III Period'. *Bulletin on Sumerian Agriculture*, Vol. 1: 73–96.

—— 1990 'Cultivation Methods in the Ur III Period'. *Bulletin on Sumerian Agriculture*, Vol. 5, Part 2: 115–145.

Nissen, H. J. 1988 *The Early History of the Ancient Near East 9000–2000 BC*. Chicago, IL and London: The University of Chicago Press.

Nützel, W. 1981 'Zur archäologischen Auswertung des mesopotamischen Rekultivierungs-programmes von William Willcocks'. *Mitteilungen der Deutschen Orient-Gesellschaft* 113: 99–110.

—— 2004 *Einführung in die Geo-Archäologie des Vorderen Orients*. Wiesbaden: Reichert Verlag.

Pemberton, W., Postgate, J. N. and Smyth, R. F. 1988 'Canals, Bunds, Ancient and Modern'. *Bulletin on Sumerian Agriculture*, Vol. 4, Part 1: 207–221.

Pettinato, G. 1967 *Untersuchungen zur neusumerischen Landwirtschaft I/1–2*. Naples: Istituto Orientale di Napoli.

—— and Waetzoldt, H. 1975 'Saatgut und Furchenabstand beim Getreideanbau'. *Studia Orientalia* 45: 259–290.

Postgate, J. N. 1984 'The Problem of Yields in Sumerian Texts'. *Bulletin on Sumerian Agriculture*, Vol. 1: 97–102.

Powell, M. 1984 'Sumerian Cereal Crops'. *Bulletin on Sumerian Agriculture*, Vol. 1: 48–72.

—— 1984a 'Late Babylonian Surface Mensuration'. *Archiv für Orientforschung* 31: 32–66.

—— 1985 'Salt, Seed and Yields in Sumerian Agriculture. A critique on the theory of progressive salinization'. *Zeitschrift für Assyriologie* 75: 7–38.

—— 1988 'Evidence for Agriculture and Waterworks in Babylonian Mathematical Texts'. *Bulletin on Sumerian Agriculture*, Vol. 4: 161–168.

Renfrew, J. M. 1984 'Cereals Cultivated in Ancient Iraq'. *Bulletin on Sumerian Agriculture*, Vol. 1: 32–44.

—— 1985 'Pulses Recorded from Ancient Iraq'. *Bulletin on Sumerian Agriculture*, Vol. 2: 67–71.

Renger, J. 1990 'Rivers, Watercourses and Irrigation Ditches'. *Bulletin on Sumerian Agriculture*, Vol. 5, Part 2: 31–46.

Salonen, A. 1968 'Agricultura Mesopotamica'. *Annales Academiae Scientiarum Fennicae*, Ser. B, Tom 149.

Selz, G. 1993 'Eine Notiz zum Tiergespann aus vier Arbeitstieren'. *Archiv orientální* 61: 11–12.

—— 2002 'Der "Garten Eden" im dritten Jahrtausend. Einblicke in das Leben städtischer Gesellschaften in Südmesopotamien zur frühdynastischer Zeit (ca. 2850–2350 v.Chr.)'. *Freiburger Universitätsblätter* 156: 21–30.

Steinkeller, P. 1981 'The Renting of Fields in Early Mesopotamia and the Development of the Concept of "Interest" in Sumerian'. *Journal of the Economic and Social History of the Orient* 24: 113–145.

—— 1988 'Notes on the Irrigation System in Third Millenium Southern Mesopotamia'. *Bulletin on Sumerian Agriculture*, Vol. 4: 73–92.

Stol, M. 1985 'Beans, Peas, Lentils and Vetches in Akkadian Texts'. *Bulletin on Sumerian Agriculture*, Vol. 2: 127–139.

—— 1987 'Garlic, Onion, Leek. The Cucurbitaceae in the cuneiform texts'. *Bulletin on Sumerian Agriculture*, Vol. 3: 57–80, 81–92.

Vanstiphout, H. L. J. 1984 'On Sumerian Disputation between the Hoe and the Plough'. *Aula orientalis* 2: 239–251.

Van Zeist 1985 'Pulses and Oil Crop Plants'. *Bulletin on Sumerian Agriculture*, Vol. 2: 33–38.

Waetzoldt, H. 1985 'Ölpflanzen und Pflanzenöle im 3. Jahrtausend vor Chr.' *Bulletin on Sumerian Agriculture*, Vol. 2: 33–96.

—— 1987 'Knoblauch und Zwiebeln nach den Texten des 3. Jt. vor Chr.' *Bulletin on Sumerian Agriculture*, Vol. 3: 23–56.

Yamamoto, S. 1979–1980 'The Agricultural Year in Pre-Sargonic Girsu-Lagash I–II'. *Acta Sumerologica Japanica* 1–2, pp. 85–97 (I), 169–187 (II).

Zarins, J. 1986 'Equids Associated with Human Burials in Third Millenium in Mesopotamia'. In: *Equids in the Ancient World*. R. H. Meadow and H. P. Uerpmann, eds, Tübinger Atlas des Vorderen Orients, Beihefte, Reihe A 19/1. Wiesbaden: Dr. Ludwig Reichert Verlag, pp. 164–193.

CHAPTER FIVE

URBAN FORM IN THE FIRST MILLENNIUM BC

———•◆•———

Heather D. Baker

INTRODUCTION

Here we present an overview of urban form in first millennium BC Babylonia. Following a brief introduction to the sources and the state of the evidence, we consider matters of urban layout and examine why the Babylonian cities took the shape they did. In discussing the different elements of the city we will pay greater attention to the less well studied features, such as the street network and the residential areas, than to the monumental structures which have often been described in other works. Many of the issues raised here will be dealt with in greater detail in a study by the author (Baker forthcoming).

The sources

The evidence available for the study of urban form in first millennium BC Babylonia encompasses both excavated remains and written sources. Archaeological excavation has, of course, revealed the actual layout of a good many buildings, streets and other features. The textual material, on the other hand, tends to offer a more indirect kind of information, since the features referred to in the cuneiform documents very often cannot be identified on the ground, usually because they have not yet been excavated; alternatively, the details given in the tablets may not be sufficiently specific to secure their identification. Nevertheless, the contemporary cuneiform documents constitute an invaluable source on urban topography which, with careful study, can help to fill in the gaps in the archaeological record and build up a more complete model of urban form at this period. The tablets which are relevant for our purpose can be divided into two groups: the literary/topographical tablets (edited with translations by George 1992) on the one hand, and the economic documents on the other (for an introduction to these see Jursa 2005). The bulk of the latter group is made up of legal contracts usually deriving from private family archives; administrative documents play a lesser (though still significant) role. The economic documents are not evenly distributed throughout the first millennium BC; rather, they peak in the sixth and early fifth centuries, with another, smaller peak later on, in the Hellenistic period.

The present state of knowledge

Excavations of first millennium remains have been conducted at a number of Babylonian cities: Abu Qubur (ancient name uncertain); Babylon; Borsippa; Dilbat; Isin; Kish; Kissik (modern Tell al-Lahm); Kutha; Larsa; Nippur; Sippar; Ur; and Uruk. (Since we are concerned here with the urban tradition of Babylonia, the city of Seleucia-on-the-Tigris will be omitted from our account because it represents a new foundation of the Hellenistic era and has to be considered as a Greek implantation.) Despite the range of urban sites investigated, the areal extent of excavation, not to mention the technical standards applied in its execution and the quality of the published accounts, vary enormously. The result of this state of affairs is that our knowledge of urban layout is still very patchy. Traditionally, excavators in Mesopotamia have concentrated their efforts on the central, monumental sectors of the cities. Considerably less attention has been paid to residential areas and other districts or features, such as areas of industrial activity, unbuilt areas, and the street network. To some extent, textual sources can redress the balance because they provide information on the kinds of structures which have not yet been systematically excavated, such as workshops and storerooms, or which were made of perishable materials and hence would not in any case have been recovered, such as reed structures.

THE CITY AND ITS COMPOSITION

The principal elements of urban layout

The characteristic features of the Mesopotamian city have been discussed by Van De Mieroop (1999: 72–83) and can be summarised as follows: they enjoyed an elevated situation, and possessed defensive walls with gates placed at intervals; different city areas were separated by streets and canals; as well as monumental buildings, there were non-monumental areas, i.e. residential districts mixed with industrial areas, and open spaces. This scheme applies to the Babylonian city of the first millennium, though as we have seen, some elements are more accessible to us than others.

The street network

Streets play a major role in defining the character of a city; they both shape and reflect the circulatory patterns of the inhabitants (and the gods, as we shall see) and provide the link between different districts. Textual sources indicate a three-tier hierarchy of streets and alleys in the Babylonian city. The main processional ways are usually designated 'broad street, thoroughfare of the gods'. In the literary/topographical texts, their ceremonial names are also given. By contrast, the other public streets are most often known in the tablets by the generic designation 'narrow street, thoroughfare of the people'. The dead-end alleys, known generally as 'exit (passageway)', served one or more houses within a residential quarter, and were in private ownership.

Recent studies have claimed that the Neo-Babylonian cities of Babylon and Borsippa were laid out in a regular grid pattern (Van De Mieroop 1999: 86, with reference to Figures 4.7 and 4.8; Gates 2003: 181). It is worth devoting some attention to this issue because it is important, not only for our understanding of Babylonian urbanism in the first millennium BC, but also for any attempt to place the Babylonian cities in a wider historical context from the point of view of urban development.

In fact, this view that we are dealing with a grid layout has to be challenged, because it is based on a reconstructed street network which is almost entirely hypothetical and which has little basis in excavated reality. If one traces the genealogy of the city maps presented by these two authors (who are only the most recent in a long tradition), one discovers that they go back to reconstructions published by Unger in his study of the topography of Babylon in 1931 (pl. 57, fig. 64 for Babylon; pl. 18, fig. 27 for Borsippa). Unger knew from his study of the cuneiform topographical tablets concerning Babylon that certain streets bore names explicitly associating them with a specific city gate, such as 'street of the Urash Gate'. His method, so it seems, was to project a straight line from the inside of each gate (not all of whose locations were known), on a course roughly perpendicular to the line of the city wall, towards the centre of the city (or towards another projected street intersecting with the street in question). He then labelled the street accordingly. However, very nearly all of the streets reconstructed in this way are entirely conjectural and, of the nine gates marked on Unger's plan, the identification and location of only five can be defended (see below). Very few actual streets have been excavated, namely, the Processional Way and the streets of the Merkes quarter of Babylon – the latter being generally more or less straight but by no means forming a grid pattern. Stretches of streets have been found in other areas, for example to the south-east and north-west of the Ninurta temple (see Wetzel 1930: pl. 10), but these are not sufficient to enable their courses to be projected over a longer distance. One textually attested street, the Processional Way of Nabû, can be located with some certainty, since it is known to have run from the Urash Gate to Esagil, the temple of Marduk.

Following Unger, Wiseman (1985: 46, fig. 3) added further streets to the reconstruction of Babylon on the basis of his own study of the topographical tablets, but the location of these is equally conjectural and that of the gates erroneous. These additions were incorporated into the plan of Babylon presented by Gates (2003: 183, fig. 10.12). However, recent work by George has resulted in an improved scheme for identifying and locating the gates of Babylon. Therefore, the conjectural streets – which, we recall, were placed in relation to the gates with which they are associated – would have to be moved too! It is better to follow the example of George (1992: 24, fig. 4), who omits the street network altogether from his reconstruction of sixth century BC Babylon, apart from the excavated stretch of the Processional Way.

The situation as regards Borsippa is even less satisfactory. Unger's reconstruction (1932: pl. 59) shows a city that is square in outline, crossed by a grid of straight streets, with the main temple enclosure at the centre. But this is highly schematic, compared with the 1859 survey of W.B. Selby, which is reproduced by Unger (1932: pl. 55). Selby's map of Borsippa shows the ziggurat and Ezida situated near the edge of the city rather than in the centre; moreover, according to it the shape of the city was not square, and there were no visible gates that could be used in reconstructing a street grid. The only detailed, measured plan available for Borsippa is that of the ziggurat and the Nabû Temple and vicinity, as published by the German excavators (Koldewey 1911: pl. 12). A sounding was made in the city wall (see Koldewey 1911: 51 and fig. 91 for a photograph), but neither the location of the trench nor the wall itself is shown on any plan.

It seems, therefore, that previous scholars either did not realise the very great extent to which these reconstructions were conjectural, or, in the case of Babylon, they accepted the line of reasoning which assumes that streets associated with the city gates led in a straight line, without any deviation, right to the centre of the city. Once this assumption is questioned – as it surely must be – then the grounds for considering Babylon and Borsippa to have been cities planned on a regular grid layout are completely undermined.

Canals and watercourses

It goes without saying that all city dwellers needed access to water. Babylon itself was bisected by the Euphrates running approximately north–south, and there were also canals within the city. Uruk was not located directly on the river, but there is abundant textual evidence from our period for properties within the city bordering onto canals, or onto streets leading down to canals.

The city walls and gates

Babylon was enclosed by a double inner wall of roughly rectangular configuration. There is evidence that, at least as early as the eleventh century BC, the inner-most wall of the pair, Imgur-Enlil, followed the same course as its successor from the time of Nebukadrezzar II (George 1992: 344). A substantial additional area was enclosed at this later period by an outer wall which ran from the east bank of the Euphrates north of the city on a roughly triangle-shaped course with its apex east of the city, rejoining the river on the south side. Like the temples and streets, the walls of the major cities were given ceremonial names by the kings who built or rebuilt them. The explicit concern of the kings when they refurbished the city walls, according to their own rhetoric, was to protect the major shrines within the city.

Palaces

Palaces are known from a number of cities: certainly Agade, Babylon, Larsa, Sippar, Ur and Uruk, and possibly also Borsippa, Kutha and Nippur (see Jursa 2004 for details). According to documentary evidence there was also a palace in a place called Abanu in the vicinity of Uruk. Palaces outside of the capital would have served as administrative centres for the local government. In Babylon three palaces, all built by Nebuchadrezzar II, have been investigated (Miglus 2004). The most impressive of these, the 'South Palace', consisted of an arrangement of five courtyard complexes side by side. In addition to the throne room and residential suites it provided ample facilities for storage and administration.

The temples and ziggurats

Each city contained shrines not only of its principal deity (or deities) but also of lesser gods and goddesses. We may make a distinction between the temples which were themselves contained within an extensive precinct dominating the heart of the city, such as the Eanna in Uruk, and those which stood alone, often being rather more integrated into the fabric of the city, such as the temples of Ishtar of Agade and Ninurta in Babylon. The larger temples housed not only the principal deity but also contained smaller shrines and cultic daises of other gods and goddesses. The huge precincts of Eanna, Ebabbar (Sippar), Ezida (Borsippa) and of the ziggurat Etemenanki (Babylon) would not only have accommodated the religious elements of cultic practice but also much of the subsidiary 'industry' which serviced the cult, i.e. the numerous workshops and storerooms of the craftsmen and professionals in the employ of the temple.

As for ziggurats, there are tablets dating from both the Kassite and the Neo-Babylonian periods which list their ceremonial names and the cities in which they were located (see George 1993: 45–49, nos. 4–5). It is clear from these texts that there were ziggurats in a number of cities which were occupied in the first millennium BC: Agade; Babylon; Borsippa; Dilbat; Kish and Hursagkalamma; Kutha; Larsa; Marad; Nippur; Sippar; Shatir; Ur; and Uruk. Archaeological remains at the site of Tell Hammam near Umma (modern Jokhah) may also be interpreted as a ziggurat (Heinrich 1982: 327, fig. 419). In fact, some cities possessed more than one ziggurat, according to the written sources (for example, Agade and Hursagkalamma). Not all of these structures have been investigated archaeologically, but a number of them are known to have been rebuilt during this period. The kings Nebukadrezzar II and Nabonidus were especially active in this respect, as is evidenced by their inscriptions.

Usually the ziggurat was integrated into an extensive precinct (see above) which also encompassed the principal temple of the city, such as Eurmeiminanki, the ziggurat of Borsippa, which shared a precinct with Ezida, the Nabû temple of that city. A similar situation prevailed in the Eanna precinct at Uruk, and in that of Ebabbar at Sippar. Unusually, Esagil, the temple of Marduk at Babylon, was independent of the ziggurat Etemenanki and its extensive enclosure.

Residential areas

Three principal areas of first millennium housing have been excavated: in the Merkes area of Babylon (Reuther 1926: 77–122), at Ur (Woolley 1962: 43–8 and Plate 71) and at Uruk, to the west and southwest of the Eanna temple enclosure (for a plan see Kessler 1991: Beilage 1). For an excellent survey of the archaeological evidence concerning houses see the relevant sections in Miglus 1999.

Most of the Merkes houses are significantly larger than the average house of this period (ca. 417 square metres); they range in area from 190 to 1,475 square metres. They are also unusually well built, and it seems that we should be wary of assuming this district to be typical for Neo-Babylonian residential districts in general; probably we are dealing here with the dwellings of the elite in what was, after all, the capital. Houses were accessed via a single entrance opening off a public street or a private dead-end alley. In the excavated areas of housing, such alleys are actually under-represented in comparison with streets, but the abundant textual evidence for alleys confirms that the Neo-Babylonian residential districts were no different in this respect from their earlier counterparts (as at Old Babylonian Ur, for example).

The houses were built almost entirely of mudbrick, unlike those at Old Babylonian Ur, where baked bricks were used much more extensively, at least for the lower courses of walls. By this time the use of baked bricks was confined to special features, such as courtyard paving and built drains, or for protecting the bases of walls which were exposed to water. Bitumen was also used as a protection against water. The roof consisted of a mud slab laid on a support of wooden beams (of date palm or poplar) which were themselves overlain with smaller slats and reed matting; the same basic technique is still in use today in the region. House rental contracts invariably required the tenant to take care of the two most vulnerable parts of the house, namely the external wall-footings (which were vulnerable to erosion from splashing rainwater) and the mud roof, which needed regular resealing in order to maintain its resistance to water.

In plan, the house consisted typically of suites of rooms arranged around a central courtyard; larger, more complex houses could contain a couple of subsidiary courtyards in addition to the main one. The principal living room – the largest roofed space in the house – was usually situated on the south-east side of the courtyard, and was accessed directly from it. If the house possessed a bathroom (or a toilet), it was usually integrated into the suite which contained this main room (for further discussion see below under 'Sanitation'). A second living room was situated on the opposite side of the courtyard from the principal living room, and the main entrance to the house was almost invariably also on the far side of the house, leading via an indirect route to the courtyard. Staircases have rarely been found, and even then it is not certain whether they led to the roof rather than to a second storey. Textual sources rarely mention the existence of upper floors, and most cases actually relate to other kinds of structures, not to houses. The courtyard was the main (or only) source of light, and provided some protection from the sun in hot weather; it also facilitated the circulation of cool air around the house.

The identification of specific activity areas within the house has, to date, focused on the presence of fixtures (such as ovens, drains etc.) and on any special treatment of walls and floors (e.g. paving, waterproofing with bitumen). Rooms which lack any such distinguishing features are of somewhat indeterminable function, presumably having been used for general living purposes which have left no particular physical trace (according to the techniques of recovery used in their excavation). The textual sources give very little away as regards terms for particular types of rooms. However, the temptation to classify such rooms as multi-functional on analogy with contemporary dwellings in the area, whose inhabitants traditionally use a minimum of furniture, and of a type that is easily stowed away, should be resisted as the situation is not so straightforward. Contemporary dowry texts attest to the use of wooden furniture, including items such as beds, tables and chairs, which would surely have lent some specificity of function to the room in which they were placed. The reason why the terms for room types are so rarely attested probably has more to do with conventions of record keeping. Simply put, individual bathrooms or bedrooms were unlikely to be sold on their own and, when they formed part of a larger complex, there was no reason to refer to them by name. There is a small amount of textual evidence for storage taking place within certain parts of the house, or for specific activities, such as baking being carried out in a courtyard, but it is not sufficient to enable a coherent picture to be drawn up.

The documents provide evidence for other kinds of urban structures of a more flimsy character, some of them integrated into the house complex, others independent of it. For example, an annexe could be built up against a house wall, either in the courtyard or on the outside of the dwelling. The leasing of workshops and storerooms which were clearly located within residential areas is also attested, and contracts for the construction of reed structures have survived. Other evidence for the location of craft production and industry is slight, apart from those activities which we know from the textual evidence to have taken place within the temple precinct (see above). Small-scale production could well have taken place within the residential areas, in the aforementioned workshops, but those processes that were noxious (such as tanning) or required copious amounts of water would presumably have been located elsewhere; direct evidence is lacking.

Open spaces and gardens

Open spaces have not often been identified in excavations at first millennium sites. Even where they have, it is difficult to assess their extent and function. The textual corpus provides ample evidence for vacant land within the city in the form of privately owned unbuilt plots. These could be bought and sold, just like built structures, and were ripe for redevelopment. On the other hand, there is practically no reference to unbuilt land belonging to the institutions of temple and state which might have been used for dumping refuse, recreation, or any other kinds of communal activities – the lack is inevitable, since the textual record is concerned essentially with tracking the transfer of private property, and (to a lesser extent) with the exploitation of that owned by the temple. It is worth drawing attention to the sale of a remarkable 5,600 square metres of derelict land in the city of Sippar which took place in 570 BC (Jursa 1999: 89, 142–144); we assume that the buyer intended to develop the land, and it is surely no coincidence that the sale took place at a time which saw a surge in economic prosperity and, most likely, a growth in urban population.

There is textual evidence for the existence of a 'Royal Garden' within the city of Uruk, and we might speculate that this was located in the vicinity of the royal palace there, whose approximate location has been suggested by Kessler (1999: 171). There is also abundant evidence for the presence of date orchards within the city. Babylon, on the other hand, was too densely populated for orchards to be established within the walled city itself, but cultivation did take place within the area between the inner walls and the long, triangular stretch of outer wall on the east side of the city. The location of the so-called 'Hanging Gardens' remains a matter of controversy.

Sanitation

While monumental structures were equipped with well-built, sometimes elaborate drainage installations, drainage and sanitation within the residential areas were, rather, matters for the individual households to take care of. Water had to be fetched from the nearest water course and would therefore be used as sparingly as possible; activities that required a lot of water would have taken place by the canal or river. Drainage within the house, at ground floor level, was usually effected by means of soakaways, i.e. shafts dug into the floor and lined with hollow ceramic drums laid vertically one above the other. Built drains consisting of baked brick channels running through the bases of walls and draining onto the street are somewhat less common, no doubt because the level of the street outside was often higher than that of the internal floors. This difference in levels was no barrier, however, to draining rainwater off the roofs and, at Babylon, houses were occasionally equipped with vertical drains leading rainwater down an external waterpipe and into a sump dug into the adjacent street.

Bathrooms tend to be found in private houses which are of larger than average size, and only very few built toilets have been securely identified. Presumably other households made use of portable containers; waste may have been collected for use as fertiliser outside of the city, a practice that is well attested ethnographically. The built toilets consisted of baked brick fixtures over a deep vertical shaft. In the absence of a continuous and reliable water supply, it would have been more hygienic to keep the use of water in the toilets to a minimum. The toilets tended to be located in the least accessible part of the house, as viewed from its main entrance.

INFLUENCES ON URBAN LAYOUT

The 'Oriental city' – a concept which has itself been justifiably questioned in recent years (see Liverani 1997) – has often been seen as a product of haphazard, unplanned development in comparison, for example, with the allegedly more ordered urban settlements of Classical antiquity. It is now generally recognised that a much more nuanced and less Eurocentric approach is desirable in the study of ancient urbanism. On the other hand, there are certain features which the Neo-Babylonian city apparently shares both with those of other areas and periods within Mesopotamia and with later, historically documented cities of the Middle East. This applies most particularly to the residential areas: scholars have often remarked, for example, on the close similarity in character between the areas of Old Babylonian housing excavated at Ur and the residential quarters of later Islamic cities. The housing quarters of the first millennium, in so far as they have been uncovered, seem to conform in general to their earlier counterparts. It is worth noting at this juncture that some features which can be seen as responses to specific socio-cultural conditions (e.g. a strong desire for privacy on the part of the household) can equally well be interpreted as adaptive measures in the face of an extreme climate. Take, for example, the houses with their blank, windowless façades and their enclosed internal courtyards. Such a configuration both helps to ensure privacy for the family within and facilitates thermal insulation and the optimal circulation of cool air, and it seems unproductive to attempt to weigh up the relative influence here of culture versus climate. Both factors seem to have ensured the long survival of the courtyard house as the typical dwelling type throughout the region until modern times, but clearly we have to be wary of assuming (rather than demonstrating) that the underlying social structure was similar in antiquity on the basis of such longevity.

The residential areas were but one element of the Babylonian city, and a systematic analysis of urban form requires a consideration of how all of the parts functioned together. Moreover, different sectors of the city may well have been subject to different degrees of planning, and different influences on their layout. Having briefly mentioned two of the factors that contributed to shaping the configuration of the residential districts, we may now address some of the other pertinent considerations affecting the shape of the city.

The concept of urban planning implies a degree of agency, that is, an authority responsible for conceiving a plan and implementing it. Normally this would be the king. It is not possible to study the history of Mesopotamia without repeatedly confronting the king in his role as builder – of temples, palaces and other monumental structures, such as city walls, streets and gates and (usually outside of the city) canals. These activities are very well attested in the corpus of royal inscriptions for all periods of Mesopotamian history. The execution of large-scale building projects implies the mobilisation of large numbers of workers and the procuring of huge quantities of the necessary materials, not to mention the administration and supervision of both men and supplies by a host of trained officials.

But the king himself was, of course, subject to social and religious convention. A major influence on the shape of the cities was the pervasive, long-term conservatism and the high degree of resistance to change, especially with respect to the layout of religious buildings. Kings actively sought to follow earlier plans when engaged in the rebuilding of temples. The lengths to which the Neo-Babylonian rulers were prepared to go – even to the extent of conducting programmes of 'archaeological excavation' – have been nicely documented by Winter (2000). This conservatism also applied with regard to the course of ceremonial streets: there is textual evidence which indicates that diverting such a street was considered to be a sin. The positioning of palaces was not affected by such considerations.

Display and prestige are further factors to be taken into account as influences on the shape of the city. We should be mindful of the visual effect of the temples, palaces and other monumental structures, which would have towered over the areas of (generally single-storey) housing. As we have seen, monumental buildings were not necessarily confined to the city centre; temples at Babylon, for example, were distributed around the city, in the heart of residential quarters. Other features intended to impress may have included royal gardens (see above).

Finally, we have to take into account the effects of existing property boundaries on city layout. This factor was especially critical in the residential districts. Streets, as we have seen, were often very long lived, and the boundaries of the built-up *insulae* which they separated would therefore tend to be stable over considerable periods. However, within the *insulae* it was a different matter. A private alley leading to the heart of a residential block could be remodelled or even moved as individual houses, or parts of houses, changed hands, according to the requirements of the inhabitants. Property boundaries were fluid and, facilitated by the use of mudbrick, which lent itself to relatively easy modifications, houses could change shape as the household expanded or contracted and parts were sold off or neighbouring rooms acquired. At the level of the residential neighbourhood there was probably little, if any, official involvement in planning, and private residents would determine for themselves, by mutual if not by written agreement, the shape of their own immediate environment. These transformations are evident both in the archaeological record and in the legal contracts, which shed a great deal of light on the social background to them in terms of the contemporary patterns of property ownership, transmission and inheritance.

CONTINUITY AND CHANGE IN URBAN LAYOUT

When dealing with cities that were occupied over many hundreds of years, it can be difficult to distinguish truly innovative elements in urban planning from those which

Figure 5.1 Plan of Nippur, *c.*1500 BC, showing the city wall with seven of its gates, the Euphrates and two canals, as well as the enclosure of the Enlil temple on the right. (The plan is incomplete and there is no way of knowing how many gates the city had in total, but it was certainly more than the seven depicted on the preserved plan.) (Hilprecht collection, Friedrich Schiller Universität, Jena).

were merely 'makeovers' of what had gone before. Strictly speaking, in order to do so, we would have to have – for each particular element – a detailed stratigraphic investigation to determine the sequence of (or absence of) antecedents on that particular spot. But ideal, laboratory-style conditions do not apply, and we have to make the best of piecemeal data that shed light on some features but which cannot tell us much of what we really want to know. In spite of this, there are some clues available to us in trying to decide how much the first millennium cities owe to their forebears.

For Nippur, there exists a map of the city drawn on a clay tablet, with its principal features labelled in cuneiform (Zettler 1993: Plates 6–7) (see Figure 5.1). The map has been dated to the Kassite period, and some of the features depicted on it, such as three of the city gates (the Exalted, Gula and Ur-facing gates), are still attested in documents of the mid-first millennium BC. This suggests that the city wall, together with its gates, remained in use from the Kassite period through to at least the fifth century BC. In fact, excavations in the WC area of Nippur have confirmed the presence of a seventh-century city wall in close proximity to its Kassite and Ur III-period predecessors (McG. Gibson, introduction to Zettler 1993: 8–9).

Similarly, for Babylon, many of the topographical features known from texts of the first millennium are already present in the literary-topographical series Tin.tir = Babylon, a series of (originally) five tablets for which George (1992: 4–7) has proposed a dating in the late second millennium BC. Some of the topographical features mentioned in Tin.tir, such as four of the eight gates of Babylon, can be identified with excavated remains, while others can only be approximately located. Van De Mieroop prefers to attribute the reshaping of Babylon to the Neo-Babylonian kings Nabopolassar (625–605 BC) and Nebukadrezzar II (604–562 BC), perhaps following the example of the late Assyrian kings (Van De Mieroop 1999: 88). In doing so, he rejects a late second millennium date for the series Tin.tir on the grounds that it is only attested in later exemplars (the earliest ones are from the library of Ashurbanipal). However, the transmission of the series in late exemplars does not rule out a late second-millennium composition for it. Moreover, the fact that the series was already known in the time of Ashurbanipal implies that the topographical features were laid down in his reign at the latest, and yet there is no evidence for the wholesale remodelling of Babylon during the Neo-Assyrian period. An inscription of Ashurbanipal attests to his *re*building of Imgur-Enlil and Nemetti-Enlil, the paired inner walls of Babylon, implying that they were already well established by his time.

This author prefers, therefore, to be guided by George's dating of the series Tin.tir = Babylon, and believes that the basic layout of Babylon – the city walls, the gates and the major, processional streets – were essentially already in place by some time in the late second millennium. The Neo-Babylonian rulers largely fitted their extensive monumental building projects into this existing framework. It is worth noting that Reuther, writing on the street network in the Merkes area, observed that these thoroughfares invariably followed long-established courses; sometimes they could be shown to go back as far as the Old Babylonian period (Reuther 1926: 66). He also notes that the Processional Way of Nebukadrezzar II was a later insert and was not aligned precisely with the streets of Merkes.

SUMMARY AND CONCLUSIONS

In the foregoing paragraphs we have described the basic elements which made up the Babylonian city during the first millennium BC and identified some of the key factors which influenced its form. These latter include: social structure; climatic conditions; materials and the state of technical know-how, and existing property boundaries combined with patterns of ownership, transmission and inheritance. The king, as the agent of any central planning, was himself subject to social and religious tradition, and was no doubt motivated by the desire for display and the prestige that it conferred. The complex interaction of all of these factors shaped the Babylonian city and, of course, they did not operate equally across the city but, rather, each element of the urban layout was more susceptible to certain influences than to others. It would therefore be misleading to use the terms 'planned' and 'organic' as though they were mutually exclusive, opposite categories. Both elements can be found in the Babylonian city. Moreover, as we have shown, great caution has to be exercised in inferring any grand plan on the basis of the street layout, since the evidence for the existence of a regular grid of streets, as has been proposed for Babylon and Borsippa, is much more slight than has been realised up to now. In any case, the fact that the Neo-Babylonian rulers essentially worked with an existing pattern for the city hardly diminishes their great achievements in the sphere of monumental architecture, as exemplified by Nebukadrezzar's Babylon.

BIBLIOGRAPHY

Baker, H.D. (forthcoming). *The Urban Landscape in First Millennium* BC *Babylonia*.

Gates, C. (2003). *Ancient Cities. The Archaeology of Urban Life in the Ancient Near East and Egypt, Greece, and Rome*. London and New York: Routledge.

George, A.R. (1992). *Babylonian Topographical Texts*. Orientalia Lovaniensia Analecta 40. Leuven: Peeters.

—— (1993). *House Most High. The Temples of Ancient Mesopotamia*. Mesopotamian Civilizations 5. Winona Lake, IN: Eisenbrauns.

Heinrich, E. (1982). *Die Tempel und Heiligtümer im alten Mesopotamien. Typologie, Morphologie und Geschichte*, 2 vols, with the collaboration of U. Seidl. Denkmäler antiker Architektur 14. Berlin: Walter de Gruyter & Co.

Jursa, M. (1999). *Das Archiv des Bel-remanni*. Publications de l'Institut historique-archéologique néerlandais de Stamboul (PIHANS) 86. Istanbul: NINO.

—— (2004). 'Palast. A IV8.b. Neubabylonisch', *Reallexikon der Assyriologie* 10: 209–212.

—— (2005). *Neo-Babylonian Legal and Administrative Documents: Typology, Contents and Archives*. Münster: Ugarit-Verlag.

Kessler, K. (1991). *Uruk. Urkunden aus Privathäusern. Die Wohnhäuser westlich des Eanna-Tempelbereichs, Teil I. Die Archive der Söhne des Bel-ushallim, des Nabû-ushallim und des Bel-supê-muhur*. Ausgrabungen in Uruk-Warka, Endberichte 8. Mainz am Rhein: Philipp von Zabern.

—— (1999). 'Der vergessene spätbabylonische Königspalast neben Eanna', *Baghdader Mitteilungen* 30: 165–173.

Koldewey, R. (1911). *Die Tempel von Babylon und Borsippa nach den Ausgrabungen durch die Deutsche Orient-Gesellschaft*. Wissenschaftliche Veröffentlichung der Deutschen Orient-Gesellschaft 15. Leipzig: J.C. Hinrichs.

Liverani, M. (1997). 'Ancient Near Eastern cities and modern ideologies', in Wilhelm (ed.) 1997: 85–107.

Matthiae, P., Enea, A., Peyronel, L. and Pinnock, F. (eds) (2000). *Proceedings of the First International Congress on the Archaeology of the Ancient Near East, Rome, May 18th-23rd 1998*. Vol. 2. Rome: Università degli Studi di Roma 'La Sapienza', Dipartimento di Scienze Storiche, Archeologiche e Antropologiche dell'Antichità.

Miglus, P. (1999). *Städtische Wohnarchitektur in Babylonien und Assyrien*. Baghdader Forschungen 22. Mainz am Rhein: Philipp von Zabern.

—— (2004). '(Palast B.) §8.1.9 Spätbabylonische Zeit', *Reallexikon der Assyriologie* 10: 254–255.

Reuther, O. (1926). *Die Innenstadt von Babylon (Merkes)*, 2 vols. Wissenschaftliche Veröffentlichungen der Deutschen Orient-Gesellschaft 47. Leipzig: J.C. Hinrichs.

Unger, E. (1931). *Babylon: die heilige Stadt nach der Beschreibung der Babylonier*. Berlin: Walter de Gruyter & Co.

—— (1932). 'Barsippa', *Reallexikon der Assyriologie* 1: 402–429, Taf. 55–59.

Van De Mieroop, M. (1999). *The Ancient Mesopotamian City*. Oxford: Oxford University Press.

Wetzel, F. (1930). *Die Stadtmauern von Babylon*. Wissenschaftliche Veröffentlichung der Deutschen Orient-Gesellschaft 48. Leipzig: J.C. Hinrichs.

Wilhelm, G. (ed.) (1997). *Die orientalische Stadt: Kontinuität, Wandel, Bruch. 1 Internationales Colloquium der Deutschen Orient-Gesellschaft, 9.-10. Mai 1996 in Halle/Saale*. Colloquien der Deutschen Orient-Gesellschaft 1. Saarbrücken: Saarbrücker Druckerei und Verlag.

Winter, I.J. (2000). 'Babylonian archaeologists of the(ir) Mesopotamian past', in Matthiae *et al.* (eds) 2000: 1785–1800.

Wiseman, D.J. (1985). *Nebuchadrezzar and Babylon. The Schweich Lectures of the British Academy 1983*. Oxford: Oxford University Press.

Woolley, L. (1962). *Ur Excavations, Volume IX. The Neo-Babylonian and Persian Periods*. London: The British Museum and the University Museum, University of Pennsylvania, Philadelphia.

Zettler, R.L. (1993). *Nippur III. Kassite Buildings in Area WC-1*. Oriental Institute Publications 111. Chicago, IL: The Oriental Institute of the University of Chicago.

PART II

MATERIAL CULTURE

———•◆•———

CHAPTER SIX

ARCHITECTURE IN THE OLD BABYLONIAN PERIOD

———•◆•———

Harriet Crawford

INTRODUCTION

The study of ancient architecture is an extremely valuable tool because the buildings and settlements that they form are far more than a collection of bricks and mortar. The size and patterning of settlements across the landscape frequently reflects the social and political complexity of a society, while the tracks and roads between the settlements indicate the connections between them. They may also point in the direction of significant external contacts as well. The internal arrangement of the settlements relates to the values and structure of the society to which they belong and may also play an active role in promoting them. The relationship between buildings and behaviour is not straightforward, but it is widely agreed that such links exist and that the built environment both reflects the ideals of the society in question, and plays an active role in encouraging socially desirable behaviour (see, for example, the work of Hillier and Hanson 1984, of Kent 1990 and Rappaport in Kent 1990).

If we accept this premise, it follows that the structure of a settlement can offer us a glimpse into fossilised behaviour patterns, if only we can unravel their meaning. If we take the example of a typical Old Babylonian town or city, its layout will probably demonstrate which buildings were given prominence and which were most lavishly decorated, both features suggesting the importance that society attached to them. Domestic buildings will be grouped together in different ways, often with different floor areas. This can indicate whether or not the extended family played an important part in society, or if the nuclear family was the norm. A wide range of floor areas among the domestic units can tell us whether there were major differences in wealth which may, in turn, indicate whether the society was highly stratified or not. If certain members of society were secluded and protected from contact with anyone other than their own families, this too may be apparent from the house plans. Industrial areas and cottage industries should also be readily identifiable.

More prosaically, architecture provides us with important insights into the technical achievements of the Old Babylonian builders who mainly used mud brick for their constructions. It demonstrates their engineering ability, their tools and their surveying methods as well as their use of other raw materials, some of which may not be local to Mesopotamia. Their level of professional expertise, in turn, provides us with indirect information on the degree of craft specialisation within the construction industry, information which, in Babylonia, can often be supplemented by the textual record. The presence of skilled craftsmen, if they are present, in turn tells us something about the level of administration that was necessary to support and provide for these master builders and surveyors.

In this chapter we will look first at the structure of a typical Old Babylonian town, then at the major public buildings, the temples and the palaces, and finally at domestic housing. Most of the evidence will be drawn from Babylonia itself, but it will be augmented by some drawn from a little further north, from sites such as Mari and Rimah which lay on the northern edge of the Babylonian world.

THE URBAN STRUCTURE

Two important surveys of Old Babylonian cities in the last twenty years have greatly increased our knowledge of these fundamental building blocks of society (by the early second millennium many sites in the south were already old foundations and so may, in practice, reflect the values of an earlier time). The older towns and cities stood on considerable tells or mounds, but others were newly founded on 'green field sites' and had a more open configuration.[1] So important were towns in the Babylonian world view that each city and its environs were seen as property of a great god who guided its destiny and protected its citizens. Men and women were often identified in the textual record as being of such and such a city, not by a family name, and their personal names might include the name of their city god as one element, while the rulers were often referred to as simply the man of their capital city. Hammurabi, for instance, was often referred to as the man of Babylon.

Our evidence is drawn from the French survey of the great tell site of Larsa (Huot 1989), capital of one of the most important city states on the south Mesopotamian plain at the beginning of the reign of Hammurabi with an area of about 190 ha, and from that of Mashkan-Shapir (Stone and Zimansky 1995), second city of the Larsa state, a much flatter, younger, site of about 100 ha. In addition, valuable information can be obtained from two much smaller planned sites, each less than 2 ha in area: Haradum, again a French project (Kepinski-Lecomte 1992) and Harmal explored by an Iraqi team (Baqir 1946: 22–30).

All settlements on the southern plain of Mesopotamia lay on water courses, either the Tigris or the Euphrates, or on canals, because the rainfall was insufficient for agriculture or for the needs of men and beasts. The great city of Ur had access to water by means of two harbour areas on the Euphrates and one on a large canal, both of which were major arteries of communication as well. Harbours are found in many large sites and were important commercial areas known as the *Karums*, where goods were loaded and unloaded and business was transacted. Smaller canals then led water into the settlements. Most towns seem to have been walled and a study of the modern contours of a site often indicates the position of the gates which were frequently heavily fortified. At Larsa, five gates have been identified, some for wheeled traffic and some just posterns (Huot op. cit.: 40). Relations between town and country were very close in the Old Babylonian period and no clear boundary existed between the two.[2] Many inhabitants of the towns worked land on the outskirts of their settlements and intensively cultivated gardens, orchards, and plantations of date palms frequently lay within the town walls (Harris 1975: 20).

Within the gates the town was usually divided up by roadways and water courses into a number of smaller tells representing quarters or *babtums*, as they were known, which often had different characters. At Larsa, the major roads appear to converge on the religious and administrative area, lying in the centre of the city, which housed the main temple of Ebabbar and a ziggurat which must have physically dominated the city. Other areas are more difficult to identify with certainty, but specialist production areas for metal working, flint and semi-precious stone working have been identified both inside and outside the walls, while the main domestic quarter lay to the east and north (Huot op. cit.: 36–37, 45). More information can be obtained from the survey of Mashkan-Shapir which was surveyed by a combination of aerial photography and foot patrols (Stone and Zimansky op. cit.). It was, like Larsa, a walled town on a number of canals which divided the city into five quarters. Some gardens, palm groves and a cemetery all apparently lay within the wall. Unlike Larsa, the temple area, which was not excavated, lay in the south-west corner of the site rather than in the centre as in most contemporary cities. The main temple was dedicated to Nergal, god of death and disease and one might suggest that its position on the perimeter of the site was so that this warlike god could help in the defence of his town.

Close to the temple lay what was probably the administrative area, and a cemetery with another possible temple, while a large metal-working and pottery-making area lay to the south-west where the prevailing wind would blow the fumes away from the domestic quarters which seem to have been in the centre and the north-west. Pottery kilns and other metal-working areas are, however, also found widely distributed across the whole area, suggesting the presence of cottage industries as well as larger scale production in dedicated workshops. One puzzle is the position of the market place in such settlements, if one existed, as there is little room within the confines of a tell site for large open spaces. It is now thought that markets were present and may have been held at the gates of the city or just outside them, although smaller markets and shops probably stood within the walls. As we have seen, the quays of the city were the main commercial centres, although not necessarily the only ones. Mashkan-Shapir was a relatively new foundation and thus did not stand on a high tell, so the market may have been held in the open area between the walls and the built-up area to the south-east.

Haradum and Harmal are very different, not only in terms of scale, but because both seem to have been planned settlements with specialist functions. Harmal on the outskirts of modern Baghdad was a small administrative centre, while Haradum on the middle Euphrates, about 90 km south-east of Mari, was a settlement to facilitate trade up and down the river. Both were very small compared to the sites we have been looking at, neither reaching two hectares in area, but both were heavily fortified. The plan of Haradum is more regular and we can see that the town was laid out on a grid plan which looks almost Roman in its symmetry. The two main buildings, the temple and what was identified as the mayor's house, stand on a small square just north-east of the centre of the settlement. The rest of the area inside the walls was divided into blocks and seems to be taken up with houses, except for the south-eastern corner which may have had a more specialised function.

PUBLIC BUILDINGS, TEMPLES

We have seen that religious buildings were often at the centre of Babylonian cities. They usually formed an impressive group around the ziggurat or stepped tower which would have dominated the skyline. The ziggurat at Larsa seems to have been founded in the Ur III period and what remains is largely the work of the Neo-Babylonian king Nabonidus who restored the building, which was dedicated to the sun god Shamash and his wife Aya (Bachelot and Castel 1989: 56–77). We know little of the Hammurabi foundation except that it stood in its own court and its dimensions as restored were almost square, measuring 40.30 m × 43.50 m. A niche was uncovered on the east face, but no trace of the access remained and we do not know how many stages it had or if it had a triple stair like the contemporary one at Ur, a single flight of steps, or even a ramp.

The main temple, called Ebabbar, is also unexcavated and lies adjacent to the ziggurat. It may have been founded in the Ur III period like the ziggurat, but the plan seems to date to the time of Hammurabi and was carefully restored by the Kassite king Burnaburiash. Work has been carried out on a series of impressive courtyards which presumably gave access to the main shrine (Calvet *et al.* 1976: 1–28). The courts were surrounded by small rooms which may have been used as offices or even workshops. In one of them, room 13, buried below the floor, a jar was found containing what was originally thought to be a jeweller's hoard as it contained both finished items of jewellery, 65 weights and a small quantity of precious scrap metal in addition to various tools, clay sealings and an inscribed haematite seal. Its purpose has since been re-assessed and it is now considered that it may have belonged to a temple official or to a merchant (Huot 1995). The main court, Court 1, in which room 13 lay and the hoard described above was found, has a number of interesting features of which the most impressive is the decoration of the internal walls (Calvet *et al.* 1976). This is made up of engaged half columns decorated with a design that closely resembles twisted barley-sugar sticks. The pillars were made of specially moulded semi-circular bricks and at a later stage were plastered over so that eventually the decoration disappeared. The court was not completely excavated, but its overall dimensions were of the order of 46.70 m × 36 m. There was access from this court to at least two other smaller ones. An impressive doorway in the south-west wall gave access up a flight of steps to room 9. To one side of this stair lay a suite of platforms and walls coated with bitumen, known as the Construction Annexe, which the excavators thought might may have been altars or offering places. Room 9, a rectangular space, seems to have been a subsidiary sanctuary which appears to have predated the main construction of the court. Inside lay two piles of brick, perhaps also the remains of altars, set diagonally across the main axis of the room, which strongly suggests that they belong to an earlier structure and were too important to be destroyed or relocated. Their alignment is the same as that of the Construction Annexe and this structure, too, probably belongs to an earlier building.

The engaged columns of Court 1 with their barley-sugar decoration provide a distinctive decorative feature that links a number of temples of approximately this date. The Larsa courtyard is not the earliest example which we have. This is found at Ur where a king of Larsa called Warad-Sin fortified the ziggurat enclosure with a bastion on the north-west of the terrace bearing the same style of decoration, also

Figure 6.1   A hypothetical reconstruction of the temple at Tell Rimah
(courtesy of Dr Joan Oates).

made of specially moulded mud brick (Woolley 1939: 42–43, and fig. 71). The style
seems to have moved from the south of Mesopotamia northwards, perhaps via the
Jebel Hamrin, part of a long-established route east of the Tigris which linked cities
as far apart as Susa and Nineveh. A fine temple was uncovered at Tell Haddad during
rescue operations in the Hamrin valley, which unfortunately is largely unpublished,
but the interior of the courtyard was decorated in this very distinctive way.[3]

Fortunately, our next example from Tell Rimah is much better recorded. This
site lies on the north Mesopotamian Jazira about 13 km south of Tell Afar. A glance
at the topography suggests there was an upper and a lower town, something not seen
in the south, the upper town dominated by a large religious complex which was
excavated by Professor David Oates (see Oates 1982 for a summary and references).
Excavation showed that the complex was made up of a large temple and a ziggurat
dating to the time of Hammurabi, a period of considerable prosperity when Rimah
stood close to one of the routes linking the Assyrian plain with the metal-rich region
of central Anatolia, and shared in the prosperity this trade brought to the region.

The temple stood on a platform which was linked to the lower town by a fine
processional stair carried on three vaults of diminishing size. The temple itself was
just under 40 metres square, approached through a monumental gate on the east side
at the head of the stair. The gate led into a court 19 metres square in the north
corner of which stood a stair carried on a series of vaults which survived to first floor
level. Opposite the main entrance lay the door into the inner and outer sanctuaries,
rectangular rooms which had their long walls parallel to the wall of the court. The
statue of the god probably stood on the long back wall of the inner cella or sanctuary,

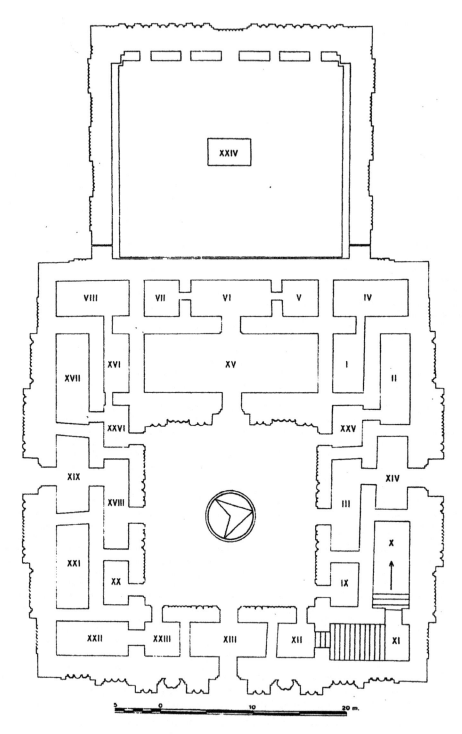

Figure 6.2   Plan of the temple at Tell Rimah
(courtesy of the British School of Archaeology in Iraq).

where it could be seen from the main entrance and had a view out over his city. The entrance to the shrine seems to have been flanked by monumental figures of a goddess and a protective spirit, but neither was found in its original position.

On the other three sides of the court lay smaller service and storage rooms, some of which seem to have been two storeys high. The interior walls of the court and the exterior walls of the building were decorated with engaged half pillars decorated like the ones which we saw at Larsa. In addition to the twisted barley sugar design there are two other patterns, one made up of a series of small diamond shapes and another of a quatrefoil. All seem to have been made of carefully carved bricks which were then assembled to form the required pattern. It has been suggested that two of the designs evoke the pattern left on the stem of a palm tree when the fronds are chopped off to prune it.

These patterns also occur at two other temples of this period in north Mesopotamia, at a site in north-east Syria called Leilan, ancient Shubat-Enlil, Samsi-Addu's new capital, where they are found on the façade of a building which has only been partially excavated, but which includes the exterior wall of a shrine. The shrine itself is also of interest as its design, with the altar on the short rather than the long wall of the cella, reverts to a plan not seen since the late third millennium (Weiss *et al.* 1995: 533, fig. 4). The final site is Mari on the middle Euphrates where similar pillars in a poor state of repair were found on the façade of the Temple des Lions (Margueron 1991: 9–10).

At Rimah, two more entrances were uncovered in the main temple court opposite each other on the north and south walls. There was no entrance on the west wall because a great high terrace or ziggurat, approximately 25 metres square was built up against the outer wall of the temple on this side. It is badly preserved and it is not clear if there was ever more than one superimposed platform, nor is it obvious where the access was. It seems likely that the only way onto the top of the terrace was from the roof of the adjacent temple which, as we have seen, could be reached by a stair in the north corner of the inner court. This makes it very different to the classic ziggurats we have seen which are free-standing in their own courts with direct access by stairs or ramps, and contrasts with the plan of the temple which is very similar to those in the south.

There was another remarkable feature found in the Rimah temple complex. Some unexpected and sophisticated techniques were employed to roof the structures. Some of the store-rooms in the temple were covered by steeply pitched radial vaults and the stair to the roof was also composed of eight transverse radial vaults of increasing height, each carrying two treads. The substructure of an apparently earlier platform adjacent to that on which the temple stood was supported on a series of pitched brick vaults one above the other (Oates 1992). Corbel-vaulting had, of course, been in use for more than a millennium before this and these innovative techniques seem to be a response to the problem posed by the lack of good timbers which could be used to support the roofs of large public buildings.

Other temples are known from the Old Babylonian period and one of the most complete is that found at the site of Ischali in the Diyala valley which was probably a provincial capital. The temple was dedicated to a manifestation of the goddess Inanna and was known as the Kititium temple. It is an impressive structure standing

Figure 6.3 'Barley sugar' pillars at Tell Rimah (courtesy of Dr Joan Oates).

on a platform with the main sanctuary raised a further two metres on a second platform. This second platform was approached by a monumental flight of steps from a
ceremonial courtyard at the lower level. This court, in turn, was surrounded by smaller
shrines and service rooms. The main shrine could also be approached directly from
the road outside and, like the earlier temples of the Ur III period and the temple at
Rimah, the cella and ante-cella lay on the far side of an internal courtyard with a
clear view of the divine statue standing in a niche in the centre of the back wall of
the cella. The cellas could be closed off by means of massive double doors. Behind
the shrine lay a number of service rooms some of which seem to have housed the
treasures of the temple which included a magnificent bitumenous bowl decorated
with the heads of wild moufflon sheep or ibis, probably from Susa, and a stamp seal
which originated in the Arabian Gulf far to the south (Hill and Jacobsen 1990).

Smaller versions of similar, but less elaborate shrines were found at the two small
sites mentioned earlier, Harmal and Haradum. At Haradum there was only one shrine
in the centre of the town laid out in a similar manner and at Harmal there were a
number apparently dedicated to scribal gods, where in at least one instance the
entrances were guarded by pairs of charming clay lions sitting on their haunches.
Scribal gods were especially appropriate in this case because Harmal is thought to
have been a small specialist administrative enclave.

Hammurabi and his contemporaries also built at the old Sumerian cities of the
south, but in many cases the remains are fragmentary. At Ur, for instance, the Giparu
or palace of the high priestess was renovated by the sister of the king of Larsa, Warad-
Sin, whom we have already met as the builder of the bastion with the palm tree
decoration at Ur (Weadock 1975: 109–110). One of the gateways into the inner
ziggurat enclosure which had been modified to serve as a sort of law court known as
the E-dub-lal-mah in the Isin-Lara period and whose inner room may have been
roofed by a dome, was also in use, although not much work was done here in the
Old Babylonian period (Woolley 1965: 9–14, figs 48 and 51). Various other subsidiary
temples were also built or refurbished outside the main temenos area.

PALACES

The remains of Hammurabi's own city at Babylon are, unfortunately, almost inaccessible
as the water table has risen too high to allow them to be explored. The problems
have now been compounded by the use of the site as a large army camp in the aftermath of the second Gulf war. For example, big trenches were dug through the archaeological levels, large areas were levelled and treated to make hard standing for lorries
etc. and sand bags filled with material from outside the perimeter of the site, some
containing archaeological items, were used for protection. Many of these bags have
now burst, mixing imported material with the indigenous remains. We will probably
never know what Hammurabi's own palace looked like and there are few other palace
buildings from this period in the south which can be used as models. One structure
from Larsa, of which only the foundations remain, was found and is thought to be
the remains of a palace built by Nur-Adad of Larsa who lived about 50 years before
Hammurabi. Sadly, it has been badly damaged by brick robbing and illegal digging
(Margueron 1982). It is a large rectangular building well separated from the temple

complex, perhaps underlining the separation of what could very loosely be called 'church' and 'state', and seems to have been built round a series of courtyards; a reception suite or throne room has been tentatively identified.

Happily for us there is an excellent and well preserved example of a palace from the city of Mari on the middle Euphrates. It was founded in the mid-third millennium, but was extensively restored in the early second millennium by Zimri-Lim who was conquered by Samsi-Addu, and the building was finally destroyed by Hammurabi towards the end of his reign. The complex web of diplomatic, cultural and economic contacts across the region at this period make it reasonable to see this building, which was much admired by contemporaries, as fairly typical of palaces across the region. It can also be suggested that the design of the palace, which was almost a city in microcosm, reflects the many and different roles that a king was expected to play in the life of his city (for a summary of the evidence see Gates 1984, Margueron 1982, and for more details M.A.R.I).

The palace is a huge fortified structure, evidence for the king's military role, covering 32 acres, indicative of his wealth and the range of his power. The main entrance lay on the north wall and gave access through a number of auxiliary rooms to a great public court with a cistern in the centre. On the far side of this is what may be a raised reception room or shrine which has traces of frescoes on the walls. It is tempting to see this area as the site of the *majlis*, or court, where local people probably had direct access to their ruler or his deputy. Here they could air their grievances or express their views on matters of great concern to them, as still happens today in some traditional Arab societies. In the north-west corner of this court an entrance led into the heart of the palace complex, the great Court of the Palm as it is designated in the texts found nearby. The name seems to have derived from the presence of a palm tree in the centre of the court whose position is today marked by a pierced stone which may have supported it. The south side of the court was shaded by a loggia supported by posts of which traces remain, while a central door gave on to the outer throne room. The south wall was also remarkable for the unique painting found adjacent to the entrance. This spectacular painting seems to represent a wall hanging with scalloped fringes along the top and bottom. It shows the investiture of a king of Mari in its central panel which is divided into two horizontally. The top half depicts the goddess Ishtar, bristling with weapons, her foot on her lion, presenting the king with the traditional symbols of kingship, the so-called rod and ring. Behind him stands a protective minor goddess while Ishtar is attended by another similar goddess and a god who is probably Amurru god of the west. The lower half of the panel shows two goddesses with flowing vases, traditional symbols of fertility in this barren region. The central panel is flanked on each side by mythical beasts, trees and two more protective goddesses (Margueron 1990: 115–125).

The entrance in the south wall of the Court of the Palm gives onto an outer audience chamber, room 64, which holds a stepped platform, visible from the court, flanked originally by two statues. One survives today and represents a goddess holding a vase with water flowing from it, similar to those shown on the investiture painting. From here a further two doors allow access to the main throne room which has a raised niche at the east end with the bases of a number of statues in it. It has been plausibly suggested that originally this niche held statues of the king and the goddess Ishtar in a scene which mirrored that shown in the investiture painting in the court (al Khalesi 1978: 68) At the foot of the steps leading up into the niche lay the fallen statue of an earlier king of Mari. From this ceremonial complex, where no doubt the king received important foreign and local dignitaries, a stair gave access to an upper floor and to the king's private apartments.

Other important sectors within the palace compound include a large religious quarter in the south-east lying above the third millennium shrines and reflecting the king's sacerdotal duties; an extensive chancery or scribal quarter where the administrative functions of the palace were focused; storage facilities, highly necessary to provision the palace and perhaps the town in times of stress; and, finally, another sumptuous domestic suite which was probably the queen's apartments. The queen had important duties of her own and when her husband was away on official business effectively ran the day-to-day business of the palace (Dalley 1984, especially chapter 5).

DOMESTIC HOUSING

Although housing occupied much of the space within a city's wall, only two urban areas in south Mesopotamia of Old Babylonian date have been excavated over a wide area. The first was at Ur and the second at Nippur (Woolley and Mallowan 1976; Stone 1987). The Ur quarter especially gives a flavour of the character of a domestic area at this time with buildings tightly packed together, winding main roads leading to smaller streets and crowded alleyways which, in turn, gave access to individual groups of buildings. In addition to the mud brick houses, which presented blank walls to the street with narrow doors giving access to the interiors, there were small shrines which were miniature versions of some of the major religious buildings that have already been described. The entrances of these shrines were sometimes protected with clay reliefs showing protective figures of minor deities. There are also one or two buildings which may have been shops. At Ur, one of these has a hatch or window giving on to the street through which food and drink might have been sold.

The majority of the buildings at both Ur and Nippur are domestic and a high proportion are courtyard houses where the rooms lie round one, two, or occasionally three courtyards which provided light and air to the rooms and work space for the inhabitants. A recent study of the houses at Ur shows a wide variation in floor space from 9.68 m^2 to 19.25 m^2 suggesting considerable inequalities of wealth and in the number of residents per unit. It is also tempting to suggest that, while the smaller houses were lived in by nuclear families, the larger ones sheltered extended ones (Brusasco 1999–2000: 67). Similar variations in size were observed at Nippur and it is suggested that the presence of 'rich' and 'poor' houses together in close proximity may indicate that these neighbourhoods were lived in by groups who were related to each other, rather than by groups of similar economic standing (Stone 1987: 17; Brusasco op. cit.: 144). It has also been suggested that some of the blind alleys at Ur, which give access to both large and small units, may have been jointly owned by the residents who, on this hypothesis, would also have been part of the same kin group. It also seems that professions ran in certain families so that each neighbourhood may also have housed groups of professionals working in the same field. The presence of chapels in some of the larger houses at Ur has led to suggestion that the area may have been a priestly enclave. However, in the Isin-Larsa period at least one house is known, from the tablets found in it, to have been lived in by a Dilmun merchant called Ea.Nasir[4] and chapels are known from houses at other contemporary sites. Tablets found in the houses are mostly personal business archives and legal documents such as wills and land sales. Some people seem to have worked from home using one room as an office. There are also a number of school exercises leading to the proposal that, at both cities, small neighbourhood schools were present.

It is difficult to determine with certainty what individual rooms within the houses were used for and Brusasco (op. cit.: 71) stresses that most rooms were multi-functional, something that is easier in a culture where furniture is minimal and the placing of mats and cushions can easily transform a living area into a sleeping area and vice versa. Usage will also vary depending on the time of day and the weather so that in winter tasks undertaken outside will move into the interior. It is somewhat surprising that few houses had washing areas and only 6.8 per cent of the rooms at Ur contained hearths. Much of the cooking seems to have been done in the courtyard. It is not clear if the houses at Ur and Nippur had upper floors, but it seems likely that some did and there can be little doubt that the flat roofs provided useful additional storage and living space. At other towns, such as Sippar, texts record the presence of upper floors which could be sold or rented separately (Harris op. cit.: 22). We also know from the texts that inheritance laws divided property between all surviving sons with the eldest getting an additional 10 per cent and custody of the chapel and the family tomb which usually lay in it. Girls received their share as a marriage portion. This system meant that through time properties tended either to be sold and the proceeds shared between siblings or that buildings were subdivided into smaller and smaller units so that each son got their share (Stone 1981: 24–25; Brusasco op. cit.: 113, 116–117, 134).

CONCLUSIONS

The evidence that has been presented above relates to the situation in large southern urban centres. We have almost no evidence for the situation in the countryside, but we certainly cannot assume the buildings were exactly the same. Ethnographic evidence points to the presence of large walled compounds in the countryside, rather than courtyard houses, as these also provide space for at least some of the family's stock. In north Mesopotamia the situation also seems to have been rather different, although the evidence is, again, fairly sparse. Evidence from Chagar Bazar and from Hamoukar, for instance, shows that a variety of house plans were present, some similar to the southern ones as well as a considerable number of buildings composed of a single rectangular room, and others with a T-shaped configuration (Mallowan 1936: 14–16, 1937: 108–112; Gibson 2002: 23–27). At Tell Mohammed Diyab in north-east Syria, there is evidence for the use of barrel vaults to roof some of the rooms (Sauvage 1992) something that we have already noted at Tell Rimah, but for which there is no evidence in the houses in the south.

It was suggested at the beginning of this chapter that a study of the built environment could provide information in a number of fields. A striking feature of the larger sites we have looked at is that most of them were already old and their structures well established by the early second millennium. The tradition of walling them and the domination of the urban scene by temples and palaces continues. The Old Babylonian kings seem to have been well aware of the importance of tradition as the rebuilding of the great temple at Larsa and repairs at other sites also shows. At Larsa, older features such as the Construction Annexe were carefully incorporated in the new design. The continuity in the design of the urban courtyard house is also striking and must be a tribute to its suitability both environmentally and socially to the needs of the community. It has been suggested that both nuclear and extended families are present in the towns and that neighbourhoods may have been lived in by kin groups who were not only related by blood, but also by profession. The technical abilities of the builders are also clear and the presence of the dome at Ur and a wide variety of vaulting techniques in the north is impressive, as is the ability of the builders to use mud brick in a variety of ways to decorate major public buildings. It should therefore be no surprise to note that the texts show us that professional builders and architects were present in society (Postgate 1992: 236; Crawford 2002: 69).

This study of the built environment has, as we hoped, produced a number of models for the workings of society in the second quarter of the second millennium BCE and these models can be tested against the evidence presented in other studies in this book.

NOTES

1 In the north the configuration was often different and showed an upper and a lower town.
2 For an excellent study of the Mesopotamian city see Van De Mieroop 1997.
3 I am grateful to Professor Michael Roaf for this information.
4 No. 1 Old Street.

BIBLIOGRAPHY

Al Khalesi, Yasin M. 1978. *The court of the palms: a functional interpretation of the Mari palace.* Bibliotheca Mesopotamica volume 8. Malibu.

Bachelot, L. and C. Castel. 1989. Recherches sur la ziggurat de Larsa. In: Huot ed. 1989, pp. 53–77.

Baqir, T. 1946. Tell Harmal: a preliminary report. *Sumer* vol. 2: 22–30.

Brusasco, Paolo. 1999–2000 Family archives and the use of space in Old Babylonian houses at Ur. *Mesopotamia XXXIV–V*: 3–174.

Calvet, Y., D. Charpin, S. Cleuziou and J.-D. Forest. 1976. In: J.-Cl. Huot ed., Larsa: rapport préliminaire sur le 6eme campagne de fouilles. *Syria* LIII: 1–28.

Crawford, Harriet. 2004. *Sumer and the Sumerians.* 2nd edition. Cambridge.

Dalley, S. 1984. *Mari and Karana.* London.

Gates, M. 1984. The palace of Zimri-Lim at Mari. *Biblical Archaeologist* 47.2: 70–87.

Gibson, McG. ed. 2002. Hamoukar: a summary of three seasons of excavation. *Akkadika* 123: 11–34.

Hill, H. and T. Jacobsen. 1990. *Old Babylonian public buildings in the Diyala region.* Oriental Institute Publications 98. Chicago.

Hillier, B. and J. Hanson. 1984. *The social logic of space.* Cambridge.

Huot, J.-L. ed. 1989. *Larsa: travaux de 1985.* Edition Recherches de la Civilisations. Memoire 83. Paris.

—— 1995. A propos du trésor de Larsa. In: U. Finkbeiner *et al.* eds, *Beiträge zur Kulturgeschichte vorderasiens. Festschrift für Rainer Michael Boehmer.* Von Zabern Mainz: 267–269.

Kent, S. ed. 1990. *Domestic architecture and the use of space.* New Directions in Archaeology. Cambridge.

Mallowan, M.E.L. 1936. Excavations at Chagar Bazar. *Iraq III*: 1–86.

—— 1937. Excavations at Chagar Bazar & an archaeological survey of the Habur region. In: *Iraq IV*: 91–154.

Margueron, J. 1982. *Recherches sur les palais mesopotamiens de l'âge de bronze*. Paris.

—— 1990. La peinture de l'investiture et l'histoire de cour 106. In: O. Tunca ed., *De la Babylonie à La Syrie*. Liege, pp. 115–125.

—— 1991. Recherches en cours. *Orient-Express* 1991: 9–10.

M.A.R.I (Mari: annales de recherches interdisciplinaires.) This carries the most up to date information.

Oates, David. 1982. Tell al Rimah. In: J. Curtis ed., *50 years of Mesopotamian discovery*, pp. 86–98. British School of Archaeology in Iraq. London.

—— 1992. Innovations in mudbrick decorative and structural techniques in ancient Mesopotamia. *World Archaeology* 21.3: 388–404.

Postgate, C., D. Oates and J. Oates. 1997. *The excavations at Tell Rimah: the pottery*. Iraq Archaeological Reports 4. British School of Archaeology in Iraq. London.

Postgate, J.N. 1992. *Early Mesopotamia*. London.

Rappaport, A. 1990. Systems of activities, systems of settings. In: S. Kent ed., *Domestic architecture and the use of space*. New Directions in Archaeology. Cambridge, pp. 9–20.

Sauvage, Martin. 1992. L'utilisation de la voûte dans l'habitat à Mohammed Diyab. J.M. Durand ed., *Recherches en Haute Mesopotamie: Tell Mohammed Diyab campagnes 1990 et 1991*. Paris, pp. 23–30.

Stone, E. 1981. Texts, architecture and ethnographic analogy; patterns of residence in Old Babylonian Ur. *Iraq XLIII* part1: 19–34.

—— 1987. *Nippur neighbourhoods*. Studies in Ancient Oriental Civilization 44. Oriental Institute. Chicago.

—— 2004. *The anatomy of a Mesopotamian city: survey and soundings at Mashkan-Shapir*. Winona Lake.

Stone, E. and P. Zimansky. 1995. The tapestry of power in a Mesopotamian city. *Scientific American* April: 92–97.

Van De Mieroop, M. 1997. *The ancient Mesopotamian city*. Oxford.

Weadock, P. 1973. The *Giparu* at Ur. *Iraq XXXVII* part 2: 101–128.

Weiss, H., P. Akkermans, Gil J. Stein, D. Parayre and Robert Whiting. 1990. 1985 excavations at Tell Leilan, Syria. *American Journal of Archaeology* 94: 529–569.

Woolley, Sir Leonard. 1939. *The ziggurat and its surroundings*. Ur Excavations vol. V. London and Philadelphia.

—— 1965. *The Kassite period & the period of the Assyrian kings*. Ur Excavations vol. VIII. London and Philadelphia.

—— and Sir Max Mallowan. 1976. *The Old Babylonian period*. Ur Excavations vol. VII. London and Philadelphia.

CHAPTER SEVEN

BABYLONIAN SEALS[1]

Dominique Collon

THE OLD BABYLONIAN PERIOD

The kingdoms set up by the Semitic Amorite rulers of Mesopotamia after the fall of the Third Dynasty of Ur inherited cuneiform writing on clay and the administrative practices of their Sumerian predecessors, adapted for their own language and requirements. They also adopted the cylinder seal for ratifying documents.

Until then, writing, and therefore sealing, had been restricted to those involved in a highly centralised administration. With the multiplication of small kingdoms, there was an explosion in literacy and a concomitant use of seals. There are far more cylinder seals preserved for the 400 years of the Old Babylonian period (here understood to include the dynasties of Isin and Larsa), than for any other period in the history of the cylinder seal, and there is also far more evidence for the rules governing the administrative use of the seals than at any other period.

Cylinder seals were a particularly Mesopotamian sealing device used from about 3400 BC for some 3,000 years for marking ownership, protecting property and later, particularly in the Old Babylonian period, for sealing letters and contracts written on clay. Under Mesopotamian influence their use and iconography were adapted in neighbouring countries. They are, as the name implies, cylinders, perforated vertically so that they could be worn on a pin or cord. They were generally made of stone, carved in *intaglio* with a design, and sometimes an inscription, in reverse, that would appear as a repeating relief in positive when the seal was rolled out on clay (see Figures 7.1 and 7.2).[2] Over the millennia, the designs changed, and provide insights into various aspects of contemporary life. Cylinder seals could also be used as amulets and items of jewellery.

The Amorites inherited the extremely formalised glyptic of the Third Dynasty of Ur, when seals had generally been carved from dark chlorite, although haematite – a term used to include other visually similar iron oxides such as goethite and magnetite – was just beginning to make its appearance. Haematite, probably obtained from south-eastern Turkey, is difficult to work, but it is a fine-grained, hardwearing material that produces extremely clear images, and it is therefore still used for modern signet rings. It can be highly polished to achieve a metallic grey-black lustre and the design is clearly visible on the actual seal and not just on the impression (Figure 7.3 a–e).

Figure 7.1 Warrior king, Lama and small naked woman. Inscribed 'Imibanu,
son of Enlil-mansum, servant of the god Enlil'. Haematite. 2.45 × 1.05.
BM ANE 108846 (1914-4-7, 12) (Collon 1986, no. 271).

The 665 Old Babylonian seals in the British Museum's collections are probably
representative of the materials used in the Old Babylonian period (M. Sax in Collon
1986: 4–11, especially p. 5).[3] The 351 haematite and 84 other iron oxides accounted
for 68 per cent, while the remainder were fairly evenly distributed between quartzes
(jasper, rock crystal, agate, carnelian), calcite minerals (mostly limestone), hydroxy
magnesium silicates (mostly serpentinite and chlorite, the most widely used materials
for, respectively, Akkadian and Ur III seals), and a variety of other materials. Haematite
was adopted for seals in contemporary Assyria, Syria and Anatolia, but was rarely
used in later periods, except for elite Cypriote seals in the fourteenth century BC and
for Sasanian stamp seals of the third to early seventh centuries AD. The rarity of lapis
lazuli (ten seals) may indicate that access to the mines at Badakhshan in northern
Afghanistan was difficult or impossible (but see Figure 7.4 – a royal-name seal).

The cylinder seal was predominantly an administrative tool in the Old Babylonian
period, and it was therefore the optimum size and shape for rolling out on clay,

Figure 7.2 Lama, the warrior king and the goddess Ishtar.
Inscribed 'Ur-mesukkina, son of Za, servant of the god Shulpae'. Haematite. 2.8 × 1.5.
BM ANE 89169 (1894-5-20, 2) (Collon 1986, no. 387).

(a)   (b)   (c)   (d)

(e)   (f)

Figure 7.3   Representations of the Lama goddess photographed on actual Old Babylonian cylinder seals (Collon 1986, nos. 73, 388, 394, 237, 588, 488, respectively):

(a) Haematite. 2.35 × 1.15. BM ANE 102046 (1905-11-14, 5);
(b) Haematite. 2.7 × 1.5. BM ANE 130694 (1945-10-15, 21);
(c) Haematite. 2.7 × 1.5. BM ANE 129528 (1945-10-13, 73);
(d) Goethite. 2.7 × 1.2. BM ANE 89083 (1891-1-23, 2);
(e) Haematite, some magnetite and goethite. 2.8 × 1.2. BM ANE 89191 (1894-6-11, 57);
(f) Red and white jasper. 3.3 × 2.1. BM ANE 89076 (1870-11-1, 2).

generally a cylinder 2.5 to 3.0 centimetres high, with the diameter typically half the height. A few seals are very slightly concave sided. Seals of variegated stones, mainly quartzes, sometimes belonging to women, are usually larger, but the designs are simple and often show one or two figures facing an inscription (Figure 7.5), frequently crudely executed, but the quality of the cutting would have been less easy to see on variegated stone (Figure 7.3f; Collon 1986: 199–200, pls XL–XLIV). Several of the carnelian and agate seals are basically barrel-shaped and were probably imported as beads and subsequently carved as seals (Collon 1986, pl. IV bottom row).

Figure 7.4 Presentation scene before seated king (note the small dancing lute-player). Inscribed 'Sin-Ishmeanni, son of Sin-iddinam, servant of Sumu-Yamutbala [attested as ruler of a city in northern Babylonia from 1855-1843 BC]'. Lapis lazuli. 2.48 × 1.45. BM ANE 134757 (1966-2-18, 18) (Collon 1986, no. 56).

(a)

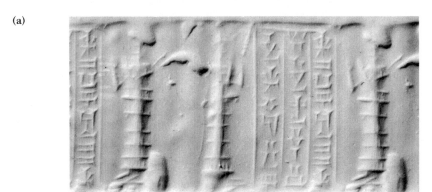

(b)

Figure 7.5 Impressions of seals, probably of the seventeenth century BC, showing the use of cutting wheel and drill: (a) Lama goddesses. Inscribed 'Abagal-dayyan, son of Taribum, servant of the god Nergal'. Quartz with minor feldspar and chlorite. 2.8 × 1.3. BM ANE 89045 (1863-4-21, 12) (Collon 1986, no. 579); (b) seventeenth-century BC version of the goddess Lama, nude hero, robed king and ascending god with standard. Haematite. 2.25 × 1.0. BM ANE 89436 (1851-10-9, 19) (Collon 1986, no. 432).

Figure 7.6 Envelope fragment from Sippar with impressions of a Babylonian presentation scene (cf. Figs 7.2 and 7.11), and a seal combining Babylonian and Syrian motifs (for the twisted legs above the chariot see Fig. 7.9). Clay. 6.7 × 4.5. BM ANE 16815A, dated to 1779 BC and recording the sale of land by a *naditu* priestess from Sippar (Collon 1987, no. 730).

The Old Babylonian period is particularly important because it was at this time that the technology for cutting hard stones was developed, using horizontally mounted cutting wheels and drills, although previously it had been claimed that this technological breakthrough could be attested as early as the late fourth millennium BC (Nissen 1977). This has been demonstrated in a series of studies, backed up by experimental work, carried out by Margaret Sax of the British Museum Department for Scientific Research (Sax *et al.* 2000). Prior to this seals had been cut with hand-held tools, and although the drill was used in cutting the designs, this was hidden beneath overcutting. However, the new technology often resulted in a simplification of designs and deterioration in technique particularly evident on Figures 7.3d–e and 7.5a–b (compare the different ways the goddess Lama is depicted in Figure 7.3). The perforations were, and continued to be, drilled from both ends to avoid overheating and possible fracture of the stone. There is some evidence for the use of decorative caps on the seals, particularly in Syria, but in Mesopotamia only towards the end of the period, especially during the reign of Ammiṣaduqa (1646–1626 BC); however, these have rarely survived, probably because they were mostly made of gold, and they are attested predominantly by their impressions (Colbow 2002, nos. 150, 266, 321, 334, 383, 425).

The seals were sometimes rolled out on clay tablets, particularly towards the end of the period, but more often on the clay envelopes that enclosed the tablets. Generally only documents that had to be witnessed were sealed. The text was written on the tablet and included the list of officials and witnesses present. The tablet was then allowed to dry, presumably in the presence of the witnesses, and was wrapped in an envelope of clay on which a summary of the contents was written, and the seals were rolled out in a special order, with some pressure being exercised in order to produce a clear impression. In some cases, where a seal was uninscribed, or the person using it was not that named in the seal inscription, an annotation or *Beischrift* in cuneiform supplied the missing information (Teissier 1998: 111–12, 2.2). A study (Teissier 1998) of sealing practices of 177 documents of the reign of Hammurabi of Babylon (1792–1750 BC) from Sippar, south of Baghdad, has shown that the upper obverse left or upper edge of an envelope was reserved for persons of status should they be present (Figure 7.6). Envelopes were sealed at right angles to the text except on the upper and lower edges. Generally the inscription on a seal was given priority over the design. The complexity of sealing practice is apparent from the archives of the Assyrian merchant colonies in central Anatolia (modern Turkey); these are beyond the scope of this chapter but are contemporary and therefore of interest (Teissier 1994). Sometimes an individual who did not own a seal could arrange to have an unperforated *purkullu* seal cut in a soft material (gypsum, clay), presumably on the spot, with his name, patronymic and profession (Collon 1986, p. 218; Figure 7.7).

Another use of seals was on devices for locking storerooms. These are best attested at this period for the city of Mari, on the Middle Euphrates in eastern Syria. A door would be closed by means of a string linking it to a knob in the adjacent door-jamb; the string would be wrapped around the knob and coated with clay over which the officials responsible rolled their seals. Only by breaking the sealing or cutting the string would the store be accessible, thus providing a deterrent to theft (Collon 1987, no. 494).

Figure 7.7 Impression of *purkullu* seal. Inscribed 'Adda, son of Dudu'. Ceramic. 3.0 × 0.95.
BM ANE 122549 (1929-10-17, 361) excavated at Ur (Collon 1986, no. 649).

Figure 7.8 Nude hero fighting bull-man; nude hero fighting lion; naked woman; Ishtar; filling motifs. Haematite. 2.45 × 1.4. BM ANE 86267 (1899-4-18, 9) (Collon 1986, no. 122; Collon 1993 for possible Sippar provenance).

Finally, a large number of bullae or dockets are known: lumps of clay carefully shaped around the knots in the strings securing containers and packages, or issued to hired workers who wore them as entitlement to rations (Weitemeyer *et al.* 1962: 137–45). These bullae, in a variety of shapes, were sealed and sometimes annotated in cuneiform. Groups of bullae often provide indications of long-distance trade. For instance the bullae found at Acemhöyük, in central Turkey, and dating to the early eighteenth century BC, bore the impressions not only of local seals, but also of seals naming Aplahanda, king of Carchemish on the border with Syria, Samsi-Addu, king of Upper Mesopotamia, the sister of Iahdun-Lim, king of Mari on the middle Euphrates, and even of an Egyptian scarab of a type attested at Megiddo and Jericho in Palestine (Özgüç 1980).

On the miniature reliefs produced by the impressions of cylinder seals, the head and legs are shown in profile and the torso, frontally. In low relief it is difficult to depict a face convincingly without the features – particularly the nose – appearing as flattened. Nevertheless, certain figures are consistently shown frontally in Mesopotamian art: the goddess Ishtar, the bull-man, the nude bearded hero (Figure 7.8) and the demon Humbaba (whose head appears on Figure 7.9). Apart from Ishtar (see below), the others are protective, generally beneficent figures, so that frontality was probably used to allow the viewer to catch their attention and communicate with them. The direction of presentation scenes on the impressions (and on sculpture) is almost always from left to right towards the most important person (king or deity). These became highly formalised during the Third Dynasty of Ur.

After the fall of Ur in 2004 BC, these designs continued (Collon 1986, pls V–VI), with a high official being led by the interceding goddess Lama before a seated goddess, as on the poorer seals of the previous period. The inscription is short, occupying a

Figure 7.9 Four winds; small storm god on lion-dragon; small priest; filling motifs. Haematite and some quartz. 2.8 × 1.6. BM ANE 134773 (1966-2-18, 34), possibly from near Borsippa, south of Baghdad (Collon 1986, no. 451).

box at the end of the scene, and typically naming the sun god Shamash and his bride Aya (Figure 7.10); it is frequently replaced by symbols, conventionally referred to as 'filling motifs', many of which are new.

During the nineteenth century BC, there was a return to the better-quality Ur III presentation scene, with a high official, often a scribe, standing before the deified king in ceremonial robes (not a specific king but a symbol of royalty), who is seated on a padded stool and holds a cup beneath a crescent moon; the interceding goddess Lama no longer leads the owner of the seal, but stands, with both hands raised, behind him. The three-line inscription is in a box at right-angles to the scene, and gives the name of the owner, his father's name, his profession and the deity or, very rarely, the

Figure 7.10 Presentation scene before seated goddess. Inscribed 'Shamash, Aya'.
Goethite. 2.3 × 1.55. BM ANE 103331 (1911-4-8, 21) (Collon 1986, no. 1).

ruler he serves (Figure 7.4) although, paradoxically, in the design the king is only occasionally replaced by a seated deity (Collon 1986, pl. VII).

During the nineteenth century, the seated king in ceremonial robes was gradually replaced by a standing king in a warrior's kilt, facing the interceding goddess Lama (Figure 7.1), with his right hand by his side, and holding a mace, head down at waist level, in his left hand. The inscription still typically consisted of three lines, and the remaining space was either left blank or was cut with filling motifs (Collon 1986, pls XV–XXIII). Often, towards the end of the nineteenth century BC, a frontal naked woman, depicted with shoulder-length hair but without the horned headdress of a deity, stands in diminutive form between the figures, or full size at the end of a scene. Her identity has been much disputed, but she may, in some cases, be Shala, the consort of the storm god Adad (Figures 7.1 and 7.8; Collon 1986: 131–2).

From the middle of the nineteenth century more complex scenes appear with further deities standing and receiving offerings and with a space for an inscription, although this was not always cut. The most popular were still three-figure scenes with the goddess Lama with both hands raised on the left, facing right and standing behind the royal figure who is either kilted as a warrior, or wearing ceremonial robes with one hand raised, or pouring a libation, or carrying an animal offering before a standing deity. The god most frequently the focus of these scenes is the sun god Shamash, who is no longer shown with rays as in Akkadian times (and on the Code of Hammurabi, see Figure 10.2); instead, he generally holds the saw-toothed knife with which he cuts his way through the mountains at dawn (Figure 7.11), but occasionally, he holds

Figure 7.11 Lama; king with offering; the sun god Shamash; lightning fork of the storm god Adad. Inscribed 'Ili-turram, son of Ipqu-Adad, servant of Adad'. Haematite. 3.0 × 1.65. BM ANE 89228 (1814-7-5, 1 – ex-Townley Collection) (Collon 1986, no. 344).

Figure 7.12 Warrior god; priest on dais with cup and bucket; warrior god; warrior god brandishing sword, whirling mace and treading on fallen enemy. Inscribed 'Hali-ilu, son of Hunnubum, servant of Abi-maras'. Haematite. 2.7 × 1.6. BM ANE 89011 (1843-11-17, 2), found at Babylon in 1829 by Sir Keith Jackson (Collon 1986, no. 420).

the rod and ring of divinity and justice. He stands in what has been termed the 'ascending posture', with his long skirt hanging open to allow freedom of movement, and with one foot on a small stylised, box-like mountain, or on a reclining human-headed bull (Collon 1986: 138–40, pls XXIV–XXVIII).

The warrior goddess Ishtar often replaces Shamash. Above the waist she is shown frontally, but her legs are in the ascending posture, with her robe hanging open and her foot resting on a diminutive lion, only the front of which is depicted (Figure 7.2; see also Figure 23.3, and cf. Figure 7.8). The seal cutter may have been attempting to represent a famous cult-statue of the frontal goddess with one foot on her lion, of which only the forepart would have been visible to the approaching worshipper. The goddess holds a scimitar in her lowered left hand and a double-lion-headed mace in her raised right hand, sometimes together with a rope leading to her lion. Occasionally a god, depicted in profile, replaces her, holding the double-lion-headed mace, a whirling mace (Figure 7.12), or some other weapon (Collon 1986: 156–8, pls XXIX–XXXI).

The storm god Adad is also the focus of three-figure scenes, but many of these seals are arranged in a non-canonical fashion, with added figures and Adad often facing right instead of left (Figures 7.9 and 7.13). He too stands in the ascending posture, sometimes on his bull, holding his forked lightning, often with another weapon which he brandishes in the so-called 'smiting posture' (Collon 1986: 165–7, pls XXXII–XXXIII). It should be noted that Shamash, Ishtar and Adad are the three deities who receive animal offerings from the king in ceremonial robes, and these are the three deities who are associated in texts with divination. It is, therefore, possible that the animals are destined for haruspicy (liver omens) and the purpose of the seals is to obtain good omens for the king, the kingdom and the owner of the seal. Priests can be added to the scene (Figure 7.12): they are often naked or kilted, with heads

Figure 7.13 The gods Amurru (with crooks) and Adad; robed king with offering; robed god. Haematite. 2.35 × 1.25. BM ANE 89521 (1841-7-26, 113) (Collon 1986, no. 446).

shaven apart from a forelock, and they can hold a pail, and a libation cup or a frond – the Babylonian equivalent of the aspergum that is still used today.

Unidentified deities also appear on seals that are based to a greater or lesser degree on this three-figure presentation scene. Some wear the horned headdress and tiered ('flounced') garments of deities but do not hold an attribute; one particularly popular figure of this type stands with his hand extended like the sun god, but the knife is missing (Collon 1986, p. 25, pls XXXIV, XXXVI–XXXVII). Several show a god who wears a distinctive robe with a ladder-pattern down the front (Figure 7.14; Collon 1986: 27–8, pl. XXXV). It is often difficult to identify the deities depicted on the seals because it seems that there was a conscious effort to enlist as many deities as possible in the protection of the owner of the seal and his business transactions. As a result, the deities invoked in the inscriptions are not generally those depicted, and nor are they necessarily those whose symbols appear scattered in the field of the design (see especially Figures 7.8 and 7.9; Collon 1986: 22–4; Braun-Holzinger 1996).

The stereotyping and repetition of these scenes make it possible to draw some conclusions regarding general trends and regional characteristics, and to isolate the work of different craftsmen. In this respect, the prolific output of the two main workshops at Sippar, south of Baghdad, is particularly revealing (al-Gailani and Al-Jadir, n.d.; Buchanan 1970; al-Gailani Werr 1980, 1981, 1988; Van Lerberghe and Voet 1991; Blocher 1992a, b; Colbow 1995a, b, 2002; Teissier 1998). They are differentiated by the way the tiered garments of deities are depicted, either with straight lines or with undulating lines, often in deeper relief and in groups (Figure 7.3a–c). The inscriptions were often written in separate lines between the figures.

Figure 7.14 Lama; warrior king; god with ladder-patterned robe; filling motifs. Haematite. 2.65 × 1.4. BM ANE 89072 (1867-11-15, 5) (Collon 1986, no. 490).

The craftsmanship is exceptional, particularly if we consider that seals produced before about 1740 BC were made with hand-held tools. Whereas the rare Old Babylonian contest scenes showed lions or lion-griffins dominating kneeling figures and animals (a complete reversal in the treatment of the subject on Akkadian seals where the hero and lion were equally matched), work typical of Sippar craftsmen shows both types (Figures 7.8 and 7.15; Collon 1993; see Collon 1986: 87–90, pls XII–XIV for the subject and especially nos. 121–2 and 132–4 which were probably made at Sippar or by Sippar craftsmen).

As Sippar was situated on the Euphrates south of Baghdad and the river provided a trade route with Syria and Turkey in the north and with southern Babylonia and the Gulf in the south, its workshops also specialised in unusual subjects for a foreign clientele, and it is probable that craftsmen from Sippar influenced the development of high-quality glyptic throughout Syria in the eighteenth century BC (Collon 1982).

Figure 7.15 Lion-griffins attacking goat; lion attacking one of two nude heroes fighting lion. Haematite (chipped). 2.45 × 1.45. BM ANE 26175 (1898-2-16, 1229) (Collon 1986, no. 137; Collon 1993 with evidence for probable Sippar provenance).

An extraordinary seal of Sippar type (Figure 7.9), and impressions from Sippar itself, Babylonia and Syria, depict personifications of winds, winged, with wind-blown hair, one of which has twisted legs probably representing a whirlwind (Collon 1986, no. 451 for references). The horizontal twisted legs of a similar figure are visible above the chariot which a king is driving like the proverbial whirlwind on the Sippar envelope in Figure 7.6; however, the troops the king leads into battle are depicted in typical Syrian manner.

KASSITE AND POST-KASSITE SEALS

The fall of the First Dynasty of Babylon to the Hittites is dated 1595 BC according to the Middle Chronology. There has been much debate as to whether this chronology, which is generally accepted for convenience, should be replaced by a higher or a lower chronology. From the point of view of glyptic development, a low chronology would be preferable as a gap of almost two centuries between the last seals of the Old Babylonian period and the first dated seals of the succeeding Kassite Dynasty is too large, considering that the main technical, compositional and stylistic characteristics were already in place (see note 1; Collon 1987: 50–2; Matthews 1990: 27–54; Colbow 2002).

The Kassites ruled Babylonia for about 500 years, but fewer than 400 known seals can be attributed to this period (Matthews 1990, p. 55). The considerable continuity with earlier periods, manifest in other fields of activity, is reflected in Kassite glyptic (Figure 7.16). The three main glyptic styles have long been recognised (see Collon 1987: 58–61), but were reassessed by Donald Matthews (1990) who demonstrated that inscribed seals naming rulers extend only from the reign of Karaindash in the late fifteenth century BC to that of Nazi-Maruttash (1307–1282 BC) (Matthews 1990, nos. 1 and 33).

Figure 7.16 Two figures (cf. Figure 7.1); filling motifs. Inscribed with a prayer to three deities. Eyed agate. 3.1 × 1.4. BM ANE 89182 (1843-11-17, 5) (Matthews 1990, no. 88).

Figure 7.17 Seated god; filling motifs. Inscribed with a prayer by Sha-ilimma-damqa, son Lugal-mansi, to the sun god Shamash. Chalcedony. 4.4 × 1.9. BM ANE 89128 (before 1900) (Collon 1987, no. 238; Matthews 1990, no. 34).

First Kassite seals (Figure 7.17) are characterised by seated deities or elongated figures of a deity and worshipper, and a long votive prayer. Matthews (1992) divided the First Kassite seals into a Central group (based on dated documents from Nippur) and a Northern group (impressed on the tablets from Nuzi, near Kirkuk); these groups use different figure combinations and filling motifs. Matthews also isolated a Pseudo-Kassite group derivative from Northern, with Elamite connections: many actual seals have been excavated at Susa and Choga-Zanbil in south-western Iran (Figure 7.18). His subsequent work on sealed documents from Nippur led Matthews to speculate as to whether the Northern group was actually a later phase of the Central group and whether Pseudo-Kassite was what happened to First Kassite when the seals were carved in a material, such as faience, which was softer than the customary quartzes (Matthews 1992).

Two interesting variations of the First Kassite style deserve mention although they are not really Babylonian. They are rock crystal seals (an exceptional material for this period) and were recovered from a ship that sank around 1300 BC off Uluburun on the south coast of Turkey (Collon 1987, no. 571). A further extraordinary seal was recovered from a grave at Metsamor in Georgia (Figure 7.19).

Second Kassite seals (Figure 7.20) are less stereotyped and correspondingly more attractive. The scene is arranged around a central figure (mountain god, nude hero

Figure 7.18 Worshipper with fan before seated figure with cup; filling motifs. Inscribed 'It is the god who (gives) life; it is the king who saves'. Faience. 5.02 × 1.7. (Collon 1987, no. 291).

Figure 7.19 Scene based on Egyptian depictions of Levantines; the vessels are Mycenaean stirrup jars. Inscribed in crude Egyptian hieroglyphs 'Great Prince of Sangar, Kurigalzu', presumably Kurigalzu II (1332–1308 BC); Sangar was an Egyptian name for Babylonia. Carnelian. Dimensions not given. Excavated at Metsamor in Georgia. Drawing (not to scale) by D. Collon after the photograph in Brentjes 1991.

Figure 7.20 Water god, with flowing vases, between mountains and flowers. Inscribed 'Kidin-Marduk, son of Sha-ilimma-damqa [see Figure 7.17], *sha-reshi* official of Burnaburiash [1359-1333 BC], king of the world'. Lapis lazuli. 4.2 × 1.5. Excavated at Thebes in Greece (Porada 1981, No. 26; Collon 1987, No. 240 and see No. 239 for another seal of Kidin-Marduk, and No. 241 for the seal of his son; Matthews 1990, No. 130).

or winged demon) framed by a terminal tree or inscription (although sometimes the inscriptions are written horizontally). Second Kassite developed from 'a Classic fourteenth century beginning [around 1350 BC], through a vibrant chaos of invention at the beginning of the thirteenth century, to a formal heraldic phase [ending around 1200 BC]' (Matthews 1992: 9). A hoard of lapis lazuli cylinder seals, including several very fine Kassite examples (see Figure 7.20) was excavated at Thebes in Greece (Porada 1981).

Third Kassite seals (Figure 7.21) are not attested in the Nippur archives, which end around 1200 BC; they are probably later, and are also often named after the Second Dynasty of Isin (1157–1026 BC) which replaced the Kassite dynasty. The main design consists of confronted animals flanking a tree within a border of hatched triangles mimicking the elaborate gold settings that decorated First and Second Kassite seals, as shown on the impressions from Nippur. The fact that the seals are made of soft stones and easily cut, artificial materials indicates that this is, indeed, a decadent phase. What happened to Babylonian glyptic in the following couple of centuries is not clear because of the dearth of archives and inscribed seals.

NEO-BABYLONIAN SEALS

The seals discussed here cover the first half of the first millennium BC, from about 1000 to 500 BC. Unfortunately, there is even less evidence for the use, and therefore the dating, of seals than in Kassite times. Furthermore, seals were very rarely inscribed,

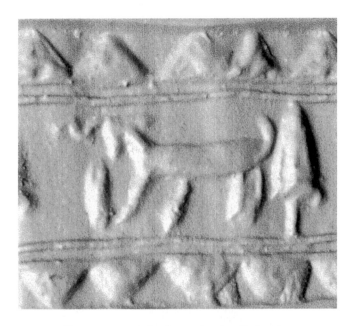

Figure 7.21   Animal; tree; border of triangles.
Vitrified faience. 4.1 × 1.5. BM ANE 89518 (1859-10-14, 191).

and only a few have inscriptions of any length or historical import (Figures 7.22 and 7.23; and see Figures 7.27 and 7.28; see also Watanabe 1995). It should be noted that inscriptions were now cut so as to be read on the actual seal – i.e. reversed on the impression – an indication that the impression of the seal was of secondary importance.

Attempts at establishing a chronology are extremely tentative (Porada 1947; Boehmer 1973; Wittmann 1992; Collon 2001: 154–5) and it is even difficult to define criteria for differentiating Babylonian from Assyrian seals, particularly from the late eighth century onwards. It seems, however, that in Babylonia more use was made of hard stones than in Assyria, and Babylonian technical expertise was correspondingly superior. The terms Neo- and Late Babylonian are often used interchangeably, although there is a tendency to adopt the latter term for the Chaldaean dynasty that ruled briefly from 625 to 539 BC. Here the term 'Neo-Babylonian' will be used for the whole period under consideration, from its arbitrary initial date of 1000 BC.

There is no way of knowing for how long the designs, isolated above as being possibly distinctive of the Second Dynasty of Isin, may have continued into the first millennium. Two groups appear to be distinctive of the early first millennium BC; both, paradoxically, are derived from Middle Assyrian styles of the thirteenth century BC. This may indicate continuity, but it is possible that Babylonian craftsmen consciously turned to the lively styles of Assyria for inspiration after the stagnation of Third Kassite (see Figure 7.21). The first group is cut with animals or monsters pursuing each other around the seal (Figure 7.24), worked not only with cutting wheel and drill, but also filed, thus producing the distinctive diagonal direction of the design (cf. Collon 1987, nos. 285–6 for Middle Assyrian prototypes). They are small hard-stone cylinders from sites in southern Babylonia such as Ur and Uruk,

Figure 7.22   Robed figure holding staff. Inscribed '(Seal) of Marduk-shakin-shumi, son of Marduk-zera-uballit, descendant of Yakin, of/governor of the town of Usur-Marduk'. Variegated black and white diorite. 3.35 × 1.4. BM ANE 129532 (1945-10-13, 76) (Collon 2001, no. 388).

(a)   (b)

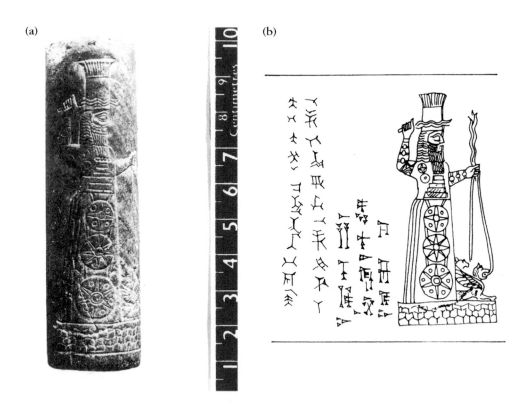

Figure 7.23   Votive seal carved in relief (NB). The storm god Adad on a dais. Inscribed (middle short line), probably in the ninth century BC, 'The seal of the god Adad'; straddling short lines added: 'Property of the god Marduk' and 'of the Esagila' (i.e. the temple of Marduk in Babylon). Long lines added: 'To the god Marduk, great lord, his lord, Esarhaddon, king of the universe, king of Assyria [680–669 BC], has given (this seal) for his life'. Lapis lazuli. 12.5 × 3.2. Berlin, Vorderasiatische Museum, VA Bab 647. Excavated in Babylon (Collon 1987, no. 563).

Figure 7.24   Bird-griffin and winged gazelle. Streaked carnelian.
1.9+ (bottom end broken) × 0.75. BM ANE 130620 (1928-10-10, 902).
Excavated at Ur (Collon 2001, no. 59).

and a probable date range from the ninth to eighth centuries BC (Collon 2001: 49–50, nos. 54–65).

Seals of the second group, the Neo-Babylonian contest scene (Figure 7.25; cf. Matthews 1990, nos. 364–5), were cut on larger hard-stone seals. They depict a distinctive hero who holds a sickle-sword in one lowered hand (generally the one nearest the viewer) and, with the other, grasps the raised foreleg of a rearing beast; sometimes he places his foot on the back of a small animal between them. Generally the beast is a lion, but the winged griffin, winged human-headed lion (i.e. a sphinx), bull and winged bull are also depicted. That this contest scene is Babylonian can be demonstrated by the concentration of provenanced examples in such sites as Babylon, Ur and Uruk. Because of Middle Assyrian parallels, it has been suggested that the Babylonian contest originated in the second millennium, but there is neither the evidence nor a sufficient number of surviving examples to support such a long floruit (see Collon 2001: 154–64, nos. 294–305). Indeed, a date in the tenth to ninth centuries seems more probable. Sometimes the Babylonian hero approaches an ostrich and holds up an object that may be an ostrich egg, possibly a way of hunting the bird; this form of contest seems to have been most popular in the eighth century and is also attested on later stamp seals (Figure 7.26; Collon 1998). There is a particularly elaborate example of the Babylonian contest which is inscribed with the name of Marduk-apla-iddina (the Merodach-Baladan of the Bible) who reigned twice, between 721 and 710 BC and in 703 BC (Figure 7.27). This Babylonian contest survived, or was revived, in Achaemenid Persian times (e.g. Garrison and Root 2001, pl. 244b, d, g, i, j). Another spectacular seal is a mythical scene showing a god riding on a bovine monster and aiming an arrow at a leonine monster (Figure 7.28). The motif was known in Assyria (where the god was Ninurta), but the dynamic movement and the very fine cutting are characteristic of Babylonian art (where Marduk assumed Ninurta's role), and although the inscription mentions a forebear of Merodach-Baladan, the seal probably also dates to the latter's reign.

Two particularly fine symmetrical variants of the Babylonian contest seem to have developed during the eighth century BC, with two heroes, now generally with four wings of equal length (Figure 7.29), or one four-winged hero between two beasts,

Figure 7.25 Hero fighting lion. Inscribed '(Seal) of Haza-ilani'. Pale brown chalcedony. 3.8 × 1.5. BM ANE 89023 (1851-1-1, 212). Excavated or obtained by W. K. Loftus at Uruk (Collon 2001, no. 296).

Figure 7.26 Hero and ostrich. Chalcedony. 1.65 × 1.0. BM ANE 141639 (1996-10-2, 8) (Collon 2001, no. 323).

Figure 7.27 Hero fighting lion. Inscribed 'For his Lord, Marduk-apla-iddina'. Chalcedony. 3.6 × 1.6. Baghdad, Iraq Museum IM 67920. Photograph courtesy of L. al-Gailani Werr (Collon 1987, no. 369; Collon 2003: 10*–12*, Fig. 1).

Figure 7.28 A god (Ninurta or Marduk?) and mythical beasts. Erratic seven-line dedicatory inscription to Nabu fitted around the design, with a later two-line dedication naming 'Eriba-Marduk, the king' added in larger, untidy script, perhaps by Merodach-Baladan (his son or grandson), in whose time the seal must have been cut. Chalcedony. 3.5 × 1.71. Mossène Foroughi collection (Porada 1993: 578–81, Fig. 46; Collon 2003: 12*–13*, Fig. 2).

generally rampant but occasionally inverted (Figures 7.30 and 7.31). It was this design – the three-figure contest – that was reintroduced into Assyria, after a long absence (cf. Collon 1987, no. 288 for a Middle Assyrian prototype), and I have suggested that Babylonian craftsmen, who had been carried into exile by Tiglath-pileser III in 729 BC and by Sargon II in 710 BC, were responsible for this (Collon 2001: 165–7; Collon 2003). With their greater expertise in the cutting of hard stones, these craftsmen revolutionised Assyrian seal cutting, with the fusion of the two traditions producing some of the finest glyptic in the 3,000-year history of the cylinder seal (e.g. Collon 2001, pls XXXVIII and XXXIX top). Babylonian versions can be identified because of the very fine tools used (Figure 7.32) and the fact that the four wings are of equal length, whereas in Assyria the lower wings are longer. The same features appear on scenes showing winged figures flanking a distinctive type of stylised rosette tree (Figure 7.33). These seals may belong to the seventh century BC, but examples are difficult to date as there is a dearth of surviving archives.

By the end of the seventh century, however, there seems to have been a decline, both in seal-cutting techniques and in creative imagination, that extends throughout the sixth century, long after the fall of Babylon to the Achaemenid king, Cyrus the Great, in 539 BC and at least until year 22 of Darius I (500 BC) (Zettler 1979; Graziani 1989). The types used are illustrated by impressions on tablets from a number of Babylonian administrative archives, several of which have been published. The principal ones are those of the Egibi family of bankers active in Babylon between around 585 BC for about a century (Wunsch 1993, 1997–98, 2000a, b), those of the Ebabbar Temple in Sippar (MacGinnis 1995), and those of the Eanna Temple in

Figure 7.29 Winged heroes with bird and sphinx; filling motif. Grey chalcedony. 3.6 × 1.6. BM ANE 100674 (1905-10-14, 2) (Collon 2001, no. 327).

Figure 7.30 Winged hero between ibex-horned, winged sphinxes; filling motifs. Green-blue and black jasper. 3.75 × 1.4. BM ANE 103319 (1911-4-8, 9) (Collon 2001, No. 332).

Figure 7.31 Winged hero fighting inverted lions; filling motifs. Blue-green jasper. 3.75 × 1.45. BM ANE 129559 (1945-10-13, 103) (Collon 2001, no. 328).

Figure 7.32 Winged hero between bird-griffins.
Inscribed '(May the) god Nabu preserve life, grant health'. Carnelian. 2.4 × 1.55.
BM ANE 89019 (1846-5-23, 324) (Collon 2001, no. 347).

Figure 7.33 Tree flanked by winged heroes with cone and bucket.
Blue chalcedony. 2.55 × 1.35. BM ANE 89307 (1870-5-11, 2) (Collon 2001, no. 179).

Figure 7.34 Priest with cup and bucket before offering table and altars with symbols. Blue chalcedony. 3.85 × 2.0. BM ANE 89311 (1856-4-24, 7) (Collon 2001, no. 391).

Figure 7.35 Pyramidal seal. Priest before altar with symbols. Chalcedony. 3.3 × 2.4 × 1.4. BM ANE 102575 (1908-4-11, 83).

Uruk (Ehrenberg 1999). However, sealed documents are in a minority, accounting for only two per cent at Uruk. The main subject on the cylinder seals was the figure of a priest before a series of altars bearing divine symbols (Figure 7.34). Stamp seals were also popular, particularly tall, so-called pyramidal or ellipsoid seals generally showing a priest with a single altar; impressed examples at Uruk are generally of good quality, but surviving examples are often highly schematised (Figure 7.35; cf. Ehrenberg 1999, nos. 45 and 49). Babylonian three-figure contest scenes either continued to be produced or were reused, and some appear alongside the Achaemenid three-figure contests in the Fortification archive in Persepolis (Garrison and Root 2001, e.g. pl. 176 and note that the wings are of equal length in the Babylonian manner). Actual examples of all these seals are generally made of chalcedony.

BABYLONIAN SEALS FROM 500 TO 200 BC

After the death of Darius I in 486 BC, the Achaemenid administration seems to have abandoned cuneiform writing on clay tablets for the recording of its transactions, and switched to documents written on parchment or papyrus, secured with sealed clay bullae. The latter survive but the documents they sealed have long vanished, and with them the evidence of content and date. However, the famous Murashu family of bankers, who were active in the city of Nippur, south of Baghdad, in the reigns of Artaxerxes I and Darius II (464–405 BC), still used clay tablets for their transactions. Although some of their seals were Babylonian, of the types known in the sixth century, their documents were primarily sealed with Achaemenid stamp seals, and some Greek seal ring impressions appear (Legrain 1925: 45–8, nos. 801–1001; Bregstein 1993, 1996; Donbaz and Stolper 1997). Few metal seal rings have survived as they have

Figure 7.36 Enlarged ancient impressions, made by two Babylonian seals (cf. Figures 7.27 and 7.34), from a grave excavated at Ur (Collon 1996, Fig. 1e and g; BM ANE 1932-10-8, 318 and 196).

mostly corroded in the saline environment of Babylonia or been melted down for reuse. An interesting series of impressions on almost 200 very small lumps of clay were found in a coffin at Ur, in southern Iraq, possibly that of a jeweller (Figure 7.36). They illustrate motifs from Assyrian, Babylonian, Achaemenid and Greek seals and from Greek coins, and range in date from the eighth to the fourth century BC (Legrain 1951, Nos. 701–841; Porada 1960; Collon 1996).

The site of Uruk is the main source of published sealed documents for southern Babylonia in the Hellenistic period (from 330 BC), both cuneiform tablets and bullae (Wallenfels 1994, 1996; Lindström 2003). Seal-ring impressions are in the majority, many with zodiacal signs, but there are impressions of some fine circular official portrait seals based on coin-types. However, at the Seleucid capital of Seleucia-on-the-Tigris, where a public archive building was excavated, the texts had been written on perishable materials and all that remains are some 25,000 sealed bullae (Invernizzi 1996), mostly with impressed with Greek seals, but some still bearing Babylonian motifs (Invernizzi 1994).

NOTES

1   In this chapter I have used the Middle Chronology, according to which Hammurabi of Babylon reigned from 1792 to 1750 BC. A Low Chronology is advocated later in the chapter, but any change in chronology has to take into account the varying dating schemes of the whole Eastern Mediterranean, the Near East and beyond. It is to be hoped that dendrochronology and ice-core dating may soon produce the absolute dates that will settle the problem of High, Middle or Low.

2   In the figure captions the dimensions of the seals are given in centimetres, height × diameter, or height × length × width. Unless otherwise stated the seals are cylinder seals in the British Museum, the photographs are reproduced courtesy of the Trustees of the British Museum and the designs are from modern impressions.

3   The materials of the British Museum's collection of Near Eastern cylinder seals and Sasanian stamp seals, covering over 4,000 years, have been subjected to analysis using the same methods and nomenclature, thus providing a unique tool for a study of the development of techniques for cutting increasingly hard materials.

BIBLIOGRAPHY

Al-Gailani Werr, L. 1980: 'Chronological table of Old Babylonian seal impressions', *Bulletin of the Institute of Archaeology* 17: 33–84.

—— 1981: 'Seals from Sippar, Part I', *Sumer* 37: 129–41.

—— 1988: *Studies in the Chronology and Regional Style of Old Babylonian Cylinder Seals* (Bibliotheca Mesopotamica 23), Malibu (Undena Publications).

—— and Al-Jadir, W. n.d.: 'Seals from Sippar, Part II', *Researches on the Antiquities of Saddam Dam Basin Salvage and other Researches* (State Organisation of Antiquities and Heritage), Baghdad, pp. 163–70.

Blocher, F. 1992a: *Siegelabrollungen auf frühaltbabylonischen Tontafeln in der Yale Babylonian Collection* (Münchener Vorderasiatische Studien 9), Munich.

—— 1992b: *Siegelabrollungen auf frühaltbabylonischen Tontafeln im British Museum* (Münchener Vorderasiatische Studien 10), Munich.

Braun-Holzinger, E. A. 1996: 'Altbabylonische Götter und ihre Symbole', *Baghdader Mitteilungen* 27: 235–359.

Bregstein, L. B. 1993: *Seal Use in Fifth Century B.C. Nippur, Iraq: A Study of Seal Selection and Sealing Practices in the Murašû Archive* (Ph.D. Dissertation, University of Pennsylvania), Ann Arbor (UMI).

—— 1996: 'Sealing practices in the fifth century B.C. Murašû archive from Nippur, Iraq', in Boussac, M.-F. and Invernizzi, A. (eds), *Archives et sceaux du monde hellénistique – Torino, Villa Gualino 13–16 gennaio 1993* (Bulletin de correspondence hellénique, Supplément 29), pp. 53–63.

Brentjes, B. 1991: 'Rollsiegel aus dem südkaukasischen Bereich', *Baghdader Mitteilungen* 22: 331–3.

Buchanan, B. 1970: 'Cylinder seal impressions in the Yale Babylonian Collection illustrating a revolution in art circa 1700 B.C.', *Yale Library Gazette* 45: 53–65.

Colbow, G. 1995a: *Die spätaltbabylonischen Glyptik Südbabyloniens* (Münchener Vorderasiatische Studien 17), Munich.

—— 1995b: 'Samsu-iluna-zeitliche Abrollungen aus nordbabylonischen Archiven ausserhalb Sippars, *Revue d'Assyriologie* 89: 149–89.

—— 2002: *Tradition und Neubeginn – Eine ausführliche Bearbeitung der spät{alt}babylonischen Abrollungen aus Sippar und ihres Beitrags zur Glyptik der Kassiten*, Munich (Profil Verlag).

Collon, D. 1982: 'The Aleppo workshop: A Syrian seal-cutting workshop of the 18th century B.C.', *Ugarit Forschungen* 13: 33–43.

—— 1986: *Catalogue of the Western Asiatic Seals in the British Museum – Cylinder Seals* III. *Isin-Larsa and Old Babylonian Periods*, London (British Museum Publications).

—— 1987: *First Impressions – Cylinder Seals in the Ancient Near East*, London (British Museum Press).

—— 1993: 'Another Old Assyrian document from Sippar', in Mellink, M., Porada, E. and Özgüç, T. (eds), *Aspects of Iconography: Anatolia and its Neighbours – Studies in Honor of Nimet Özgüç*, Ankara (TTK), pp. 117–9 and Pls 18–19.

—— 1996: 'A hoard of sealings from Ur', in Boussac, M.-F. and Invernizzi, A. (eds), *Archives et sceaux du monde hellénistique – Torino, Villa Gualino 13–16 gennaio 1993* (Bulletin de correspondence hellénique, Supplément 29), pp. 65–84.

—— 1998: 'First catch your ostrich', *Iranica Antiqua* 33 (Festschrift D. Stronach), pp. 25–42.

—— 2001: *Catalogue of the Western Asiatic Seals in the British Museum – Cylinder Seals* V. *Neo-Assyrian and Neo-Babylonian Periods*, London (British Museum Publications).

—— 2003: 'Seals of Merodach Baladan', *Eretz-Israel* (Hayim and Miriam Tadmor Volume), pp. 10*–17* (* = English section).

Donbaz, V. and Stolper, M. W. 1997: *Istanbul Murašû Texts*, Leiden (Uitgaven van het Nederlands Historisch-Archaelogisch Instituut te Istanbul LXXIX).

Ehrenberg, E. 1999: *Uruk – Late Babylonian Seal Impressions on Eanna-Tablets* (Ausgrabungen in Uruk-Uruk Endberichte 18), Mainz am Rhein (Philipp von Zabern).

Garrison, M. B. and Root, M. C. 2001: *Seals on the Persepolis Tablets* I. *Images of Heroic Encounter* (Oriental Institute Publications 117), Chicago (2 vols).

Graziani, S. 1989: 'Le impronte di sigilli delle tavolette mesopotamiche del British Museum, pubblicate da J. N. Strassmeier, datate da Ciro, Cambise, Dario e Serse', *Annali dell'Istituto Orientale di Napoli* 49: 161–200.

Invernizzi, A. 1994: 'Babylonian motifs on the sealings from Seleucia-on-the-Tigris', in Sancisi-Weerdenburg, H. and Kuhrt, A. (eds), *Achaemenid History* VIII. *Continuity and Change*, Leiden (Brill), pp. 353–64.

—— 1996: 'Gli archivi pubblici di Seleucia sul Tigri', in Boussac, M.-F. and Invernizzi, A. (eds), *Archives et sceaux du monde hellénistique – Torino, Villa Gualino 13–16 gennaio 1993* (Bulletin de correspondence hellénique, Supplément 29), pp. 131–43.

Legrain, L. 1925: *The Culture of the Babylonians from their Seals in the Collections of the Museum* (University of Pennsylvania The University Museum, Publications of the Babylonian Section XIV), Philadelphia (2 vols).

Lindström, G. 2003: *Uruk – Siegelabdrücke auf hellenistischen Tonbullen und Tontafeln* (Ausgrabungen in Uruk-Uruk Endberichte 20), Mainz am Rhein (Philipp von Zabern).

MacGinnis, J. 1995: *Letter Orders from Sippar and the Administration of the Ebabbara in the Late Babylonian Period*, Poznan.

Matthews, D. M. 1990: *Principles of Composition in Near Eastern Glyptic of the Later Second Millennium B.C.* (Orbis Biblicus et Orientalis Series Archaeologica 8), Freiburg Schweitz and Göttingen.

—— 1992: *The Kassite Glyptic of Nippur* (Orbis Biblicus et Orientalis 116), Freiburg Schweitz and Göttingen.

Nissen, H. J. 1977: 'Aspects of the development of early cylinder seals', in Gibson, McG. and Biggs, R. D. (eds), *Seals and Sealing in the Ancient Near East* (Bibliotheca Mesopotamica 6), Malibu (Undena Publications), pp. 15–23.

Özgüç, N. 1980: 'Seal impressions from Acemhöyük', in Porada, E. (ed.), *Ancient Art in Seals*, Princeton (University Press), pp. 61–100.

Porada, E. 1947: 'Suggestions for the classification of Neo-Babylonian cylinder seals', *Orientalia* 16: 145–65.

—— 1981: 'The cylinder seals found at Thebes in Boeotia', *Archiv für Orientforschung* 28: 1–78.

—— 1993: 'Why cylinder seals? Engraved cylindrical seal stones of the Ancient Near East, fourth to first millennium B.C.', *The Art Bulletin* 75/4, pp. 563–82.

Sax, M., Meeks, N. D. and Collon, D.: 'The early development of the lapidary engraving wheel in Mesopotamia', *Iraq* 62: 157–76.

Teissier, B. 1994: *Sealing and Seals on Texts from Kültepe* karum *Level 2* (Uitgaven van het Nederlands Historisch-Archaeologisch Instituut te Istanbul LXX), Leiden.

—— 1998: 'Sealing and seals: Seal impressions from the reign of Hammurabi on tablets from Sippar in the British Museum', *Iraq* 60: 109–86.

Van Lerberghe, K. and Voet, G. 1991: *Sippar-Amnanum – The Ur-Utu Archive* (Mesopotamian History and Environment III, Texts 1), Ghent.

Wallenfels, R. 1994: *Uruk – Hellenistic Seal Impressions in the Yale Babylonian Collection I. Cuneiform Tablets* (Ausgrabungen in Uruk-Uruk Endberichte 19), Mainz am Rhein (Philipp von Zabern).

—— 1996: 'Private seals and sealing practices at Hellenistic Uruk', in Boussac, M.-F. and Invernizzi, A. (eds), *Archives et sceaux du monde hellénistique – Torino, Villa Gualino 13–16 gennaio 1993* (Bulletin de correspondence hellénique, Supplément 29), pp. 113–29.

Watanabe, K. 1995: 'Beschriftete neubabylonische Siegel', in H.I.H. Prince Takahito Mikasa (ed.), *Essays on Ancient Anatolia and its Surrounding Civilizations*, Wiesbaden (Harrassowitz), pp. 225–34.

Weitemeyer, M., Porada, E. and Lampl, P. 1962: *Some Aspects of the Hiring of Workers in the Sippar Region in the Time of Hammurabi*, Copenhagen.

Wittmann, B. 1992: 'Babylonische Rollsiegel des 11.-7. Jahrhunderts v. Chr., *Baghdader Mitteilungen* 23: 169–289.

Wunsch, C. 1993: *Die Urkunden des babylonischen Geschäftsmannes Iddin-Marduk. Zum Handel mit Naturalien im 6. Jahrhundert v. Chr.* (Cuneiform Monographs 3), Groningen.

—— 1997–1998: 'Und die Richter berieten . . . – Streitfälle in Babylon aus der Zeit Neriglissars und Nabonids', *Archiv für Orientforschung* 44–45: 59–100.

—— 2000a: 'Die Richter des Nabonid', *Alter Orient und Altes Testament* 252 (Festschrift J. Oelsner), pp. 557–97.

—— 2000b: *Das Egibi-Archiv* (Cuneiform Monographs 20A-B), Groningen.

Zettler, R. L. 1979: 'On the chronological range of Neo-Babylonian and Achaemenid seals', *Journal of Near Eastern Studies* 38: 257–70.

CHAPTER EIGHT

BABYLONIAN SOURCES OF EXOTIC RAW MATERIALS

——— •◆• ———

D. T. Potts

INTRODUCTION

'Belonging to another country, foreign, alien'. This is how the *Oxford English Dictionary* defines exotic. It is interesting to note that the intrinsic worth of an object or resource plays no role in determining whether or not it is exotic. This is particularly apt in the case of ancient Babylonia since, for the most part, the goods we think of as exotic were not necessarily valuable, either in a financial sense (something of an oxymoron in discussing a pre-monetary economy) or in a functional sense (as in the case of something which was essential to a particular industry, timber being perhaps the most obvious exception). Rather, for the most part, the exotics which were imported played a symbolic role, imbuing their owner – whether a deity's cult image in a temple, a merchant, or a member of a royal household – with a set of attributes capable of conveying messages to any discerning observers. The colour of a semi-precious stone, its religious aura and associations with specific deities; the distance travelled by a material; the hardships involved in its procurement; the status of the bearer – these and other overtones were undoubtedly heard and understood by those who witnessed the conspicuous display of materials which came to Mesopotamia from, in many cases, great distances.

While materials probably flowed into Babylonia from all directions, this chapter will concentrate on those that arrived from the east and the south, either overland through what is today Iran, or by sea up the Persian Gulf. For convenience these may be classified as inorganics and organics. In the first category belong metals and stones, while in the latter are materials such as shell, ivory, timber and aromatics.

INORGANICS

Base metals: copper and tin

Copper

The Babylonian use of base metals was part of a pattern of great antiquity. Leaving aside a malachite pendant from a ninth millennium BC context at Shanidar cave in

Figure 8.1 The so-called 'Loftus Hoard', a collection of copper and some bronze tools discovered in 1854 by W.K. Loftus at the site of Tell Sifr, ancient Kutalla. The hoard was carefully hidden away, indicative of the value that was attributed to metal tools, and was found alongside the archive of a local businessman, who seems to have buried his valuables in the tenth year of Samsuiluna (1740 BC), shortly before the occupation of his home town came to an end (courtesy of the Trustees of the British Museum).

north-eastern Iraq, which may or may not have been worked, the earliest copper objects in Mesopotamia are a cold-hammered awl from Tell Maghzaliyeh, of seventh millennium BC date, and two roughly contemporary beads from Tell Sotto, sites located in northern Iraq. From this point onward we can document a gradual increase in the number of copper beads, pins and spatulae at sites dating to the sixth millennium BC The range of small, personal objects of copper, to which we may add buttons, was augmented during the fifth and early fourth millennia BC by tools (adzes, axes, chisels) and weapons (spear- or lanceheads). By the late fourth and early to mid-third millennium BC, copper was being incorporated into architectural decoration in Mesopotamia. Ringed poles set up in the Stone Cone Temple (*Steinstifttempel*) at Uruk were covered with copper sheeting, and the famous relief showing stags and a mythical lion-headed bird found at Tell al-Ubaid was cast in copper. By the time of the Royal Cemetery at Ur (*c.*2500 BC), the variety of copper (and bronze, see below) tools, weapons and vessels in the Mesopotamian repertoire had increased markedly, while cast (lost wax or *cire perdu*) copper statues and statuettes were becoming increasingly common. Throughout the later periods copper continued to be important, even though the advent of iron metallurgy greatly diminished its role from the first millennium BC onwards.

Table 8.1 Sources of Mesopotamian copper through the millennia

Region	Location	4th	3rd	2nd	1st millennium BC
Dilmun	Bahrain/ NE Arabia	*	*	*	?
Magan	Oman	*?	*	*	?
Meluhha	Indus valley		*		
Kimash	Iran?		*		
Nairi	NE Anatolia				*
Jamanu	Ionia?				*

Where did the copper come from? Geological and archaeo-metallurgical surveys in Anatolia (especially around Ergani Maden in what is today central Turkey), on Cyprus, in the Sinai peninsula and parts of southern Jordan, on the central plateau of Iran (Anarak-Talmessi, Veshnoveh, Arisman), and in the mountains of Oman in south-eastern Arabia have identified numerous areas of copper mineralization that were exploited in antiquity. Not all of these areas were equally important, nor does their existence alone ensure that they actually supplied Mesopotamia with copper (and even when they did, this did not necessarily occur on a continuous basis). Unfortunately, there is still a surprising lack of analytical data available on Mesopotamian metallurgy which could help identify the source areas exploited by a particular site or in a given period. Moreover, the tendency of metalsmiths to recycle old metal, melting down various fragments or unwanted objects and recasting the molten mixture, means that source areas which might have distinctive compositional 'signatures' can be masked by admixture of metal from various sources.

One way of trying to better understand which source areas were actively exploited in which periods of Mesopotamian history is to combine our geological knowledge of copper mineralization across Western Asia with the evidence of cuneiform sources. From the late fourth millennium BC onwards, a variety of lexical, economic, royal and literary texts refers to regions which supplied Mesopotamian consumers with copper, or to copper named after those regions. The most important of these are listed in Table 8.1 and although we are not 100 per cent certain of the locations of all of the regions that were associated with copper, we have a very good idea of where most of them were situated.

Dilmun appears at the head of the list because it is, chronologically speaking, the first foreign land associated with metals to appear in the Mesopotamian written record. The earliest texts yet discovered – the so-called 'Archaic' texts from Uruk – include lexical documents (word lists), one of which is a list of metals (Englund 1983: 35). 'Dilmun axe' appears in four examples of this list datable to c.3000 BC, and although it is not specifically identified as a copper axe, it is highly probable, particularly given the later link between Dilmun and copper. A particularly vivid series of texts from the important site of Ur charts the activities of a copper merchant named Ea-nasir, one of the *alik Tilmun* or 'Dilmun merchants', around 1850 BC. Yet, it is important to underscore the fact that Dilmun itself was not a source area but a *purveyor* of copper. Centred on the island of Bahrain in the Persian Gulf, and encompassing the mainland opposite in what is today the Eastern Province of Saudi Arabia,[1] Dilmun was an emporium which transhipped copper from further east, principally from Magan.

In the Old Akkadian period (*c.*2350–2200 BC) Mesopotamian royal inscriptions refer to Magan as a place with metal mines, and in the Ur III period (2100–2000 BC) a merchant at Ur named Lu-enlilla was actively involved in importing copper from Magan to Ur in return for textiles (often of a very coarse quality). The supposition is strong that even though Magan is not mentioned during the early second millennium, it was, in fact, the source of the copper sold by Dilmun's merchants. Although some scholars long believed that Magan (Akkadian *Makkan*) could be identified with Makran (south-eastern Iran and the adjacent portion of south-western Pakistan), the evidence for its identification with the Oman peninsula (south-eastern Arabia) is compelling.[2] From the late fourth to the early first millennium BC, the output of finished copper weapons, tools, jewellery and ingots in Oman was prodigious and hundreds of sites with slag, testimony to millennia of copper smelting, have been located in the northern United Arab Emirates (Fujairah) and Oman (Potts 1990; Weeks 2003).

Although ships from Meluhha docked at the capital of Agade during Sargon of Agade's reign, we are not told what they transported (but see below). A few centuries later, however, copper from Meluhha is attested at Ur and in lexical sources naming different sorts of copper. The location of Meluhha is not as certain as that of Dilmun and Magan, but because of its association with carnelian (abundant in Gujarat around Khambat) and ivory (which in most cases came from the Indian elephant), and because it seems to have lain further east than Magan, most scholars have identified it with the Harappan or Indus Valley civilization. Small numbers of typical Harappan artefacts – principally seals and beads – have been found in southern Mesopotamia, attesting to the existence of contact between the two civilizations.[3]

Kimash is mentioned twice in the inscriptions of Gudea, governor of Lagash around 2100 BC, as a mountain range where copper was mined. Although the location of Kimash is uncertain, it is likely to have been in western or central Iran. While earlier suggestions favoured a location somewhere in the western Zagros mountains, this is not an area particularly rich in copper. On the other hand, the Anarak-Talmessi region on the central Iranian plateau, south of Tehran, which has been exploited for its copper, antimony, arsenic, cobalt, iron, lead and nickel since antiquity (Ladame 1945: 299), has recently been suggested as the possible location of Kimash (Lafont 1996). Metallurgists have long recognized that the copper of the Anarak-Talmessi sources in Iran, which is particularly rich in arsenic, constituted in effect a 'natural' bronze (often referred to as 'arsenical bronze') which was used for thousands of years.

Finally, the Old Akkadian king Rimush is said in one royal inscription to have dedicated 36,000 *minas* (roughly 18,000 tons) of copper to the god Enlil following a campaign against Marhashi. Although not otherwise attested as a regular source of copper, Marhashi – which new evidence suggests can be located in eastern Kerman on the Iranian plateau[4] – could well have supplied that much copper since there are extensive areas of copper mineralization in Kerman province (Ladame 1945).

When we enter the period after the mid-second millennium BC we have very little information on actual sources. Cyprus is scarcely attested as a source of copper used in Mesopotamia (Millard 1973) and while the Nairi-lands of eastern Anatolia (which included Lake Van) yielded large quantities of copper and metal objects as booty to Assyrian kings such as Ashurnasirpal II (Moorey 1994: 246), this really only indicates that the area had a flourishing local industry. It says nothing about its role as a regular supplier of copper to Mesopotamia. Similarly, the references to copper from Jamanu in two sixth-century texts from Uruk are difficult to interpret. Was Jamanu a source area, or was it perhaps transhipping copper from another region, such as Cyprus?

Tin

Bronze is an alloy of copper mixed with a variable quantity (from a few per cent to 15–20 per cent) of tin. Although archaeologists commonly speak of the Bronze Age, the reality is that, whereas copper is relatively common, tin is rare in Western Asia. While much research in the past two decades has focused on Kestel in the Taurus mountains of southeastern Turkey (Weeks 2003: 167–169), and this was a probable tin source for Anatolia, it seems unlikely that Mesopotamia's tin came from this area. Rather, it is far more likely that the tin used in Mesopotamia, Iran and the Gulf region (and indeed further west at sites like Troy) came from the southern Afghan sources identified in the 1970s by Soviet geologists. This is undoubtedly the 'Meluhha tin' mentioned in an Ur III text from Ur, and the tin used at Tell Abraq in the Persian Gulf. Moreover, it is likely to be the tin traded by Assyrian merchant houses at Kanesh (Kültepe) in Anatolia, along with Babylonian textiles, in return for Anatolian silver and gold. We know from the Mari archive that Elam, Iran's major political power prior to the foundation of the Persian empire in the sixth century BC, was an important purveyor of tin to the Mari and its vassal states in Syria (Potts 1999: 166ff.) and Elam's political relations with Assyria during the early second millennium BC almost certainly account for the ready supply of tin available to Assyrian merchants. While this probably moved from the southern Afghan sources via overland routes, the same source area may well have fed tin into a maritime network of trade, which Meluhhan merchants, at the mouth of the Indus River or in Gujarat, trans-shipped up the Persian Gulf to Magan, Dilmun and Ur.

In some respects the expectation that ancient metalsmiths would have used tin to improve casting fluidity and for a hardening effect, while technically correct, is probably historically unrealistic. Much ancient metalwork was made from recycled metal, well exemplified by a hoard of metal tools and vessels discovered by W.K. Loftus in the nineteenth century at the Old Babylonian site of Tell Sifr (ancient Kutalla) in southern Iraq. Analyses have shown that an axehead from Tell Sifr contained 2.6 per cent tin while a mattock and an adze contained 7 per cent and 4.5 per cent, respectively (Moorey *et al.* 1988: 44). It is highly unlikely that the Tell Sifr metalsmiths could control tin content, or even bothered to try, probably because they were always working with scrap metal, which they recycled. It is doubtful whether they ever really knew the tin content of the old tools and vessel fragments that they regularly recycled.

Precious metals

Gold

Because of their richness, the gold offerings recovered in the Royal Cemetery at Ur, of mid-third millennium BC date, have received considerable attention, but what of gold use in Babylonia after 2000 BC? Old Babylonian sources attest to the circulation of considerable quantities of gold. At Sippar, the craftsman most frequently mentioned in cuneiform sources was the *kutimmum*, a goldsmith or jeweller, perhaps because the 'the merchants of Sippar would hoard their wealth and riches in the form of golden jewellery' (Renger 1984: 89). Old Babylonian dowry documents often mention gold jewellery, whether armlets, earrings, nose-rings or finger-rings (Dalley 1980). Some Kassite period private accounts also reveal the ownership of considerable quantities of gold (e.g. Kessler 1982: 65). This is perhaps not surprising since gold, along with silver, functioned as an established exchange commodity in Babylonia at this time. Gold, however, was four times as costly as silver (Müller 1982: 271). An interesting sixth-century BC text from Uruk discusses the cleaning and repair of gold jewellery worn by the statues of the Lady of Uruk and Nanâ. The high regard of the Uruk goldsmiths is shown by the fact that jewellery from cult statues in the Esagila at Babylon was sent to Uruk for treatment there (Sack 1979). The lavish abundance of gold in the Esagila is also illustrated a few centuries later in Herodotus' description (*Hist.* 1.183) of a golden statue of Marduk (Zeus) and a golden altar in his temple at Babylon (Dandamaev 1993: 41). On the other hand, gold beads appear in graves of virtually all periods (Limper 1988), showing that gold was accessible to a relatively broad segment of society and was by no means limited to those associated with the temple or palace estates.

Where should one look for the gold sources of the ancient Babylonians? The answer is far from clear. Considerably more is known about the gold used in early Egypt (Forbes 1939: 241ff.; Mallory-Greenough *et al.* 2000) and Europe (Muhly 1983), but the spurious use of white platiniridium inclusions in objects from Ur, Tell Brak, Alalakh, Crete and elsewhere as evidence of a source in the Pactolus valley of Anatolia has been discredited (Muhly 1983). Evidence for gold extraction from auriferous lead has been cited at Kestel and Göltepe in Anatolia by several different authorities (for references, see Weeks 2003: 168) and Assyrian merchants exported both gold and silver from Anatolia in return for textiles and tin during the early second millennium BC. By the Achaemenid period, gold could have come from an even wider array of sources. In boasting about the construction of his palace at Susa, Darius I stated that the gold used there came both from the Lydian capital of Sardis, in Asia Minor, and from Bactria (modern southern Uzbekistan and northern Afghanistan) (Kent 1953: 144, s.v. DSf).

Silver

The fact that the Assyrians were able to acquire silver from their Anatolian trading partners obviously suggests that Anatolia may also have been a source of Mesopotamian silver. In fact, Mesopotamia's silver sources, although conspicuous by their absence in the cuneiform sources, almost certainly did lie in Anatolia (Moorey 1994: 234), although Magan is another possibility since silver has been mined in the recent, pre-modern past in Oman (Potts 1990: 116, n. 106). Argentiferous lead is common in Iran and may have been smelted in antiquity to acquire silver. Certainly Elam, the most powerful state in western Iran, on at least one occasion sent silver to Mari in Syria (Potts 1999: Table 6.2). But silver could also come from much further afield. In the Achaemenid period, the Persians imported silver from Egypt (Kent 1953: 144).

In Babylonia, silver acted as an equivalence or standard in determining value and as such must have been relatively abundant. During the Kassite period, silver seems to have functioned as a standard in private transactions, often dealing with smaller amounts of commodities, in contrast to gold which seems to have been the precious metal used as an official standard (Müller 1982: 270). Everything from fish and wine to copper, wool, barley, dates and oil had a 'price' in silver shekels (Renger 1984: Table 1). At Eshnunna (Tell Asmar) in the Diyala river valley, east of modern Baghdad, it was the jeweller's (*kutimmum*) job to weigh out the silver purchase price in land and house sales (Bjorkman 1993: 4, n. 12). In addition to silver jewellery and vessels (e.g. in some of the royal graves at Ur), a number of hoards of scrap silver have been excavated (Tell Asmar, Tell Agrab, Khafajah, Tell Brak, Tell Chura, Tell Taya – all Early Dynastic in date; Larsa – Old Babylonian; Nippur, Assur – Neo-Assyrian). Rather than representing, as sometimes assumed, ancient silversmiths' hoards, these probably represent the 'cash' of a person or family in a pre-monetary economy when value, in silver, was determined simply by weight without the need for minted coinage (Moorey 1994: 238; Bjorkman 1993).

Stones

Semi-precious (lapis, carnelian, haematite, agate, onyx)

Semi-precious stones were powerful status symbols in Babylonia, particularly when used in jewellery, inlays and in the manufacture of elite cylinder seals (Gorelick and Gwinnett 1990). For the most part, the exotic semi-precious stones most favoured in Babylonia came from the East.

In spite of the fact that lapis lazuli is found in many parts of the world (von Rosen 1988), Badakshan in northern Afghanistan remains the only source known to have been accessed by the peoples of the Ancient Near East (von Rosen 1990; Casanova 1999; Michel 2001). Much has been written about the ways and means by which lapis travelled from its source area to the consumers of the West and this undoubtedly varied from period to period. It is unlikely that, in any period, trading expeditions set out from Mesopotamia to make the trek all the way to Badakshan, but whether by peddlers, caravans or trading families, it is undoubtedly the case that lapis did reach the elite of Mesopotamia, as witnessed by the many rich grave offerings made of lapis which appear in the Royal Cemetery at Ur. The fact that many of the objects made of lapis are purely Mesopotamian in style, however, strongly suggests that the raw material arrived unworked (though no doubt trimmed) in Mesopotamian workshops, where it was then fashioned into typically Mesopotamian beads, amulets (e.g. in the shape of frogs and flies), figurines, eyes for anthropomorphic statues of deities and vessels.

Lapis was also an important stone for cylinder seals. Interestingly, 35 of the Royal graves at Ur which contained gold objects also contained lapis seals (Rathje 1977: 27). On the other hand, lapis seals were also present in some of the poorer graves (Gorelick and Gwinnett 1990: 53), and lapis beads are attested in graves of many periods at Uruk (Limper 1988). That individuals of comparatively lower status could acquire such a rare commodity is interesting for a number of reasons, suggesting both that there was more in circulation than one might think (perhaps some of it in the hands of craftsmen who produced for a less elite clientele) and that emulation of high status individuals by those of lower status may have been a potent mechanism for the appearance of lapis across a broad social spectrum.

Carnelian (Mohs 6.5), on the other hand, seems to have arrived after manufacture in the workshops of India. Gujarat remains the most important source of carnelian in the world (Tosi 1980: 448), and most of the long, barrel-shaped and smaller, etched beads that appeared in Mesopotamia during the late third millennium BC are without doubt actual products of Harappan (Indus Valley civilization) craftsmen (Reade 1979). The warm, almost blood-red colour of carnelian beads has made them popular for millennia, and some of the rich burials in the Royal Cemetery at Ur, for example, contained hundreds of them. Less well known, however, is the fact that carnelian beads were extremely common in the Neo-Babylonian period as well (Limper 1988), a time for which we otherwise lack sources on Indus–Babylonian trade.

The ability to work hard stones developed in Babylonia through time. It is clear, for example, that softer stones, such as calcite (Mohs 3) and marble, were used more frequently for cylinder seals in the late fourth and early third millennia BC, and that these were probably engraved using stone drill bits (Gorelick and Gwinnett 1989: 46). By the Old Babylonian period, haematite (Mohs 6.5) accounted for over three-quarters of all cylinder seals, and these can only have been fashioned using metal (bronze) drill bits aided by the introduction of emery as an abrasive (Gorelick and Gwinnett 1990: 53).

White-striped agate was frequently used to fashion so-called 'eye stones'. These circular discs of stone, cut so that the white stripe runs around the perimeter of the other, often brown, stone, were commonly used as votive offerings, clearly demonstrated by the inscribed dedications to deities. The elite nature of such eye stones is demonstrated by the fact that a number of them were dedicated by Old Babylonian (Warad-Sin, Abi-eshuh), Kassite (Kurigalzu, Kadashman-Enlil), Assyrian (Sargon II) and Babylonian (Nebuchadnezzar II) kings to a variety of deities (e.g. Nanna, Ningal, Ninurta, Ninlil, Adad, Nusku, Marduk, Nergal, Sarpanitum, Nabu and Enlil; see Lambert 1969). Similarly, onyx beads were also known in Babylonia. An inscription on one such bead shows that it was received as a gift from the son of the rebellious Chaldaean chieftain Merodach-Baladan by the palace of Sennacherib (Frahm 1999: 90). It is unclear where the Chaldaeans acquired their onyx but the fact that other, comparable beads of agate, chalcedony and onyx were acquired by the Assyrians from Arabian chieftains suggests that the Arabian peninsula may have provided the sources for these semi-precious stones.

As the evidence of cylinder seals and beads made of rare stones (not necessarily semi-precious, but geologically rare) attests, many other stones from outside of Babylonia were put to use in antiquity, but although a modern mineralogical identification may be possible, the majority of the ancient names for different types of stones mentioned in cuneiform sources remain unidentified (cf. al-Rawi and Black 1983). A first-millennium BC text known as 'The stone whose nature is . . .' gives us some tantalizing descriptions of stones 'whose nature is like the coat of a date-palm', 'whose nature is like an owl's coat', 'whose nature is like a clear sky', or 'whose nature is like a mouse's ear' (Postgate 1997: 217), along with their Akkadian names, but we are far from being able to attach a petrological designation to these poetically described minerals.

Non-precious (calcite/alabaster, chlorite)

Of the non-precious stones, calcite and its finer, veined variant commonly called alabaster, and chlorite or steatite, one of a number of softstones ('soapstone'), were by far the most important. Both were used for vessels and, on analogy with what we know from the later Greco-Roman era, both were probably employed to hold fatty unguents, aromatics, perfumes and similar substances.

Limestone is not particularly rare in the Near East but there were relatively few centres of vessel production. Leaving Egypt aside, the most important area was probably eastern Iran and the Indo-Iranian borderlands (Casanova 1991). Excavations at Shahr-i Sokhta in Iranian Seistan have revealed evidence of calcite vessel manufacture and the shapes produced there occur in the Royal Cemetery at Ur, in the Barbar temple on Bahrain, at Tell Abraq in the United Arab Emirates and at sites elsewhere in Iran (e.g. Shahdad) and Afghanistan (e.g. Mundigak).

Chlorite, on the other hand, came principally from two regions, south-eastern Iran and south-eastern Arabia. Excavations at Tepe Yahya in Kerman province, Iran, between 1967 and 1975 revealed clear evidence of chlorite vessel production (Kohl 2001). Raw lumps of chlorite, semi-worked pieces showing clear chisel marks, thousands of small flakes or off-cuts (*débitage*) and finished objects, all attest to a thriving industry in the late third millennium BC. In addition, archaeologists from Harvard University were able to locate several chlorite outcrops where the stone had, in fact, been quarried. The second area where chlorite vessels were produced in large quantities is south-eastern Arabia (Potts 1993). Besides being rich in copper, the mountains of Oman contained an abundance of chlorite (and other varieties of softstone). From *c.*2300 BC until the Hellenistic period a prodigious, local industry turned out thousands of vessels in a wide variety of shapes, many of them decorated with a dotted double-circle, sometimes combined with bands of horizontal lines in diagonal patterns (David 1996).

The most well-known chlorite vessels in Babylonia appear in temples around the middle of the third millennium BC. These are normally quite large, with deeply carved animals (humped bulls (*Bos indicus*), felines, snakes, scorpions) or patterns (mat-weave, imbricate, guilloche). While all of the known decorations found on Mesopotamian sites can be found in the repertoire at Tepe Yahya, a large quantity of similar material has long been known from the small island of Tarut on the Persian Gulf coast of Saudi Arabia (Zarins 1978). Recently, dozens of similar vessels have been found by clandestine excavations near Jiroft in south-eastern Iran (Majidzadeh 2003). It seems highly probable that the Mesopotamian and Arabian examples (a few more pieces have turned up on sites in the United Arab Emirates) all emanated from south-eastern Iran and that this was the area known in cuneiform sources as Marhashi. As noted above (n. 4), one fragment, inscribed by the Akkadian king Rimush as 'booty of Marhashi' (or in Sumerian, Barakhshum), is identical to the material known from Tepe Yahya and Jiroft. This is a strong indication that Marhashi should be located in what is today eastern Kerman.

Later in the third and early second millennia, the simpler bowls with dotted-circle decoration produced in the Oman peninsula appear in Mesopotamia in small numbers, e.g. at Ur (Reade and Searight 2001).

The function of such vessels is, unfortunately, unclear. If the vessels were used to hold fatty substances (aromatics, perfumes, resins mixed with oil or a soluble liquid), as was certainly the case with softstone and alabaster vessels in the Greco-Roman era (their properties for doing so were extolled by ancient authors such as Pliny and Strabo), then the chances are good that the stone itself would have absorbed the contents. This being the case, analysis by gas chromatography ought to be able to produce a spectrum that could give some indication, at least broadly speaking, of the nature of those contents. To date, such work has not been carried out on the Iranian or Omani softstone found on sites in Mesopotamia. It is likely, however, that the vessels themselves arrived in Mesopotamia as containers for something that was a desired commodity. In other words, the contents were probably of greater interest to ancient Mesopotamian consumers than the containers themselves, even though the latter have been the focus of modern archaeologists' attentions.

ORGANICS

Wood

Archaeologists working outside of hyper-arid regions such as Egypt or the coastal desert of Peru traditionally have much more difficulty identifying organic than inorganic materials. To some extent this problem is alleviated in Mesopotamia because of the rich corpus of texts. Nevertheless, even in the generally humid conditions of Iraq, wood has been known to survive across the millennia, as discoveries in the Royal Cemetery and some of the private graves at Uruk attest.

Mesopotamia was not nearly as devoid of wood as most people think. The Tigris and Euphrates supported not only marshy areas with important stands of reeds (principally *Phragmites australis*) but also 'gallery forests' with willow, poplar, tamarisk, boxwood and other species. Nevertheless, foreign woods were imported into Mesopotamia as well. Around 2500 BC, Urnanshe, king of Lagash, boasted that 'ships of Dilmun' brought 'timber from foreign lands' to him. We have no real idea what type of timber may have been involved, but it is likely to have been a higher grade wood than that which was available locally. One is reminded of the flourishing trade in mangrove poles (Prins 1966: 6–11) which, prior to the oil boom in the Persian Gulf, brought mangrove logs from the Lamu coast of east Africa to Sur in Oman and Kuwait at the head of the Gulf for the building industry.

While nothing suggests that east Africa was a source of wood for Mesopotamia in the third millennium BC, the coasts of India may well have been. As with the copper and tin trade, however, the fact that the cuneiform texts record Dilmun as the source of the timber imported by Urnanshe does not oblige us to think of native timber that may have grown on Bahrain (in which case, date palm (*Phoenix dactylifera*) would be the most likely candidate). Rather, Dilmun was probably transhipping timber from further east, just as it did with copper.

Among the rarer, foreign woods that appear in Babylonian sources are sissoo wood (*Dalbergia sissoo*, commonly called Pakistani rosewood), which grew in the Indo-Iranian borderlands, and which appears, for example, in Old Babylonian dowry documents (Dalley 1980: 66), and ebony, a wood attested in contemporary inheritance documents (Groneberg 1997: 54). Texts from Mari reveal just how expensive ebony was. In one instance 14 minas (roughly 14 × 500 g) of ebony were valued at 20 shekels of silver (Kupper 1982: 116).

Ivory

Although very few ivory objects have been excavated on archaeological sites in Mesopotamia, their presence – probably always as rarities and luxuries – is confirmed by a small but important number of cuneiform texts which refer to figurines, combs, rings and other unidentified items as well as raw (i.e. uncarved) ivory. Theoretically the ivory used in Mesopotamia could have been from the tusks of either African or Indian elephants but the marked absence of evidence for close ties between Mesopotamia and Egypt (or the Horn of Africa), prior to the Kassite period,[5] combined with the far more compelling evidence of contact with the Harappan civilization during the late third and early second millennia BC, suggests that the ivory known to the Mesopotamians of the earlier periods was Indian in origin.

Ivory figurines were already being imported to Lagash during the late Early Dynastic period (*c.*2400 BC) and in the reign of Gudea, governor of Lagash around 2100 BC, raw ivory made its first appearance. Slightly later texts from the time of the Third Dynasty of Ur (2100–2000 BC) refer to the import of about 10.58 kg of unworked ivory, and to an ivory object (unfortunately unidentifiable because of damage on the tablet to the name of the item) weighing about 19 kg, which may, in fact, have been a complete tusk (Heimpel 1987: 55). Mesopotamian woodworkers (carpenters, cabinet makers, makers of musical instruments) used ivory for inlaid decoration in a variety of settings, and carvers of figurines and statuettes fashioned objects such as goats and 'Meluhha birds' (During Caspers 1990). Ivory objects also appear in the dowry of a Marduk priestess at Babylon during the Old Babylonian period (Dalley 1980: 66), but it is unlikely that ivory was widely available in Babylonia outside of elite circles. Very few ivory objects from this period have been recovered in excavation, though a small number of pieces were recovered at Babylon in a sixth-century context (Moorey 1994: 121, 125). Certainly Babylonia never seems to have had access to nearly as much ivory as the Assyrians were able to acquire as tribute or the Persians were able to extract from their African and Asian satrapies.

Shell, mother-of-pearl and tortoise shell

A variety of shells coming from the Persian Gulf, the Arabian Sea and the western Indian Ocean were used in Mesopotamia for the manufacture of jewellery, cylinder seals and inlays (like ivory, on furniture and musical instruments, including the famous lyres found in the Royal Cemetery of Ur). Shell lamps made of *Lambis truncata sebae*, a large gastropod common along the coasts of Oman, have been excavated at Tello and Ur, while large cylinder seals made of *Turbinella pyrum*, a gastropod found on the coasts of India and Pakistan, were found in the Royal Cemetery at Ur (Gensheimer 1984). Many more molluscan species common in the Indo-Pacific region (*Engina mendicaria*, *Oliva bulbosa*, *Strombus decorus persicus*, *Conus ebraeus*, *Dentalium* sp., *Pinctada margaritifera*, *Chicoreus ramosus*) have been found on sites in Mesopotamia and are likely to reflect trade either with the peoples of the Persian Gulf littoral (Dilmun, Magan and the Iranian side of the coast) or the Indus Valley (Meluhha).

In addition, tortoise shell also appears in the cuneiform record (Leemans 1960: 25). On analogy with sites in eastern Arabia, this is likely to have derived from the carapace of the green sea-turtle (*Chelonia mydas*) although the Mesopotamian sources are very unspecific (Farber 1974; Frazier 2003).

Hardened resins

Two hard resins, originating in opposite ends of the Old World, have been found in Mesopotamia. Beads of Baltic amber (Todd 1985; Heltzer 1999) are known in small numbers from Neo-Babylonian and Achaemenid or Seleucid graves at Babylon (Reuther 1926: 211, 223, 264). While a series of transactions (rather than direct trade) may have been responsible for the diffusion of Baltic amber to the Mediterranean or Anatolia and eventually to Babylonia, the identification of a copal pendant at Tell Asmar (ancient Eshnunna) in the Diyala region in a third-millennium context is much harder to explain. This piece, once incorrectly identified as amber, is made of a hardened resin that originated in East Africa, probably in Mozambique, Zanzibar or Madagascar (Meyer *et al.* 1991: 289).

Aromatics

Although 'incense' – most often but not exclusively frankincense (*Boswellia sacra*) or myrrh (*Commiphora myrrha*) – is normally associated with the ancient South Arabian kingdoms (Saba, Qataban, Ma'in, Himyar) of the first millennia BC and AD in what is today Yemen, whence it was traded overland and by sea to many corners of the ancient world, the ancient Mesopotamians also had a wide range of terms for aromatic substances. Some of these have been identified with frankincense (Sumerian ŠIM.GIG = Akkadian *kanaktum*; Sumerian ŠIM.HI.A = Akkadian *labanatu*), and traders specifically associated with the substance are attested in third-millennium texts (Zarins 1997: 261). Another term, linked with Dilmun (ŠIM.DILMUN) which occurs at Fara in texts dating to *c.*2500 BC, is unidentified but should perhaps be linked with the word for bdellium (Sumerian ŠIM.BI.ZI.DA = Akkadian *guḫlu*), 5.28 tons of which were seized by one of Assurbanipal's generals in the seventh century BC. According to the account of this confiscation, the *guḫlu*, which belonged to a rebel chieftain in southern Babylonia named Nabu-bel-sumate, came from Dilmun (Potts *et al.* 1996). Although *guḫlu* has, in the past, been identified with substances as diverse as antimony, *kohl* (eye make-up) and bdellium – the aromatic gum exuded by *Commiphora mukul* – this latter identification seems confirmed by a comparison of Assyrian *guḫlu* and Sanskrit *guggulu* which, in all probability, was borrowed from Akkadian in the first millennium BC. *Commiphora mukul* has a wide distribution, extending from Dhofar in the southern part of the Arabian peninsula to India. As with so many other commodities discussed above – whether tin, ivory or carnelian – it is entirely possible that aromatic resins were also imported into Mesopotamia during the third millennium BC from the Harappan world. At that early date, it is also possible that South Arabian frankincense and myrrh may have reached the temples of Babylonia and Assyria by land to Oman and by sea up the Persian Gulf, but direct transport overland from Yemen via camel caravan is unlikely to have occurred before the first millennium BC. Texts from Sur Jar'a (ancient Anat) on the Middle Euphrates in Iraq, the capital of Suhu, attest to caravan traffic between that region, Tayma (in north-western Arabia), and Saba, the most powerful state of the period in what is today Yemen (Cavigneaux and Ismail 1990: 351) and the most important source of frankincense and myrrh in antiquity. The increasing use of aromatics in Babylonia at this time is well illustrated by the number of square, four-legged incense burners found at Uruk and Babylon, the majority of which date to the Neo-Babylonian period (Ziegler 1942: 230–231).

CONCLUSION

This chapter should not be considered a complete guide to all of the exotic goods that entered Mesopotamia from foreign parts. Many more, about which we know even less, could be added to the list of those discussed above. The presence of such materials in Mesopotamia – all of which were imported – demonstrates that while the essentials of existence were all readily available in the Tigris–Euphrates basin, a wide range of exotics, needed to articulate the cultural messages of Mesopotamian social dialogue, were imported from far and wide. Furthermore, it is important to remember that Babylonia was far from monocultural, and this undoubtedly had a bearing on the sources and types of exotics imported. In the Old Babylonian period, for example, Kassites, Elamites, Suteans, Suheans, Gutians and Subarians – peoples from the north-east, the north, and the west – are all attested at Sippar (De Graef 1999). By the first millennium, the level of diversity in Babylonian cities had increased markedly. Scythians (Dandamaev 1979), Persians, Medes, Choresmians, Indians and other Iranian peoples (Zadok 1977), as well as Syrians, Urartians, Kassites, Egyptians (Zadok 1979), Jewish colonists (Dandamaev 1982: 41) and others, made Babylonia a thoroughly multi-cultural society. Translators, already attested in the third millennium BC (Gelb 1968), must have been increasingly common. The diversity of exotic materials attested at sites such as Uruk and Babylon in the first millennium suggests that Babylonia was like a great harbour in a vast sea of resources, extending from Africa to Inner Asia, and from the borders of Europe to South Asia. It was a harbour in which a multitude of peoples, goods and ideas mixed on a daily basis; where gold from Africa, lapis from Afghanistan, amber from the Baltic, and carnelian from India, changed hands on a regular basis. Babylonia was, by this time, truly a land open to more cross-cultural possibilities than it had ever known in its long and complicated history.

NOTES

1   The identification of Bahrain with Dilmun dates to the nineteenth century and is based on a number of lines of evidence. Greek sources dating to the time of Alexander the Great's expedition and slightly later refer to a large island in the Persian Gulf called Tylos, which was adjacent to a smaller island called Arados. Arados can be identified with the smaller of the two main islands of Bahrain, Muharraq, where the name 'Arad' survives to this day. Tylos is a Graecized form of Akkadian Tilmun (Sumerian Dilmun). The only qualification to this equation concerns the earliest periods in which Dilmun is mentioned, for between c.3000–2300 BC there is little evidence of substantial occupation on Bahrain, whereas the mainland of eastern Saudi Arabia (as well as the offshore island of Tarut) has abundant evidence of ceramics and stone vessels which can be paralleled in southern Mesopotamia. This suggests that Dilmun may originally have denoted the mainland (around Dhahran and al-Qatif) and that its centre may have shifted to the Bahrain islands towards the end of the third millennium BC. From that point on, as the substantial settlements at Qalat al-Bahrain and Saar, and the important temple complex at Barbar attest, Bahrain must have been Dilmun. From the mid-second millennium BC, when Dilmun fell under the control of the Kassite kings of Mesopotamia, we have Kassite cuneiform texts from Qalat al-Bahrain and from Nippur in central Iraq which confirm the identification.

2   Sumerian *Magan*, Akkadian *Makkan*, Old Persian *Maka*, and Elamite *Makkash* all refer to the
    same place. The trilingual Achaemenid royal inscriptions give Qade as the Akkadian equivalent
    for Old Persian Maka. In the Neo-Assyrian period, Assurbanipal received tribute from Pade,
    king of Qade, who is said to have lived in Iskie. Iskie is without question the town of Izki,
    in central Oman, reputed in local oral tradition to be the oldest town in Oman. Moreover,
    the accounts of the Akkadian king Manishtusu's campaign against Magan, which he reached
    by sailing across the Persian Gulf from Sherikhum in southern Iran (perhaps near the head of
    the Gulf, above Bushire), in which he is said to have advanced as far as the 'metal mines', like
    that of his son Naram-Sin, who quarried large blocks of diorite in the mountains of Magan,
    certainly remind one of the Oman mountains. Finally, while there is copper in Kerman province,
    the Makran region is not noted as a copper-rich area (Ladame 1945: 248, refers to a few small
    areas of copper mineralization in the country 'behind' Minab), whereas the ophiolite (ancient
    sea crust) of Oman is one of the world's most important copper-bearing deposits.

3   A trail of evidence of Harappan contact can be followed from Ras al-Jinz, the easternmost
    point on the Oman peninsula, where Harappan ceramics and seals have been found, to Tell
    Abraq and Shimal on the Gulf coast of the United Arab Emirates, where Indus weights and
    ceramics occur, to Bahrain, where weights and ceramics have been found, and on to Failaka
    island, off the coast of Kuwait, where a seal with characters in the Harappan script (as yet
    undeciphered), has been found.

4   A chlorite bowl fragment (Klengel and Klengel 1980; Steinkeller 1982) inscribed by Rimush
    'booty of Marhashi (Barahshum in Sumerian)' belongs to a style which is now known to have
    been produced in south-eastern Iran. Tepe Yahya was one such production centre and clandestine
    excavations at a cemetery near Jiroft have yielded hundreds of further examples. This evidence
    makes it extremely likely that the area of eastern Kerman, including the sites of Tepe Yahya,
    Shahdad (?) and those near Jiroft constituted the land known in cuneiform sources as Marhashi.

5   There is evidence from the late fourth millennium BC of contact between Mesopotamia and
    Susa in south-western Iran and pre-Dynastic Egypt, probably overland via the Euphrates and
    Syria. In the Kassite period (*c.* seventeenth to twelfth centuries BC), the royal houses of Kassite
    Babylonia and Egypt were in more regular contact, as evidenced by the well-known Amarna
    letters. In the Neo-Assyrian period, when Assyrian armies pushed westward into what is today
    Lebanon, southern Syria, Palestine, Israel and even Egypt itself, African ivory undoubtedly
    entered Mesopotamia, but this does not seem very likely during the third millennium.

BIBLIOGRAPHY

Al-Rawi, F. and Black, J.A. 1983. The jewels of Adad. *Sumer* 39: 137–143.

Bjorkman, J.K. 1993. The Larsa goldsmith's hoards – new interpretations. *Journal of Near Eastern Studies* 52: 1–23.

Casanova, M. 1991. *La vaiselle d'alabâtre de Mésopotamie, d'Iran et d'Asie centrale aux IIIe et IIe millénaires*. Paris: Mémoires de la Mission archéologique française en Asie centrale 4.

—— 1999. Le lapis-lazuli dans l'Orient ancien. In: A. Caubet ed., *Cornaline et pierres précieuses: La Méditerranée de l'Antiquité à l'Islam*. Paris: Musée du Louvre, pp. 189–210.

Cavigneaux, A. and Ismail, B.K. 1990. Die Statthalter von Suhu und Mari im 8. Jh.v.Chr. *Baghdader Mitteilungen* 21: 321–411.

Dalley, S. 1980. Old Babylonian dowries. *Iraq* 42: 53–74.

Dandamaev (Dandamayev), M.A. 1979. Data of the Babylonian documents from the 6th to the 5th centuries B.C. on the Sakas. In: J. Harmatta ed., *Prolegomena to the sources on the history of Pre-Islamic Central Asia*. Budapest: Akadémiai Kiadó, pp. 95–109.

—— 1982. The Neo-Babylonian elders. In: M.A. Dandamayev, I. Gershevitch, H. Klengel, G. Komoroczy, M.T. Larsen and J.N. Postgate eds, *Societies and languages of the Ancient Near East: Studies in honour of I.M. Diakonoff*. Warminster: Aris & Phillips, pp. 38–41.

—— 1993. Xerxes and the Esagila temple in Babylon. *Bulletin of the Asia Institute* 7: 41–45.

David, H. 1996. Styles and evolution: Soft stone vessels during the Bronze Age in the Oman peninsula. *Proceedings of the Seminar for Arabian Studies* 26: 31–46.

De Graef, K. 1999. Les étrangers dans les textes paléobabyloniens tardifs de Sippar (Abi-ešuḫ – Samsuditana), 1ière partie: Sur les inconnus 'connus': Cassites, Elamites, Sutéens, Suhéens, Gutéens et Subaréens. *Akkadica* 111: 1–48.

During Caspers, E.C.L. 1990. . . . and multi-coloured birds of Meluhha. *Proceedings of the Seminar for Arabian Studies* 20: 9–16.

Englund, R.K. 1983. Dilmun in the Archaic Uruk corpus. In: D.T. Potts ed., *Dilmun: New studies in the archaeology and early history of Bahrain*. Berlin: Berliner Beiträge zum Vorderen Orient 2, pp. 35–37.

Farber, W. 1974. Von **ba** und andere Wassertieren: *Testudines sargonicae? Journal of Cuneiform Studies* 26: 195–207.

Forbes, R.J. 1939. Gold in the ancient Near East. *Jaarbericht Ex Oriente Lux* 6: 237–254.

Frahm, E. 1999. Perlen von den Rändern der Welt. In: K. Van Lerberghe and G. Voet eds, *Languages and cultures in contact: At the crossroads of civilizations in the Syro-Mesopotamian realm.* Leuven: Orientalia Lovaniensia Analecta 96, pp. 79–99.

Frazier, J. 2003. Prehistoric and ancient historic interactions between humans and marine turtles. In: P.L. Lutz, J.A. Musick and J. Wyneken eds, *The biology of sea turtles*, vol. 2. Boca Raton: CRC Press, pp. 1–38.

Gelb, I.J. 1968. The word for dragoman in the Ancient Near East. *Glossa* 2: 93–104.

Gensheimer, T.R. 1984. The role of shell in Mesopotamia: Evidence for trade exchange with Oman and the Indus Valley. *Paléorient* 10: 65–73.

Gorelick, L. and Gwinnett, A.J. 1989. 'Collars' in the holes of Near Eastern cylinder seals. *Archeomaterials* 3: 39–46.

—— and —— 1990. The Ancient Near Eastern cylinder seal as social emblem and status symbol. *Journal of Near Eastern Studies* 49: 45–56.

Groneberg, B. 1997. Eine altbabylonische Erbteilungsurkunde aus der Sammlung Dr. Martin. *Altorientalische Forschungen* 24: 49–56.

Heimpel, W. 1987. Das untere Meer. *Zeitschrift für Assyriologie* 77: 22–91.

Heltzer, M. 1999. On the origin of the Near Eastern archaeological amber. In: K. Van Lerberghe and G. Voet eds, *Languages and cultures in contact: At the crossroads of civilizations in the Syro-Mesopotamian realm.* Leuven: Orientalia Lovaniensia Analecta 96, pp. 169–176.

Kent, R.G. 1953. *Old Persian: Grammar, texts, lexicon.* New Haven, CT: American Oriental Series 33.

Kessler, K. 1982. Kassitische Tontafeln vom Tell Imliḥiye. *Baghdader Mitteilungen* 13: 51–116.

Klengel, H. and Klengel, E. 1980. Zum Fragment eines Steatitgefäßes mit einer Inschrift des Rimuš von Akkad. *Rocznik Orientalistyczny* 41: 45–51.

Kohl, P.L. 2001. Reflections on the production of chlorite at Tepe Yahya: 25 years later. In: D.T. Potts, *Excavations at Tepe Yahya: The third millennium.* Cambridge: Bulletin of the American School of Prehistoric Research 45, pp. 209–230.

Kupper, J.-R. 1982. Les prix à Mari. In: J. Quaegebeur ed., *Studia Paulo Naster oblata II. Orientalia antiqua.* Leuven: Orientalia Lovaniensia Analecta 13, pp. 115–121.

Ladame, G. 1945. Les resources métallifères de l'Iran. *Schweizerische mineralogische und petrographische Mitteilungen* 25: 166–303.

Lafont, B. 1996. L'extraction du minerai de cuivre en Iran à la fin du IIIe millenaire. In: O. Tünca and D. Deheselle eds, *Tablettes et images aux pays de Sumer et d'Akkad.* Leuven: Peeters, pp. 87–93.

Lambert, W.G. 1969. An eye-stone of Esarhaddon's queen and other similar gems. *Revue d'Assyriologie* 63: 65–71.

Leemans, W.F. 1960. *Foreign trade in the Old Babylonian period.* Leiden: Brill.

Limper, K. 1988. *Uruk: Perlen, Ketten, Anhänger.* Mainz: Ausgrabungen in Uruk-Warka End-berichte 2.

Majidzadeh, Y. 2003. *Jiroft: The earliest Oriental civilization.* Tehran: Printing and Publishing Organization of the Ministry of Culture and Islamic Guidance.

Mallory-Greenough, L., Greenough, J.D. and Fipke, C. 2000. Iron Age gold mining: A preliminary report on camps in the Al Maraziq Region, Yemen. *Arabian Archaeology & Epigraphy* 11: 223–236.

Meyer, C., Todd, J.M. and Beck, C.W. 1991. From Zanzibar to Zagros: A copal pendant of Eshnunna. *Journal of Near Eastern Studies* 50: 289–298.

Michel, C. 2001. Le lapis-lazuli des Assyriens au début du IIe millénaire av. J.-C. In: W.H. van Soldt ed., *Veenhof Anniversary Volume: Studies presented to Klaas R. Veenhof on the occasion of his sixty-fifth birthday.* Leiden: Nederlands Instituut voor het Nabije Oosten, pp. 341–359.

Millard, A.R. 1973. Cypriot copper in Babylonia, c. 1745 BC. *Journal of Cuneiform Studies* 25: 211–213.

Moorey, P.R.S. 1994. *Ancient Mesopotamian materials and industries: The archaeological evidence.* Oxford: Clarendon Press.

——, Curtis, J.E., Hook, D.R. and Hughes, M.J. 1988. New analyses of Old Babylonian metalwork from Tell Sifr. *Iraq* 50: 39–48.

Muhly, J. 1983. Gold analysis and the sources of gold in the Aegean. *Temple University Aegean Symposium* 8: 1–14.

Müller, M. 1982. Gold, Silber und Blei als Wertmesser in Mesopotamien während der zweiten Hälfte des 2.Jahrtausends v.u.Z. In: M.A. Dandamayev, I. Gershevitch, H. Klengel, G. Komoroczy, M.T. Larsen and J.N. Postgate eds, *Societies and languages of the Ancient Near East: Studies in honour of I.M. Diakonoff.* Warminster: Aris & Phillips, pp. 270–278.

Postgate, J.N. 1997. Mesopotamian petrology. *Cambridge Journal of Archaeology* 7: 205–224.

Potts, D.T. 1990. *The Arabian Gulf in antiquity*, vol. 1. Oxford: Clarendon Press.

—— 1993. Soft-stone from Oman and eastern Iran in cuneiform sources? *Res Orientales* 5: 9–13.

—— 1999. *The archaeology of Elam: Formation and transformation of an ancient Iranian state.* Cambridge: Cambridge University Press.

——, Parpola, A., Parpola, S. and Tidmarsh, J. 1996. Guḫlu and Guggulu. *Wiener Zeitschrift für die Kunde des Morgenlandes* 86: 291–305.

Prins, A.H.J. 1966. The Persian Gulf dhows: Two variants in maritime enterprise. *Persica* 2: 1–18.

Rathje, W. 1977. New tricks for old seals: A progress report. In: McG. Gibson and R.D. Biggs eds, *Seals and sealing in the Ancient Near East.* Malibu: Bibliotheca Mesopotamica 6, pp. 25–32.

Reade, J.E. 1979. *Early etched beads and the Indus-Mesopotamia trade.* London: British Museum Occasional Paper 2.

—— and Searight, A. 2001. Arabian softstone vessels from Iraq in the British Museum. *Arabian Archaeology & Epigraphy* 12: 156–172.

Renger, J. 1984. Patterns of non-institutional trade and non-commercial exchange in Ancient Mesopotamia at the beginning of the second millennium BC. In: A. Archi ed., *Circulation of goods in non-palatial context in the Ancient Near East.* Rome: Edizioni dell'Ateneo, pp. 31–123.

Reuther, O. 1926. *Die Innenstadt von Babylon (Merkes).* Leipzig: Wissenschaftliche Veröffentlichungen der Deutschen Orient-Gesellschaft 47.

Sack, R.H. 1979. Some remarks on jewelry inventories from sixth century BC Erech. *Zeitschrift für Assyriologie* 69: 41–46.

Steinkeller, P. 1982. The question of Marḫaši: A contribution to the historical geography of Iran in the third millennium BC. *Zeitschrift für Assyriologie* 72: 237–264.

Todd, J.M. 1985. Baltic amber in the Ancient Near East: A preliminary investigation. *Journal of Baltic Studies* 16: 292–301.

Tosi, M. 1980. Karneol. *Reallexikon der Assyriologie* 5: 448–452.

Von Rosen, L. 1988. *Lapis lazuli in geological contexts and in ancient written sources.* Partille: Paul Åströms Förlag.

—— 1990. *Lapis lazuli in archaeological contexts.* Jonsered: Paul Åströms Förlag.

Weeks, L.R. 2003. *Early metallurgy of the Persian Gulf: Technology, trade, and the Bronze Age world.* Boston, MA and Leiden: Brill.

Zadok, R. 1977. Iranians and individuals bearing Iranian names in Achaemenian Babylonia. *Israel Oriental Studies* 7: 89–138.

—— 1979. On some foreign population groups in first-millennium Babylonia. *Tel Aviv* 6: 164–181.

Zarins, J. 1978. Steatite vessels in the Riyadh Museum. *Atlal* 2: 65–93.

—— 1997. Mesopotamia and frankincense: The early evidence. In: A. Avanzini ed., *Profumi d'Arabia*. Rome: L'Erma di Bretschneider, pp. 251–272.

Ziegler, L. 1942. Tonkästchen aus Uruk, Babylon und Assur. *Zeitschrift für Assyriologie* 47: 224–240.

CHAPTER NINE

CLOTH IN THE
BABYLONIAN WORLD

——·◆·——

Irene Good

Babylonia bore the signature of Sumerian culture during the reign of Ibbi-Sîn. This was just before the Amorites came into the consciousness of Mesopotamians at the very beginning of the second millennium BC. Temple architecture, agrarian life and even commerce had not radically changed from earlier times. This tenacity to the Mesopotamian *gestalt* was vividly reflected in dress. The *kaunakes* garment, for example, was worn since early Uruk times, and also the diagonal spiral-wrapped panel dress was prevalent as a royal or elite garment, since the early third millennium BC (Figure 9.1).

Later, particularly during the second millennium, more differentiation in regional style and more incorporation of those styles within the Babylonian persona were effected. This was due to political expansions and increased commerce and trade with surrounding regions, even from far off places such as northeastern Iran and the Persian Gulf, Egypt and the Mediterranean. Cloth was also a main item of export. These increases in external contacts from diverse groups influenced dress, with a substantive change in the style of wearing garments as well as an increase in the woven repertoire. This change is reflected in texts, but also in the depictions of people in art; principally glyptic and figurative sculpture (see Figure 10.5).

By the first millennium; an even more cosmopolitan Mesopotamian emerged; as taste for foreign materials arose after more than a millennium of continuous and intense interaction from the West and the East. The appetite for imported cloth, especially from the Syria-Levant region, is well attested in economic and personal texts and reflected too in modes of dress.

What does the study of cloth and clothing tell us, and why is it important? It is universal that social groups and social rank are marked by cloth, clothing and mode of dress. Through the thoughtful study of ancient textiles, fibers, weaving and spinning implements, viewed within their social and physical environmental contexts, we can witness not only ancient technology and the role of cloth production in the economic sphere, but also the relevance of cloth in the definition and production of social boundaries. The comprehensive study of ancient textiles can help us to understand some of the social processes that underlie cloth production, exchange, and use: the generation and regeneration of style, genre, aesthetic and the generation of symbolic

Figure 9.1 Seal of a presentation scene of a figure being led by a goddess to a seated male deity. The goddess wears a spiral-wrapped panel dress of tiered fringe (courtesy of the Trustees of the British Museum).

communication in material culture. Observing these processes archaeologically offers us important understanding of ancient society which might otherwise be obscured. Cloth, clothing and modes of textile production, even particular types of fiber, are regionally distinct elements of material culture. The role of textile production in ancient society can be observed through the transformation in organization of production from *domos* to specialized craft. Cultural interactions through the exchange of goods, including textiles, brought about technical innovation and social change.

STORIED HISTORY

The study of mythology can inform much about cloth and its significance within the social sphere. Stories offer a unique perspective, revealing traditional and indigenous perceptions concerning cloth, even fiber. In the tale of Gilgamesh, Enkidu was a primitive, uncivilized man who was tamed by a woman. His entry and acceptance into Uruk and civil life was symbolically initiated by washing his filthy hairy body then clothing himself in a robe and donning a sash (Gray 1982: 9–10). Here in this story we see how the body clothed takes on a new identity: transformed from the natural world to the civilized world.

Evidence for the renown of textile manufacturers, particularly the differences in textile production between pastoral and agricultural economies, can also be found in literary texts from Sumer. In the Sumerian tale of Dumuzi and Enkimdu (Wolkstein and Kramer 1983: 30–31), a few basic and important differences in textile production are explicitly stated within a literary form, showing us how aware ancient Mesopotamians were about the stark difference in different types of cloth, as representative of the different socio-economic worlds of pastoralists and agriculturists. In the tale, the Queen of Heaven, Inanna, is courted by both Dumuzi, a shepherd, and Enkimdu, a farmer. Inanna's brother, the sun-god Utu, tries to persuade her to choose Dumuzi, who can offer her milk and butter and woolen garments. Inanna, however, chooses Enkimdu because his lentils and grain are more stable sustenance; and he can provide fine linen clothes.

This story reveals a perceived difference in qualities between textiles manufactured by pastoralists and those of settled agriculturists. It also suggests that the different economic framework is the reason for these differences. Perhaps the most striking aspect of the story, however, is the reputation of the agricultural community's textile production: it is *superior* to that of pastoralists. This difference is based on the procurement of different types of fiber, which is the basis of cloth becoming a commodity of trade. On another level, the notion that Inanna's decision of a marriage partner was based on his offer of finer cloth, suggests the importance of cloth as a social codifier. In a verse describing Inanna's courtship with Dumuzi, she converses with her brother Utu. He says that the fields of flax are ripe and that he will bring flax to her. In this verse the whole process from flax harvest to weaving a bridal sheet is relayed.

The investigation of myth can also reveal rather detailed aspects of the division of labor, of power structures, trade and other aspects of the economic organization of ancient societies. This has recently been done with particular regard to long-distance exchange in the Ancient Near East with Eastern Iran and Central Asia through the study of the myth of Enmerkar and the lord of Aratta (Vanstiphout 1991: 217–240; see also Good, 2005).

Dress, investiture and adornment are associated with rank, but also take on a symbolic and cosmological role and carried mystical meaning through ritual in ancient Mesopotamia. A central theme in ancient Mesopotamian life was the clothing of deities. The practice of ritual dressing may also be understood to carry meaning on all levels in Babylonian society. Protection, evocation of fertility and other apotropaic forces were met through elements of garment structures and design (see Figure 9.2). How were these features created?

TEXTILE TECHNOLOGIES

Fibers

Cloth, both in its manufacture and in its organization of production, played a key role in the process of economic and social development of early complex society. First, let us start with fiber. Linen and wool fiber were both important resources in ancient Babylon. Their use involved both local production and consumption as well as production (and eventually commoditization) for export. Specialized fiber types were developed by the Old Babylonian period and played a significant role in economic development in this early complex society (see Van Koppen, this volume, for discussion of the early economy of Babylon). These specialized fibers, in fact, were an important aspect of the developing complexity of early Babylonian society.

Linen, from the domesticated flax plant, *Linum usitatissimum* L., is a bast fiber requiring much labor to process. Bast fibers are the fibrous cells from the stem of a

Figure 9.2 Scene from a wall painting found at the palace of Mari, showing multi-colored wrap garments (after A. Parrot, *Sumer* No. 348b).

woody/herbaceous plant. Many plants have basts, but only a few have the desirable characteristics of sheen, strength, structural uniformity and length. The plant has two domestic varieties, one best for oil, and the other best for its bast. The genetics of the early domestication of this plant are not yet well understood but we know that the bast variety was used in Mesopotamia from early times.

Wool was very developed by the time of the Babylonians, but not to the extent that it was in the subsequent millennium. Fine wool such as that of the merino sheep did not yet exist. Interestingly, we find references to sheep and goats as described by their coats – their colour as well as the quality of their wool. For example, in the texts from Drehem, we see categories of sheep; also notable is the way sheep and goats were defined by their regional affiliation. This was a significant aspect of the now burgeoning economic complex that was developing in Babylonia, exemplified by the Karum of Kanish at Kültepe, where numerous texts describe the exchange of textiles.

From third-millennium texts we can glean important information regarding wool. In the third millennium BC at Ur, there are three main wool types according to the animals which bear the fleece, namely fat-tailed (kungal-la?-ke-ne), native *uligi* (uli-gi-ra-ke-ne), and goat (Jacobsen 1948: 173; Waetzoldt 1972: 40–44). The breed of sheep denoted *uligi* was considered to be a sheep graded below fat-tailed sheep, having wool fleece graded below that of standard wool sheep but above black sheep (Steinkeller 1995: 64 n. 30). The wool itself is first distinguished by the breed of sheep from which it derived, and then by whether it was graded at Ur or at the time of plucking. Jacobsen's paper does not discuss wool grades in any detail. Suffice it to say that to some degree, wool grades were already in place during Ur III times according to thickness of fiber, as well as sheep breed, and that the breeds did in fact produce different grades of wool.

The earliest historical records in Mesopotamia relevant to the procurement of wool date to the beginning of the second millennium BC. These texts clearly describe sheep being plucked. Barber (1991: 29 n. 14) points out that both plucking and shearing were practiced, evinced by two separate words *baqamu* (plucking); and *gazazu* (shearing). A close inspection of the etymologies of these words reveals that *gazazu* (shearing) only appears about 500 years later (by the second half of the second millennium BC) in reference to obtaining wool from sheep (Åke Sjøberg, personal communication 1996). Shearing was presumably inefficient, being done with a single blade of bronze.

From Ur III times, there are a number of textual sources that relate to sheep and goat terminology (Steinkeller 1995; Waetzoldt 1972). The sources relate to categories from ancient Puzrish-Dagan, founded by king Shulgi *c.*2050 BC as a center for the distribution of both domestic and wild animals (Steinkeller 1995: 49). Interestingly, the categories differ from those of neighboring Lagash (Steinkeller 1995: 54). Designations of fleece and goat hair now consist of wool from "native" sheep, and foreign or mountain sheep, long-fleeced sheep, Shimashki sheep, black sheep and goat hair (Steinkeller 1995: 57). Colors range from white, black, reddish brown, yellow and mottled. Some texts refer to different colors of wool available in Anatolia during the second millennium BC: white, yellow, bright red, reddish, and "dark"' (Veenhof 1972: 137, 186–188).

Special note on silk

Textual evidence for silk in ancient Mesopotamia is tantalizing. There is reference to what has been translated as silk (Heb. *meeshe*) in writings that date to the beginning of the first millennium BC ("She maketh herself coverings of tapestry; her clothing silk and purple" Proverbs 31: 22 KJV) as noted by Oppenheim in his paper on overland trade (1969). Oppenheim also notes a special kind of imported thread (Middle Babylonian GADA *tumanu* and *tibu* GADA), in which the determinative "GADA" might be interpreted as possibly meaning silk. Indeed, archaeological evidence is emerging for both wild silks and the use of "sea silk" (*byssus*) in the Mediterranean in the early first millennium BC and even earlier (see Good 1995 for overview).

Equipment

Spinning was done by use of a spindle, often with the aid of a whorl for added torsion. We have evidence for both middle- and low-weight spindles for the Babylonians. Interestingly, there is increasing evidence through the study of burials for the craft of spinning as associated with women of status. This becomes the norm in later Iron Age Elam, Europe and Anatolia, though not as much attention has been paid to the evidence for this type of hierarchical display in female graves in Mesopotamia.

Spinning flax requires a slightly different technology from that of wool; as flax fibers are smooth, and do not tend to naturally adhere to each other as does sheep's wool. Flax, therefore, needs to be wet when spun, allowing the natural mucilage gum to adhere to adjacent fibers. On the other hand, the staples (length of individual fibers) is generally longer and flax does not need to be twisted as much as does wool in order to stay coherent in a thread; therefore, the "draw," or amount of pull while twisting, is not as great as for wool. This makes it technically easier to spin very fine thread.

At Abu Salabikh, to the northeast of Nippur, we have what may be the first concrete evidence for the distaff (Barber 1991: 57; Postgate and Moon 1982), dating to ED III: a copper rod with a flattened nail-like head, associated with a copper spindle. Another similar item was found in ED III levels at Choga Mish. Interestingly, the distaff, while attesting to the use of flax for spinning, also suggests that it was not part of a heavy "production" line, but rather individual or *domos* style level of production. While the distaff saves time and makes holding onto scutched and hackled flax easier to access quickly while spinning; the lack thereof might actually imply the "assembly-line" approach, with several people nearby handing out small-sized portions of flax ready to spin as needed (see Barber 1991: ch. 2).

Loom

The Babylonians used the horizontal ground loom. The types of weave were evidently not too variable, though the types of cloth were, indeed, quite variable. This variation had less to do with weave structure and more to do with decorative techniques. The horizontal ground loom is a simple instrument, yet it has the capacity to produce a wide variety of types of cloth. Pile, supplemental warp and complementary warp are each possible through this type of loom, which consists of four anchoring stakes, holding two beams, fore and aft, in tension, for the warp (the vertical threads of cloth).

We know that the upright loom was also used in parts of the Near East in the second millennium BC: it was used in Egypt as early as the Eighteenth Dynasty and was also known in Anatolia. We are not certain about its earliest date or its distribution in Mesopotamia, though it may have been used there for tapestry weaving in the second millennium BC or earlier. Glyptic art does not help answer this problem directly. Representational art of the period does not directly portray anything in the way of weaving during the Old Babylonian period. Nor do later depictions show clear evidence for a vertical (upright) type of loom east of the Mediterranean.

Sometimes concrete technical information on loom type and weave can be gleaned from careful examination of artwork; though more often than not this is only speculative and it is not possible to tell with certainty.

WOVEN DECORATIVE TECHNIQUES

Dress structures – loomed shapes, curves and fringes

We have many types of dress represented in relief sculpture from second-millennium Mesopotamia, from Kar-Tukulti-Ninurta and Dur-Kurigalzu; and later even more examples from Khorsabad and Nineveh (Figure 9.3). Wall paintings from the Kassite palace at Dur-Kurigalzu are particularly rich in depictions of dress; as are some of the historical narrative captured in scenes from Khorsabad showing distinct peoples and activities. This kind of art gives us insight not only into how people distinguished themselves from each other via dress but also how these distinctions were perceived and rendered by the artist, and, by extension, the cultural context of the artist.

In Old Babylonian times, dress was a means of distinction within and between social class and profession, and between genders. *Fashion* as we think of it did not exist; but style was important, and served many purposes. Style was more static. Indeed, some of the early Babylonian modes of dress are direct descendants of earlier Akkadian style, which, in turn, directly relate to Sumerian forms. Specifically Babylonian dress shares common features throughout the Babylonian period: aside from decorative features, we see the use of layers in male formal dress, knee-high kilt and cloak; also full length kilt with fringed edge under another layer; an overdress with tailored sleeves. The sleeves seem to be depicted as attached cylinders of cloth, but may actually be woven into the dress.

An important feature of Babylonian textiles was edgework. The techniques used in finishing fall into several categories (as judged from artwork and thus are not certain in terms of method of execution). One type of edgework design may have been done with brocade. Another, more likely, technique was tapestry. A third type was plaiting and braiding. Finally, the addition of fringed strips to plain cloth was used. One feature of importance is the use of fringe on the diagonal worn across the chest. This is a distinct dress style that emerged with the Kassites.

There are many variations that can be achieved in plain woven cloth, from densely packed to fine gauzy open weave; from warp-faced to weft-faced; from tabby to napped pile carpet. We do have tantalizing hints for the possible manufacture of pile cloth in the form of garments (see Figure 9.4) and possibly carpets in Mesopotamia. Akkadian words *kamidu* and *kasiru* ("knotter") hint at the possibility that carpet was being made in Mesopotamia in the second, possibly the third, millennium BC. Other evidence

Figure 9.3 Relief sculpture from Khorsabad showing fringed skirt
(courtesy of the Trustees of the British Museum).

Figure 9.4 Seal depicting a hero fighting wild animals. Note contrast between inside and outside of garment revealing the use of pile technique (JP Morgan Library).

Figure 9.5 Assyrian palace relief sculpture of a threshold with fringe outer border, from Khorsabad (courtesy of the Trustees of the British Museum).

can be found in the neo-Assyrian palaces of Khorsabad and Nineveh where stone relief sculpture, as examined in detail by several scholars (see Dalley 1991; Barrelet 1977), may represent carpet in a form recognizable to us today (see Albenda 1978) (Figure 9.5).

The study of the decoration of these stones also suggests a design relationship with the famous Pazyryk carpet from Siberia (Rudenko 1970) which contained concentric square registers of animals and four-pointed star design on the outer border (see also the four-pointed star motif in residence frescoes at Khorasabad). Many of the design elements found in Babylonian cloth are shared with other components of material culture, such as chariots and furniture and architectural details.

Clothing is an extension of the self. It is protection, but has also had a protective element of a supernatural nature as well, and this was especially true in ancient Babylon. From textual references, we can begin to see how these design elements carried symbolic meaning and apotropaic power. For example, the petalled rosette was applied to royal and sacred garments (in the form of sheet metal, often of gold) to ward off evil (Oppenheim 1949). This practice is seen in vestigial form today in liturgical garments. Special types of weave and special forms of thread were reserved for sacred garments and cloth.

OTHER DECORATIVE TECHNIQUES

Color – dyes and dyeing

Texts reveal several types of colorant used for the manufacture of cloth garments. Principally blue (woad), red (kermes and madder) and purple (*Purpura* or *Murex* snail).[1] This is the dominant color scheme in Mesopotamian textiles, though greens and yellows were also known. Not surprisingly, we see this dominant color scheme also reflected in some of the preserved Assyrian wall frescos at Nimrud and Til Barsip; as well as the Kassite wall paintings of Dur-Kurigalzu. We have perhaps a chance to see how techniques and craftsmanship converge with aesthetic; as blue also is a dominant color in the new art of faience; and faience beadwork was an important aspect of manufacture for royal and sacred garments as well as accoutrements for chariotry (see Dalley 2000).

When evaluating these different features in tandem, we can begin to gain a sense of how the social world was built, and how cloth and dress participated in building the structure of social forms.

THE IDEA OF THE INDIVIDUAL

Dress is evidence for social complexity. Types of dress, from sacred to royal to servile, developed in ancient Babylon as an index of social station. At some point in Babylonian history, around the time of Hammurabi, the idea of the individual emerged, and the expression of this can also be found in dress. Fringed garments were a notable feature of a person's appearance. A person's garment featured a fringe that was exclusive enough to be used as a mark of individuality. Fringe became a signature, quite literally, as it was used sometimes in place of a person's seal to mark documents and goods (Dalley 1991).

TEXTILE PRODUCTION IN MESOPOTAMIA –
MODES AND INSTITUTIONS

Much of what we know of Babylonian textile production is gained from economic texts, though we also have been able to glean some information from archaeological excavation. The type of information ranges from architectural indices to small artifact distribution (principally spindle whorls, as they are often the object that remains well preserved). Historical references to the production of textiles are plentiful in documents from Ebla (Pettinato 1991) and the Old Assyrian trading colonies in Anatolia (Veenhof 1972, 1977). Of particular interest are some economic texts from the Ur III period which describe the textile industry under Ibbi-Sîn. These texts attest to the primary importance of the textile industry in the royal economy as well as document the economic mechanisms in place during the early third millennium BC for textile production (Jacobsen 1948: 172). They also describe in great detail the different stages of textile manufacture, from wool and linen processing to cloth fulling and bleaching, and finally weaving. Technical descriptions of various stages of textile production are sometimes detailed in texts that give specifications for different types of cloth. For example, there are texts that describe coarse cloth, fulled on the one side (Veenhof 1972: 92–93, 104). Other texts describe cloth made of two colors, but not dyed (Old Assyrian *barmum*) (Veenhof 1972: 186–187).

TEXTILES IN EXCHANGE

From textual evidence, it is well known that textiles were a widely traded item in western Asia during the third and second millennia BC (Leemans 1960; Veenhof 1972). Textiles were a component of what Crawford (1975) termed "invisible exports," as their importance in trade is known solely from texts. Textile products were one of the main items of export from southern Mesopotamia. Although there is virtually no direct archaeological evidence remaining of textile production in Mesopotamia, the export of textiles is well documented, especially by certain economic texts from Larsa, Lagash, Ebla and Babylonia. For example, the Garment Texts from Lagash account garment distribution among dignitaries during the reign of Gudea in the second Lagash Dynasty *c.*2200 BC. Fabrics were exported from Ur to Magan during the Third Dynasty, and were also exported to Dilmun (Leemans 1960).

Texts relating to the Old Assyrian trading colonies are comprised of archives of economic texts regarding the sale of textiles and wool, as well as letters, often personal letters between husbands and wives, which discuss transactions in textiles between the Karum and Assur. These texts reveal that there are different types of cloth denoted by region, for example *abarnium* cloth, which denotes cloth from somewhere called "Abarna." Sometimes, these cloths were actually manufactured in Assur (Veenhof 1972), apparently after their type was sufficiently well known to become signate. The practice of naming types of articles by the region from which they came also held true for species or breeds of animals, for example the Shimashki sheep or the Magan goat (Steinkeller 1995: 50, 59).

Textiles were apparently traded in bolts (by weight) as standard sizes, not as finished garments in the Old Assyrian trading colonies. The differentiation between various qualities and values of cloth is well documented here as well. Interestingly, there is a category for cloth to be used as wrapping for the transport of other goods (Veenhof 1972).

CONCLUSION

Future archaeological investigations will continue to add new textile evidence for Babylonian textile technique, through careful and refined recovery of textile fragments, and careful study of ceramic and plaster impressions and other types of direct archaeological textile evidence. Indeed, the excavations at Ur in the 1920s and 1930s produced an abundance of perishable remains. Though the region that was Mesopotamia has reputedly very poor preservation conditions for this type of material, with care and a bit of good fortune, indeed, there does come important evidence of this kind to light, as evidenced at Ur, and in the north at Abu Salabikh (Figure 9.6).[2] In Iran textiles have been recovered from sites in the Solduz Valley and in Kirman, and further east in the desert sands of Seistan. When we don't think they will be there, we don't see them when they are there.

Cloth and textiles are central to society and, therefore, their archaeological remnants should be sought and recognized for their informational value. Although the recovery of clothing in archaeological contexts is rare, it does occur. When well preserved and from good context, archaeological textiles hold a rich store of information on a wide array of topics.

Figure 9.6   Close-up of textile pseudomorph from Abu Salabikh
(photo: courtesy of J.N. Postgate)

NOTES

1　The latter evidenced at Ugarit by characteristically crushed shell; seen also at the port Minet al Beida *c*.1500–1300 BC.
2　N. Postgate, personal communication. Textile pseudomorphs as well as extant cloth have been recovered from Grave 16 (ASE 2, Graves 1–99 pp. 58–59, no. 7). Grave 112 (see *Iraq* 40, 78 with pl. XIIIa). Grave 182 (see *Iraq* 49, 96–97).

BIBLIOGRAPHY

Albenda, Pauline, 1978. "Assyrian Carpets in Stone," *The Journal of the Ancient Near East Society* (New York, Columbia University), vol. 10 (1984), pp. 1–34.

Barber, E.J.W., 1991. *Prehistoric Textiles: The Development of Cloth in the Neolithic and Bronze Ages, with Special Reference to the Aegean.* Princeton University Press, Princeton, NJ.

Barrelet, Marie Therese, 1977. "Un inventaire de Kar Tukulti Ninurta: Textiles Décorés Assyriens et Autres," *Revue d'Assyriologie et d'Archéologie orientale*, vol. 71/1: pp. 51–92.

Bier, Carol, 1995. "Textile Arts in Ancient Western Asia," in J. Sasson and K. Rubinson (eds) *Civilizations of the Ancient Near East*, Charles Scribner's Sons, New York, pp.1567–1588.

Crawford, H.E.W. 1975. "Mesopotamia's invisible exports in the third millennium BC," *World Archaeology* 5(2).

Crowfoot, Grace, 1931, *Methods of Handspinning in Egypt and the Sudan.* Bankfield Museum Notes series 2, # 12. Halifax, Nova Scotia.

Dalley, Stephanie, 1977. "Old Babylonian Trade in Textiles at Tell al Rimah," *Iraq* 39, pp. 155–159.

—— 1991. "Ancient Assyrian Textiles and the Origins of Carpet Design," *Iran*, vol. XXIX, London (1991), pp. 117–135.

—— 2000. "Hebrew *Tahas*, Akkadian *dushu*, Faience and beadwork," *Journal of Semitic Studies*, vol. XIV (1): 1–20.

Ellis, Richard, 1976. "Mesopotamian Crafts in Modern and Ancient Times: Ancient Near Eastern Weaving," *American Journal of Archaeology*, vol. 80, pp. 76–77.

Emery, Irene, 1966. *The Primary Structures of Fabrics: An Illustrated Classification.* The Textile Museum, Washington, DC.

Fiske, Patricia L. (editor), 1974. *Archaeological Textiles*, The Irene Emory Roundtable on Museum Textiles. The Textile Museum, Washington, DC.

Geijer, Agnes, 1979. *A History of Textile Art.* Sotheby Parke Bernet, New York.

Good, Irene, 1995. "On the Question of Silk in Pre-Han Eurasia," *Antiquity* 69: 945–958.

—— 2005. "Invisible Exports in Aratta: Enmerkar and the Three Tasks. Textiles in Ancient Society." In Marie-Louise Nosch and Carol Gillis eds, *Ancient Textiles: Production, Craft and Society*, 2006. Obow Books, Oxford.

Granger-Taylor, Hero, 1983. "The Textile Fragments from PG16," *Anatolian Studies* 33: 94–95.

Gray, John. 1982. *Near Eastern Mythology.* Peter Bedrick Books, New York.

Jacobsen, Thorkild, 1948. "On the Textile Industry at Ur Under Ibbi-Sîn," in *Studia Orientalia Ioanni Pedersen*, Einar Munksgård, Copenhagen, pp. 172–187.

Kawami, Trudy, 1992. "Archaeological Evidence for Textiles in Pre-Islamic Iran," *Iranian Studies* 23(3–4): 1–12.

Khlopin, I.N. 1982. "The Manufacture of Pile Carpets in Bronze Age Central Asia," *Hali*, 5(2): 116–119.

Kirby, Richard Henry. 1963. *Vegetable Fibers: Botany, Cultivation and Utilization.* Leonard Hill Books, London.

Milgrom, J. 1983. "Of Hems and Tassels," *British Archaeological Reports* 9 pp. 61–65.

Moorey, P.R.S. 1977. "Bronze Rollers and Frames from Babylonia and Eastern Iran: Problems of Date and Function," *Revue Assyriologique*, 71, pp. 137–150.

Oppenheim, A.L. 1949. "The Golden Garments of the Gods," *Journal of Near Eastern Studies* 8: 172–193.

—— 1969. Essay on Overland Trade. *Special volume honoring Albrecht Goetze*. Ed. E.A. Sachs. *Journal of Cuneiform Studies*. American Schools of Oriental Research, Cambridge, MA.

Pettinato, Giovanni. 1991. *Ebla: a New Look at History*. Johns Hopkins University Press, Baltimore.

Postgate, Nicholas. 1985. *Abu Salabikh Excavations* vol. 2. Graves 1–99. British School of Archaeology in Iraq.

—— and Moon, J. 1982. *Excavations at Abu Salabikh, 1981. Iraq* 44: 103–136.

Reade, Julian. 1991. *Mesopotamia*. British Museum Press, London.

Rudenko, Sergei. 1970. *Frozen Tombs of Siberia*. University of California Press, Berkeley.

Sollberger, Edmond. 1986. *Administrative Texts Chiefly Concerning Textiles. Archivi Reali di Ebla*, Testi VIII. Missione archeologica italiana in Siri, Roma.

Steinkeller, Piotr. 1995. "Sheep and Goat Terminology in Ur III Sources from Drehem," *Bulletin of Sumerian Agriculture* 8: 49–56.

Stone, Elizabeth. 1978. "Neighborhoods in Old Babylonian Nippur," *Iraq* 40.

Stronach, David. 1993. "Patterns of Prestige in the Pazyryk Carpet: Notes on the Representational Role of Textiles in the First Millennium BC," *Oriental Carpet and Textile Studies*, vol. IV, edited by Murray L. Eiland, Jr, Robert Pinner and Walter B. Denny, San Francisco Bay Area Rug Society and OCTS Ltd, Berkeley, pp. 19–34.

Van De Mieroop, Marc. 1987. "Crafts in the Early Isin Period," *Orientalia Lovaniensia Analecta* 24, pp. 35–36.

Veenhof, Klaas. 1972. *Aspects of Old Assyrian Trade and its Terminology*. Brill, Leiden.

—— 1977. "Some Social Effects of Old Assyrian Trade," *Iraq* 39: 109–118.

Vogelsang, M.E. 1986. "Meaning and Symbolism of Clothing in Ancient Near Eastern Texts," in H. Vanstiphout ed., *Scripta signa vocis*, pp. 265–284.

Waetzoldt, Hartmut. 1972. *Untersuchungen zur neusumerischen Textilindustrie*. Studi Economici e tecnologici, n. 1. Istituto Italiano per il Medio ed Estremo Oriente, Rome.

Wolkstein, S. and Kramer, S.N. 1983. *Inanna Queen of Heaven and Earth – Her Stories and Hymns from Sumer*. Harper & Row, New York.

Woolley, C.L. 1934. *Ur Excavations vol. I The Royal Cemetery*. Ch. XI pp. 238–248.

Wulff, Hans E. 1966. *The Traditional Crafts of Persia*. MIT Press, Cambridge, MA.

CHAPTER TEN

THE BABYLONIAN
VISUAL IMAGE

———·◆·———

Zainab Bahrani

THE BABYLONIAN IMAGE

When Ashurbanipal had a stele made for the sacred precinct of Esagila in Babylon he chose an archaising formula, derived from what was by then, already, antiquity. On the obverse of the flat slab of sandstone the king stands, centrally and frontally positioned. His wrapped and fringed garments and his *polos* shaped headdress are clearly those of an Assyrian king, as is his hairstyle and his rectangular blunt-cut beard composed of neatly arranged rows of curls. The king stands with his arms upraised, his large hands keep a reed basket in place, balanced on his head. The depicted act is an ancient one; it is the act of the king as builder. The king carries on his head the basket of earth for the ritual moulding of the first brick, an act that he performs himself as a central part of the building ritual. The first brick initiates a series of bricks for the sacred construction, each of which are moulded in a matrix of ivory, or of special wood, such as maple, boxwood or mulberry, which had writing fixed against the sides. Oil, honey and wine were poured upon the foundations, under the first course of brickwork. Similar images of rulers had existed since the relief of the Sumerian ruler Urnanshe of the mid-third millennium BC, approximately two thousand years before the reign of Ashurbanipal. Ashurbanipal's stele, however, is deliberately archaising, and perhaps also deliberately Babylonianising. It is an image of kingship that is both local and ancient.

Why does Ashurbanipal, a formidable Assyrian monarch, choose to, or agree to, have himself depicted in this manner? Babylon was under the control of Assyria. At the time of the making of the stele, his brother, Shamash-shumu-ukin, had been placed as ruler of Babylon, but it was Ashurbanipal who was, in fact, in political control. It is true that at a later date, sometime after the making and the deposit of the stele in the temple precinct, Babylon rebelled, but was the political uncertainty of the king of Assyria over Babylon the reason for the creation of a truly Babylonian image as a form of legitimacy?

The stele was discovered in the nineteenth century in an area of the temple of Marduk in Babylon. It bears an inscription that covers both sides (Luckenbill 1927: 375–376; Frame 1995: 199–202). On the obverse, the inscription is carved straight

Figure 10.1 Stele of Ashurbanipal, 668–652 BC. Sandstone, height 37 cm
(courtesy of the Trustees of the British Museum).

over the lower part of the body of the king. Therefore, we can say that the object itself is something of a hybrid between a written text and a sculpted monument. One might make an argument here for the primacy of the position of the text. The image appears to be inserted into a monument that was conceived of as a written memorial, yet the image is actually integral to the logic of the monument.

The image of the king bearing a basket of bricks is a trace of an ancient ritual of building. The ruler is decreed as the builder of the temple by the gods. He also describes himself as the conservator and preserver of the structures of earlier times. The building process begins with a ritual that inaugurates the construction by the act of the king making the first brick from the ritual mould, and laying the first foundation brick. As is standard in ritual procedures, this act itself is performative (Bahrani 2001, 2002). In other words, by going through the process of the act itself, the temple's sacred quality is achieved. The structure is no longer a brick wall, but a sacred edifice made of bricks moulded in the mould of boxwood, maple and ivory; placed upon foundations laid into wine and honey libations, no doubt accompanied by prayers and incantations. In the third millennium, the Sumerians had practised such a ritual. Representation was pivotal to the process of ritual performances. The ritual was made tangible and permanent by the insertion of foundation deposits into the earth (Ellis 1968). The deposits consistently included an image of a minor deity and, later in the third millennium, a figurine of the king, together with a written tablet. The tablet used in such a building deposit was a monumentalised text, translated from clay to more enduring materials.

Foundation deposits including figurines and inscribed tablets had to be placed at specific points in the structure, according to another set of ritual procedures. In the case of the Ashurbanipal stele we can say, therefore, that the visual image was a functional part of the monument's efficacy. As a text alone, deposited into the foundation of the temple precinct it would not suffice. The monument required both the historical text, recording the process of the building and the preservation of ancient structures, as well as the image of the king that the text describes as the 'image of kingship'.

Ashurbanipal begins his inscription by describing himself as 'the great king, the mighty king, king of the universe, king of Assyria, king of the four regions of the world, king of kings . . . who adorns Esagila, the temple of the god . . . who repaired the damage to the sanctuaries', and then goes on to describe how the wall of Ezida had become old and the foundations had become weak, and he had them restored and made the foundations firm. He calls upon the god Nabu to 'make my royal throne firm' as a reciprocal act for Ashurbanipal's preservation of the temples. The text ends with a call for future rulers of the land to restore and preserve the ruins of the sacred precinct and to protect this stele and the image of Ashurbanipal upon it (Luckenbill 1927: 376).

Ashurbanipal's stele is a Babylonian object. It is not only the fact of its find-spot in the Esagila that makes the stele Babylonian, nor simply its function as a deposit in a Babylonian temple. It is the formulation of the image itself that is Babylonian, despite the fact that it is commissioned by an Assyrian king. According to the inscription, Shamash-shumu-ukin was still the ruler of Babylon at the time that the stele was carved. What, then, is the Babylonian visual image, as opposed to an Assyrian visual image? In what follows, I will discuss a number of distinctive works of art as exemplary of Babylonian visual images. The choice is made not simply on the basis of the commissioner or patron, since we have seen that the identity of the patron does not necessarily dictate the choice, nor is the choice made on the basis of find-spot, since objects sometimes travelled far across geographical borders in antiquity. One such monument that travelled in antiquity is the stele known as the Law Code of the Babylonian King Hammurabi (1792–1750) (Figure 10.2). This monument is, perhaps, considered more exemplary of Babylonian art than any other, and yet it was found in Susa in Iran, where it had been carried off as war booty in the twelfth century BC (André-Salvini 2004). It was discovered in 1902 at the site of Susa, where it had been taken, after being removed from the Babylonian city of Babylon by the troops of the Elamite king, Shutruk Nahunte.

THE PUBLIC MONUMENT

The Codex Hammurabi is not, in fact, a code of laws (Bottéro 1987). It is, nevertheless, a stele that depicts the Law, or rather Jurisprudence, as an abstract phenomenological concept. It is a large stele, more than two metres in height, and made out of a black basalt monolith. The larger part of the oblong monument is covered with cuneiform script. Twenty-three columns of writing appear on the front, the last seven of which were erased by the Elamites in the twelfth century, and twenty-eight columns of writing appear on the back. Five columns at the beginning and at the end are written as a prologue and an epilogue to the list of laws. Here Hammurabi explains that he was chosen by the gods and recites his military conquests in succession. The gods also chose him to govern and to regulate the law. Because the laws compiled on the inscription cannot be said to cover all areas of jurisprudence, and because these laws are limited to a few areas of life, the stele's identification as a Law Code is no longer accepted. The monument is now defined as one that represents Hammurabi as a king of justice, listing some legal decisions, without being a complete code of laws (Bottéro 1992: 156–184).

At the top part of one side, a scene carved in relief appears above the text (see Figure 10.2). Here, Hammurabi is shown in front of the god Shamash. He enters his world. The space of the sacred and the profane is merged in ways that are perhaps more alarming than in earlier works of Mesopotamian kings where there is a transfiguration of the king into a divinity. Here, Hammurabi has come face to face with the god. He is smaller than the Shamash figure, yet very like him in many respects.

Shamash is seated on the right. He wears a multiple horned crown, and rays of sunlight emerge from his shoulders. He wears a layered garment that reveals a bare right shoulder and arm that are muscular and strong. Shamash is seated on a throne that is in the form of a temple structure, and beneath his feet is the scale pattern of the standard iconographic mountain motif, appropriate for the mountains from which the sun emerges. With his right hand he gives the emblems of rule to Hammurabi, who stands before him. Hammurabi holds his right hand up to his lips, in a gesture of worship. He wears the attire and headdress of a mortal king. There is nothing about him that would indicate a body that is more than human. Physically, Hammurabi is mere man. He holds none of the weapons of the warrior king, despite the fact that the prologue describes his military conquests. Here, the king is mortal, but he is

Figure 10.2   Stele of Hammurabi, 1760 BC. Basalt, height 225 cm, weight 4 tons
(Musée du Louvre).

nevertheless in the space of the god. We might say then that the justice stele of
Hammurabi is a monument that configures the place of the ruler in relation to the
law (Bahrani 2008).

Hammurabi's power is subtly expressed. It is the power to decide punishment that
may include the power to end the identity and the life of a citizen. Hammurabi
points to the actions that fall outside the social pact that would disqualify the man
as a normal citizen. These are the actions that put him outside the accepted forms
of social or civilised behaviour.

The stele of Hammurabi, therefore, constitutes a horizon of juridical certainty, even if it is not a Codex of laws. The text reads in a formulation of protasis and apodosis: 'if X then Y' (Bottéro 1992: 158). It is a scientific (and, one could say, even a metaphysical) formulation of justice. As a monument, its presence articulates the rule of law as transcendental, even beyond the actual cases mentioned in the more than three hundred specific examples. It is not each case that is at issue here, but law itself. Therefore, we can say that the subject of this monument is Law itself, as an abstract phenomenological concept. The Codex Hammurabi, then, demonstrates the seventeenth-century French philosopher Blaise Pascal's observation, in his *Pensées*, that 'the law is based only in the act of its own enunciation' (1966: 46). The monument of Hammurabi can thus be read as an enunciation of the law. Considered in this way, one can imagine the reasons that the Elamites took this stele along with the stelae of earlier kings, despite the fact that the monument's weight, at four tons, would have been a great burden to transport. As historical monuments of ancestral kings that were centuries old, the monuments that were taken to Susa all had a totemic power for the Babylonians (Bahrani 1995). But the Codex Hammurabi was, further-more, a monument of law, of authority and of sovereign rule itself.

THE VOTIVE PORTRAIT

A small copper statue dating to the same time as the reign of Hammurabi is a fine example of the Babylonian votive portrait (see Figure 10.3). The statue stands 19.6 cm in height. It portrays a man, kneeling on his right knee, and with his right hand held up to his face, with thumb and forefinger pressed together. The figure is made out of copper, in the lost wax method, and has a gold leaf covering on the hands and the face. The man depicted wears a tunic with fringed edges that end at the knees. A simple woollen cap covers his head. His short beard, close to the face, is indicated by rows of grid-like curls. The figure kneels upon a base, cast in copper with the figure. At the front of the base, a small basin is placed for receiving oil or incense. The base bears a cuneiform inscription. It states that Lu-Nanna, son of Sin Le'i, dedicated this votive to Martu/Amurru for the life of Hammurabi, king of Babylon (Frayne 1990: 360). The inscription also states that the statue is a suppliant, made of copper, and that its face is plated with gold. The text thus describes the statue and the materials out of which it is made on the base itself. In front of the inscription, at the right side, below the worshipper, an image appears moulded in relief on the base. It depicts what can be recognised as an enthroned deity with a multi-tiered gown and long beard. This is Martu/Amurru. In front of the god is the kneeling worshipper, in the same pose and with the same gesture as the figure of the statue itself. The opposite side of the base bears a relief of a recumbent lamb.

The object refers to itself and its own function as a votive offering, in the relief as in the text. The votive image depicts its own positioning in front of the deity, to pray for Lu-Nanna and for Hammurabi. The image is an offering to the god. On the opposite side, the lamb, too, is an offering to the god. The object can therefore be described as a self-referential image, a type of image that begins with the very earliest forms of representation in Mesopotamia as exemplified by the famous Uruk Vase of 3100 BC (Bahrani 2001, 2002). This is a sophisticated conception of an image that has the effect of continuously referring back to itself in an endless process of mirroring.

Figure 10.3 Lu-Nanna votive portrait, 1792–1750 BC.
Copper and gold. Height 19.6 cm (Musée du Louvre).

What is depicted here is the magic of representation itself, as a process of referentiality. This kind of 'image magic' was fundamental to Babylonian ritual and religious practices.

A votive portrait is an image that represents the worshipper in an act of prayer before the god for all time. Because, according to the Mesopotamian system of belief, the image was a valid substitute for the person, a place in which the essence of the represented person was manifest, the votive portrait became a double of the individual represented and could become a form of presence, a substitute, praying in place of that person, for all time (Bahrani 1995, 2003). The referential process that is underscored in the imagery of this votive sculpture was essential for ritual in Babylonian religion. Image making was, therefore, a necessary part of religious beliefs and social rituals in Babylonia. Visual images were able to effect change in their own right, and did not simply reflect, or depict, the world of the Babylonians, but took part in the creation of that Babylonian world.

THE BOUNDARY STONE

The genre or category of monument known as Kassite Kudurru to archaeologists is one that is associated with the Kassite dynasty of Babylonia (fifteenth–twelfth centuries). This categorisation is in fact problematic, however. A variety of objects have been categorised as Kudurru in museums around the world and in popular books on Mesopotamian art and archaeology, yet the majority of these artefacts were made after the end of the Kassite dynasty (Brinkman 1980–1983; Seidel 1980–1983, 1989; Slanski 2003). It is therefore best to refer to the monuments in question as Babylonian Kudurru stones.

The term Kudurru is an ancient one (CAD vol. 8: 495). It is a term usually translated as boundary stone. But the grouping of a number of objects under this genre is a result of the working method of modern scholarship. The Kudurrus (Aakkadian plural is Kudurreti or Kadaru) are polished boulders of an irregular cylindrical shape, ranging from about 30–70 cm in height, carved in relief all the way around with symbols or sacred objects. They are usually made of a hard stone such as black basalt or limestone, or of diorite, and are carved with cuneiform texts and numerous symbols of the gods. These stones seem to record decrees of land to officials by the Babylonian king. The standard iconography of the reliefs consists of the deity symbols and, in several examples, images of the people involved in the land grant; namely, the ruler and the recipient of the land.

The Kudurrus are described as boundary stones, yet they have not been uncovered by archaeologists in locations that can lead to any conclusions about their use as boundary markers in fields. The Kudurrus have been discovered only in the south of Iraq and are thus a Babylonian type of monument. A large number of the Babylonian Kudurrus were taken as war booty from Babylonia to Iran and were, therefore, discovered in a secondary context, in Susa (Harper *et al.* 1992: 178–182). Furthermore, it has been argued that the surfaces of the Kudurru stones, even those that have been found in Babylonia, do not appear to have been exposed to the elements for any extended amount of time. This condition of the surfaces has led scholars to conclude that the Kudurrus must have been placed in temples, where they stood as copies of boundary stones that were placed outdoors, in fields.

The function of the Kudurru is first and foremost administrative, yet it is also religious and historical. It is an administrative document turned into a monument. It records a transaction and guarantees that transaction through the existence of this permanent record. Under Kassite rule the transfer of land changed. The artefacts, which began to appear at that time, may have been first introduced by the Kassites but they continued to be used until the Neo-Babylonian period (seventh century BC).

The iconography of Kudurrus is distinctive to this particular type of artefact. Scholars, therefore, speak of Kudurru iconography as a genre that can be catalogued and analysed on its own terms. While some of the iconography and symbols on Kudurrus appear elsewhere on Mesopotamian images, nowhere do we see quite the same combination of symbols, and no group of artefacts bears the same accumulation of symbols. Some of the abstract symbols, furthermore, are known only from the iconography of Kudurrus. If we examine one such monument closely we see that a large part of the iconography is made up of these abstract deity symbols.

The Kudurru of Nebuchadnezzar I (1125–1104 BC) was found in the temple of the god Shamash at Sippar in 1882 by Abd al Ahad Thoma. It is currently in the British Museum (Figure 10.4). It is a limestone boulder, 65 cm in height bearing an inscription on the back, and six registers of divine symbols appear on the front. The inscription records that Nebuchadnezzar I granted freedom and tax exemption to the region from the province of Namar to the villages of Bit-Karziabku as a reward for the bravery of its chief, Sitti-Marduk, during a campaign against Elam (Foster 1993: 297–298; Frame 1995: 33–345).

The Kudurru is covered with closely placed deity symbols in each register carved on the surface. At the top register we see the star of Ishtar (goddess of love and war), the crescent of Sin (moon god), and the sun-disc of Shamash (sun god/god of justice). Below, there are altars with horned crowns upon them representing the gods, Ea (water), Anu (sky) and Enlil (kingship). The third register depicts altars with a spade and dragon emerging, for Marduk god of Babylon, and another altar bearing a wedge and stylus with a goat-fish emerging for Nabu, god of writing. On the fourth row there are beast-headed weapons (Nergal, underworld), and an altar with a horse head under a rainbow. The latter may be an emblem of the constellation Andromeda. A bird on a perch may be a Kassite deity. Below, we see a seated goddess and her dog. This is Gula, goddess of medicine and healing. The scorpion archer before her represents the constellation Sagittarius or Scorpio. At the lowest part of the stele, a recumbent bull with a lightning fork emerging from his back is associated with Adad, the storm god. The turtle invokes Ea (water), the scorpion (Ishara, oath goddess) and a lamp on a stand is the emblem for Nusku, god of light and fire. Finally, an undulating snake climbing up the side of the monument represents Nirah or Ishtaran, the minister of the gods. The deity symbols appear to provide divine sanction for the administrative act of the land grant, and perhaps worked to anchor the legal decree into the permanence of the monument.

As the iconography of Kudurrus developed over time, images of the people involved in the transfer of the land came to be represented also. A Kudurru bearing such a portrait is the Kudurru of Marduk Nadin Ahhe in the British Museum in London (Figure 10.5). He wears elaborate royal attire of embroidered clothes and feathered crown and carries a bow and two arrows. A caption next to the figure describes the Babylonian ruler as 'The Avenger of his People'.

Figure 10.4 Kudurru of Nebuchadnezzar I, 1125–1104 BC.
Limestone, height 65 cm (courtesy of the Trustees of the British Museum).

Figure 10.5   Kudurru of Marduk Nadin Ahhe, 1099–1082 BC.
Limestone, height 61 cm (courtesy of the Trustees of the British Museum).

Figure 10.6 Throne room wall of Nebuchadnezzar II, 604–562 BC. Glazed brick with relief sculpture (Vorderasiatische Museum, Berlin).

Figure 10.7 Portrait of a woman, third–second centuries BC.
Alabaster, height 46 cm (courtesy of the Trustees of the British Museum).

167

Besides the text that narrates the events of the legal transfer of land and property rights, labels are at times written next to the deity symbols. Sometimes the inscriptions specifically call on the gods to sanction or oversee the agreement calling on 'all the gods who are invoked by name on this kudurru' (CAD: 495). Finally, curses are invoked upon those who break the agreement.

In some examples of kudurrus, the text states that the monument itself has a name. For example, 'Establisher of Perpetual Boundaries' or 'Do not cross the border, do not obliterate the boundary, hate evil and love good' (Brinkman 1980–1983: 271). These names on the Kudurrus can give us an indication of their function. According to Babylonian religion and mythology, names were never random or external. In the Babylonian epic of creation, a thing does not exist until it is named and, therefore, names were considered to be in the essence of things in the world. This naming of monuments with proper names that invoke the protection of the gods is an ancient tradition in southern Babylonia, and appears in the earliest public monuments set up by Sumerian rulers. It is thus a continuation of a tradition that was ancient and traditional in the south of Babylonia.

THE CITY: BABYLON

The legendary walls of Babylon described by Herodotus and celebrated among the wonders of the ancient world can also be seen within the ancient tradition of image making in Mesopotamia. Babylon itself, it can be said, was a monument to rival all others. Its walls were counted among the wonders of the ancient world. The city walls were massive and the gates were decorated with magical apotropaic animals and hybrid mythical beasts. The bricks were moulded with relief figures. Images of the dragon of Marduk, the lion of Ishtar and the bull of Adad covered the walls of the Ishtar gate and the palace of Nebuchadnezzar II (604–562 BC) (Figure 10.6). These magical beasts protected the walls and invoked the protection of the gods in the same way as the images on other types Babylonian monuments. In the famed blue glazed upper parts of the Ishtar gate, now in the Berlin Museum, the lapis and turquoise colour and the shining glazed surfaces bring to mind the description of Babylon as 'a gemstone suspended from the neck of the sky' (Van De Mieroop 2003). This consciously chosen decorative program was in the tradition of Babylonian monumental arts, but applied to a city that was itself a monument.

THE GRAECO-BABYLONIAN IMAGE

Babylonian art is generally considered to end with the arrival of Alexander's troops in 331 BC. However, a close analysis of arts produced during the late fourth and third centuries BC reveals that Babylonian iconographies and styles continued to be produced under the Macedonian and Seleucid rule. This continuity of traditional forms occurred alongside new styles that appear to mix the local preference for mixed media and decorative patterning with the idealising naturalism and smooth stone surfaces of Greek sculpture. Imported Greek works and styles begin to appear soon, but these are recognisable as different from the local works, and existed alongside a specifically local production. The hybrid mix between the Greek and the Babylonian produced a new style, one that we might define as Graeco-Babylonian. One such example is the statue of a woman in the British Museum (Figure 10.7).

The alabaster statue was excavated at Borsippa, near Babylon, by the Iraqi archaeologist, Hormuz Rassam. It is a figure of a woman, dressed in a pleated garment and a shawl. She holds her right hand at her breast and with her left hand, she pulls at the shawl that is placed diagonally across her body. The sculpture is made out of alabaster, but the eyes are hollowed to receive an inlay and dark pigment gives emphasis to the rims of the eyes. This use of pigment and inlay is an ancient local tradition, as is the preference for a female ideal with full cheeks, large eyes, and a small mouth. There are traces of pigment elsewhere on the statue, and the rim of the cloak and the crescent shaped ornament she wears around her neck are added in plaster. The sculpture of a woman is very much in the tradition of Hellenistic portrait sculpture of the third–second centuries BC. The garments she wears are identifiable as the Greek *chiton* and *himation*. The manner in which she wears the garments and holds the cloak out to the side is also known from Greek sculpture of the west. However, the nipples and navel are perforated into the dress, an aspect that would have been unacceptable in a Greek counterpart in the west. The crescent-shaped ornament around her neck is an emblem of the moon god, Sin, and may indicate that this was a priestess; however, at this time the crescent ornament is also the emblem of the Greek goddess, Artemis. These details, as well as the treatment of the eyes, the use of pigment and plaster, are all local translations of a portrait type that is typically Hellenistic, indicating that Greek styles and techniques were readily mixed with the local traditions. The Graeco-Babylonian image continued to be produced under the Parthian rulers of Mesopotamia in the following centuries, but was gradually transformed in both its distinctive forms and functions after that time.

REFERENCES

Bahrani, Z. (1995) 'Assault and Abduction: the Fate of the Royal Image in the Ancient Near East' *Art History* 18(3), 363–382.

—— (2001) *Women of Babylon: Gender and Representation in Mesopotamia*, London: Routledge.

—— (2002) 'Performativity and the Image: Narrative, Representation and the Uruk vase' in *Leaving No Stone Unturned: Studies in Honor of Donald P. Hansen*, E. Ehrenberg ed. Winona lake: Eisenbrauns, 15–22.

—— (2003) *The Graven Image: Representation in Babylonia and Assyria*, Philadelphia: University of Pennsylvania Press.

—— (2008) *Rituals of War: The Body and Violence in Mesopotamia*, New York: Zone Books.

Bottéro, Jean (1992) *Mesopotamia, Writing, Reasoning and the Gods*, trans. Z. Bahrani and M. Van De Mieroop, Chicago, IL: University of Chicago Press.

Brinkman, J.A. (1980–1983) 'Kudurru: philologisch' *Reallexikon der Assyriologie* 6 Band, Berlin Walter de Gruyter, 268–274.

CAD: *The Chicago Assyrian Dictionary*, vol. 8, M.Civil, I.J. Gelb, A.L. Oppenheim and E. Reiner eds. Oriental Institute, The University of Chicago, 1971.

Ellis, Richard (1968) *Foundation Deposits in Ancient Mesopotamia*, Yale Near Eastern Researches 2, New Haven, CT.

Foster, B. (1993) *Before the Muses: An Anthology of Akkadian Literature*, Bethesda, MD: CDL Press.

Frame, Grant (1995) *The Royal Inscriptions of Mesopotamia Babylonian Periods, vol. 2: Rulers of Babylonia from the Second Dynasty of Isin to the End of Assyrian Domination (1157–612 BC)*, Toronto: University of Toronto Press.

Frayne, Douglas R. (1990) *The Royal Inscriptions of Mesopotamia Early Periods vol. 4, Old Babylonian Period (2003–1595 BC)*, Toronto: University of Toronto Press.

Harper, P.O. *et al.* (1992), *The Royal City of Susa*, New York: The Metropolitan Museum of Art.

Luckenbill, D.D. (1927) *Ancient Records of Assyria and Babylonia* vol. 2, Chicago, IL: University of Chicago Press.

Seidl, U. (1980–1983) 'Kudurru: Bildschmuck' *Reallexikon der Assyriologie* 6 Band, Berlin Walter de Gruyter, 275–277.

—— (1989) *Die Babylonischen Kudurru Reliefs*. Orbis Biblicus et Orientalis 87, Freiburg: Universitätsverlag.

Slanski, K.E. (2003) *The Babylonian Entitlement Narus (kudurrus): A Study in their Form and Function*, Boston, MA: American Schools of Oriental Research, 2003.

Van De Mieroop, M. (2003) 'Reading Babylon' *American Journal of Archaeology* 102: 257–275.

CHAPTER ELEVEN

FOOD AND DRINK
IN BABYLONIA

——— .◆. ———

Frances Reynolds

šūkil akalu šiqi kurunnu
erišti qīši epir u kubbit
ana annîmma ilšu ḫadīš
ṭābi eli šamaš irâbšu dumqu

Give food to eat, give beer to drink,
  Provide what is asked for, supply food, and honour your guests!
For this a man's god is happy with him;
  It is pleasing to Shamash [the Sun God] – he will reward him.
                    Counsels of Wisdom, 61–64 (Lambert 1960: 102;
                    Foster 2005: 413; translation author's own)

TYPES OF EVIDENCE

Investigating life in Babylonia involves assessing two main types of evidence: the evidence of archaeology, including representations in ancient art, and the evidence of texts, predominantly written in cuneiform script in the Akkadian language. In the case of food and drink modern scholars rely mainly on Akkadian texts, since the evidence from the archaeological record is more limited. Little work has been done in the following areas of Babylonian archaeology: the analysis of human skeletal remains, a potential source of information about diet; the study of animal remains; and the study of plant remains, many of which do not survive (Nesbitt 2003: 26–30). Archaeology is more revealing about food technology, the equipment and facilities used for storing, preparing and eating food, but the picture is far from complete. The extensive and varied textual record includes administrative texts, letters, lexical texts, literature and even some recipes. However, it too gives only a partial picture. Texts do not reflect society as a whole, since cuneiform literacy was restricted to highly trained professional scribes, and we cannot identify many Akkadian words for foodstuffs, including names of plants and fish, or how many of them were used (Powell 2003: 14–15). On balance, however, most of our knowledge about Babylonian food and drink derives from Akkadian texts rather than archaeological sources.

Combining all the available sources still leaves many gaps in terms of time and place for the whole of Babylonia during the period *c.*2000–200 BC. It has to be emphasised that we are dealing with sporadic pieces of evidence and that a coherent picture is beyond our reach. There is a concentration of evidence dating to the Old Babylonian period (*c.*2000–1595 BC) and this will be the chronological focus of the present study. The geographical scope is Babylonia itself and the city of Mari upstream on the Euphrates to the north-west. In the Old Babylonian period, Mari was culturally very close to Babylonia, although it was the capital of an independent state, and Akkadian texts and archaeological remains found there give valuable information about food and drink.

SOURCES OF FOOD AND DRINK

Any study of food and drink is intimately connected with the environment (Postgate 1992: 14–18, 157–90). Babylonia lay on an alluvial plain crossed by the Euphrates and Tigris rivers. The late spring floods of the Tigris and Euphrates fed by melt-water from Anatolia were pivotal events in the agricultural year. Summers were hot and dry. Babylonia was south of the rain-fed agricultural belt, so irrigation was necessary to sustain agriculture on any sizeable scale.

The rivers and their channels, ponds and marshes provided habitats for a variety of food resources, including fish, the meat and eggs of birds and turtles, and wild boar. Water collected directly or via wells had many uses including drinking, brewing beer and cooking. The combination of environment and climate made salt readily available. Orchards and gardens near water supported date palms, fruit trees, vegetables, including onions and cucumbers, and spices. Irrigated fields were planted with cereals, predominantly barley, as well as with legumes, including pulses and sesame. The most common domesticated animals were sheep accompanied by goats, which could graze on fallow fields and the steppe. Animals kept nearer or in settlements included cattle, pigs, ducks and geese. The uncultivated steppe provided food for those who hunted for it, such as game and truffles.

Most Babylonian food and drink was local in origin but imports also played a role, including wine, nuts and olives from the north, where the rainfall was greater and the terrain hillier.

FOOD AND DRINK IN SOCIETY

Most of our evidence for Babylonia relates to people who lived in cities rather than in the countryside, either in villages or in nomadic groups, and concerns the higher echelons of the social hierarchy rather than the mass of ordinary people.

Eating and drinking practices were seen as a marker of Babylonian civilisation. In the Old Babylonian version of the Epic of Gilgameš, the civilising of the wild man Enkidu by the prostitute Šamkatum includes introducing him to the proper ways of eating and drinking: 'Enkidu did not know how to eat bread (*aklum*), how to drink ale (*šikarum*) he had never been shown' (Old Babylonian Epic of Gilgameš II 90–93; George 2003: 176–77).

Enkidu is an enthusiastic pupil and ends up drunk on seven jugs of ale. Before this incident, as a member of the wild animal herds, he shared their food and drink:

accordingly he drank milk from the udder as a baby and ate grass and drank water as an adult (George 2003: 176–77, 544–45, 650–51). Thus, the animals' grass and water correspond to the civilised humans' bread and beer. In each case civilisation transforms raw materials, foods in their natural state, through complex processing, the application of food technology. There is a profound difference between eating and drinking solely to sustain life and doing so with the aim of enhanced pleasure, in other words, between functional consumption and gastronomy.

The nature of food and drink varied according to social context. The Babylonian diet was plant based and animal products were a relative luxury. Beer produced locally from barley was more readily available than imported wine. In general, wealthier people had a more varied diet and greater access to highly perishable foodstuffs such as fresh meat.

Women were normally economically dependent on men. According to the Laws of Hammurabi, a Babylonian woman with no food at home whose husband was a prisoner of war was entitled to join the household of another man (Laws of Hammurabi §§133a–136; Roth 1997: 106–07). Within domestic households women acted as cooks and brewers. This is reflected by the household equipment listed in brides' dowries in the Old Babylonian period. On tablets from Sippar, one dowry includes a 20-litre copper kettle, two stone grinding slabs, six chairs, a table, a bronze pot, a mortar and four small spoons (Dalley 1979: no. 15; Stol 1995: 486) and another dowry two stone grinding slabs for barley flour, finely ground in one case, a mortar, two containers of oil, five chairs, a table, two large spoons and five small spoons (Ranke 1906: no. 101; Schorr 1913: 291–92; Bottéro 2004: 78). An Old Babylonian bilingual wisdom text in Sumerian and Akkadian contrasts a disruptive female neighbour with a domestic paragon who provides her household with everyday food and drink. The damaged Akkadian description reads:

> *bīt šikaru ibaššû mazzaltūša*
> *bīt diqāru ibaššû kūtūša*
> *bīt aka{lu i}baššû naḫatimmatum rabītum*

> The house with beer: her position is there.
> The house with a pot: her jug is there.
> The house with food: the chief female cook is there.
>> (Scheil 1927: 36; van Dijk 1953: 90–91;
>> Bottéro 2004: 77; translation author's own)

Women's dealings with food and drink were not, however, limited to the home. In an Old Babylonian letter from an unknown site, a woman called Ḫuzālatum who lives in a village writes to a woman called Bēltani:

> They brought me 100 litres of coarse barley flour (*tappinnum*), 50 litres of dates (*suluppū*) and 1½ litres of sesame oil (*šamnum*) with the earlier caravan; 10 litres of sesame (*šamaššammū*) and 10 litres of dates this time. I have sent you 20 litres of good quality flour (*isqūqum*), 35 litres of fine barley flour (zì.gu), 2 combs and 1 litre of sauce (*šiqqum*). In order to supply her provisions and as her food ration

give her 10 litres of barley (*ûm*) and 10 litres of coarse barley flour. There are no 'spiny' fishes (*ziqtū*) here. Send me 'spiny' fishes, so I can put up sauce for fermenting for you and they can bring it to you.

(Schroeder 1917: no. 22; Frankena 1974: no. 22;
Bottéro 2004: 19; translation author's own)

Women were also active running the Babylonian equivalent of pubs and selling beer, as attested by the Laws of Hammurabi §§108–11 (Roth 1997: 101–02).

Some foods were far from being part of the staple diet. A man called Šamaš-nāṣir wrote of a taste sensation in an Old Babylonian letter from Larsa:

Tutu-māgir sent me seven *ušummū*-mice from Tur-Ugalla and I sent six on to Šamaš-lamassašu, the zabardab-official. I kept just one to eat myself, and it tasted excellent! Had I known how good they were, I'd not have sent a single one to Šamaš-lamassašu!

(Dossin 1933: no. 13; based on Englund 1995: 47)

Food and drink would be more lavish on special occasions, including marriages (Postgate 1992: 101–02). Gastronomy at its finest would be practised in the kitchens of royal palaces. Administrative records and letters from Zimri-Lim's palace at Mari give us a wealth of information about food and drink, especially that served at meals attended by the king (Dalley 2002: 78–96; Sasson 2004). In daily and monthly records, the term 'the king's meal' (*naptan šarrim*) is applied to many outlays of food, probably issued for processing in the palace; such outlays are the subject of an estimated 1,300 entries dated to Zimri-Lim's reign (Sasson 2004: 182–83, 196). Zimri-Lim's palace staff included a range of specialist food processors, both male and female, and professions included the pantrymaid (*abarakkatum*), whose duties included producing fruit conserves and pickles, and the female baker (*ēpītum*), who produced a wide variety of breads (Sasson 2004: 189). The king, accompanied by his retinue, hosted ceremonial banquets for 26 to 562 people with elaborate presentation and etiquette in order to secure or strengthen his guests' loyalty (Sasson 2004: 181, 199–202).

Among the Babylonian tablets at Yale, there are three texts consisting of Akkadian recipe collections (Van Dijk *et al.* 1985: nos 25–27; Bottéro 1995, 2004: 25–35). These tablets were written in southern Babylonia in the Old Babylonian period between 1700 and 1600 BC and were not written as a set, although an ancient scholar may have collected them together (Bottéro 1995: 3, 145–53). The three tablets contain a total of 35 recipes: 33 with meat, one with no meat but with animal fat and blood and one apparently free of animal products, although the text is badly damaged. Heating in water and fat in a pot is the predominant cooking method and one passage can occur in more than one recipe. The prevalence of meat indicates that these recipes concern the elite rather than ordinary people and there are some indications of links with religious ceremonies (Bottéro 1995: 81). The fact that these recipes were collected in writing places them in the realm of Old Babylonian scribal learning and the texts can be compared to other technical manuals, such as those for making glass or perfumes, and to medical texts (Milano 2004: 244–49). The three recipe texts are very unusual and we still do not understand all the terms for ingredients, culinary processes and equipment.

Tablet A (no. 25) contains 25 concise recipes for broth, summarised at the end as 21 meat broths (*mê šīrim*) and four vegetable (*warqum*) (Bottéro 1995: 57). For the meat broths the recipe titles are: meat broth; Assyrian; red broth; clear broth; venison broth; gazelle broth; kid broth; bitter (?); broth with crumbs (?); *zamzaganu*; dodder (?) (*kasû*-plant) broth; lamb broth; ram (?) broth; *bidšud* (?) broth; spleen broth; Elamite broth; *amursānu*-pigeon broth; thigh broth; *ḫalazzu*-plant broth; salt broth; and francolin (?) (*tarru*) broth. The vegetable ones are called *tuh'u*-beet (?); *kanašû*-plant; *ḫirṣu*-plant; and cultivated turnip. However, the first three of these also contain meat. Typically the cooking medium is water (*mû*) with added animal fat, probably sheep fat, (*lipûm*) in a pot. The tannur oven is mentioned several times. As an example, the eleventh recipe reads:

mê kasî šīrum ul izzaz šītum mê tukān lipi'am tanaddi
kasû kīma marāqi šusikillu samīdu kisibirru kamūnu karšum ḫazannum
diqāra ina tinūri kīma ḫapê meḫrum naglabi

Dodder (?) (*kasû*-plant) broth. Fresh meat is not used, but salted meat. You
    set up water; you put in animal fat;
crushed dodder (?); onion; *samīdu*-plant; coriander; cumin; leek; garlic.
The pot covers (?) the tannur: ready to eat [literally 'before the knife'].

(Bottéro 1995: 42–44; Bottéro 2004: 27;
translation author's own)

Tablet B (no. 26) contains seven complex, detailed recipes for cooking birds, involving a wide range of ingredients and cooking techniques. For example, the elaborate first recipe for a dish of small birds (*iṣṣūrū ṣeḫrūtum*) in a case of dough (*līšum*) can be summarised (Bottéro 1995: 58–73; Bottéro 2004: 29–30):

1   Birds in broth: Precook the butchered and washed birds, their gizzards (*šisūrrum*) and entrails (*esrū*) in a cauldron (*ruqqum*). Wash, wipe and sprinkle with salt (*ṭābtum*). Bring to the boil in a pot (*diqāru*) of water and milk (*šizbum*) with animal fat (*lipûm*), pieces of wood (*iṣṣū*) and rue (?) (*sibburatum*). Add onion (*šusikillu*), *samīdu*-plant, leek (*karšum*), garlic (*ḫazannum*) and water. After cooking, add mashed leek, garlic and edible crocus bulb (?) (*andaḫšu*).
2   Dough: Soak washed, fine-grade flour (*saskûm*) in milk. Knead with fish-sauce (*siqqum*) and add *samīdu*-plant, leek, garlic, milk and pot fat (*šamnum ša diqāri*). Use half the dough to bake *sebetu*-breads in the tannur. Let the other half rise and line a shallow dish (*mākaltum*) sprinkled with *nīnû*-plant (?) to make a crust to cover the birds. Knead more fine-grade flour soaked in milk and add oil (?), leek, garlic and *samīdu*-plant. Using this dough as a base for the cooked birds, line another shallow dish letting the dough protrude above the rim. Bake the base and crust on two supports on top of the tannur. Remove the crust from the shallow dish and rub it with oil (*šamnum*).
3   Presentation: Lay the birds on the base and scatter them with the entrails, gizzards and *sebetu*-breads, setting aside the broth and pot fat. Cover with the crust. Serve at table immediately.

Tablet C (no. 27) contains three damaged recipes for the pot cooking of a bird, *buṭumtu*-grain and some kind of meat (Bottéro 1995: 103–10; Bottéro 2004: 34–35).

Apart from direct human consumption, there were two other main social roles played by food and drink: offerings to the gods, commonly redistributed for human consumption, and offerings to the dead (Mayer and Sallaberger 2003: 93–102; Seidl 2003: 102–06; Bottéro 2004: 107–21).

SOME ARCHAEOLOGICAL EVIDENCE FOR COOKING AND KITCHEN EQUIPMENT

Pottery containers for storing, processing and serving food and drink were the norm. Stone grinding slabs, the so-called saddle querns, and the upper handstones that were drawn across them are common finds, sites including private houses. These hand mills were used mainly for grinding grain into flour but also for grinding other foodstuffs such as cumin and sesame seeds (Milano 1993–97b: 393–400; Ellis 1993–97: 401–04).

A cooking pit or open hearth could be used for roasting, broiling, cooking on hot stones and cooking in supported pots. The earliest type of oven used by people in the Ancient Near East was the clay tannur (*tinūrum*): an open-topped, bell-shaped oven with thick walls and an opening near the bottom for fuel (Miglus 2003: 40). The tannur was fixed into place on the floor – the fitted kitchen has a long history. Via the open top, dough was stuck onto the inside of the pre-heated walls and baked as flat bread (Curtis 2001: 207). Pots could also be placed on top of the tannur (see point 2 in the recipe above). The Akkadian word, *tinūrum*, and the modern Arabic word, tannur, are cognate and people still use this type of oven in the Middle East today. Leavened bread was baked in another type of oven, the dome oven, which had a domed chamber with one opening for fuel and food. Fuel burnt in the chamber heated the oven, the ashes were raked out and food put into the chamber to cook (Curtis 2001: 208). Good examples of dome ovens from the Old Babylonian period have been excavated at Ur and Mari. In Ur, a private house (dubbed No. 1B Baker's Square by its excavator Woolley) contained three mudbrick circular dome ovens with their openings set into two walls of Room 3 and their chambers in two adjacent rooms (Woolley and Mallowan 1976: 158–59, pl. 50). Big ovens of this type were probably used for large-scale baking, both directly for people and for offerings made to the gods in temples (Miglus 2003: 40).

Archaeological evidence from Zimri-Lim's palace at Mari includes ovens, hearths and highly decorative kitchen equipment. Room 70 near the throne room contained the remains of two dome ovens, both opening into the room; during a kitchen refit the large circular oven replaced the smaller quarter circle one in the corner (Parrot 1958: 230–35; Margueron 2004: 492). In the adjoining Room 77, the excavators found 49 decorated terracotta objects, probably moulds for food destined for the king's table (Parrot 1958: 222–27; Bottéro 1985: 38; Margueron 2004: 430, 515–16). Many of these moulds are round but some are rectangular and some animal-shaped, representing either a fish or a lion lying down (its pose reminiscent of a modern rabbit-shaped mould for jelly). The motifs on the round moulds are geometric or figurative. Concentric circles are common and can be combined with either circles of animals, such as fish, nose to tail or a central scene. Such scenes include humanoid figures, lions, bulls and the well-known motif of two rearing goats flanking a tree.

Among scenes on rectangular moulds are a man holding a stag by its antler with his dog in attendance, a lion attacking a humped bovine from the rear, and a seated female figure, naked except for headdress and jewellery. Other animals represented on the moulds include gazelles, birds and hedgehogs. Near the palace entrance, Room 167 contained a cooking range. A rectangular mudbrick bench incorporated a row of five hearths. Each has a bottom opening for fuel in the front of the bench and an opening for cooking in the top of the bench; presumably cooking pots would have rested on a support (Parrot 1958: 24–26; Margueron 2004: 492).

WHAT DID THE BABYLONIANS EAT AND DRINK?

The following list does not aim to be exhaustive but to give a general picture of the types of identifiable foods and drinks consumed in Babylonia in the Old Babylonian period. Ancient lists of terms for items of food and drink are preserved on Tablets 23–24 of the thematic lexical series called Ur₅.ra = *ḫubullu* and their Old Babylonian 'forerunners' (Reiner 1974: 67–90, 109 ff.). Tablet 23 lists soups, beers, brewing products, flours and breads; Tablet 24 sweeteners, fats, herbs and spices, milk products, legumes, grains, fruits and vegetables.

Plant-based foods

Plants and their products dominated the Babylonians' diet. Staple foods and drinks included barley, beer, garlic, onions, dates and sesame oil. Other vegetables and fruits were also important. Many Akkadian (and Sumerian) terms for plants and plant-based foods resist identification and, even when a plant is identified, it can be uncertain which part was used (Powell 1998: 290–91).

Cereals

Barley (*ûm*; *Hordeum* spp.) and, less frequently, wheats including emmer (*kunāšum*; *Triticum dicoccum*) featured in the Babylonians' diet as whole grains and, after milling, as various types of flour (*qēmum*) and coarser groats (*mundum*); cereal products were consumed in many types of beers, soups, porridges, cakes and breads (e.g. Milano 1993–97a: 22–31; Powell 2003: 13; Sasson 2004: 187, 190). We have a relatively detailed knowledge of the ingredients of a cake called *mersum*: it was based on flour, usually combined with some kind of fat, and in texts from Mari additions include dates, terebinth nuts, garlic, cumin, black cumin, coriander and fruit syrup or possibly honey (Bottéro 1995: 22–23; Bottéro 2004: 23–24). Cereal products in the Yale recipes include a malted barley product called *bappiru*, also used in brewing beer, which is often translated as beer bread but was probably a powder (Bottéro 1995: 40; Curtis 2001: 215–16).

Vegetables

The following list based on cuneiform sources is derived from Powell (2003: 13–15, 19–22). The long-lasting bulbs of garlic (*šūmū* or *ḫazannum*; *Allium sativum*) were central to the diet; the bulbs of onion (*šuškillu* or *šamaškillum*; *Allium cepa*) and of leek (*karašum*; *Allium porrum*) were common foodstuffs. The green tops of all three were probably also eaten and all three could be dried (Charpin *et al.* 2004: 856). Other vegetables included: lettuce (*ḫassu*; *Lactuca sativa* (?)); probably some kind of Brassica; the cucumber (*qiššum*; *Cucumis sativus* (?)); the roots, and probably the tops, of the turnip (*laptum*; *Brassica rapa* ssp. *rapa*); the radish (*puglu*; *Raphanus sativus*); and possibly the beet (*šumuttum*; *Beta vulgaris*) and an edible crocus bulb (*andaḫšum*). Legumes were important and probably *ḫallūrum* is the broad bean (*Vicia faba*), *kakkûm* the common pea (*Pisum sativum*) and/or the lentil (*Lens culinaris*), and *appānum* the chick pea (*Cicer arietinum*) (Charpin *et al.* 2004: 857–58). In the Yale recipes, alliaceous vegetables are very common, including garlic, leek and onion; other vegetables include the edible crocus bulb and the turnip (Bottéro 1995: 56–57, 161).

Fruits

This list is based on cuneiform sources and derived from Powell (2003: 13–19). Dates (*suluppū*; cf. *uḫinnum*, 'unripe, green dates') from the date palm (*gišimmarum*; *Phoenix dactylifera*) were Babylonia's most important fruit and the palm heart (*uqūrum*) was also eaten. Other basic fruits include the fig (*tittum*; *Ficus carica*) and the grape (*karānum*; *Vitis vinifera*), which was probably cultivated in Babylonia more for raisins (*muzīqu*) and juice, than for wine as in the northern uplands. Sugar came mainly from dates, followed by pricier grapes and figs; all three could be processed to produce syrup (*dišpum*). The other basic fruits are the apple (*ḫašḫūrum*), probably the domesticated apple (*Malus pumila*) but possibly also the wild crab apple (*Malus sylvestris*), and the pomegranate (*nurmû*, *lurmûm* or *lurimtum*; *Punica granatum*). Northern fruits include the olive (*serdum*; *Olea europaea*), mainly grown for its oil, the pear (*kamiššarum*; *Pyrus communis*) and a fruit called *šallūrum*, possibly a type of pear or plum. All these fruits (or their trees) occur in Mari texts (Sasson 2004: 188–89).

Nuts

The main nuts were the almond (*šiqdum*, *šāqidum* or *šaqīdum*; *Amygdalus communis* (?)), which may have been grown in Babylonia, and the terebinth (*buṭnu* or *buṭuttu*; *Pistacia* spp.), an upland tree (Nesbitt and Postgate 2001: 633–34).

Herbs and spices

Identification is particularly difficult, sometimes including the part of the plant used (Bottéro 1995: 161; Nesbitt and Postgate 2001: 635; Powell 2003: 14, 19–20; Charpin *et al.* 2004: 856–57; Sasson 2004: 191–92). Old Babylonian sources refer to many plants that added flavour to foods and drinks, such as the peppery seeds of cress (*saḫlû*; *Lepidium sativum* (?)); coriander seeds and possibly leaves (*kisibirrum*; *Coriandrum sativum*); cumin seeds (*kamūnum*; *Cuminum cyminum*); the unidentified *samīdum*; saffron (?) (*azupīrum* or *azupirānum*); toothpick plant (?) (*nīnûm*); seeds of dodder (?) (*kasû*); and in the north seeds of black cumin (*zibûm*; *Nigella sativa*) and juniper kernels (*kikkirênū*; *Juniperus* spp.) Other additives included products from cypress (*šurmēnum*) and myrtle (*asum*).

Oils

The staple fat (*šamnum*) in the Babylonians' diet was oil from the pressed seeds of the sesame plant (*šamaššammū*; *Sesamum indicum*) (Charpin *et al.* 2004: 941–43, 975; Powell 1991). Sesame oil also had its elite uses, as in the Yale recipes and a dish of ostrich eggs for the king's table at Mari (Bottéro 1995: 161; Sasson 2004: 187). Olive oil was imported into Mari from the west, although not always as a foodstuff (Stol 2003: 33).

Vinegars

Vinegar (*ṭābātum*) could be fermented from barley or grapes and was a household staple often grouped together with sauce (*šiqqum*) (*CAD* Š/3, 99–100; *AHw*, 1376). Vinegar is used in the Yale recipes (Bottéro 1995: 161).

Animal-based foods

Foods derived from animals, whether domesticated or wild, were secondary to plant-based ones and featured more in the diet of the elite and as offerings to gods or the dead. Most domesticated animals were not kept with the primary aim of killing and eating them. High-maintenance cattle were kept primarily for their strength as draught animals, and sheep, and to a lesser extent goats, for their wool, although cows and goats were also milked (Charpin *et al.* 2004: 949–72). Fish were naturally abundant, served primarily as a food and were more widely eaten. Fresh milk and fresh milk products, as well as fresh meat and offal (whether of mammals, birds, fish or insects), did not keep well, so fresh products were higher status and preserved products the norm (Sasson 2004: 192–95, 206–09).

Mammals: milk and its products

This section, based on Stol (1993) and Stol (1993–97), mainly draws on evidence predating the Old Babylonian period. Fresh milk (*šizbum*) and cream (*lišdum*) did not keep well and were not part of the normal diet. Milk from cows and goats only was processed into sour milk. This was churned into buttermilk and butter (possibly *itirtum*), which was usually clarified into longer-lasting ghee (*ḫimētum*). Dried cheese made from sour milk or buttermilk could be stored and mixed as powder with water to make reconstituted sour milk. True cheese (*eqīdum*) was made by curdling milk, and *kisimmum*, a solid milk product, may be a true cheese. The Yale recipes include *šizbum*, *itirtum*, *ḫimētum* and *kisimmum* (Bottéro 1995: 161).

Mammals: meat, offal, fat and blood

Meat came from a wide range of animals (Potts 1997: 86–89; Curtis 2001: 233–34; Sasson 2004: 206–10). Sheep were the most common domesticated animal but goats, cattle and, to a lesser extent, pigs were also eaten. Wild animals, although these were sometimes at least semi-domesticated, included wild boar, hares (*arnabātum*), deer (*nālū*), stags (*ayalū*) and gazelle (*ṣabītum*). A type of mouse (*ušummum*) was a great delicacy (Charpin *et al.* 2004: 974; Englund 1995). The luxurious Yale recipes mainly use unspecified meat (*šīrum*) but include lamb broth (*mê puḫādi*), kid broth (*mê unīqi*), venison (stag) broth (*mê ayali*) and gazelle broth (*mê ṣabītim*) (Bottéro 1995: 36–38, 44). Recipe ingredients include offal, specifically blood (*dāmu*), fat (*lipûm*), *persu*-entrails, stomach (*karšu*) and spleen (*ṭulīmu*) (Bottéro 1995: 31, 46, 161). The sheep is probably the source of the fat and possibly all the offal.

Birds

The goose (*ūsum*) and the duck (*paspasu*) were domesticated and fed on grain; trapped wild birds included marsh birds, the francolin (?) (*tarru*) and the *amursānu*-pigeon (Unger 1957–71: 140; Dalley 2002: 81–82; Sasson 2004: 193). Many Old Babylonian bird names cannot be identified. We have references to duck eggs and eggs in general and a cluster of information about the ultimate egg served to the king of Mari, that of the ostrich (*lurmum*), which could be prepared using oil; eggs were also boiled (*CAD* P: 320–21; Sasson 2004: 187–88). Ten of the 35 Yale recipes probably concern bird dishes, including *amursānu*-pigeon broth (*mê amursānu*) and francolin (?) broth (*mê tarri*), and two of these recipes involve birds' gizzards (*šisūrrum*) and entrails (*esrū*) (Bottéro 1995: 48, 52, 73–80).

Fish

The Babylonians ate many different freshwater fish, including those raised in manmade ponds or moats, and some saltwater fish (*CAD* N/2: 338–39; Dalley 2002: 81–82; Charpin *et al.* 2004: 822–23; Sasson 2004: 194). At Mari fish is mentioned in general (*nūnum*) and by particular names, including carp (?) (*arsuppum*), large carp (*purādum*), eel-like fishes (*kuppûm*; *girītum*) and, most frequently, the highly prized *kamārum*-fish (Reynolds 2002: 222; Sasson 2004: 193–94). Many fish names remain unidentified.

Fish could be preserved by salting, drying, smoking or making the fermented sauce *šiqqum*, a household staple also made from locusts (Charpin *et al.* 2004: 823; *CAD* Š/3: 99–100). Four of the Yale recipes use this sauce (Bottéro 1995: 161).

Other animals

Locusts, or grasshoppers when in their migratory stage, were a relatively common foodstuff (types or stages: *erbûm*; *ṣanṣar* or *ṣarṣar*; *erḫizzum*; *ergilatum*) and at Mari they could be brought to the palace still alive in reed cages or already preserved (Sasson 2004: 193). They could be processed into a fermented sauce (*šiqqum*) (see Fish above). Honey from wild bees was a luxury item; (Curtis 2001: 240–41; Sasson 2004: 188; for the usual sweeteners see Fruits, above). People ate crayfish or shrimp (*ereb tâmti*; *erbum*) and there is evidence that turtles (*raqqum*; *šeleppûm*) were caught (Lion *et al.* 2000; Dalley 2002: 82; Charpin *et al.* 2004: 822–23; Sasson 2004: 194).

Fungi

Most of our information comes from Mari where the highly prized seasonal truffles (*kam'ātum* or *kam'û*) and the similar *gib'û* grew after rain and were sent to the palace by regional officials (Sasson 2004: 187).

Figure 11.1 Assyrian palace relief showing a fisherman
(courtesy of the Trustees of the British Museum).

Minerals

Given the climate, salt (*ṭābtum*) was an important element in the Babylonians' diet and was collected from salines, briny lakes or marshes, after natural evaporation (Potts 1997: 103–06). Salt was important for preserving meat and fish and this may lie behind the large quantities of kinds of salt coming into the palace in Mari (Bottéro 1980–83: 194–95; Sasson 2004: 195). Salt is an ingredient in 17 of the 35 Yale recipes (Bottéro 1995: 161).

Drinks

Water

Water (*mû*) was the basic drink but, although abundant, it was exploited in many different ways and establishing an accessible source of clean drinking water could be difficult (Van De Mieroop 1997: 158–61; Margueron 2004: 495–500). Water in the form of ice (*šurīpum*) was used to chill drinks in northern Mesopotamia (Margueron 2004: 493–94; Dalley 2002: 91–93).

Beer

'Beer is food' certainly applies to the many varieties of highly nutritious Babylonian barley beer (*šikarum*). Most of our sources for the brewing process predate the Old Babylonian period (Powell 1994: 93). Barley was moistened, allowed to sprout and dried, thereby forming malt (*buqlum*). The malt was ground and mixed with another malted product called *bappirum*, probably a powder rather than a bread. The resulting dry mixture (*isimmānum*) was, in effect, powdered beer and travellers carried it as part of their provisions. Beer was brewed by adding water and letting the liquid mash ferment. This resulted in dense beers that needed straining or filtering, long straws being one solution. Herbs, spices and sweet date syrup were among possible additions during brewing. Sumerian types of beer included golden beer, dark beer and ruby beer and people blended different beers (Powell 1994: 91–119; Stol 1995: 497; Sasson 2004: 191–92). Four of the Yale recipes include beer (Bottéro 1995: 161).

Wine

Wine (*karānum*) was imported into Babylonia from the north down the Euphrates and was a luxury item, much less widely drunk than local beers. Not surprisingly, wine is more in evidence at Mari, and Zimri-Lim, King of Mari, records that he sent ten jars of his favourite wine to Hammurabi, King of Babylon. As with beers, herbs and spices could be added to wines and different wines could be blended to suit personal taste (Dalley 2002: 90–91; Sasson 2004: 191–92, 206).

BIBLIOGRAPHY

Bottéro, J. 2004 *The Oldest Cuisine in the World: Cooking in Mesopotamia*. Chicago and London.
—— 1995 *Textes culinaires Mésopotamiens: Mesopotamian Culinary Texts*. Mesopotamian Civilizations 6. Winona Lake.
—— 1985 'The Cuisine of Ancient Mesopotamia' in *Biblical Archaeologist* 48, 36–47.
—— 1980–83 'Konservierung' in E. Weidner and W. von Soden (eds) *Reallexikon der Assyriologie und Vorderasiatischen Archäologie* 6, 191–97. Berlin and New York.
Charpin, D., Edzard, D.O. and Stol, M. 2004 *Mesopotamien: Die altbabylonische Zeit*. Orbis Biblicus et Orientalis 160/4. Fribourg and Göttingen.
Curtis, R.I. 2001 *Ancient Food Technology*. Technology and Change in History 5. Leiden, Boston and Cologne.
Dalley, S. 2002 *Mari and Karana: Two Old Babylonian Cities*. 2nd edition. Piscataway.
—— 1979 *A Catalogue of the Akkadian Cuneiform Tablets in the Collections of the Royal Scottish Museum, Edinburgh, with Copies of the Texts*. Art and Archaeology 2. Edinburgh.
Dossin, G. 1933 *Lettres de la première dynastie babylonienne*. Musée du Louvre, Département des Antiquités Orientales, Textes cunéiformes 17. Paris.
Ellis, R.S. 1993–97 'Mühle. B. Archäologisch' in D.O. Edzard (ed.) *Reallexikon der Assyriologie und Vorderasiatischen Archäologie* 8, 401–04. Berlin and New York.
Englund, R.K. 1995 'There's a Rat in my Soup!' in *Altorientalische Forschungen* 22, 37–55.
Foster, B.R. 2005 *Before the Muses: An Anthology of Akkadian Literature*. 3rd edition. Bethesda.
Frankena, R. 1974 *Briefe aus dem Berliner Museum*. Altbabylonische Briefe in Umschrift und Übersetzung 6. Leiden.
George, A.R. 2003 *The Babylonian Gilgamesh Epic*. Oxford.
Lambert, W.G. 1960 *Babylonian Wisdom Literature*. Oxford.

Lion, B., Michel, C. and Noël, P. 2000 'Les crevettes dans la documentation du Proche-Orient Ancient' *Journal of Cuneiform Studies* 52: 55–60.

Margueron, J.-C. 2004 *Mari: Métropole de l'Euphrate au IIIe et au début du IIe millénaire av. J.-C.* Paris.

Mayer, W.R. and Sallaberger, W. 2003 'Opfer.A. I' in D.O. Edzard (ed.) *Reallexikon der Assyriologie und Vorderasiatischen Archäologie* 10 1/2, 93–102. Berlin and New York.

Miglus, P.A. 2003 'Ofen' in D.O. Edzard (ed.) *Reallexikon der Assyriologie und Vorderasiatischen Archäologie* 10 1/2, 39–42. Berlin and New York.

Milano, L. 2004 'Food and Identity in Mesopotamia: A New Look at the Aluzinnu's Recipes' in C. Grottanelli and L. Milano (eds) *Food and Identity in the Ancient World*. History of the Ancient Near East, Studies 9, 243–56. Padua.

—— 1993–97a 'Mehl' in D.O. Edzard (ed.) *Reallexikon der Assyriologie und Vorderasiatischen Archäologie* 8, 22–31. Berlin and New York.

—— 1993–97b 'Mühle. A. I. In Mesopotamien' in D.O. Edzard (ed.) *Reallexikon der Assyriologie und Vorderasiatischen Archäologie* 8, 393–400. Berlin and New York.

Nesbitt, M. 2003 'Obst und Gemüse (Fruits and Vegetables). B. Archäobotanisch' in D.O. Edzard (ed.) *Reallexikon der Assyriologie und Vorderasiatischen Archäologie* 10 1/2, 26–30. Berlin and New York.

—— and Postgate, J.N. 2001 'Nuss und Verwandtes (nuts)' in D.O. Edzard (ed.) *Reallexikon der Assyriologie und Vorderasiatischen Archäologie* 9 7/8, 633–35. Berlin and New York.

Parrot, A. 1958 *Le Palais: Architecture*. Mission archéologique de Mari. Paris.

Postgate, J.N. 1992 *Early Mesopotamia: Society and Economy at the Dawn of History*. London and New York.

Potts, D.T. 1997 *Mesopotamian Civilization: The Material Foundations*. London.

Powell, M.A. 2003 'Obst und Gemüse (Fruits and Vegetables). A. I.' in D.O. Edzard (ed.) *Reallexikon der Assyriologie und Vorderasiatischen Archäologie* 10 1/2, 13–22. Berlin and New York.

—— 1998 'Review of J. Bottéro "Textes culinaires Mésopotamiens: Mesopotamian Culinary Texts"' in *Journal of the American Oriental Society* 118, 290–91.

—— 1994 'Metron Ariston: Measure as a Tool for Studying Beer in Ancient Mesopotamia' in L. Milano (ed.) *Drinking in Ancient Societies: History and Culture of Drinks in the Ancient Near East*. History of the Ancient Near East, Studies 6, 91–119. Padua.

—— 1991 'Epistemology and Sumerian Agriculture: The Strange Case of Sesame and Linseed' in *Aula Orientalis* 9, 155–64.

Ranke, H. 1906 *Babylonian Legal and Business Documents from the Time of the First Dynasty of Babylon Chiefly from Sippar*. The Babylonian Expedition of the University of Philadelphia Series A: Cuneiform Texts 6/1. Philadelphia.

Reiner, E. 1974 *The Series ḪAR-ra = ḫubullu Tablets XX–XXIV*. Materials for the Sumerian Lexicon 11. Rome.

Reynolds, F.S. 2002 'Describing the Body of a God' in C. Wunsch (ed.) *Mining the Archives: Festschrift for Christopher Walker on the Occasion of His 60th Birthday*, 215–27. Dresden.

Roth, M.T. 1997 *Law Collections from Mesopotamia and Asia Minor*. Society of Biblical Literature, Writings from the Ancient World 6. 2nd edition. Atlanta.

Sasson, J.M. 2004 'The King's Table: Food and Fealty in Old Babylonian Mari' in C. Grottanelli and L. Milano (eds) *Food and Identity in the Ancient World*. History of the Ancient Near East, Studies 9, 179–215. Padua.

Scheil, V. 1927 'Carptim' in *Revue d'assyriologie* 24, 31–48.

Schorr, M. 1913 *Urkunden des Altbabylonischen Zivil- und Prozessrechts*. Vorderasiatische Bibliothek 5. Leipzig.

Schroeder, O. 1917 *Altbabylonische Briefe*. Vorderasiatische Schriftdenkmäler 16. Leipzig.

Seidl, U. 2003 'Opfer. B.I.' in D.O. Edzard (ed.) *Reallexikon der Assyriologie und Vorderasiatischen Archäologie* 10 1/2, 102–06. Berlin and New York.

Stol, M. 2003 'Öl, Ölbaum. A' in D.O. Edzard (ed.) *Reallexikon der Assyriologie und Vorderasiatischen Archäologie* 10 1/2, 32–33. Berlin and New York.

—— 1993–97 'Milch(produkte). A' in D.O. Edzard (ed.) *Reallexikon der Assyriologie und Vorderasiatischen Archäologie* 8, 189–201. Berlin and New York.

—— 1995 'Private Life in Ancient Mesopotamia' in J.M. Sasson (ed.) *Civilizations of the Ancient Near East*, 485–501. New York.

—— 1993 'Milk, Butter, and Cheese' in *Bulletin on Sumerian Agriculture* 7: 99–113.

Unger, E. 1957–71 'Gans' in E. Weidner and W. von Soden (eds) *Reallexikon der Assyriologie und Vorderasiatischen Archäologie* 3, 140. Berlin.

Van De Mieroop, M. 1997 *The Ancient Mesopotamian City*. Oxford.

Van Dijk, J., Goetze, A. and Hussey, M.I. 1985 *Early Mesopotamian Incantations and Rituals*. Yale Oriental Series: Babylonian Texts 11. New Haven, CT and London.

Van Dijk, J.J.A. 1953 *La Sagesse Suméro-accadienne*. Leiden.

Woolley, C.L. and Mallowan, M. 1976 *The Old Babylonian Period*. Ur Excavations 7. London.

PART III

ECONOMIC LIFE

———•◆•———

CHAPTER TWELVE

ECONOMY OF ANCIENT MESOPOTAMIA

A general outline

——·◆·——

Johannes Renger

Ancient Mesopotamia's economy was based on agriculture with integrated animal husbandry. Manufacture and the production of crafted goods were of supplementary importance. For lack of own resources, goods and materials necessary for the reproduction of the society as a whole had to be obtained through long-distance trade from the outside world. This comprised tin and copper for the making of bronze, iron, gold and silver for prestige articles, as well as for payments or exchange, timber for use in the construction of ostentatious public buildings (temples and palaces), semi-precious and other stones for building and art purposes. The digging of canals and the maintenance of an extensive irrigation system that encompassed the entire alluvial plain, the building of numerous public buildings and structures, the support of a complex administration and an army, were only possible thanks to the surplus production of agriculture and animal husbandry.

Knowledge of the processes and institutions that gave structure to the economy of ancient Mesopotamia is based on about 200,000 published legal and administrative documents, letters and collections of laws. The earliest administrative documents date to around 3200 BC, the latest to the Hellenistic and Arsacid periods (third century BC and later). In addition, archaeological artefacts permit the reconstruction of the material culture of ancient Mesopotamia and add to our perception of economic facts.

ECONOMIC THEORIES AND PREMISES

The nature of an ancient economy such as that of ancient Mesopotamia has been the subject of theoretical discussion in which two opposing views play a role: Karl Polanyi, the American economic historian, has argued for a fundamental difference between modern economies governed by price-fixing markets and traditional and non-industrialized, ancient as well as medieval economies, where the social embeddedness of the economy determines economic activities, behaviour and motivation. Polanyi maintains that such difference requires an adequate analytical approach to understand the specific nature of ancient economies. For him, it is inappropriate to understand pre-modern economies on the basis of an analytical framework derived from the experience with an economy determined by price-fixing markets. Polanyi's position stands in contrast to the views held by many historians of ancient Mesopotamia who – without regarding the theoretical implications – apply unconsciously their experiences with today's market-oriented economy to ancient economies (Stol 2004: 904–909).

Several statements made by Polanyi to substantiate his theory are no longer tenable (Renger 1984). Nevertheless, the question remains whether such arguments affect his entire theory concerning marketless trading, modes of exchange, the ways the populace acquires its daily necessities or, more generally, the character of ancient economies. This appears not to be the case. One also has to reckon that quite a number of scholars of different theoretical and factual orientation have emphatically insisted on the difference between ancient or premodern economies and modern economies – some of them long before, others after Polanyi's theory was subject to dispute. And they have shed doubt on economic theories that conceive and analyse ancient economies as well as peasant economies in terms of neo-classical market-oriented economic theory (Renger 1994b). One should just mention Thorstein Veblen (1899) and Siegfried Morenz (1969) applying Veblen's ideas to the economy of Ancient Egypt, Victor Kula (1976) offering an explanation of the feudal economy in Poland in the seventeenth and eighteenth centuries, disregarding neo-classical market theories. Based on his experience in developing countries, Chris Gregory (1982), a representative of traditional political economic theory, also argued in this direction. Moses Finley (1985) explained the economy of Ancient Greece in Polanyian terms. Douglas C. North (1981), the Nobel laureate, who basically adheres to positions of neo-classical economic analysis, concedes that several phenomena of ancient economies defy an explanation in neo-classical terms. Nor should one forget Wallerstein, Godelier or Sahlins.

Of interest in the present context is the impact Polanyi has had on the study and conception of the economy of ancient Mesopotamia. Under A. L. Oppenheim's direction, Sweet wrote his Chicago dissertation (1968) 'On Prices, Moneys, and Money Uses in the Old Babylonian Period'. As indicated not only by the title but also *expressis verbis* in the introduction, the dissertation was a case study with respect to Polanyi's theories. Oppenheim, himself, refers approvingly to Polanyi, although he is more cautious regarding the non-existence of markets all over the Ancient Near East when he states that 'one gains the impression that the institution of the market was at home outside Mesopotamia, in Elam, and in Anatolia . . . In Mesopotamia it seems to represent a late development . . . and was clearly of limited and marginal importance' (Oppenheim 1977: 129). The central concerns of Polanyi were what he termed marketless trading, administered trade and the role of ports-of-trade. For him the overland trade of Assyrian merchants from Assur with Cappadocia (twentieth–eighteenth centuries BC) constituted a striking example of administered trade. Klaas Veenhof (1972) could falsify Polanyi's assumptions regarding the Old Assyrian trade with Cappadocia as administered trade on the basis of a more intimate knowledge of the primary sources, now more plentiful than at the time when Polanyi formulated his theses. It was only in the 1980s that Polanyi's theories became an issue for those studying the Mesopotamian economy. Some were approving, others sceptical or even extremely critical[1] towards Polanyi's tenets. Vargyas (1987) argues from a viewpoint that is basically determined by neo-classical theory and without taking cognicance of the critique voiced also by economists, that a different approach is needed when analysing premodern economies. The critique of Polanyi's tenets by Gledhill and Larsen (1982) neglects the analytical value of Polanyi's paradigm regarding the concept of 'embeddedness', as well as his methodological position that premodern economies should be studied with analytical tools other than those derived from the study of modern, market-oriented economies. A view different from that offered by Gledhill and Larsen seems possible by taking into account the dialectical relationship between the 'state' and the individual entrepreneur or trader. Especially Larsen's emphasis on private business appears to be perceived too much from the vantage point of the Old Assyrian traders who clearly represent an exceptional case that has to be seen against the background of the oligarchic constitution of the Old Assyrian state. In fact, the Old Assyrian trade represents a striking example for the dependence of economic organization on the societal structures into which it is embedded.

On the other hand, scholars in economic anthropology as well as in Ancient Near Eastern studies have been influenced by Polanyi's ideas and have developed them further on the basis of a plethora of written documentation not available to Polanyi in the early 1950s.[2]

Polanyi emphasized different forms determining the access to the daily necessities of life – reciprocity, redistribution and market exchange. It has become necessary, however, to investigate and describe also other forms of economic organization and processes that are characteristic for the economy of ancient Mesopotamia. Most often, the term 'palace economy' is being used. It describes a form of economy organized by, and centred around, institutional households. It is characteristic for societies where the economy is organized in an autocratic-monarchic state and in which a considerable part, or even the entire, population are dependent on institutional households (temple, palace). Such dependency can have different forms – either by direct and total integration as dependent labourers into such household(s) or indirect dependency in the form of tributary or service obligations towards the palace.

A somewhat different perception of the ancient Mesopotamian economy emphasizes the importance and more decisive role of communal, individual or private economic activities throughout the entire history of ancient Mesopotamia, clearly set apart from the economic activities of the great institutional households. Which form of non-institutional economy is dominant depends on the societal organization at a given time and in a given ecological environment. This raises the question of how persons operating in economic independence from the palace and the ruler related to the palace and the ruler, given that in any autocratic-monarchic society the populace as a whole is regarded as subject to the king. This could be answered in reference to the general patrimonial system.

FORMS OF ECONOMIC ORGANIZATION

It is a plausible assumption that in the late fifth and partly in the fourth millennium agricultural production in lower Mesopotamia was based on common property of the arable land by village communities. Work connected with irrigation installations required cooperation and reciprocal help. The process of the integration of rural communities into the patrimonial system took place over a long time. The growth of the centrally organized irrigation networks led to a rapid integration of the rural population into institutional households. An additional factor is a concomitant process of social stratification, often accelerated by natural causes (bad harvest, diseases among livestock) which led to the impoverishment of large segments of the population and eventually resulted in indebtedness and loss of control over their agricultural holdings (Renger 1995b, 304–308). This could mean that more or less all arable land and therefore the entire agricultural production came under institutional control. As a consequence the dominant mode of production was determined by large urban institutional households (*oikoi*). Once this stage was reached there remained little room for societal and economic structures outside the palace.

Oikos economy during the fourth and third millennia

The *oikos* economy as an ideal-typical concept of economic organization was first described by Karl Rodbertus, later by Karl Bücher and Max Weber. Eventually the *oikos* concept was applied to ancient Mesopotamia by Gelb (1979) and most succinctly by Grégoire (1981; 1992). Oppenheim (1977: 95) speaks of temple and palace as the 'great organisations' which control most of the means of production, i.e. the arable land. The *oikos* economy was the dominant economic organization in Mesopotamia during the later part of the fourth and the third millennia. It has two major characteristics. First, the patrimonial household (*oikos*) of the ruler is identical in institutional as well as in spatial terms with the 'state'. Integrated into it is more or less the entire population which provides the necessary labour needed for the reproduction of the state and its institutions. Second, these self-sufficient households produce everything necessary, except for a few strategic needs such as metal or prestige goods that must be obtained from the outside. Characteristic for the *oikos* economy is the redistributive mode of production by which the results of collective labour in agricultural and non-agricultural activities are appropriated by a central authority, i.e. the ruler, and subsequently redistributed among the producers, i.e. the entire populace of the state – we thus speak of a redistributive *oikos* economy.

Redistribution has the form of daily or monthly rations in kind, supplemented for certain groups of the labour force and the administrative personnel by the assignment of small plots of fields. Together with rations, they assure the subsistence needs of a person or family. In this type of redistributive economy, individual property on arable land does not play any decisive economic role.

During the earlier parts of the third millennium BC, the household (*oikos*) of the ruler of small territorial entities is, in organizational and functional terms, less complex or differentiated than during the Third Dynasty of Ur. The household of the ruler of the Ur III state now encompasses the entire realm and the patrimonial household of the ruler is characterized by five different types of *oikoi* (Grégoire 1992: 323f.) They are:

- Agricultural domains of 50 to 200 hectares each (Renger 1995b, 285) managed by the temples but also by palace-dependent households. The temple domains were administered by a substantial managerial personnel, usually organized in three tiers.
- Workshops e.g. for textile production, grain processing, or for producing crafted goods, all organized as *ergasteria* (workhouses) managed by the palace, sometimes employing 1,000 or more male and female workers.
- Distribution households.
- Households supporting the administrative activities of the state.[3]

- Individual households of the ruler, members of the royal family, high priests and the highest officials of the realm for their personal support.

The early second millennium: the emergence of the tributary economy

External and internal factors, such as the influx of tribal groups, military attacks from Elam, political rivalries, over-extension of the *oikos* system, and salinization in the south of Babylonia, led to significant political and socio-economic changes during the twentieth century BC. As a result, the household or *oikos* system of the third millennium gradually lost its predominance as a decisive economic factor. It was replaced by a system in which a large proportion of economic activities that hitherto took place within large institutional households were assigned to individuals farming small plots of land, or to entrepreneurs. This concerned activities such as large-scale cereal production, date palm cultivation, animal husbandry, as well as the exploration of natural resources (fishing, fowling, harvesting of reed, brickmaking). It also comprised services such as the collection of dues and revenues, the transportation of agricultural goods, storage of cereals, long-distance trade, as a kind of franchise often labelled 'enterprise of the palace' (German: *Palastgeschäft*). Since the entrepreneur had to pay the palace in kind or in silver, this is known as tributary economy (Renger 2000a). Most of the entrepreneurs were members of the administrative elite. The risk of the enterprise was carried by the entrepreneur. This meant that, more often than not, they were not able to deliver the promised service, due to various factors, such as bad harvests, diseases among herds. Since the palace was dependent upon the services of the entrepreneurs, the accrued debt could be remitted by so-called edicts (Renger 2000b).

Agricultural production was now largely in the hands of individuals. As before they were still subjects of the ruler, but instead of daily or monthly rations in kind they were given a house, an orchard, and fields[4] for their subsistence in exchange for rendering various types of corvée or to pay rental dues in kind.[5] Besides subsistence and rental fields assigned to individuals by the palace, privately held property of arable land also existed in certain parts of Babylonia from the nineteenth to the seventeenth century BC. However, it is not possible to quantify the relationship between both types of land holdings (Renger 1995b).

Many aspects of societal and political organization find their plausible explanation only when one considers the dominant role played by the *oikos* as well as the tributary economies during certain periods of Mesopotamian history (Renger 2000b).

Cereal agriculture and date palm cultivation

From early in the fourth millennium onwards, agriculture attained extraordinary accomplishments, not so much because of technological advances but through highly developed managerial means, such as the highly effective mobilization of human labour. Agronomic skills and the optimal use of animal labour by employing draught animals (oxen) trained to work in teams of four, were major factors in handling agricultural work on large tracts of land on the institutional domains.[6] Babylonian cereal agriculture was barley monoculture. Since no natural fertilizer was used, the fertility of fields was maintained by a rigid fallow system. The hazards of salinization caused by artificial irrigation were met by leaching and drainage. Unparalleled in antiquity is the high seed–yield ratio of 1 : 16 up to 1 : 24 and yields of roughly 750 kilograms per hectare.[7] Second to cereal agriculture was date palm cultivation.

Animal husbandry

Typical of Mesopotamian animal husbandry was the herding of sheep and – to a lesser degree – goats. Sheep provided wool for high-quality textile production, the main Mesopotamian staple for trade with the outside world. Cattle served in Mesopotamia mainly as plough animals. Besides sheep, goats and cattle, donkeys and mules were important for transport needs, especially for caravans in long-distance trade. Pigs, ducks and geese were kept among individual households. Animal husbandry, with its very high levels of breeding and herding, was interdependent with agricultural production.[8] However, the need for pasture also competed for available land where herding took place in more densely inhabited and agricultural areas. Especially cattle made great demands for green pasture, since unlike sheep and goat they could not find sufficient food in the steppe areas (Renger 1994a).

Reciprocity and redistribution

While the modes of allocation or the manners of acquisition of the daily necessities of life took specific forms in Mesopotamia they gave rise to considerable debate between economic anthropologists, economic historians and historians of the Ancient Near East. For Polanyi (1977: 35f.) the difference between a premodern and a modern, capitalist, market-oriented economy becomes especially evident with regard to particular modes of exchange. Reciprocity and redistribution were rather easily accepted even by Near Eastern scholars adhering to economic concepts that apply the market principle to economic analysis. They do so despite the fact that reciprocity and redistribution are essential parts of Polanyi's concept of marketless trading, a concept that denies the existence of markets in ancient societies and their economies. It should be noted, however, that Polanyi does not totally deny the existence of trading, of exchange mechanisms that he called market substitutes and market elements (1977: 125f.). But his basic assumption remains valid that the exchange of goods (and services) takes place predominantly under reciprocal or redistributional conditions and not necessarily in the form of market exchange governed by a supply-demand-price mechanism.

The redistributive nature of Mesopotamian society and economy is most obvious in the fourth and third millennia BC but the reciprocal modes of exchange are much more difficult to detect in the written records of this period. Official and private letters from the eighteenth to seventeenth centuries BC, however, attest such reciprocal exchange (Renger 1984) which opens the possibility that it also existed in earlier periods. Moreover, considering the general context of these letters it becomes obvious that reciprocity was operative only in parts, in segments of society. Other segments were determined by redistribution. Reciprocity and redistribution as the primary modes of exchange in ancient Mesopotamia should, therefore, not be seen in an evolutionary context since they existed side by side during the entire history of

Mesopotamia. Besides redistributive elements we encounter tributary elements – agricultural land assigned for services rendered or on condition that part of the yield be given to the palace.

Thus, one has to reckon with two separate – although interacting – economic spheres (Renger 1990a). One is based on subsistence agriculture performed on small lots, characterized by life in small villages and hamlets of the Babylonian countryside. Reciprocal exchange and traditional solidarity are the dominant principles governing social and economic relations in the rural sphere. The other is determined by the economic organization of the large institutional households and its redistributive system and is characteristic of the Mesopotamian urban society. Nevertheless, reciprocal modes of exchange also play a role in the urban sphere, as is the case of the redistributive system infringing on the rural sphere.

Market exchange

For Polanyi, market exchange is the latest stage in his sequence of modes of exchange. However, before one assumes the existence of market exchange as a decisive economic factor for ancient economies, one should clarify the role of market exchange (Renger 1993) since the abstract term 'market' denotes a complex process relating to the exchange of goods and services – in short, the three-fold relations between supply, demand and resulting price (Wallerstein 1990). As for ancient Mesopotamia: was there enough demand for a sizeable market exchange? A number of questions need to be asked. Were there institutionalized markets on a periodical basis, or markets of an irregular yet institutionalized nature? Was it determined by the type of goods offered or determined by its function, such as to serve the allocation of daily necessities or to fulfil other expectations? When discussing the need for market exchange, one has to ask: who were the participants; who would supply a market with what kind and amounts of goods; with what kind of money would recipients pay and where would the money come from; to what quantitative degree would such a market take care of the dietary requirements of the populace; and what other means existed to sustain a person's livelihood, i.e. subsystems (rations, reciprocal exchange) and what would such system cover (Renger 1984)?

Furthermore, one has to ask whether and in what manner market exchange was possible and necessary to provide for the livelihood of the populace. In the redistributive era of the fourth and third millennia, economy and society were organized as the *oikos* of the patrimonial ruler. All agricultural land was controlled by the great institutional households of that time into which practically the entire population was integrated and provisioned through a redistributive ration system. Since the second millennium, subsistence agriculture on family-farmed plots produced everything needed, just about securing the livelihood of the producers. Practically no marketable surplus was left to supply a market in the true sense, there was no need to provision oneself via a market. Producing for one's own needs limits demand, total or near total consumption of one's production limits supply (Renger 1993: 101). Besides the need to satisfy the basic nutritional necessities, the necessity to provide for one's clothing – this being part of the rations in redistributive systems – and shelter, there exists a need for tools and utensils. Utensils such as agricultural tools were either produced within individual households or, like pottery, in a cooperative way within a village. Only tools and utensils made from metal could be obtained from outside by those who could afford them, although it is by no means clear to what extent metal tools were actually used in individual rural households. The great institutional households, however, relied on production of pottery, utensils and tools within their own workshops (Steinkeller 1996).

The general principle of the institutional economy of the fourth and third millennia BC was self-sufficiency. Only very few products had to be obtained from outside Mesopotamia through long-distance trade organized by the institutional households and operated by mercantile agents (entrepreneurs) who were dependent members of these households. Goods and objects available within Mesopotamia, such as plough animals, donkeys, sheep and goats, and also cereals, which were not available or in short supply in a particular institutional household, were acquired through institutional exchange between these households. Some of the equivalent for the goods received was given in silver.

Economic growth

The important question of economic growth in ancient Mesopotamian economy has, so far, not been the subject of much discussion. Several factors were decisive in letting economic growth remain at, or near, a level of zero per cent. Once basic technological breakthroughs in metallurgy, pottery and textile production, as well as in building and agricultural techniques and the organization of labour, had been achieved (fifth–fourth millennia BC), no further substantial developments that could have generated a significant quantitative productive output can be observed for the following periods of Mesopotamian history.

The agricultural area was limited because the water supply for irrigation from the Euphrates was limited. This resulted in limited population growth which, in turn, had repercussions for the amount of manpower available for production. A further delimiting factor was the competition for the use of land between animal husbandry and cereal production. Natural disasters and man-made factors, such as warfare and intruding nomads, limited growth in the short term, while salinization of the arable land caused by irrigation and a climatic change around 1200 BC affected long-term development.

Economic growth also depends on available sources of energy and of material resources. For Mesopotamia, they were only sufficient to support the economic *status quo*, but not enough to sustain a measurable growth. The main sources of energy for agricultural work were human labour and animal power. For transportation purposes three sources of energy existed: man power (carriers, gangs for towing boats); animal power (plough-oxen, donkeys for overland trade); water(ways) as a means to move boats with bulky goods and the open sea by ships taking advantage of wind.

Of fundamental importance for sustaining an economy, besides a sufficient energy input and demographic factors, is the availability of natural resources. Foremost for an agrarian economy, they are cultivable soil, water (either rain or irrigation water), and a suitable climate, supplemented by additional nutritional natural resources (fish, fowl, game and anything not produced as agricultural crops). One of the basic natural resources in ancient Mesopotamia was clay. It was used as the main building material and for the production and the manufacture of ceramics and utensils (e.g. clay sickles for use in harvesting).

The role of money, credit and surplus

Silver money played a limited role in the economy of ancient Mesopotamia. Credit as a monetary instrument enabling investment for productive purposes is absent. Pierro Scraffa's (1960) theory of producing commodities by means of commodities has been applied to the economy of Ur III Mesopotamia by Kurz (2000: 101–104). He speaks of a 'corn-model' since the basic commodity in Mesopotamia was corn (barley). In respect to this model, two different situations regarding agricultural productivity have to be considered. The first concerns subsistence economy that just permits the material reproduction of those producing the agricultural product, thus sustaining a society as a whole. Subsistence economy of this type applies to agricultural regimes with a seed–yield ratio of 1:2 to approximately 1:6. A yield on such low levels leaves practically nothing as a surplus after accounting for next year's seed and the consumptive needs of those working the land. In contrast, Mesopotamian agrarian economy produced seed–yield ratios ranging from 1:16 to about 1:24 and thus achieved a substantial surplus whose exact amount may vary according to actual harvest figures and the demographic situation (Renger 1994a). Such surplus was produced by only part of the populace. Thus only a part of the workforce, including managerial personnel, produced more than was needed for their reproduction. The surplus could therefore be used to feed other segments of society, for instance large numbers of workers in weaving establishments. They produced, in a very time-consuming process, textiles of extraordinary quality which were not only used for internal prestige purposes but also as a very much sought-after export commodity. In exchange, other luxury goods, but also commodities such as silver, gold or strategic goods such as copper and tin for bronze production, or timber were brought back to Mesopotamia. This surplus generated by production of commodities (textiles) by means of commodities (corn/barley) served exclusively ostentatious and prestige purposes. It was not 'invested' to generate economic surplus.

Despite its enormous achievements in quantitative as well as qualitative terms the economy of ancient Mesopotamia was, for inherent and systemic reasons, a stagnant economy, an economy without measurable growth. It provided just for the daily requirements of the majority of the populace and plenty for the elite.

NOTES

1   Silver 1985, see the critique in Renger 1994b refuting emphatically Silver's assumptions.
2   Janssen, 1975; Liverani, 1990: 19–21; Renger 1994b; Robertson 1993; Zaccagnini 1983.
3   E.g. the messenger household é.sukkal headed by the sukkal-maḫ.
4   Minimum size ca. 6 ha.
5   This system has been labelled in Mesopotamian terms as *ilku*.
6   Renger 1990b: animals.
7   Classical Attica 1:7; Apulia 1:10, medieval central Europe 1:3.
8   The organization of animal husbandry shows a very complex system of herding. Documents from the beginning of the third millennium through the eighteenth century BC attest expected goals for the managers of a flock (Kraus 1966). They were obliged to report a growth rate of a herd of 80 animals per 100 mother sheep (Renger in Hrouda: 190–193; Renger 1991; for cattle (*Rinder*) Nissen 1990: 139–146). Whenever a herdsman had a surplus, the animals went into his own, private herd.

BIBLIOGRAPHY

Finley, M.I. 1985 *The Ancient Economy*. Berkeley and Los Angeles, University of California Press.

Gelb, I.J. 1979 'Household and Family in Early Mesopotamia', in: E. Lipinski (ed.), *State and Temple Economy in the Ancient Near East* I, 1–97. Leuven, Departement Orientalistiek.

Gledhill, J. and Larsen, M.T. 1982 'The Polanyi Paradigm and a Dynamic Analysis of Archaic States', in: C. Renfrew *et al.* (eds), *Theory and Explanation in Archaeology*, 197–230. New York, San Francisco, London, Academic Press.

Grégoire, J.-P. 1981 'L'origine et le développement de la civilisation mésopotamienne', in: C.-H. Breteau *et al.*(eds), *Production, Pouvoir et Parenté dans le monde méditerranéen*, 27–101. Paris, P. Geuthner.

——— 1992 'Les grandes unités de transformation des céréales: l'exemple des minoteries de la Mésopotamie du Sud à la fin du IIIe millénaire avant notre ère', in P.Ch. Anderson (ed.), *Préhistoire de l'Agriculture: Nouvelles Approches Expérimentales et Ethnographiques* (= Monographie du CRA no. 6, édition CNRS, Paris), 321–339.

Gregory, Chris A. 1982 *Gifts and Commodities – Studies in Political Economy*. New York, San Francisco, London, Academic Press.

Janssen, J.J. 1988 'Prices and Wages in Ancient Egypt', in: *Altorientalische Forschungen* 15 (Berlin, Akademieverlag) 10–23.

Kula, W. 1976 *An Economic Theory of the Feudal System – Towards a Model of the Polish Economy 1500–1800*. London, NLB.

Kurz, H.D. 2000 'Das Kornmodell und seine Folgen', in: S. Ryll and A. Yenal (eds), *Politik und Oekonomie. Problemsicht aus klassischer, neo- und neuklassischer Perspektive*. FS G. Huber (Marburg, Metropolis Verlag) 99–117.

Liverani, M. 1990 *Prestige and Interest*. Padua, sargon srl.

Moeller, A. 2004 'Zur Aktualitaet der Wirtschaftsanthropologie Karl Polanyis', in R. Rollinger and C. Ulf (eds), *Commerce and Monetary Systems in the Ancient World*, 218–239. Wiesbaden, Franz Steiner Verlag.

Morenz, S. 1969 *Prestige-Wirtschaft im alten Ägypten*. Munich, Verlag der Bayerischen Akademie der Wissenschaften.

North, D.C. 1981 *Structure and Change in Economic History*. New York and London, W.W. Norton & Comp.

Oppenheim, A.L. 1972 *Ancient Mesopotamia – Portrait of a Dead Civilization*. Chicago, IL, University of Chicago Press.

Polanyi, K. 1977 *The Livelihood of Man*. New York, San Francisco, London, Academic Press.

Renger, J. 1984 'Patterns of Non-institutional Trade and Non-commercial Exchange in Ancient Mesopotamia at the Beginning of the Second Millennium BC', in: A. Archi (ed.), *Circulation of Goods in Non-Palatial Context in the Ancient Near East*, 31–123. Rome, Edizioni dell'Ateneo.

——— 1986 'Überlegungen zur räumlichen Ausdehnung des Staates Ebla an Hand der agrarischen und viehwirtschaftlichen Gegebenheiten', *Istituto Universario Orientale, Napoli, Series Minor* 27, 293–311.

——— 1990a 'Different Economic Spheres in the Urban Economy of Ancient Mesopotamia – Traditional Solidarity, Redistribution and Market Elements as the Means of Access to the Necessities of Life', in: E. Aerts and H. Klengel (eds), *The Town as Regional Economic Centre in the Ancient Near East*, 20–28. Leuven, Leuven University Press.

——— 1990b 'Report on the Implications of Employing Draught Animals', in: *Irrigation and Cultivation in Mesopotamia*, Part II (Bulletin on Sumerian Agriculture 5 (Cambridge, England, Sumerian Agriculture Group, Faculty of Oriental Studies)), 267–279.

——— 1993 'Formen des Zugangs zu den lebensnotwendigen Gütern: Die Austauschverhältnisse in der altbabylonischen Zeit', *Altorientalische Forschungen* 20 (Berlin Akademieverlag), 87–114.

—— 1994a 'Landwirtschaftliche Nutzfläche, Einwohnerzahlen und Herdengröße', in: *FS Léon de Meyer*, 251–253. Leuven, Peeters.

—— 1994b 'On Economic Structures in Ancient Mesopotamia', *Orientalia NS* 63, 157–208. Rome, Pontifical Biblical Institute.

——1995a 'Subsistenzproduktion und redistributive Palastwirtschaft: Wo bleibt die Nische für das Geld?', in: W. Schelkle, M. Nitsch (eds), *Rätsel Geld – Annäherungen aus ökonomischer, soziologischer und historischer Sicht*, 271–324. Marburg, Metropolis Verlag.

—— 1995b 'Institutional, Communal, and Individual Ownership or Possession of Arable Land in Ancient Mesopotamia', in: *Chicago-Kent Law Review* 71, 269–319. Chicago, Chicago-Kent Law School.

—— 2000a 'Das Palastgeschäft in der altbabylonische Zeit', in: A.C.V.M. Bongenaar (ed.), *Interdependency of Institutions and Private Entrepreneurs*, 153–183. Leiden, Nederlands Instituut voor het Nabije Oosten.

—— 2000b 'Royal Edicts of the Old Babylonian Period', in: M. Hudson and M. Van De Mieroop (eds), *Debt and Economic Renewal in the Ancient Near East*, 139–162. Bethesda, MD, CDL Press.

Robertson, J.F. 1993 'On Profit-seeking, Market Orientation, and Mentality in the "Ancient Near East"', in *Journal of the American Oriental Society* 113, 437–443.

Sahlins, M. 1972 *Stone Age Economics*. Chicago, IL, Aldine & Athertone.

Saller, R. 2002 'Framing the Debate over Growth in the Ancient Economy', in W. Scheidel and S. von Reden, *The Ancient Economy*, 251–269. Edinburgh, Edinburgh University Press.

Scraffa, P. 1960 *Warenproduktion mittels Waren* (engl. Production of Commodities by Means of Commodities). Frankfurt/Main, Suhrkampverlag.

Sigrist, M. 1992 *Drehem*. Bethesda, MD, CDL Press.

Silver, M. 1985 *Economic Structures of the Ancient Near East*. London and Sidney, Croom Helm.

Steinkeller, P. 1996 'The Organisation of Crafts in the Third Millennium Babylonia: The Case of Potters', *Altorientalische Forschungen* 23 (Berlin, Akademieverlag), 232–253.

Stol, M. 2004 'Wirtschaft und Gesellschaft in altbabylonischer Zeit', in P. Attinger *et al.* (eds) *Mesopotamien. Die altbabylonische Zeit*, 643–975. Universitätsverlag Freiburg Schweiz & Vandehoek & Rupprecht, Göttingen.

Sweet, R.F.G. 1968 *On Prices, Moneys, and Money Uses in the Old Babylonian Period.* Chicago, Chicago University Dissertation.

Vargyas, P. 1987 'The Problem of Private Economy in the Ancient Near East', *Bibliotheca Orientalis* 44, 376–385. Leiden, E.J. Brill.

Veblen, Th. 1899 *The Theory of the Leisure Class – An Economic Study of Institutions*. New York, Kelley.

Veenhof, K.R. 1972 *Aspects of Old Assyrian Trade and its Terminology*. Leiden, E.J. Brill.

Wallerstein, I. 1990 'Capitalist Markets: Theory and Reality'. Paper read at the Xth International Congress of Economic History, Leuven August 20–24, 1990. Published by the Fernand Braudel Center for the Study of Economies, Historical Systems, and Civilizations, State University of New York, Binghamton, NY.

Warburton, D.A. 2003 *Macroeconomics from the Beginning. The General Theory, Ancient Markets, and the Rate of Interest*. Neuchâtel-Paris, Recherches et Publications.

Wilcke, C. 2006. 'Markt und Arbeit im Alten Orient am Ende des 3. Jahrtausends v. Chr.', in: W. Reinhard and J. Stagl (eds) *Menschen und Märkte. Studien zur historischen Wirtschafts anthropologie*, 71–121. Wien, Köln, Weimar, Böhlau Verlag.

Zaccagnini, C. 1983 'On Gift Exchange in the Old Babylonian Period', in O. Carruba (ed.), *Studi Orientalistici in Ricordo di Franco Pintore*, 189–253. Pavia, GJES Edizioni.

CHAPTER THIRTEEN

THE OLD BABYLONIAN ECONOMY

———.◆.———

Anne Goddeeris

INTRODUCTION

The Old Babylonian period witnesses some fascinating economic developments, which deserve a separate treatment in this volume. For the first time in Babylonian history, the three traditional sectors of the economy, palace, temple and private citizenry, are well represented in the written documentation. However, many of the private citizens keeping an archive had connections with one of the patrimonial households.

Thus, despite the numerous 'private' contracts that are known from this period, this chapter will chiefly focus on the characteristic ways in which the Old Babylonian rulers attempted to integrate the existing self-sufficient households into a patrimonial economy. Therefore, I will first establish the political framework before addressing the economic institutions. Although the characteristic institutions discussed at the end of this chapter existed in both regions, the north and south of Babylonia are treated separately because the ecological factors were different and they had a different historical outset and outcome.

THE POINT OF DEPARTURE: THE THIRD MILLENNIUM

In the course of the fourth and third millennia BC, one can observe a gradual centralization of economic resources by temple and palace households in the archaeological and textual evidence. In order to manage these resources and provide their power with an economic basis, the households developed organizational and administrative structures. However, after two or three generations, the systems always seem to have disintegrated into local entities centred around city-states. Of course, the new administrative institutions remained embedded in these city-states and played a role when a ruler made a fresh attempt towards centralization.

At the end of the fourth millennium BC, the Uruk state and its colonies reached a first high point in this development. In the frame of this system, which was controlled by the temple complex of Uruk, the cuneiform writing system developed. After the Uruk state disintegrated, the city-states in southern Babylonia were managed by their temples. As pointed out by Renger in the previous chapter, the households operated more or less autonomously and maintained huge gangs of labourers through a ration system.

Competition between the city-states intensified in the course of the third millennium, as the defensive structures excavated at sites from around 2500 BC illustrate. First Sargon of Akkad, and, two centuries after him, Ur-Nammu and his son Shulgi of Ur, succeeded in conquering a territorial empire covering the largest part of Mesopotamia and founding a dynasty. They integrated the rich local temple organizations into their royal administration so as to redirect the surpluses to royal destinations. Especially Shulgi, the second king of the Ur III dynasty, instigated some large-scale centralization projects. Thus, the settlement Puzrish-Dagan, near Nippur, the major cult centre of Babylonia, was set up to control the delivery and processing of cattle and livestock sent as tribute to Nippur from the different provinces. All the aspects of the processing, from the actual delivery to the allocation of the meat, the tendons and other parts of the cadaver, as well as the labourers involved in the further handling of these parts, are accounted for in the administration of the central household by a chain of delivery and receipt records. Other households recorded aspects of their economical management, such as the administration of labourers in workshops and the collection of wood, in a comparable, detailed manner (Steinkeller 2003).

However, these innovations pertained to the centralization of the surpluses rather than bringing about economic integration of the temple households and other local economic powers. Especially outside the core area of southern Babylonia, which had been Ur III governmental control seems to have been restricted to the extraction of tribute. Thus, when the Ur III empire disintegrated under the reign of Ibbi-Sîn, provincial governors or high officials of the temple households had easy access to a sound economic basis.

Written evidence of the third millennium BC concentrates on the management of these households or 'great organizations', as Oppenheim labelled the Mesopotamian palace and temple households. The class of individuals living independently of the 'great organizations' in the countryside, are only hinted at in the documents. The relative importance of this economic class cannot be assessed.

SOUTHERN BABYLONIA

The early Isin-Larsa period (ca. 2002–1831 BC)

After the disintegration of the Ur III empire, some of the governors of the provincial centres, such as Isin and Eshnunna, were able to establish their power over the city and its environments and to found a dynasty. In the southern part of Babylonia, which had been the core of the Ur III empire, the dynasty of Isin attempted to continue the Ur III institutional and economic traditions on a smaller scale. The rulers of Isin were able to control southern Babylonia during the twentieth century BC. After that time, they gradually lost power in favour of the kings of Larsa who finally annexed Isin at the beginning of the nineteenth century BC.

Only few archives date from the twentieth century BC. The Isin craft archive (Van De Mieroop 1987) is the major source for the economy of this period. This means that only a small section of the economy of Isin is documented. At first sight, the archive of the craft workshops originates from what seems to be a continuation of the royal craft workshops in Ur from the previous century. This was the capital of the Ur III dynasty and has yielded a fascinating archive documenting the activities of a craft workshop producing luxury items. But we are dealing with different aspects of the craft industry here. Whereas the Ur workshops handled precious and exotic materials, the Isin craft archive documents the manufacture of practical utensils in the carpentry, reed, leather and felter workshops. Probably, the manufacture of precious goods was not as important in Isin as it was in Ur. Moreover, the craftsmen worked only part-time for the Isin workshop, compared to full-time in Ur. The destinations of the products show that the workshops were managed by the central household of Isin, probably the palace. They include the palace (the most important consumer) and the royal family (furniture and utensils, also for royal servants), temples (furniture for gods, furniture and utensils for temple personnel), central storehouses (furniture and building material), other workshops (for further completion) and administrative units (utensils, e.g. oil jars and oil bags for the house of the oil pressers), illustrating the integration of the economic sectors in the town. Some finished products were sent as official presents to other countries (e.g. Elam, Dilmun, Mari) and to other towns of the kingdom of Isin. A few texts from the archive of the Inanna temple in Nippur dating to this period display prosopographical parallels with the Isin craft archive.

The offering lists of the Ninurta temple in Nippur (Sigrist 1984) cover the complete nineteenth century BC. The reverses of these lists state to whom the food offerings were redistributed after they had been placed in front of the gods, most often to priests, temple functionaries and artisans responsible for the provision of the offerings, such as brewers or bakers. These administrative texts form one of the earliest testimonies of the institution of temple prebends in Babylonia. Other archives from a somewhat later date illustrate other aspects of prebends. Therefore, the institution will be discussed more thoroughly below. Together with some other administrative texts from Nippur, the offering lists illustrate that the temples did not control their own assets, but that the economic basis of the temples was administered centrally for the whole city, something that can be observed in Ur as well and which was customary probably since the Akkad or the Ur III period.

The written evidence from Ur offers the most diverse picture of the economic proceedings of an Old Babylonian city (Van De Mieroop 1992). The preserved part of the administration of the temple complex of Nanna and Ningal only really starts around the time when Larsa gains supremacy over the town (ca. 1926 BC) and disappears during the reign of Warad-Sîn (1834–1823). The temple must have been the most influential economic factor of Ur during that period, owning huge herds and large tracts of land and marshes. For the actual exploitation of these resources, the temple engaged private individuals through lease and herding contracts, placing the responsibility and the risk with the farmers and herdsmen and securing a regular income. The herdsmen kept the institutional cattle or livestock assigned to them, together with their own flock. Yearly, when the wool was shorn and delivered to the temple, the heads of sheep and cattle were counted. Depending on the number of ewes, the temple required a quota of newborn lambs. Any arrears or surpluses were evened out with heads of their own flocks. The herdsmen also had to deliver dairy products on a regular basis. Surplus dairy products could be sold or bartered locally.

Throughout the Old Babylonian period, the 'great organizations' were to apply the principle of herding contracts for their flocks. Fishing grounds in the marshes were leased out in a comparable way. In return for a fixed amount of fish and reed, the fishermen were assigned a subsistence plot for the cultivation of barley and were allowed to hunt their swamp for fowl and fish. Much of the temple land was probably assigned to temple dependents as subsistence plots. The dependents then leased out their plot to farmers living in the countryside.

The south under Warad-Sîn and Rim-Sîn of Larsa and under Babylonian domination (ca. 1834–1919BC)

Until the reign of Warad-Sîn, the temple personnel directly supervised the management of the economic assets and the preparation of the offerings. From then on, the documents originating from the temple administration diminish in number, and archives of private townsmen illustrate how they were responsible for directing the flow of income towards the temple. This development must probably be related to the fragmentation of prebendary temple offices. Some lucrative temple offices were included in the inheritance divisions until they covered only a month or even a few days a year. The offices could even be leased and sold. Thus, the execution of the task became separated from the income attached to it, consisting of a share in the offerings and/or a subsistence plot. A few important temple offices, however, were not fragmented and remained related to the execution of managerial or cultic tasks.

Also until the reign of Warad-Sîn, the Ningal temple controlled the oversea trade to Dilmun by levying ten per cent on the incoming products. Warad-Sîn seems to have transferred this tax to the palace. Through trade with Dilmun, a location in the Persian Gulf, the Babylonians imported copper, semi-precious stones and spices, in return for silver, wool and garments, sesame (oil) and wheat. The Gulf trade formed a monopoly of Ur during the Old Babylonian period. Private merchants executed the journeys and financed their enterprises by collecting investments from different households and individuals through loans and partnerships.

After the conquest of the south by Hammurabi, the private archives from Ur contain hardly any signs of institutional activity. The administration of the province of Larsa, to which Ur belonged, was centred at Larsa. Even the 'Overseer of the Merchants of Ur', the important local official responsible for the collection of the share of the Babylonian palace in the economic assets, for its conversion into silver and for its actual delivery to the Babylonian crown, seems to have resided in Larsa.

Just like Ur, the towns of Nippur and Kutalla have produced several archives from residential quarters, mainly from the period of domination by Larsa and Babylon. They all contain chains of title deeds, relating to houses, date-palm orchards, prebends with the sustenance fields attached to them and slaves, which all could be rented out. Besides, most archives contain some documents referring to business activities and investments. These may cover entrepreneurial activities for the temple or the palace, not only collecting dues and converting them into silver, but also investing temple and palace silver in loans together with their own silver and organizing craft activities. Before delivering the silver to the palace or temple household, the entrepreneurs kept it as long as possible and used it to augment their own capital. The accumulated silver could be invested in loans for consumptive purposes (issued to fishermen and herdsmen who could not fulfil their quota) and for commercial purposes.

The three major Old Babylonian archives from Larsa itself, the archive of Balmunamhe, the one of Shep-Sîn and the letter archive of Shamash-hazir and Sîn-iddinam, all date from the period of domination by Hammurabi and Samsuiluna. Apart from the fact that dues were redirected to the palace in Babylon and a definite increase in scale, they exhibit much continuity with the previous period.

It is still not clear how far the activities of Balmunamhe, the most famous inhabitant of the area of large residences excavated in Larsa, extended (the cuneiform tablets were excavated illicitly before the official French excavations started). This businessman was involved in slave purchases and real estate transactions. A village from which revenues was extracted was named after him, just as another village was named after his father. A study by Dyckhoff (1998) situates the activities of Balmunamhe in the management of the Enki temple of Larsa. However, the barley revenues of his village (or rather, the agricultural district under his supervision) and the one of his father were brought to the central storehouse of Larsa. This reconstruction confirms and illustrates how the palace used the existing structures – in the south, the temple households – to control the local economy and extract its surpluses.

The archive of Shep-Sîn consists of two files. On the one hand, the file of mainly loan documents dating from before and after Shep-Sîn's official function as Overseer of the Merchants in Larsa, forms his private archive. Another file, consisting of administrative texts dated between Hammurabi 36 and Hammurabi 42, documents the responsibilities of Shep-Sîn as overseer of the merchants. These official documents must have been kept in his private archive, a practice not uncommon in Babylonia. In his function as Overseer of the Merchants, Shep-Sîn was responsible for the retail of dates from the palace orchards around Larsa. The merchants selling the dates owed an amount of silver to the palace equivalent to one-third of the value of the dates, to be collected and delivered to (the delegate of) the palace in Babylon by Shep-Sîn. Accordingly, the merchants had a profit margin of two-thirds of the value of the dates. The retail of fish from the palace marshes also fell under Shep-Sîn's responsibility.

The correspondence of Hammurabi with Shamash-hazir and Sîn-iddinam concerns the managment of royal land in the province of Larsa after Hammurabi's conquest of the region. Since this is our main source for the practice of assigning subsistence plots, it will be discussed below.

NORTHERN BABYLONIA

Ur III control over the northern part of Babylonia and the Diyala region seems to have been largely restricted to the extraction of tribute. Since no archives from Ur III 'great organizations' have been recovered, continuity cannot be detected. After the downfall of the Ur III kingdom, the local palaces could not fall back on temples or other households with a well established economic basis, as in the south.

Political developments

In the Diyala-region, written (though largely unpublished) documentation continues after the fall of the Third Dynasty of Ur. Already at the beginning of Ibbi-Sîn's reign, the governor of Eshnunna, Shu-ilija, declared himself independent and founded a local dynasty.

At the beginning of the nineteenth century BC, written documentation suddenly appears in several northern Babylonian towns, each referring to its own Amorite petty ruler (Charpin's (2003) 'second Amorite wave'). After only about two decades, the northern Babylonian petty kingdoms were incorporated in the expansive kingdom of Sumu-la-el of Babylon (ca. 1880–1845), who introduced concepts and institutions that were to shape the economy of the following centuries, such as the royal edicts, the *ilkum* duties, and the engagement of entrepreneurs to manage royal assets.

During the rest of the nineteenth century, Babylonia was one of the political major powers of Syro-Mesopotamia, entertaining diplomatic relations with, and switching alliances between, its neighbours, Larsa, Eshnunna, Mari, Elam and Upper-Mesopotamia. International correspondence from this period between the rulers and their high officials illustrates how the borders of the kingdoms fluctuated and how coalitions were forged and broken (see Warburton in this volume).

During the latter half of Hammurabi's reign (ca. 1792–1750), after the disappearance of the Upper-Mesopotamian empire, he eliminated his rivals, Larsa, Eshnunna and Mari (all of whom, at a certain point, had been his allies) one after the other. In Hammurabi's thirty-second regnal year, the Babylonian empire stretched from the Persian Gulf to Mari in the West, Assur in the North and Eshnunna in the East. However, in his eighth regnal year, Hammurabi's son Samsuiluna had already lost control over the most southern towns of the empire. After Samsuiluna 11, all written and archaeological documentation disappears from southern Babylonia for several centuries. Apparently, a large part of the population fled to northern Babylonian towns, where the cults from Uruk and Lagash were reinstalled in Kish, those from Larsa and Nippur in Babylon, and the one from Isin in Sippar. The cause of this collapse must at least partly be sought in environmental factors.

In the course of his reign, Samsuiluna's territory further shrank with the loss of northern Sumer (the region of Nippur and Isin) in his thirtieth year and the varying attachment of Eshnunna to the Babylonian kingdom, which was lost definitively in his thirty-fifth year. The political and territorial history of the 'late Old Babylonian' rulers during the subsequent century is not well known. Their year-names refer to votive donations rather than to military achievements and the royal correspondence concerns internal and mainly economic affairs. However, the economic texts pertaining to the royal assets hardly ever refer to assets or income from outside northern Babylonia. Therefore, the Old Babylonian kingdom seems to have shrunk back to its old borders, which had been more or less stable for about a century already between the reigns of Sumu-la-el and Hammurabi.

The final collapse of the Old Babylonian kingdom must be attributed to a Hittite invasion. However, an increasing social and economic weakness can be observed during the thirty-year-long reign of Samsuditana, the last king of the first dynasty of Babylon. First, there was a drastic decline in the number of texts under his reign. More precisely, only very few archives continue after the accession of Samsuditana. In a study of the collapse of the Old Babylonian kingdom (Richardson 2002), the decline has been situated in the newly founded garrison towns. Many of the inhabitants of these towns were of foreign origin, mainly Kassites, who had invaded northern Babylonia in several waves during the second half of the Old Babylonian period. Some of the Kassites integrated into Babylonian society, others earned their living as mercenaries, but as a group they became increasingly important, just as the Amorites did during the Ur III period. The silver extracted by the crown from the traditional northern Babylonian towns Sippar, Dilbat, Babylon and Kish was redirected to the garrison towns, which caused instability in the long-established urban centres.

Thus, the Babylonian kingdom, falling victim to the Hittite raid in 1595 BC, was internally weakened.

The three economic sectors

For the periods of greatest territorial expansion (the reigns of Rim-Sîn of Larsa and of Hammurabi of Babylon), it becomes increasingly difficult to separate the sectors through which the Mesopotamian economy is traditionally studied – the palace, the temple and the private or communal sector – from each other. This situation continues during the last two centuries of the era. Nearly all the private individuals who kept accounts of their economic activities were involved with palace, temple or other religious institutions as entrepreneurs, prebend holders, nuns or officials. The temples and palaces contracted private individuals to manage their assets and the temple surpluses were redirected to the palace as much as possible.

Sumu-la-el, the first king of the First Dynasty of Babylon, took the first steps towards economic integration in northern Babylonia. For the most clearly distinguished sectors, we must turn to the early Old Babylonian petty kingdoms.

Palace households

Two examples of the administration of (part of) the household of a petty ruler have been recovered from Sippar and Kisurra respectively. It appears that initially the king controlled only a fraction of the agricultural land in these towns. However, his administration acquired more lands through the acquisition of fields pledged for unpaid debts. As for the cultivation of the agricultural assets, royal letters from the Sippar archive refer to the assignment of subsistence plots attached and to *ilkum* service, whereas an administrative document from Kisurra lists farmers of royal land, most of whom are known as previous owners of land sold to the royal household. Also, there are allusions to substitute workers, rations and cattle management, elements that are well known from more extensive royal or temple administrations. The surpluses were invested in metal industry, cultic and diplomatic obligations, trade and large building projects.

Since the Old Babylonian layers of Babylon, the capital, are situated below the water table, no other palace administration has been recovered from northern Babylonia. Only where the palace economy interfered with the private sector – in the frame of the edicts and the engagement of entrepreneurs – did it leave traces in our documentary evidence. Other direct information concerning the royal economic policies is contained by letters from kings to their local agents, such as the correspondence of Hammurabi with Shamash-hazir and Sîn-iddinam.

Temple households

The administration of two early Old Babylonian temple households from the Diyala region, of the Sîn-temple in Khafaja and of the temple of Ishtar-Kititum in Ishchali, demonstrates some significant differences with that of the southern temples. Both temple households did not own large tracts of land at the outset, but acquired control over land and labour through unpaid debts. The *sangu* of the Kititum temple issued loans together with the god Sîn, who had a temple in a nearby locality. Moreover, his seal qualified him as a servant of the king rather than of Ishtar-Kititum. Thus, also in Northern Babylonia, temple households seem to be integrated to some degree in the centralized royal management.

The gods Shamash, Nanna and Sîn issued numerous loans that cannot be situated in an archival context. The Assyriological attempts to attribute a charitable rather than a usurious nature to this practice have not been successful. Interest rates on these loans could be just as high (25 to 33 per cent) as on 'normal' loans.

Part of the administration of the Annunitum temple in Sippar-Amnanum has been recovered from the house of Ur-Utu, the gala-mah of Annunitum during the reign of Ammi-saduqa, the penultimate ruler of the Old Babylonian dynasty. As observed above for the temples of Ur, the temple management at this time was supervised by high ranking priests, such as the gala-mah, but the execution of actual tasks such as the preparation of offerings and cultivation of the fields, was managed through entrepreneurs.

Private townsmen

Most of the cuneiform tablets from the early period in northern Babylonia document the activities of private individuals living in the Northern Babylonian towns. In Sippar, Dilbat, Kish and Kisurra, townspeople sold, leased, inherited and bought fields, house plots and gardens. Unlike in the south, it was possible to sell fields in northern Babylonia. Still, in many instances where the context of the sale is well documented, seller and purchaser appear to be related, or the field is sold to cover unpaid debts to be redeemed later. Especially the so-called 'Manania'-archives from the region of Kish, which cover only one generation, record how real estate sales were embedded in a context of indebtedness and how the previous owner became a dependant (slave or lessee) of his creditor. Thus, the real estate market may not have been as free as the numerous sale documents, kept in the family archives for generations as title deeds, suggest. Since the agricultural lands often formed the economic basis, and the house the social basis of the family estate, it could not easily be dispensed with. From the reign of Hammurabi on, real estate sales gradually disappear from the textual record and are replaced by lease contracts.

Just as in the south, the well-off townspeople used their assets to give out loans, for consumptive as well as commercial purposes. When the debtors were unable to repay their debts, the creditor could accumulate lands and labour force and thus acquire considerable wealth. However, because of the principle of partitive inheritance which operated in Babylonia, the estate of a large family could sometimes be dissolved within a few generations.

SOME CHARACTERISTIC OLD BABYLONIAN ECONOMIC INSTITUTIONS

The *gagûm*

The principle of partitive inheritance operating in Babylonia, brings about a fragmentation of the paternal estate. The patrilocal system allows the sons to manage the paternal estate collectively, but, on the other hand, forces the daughters to take their share into the family of their husbands as a dowry. A *paterfamilias* could reduce the effects of this development by letting his daughter enter the *gagûm*, the 'cloister' of Shamash, in Sippar as a *nadītum*, who was not allowed to marry. The numerous archives of these ladies contain title deeds of house plots in the *gagûm*, fields and 'ring silver', a means of payment reserved for the *nadītum* priestess. Field leases constitute the other major type of text in these archives.

The Codex Hammurabi (§178) states that the estate of these women, consisting of the dowry which was bequeathed to them on their entering in the cloister, must be managed by their father or their brother. This practice only rarely appears from the legal documents since the *nadītum* acts as the nominal owner of her possessions. Some inheritance documents specify that the brother is obliged to give rations to his *nadītum* sister.

On the surface, the numerous adoption-support documents seem to imply that these women were able to assign it to the heir of their choice. However, when we are able to establish her family relations, it appears that the heir of a *nadītum* of Shamash was very often the daughter of one of her brothers, who was also ordained as a *nadītum* and that the dowry remained in the hands of the family in this way.

The role of entrepreneurs

As illustrated in the above discussion of the temple management in Ur (the herding contracts and the exploitation of the marshes) and the responsibilities of Shep-Sîn, 'Overseer of the Merchants' of Larsa, the 'great organizations' increasingly assigned economic activities to private individuals as a kind of franchise in the course of the Old Babylonian period (Renger 2000). This practice is traditionally labelled '*Palastgeschäfte*' in Assyriological circles. Its purpose was to escape the costs of permanent maintenance of the personnel, to transfer the economic risks onto the shoulders of the 'entrepreneur' and to keep the administration of the whole organization relatively simple by laying the responsibility of the whole scheme on a few managers, such as the 'Overseer of the Merchants' in the case of fish and date retail.

Nearly all the aspects of the palace and temple economy would eventually be managed through one or other variant of this principle, from agricultural production and stock-breeding, to fishing and craftsmanship, tax-farming, the recruitment of labourers and the retail sale of agricultural and other products. Freed from the obligation to provide rations for its dependants, the palace was far more interested in stocks of silver than in supplies of staple products.

The most extensive Old Babylonian documentation concerns the conversion of wool staples (and, to a lesser degree, oxen and sesame) into silver. From the reign of Ammi-saduqa, an archive concerning the responsibilities of Utul-Ishtar is preserved. Combined with other texts such as letters concerning the annual shearing of the sheep, we are able to reconstruct the complete course of events. Right after it was shorn, the wool was kept in a storehouse of the palace, the 'New Year house', and later distributed to local merchants. The palace kept track of its assets through loan contracts, in which the merchant declared that he owed an amount of silver, representing the amount of 'wool of the palace', to the palace. The silver had to be repaid at a time specified by the palace (on one occasion only seven years later). The whole transaction involved two middlemen: the 'Overseer of the Merchants' on the part of the merchants, and Utul-Ishtar on the part of the palace.

Silver loans labelled as 'wool of the palace' or containing the phrase 'to be repaid when the palace requests its profits' occur in Kish and Kisurra as early as the reign of Sumu-la-el, the earliest ruler of the Old Babylonian dynasty. A few decades later, tablets from Sippar and Babylon contain references to the practice as well. This shows that entrepreneurs play a major role in the economy throughout the Old Babylonian period.

Edicts

Several year-names of Old Babylonian rulers refer to the proclamation of a *mīšarum* ('redress') edict (Charpin 1990). These decrees do not contain reforms but, rather, measures with a temporary effect. A *mīšarum* edict orders that the people involved in the production of palace assets (cultivators, herdsmen and flayers) and the merchants selling the palace surpluses get a remission of the arrears they owe to the palace. The edicts interfered in the relations between private citizens as well. All non-commercial debts were cancelled. The application of this measure can be observed in loans issued shortly after the *mīšarum* proclamation, which contain a clause assuring that the loan is concluded after the proclamation and, therefore, cannot be subject to it. Also several archives display a concentration of many unpaid debts (therefore, not destroyed) in the years preceding the proclamation of an edict. Some debtors were forced to sell their land or their relatives in order to get their previous possessions back. Self-sales because of unpaid debts are annulled as well. Therefore, sale documents, too, may contain the clause that they have been concluded after the proclamation.

The recurring proclamation of a *mīšarum* was necessary during the Old Babylonian period because the economic risks were carried by the producers and the lowest levels of the entrepreneurs. They did not have any reserves to fall back on, as would the creditors and the 'great organizations' who called in the entrepreneurs.

Most often a king promulgated a *mīšarum* at his accession. Often he repeated this in the course of his reign. However, he did not do so at regular and predictable intervals, because that would have rendered the edicts ineffective.

The *ilkum* institution

The Code of Hammurabi distinguishes two major classes of individuals: the *muškēnūm*, who had no obligations to the crown, and the individuals obliged to fulfil an *ilkum*-duty. Administrative and legal documents may refer to the persons carrying out their *ilkum* assignment with the term *rēdûm*, most often translated as 'soldier', although *rēdûm* may have worked in public projects as well. In return for this duty, which could consist of military service, participation in public building or irrigation projects, transportation of barley or dates, agricultural work, flaying or fishing, to name just some of the public tasks, they received rations or could cultivate a subsistence field, a so-called suku field.

Hammurabi's correspondence with Shamash-hazir and Sîn-iddinam, two high officials who were situated in Larsa after its conquest, for a large part concerns the assignment of suku land in the southern region. It appears that the ration system was increasingly replaced by assignment of subsistence fields. Most often, the fields were cultivated through lease contracts, frequently by *muškēnum*.

Although forbidden by the Codex Hammurabi (§26), individuals often sent substitutes to fulfil their duty. Often, the substitutes were members of the same family or household. Otherwise, they belonged to the poorer classes of the towns.

The service could also be paid off with an amount of silver, the *kasap ilkim*. During the late Old Babylonian period, the collection of *kasap ilkim* by entrepreneurs from the holders of suku fields (also an entrepreneurial activity) probably became the norm. With this silver, the palace could hire labourers, fishermen and soldiers, which proved to be an efficient system. By this time, the suku fields were considered part of the family property.

CONCLUSIONS

In order to provide their power with an economic basis, the Old Babylonian rulers integrated the existing economic units in a way markedly different from the preceding dynasties. Instead of establishing a centralizing bureaucracy, which controlled all the details, and fully sustaining the labour force and the administrative apparatus, the palace delegated as many tasks as possible. Thus, it shifted the economic risks to the producers and the entrepreneurs. For certain sectors, such as trade, this tendency can be observed already in the Ur III period. These practices minimized the official administration and left more room for private initiative. While the dynasty was able to remain in power for a longer time, it also necessitated the recurring cancellation of debts through *mīšarum* edicts.

BIBLIOGRAPHY

Charpin, D. 1990 'Les édits de "restauration" des rois babyloniens et leur application' in Cl. Nicolet (ed.) *Du pouvoir dans l'antiquité: mots et réalités*. Geneva: Librairie Droz, 13–24.

Dyckhoff, C. 1998 'Balamunamhe von Larsa – eine altbabylonische Existenz zwischen Ökonomie, Kultus und Wissenschaft' in J. Prosecky (ed.) *Intellectual Life of the Ancient Near East. Papers Read at the 43rd Rencontre Assyriologique Internationale, Prague, July 1–5, 1996*. Prague: Academy of Sciences of the Czech Republic. Oriental Institute, 117–124.

Goddeeris, A. 2002 *Economy and Society in Northern Babylonian in the Early Old Babylonian Period (ca. 2000–1600 BC)*. Leuven: Peeters.

Kraus, F.R. 1984 *Königliche Verfügungen in altbabylonischer Zeit*. Leiden: Brill.

Renger, J. 2000 'Das Palastgeschäft in der altbabylonische Zeit', in A.C.V.M. Bongenaar (ed.) *Interdependency of Institutions and Private Entrepreneurs*. Istanbul: Nederlands historisch-archeologisch instituut, 153–183.

—— 2002 'Royal Edicts of the Old Babylonian Period' in M. Hudson and M. Van De Mieroop (eds) *Debt and Economic Renewal in the Ancient Near East*, Bethesda, MD: CDL Press, 139–162.

Richardson, S. 2002 *The Collapse of a Complex State: A Reappraisal of the end of the First Dynasty of Babylon, 1683–1597 BC*, Ph.D. Columbia University.

Sigrist, M. 1984 *Les šattukku dans l'Ešumeša durant la période d'Isin et Larsa*. Malibu, CA: Undena.

Steinkeller, P. 2003 'Archival Practices at Babylonia in the Third Millennium' in M. Brosius (ed.) *Ancient Archives and Archival Traditions, Concepts of Record-Keeping in the Ancient World*. Oxford: University Press, 37–58.

Stol, M. 2004 'Wirtschaft und Gesellschaft in Altbabylonischer Zeit' in P. Attinger, W. Sallaberger and M. Wäfler (eds) *Mesopotamien. Die Altbabylonische Zeit*. Göttingen: Vandenhoeck & Ruprecht: 643–975.

Van De Mieroop, M. 1987 *Crafts in the Early Isin Period: A Study of the Isin Craft Archive from the Reigns of Išbi-Erra and Šū-ilišu*. OLA 24, Leuven: Peeters.

—— 1992 *Society and Enterprise in Old Babylonian Ur*. Berlin: Dietrich Reimer Verlag.

van Driel, G. 2002 *Elusive Silver. In Search of a Role for a Market in an Agrarian Environment. Aspects of Mesopotamia's Society*. Leiden: Brill.

CHAPTER FOURTEEN

ASPECTS OF SOCIETY AND ECONOMY IN THE LATER OLD BABYLONIAN PERIOD

———•◆•———

Frans van Koppen

INTRODUCTION

The Old Babylonian period is a convenient designation for the first four centuries of the second millennium BC, but as the term hints at a prominent role of the city of Babylon, one could argue that it should be reserved for the period that started with the unification of Lower Mesopotamia in the later part of the reign of Hammurabi.[1] The kingdom of Babylon, at first just one among several states, rapidly became the unrivalled overlord of the region between the Persian Gulf and the Jezirah plateau. This unity was a singular achievement, as it would remain the only instance in a period of more than five centuries that all of Lower Mesopotamia recognized a single ruler. Being the product of exceptional circumstances, the expanded state was also vulnerable, and a series of political and economic problems led to the contraction of the Babylonian realm within a few decades following the death of its founder.

Even though Hammurabi's 'empire' may be deemed ephemeral, it could be considered as the beginning of a distinct era in Mesopotamian history. The rise of Babylon was just one aspect of a more comprehensive geopolitical rearrangement in the Mesopotamian and Syrian areas, with important consequences for patterns of long-distance trade. Moreover, when the social and economic factors that had weakened Babylon's neighbours and paved the way for Hammurabi's successes finally afflicted Babylon itself, the crisis precipitated the emergence of a much smaller and strongly centralized Babylonian state that survived for centuries and passed with no major disruption to the Kassite heirs of the throne.

The archival documentation for the Old Babylonian period is rich but also quite fragmentary, so that current descriptions of its economic system draw on disparate groups of texts, with each group illuminating particular elements of a system within specific geographical and historical settings. Diachronic developments and local particularities are therefore often obscured. While the basic traits of early second-millennium economy were determined by the timeless constants of the Mesopotamian landscape and by the enduring managerial strategies of the state institutions as they are described by Goddeeris in the previous chapter, the purpose of this chapter is to look more closely at aspects that may be considered distinctive for the period of time that followed Hammurabi's experimental unification of North and South. Modern perceptions of ancient Mesopotamian history have been strongly affected by the customary periodization, and the recognition of a so-called 'Dark Age'[2] after the reign of Babylon's last king, Samsuditana, has added weight to the opinion that the Fall of Babylon in 1595 BC was also the end of a distinct period in socio-economic history. This chapter aims to show that the Old Babylonian period in the general sense of the word was far from homogeneous but may be subdivided in proportion to different developments that can be observed in this period of time. Since socio-economic conditions did not change significantly over the Fall of Babylon, the early Kassite kings should be seen as the heirs rather than the vanquishers of the First Babylonian Dynasty: the documentary evidence for its final phase can thus shed some welcome light on a problematical dark spot in Mesopotamian history.

GEOPOLITICS AND FOREIGN TRADE

The rise of Babylon roughly coincided with the arrival of Yamhad, the kingdom with the city of Aleppo as its capital, as the foremost power in present-day Syria. In the early centuries of the second millennium BC, the kingdom of Qatna, near the modern town of Homs, had been dominant in that area and a long-time ally of the Middle Euphrates kingdom of Mari. Together they monopolized all Mesopotamian–Mediterranean traffic via the land route passing through the Palmyra oasis. Qatna's political influence, however, was waning when the Mari palace archive sets in, and these sources illustrate how Samsi-Addu, who was then in control of all of Upper Mesopotamia, shifted alliance towards Yamhad, the new rising power in Syria. The disintegration of Samsi-Addu's realm shortly afterwards allowed Yarim-Lim of Yamhad to gain influence in Upper Mesopotamia and to secure the throne of Mari for his follower Zimri-Lim.

Lower Mesopotamia, meanwhile, was the domain of three important states: Larsa, encompassing the southern alluvial basin of ancient Sumer; Eshnunna, in control of the Diyala region and the middle course of the Tigris and Euphrates rivers; and Babylon, occupying the central alluvial zone. The first two were long-standing strategic partners, with a vested interest in all traffic passing between Elam and the Persian Gulf and the regions accessible from the upper courses of the Tigris and the Euphrates. Eshnunna constituted a considerable military power and had been ally as well as opponent of Samsi-Addu's Upper Mesopotamian kingdom, but the once powerful state of Larsa was now in economic decline. Larsa's ruling house was of Elamite descent, and it is likely that their realm came close to a protectorate of the omnipotent king of Elam, the Iranian state which, at that time, had reached a high point of influence throughout the southern Zagros Mountains and the Iranian highland.

Babylon's connections with foreign markets were consequently fully determined by the neighbouring states of Eshnunna and Larsa, and attempts to undo this by occupying parts of the main watercourses had so far been unproductive. However, this changed unexpectedly when Elam – for reasons still unknown – decided to conquer Eshnunna. The subsequent manoeuvres of Babylon, which first headed the anti-Elamite coalition, then conquered the now exposed kingdom of Larsa, and finally consolidated its sway over the Sinjar region before turning against Mari itself (1765–1761 BC), are well documented by the Mari palace archive. In order to secure its territorial gain and profitable access to the trade routes, Babylon's prime concern was now to neutralize Eshnunna. This weakened but still formidable power was situated close to a strategic knot in the riverine routes of northern Lower Mesopotamia. Eshnunna's subjugation was a main objective of Hammurabi's campaigns in the last decade of his rule, and would remain a perennial problem throughout the later history of his dynasty.

We can see that a crucial aspect of Hammurabi's legacy was thus that an unobstructed trade route connecting the Persian Gulf and adjacent regions with Syria and the Mediterranean Sea via the Euphrates river had been fully integrated in the territories of Babylon and Yamhad. Both states benefited a great deal from this flow of merchandise, as is particularly clear from the sources from the city of Sippar. This Babylonian mercantile centre on the Euphrates was the home of a group of traders who specialized in river-borne trade, and whose correspondence allows a glimpse of their business at the end of the reign of Hammurabi and the first decade of Samsuiluna (van Soldt 1990: ix–x). Babylon and Yamhad were now united by strong strategic and commercial ties, and their alliance, as well as the importance of the Euphrates trade artery, would persist throughout the Old Babylonian period. The final destruction of Mari, a few years after the Babylonian conquest, liberated the Euphrates allies from a potential obstacle to free passage. It certainly spelled the end for the land traffic over the Palmyra route and thereby sealed the fate of the former power Qatna, which now wholly submitted to Yamhad. The city of Emar, located in the bend of the Euphrates, became the single most important port of transit for the kingdom of Yamhad and attracted many Babylonian residents. This had a lasting impact on the local scribal conventions since as late as fourteenth-century BC texts of the so-called 'Syrian type' from Emar and nearby sites preserve distinctive Babylonian traits.

However, a negative effect of Mari's disappearance was that trade caravans passing through the Euphrates valley were no longer adequately protected. This was already felt at the end of Hammurabi's reign, when shareholders of a plundered caravan went to court about the division of the reimbursement payment that Hammurabi had obtained for them from the king of Yamhad.[3] This situation led Samsuiluna to improve military control over the Euphrates valley by building strongholds and extending his control upstream to Terqa whose local dynasty acknowledged later Old Babylonian kings as their overlords. Hammurabi, or one of his successors, had set up colonies of foreign mercenaries, known as the 'Kassite houses', to protect the Middle Euphrates area. Many years later these military settlements developed into semi-independent polities which ultimately waged war against Ammisaduqa (ca. 1630 BC), an episode that brought Euphrates trade to a temporary stop. When the conflict settled down, trade was resumed again, and a new type of legal text emerged, investment loans in 'Euphrates expeditions', suggesting that new rules for such trips, regarding matters such as liability, had been introduced.

The Euphrates can be considered the lifeline of the later Old Babylonian state, since other routes could no longer sustain a reliable flow of merchandise. This is readily understood for the trade with Dilmun (the island of Bahrain), a port of trade for a variety of goods from the Persian Gulf, which had been a long-established element of the southern Mesopotamian economy. This trade had been highly profitable, for example with copper from Oman that was bought at the time of Rim-Sin for the lowest prices recorded in Mesopotamian history (Powell 1990: 83f.), but is no

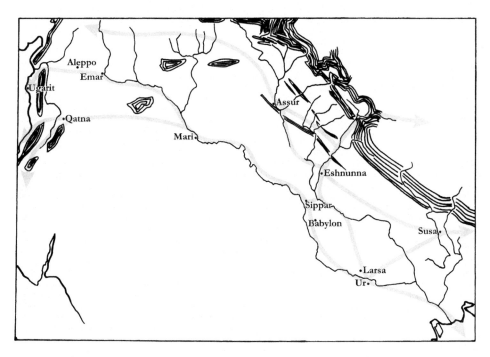

Figure 14.1   Map showing changes in the main inter-regional trade routes
of the early second millennium BC.

longer documented under Babylonian rule, and certainly came to a halt when the
southern Mesopotamian cities were depopulated. Alternative, but also more expensive,
sources for the same vital commodity were the markets of Yamhad, where Cypriot
copper and 'mountain copper', possibly from Anatolia, could be bought. The fabled
'tin route' also underwent restructuring: the Old Assyrian traders in the nineteenth
century BC had obtained their tin from Larsa and ultimately Elam, but Eshnunna
did not partake in this trade, presumably because it experienced a decline in power
at that time (Dercksen 2004: 25–31). Tin has become much more scarce when the
Old Assyrian sources resume again in the eighteenth century BC, no doubt because
the once more powerful state of Eshnunna again controlled the flow of this commodity
(Dercksen 2001: 64f.). Very little information is yet available about later tin trade,
but the Babylonian cities still maintained commercial ties with Elam, and the main
westward route of tin may now have followed the Euphrates; this must have harmed
the Old Assyrian trade and presumably contributed to the decline of Assur that is
revealed by the fact that its trade with Anatolia was not resumed again when *kārum*
Kanesh had been destroyed for a second time (ca. 1725 BC), but explicit texts to
prove this are still lacking.

POPULATION AND ARMED FORCES

According to the conventional text of the redress decree of the kings of Babylon,
whose best-preserved copy was issued by Ammisaduqa, certain rulings applied to

Figure 14.2 Two impressions of the same seal on a tablet from Hursagkalama dating to the eighteenth year of Ammisaduqa (YOS 13 217) depicting an archer (left) and a warrior with shield and dagger in combat (Yale Babylonian Collection).

'Akkadians and Amorites', and it would seem that everybody in the realm was included under these terms. Both names were traditional and could be used in varying shades of meaning. Akkad was the name of the capital city and the country of Sargon, the founder of the Akkad Dynasty, and the terms 'land of Akkad' and 'Akkadians' in a comparable narrow sense were applied in the Old Babylonian period to the kingdom of Eshnunna. Second, it designated a language, and could accordingly be used in a broader geographical meaning, which occurs in the pairing 'Sumer and Akkad' first attested in the late third millennium BC, when the whole of Lower Mesopotamia could be described as a Sumerian-speaking southern, and an Akkadian-speaking northern part; the concept was maintained throughout the second millennium BC, when Sumerian as a spoken language had long died out.

Amorites, the second term, is another third-millennium appellation and was originally used for people who, from a Mesopotamian perspective, came from the 'West'; the term also stood for one of the cardinal points. The same meaning is sporadically attested in Old Babylonian texts from Lower Mesopotamia, but another secondary meaning occurs there as well: Amorites had been an important constituent of the Ur III army and were the founders of subsequent dynasties, so that the term acquired distinct martial connotations and came to denote the political and military elite, and the rural component of the population that supplied the greater part of the armed forces in general (Weeks 1985). The term in this meaning does not occur frequently either, and instead one encounters specific ethnic labels to designate these groups: Amnanum and Yahrurum, for example, were the tribal groups that constituted the core of the Babylonian army. Amorite was, furthermore, the name of a Semitic language entirely different from Akkadian, and members of the political and military elite in the Old Babylonian period habitually bore names in this language. This choice was governed by tradition and prestige and is therefore no valid pointer to their spoken language, and one observes furthermore that the Amorite onomasticon was reserved for males only.

The particular meaning established for the second term allows us to see in 'Akkadians and Amorites' a description of the population of the Babylonian state in two parts: the Akkadian-speaking, urban population on the one hand, and the rural population that provided military service on the other; it is unlikely that the pairing should also imply a distinction in speech. This passage was presumably included in the redress decree as it was first issued by Hammurabi, when it conceivably already had a traditional ring, and was maintained in the edicts of the later Babylonian kings, even when it eventually lost its accuracy with regard to the social constitution of their state. This demographical makeover, which entailed the disappearance of the Amorites and the emergence of a society that is described as comprising 'Kassites and Akkadians' in a royal inscription of the early Middle Babylonian period,[4] was the outcome of migrations that seem to have begun under Hammurabi.

The main thrust in population movements at that time led from the Zagros Mountains into the Mesopotamian lowlands. The sources from the time of the Upper Mesopotamian kingdom of Samsi-Addu show vividly how this migration was initially triggered by inter-Zagros conflicts, but then inadvertently escalated as a result of military intervention of the Mesopotamian kingdoms (Eidem and Læssøe 2001). The causes underlying these conflicts are not articulated in the texts, but it may be that ecological deterioration led to inter-state competition over scarce resources, as well as mass departures in search of new livelihoods; that the environmental factor should be considered here is apparent when the widespread de-urbanization throughout the Iranian highlands at the end of the Middle Bronze Age is taken into account (Lamberg-Karlovski 1985: 68f.). The defeat of buffer states at or near the Zagros foothills – such as the kingdom Qabrā at the time of Samsi-Addu and the kingdom of Eshnunna by Hammurabi – opened the door to a surge in ethnic displacement into the lowlands, which the military campaigns against Zagros population groups that are recorded for Hammurabi's later years could not halt; on the contrary, these operations led to the deportation of large numbers of prisoners of war who were settled in the Babylonian countryside (Charpin 1992).

The duration and intensity of this resettlement process remain to be determined, but its consequences for the Mesopotamian demography and political landscape are evident from a variety of evidence. There were, on the whole, two options for recent immigrants in Mesopotamian alluvium. Ethnic groups could organize themselves into new political entities in the peripheral areas out of reach of the established kingdoms, with the influential, but presumably short-lived, Turukkean kingdom in the east-Tigris country during the second half of the reign of Hammurabi as the best-known example (Eidem and Læssøe 2001: 55–58). Alternatively, they could subject themselves to the authority of the Mesopotamian states and seek a livelihood as labourers and, especially, mercenaries. This strategy is again attested for the Turukkeans, when we read how groups of them were resettled under Samsi-Addu in the core of his kingdom and admitted into his army (Charpin 2004: 177). These well-documented cases can serve as a paradigm to explain the appearance of other ethnic groups on the Mesopotamian scene.

The Kassites were the most famous and influential of these groups. This ethnic label was of Babylonian coinage but derives probably from a Zagros toponym (Eidem and Læssøe 2001: 28), and there is more evidence to support the idea that at least some of them indeed came from the highlands. They appear for the first time in the ninth year-name of Samsuiluna, where it is said that the king 'tore out the roots of the Kassite army [at] Kikalla'. There is no further information about this event, but since Kikalla, a town in the vicinity of Kish, is known for its military field holders, it is possible that the year-name refers to the suppression of an uprising of mercenary forces who had been settled in the area – an interpretation for which the rebellion of the Turukkean army under Samsi-Addu offers a direct parallel. Yet again in subsequent generations, one hears repeatedly of incidents with hostile Kassite forces, but whatever impact these events may have had, it is clear that a Kassite participation in the Babylonian army had become an established phenomenon already at the time of Samsuiluna, and is well attested until the end of the Old Babylonian period (Sassmannshausen 2004a). In fact, the marked military character of the Kassites throughout the period leads us to believe that the term may have been used in a fairly broad sense for warriors of highland extraction, rather than for people of a specific ethno-linguistic background. A similar degree of ambiguity concerns other foreigners in Babylonian service: Gutean and Elamite troops are also well attested, but since these people had long been highly regarded as professional soldiers, it is quite impossible to decide whether these labels refer to individuals of a specific ethnic background, or to professionals with particular skills (Eidem and Læssøe 2001: 31f.). Other ethnic labels occur more sporadically, such as the Hurrian-speaking troops from Hanigalbat and those from faraway Tukris beyond the Zagros mountains who are mentioned under the last kings of Babylon, but in these cases there is no reason to doubt that these bands were really of foreign descent.

All this indicates that the proportion of foreigners in the Babylonian army increased radically ever since the reign of Samsuiluna. Their recruitment not only neutralized what would otherwise be a potentially destabilizing element in society, but, more importantly, these mercenaries were undoubtedly better warriors than the conventional forces of conscripted non-professionals that had constituted the main part of the army under Hammurabi. Also, the development of new military techniques, above all the effective implementation of the light horse-drawn battle chariot under Hammurabi's successors, required skills that only professional specialists could provide; one may furthermore assume that foreign mercenaries played a part in the transmission of these technological innovations (Moorey 1986). This increasing professionalism meant that the need for untrained conscripted infantry troops decreased, while more money was needed for the treasury to finance the mercenary forces, and this shift is manifest since the reign of Abi-eshuh, when the obligatory service performance that was linked to the usufruct of a service field was increasingly replaced by a silver tax.

The source situation dictates that the ethnic newcomers in the Mesopotamian lowlands who did not enter into state service remain virtually invisible, but their presence is revealed when one takes note of polities in the peripheral regions, outside of the Babylonian state, that emerged by the amalgamation of groups of various ethnic and social backgrounds. This is best observed at the Middle Euphrates, a frontier region where, under Hammurabi or one of his successors, mercenary forces in Babylonian pay had been settled in the already mentioned 'Kassite houses'. What happened afterwards is not documented, but a few generations later, when the 'Kassite houses' survived only as a toponym, several autonomous powers were found in the area, with the Samharû as the most prominent constituent, a name that in the Middle Babylonian period was used by some as the designation for the Kassite dynasty on the Babylonian throne (van Koppen 2004). A similar course of events can be assumed to occur in the Diyala region, but here we must largely rely on later evidence, when we observe that the elite of the Kassite dynasty maintained particularly close ties with this area, and note that the Nuzi texts (fourteenth century BC) refer to it as the 'Kassite land'. Nonetheless, there are good reasons to accept that already at the time of Samsuditana, the Diyala region, including the city of Eshnunna, constituted a kingdom whose rulers were counted in later tradition among the ancestors of the Kassite royal lineage. These peripheral political entities no doubt contributed to the growing destabilization that was felt towards the end of the Old Babylonian period, and may be brought forward, in conjunction with incidents of mutiny of the regular mercenary forces, to explain the allusions to Kassite hostility that occur throughout the Old Babylonian period.

SETTLEMENT

When Hammurabi conquered the kingdom of Larsa, he took over a country in economic decline. The high incidence of redress acts under Larsa's last king, Rim-Sin, points to widespread impoverishment in his time, which in all probability was rooted in a drop in agricultural productivity due to diminishing water supplies, a phenomenon that the major canal repair works of Rim-Sin's reign evidently failed to remedy. Hammurabi claims in official statements that he honoured the royal duty to care for the land's hydraulic infrastructure, but his correspondence with his servants in Larsa shows that the situation, in reality, was close to disastrous. Much evidence has survived about Babylonian economic policy in the newly established 'Lower Province', but its interpretation so far allows only provisional conclusions about its substance and effects. It is evident that the income from large tracts of state land, so far enjoyed by the local elite, were now set aside for Babylonian officials. The Babylonians also tried to cut expenses for rations by increasing the number of subsistence field holders, which, in the light of the declining yields, may have been unfavourable for many beneficiaries. The collection of revenues in kind due to palace and temple, and its conversion into silver, had traditionally been the job of entrepreneurs and continued to be so under Babylonian rule, but an unusual arrangement is now in place: the palace farmed out its tax income for one-third of its nominal value in silver, and occasionally for even less (Stol 1982). This arrangement, which parallels land leases in regard to the division of labour and profit, is only attested in this period and may have been a Babylonian adaptation of the local system, but we lack comparable texts of earlier date to confirm this impression. As regards its economic motive, the sharp discount may indicate that the expected volume of revenue could no longer be realized, so that extra incentive for the entrepreneurs was required to ensure a steady, though less than maximum, supply of silver to the capital; after all, the palace of Babylon was solely interested in receiving silver and barley from its new territories.

It is against this backdrop of low prosperity, failing agriculture and high taxation that the southern revolts against Samsuiluna must be understood. The king of Babylon reacted brutally, and the sudden abandonment of cities is the well-known outcome of the war. Urban life in the south had been faltering before, as is revealed by the concentration of governmental and cultic offices in the capital city of Larsa during the reign of Rim-Sin, but the breakdown accelerated rapidly at this time, possibly as a consequence of intentional diverting of water at an upstream position, with the result that some cities were not rebuilt after warfare damage, while others were evacuated without overt signs of violence (Gasche 1989); the ensuing northward migration of elites and cults is well documented (Charpin 1992). Without the urban basis, the southern countryside permanently escaped Babylonian control, but somewhere in the marshlands the Sealand must be sought, whose king is first attested in the ninth year of Samsuiluna[5] and played a decisive role in the warlike events of his later years. The First Sealand Dynasty lasted into the Middle Babylonian period, but almost no textual sources shed light on their state, and its part in a vibrant trade network at the head of the Persian Gulf is only known from archaeological evidence (Højlund 1989).

Unlike the southern alluvium, the de-urbanization in the east-Tigris lands around the time of Hammurabi is not illuminated by contemporary textual evidence, but is suggested by research in the Diyala and Hamrin regions, where almost all larger sites disappear around that time; here, social factors are the likely cause, as it would seem that the demographical instability discussed above negatively affected permanent settlement. Some urban centres, nevertheless, survived as political focal points, such as Eshnunna, a site where the upper occupation levels are lost to erosion, but which is known from textual evidence to persist as an administrative centre until the end of the Old Babylonian period.

The environmental factor that lies at the root of the urban crisis of the South did not leave the Babylonian heartland unaffected. Barley–silver equivalences indicate that agricultural productivity had peaked at the turn of the second millennium BC. The price of barley then moved upwards, but this process may have been quite gradual, if one disregards episodic shortages that are bound to occur in a traditional agricultural regime. Even by the time of Hammurabi, when the traditional equivalence 1 shekel of silver = 300 litres of barley has lost its validity (Powell 1990: 92), real barley prices were only slightly higher, until they rose sharply under Samsuiluna, and henceforth seem to stay at a high level. Much around the same time, the price of arable land dropped – at least at Sippar, which has produced most evidence. That these sudden price movements are signs of a food crisis is clear from the explicit evidence for famine in the later years of Samsuiluna, an episode that may well have inspired the graphic descriptions of starvation in the contemporary Atrahasis myth (Wilcke 1999).

It may be that this period of famine was triggered by the political turmoil at the time, but the root cause of the declining yields was a change in the Euphrates system that, perhaps quite suddenly, brought about a permanent failure of the Euphrates branch that runs through Kish and Nippur to carry sufficient water (Cole and Gasche 1998: 27). This led to the evacuation of the city of Nippur, but also to the decline of Uhaimir, ancient Kish, an important town until it was largely, if not completely, deserted under Samsuiluna's successors, while the archives of nearby Ingharra, known as Hursagkalama but also as Kish, last until the end of the Old Babylonian period; no doubt other sites dependent on the same water course suffered as well. Other cities also declined, with no evident correlation with the failing Kish branch: the built-up area inside the walls of Abu Habbah, one of the twin cities named Sippar, contracted under Samsuiluna, whereas Tell ed-Der, the other Sippar, was given up altogether after its wartime conflagration under Ammisaduqa. These sites had for centuries been our main source of texts, but when finally, late in Samsuditana's reign, even the textual output of Abu Habbah and Ingharra came to an end, all sources fall silent and a Dark Age begins.

This process of site abandonment has profoundly shaped our perception of the Old Babylonian period. The archaeological survival of our sources is wholly determined by it, and their total cessation invokes an image of a cycle coming to an end. We should, however, realize that the available evidence does not tell the whole story, because the most prosperous and densely inhabited part of the Babylonian state is seriously under-represented in the documentary record and unmapped by archaeological reconnaissance. This is the land along the Arahtum, the branch of the Euphrates that flowed through Babylon, where second-millennium BC sites are often buried by sedimentation and only few archives have come to light (Hritz 2004). When the Kish branch stagnated, intensive agriculture continued along the Arahtum and drew a population shift from the eastern branch, while the growth and prosperity of the city of Babylon may have attracted even more people from the dwindling towns in the country.

The strip of alluvial plain north and south of Babylon thus came to be the core of the later Old Babylonian state, and it is here that urban life almost certainly continued beyond the end of the First Dynasty. In the early Middle Babylonian period, a grand programme was carried out to bring the eastern lands, which the clogged Kish branch had left dry, under cultivation again. To this end canals were dug that irrigated the hinterlands of Nippur, Isin and Uruk from the Arahtum or other western Euphrates channels (Armstrong and Brandt 1994: 261); since the cults at these sites had been restored by the time of Kurigalzu I (Clayden 1996), the main effort of this enterprise can be dated to the fifteenth century BC.

THE ROLE OF BABYLON

First-hand evidence about Old Babylonian Babylon is solely based on the limited deep soundings of the German excavations (Pedersén 1998), but its paramount role in the administration of the kingdom is clearly perceptible in the textual record from provincial sites. The city expanded greatly, and may have reached the dimensions of the later Nebuchadnezzar city walls in the middle Old Babylonian period.[6] Babylon benefited from the political successes of its kings, but also from the subsequent urban crisis, as this led to a concentration of cults and offices of the ruined regional centres within its walls. Babylon's victories had shaped the theology of the city god Marduk (Wiggermann 1989), and the reception and embellishment of uprooted cults were, again, ideologically important, and may have some bearing on the theological elevation of Babylon and the promotion of Marduk to the head of the pantheon at a later date. Both organizationally and ideologically, the city thus developed into the only supra-regional centre of Lower Mesopotamia in the centuries that followed the reign of Hammurabi.

The palace of Babylon strongly influenced private economic behaviour, as the prevailing model of kingship was paternalistic – the king being the 'good shepherd', an attitude that materialized in the royal administration of justice. Hammurabi was, in this respect, again a transitional figure, as his famous Law Code was the last example of a specific genre of royal proclamations of just rules set on stone monuments. While earlier examples include legal provisions of universal applicability (nowadays referred to as 'laws') as well as a description of social and administrative reforms, Hammurabi reserved only the former category for his monument, incorporating the latter in another type of legal proclamation: a royal decree that was not inscribed in stone but circulated on clay tablets only (Wilcke 2002: 301). This practice was taken over by his successors, whose decrees incorporated and expanded Hammurabi's text, and the best-preserved issue is now known as the 'Edict of Ammisaduqa'. Hammurabi's decree accompanied the celebration of a redress act, a highly ideological and time-honoured event that aimed at establishing equity in the country by the redress of wrongs that had transpired in the past. His successors performed similar acts, and copies of the redress decree were distributed to announce the occasion. The relation between the act and the decree is, however, ill-matched, because the act is known to have affected various kinds of economic activities that are not described in the decree and, conversely, much of its traditional text lost its validity in the course of time: the ritualistic nature of the document in the later Old Babylonian period should therefore be emphasized. The redress acts were, however, entirely real and are an important factor to explain the composition of the surviving archives (Charpin 2000).

These redress decrees must be kept strictly apart from another type of royal decree, one that introduced specific elements of permanent legislation in response to acute problems presented to the court (Veenhof 2001). These decrees of the second type had an immediate effect on the day-to-day dealings of the population and affected the phrasing of legal texts: sometimes explicit reference to them is made in contracts ('in accordance with the royal decree'), but more often these regulations can be only detected through changing patterns in the documentation, as they harmonized legal forms in the different cities of the kingdom and shaped their development over time. By means of such regulations, the king interfered in customary law, for example in the laws of sale and credit, or when a status investigation for chattel slaves was stipulated in order to protect indebted civilians (van Koppen 2004), but also when lower fixed yield rates for field leases appear – presumably in reaction to a declining productivity. This form of legislation peaked under Samsuiluna and Abieshuh and addressed social problems that may have worsened because of the recent hydraulic crisis. After a while, economic reality found ways around some of these rulings, but their influence on the common types of legal texts was permanent.

In the course of the Old Babylonian period, the control of the ruling class of Babylon over the provincial resources and wealth increased markedly at the expense of the traditional local elites. The class of palace officials expanded and their titles multiplied, while the development of epistolary forms reveals how class-consciousness heightened. The rich evidence from Sippar shows how local families were recruited as acting managers for hereditary lineages of court officials, and occasionally were tied by matrimonial bonds. The patrimonial character of the state administration meant that the elite's increasing economic power was inextricable from that of the palace, and high officials profited from the much-studied palace transactions. At a local level, this effected that erstwhile forms of autonomy waned and government appointees came to dominate the administration, visible, in Sippar for example, in the decline of the traditional institutions of *kārum* and *gagûm*.

CONCLUSION

Given that the fortune of Aleppo and Babylon had been much like two sides of the same coin, it does not surprise that the Hittite conquest of Aleppo finally led to an attack on Babylon, perhaps in an offbeat attempt to control the profitable Euphrates route. That Babylon suffered from this event is clear from the fact that the excavated parts of the city show signs of a hiatus in occupation, but the city remained the capital of the land, and the new Kassite rulers began to date their years by an era starting with the year 'when (the country of) Babylon was resettled'. The dynastic change had brought the leaders of the former mercenary forces to power, and the limited evidence that is presently available suggests, as may be expected from analogous cases, that at first no major social and economic changes occurred. A few decades later, the new rulers began to extend the limited territories of Babylon, first subjugating their rival in Eshnunna and then pushing south until, in the beginning of fifteenth century BC, the Sealand was conquered and their authority was recognized as far as Dilmun (Sassmannshausen 2004b). Lower Mesopotamia had once more been united and another distinct historical era – that of the Kassite kingdom of Karduniash – begins.

NOTES

1 This chapter is based on research undertaken with funding of the *Jubiläumsfonds der Österreichischen Nationalbank*. The size limit of this chapter precludes giving full evidence in support of the arguments that are brought forward, but the recent manuals of Charpin 2004 and Stol 2004 contain all relevant facts. The article follows the customary Middle Chronology, with the Fall of Babylon in 1595 BC; this is certainly wrong, but the real date of the event (sometime in the second half of the sixteenth century BC) cannot yet be determined.

2 A cessation of textual evidence for an unknown period of time.

3 Unpublished tablet BM 16469 (Hammurabi 42).

4 The so-called 'Agum-kakrime Inscription' I 31–32.

5 OECT 15 78.

6 George 1992: 15–19; this date for the creation of the (predecessor of the later) Imgur-Enlil wall is suggested by the fact that in Old Babylonian sources the Ishtar (Szlechter TJA UMM G 18) and Urash (Stol 1982 no. 28) gates constitute the northern and southern city borders.

BIBLIOGRAPHY

Armstrong, J.A. and Brandt, M.C. 1994. Ancient dunes at Nippur, 255–263, in: H. Gasche *et al.* (eds), *Cinquante-deux réflexions sur le Proche-orient ancien offertes à Léon De Meyer*, MHEM 2, Leuven: Peeters.

Attinger, P., Sallaberger, W. and Wäfler, M. (eds) 2004. *Mesopotamien. Die altbabylonische Zeit. Annäherungen* 4. OBO 160/4. Fribourg: Academic Press; Göttingen: Vandenhoeck & Ruprecht.

Charpin, D. 1992. Immigrés, réfugiés et déportés en Babylonie sous Hammu-rabi et ses successeurs, 207–218, in: D. Charpin and F. Joannès (eds), *La circulation des biens, des personnes et des idées dans le Proche-Orient ancien. Actes de la XXXVIIIe Rencontre Assyriologique Internationale* (Paris, 8–10 July 1991). Paris: ERC.

—— 2000. Les prêteurs et le palais: les édicts de *mîsarum* des rois de Babylone et leur traces dans les archives privées, 185–211, in: H. Bongenaar (ed.), *Interdependency of Institutions and Private Entrepreneurs. Proceedings of the second MOS symposium (Leiden 1998)*. MOS Studies 2. PIHANS 87. Leiden: NINO.

—— 2004. Histoire politique du Proche-Orient amorrite (2002–1595), 23–480, in: Attinger *et al.* 2004.

Clayden, T. 1996. Kurigalzu I and the restoration of Babylonia, *Iraq* 58: 109–121.

Cole, S.W. and Gasche, H. 1998. Second- and first-millennium BC rivers in Northern Babylonia, 1–64 in: H. Gasche and M. Tanret (eds), *Changing Watercourses in Babylonia. Towards a Reconstruction of the Ancient Environment in Lower Mesopotamia Volume 1*. MHEM 5/1. Ghent: University of Ghent; Chicago, IL: Oriental Institute.

Dercksen, J.G. 2001. 'When we met in Ḫattuš'. Trade according to Old Assyrian texts from Alishar and Boğazköy, 39–66, in: W.H. van Soldt *et al.* (eds), *Veenhof Anniversary Volume. Studies presented to Klaas R. Veenhof on the occasion of his sixty-fifth birthday*. PIHANS 89. Leiden: NINO.

—— 2004. *Old Assyrian Institutions*. MOS Studies 4. PIHANS 98. Leiden: NINO.

Eidem, J. and Læssøe, J. 2001. *The Shemshara Archives 1: The Letters*. Kongelige Danske Videnskabernes Selskab Historisk-filosofiske Skrifter 23. Copenhagen: Kongelige Danske Videnskabernes Selskab.

Gasche, H. 1989. *La Babylonie au 17e siècle avant notre ère: approche archéologique, problèmes et perspectives*. MHEM 1. Ghent: University of Ghent.

George, A.R. 1992. *Babylonian Topographical Texts*. OLA 40. Leuven: Peeters.

Højlund, F. 1989. Dilmun and the Sealand, *NAPR* 2: 9–14.

Hunger, H. and Pruzsinszky, R. (eds), *Mesopotamian Dark Age Revisited. Proceedings of an International Conference of SCIEM 2000, Vienna 8–9 November 2002*. Contributions to the Chronology of the Eastern Mediterranean 6. Österreichische Akademie der Wissenschaften Denkschriften der Gesamtakademie 33. Vienna: Verlag der Österreichischen Akademie der Wissenschaften.

Hritz, C. 2004. The hidden landscape of Southern Mesopotamia, *Akkadica* 125: 93–106.

Koppen, F. van 2004. The geography of the slave trade and Northern Mesopotamia in the late Old Babylonian period, 9–33, in: Hunger and Pruzsinszky 2004.

Lamberg-Karlovsky, C. 1985. 'The *longue durée* of the Ancient Near East', 55–72, in: J.-L. Huot, M. Yon and Y. Calvet (eds), *De l'Indus aux Balkans. Recueil à la mémoire de Jean Deshayes*. Paris: ERC.

Moorey, P.R.S. 1986. The emergence of the light, horse-drawn chariot in the Near-East c. 2000–1500 BC, *World Archaeology* 18: 196–215.

Pedersén, O. 1998. Zu den altbabylonischen Archiven aus Babylon, *AoF* 25: 328–338.

Powell, M.A. 1990. Identification and interpretation of long term price fluctuations in Babylonia: More on the history of money in Mesopotamia, *AoF* 17: 76–99.

Sassmannshausen, L. 2004a. Kassite nomads: Fact or fiction?, 287–305, in: C. Nicolle (ed.), *Nomades et sédentaires dans le Proche-Orient ancien. Compte rendu de la XLVIe Rencontre Assyriologique Internationale (Paris, 10–13 July 2000)*. Amurru 3. Paris: ERC.

—— 2004b. Babylonian chronology of the 2nd half of the 2nd millennium BC, 61–70, in: Hunger and Pruzsinszky 2004.

van Soldt, W.H. 1990. *Letters in the British Museum*. AbB 12. Leiden: Brill.

Stol, M. 1982. State and private business in the land of Larsa, *JCS* 34, 127–230.

—— 2004. Wirtschaft und Gesellschaft in altbabylonischer Zeit, 641–975, in Attinger *et al.* 2004.

Veenhof, K.R.V. 1997–2001. The relation between royal decrees and 'law codes' of the Old Babylonian period, *JEOL* 35–36: 49–83.

Weeks, N. 1985. The Old Babylonian Amorites: Nomads or mercenaries?, *OLA* 16: 49–57.

Wiggermann, F.A.M. 1989. Tišpak, his seal and the dragon *mušḫuššu*, 117–133, in: P.M.M.G. Akkermans, H.H. Curvers and O.M.C. Haex (eds), *To the Euphrates and Beyond. Archaeological Studies in Honour of Maurits N. van Loon*. Rotterdam: Balkema.

Wilcke, C. 1999. Weltuntergang als Anfang. Theologische, anthropologische, politisch-historische und ästhethische Ebenen der Interpretation der Sintflutgeschichte im babylonischen *Atram-ḫasīs*-Epos, 63–112, in: A. Jones (ed.), *Weltende. Beiträge zur Kultur- und Religionswissenschaft*. Wiesbaden: Harrassowitz.

—— 2002. Der Kodex Urnamma (CU): Versuch einer Rekonstruktion, 291–333, in: T. Abusch (ed.), *Riches Hidden in Secret Places. Ancient Near Eastern Studies in Memory of Thorkild Jacobsen*. Winona Lake: Eisenbrauns.

CHAPTER FIFTEEN

THE BABYLONIAN ECONOMY IN THE FIRST MILLENNIUM BC

——— •❖• ———

Michael Jursa

SOURCES

The first millennium BC is one of the best documented periods of Mesopotamian history. Both archaeological remains and textual sources are available in abundance, but their diachronic distribution is uneven.[1] The first two centuries are only very scarcely documented and contemporary texts are rare. Assyrian sources and later chronicles suggest that this was a period of unrest, collapse of central authority and general economic decline. The eighth and especially the seventh century have yielded slightly richer documentation, for instance an eighth-century letter archive from central Babylonian Nippur (Cole 1996). This is also the period at the end of which a gradual increase both of the number and the size of settlements first becomes perceptible in the archaeological record. From about 700 BC onwards, demographic growth and increasing urbanisation are the decisive economic trends, especially for northern Babylonia, well into the Sassanian period. At the culmination of this development, in the first centuries AD, probably the entire agriculturally usable area of the southern alluvium had been taken under the plough.

However, this development, suggested primarily by one large-scale archaeological survey (Adams 1981), might not be quite so continuous and unidirectional as has been suggested. Temporary and locally limited discontinuities, even reversals of the general trend, may have occurred. In the absence of additional survey data, the textual sources must be sifted for pertinent evidence. This is possible primarily during the sixth and fifth centuries from which tens of thousands of tablets are known. From the fourth century onwards, and especially after the Macedonian conquest, not only is a gradual decline in the number of tablets found noticeable; increasingly fewer subjects were treated in these texts as well. This is owed to the gradual rise of Aramaic – written on perishable materials – and partly also of Greek as the official language of the Macedonian and Seleucid administrations.

In addition to the uneven diachronic distribution of the textual sources, another limitation has to be mentioned: of the two traditional institutional agents of the Mesopotamian economy, the household(s) of the ruler and the temples, only the latter are well attested. Information on the royal establishment has to be culled from sources of other origin. As for the private sector of the economy, only propertied city dwellers tend to be directly documented by their own archives. The texts remain silent regarding the lower strata of urban society, especially the rural population without institutional affiliations.

THE ECONOMY OF BABYLONIA IN THE FIRST MILLENNIUM BC: BASIC CHARACTERISTICS

The first millennium does not differ from earlier periods of Mesopotamian history with regard to the fundamental features of economic life. The environmental conditions determined, to a large extent, the economic activities. Four principal ecological zones can be distinguished: the central alluvial plain, criss-crossed by rivers and irrigation canals, swampy river deltas and generally deeper lying areas with little or no drainage; the reed forests in which hunters, fishermen and bird catchers operated; the steppe bordering on the alluvium – the realm of the shepherds; and the cities. The corresponding principal ways in which these zones were exploited, namely, agriculture, hunting and fishing, sheep breeding and artisanal and other city-based non-agricultural activities, will now be reviewed in turn, as will be their social setting.[2]

AGRICULTURE IN THE CENTRAL ALLUVIUM: LAND USE AND LAND OWNERSHIP

As in all other periods, Babylonia in the first millennium BC was a predominantly agrarian society dependent on irrigation agriculture. The most distinctive trait of arable farming consisted in the usage of the seeder plough, an ingenious implement allowing high returns on seed. Cereal farming (producing barley, mostly) was, therefore, an extensive form of cultivation, economising on scarce resources – water, seed and labour – while making comparatively lavish use of land. On the other hand, date gardening, the second distinctive agrarian regime abundantly attested in this period, implied a far more intensive use of land (and water). Typically, date groves were used also for vegetable gardening, fruit trees and even grain farming. Returns – in comparison to the land used – were naturally far higher than in the case of simple arable farming, as were labour requirements, of course.[3]

The fact that, from the seventh century onwards, the importance of date gardening greatly increased in comparison to earlier periods is one of the clearest indications of demographic and, generally, economic growth; a widespread shift to a much more intensive form of cultivation must mean that there was pressure towards economising on land and that sufficient labour was available. This trend, however, was not universal. It can be clearly recognised in archives from northern Babylonian cities such as Sippar, Borsippa and Babylon. There, propertied city dwellers much preferred to invest in date groves; fields were turned into gardens everywhere. Institutional land holders – temples and the king – continued to occupy themselves with simple arable farming on a large scale, but even they moved into date gardening whenever possible. In central Babylonia on the other hand, for instance in Nippur, this trend was far weaker. There, private land holders continued to be involved in arable farming and institutional land was predominantly used for cereals. In the south, especially in the Uruk area, cereal farming always remained the principal agricultural activity; date gardening in the vicinity of urban centres, while still important and yielding high returns, was only of secondary importance overall. These differences are one of several indications suggesting an economic dichotomy between northern Babylonia and the central and southern parts of the country.[4] Another important distinction is that between the agricultural landscape in close vicinity of the cities and that in more remote parts of the country. Land use around the cities was always much more intensive and geared towards supplying the urban centres and less towards subsistence agriculture for the benefit of the rural population. It can be shown, for instance, that the immediate hinterland of Babylon was characterised by very intensive market gardening.

The single most important land owners were the institutions. The majority of the temples' holdings – far better attested than royal land – were concentrated around their home cities, but in the case of the two best-known temples, the Ebabbar in northern Sippar and the Eanna in southern Uruk, it can be demonstrated that numerous estates were, in fact, situated at a considerable distance from the urban centre. The Ebabbar, for instance, owned fields and gardens in the vicinity of Borsippa and Dilbat, south of Babylon. The cultivation of temple estates was achieved partly by the temples' own dependants, ploughmen and gardeners, who were, in all likelihood, unfree serfs (Akkadian *širku*). However, their number was always insufficient for the agricultural needs of the temples. Therefore, at all times, the land that had to be rented out to share croppers, free gardeners and other contractors exceeded the part of the temple domain that was under direct management. Not infrequently, large-scale leasing and sub-leasing took place. In this way, private entrepreneurs took part in the cultivation of institutional land. The so-called rent farmers were contractors undertaking the management of significant parts of the temple estates (or even of the entire holdings of a temple) against the payment of a predetermined rent. Initially, these men, who first appear late during the reign of Nebuchadrezzar II, in the first half of the sixth century, were royal protégées, later, during the rule of the Achaemenids, they could also originate in the temple households themselves. In theory, such entrepreneurs were supposed to be supplied with the necessary means for cultivating the land entrusted to them by the temples, but in practice they always had to invest at least part of their private means (which therefore had to be considerable) as well. The temples (and thus, indirectly, the crown) expected from such contractors not only a simplification of the bureaucratic tasks of supervising cultivation and the payment of rents and dues, but also the availability of outside capital. The entrepreneurs, of course, hoped to make a profit beyond the fixed rent that was expected of them.

As far as we can tell from the not over-abundant sources, royal estates and holdings of members of the king's family and of high officials were managed along the same lines as lands of the temples, which could not really be considered as totally independent since their resources could always be drawn upon by the royal administration when necessary. In addition to direct management and farming out, royal land could be exploited in a third way, for instance by apportioning it to royal dependants who, in return, owed the state labour or military service and/or tax payments. Frequently, such estates were granted to various collectives, sometimes of a certain professional background, but more frequently of common, usually non-Babylonian, origin. The land-for-service scheme was the easiest way by which the royal administration could integrate outsiders into Babylonian society.[5] Such settlements of non-Babylonians already existed in the Chaldean period, but they are most amply attested in the fifth century thanks to a group of texts, the so-called Murashû archive, named after a family-based firm of entrepreneurs that operated in the rural hinterland of Nippur. At least in part such estates seem to have been situated on previously temple-owned lands. In general, sixth-century texts suggest that the royal administration requisitioned surplus temple land for its own purposes.

The archives of propertied city dwellers contain ample information on private ownership of agricultural land; fields and gardens in private hands could be bought and sold freely. In the sixth century, one frequently hears of land that had come into the hands of upper-class families as a result of land allotment schemes sponsored by king, temple, or city authorities. In the seventh or early sixth centuries it had been acquired in the context of the reclamation of land that had fallen into disuse in the previous period of economic decline and political unrest.[6] At least some city-based families were also part of the land-for-service system by virtue of holding titles to estates encumbered with service and tax obligations of different kinds.

Well-to-do families would normally own date groves of not much over a hectare of surface area, mostly within easy reach from the city, if not actually within the walls. Such family gardens and, particularly in the south, fields were prized assets and normally only alienated in cases of distress, since they formed the background of the subsistence strategy of their owners (even though these might pursue many different kinds of activities in the city) (see Wunsch in this volume). Gardens were most often rented out to free tenants, less frequently they were entrusted to family slaves or managed (and worked) directly by the proprietors.

Private involvement in agriculture beyond the rentier kind of property management described above is likewise attested; agricultural contracting, leasing and subleasing, occurred not just in the institutional sphere. Some city-based entrepreneurs specialised in managing estates in private as well as institutional hands or invested much money in the purchase (and amelioration) of land on a large scale. Such activities always went hand in hand with other business, such as trade in primary and processed agricultural products.

An important part of the population which left next to no traces in the written documentation were subsistence-farming villagers. Small rural settlements are normally not excavated, and textual information is usually restricted to villages which included temple estates or holdings of (rich) urbanites.[7] If these connections to the cities (and the city archives) are lacking, villages appear in the texts only in exceptional cases, for instance as places of origin of workers hiring themselves out to temples for canal or building work.[8] Nevertheless, the independent village has to be considered an important constituent part of the Babylonian agricultural landscape (see Richardson in this volume).

ANIMAL HUSBANDRY

The necessary complement to agriculture in Babylonia, sheep breeding, is amply attested in first-millennium sources of institutional origin.[9] The temples' large flocks were often entrusted to so-called herdsmen on a contractual basis. These men, who have to be considered entrepreneurs, were required to deliver a certain number of animals and a certain amount of wool at the time of the shearing.[10] These amounts were determined on the basis of the original size of the herd, employing simple rules of thumb for the prospective number of lambs and the wool to be expected per head of sheep. Animals and wool in excess of expectations would remain the property of the herdsman who, on the other hand, was expected to make up for any shortfalls as well. Normally, herdsmen probably did not tend the sheep themselves; this was done by shepherds who often were of West Semitic origin – as in other periods, animal husbandry was the sector of the economy in which the world of the (semi-)nomadic tribes encountered that of the urbanised agriculturalists most regularly.

The flocks roamed quite widely to find adequate grazing. Urukean sheep could be found in regions as far away from their home as the trans-Tigridian area north-east of Babylonia. The principal product of animal husbandry was wool, the raw material for Babylonia's textile 'industry'; meat and milk products were of lesser importance. Especially in the south, where sheep breeding overall played a larger role for the institutional economy than in the north, wool was used frequently as a means of payment. The second most important product of animal husbandry for the temples were young male lambs, the most common offering to the gods. Contrary to, for instance, the Old Babylonian period, there is very little information on the involvement of private city dwellers in sheep breeding.

Other sectors of animal husbandry were cattle and bird raising. Cattle breeding never reached the scale of sheep breeding for the simple reason that large herds of cattle could not easily be maintained in southern Mesopotamia. The principal importance of cattle lay always in their use as draught animals, especially for ploughing. There is some evidence for private persons being involved in cattle breeding; typically, single animals would be rented out or put at the disposal of a farmer or cattle minder for the purpose of profit sharing by their owners. Bird breeding, like sheep breeding, is nearly exclusively attested in temple archives. Large flocks of ducks and geese were held, and bred to contract, mostly for the purposes of the offering regime.

THE ECONOMIC USE OF THE MARSHES

Hunting, fishing and bird catching were the activities normally associated with the periodically or permanently inundated parts of the country.[11] Very little written documentation survives. Fish was occasionally offered to the gods, which made the work of fishermen of some importance for temple administrations. One also hears of payments for fishing rights and of fish ponds which were exploited commercially by entrepreneurs.

THE CITY

As in all other periods of Mesopotamian history, the city and its inhabitants are the main focus of the written record.[12] However, the documentation strongly privileges certain parts and strata of society: the propertied upper class, and the institutional sector. The latter is represented predominantly by temples (and their archives).

THE TEMPLES

First-millennium Babylonian temples were complex economic entities – households, according to the most frequently used model – with often several thousand dependants.[13] The highest echelons within the temple administrations were partly royal officials – for all practical purposes, temples were subject to royal authority – and partly recruited among the traditional leading families of the city. The same families dominated the ranks of the numerous specialist professions employed in the cult, especially for the preparation and presentation of the daily food offerings, the central religious activity in a Babylonian temple. The offices of temple butchers, bakers, brewers, singers, exorcists and so forth brought with them a regular income related to the periods of service. These so-called temple prebends constituted a vital economic link – in addition to religious/ideological factors – which bound the temple to the city and (certain parts) of its population. It is no coincidence that in the Hellenistic period, at a time when traditional Babylonian ways of life were gradually disappearing, the sphere of the temples proved to be the most resilient and conservative sector of Babylonian culture.

Below the level of the prestigious holders of temple prebends, there was a stratum of ordinary craftsmen – smiths, weavers, potters, etc. – and menial workers, mostly unfree serfs (*širku*s, literally 'oblates') bound to the temple, but living in families. Such workers were maintained primarily by regular salaries, originally paid in kind, but from the sixth century onwards, increasingly in silver.

The latter point is particularly noteworthy. A regular payment of silver wages to temple dependants does not fit the traditional model, which considers the Babylonian temple economy to have been a classical redistributive system; the temples are con-sidered to have been economically more or less autarchic, or at least to have been striving for economic independence. In fact they were nothing of the kind. To the political, and partly also economic, dependence on the crown, one has to add the effects of a permanent lack of workers, which made the temples rely on hiring inde-pendent labour to a large extent (a similar phenomenon has been mentioned above in the discussion of temple agriculture). Furthermore, the increasing monetisation of economic life caused a certain degree of economic specialisation among the temples. The Ebabbar temple in Sippar, for instance, intensified agricultural production by specialising in date gardening even more than was the rule in northern Babylonia, at the expense of the temple's grain fields. Grain was bought with money made by the sale of dates. For the Eanna temple in southern Uruk, the major cash crop was wool. In some years this temple increased its agricultural income by as much as a third through purchase of grain that was paid for with the proceeds of the wool trade. Thus, money came to play an increasingly prominent role in the temple economy, explaining the gradual replacement of the traditional ration system by money salaries.

THE URBAN BOURGEOISIE

This – deliberately anachronistic – term is used here *faute de mieux* for a certain sector of the propertied upper class inhabiting Babylonian cities which has left a particularly rich documentation. The so-called 'prebendary' families held prestigious temple offices and lived to a large extent from these benefices.[14] While the social range encompassed by this group was quite large – one finds extraordinarily rich families traditionally holding high positions in the provincial government, as well as far more humble artisanal families specialising in certain prebendary trades – there are several characteristics typical for all members of this 'class'. From a social perspective, their main point of reference was the temple and its community. This is apparent most clearly in marriage practices – group-specific 'endogamy', i.e. intermarriage between prebendary families, is the rule – but also in residential patterns and business contacts. Economically, the ownership of temple prebends supplied these families with a (comparatively) secure source of income (in kind, mostly). Prebends (and shares in prebendary income) were traded very frequently, allowing us to study patterns of ownership and economic strategies of prebendary families. While some prebendaries clearly tried to gain a prebend portfolio that was as variegated as possible, others seem to have specialised in just one profession, sometimes even aiming at monopolising the execution of one kind of prebendary service in a temple. The need to organise the actual temple service gave rise to many different types of business arrangements between members of this group, their dependants and slaves, and sometimes also free craftsmen not attached to the temple establishment: especially in the area of the preparation of the food offerings, a large part of the preparatory work incumbent on the prebendaries was actually contracted out to third parties. In this way the prebendary system benefited even people beyond the tight social boundaries delimiting the circle of its primary usufructuaries.

The second pillar of the subsistence strategy of prebendary families was land ownership. Typically, such families owned one or two date groves in the vicinity of their cities. Depending on their financial situation, they might try to increase these holdings by additional purchases (the second important source of additional land being dowries of women marrying into such families), but more often they would be content with managing and maintaining the family property. Simplifying the evidence, one could say that their economic activities were characterised by a rentier mentality. Numerous additional holdings in the hands of a family invariably meant a more varied business activity, usually with perceptible 'entrepreneurial' traits. For instance, several rich prebendary brewers also commercially exploited the yields of their date gardens by brewing and selling beer of dates, the most common alcoholic drink of this period. On the other hand, only very rarely do the business activities of prebendaries approach the complexity and variety found among the representatives of the group of city dwellers which is to be discussed now.

THE ENTREPRENEURS

These men – we have to do with single individuals without any known family back-ground far more often than is the case with representatives of the prebendary class – are less easily defined than the prebendaries.[15] The absence of tight links to temple households is a common (but not invariable) trait. More importantly, they did not rely on moderately sized rural holdings for their subsistence; agriculture at, or close to, subsistence level did not belong to their repertoire of preferred economic strategies. If they owned just a little land, its overall importance for their activities was always limited. More extensive holdings, of course, were exploited for reasons of profit, not subsistence.

As in the case of the prebendaries, the social range attested within this group is remarkably wide. In the present context, only some general remarks on the types of business attested can be made; a detailed case-study is offered in this volume by Cornelia Wunsch.

Agricultural management and the trade in agricultural staples was probably the most important occupation of Babylonian entrepreneurs. Gardeners or farmers renting land from city-based property owners on share-cropping or other terms cannot be considered to fall within this category. But there was a wide range of entrepreneurial activities going on just one level above that of the actual cultivators, and extending far up the social scale, up to the important rent farmers to whom the management of institutional land and canals was contracted out. Frequently, for instance, entrepreneurs would rent land and sublease it either to dependants or to free tenants, whom they would supply with the means necessary for their work. The profit would be shared, and only a comparatively small part of the rent would go to the land owner. Especially institutional land was often managed by a hierarchy of such businessmen who leased land from, and subleased land to, yet other entrepreneurs. Another area where private businessmen and institutions frequently interacted was animal husbandry: the temples' and king's flocks were often managed by entrepreneurs who took a share in the proceeds.

An involvement in the trade in wool, staples, and beer brewed from dates was a natural consequence of entrepreneurial activities in the areas of agriculture and animal husbandry. The available evidence is comparatively scarce, since even important cash transactions did not have to be recorded in writing. We are, on the other hand, well informed about the wider background of this trade, since businessmen frequently had to form partnerships with colleagues to acquire the necessary capital for such ventures. Partnership contracts attest a wide range of different arrangements: joint ventures of partners equally sharing work, risk and profit are just as frequent as one-sided contracts with sleeping partners or 'capitalists' (not infrequently royal officials) who invested in the business of other (often younger) men. Such partnerships could exist for decades, only to be dissolved at the death of one of the partners; they could even be handed down to the heirs of their founders.

The volume of domestic trade in primary goods cannot be quantified reliably, but it must have been significant. This is borne out by individual texts documenting very important transactions, by the evidence for large-scale cash crop agriculture, and by the fact that, in all likelihood, a numerically significant part of the urban population seems to have been dependent on a food-market for their livelihood (see below). International long-distance trade is even more difficult to get to grips with. The best-attested imported goods are slaves, iron, copper, wine, wood, alum and dyes (for the Babylonian textile industry) and prestige goods such as aromatics, scarabs and glass. Most of these came from the west. Babylonia exported slaves, barley, dates, wool and garments. It is likely that textiles were the most important export product, but this cannot be verified on the basis of the available sources.[16] The obvious monetisation of economic exchange in Babylonia means that much silver was coming into the country. The two main sources were trade and tribute, as well as booty taken by the Neo-Babylonian kings from the west, but it is impossible to tell which may have been more important. Under Achaemenid rule, taxes payable in silver caused much money to be withdrawn from circulation within Babylonia but, by and large, no clear deflationary tendencies are noticeable. This suggests that money was still flowing into the country; and in this period this must have been primarily a result of trade, government spending being of less importance under foreign rule.

Given these background conditions, it is hardly surprising that money and credit transactions of many different kinds make up a large part of the surviving written record. Straightforward lending of money at interest, however, was not a typical entrepreneurial business, although it is of course attested. More frequently such businessmen extended loans in money or in kind to agricultural producers who had to pay them back, invariably in kind, at harvest time – thereby allowing the money-lenders to profit from the lower post-harvest prices. The normal interest rate for loans was 20 per cent per annum during the sixth century; earlier it was more flexible and frequently lower, from the fifth century onwards there was a tendency towards higher interest, reaching often as much as 40 per cent per annum. In the third century BC, genuine deposit banking developed in Babylonia for the first time.

The role of money-lending in the realm of agriculture was increasingly important from the fifth century onwards, when the Persian government extracted more and more of the taxes in cash. In Nippur, the Murašû family 'firm' specialised in lending money to holders of service land (sometimes called 'fiefs'), thus enabling them to pay their dues to the king.[17] In return, the Murašû took control of the pledged estates of these men, exploiting them with their own personnel and selling the produce presumably in Nippur, thus earning the money they needed to pay the taxes the king demanded. Elsewhere in Babylonia, and already in the sixth century, various forms of tax farming developed in a similar way, thus creating another sector of the economy in which private entrepreneurial activities and the realm of the institutions, in this case the royal administration, were inextricably linked.

'LOWER' STRATA OF THE URBAN POPULATION

The mass of the urban population appears only indirectly in the sources, so generalisations are difficult to make. However, it is likely that the majority of the city dwellers in northern cities such as Babylon, Borsippa and Sippar (but maybe not to the same extent in Uruk) were not directly affiliated to one of the temple households and were, at best, indirectly dependent on the royal administration (for instance, as beneficiaries of land grants connected to service obligations). Both private and institutional archives attest to the availability of free labour for hire.[18] In a rural context, these workers will have come primarily from independent villages, in a city environment, they must have been recruited from the lower strata of urban society.

The important question to be asked is the extent to which these people depended on hiring themselves out for their livelihood, and if they had other, supplementary means of sustaining themselves, such as modest holdings of land. The available data are not sufficient to answer this question directly, but, as already mentioned above, some indications point towards the existence of a class of people for whom wage labour was the primary source of income. Newly available texts suggest that the large-scale building activities under the Neo-Babylonian kings were, to a significant extent, financed on a monetary basis and depended primarily on hired labour, not on conscripted workers.[19] This means that a large urban work-force must have found continuous employment in these undertakings for years on end, earning money wages. These men would then not have been available for primary food production and would have had to be supplied through a market since their employer, the state, did not normally supply them directly with rations. Urban market places, either in the area of the city gates or in the city centres, are clearly attested in the sources. Their importance is also apparent from the fact that from the seventh century onwards, data on prices of the most important agricultural staples were collected in a temple in Babylon. The primary purpose of these data was astrological – the prices appear together with astronomical observations – but the fact that they were worthy of such systematic attention is sufficient proof of their importance in the mind of contemporaries. A statistical analysis of these price data, a unique source of information, shows regular seasonal price differences and consistent long-term trends, but also rather volatile short-term price fluctuations suggesting poor market-integration which allowed local shortages to have dramatic short-term effects. All this, and in addition the importance of cash crop agriculture in the urban hinterland, suggests the existence of an urban 'working class', a genuine 'proletariat' of considerable size, which was embedded in a monetised economy and subsisted without a firm base in the production of primary agricultural goods.[20]

SUMMARY AND CONCLUSIONS

The economy of the Neo-Babylonian period can be considered in many ways a continuation of that of earlier periods of Mesopotamian history. The same economic agents – state, temples, the private sector – are present; the ecological background did not change fundamentally; we are still dealing with a basically agrarian society. But there are also important changes, the most important being the increasing degree of urbanisation at least in the north of the country, the concomitant intensification of agricultural production and increasing importance of cash crops, and the gradual monetisation of the economy. We probably also see a decrease of the overall importance of the institutional households; in any case, the temples were struggling to maintain their prominent position in a changing economic environment which offered a large range of opportunities to private initiative. The role of the state has not yet been investigated sufficiently. The principal areas in which its activities affected the economy are the land-for-service sector on the one hand – through land grants, new population groups could be integrated into Babylonian society – and the circulation of silver on the other. Silver came into Babylonia as tribute and booty during the time of the Chaldean monarchy and was brought into circulation by the government, for instance through the large-scale building projects. On the other hand, the state increasingly levied taxes in silver, not in kind; this accelerated the existing trend towards monetisation. The fact that the Persian government's tax policies did not lead to widespread deflation is an indirect confirmation of the assumption that Babylonia's foreign trade (in textiles, probably) contributed significantly to the increase in the amount of silver circulating in the country.

NOTES

1 Jursa 2005a contains a detailed survey of the textual data of economic content from first-millennium Babylonia, including summary treatments of all the main tablet archives. Statements on these archives here will generally be documented by reference to this book where further information can be found. Other surveys of the material and summarising descriptions of first-millennium economy include Dandamaev 1984: 6ff., Jursa 2004a and the pertinent sections

of Joannès 2002 and Briant 2002. The most important work on the archaeological record is still Adams 1981.

2 On the ecology of Mesopotamia and how it shaped (and continues to shape) its economy see e.g. Postgate 1994: 3ff., Potts 1997: 1ff. and Wirth 1962.

3 One of the best general introductions to Babylonian agriculture is Liverani 1998: 45ff. Specifically for the first millennium see Jursa 1995 and 2004b, with further references. Much of what follows depends on Jursa 2005b.

4 References for the relative importance of date gardening and cereal farming in different regions of Babylonia can be found in Jursa (in press), where additional pertinent secondary literature is cited as well.

5 See e.g. van Driel 2002: 226ff.

6 This gradual process of land reclamation started already in the mid-seventh century in the south, whereas in the north, especially in the Sippar area, this process got under way only after the final end of Assyrian rule and the establishment of the Chaldean monarchy: Jursa 1995: 236–237 for Sippar; the Uruk evidence will be treated by B. Janković (forthcoming).

7 In some Borsippa archives we hear of villages which were for all intents and purposes owned by rich city-based families; cf. e.g. Jursa 2005a: 82f.

8 See e.g. Zawadzki (in press).

9 The most important points of reference are two articles by G. van Driel: 1993 and 1995.

10 A few of these men from Uruk have left (small) private archives: Jursa 2005a: 145+1135; 142+1110 (a cattle breeder).

11 Janković 2004; Kleber 2004.

12 For the Mesopotamian city in general see Van De Mieroop 1999. Some of his conclusions do not fit the evidence from the first millennium (as presented here).

13 The best study of a Neo-Babylonian temple is Bongenaar 1997. The following argument is explored in more detail in Jursa 2005b, where references and documentation can be found.

14 See van Driel 2002: 31ff. Descriptions of some typical archives of prebend-holding families on which the following generalisations are based can be found in Jursa 2005a: 77ff.

15 Some typical archives: Jursa 2005a: 65f., 69ff., 73, 75f.,. 108f. There, references for the different types of business activities described here can be found.

16 For some anecdotal evidence for entrepreneurial investment in textile manufacture see e.g. Jursa 2005a: 130 (on FLP 667), 132 and 146.

17 Jursa 2005a: 113f.

18 On hired labour see for the time being Dandamaev 1987 and Jursa 2005b: 173ff. (where some of the following arguments are explored in greater detail).

19 See preliminarily Beaulieu (in press).

20 On market places see preliminarily Jursa 2005b: 179f. The prices in the astronomical diaries have been frequently discussed; see lastly Van der Spek and Mandemakers 2003.

BIBLIOGRAPHY

Adams, R. McC. 1981. *Heartland of Cities, Surveys of Ancient Settlement and Land Use on the Central Floodplain on the Euphrates.* Chicago, IL and London: The University of Chicago Press.

Beaulieu, P.-A. in press. 'Eanna's Contribution to the Construction of the North Palace at Babylon', in H.D. Baker and M. Jursa (eds), *Approaching the Babylonian Economy: Proceedings of the START-Project Symposium Held in Vienna, 1–3 July 2004.* Münster: Ugarit-Verlag.

Bongenaar, A.C.V.M. 1997. *The Neo-Babylonian Ebabbar Temple at Sippar: Its Administration and Its Prosopography.* Istanbul: Nederlands Historisch-Archaeologisch Instituut.

Briant, P. 2002. *From Cyrus to Alexander. A History of the Persian Empire.* Winona Lake: Eisenbrauns.

Cole, S. W. 1996. *Nippur IV. The Early Neo-Babylonian Governor's Archive from Nippur.* Chicago, IL: Oriental Institute Press.

Dandamaev, M.A. 1984. *Slavery in Babylonia from Nabopolassar to Alexander the Great (626–331 BC).* DeKalb: Northern Illinois University Press.

—— 1987. 'Free Hired Labor in Babylonia During the Sixth through Fourth Centuries BC', in M. Powell (ed.), *Labor in the Ancient Near East*. New Haven, CT: American Oriental Society, 271–279.

—— 1995. 'Cattle in the Neo-Babylonian Period', *Bulletin on Sumerian Agriculture* 8: 215–240.

—— 2002. *Elusive Silver. In Search of a Role for a Market in an Agrarian Environment. Aspects of Mesopotamia's Society*. Istanbul: Nederlands Historisch-Archaeologisch Instituut.

Janković, B. 2004. *Vogelzucht und Vogelfang in Sippar im 1. Jahrtausend v. Chr.* Münster: Ugarit-Verlag.

—— forthcoming. *Aspekte der Landwirtschaft in Uruk im ersten Jahrtausend v. Chr.* Ph.D. thesis, University of Vienna.

Joannès, F. 2002. *La Mésopotamie au 1er millénaire avant J.-C.* Paris: Armand Colin (second edition; first edition 2000).

Jursa, M. 1995. *Die Landwirtschaft in Sippar in neubabylonischer Zeit*. Wien: Institut für Orientalistik.

—— 2004a. 'Grundzüge der Wirtschaftsformen Babyloniens im ersten Jahrtausend v.Chr.', in R. Rollinger and C. Ulf (eds), *Commerce and Monetary Systems in the Ancient World: Means of Transmission and Cultural Interaction*. Wiesbaden: Franz Steiner Verlag: 115–136.

—— 2004b. 'Pacht. C. Neubabylonische Bodenpacht', *Reallexikon der Assyriologie* 10, 3/4: 172–183.

—— 2005a. *Neo-Babylonian Legal and Administrative Documents: Typology, Contents and Archives*. Münster: Ugarit-Verlag.

—— 2005b. 'Money-Based Exchange and Redistribution: the Transformation of the Institutional Economy in First Millennium Babylonia', in Ph. Clancier *et al.* (eds), *Autour de Polanyi: Vocabulaires, théories et modalités des échanges*. Paris: De Boccard: 171–186.

—— in press. 'Das Archiv von Bēl-ṭēri-Šamaš', in H.D. Baker and M. Jursa (eds), *Approaching the Babylonian Economy: Proceedings of the START-Project Symposium Held in Vienna, 1–3 July 2004*. Münster: Ugarit-Verlag.

Kleber, K. 2004. 'Die Fischerei in der spätbabylonischen Zeit', *Wiener Zeitschrift für die Kunde des Morgenlandes* 94: 133–165.

Liverani, M. 1998. *Uruk la prima città*. Rome and Bari: Laterza.

Postgate, J.N. 1994. *Early Mesopotamia. Society and Economy at the Dawn of History*. Second Edition. London: Routledge.

Potts, D. 1997. *Mesopotamian Civilization. The Material Foundations*. London: The Athlone Press.

Van De Mieroop, M. 1999. *The Ancient Mesopotamian City*. Second edition. Oxford: Oxford University Press.

Van der Spek, R.J. and Mandemakers, C.A. 2003. 'Sense and Nonsense in the Statistical Approach of Babylonian prices', *Bibliotheca Orientalis* 60: 521–537.

van Driel, G. 1993. 'Neo-Babylonian Sheep and Goats', *Bulletin on Sumerian Agriculture* 7: 219–258.

Zawadzki , S. in press. 'The Building Project North of Sippar in the Time of Nabonidus', in H.D. Baker and M. Jursa (eds), *Approaching the Babylonian Economy: Proceedings of the START-Project Symposium Held in Vienna, 1–3 July 2004*. Münster: Ugarit-Verlag.

CHAPTER SIXTEEN

THE EGIBI FAMILY

———— ·◆· ————

Cornelia Wunsch

The records of the Egibi family constitute the largest and most important private archive from the Neo-Babylonian and early Achaemenid periods (sixth and early fifth centuries BC). Local people hoping to find antiquities to sell discovered the tablets in the 1870s and 1880s among the ruins of private houses in the Babylon area. They were found in sealed earthen jars, a sure sign that they had been consciously set aside by their owners. The archive is said to have originally comprised some three to four thousand tablets, but the rough handling during excavation, shipment, and trade inevitably reduced their number. George Smith acquired the bulk of this archive for the British Museum in 1876, the rest was dispersed among many collections in Europe and America. Today about 1,700 texts can be confidently attributed to this archive, discounting duplicates and joined fragments.

The records cover five generations of members of one family (a sequence of first-born sons) over more than 100 years, from the time of Nebuchadrezzar II until the beginning of Xerxes' reign. Late nineteenth-century scholars described the family as 'bankers of Jewish origin'; this reflected contemporary ideas about Jews and their role in banking rather than actual fact. These labels are still in use today even though the notions both of 'bankers' and the allegedly Jewish ethnicity of the Egibis were shown to be inappropriate many decades ago. The family name Egibi is of straightforward Sumero-Babylonian origin,[1] and the business activities of the branch that left the famous archive fit the description of *entrepreneurship* rather than deposit banking.[2]

There is no sign that the first generation of our family branch owned or inherited any real estate or prebendary offices. The latter were the insignia of the traditional wealthy urban class and guaranteed participation in the stream of income from local temples. M. Jursa (2005: 66) described the Egibi as 'members of a socially mobile class of entrepreneurially oriented urbanites without well-established roots in the traditional establishment whose focal point was formed by the old sanctuaries'.

The documents of the first generation were drawn up for Šulaja, the son of (Nabû)-zēra-ukīn. Most of them concern wholesale trade in commodities (barley and dates) in the rural districts around Babylon. For this end, Šulaja engaged in long-term business ventures with several partners, sharing profits and risks, and built up capital as well as connections, later to be developed by his son Nabû-ahhē-iddin.

It is in the second generation that the acquired wealth was translated into assets, prestige and office. Nabû-ahhē-iddin underwent a scribal education and legal training that allowed him to act as a court scribe. From the few records that survive of this period we get a glimpse on his early career: during the late years of Nebuchadnezzar he spent some time at Opis, a royal administrative centre. There he issued, for instance, documents to royal officials on their private matters, probably as a by-product of his main occupation, serving the administration. Among his clients was the administrator of the crown prince's palace. Nabû-ahhē-iddin also is known to have arranged legal and financial issues for the purchase of a valuable house by Neriglissar (some time before the latter usurped the throne), acting as his 'lawyer' so to speak. He disentangled a complex web of creditor rights in a bancruptcy case. After Neriglissar's death he managed to advance his career under the next king, Nabonidus, when he held an influential position as royal judge in Babylon. Many of his business tasks were then delegated to his eldest son or to some skilled and well-trusted slaves.

After Nabû-ahhē-iddin's death early in the thirteenth year of Nabonidus, Itti-Marduk-balātu managed the affairs of the Egibi house in the third generation, until the end of Cambyses' reign. The Persian conquest of Babylonia occurred at this period. The political transition seems to have been smooth, though Itti-Marduk-balātu must have made some special efforts to keep the business going since a huge part of his commodity trade depended on cooperation with the royal administration. He untertook several long trips to Persia, obviously as part of a group of Babylonian business people in pursuit of the royal court and its influential personalities. As later records show, he succeeded in maintaining and expanding his position in the tax collection in the Babylon area and in providing army supplies.

He seems to have died suddenly at the beginning of Darius' reign, with his eldest son Marduk-nāṣir-apli being neither married nor introduced to his father's business affairs. Both matters were only accomplished according to Itti-Marduk-balātu's intentions by the latter's father-in-law, with whom he had a close business relationship; apparently he did not consider his own brothers trustworthy in such matters.

Marduk-nāṣir-apli stayed in charge of the family business for 14 years. At this point his two younger brothers demanded to receive their shares. The record of the inheritance division shows the wealth of the family: 16 urban properties in Babylon and Borsippa and more than 100 slaves are distributed among the brothers; gains and losses of pending business were to be shared accordingly. The fields and gardens, as well as houses in Hursagkalamma (where some business operations were based), are only mentioned in passing as they were not yet subject to division.

This inheritance division was problematic as it reduced the working capital. Marduk-nāṣir-apli can be seen pledging valuable properties for debts owed to the temple Esagila in Babylon, presumably in connection with his rent or tax farming activities. One record attests to the foreclosure on assets worth 50 minas (about 25 kg) of silver. However, despite this trouble there is no indication of a general or drastic decline in the family's fortunes.

Marduk-nāṣir-apli's son Nidinti-Bēl took over the business after the death of his father in the thirty-sixth year of Darius. Only few records remain from this time, as the archives as we know them came to an end at the beginning of Xerxes' reign during a period of political unrest. Nidinti-Bēl seems to have sifted through his tablets, keeping those of immediate interest for his business affairs while putting aside everything obsolete and outdated. It is this discarded corpus, carefully buried in jars, that has survived the millennia.

THE BUSINESS TRANSACTIONS

Transactions involving commodities (essential goods such as barley, dates, onions and wool), from their purchase in the rural area around Babylon to their transport, storage and sale, formed the mainstay of the Egibi enterprise, with little change in the forms of organization throughout the decades. Numerous smaller private archives, as well as information about other entrepreneurs in the Egibi documents demonstrate that a great number of urban, upper-middle-class people were engaged in similar activities, playing a mediating role between producers and consumers. Although they had various professional contacts to royal officials or temple personnel they did not operate in a capacity of representing an institution, but as private entrepreneurs. Business with commodities must have been lucrative, not least because of Babylon's growing population, who, attracted by the large-scale building projects under Nebuchadrezzar and Nabonidus, were not engaged in agriculture and did not have their own plots to cultivate.

Šulaja and his son began by working with other partners in so-called *ḫarrānu*-companies (*ḫarrānu* means 'street, caravan'), the equivalent of the long-lasting *commenda* enterprises known from Italy and the Hanseatic. Usually, one of the partners provided the start-up capital while the other did the work in the countryside. The farmers were given seed corn and draught animals on credit which they had to pay back in kind at harvest time. Just before the harvest, buyers would move around the fields to secure part of the harvest in advance. Barley, dates and onions had to be gathered up, the farmers then moved them to depots along the canal from whence they were loaded onto boats and taken to Babylon or other depots lining the canal. This entailed negotiations with the palace administration about canal charges, the hiring of boats and storage space, the brewing of beer from barley – all these different procedures are well documented, only the sale transactions to the final consumer are not. The provider of the capital and his active partner shared the profit (Akkadian *utru* 'surplus') equally, and the former also shared the risk. The acting partner was often not allowed to work for others on the side or to enter into business deals with others, he had to work full-time. This made the crucial difference to business transactions on the basis of normal loans where the interest was 20 per cent per year and secured by a deposit. *Ḫarrānu*-companies were, therefore, suitable for ambitious businessmen, without their own capital as well as for the wealthy, prepared to take a risk for above average profit margins. There is no doubt that the economic situation at the time of the Neo-Babylonian empire was favourable for such enterprise and some families became seriously rich quite quickly. However, there is also documentation of families who were forced to sell substantial property (houses, gardens, slaves) in one go in order to pay their creditors – not all entrepreneurs were as successful as the Egibi.

While Šulaja began by acting as managing associate with his partners' capital, Nabû-aḫḫē-iddin soon had enough funds of his own to let others work for him. He married his eldest son to the daughter of another very successful businessman, Iddin-Marduk, of the Nūr-Sîn family. This resulted not only in a dowry of 24 minas which were invested into the family fortune, but also in access to the other family's commodity business (especially onions), which was concentrated on the Borsippa canal. Iddin-Marduk had established there a network of connections to local producers and officials. He, too, had begun to do business with *ḫarrānu*-companies, on a small scale at first, then through subordinates and finally even some slaves. The latter now also worked for Itti-Marduk-balāṭu, the son-in-law, and later became part of Egibi property.

The profits seem to have been invested productively. Business accounts mention especially slaves, houses and real estate which had been purchased with company funds and then allocated to shareholding parties, sometimes by drawing lots. Lease contracts for fields and gardens, rent receipts for houses in Babylon and Borsippa, as well as payments from slave dues, all record respective incomes. Work or delivery contracts with craftsmen also show that the Egibi (and their wives) were interested in gold, silver, precious stones, sumptuous textiles and beautiful beasts – prestige objects appropriate to members of a wealthy family.

REAL ESTATE

There is no evidence that Šulaja, the representative of the first generation, had inherited or purchased fields and orchards. There is one document, however, that shows him as leaseholder of palace land somewhere near Babylon. This contract was for an unlimited period of time and obliged him to cultivate the land with date palms. Šulaja as leaseholder was to receive part (probably half) of the yield. Since the text is badly preserved and other relevant documentation is missing, we cannot be clear about details of sub-leasing and production. It was a large area, 400 metres long at the front side of the canal. Normally strips of cultivation reached one to two kilometres inland. It is likely that this royal reclamation project helped to get Šulaja's commodity business off the ground.

It was only under Nabû-aḫḫē-iddin's direction that the first town houses were purchased, and then, in quick succession during the reign of Nabonidus, agricultural plots, mainly smaller parcels of less than one hectare, but also some larger ones. Most were situated in the immediate vicinity of Babylon. In the sale contracts, they are defined at first generally according to adjacent canals and paths, the nearest city gate and the administrative district, then follow the names of neighbours on all sides. This form of localization makes it hard for us to situate these properties with any certainty; field plans were rarely transmitted and are difficult to relate to the description of extant sales contracts. Therefore it is unlikely that we will ever be able to make a map of 'Babylon environs'.

The Egibi preferred property outside the city wall in the east and south-east of Babylon, but not exclusively. In fact, their largest contiguous possession was in the north-west, outside the Enlil Gate.

It can be seen from exchange contracts that they tried to swap small isolated parcels outside the main holding for those bordering their land.

A comparison of property prices in the area of Babylon does not show an increase for the years 575 to 510, the period for which we have enough material for comparison. Date palm orchards with productive palm trees within the city walls fetched the highest price, followed by extramural ones. One shequel of silver (the monthly income of a hired man) corresponded to 22 to 75 square metres of orchard land (with a normal density of one to two trees). Orchards with a few or young trees were relatively cheaper, agricultural land up to ten times more, depending on soil quality.

It is often possible to deduce from the sales and other documents why a property was sold. Frequently it was to pay off debts, sometimes debts had accumulated for two generations, with the property being pawned, until there was no alternative to selling. Sometimes fields or orchards formed part of a communal inheritance or business partnership, and the owners wanted to sell all or part of it, because there had been a quarrel, or because the parcels had become too small through partition, or the cultivation too complicated, or when they needed the money for something else.

The cultivation of a property was effected by the leaseholders, which included slaves belonging to the Egibi. Lease contracts with special clauses document that date cultivation in the Babylon area was heavily intensified and that numerous new plantations were made along the canals. This procedure was very labour intensive and the leaseholder was compensated accordingly by high proportions of the yield over several years. Since this meant that advantages and profits only accrued after several years it proves the far-sighted and long-term investment strategies of the Egibi.

It was Nabû-aḫḫē-iddin who made the first purchase of tillable property outside the gates of Babylon, just a few months after Neriglissar had usurped the throne. As we have seen, he had already established business contacts with Neriglissar during the reign of Nebuchadrezzar and now benefited from this connection. Since the 'fate' of this field is well documented across three generations, we can use it as a case study for how the Egibi acquired and cultivated property, how it was subject to partition in each generation and how the heirs tried to consolidate their share through exchanges and re-purchase.

Nabû-aḫḫē-iddin bought an area of 24 kur (ca. 2,300 m × 140 m = 32.4 hectare), situated on both sides of the New Canal, north-west of the city. The document was signed by high-ranking witnesses: the governor of Babylon and seven royal judges who, together with the four scribes, rolled their seal along the edges of the tablet. The vendors were four brothers, facing Nabû-ahhe-iddin as the sole purchaser. The buying price, 22⅓ minas (about 11,166 kg) of silver, however, was not handed over to the four vendors but to the temple of Marduk, Esagila, who had a claim against the brothers 'on account of oxen' as it says.

The background emerges from other documents since the brothers handed the existing sale contract to the buyer, as was the custom at the time, in order to show that they had purchased the property legitimately and they were entitled to sell it on. According to this sales contract, the father of the four brothers had bought the property in the thirtieth regnal year of Nebuchadrezzar through a middle man, when he himself was acting governor of Babylon. A later, unfortunately fragmentary, text cites a directive by Neriglissar concerning our field, which he issued after his accession to the throne. Is it too fanciful to think of this as a case of corruption or enrichment in office penalized by the new ruler? After all, the governor of Babylon had considerable debts, at least to the temple of Marduk. And is it coincidence that Neriglissar's protégé, Nabû-aḫḫē-iddin got a good deal with his purchase? Although he paid a somewhat higher price than the governor had paid 15 years previously (about 17 per cent), the value of the property had also risen in the meantime because of the new date palm plantations. While at the beginning only a thirtieth of the surface, a narrow strip along the shore, had been planted with date palms, the proportion at sale was nearly a sixth, of which one half had productive and one half young trees. Land planted with date palms was worth five to ten times more than arable land. Despite the favourable conditions Nabû-aḫḫē-iddin had not been able to raise the purchase price all by himself at this time in his career. Immediately after the purchase he, therefore, made half the property over to his business partner, with whom he shared the lease income for the following years. Date cultivation alone could yield up to 30,000 litres of dates in a good year, as can be seen from the relevant obligation bills laid on the lease holder. When one takes the ideal conversion rate of dates to silver into account, which was applied, among others, for the conversion of debts in kind into silver or as equivalent in lease contracts, then this represents the considerable sum of $2\frac{3}{4}$ minas.

After Nabû-aḫḫē-iddin's death the property was divided in half, equally between his heirs and those of his business partner and henceforth cultivated separately. Nabû-aḫḫē-iddin had specified in a written document that the yield of his share should go to his wife during her lifetime. Only after her death could his three sons take possession of the property. She survived her husband by nearly 20 years and during this time she did, indeed, issue lease contracts for plots at the New Canal and received an income.

Just after her death, her three sons made a contract as to how much each could claim as his share. Itti-Marduk-balāṭu as the eldest received half as his customary preferential share, Iddin-Nabû and Nergal-ēṭir, the two younger siblings, one quarter each. This specification was necessary because Iddin-Nabû, the second eldest, was in financial difficulties. He had, among other things, already tried to sell a female slave belonging to his brother under his own name in a foreign city, and finally even his creditors were obligated not to lend him any more money without the consent of his brothers. In order to pay off at least part of his debts, he sold his share to his younger brother.

The property was at that time not divided physically and parcelled up, it was agreed that it should be administered communally and the income shared. But only two years after the mother's death, her eldest son Itti-Marduk-balāṭu died, who had heirs of his own. Now the moment had come to sort out the matter properly and to initiate a formal partition of the land because otherwise it would have been too complicated to establish ownership. The heirs of Itti-Marduk-balāṭu received the one half, their uncle Nergal-ēṭir the other. At this occasion the land was surveyed before witnesses and a schematic plan made (Figure 16.1) which details the lateral lengths and surface portions according to their agricultural usage, mentions the neighbours and even records the number of date palm trees along the river bank. These data were entered into the partition document which was issued on the same day by the same scribe, and before the same witnesses. Both texts are damaged but complement each other.

The obverse of the field plan shows a rectangle, divided lengthwise into two halves. These are subdivided horizontally into four parts each, the border between the first two is the New Canal. The lateral lengths of all plots are given, as well as their surface area, the former measured in yards, the latter in Babylonian kur to 54,000 square yards. The complicated system of calculation (1 kur = 5 pān = 30 sūt = 360

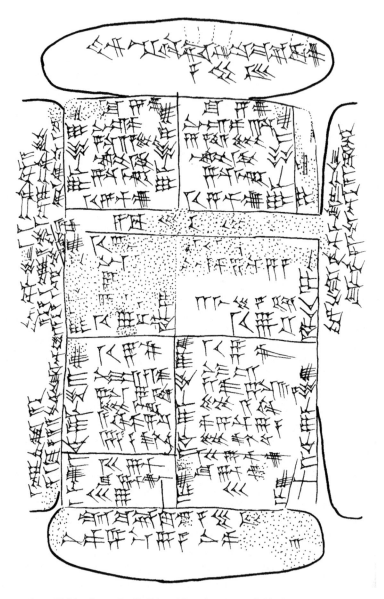

Figure 16.1 Tablet from the Egibi archive showing a field plan (copy: C. Wunsch).

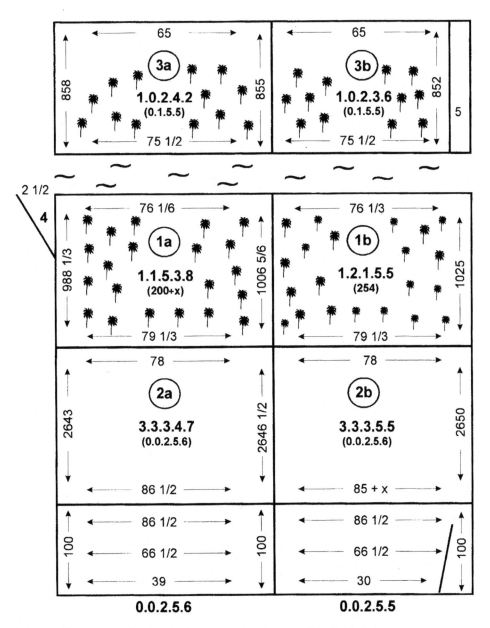

Figure 16.2 Schematic interpretation of the field plan.

qa = 3600 nindan) explains why sales contracts were only drafted by a small circle of specially qualified and privileged scribes who ratified the tablets with their seals and who must have fulfilled a position like a notary.

This plan is an abstraction since the property is 30 times longer than wide. The names of the neighbours are listed at the side. On the reverse is the description of the portions: the left is ascribed to Nergal-ēṭir, the right to his nephews. The lengthwise partition results in rather narrow strips, but since the date plantations are alongside the canal, both parties thereby receive an equal share of garden and arable land and have unhindered access to the water course and hence to irrigation devices. Since yields depended on artificial irrigation, this was a very important aspect. The plan also records details rarely found in other texts: on the southern bank of the canal (below) is an area with ca. 500 date palms on 2.5 hectares, which means that the density of the trees is one tree per 50 square metres or 200 trees per hectare. On the other canal bank, land in the form of a strip parallel to the bank has two-thirds of its surface cultivated with palms, while beyond is an area for barley. South of the canal the arable field begins after 500 metres and extends for 1.37 kilometres where it ends in a sharp triangle in a drainage basin.

Date cultivation at this time covered about a quarter of the whole surface. From the first mentioning of the property, 56 years before, the cultivation had expanded enormously and probably reached the limits of irrigation potential. This is made clear by a lease contract which allows a gardener to cultivate an additional plot of land which had to be irrigated with buckets, and therefore must have been beyond reach of the canal. This shows just how intensively fields in Babylon were cultivated at this time.

Seven years after the partition described above, the property features again in another document. Nergal-ēṭir had died without male heirs and his widow found herself in financial difficulties. She exchanged Nergal-ēṭir's share with Marduk-nāṣir-apli, her nephew, against another, smaller field and a sum of compensation which was paid to her husband's creditors. This meant that those 12 kur which used to belong to Nabû-aḫḫē-iddin, were once more in one hand, that of his grandson, Marduk-nāṣir-apli, who continued to direct business as the family head for another four years, until his brothers insisted that he surrender their inheritance, which initiated the next round of partition.

MARRIAGES AND DOWRIES

In well-to-do Babylonian families, marriage was a matter of prestige, income prospects and business connections, arranged by the father or both parents for daughters, sometimes when they were children. Grown sons could not marry without their father's consent and often did so only after his death. Neither daughters nor wives could inherit since the dowry, which was handed over to the future husband or his father, fulfilled the obligations of their own families. It was, however, up to the husband or father to make donations or last wills in favour of wives or daughters. There was no general norm as to the value of a dowry in relation to the expected inheritance share of brothers. This meant that non-material aspects such as the family's status and the social connections played a decisive role in the initial negotiations and the settlement of the dowry. The Egibi archive contains dowry contracts for women of three generations (the third to the fifth). They show a noteworthy pattern; women who married into the family brought rich property values whereas the daughters of the Egibi had comparatively modest settlements. Obviously, it must have been lucrative as well as prestigious to marry into this part of the family, at least since the third generation.

Nuptaja, the wife of Itti-Marduk-balāṭu, not only brought, as mentioned already, 24 minas of silver but also the infrastructure of her father's business; she was also assured by contract of a third of the paternal inheritance – an unusual directive, probably explicable by the fact that only one son and one daughter had to be considered. Nuptaja's eldest daughter, according to her dowry contract, was also meant to marry one of her father's business friends but only received ten minas of silver and five slaves as her dowry. Ten years later, however, another document asserts that nothing of this had yet been handed over. The woman had died in the meantime, either before the marriage was consummated, or before she had any children. Her fiancé (or husband) was now offered the second sister but she was to get only a property of one kur (= 1.35 hectare) and three slaves. This dowry corresponds to the amount specified for her in her father's will 12 years earlier, when her elder sister was still alive and she herself was not yet betrothed. On the same day the youngest daughter, who could not have been older than nine years, was promised, for the same conditions, to a man who, among other things, wrote her father's business documents.

The dowry of her sister-in-law, who was married to Marduk-nāṣir-apli, is on a quite different scale. She brought 30 minas of silver, a property of two kur, five slaves, jewellery and abundant household equipment into her marriage to the future head of the Egibi firm.

The dowry silver could be invested into business by the husband (unless it was contractully reserved for the *quppu* box of the wife) but not without transferring other property of equal value (real estate, slaves) for the wife's security. Also dowry slaves or plots had to be compensated for if the husband wanted to sell them, because while he had the right of use and income, he could not dispose of them at will. Furthermore, as long as no children had been born, the dowry belonged in principle to the wife's family and had to be given back intact if she should die without issue. This is why the handing over of the dowry or of particular items was often delayed until the birth of children. They shared the dowry after the mother's death. Dowries unite the interests of two families and three generations which explains why relatively many documents about dowry provisions, receipts and compensations have been preserved in private archives.

NABÛ-AḪḪĒ-IDDIN AS ROYAL JUDGE

Nabû-aḫḫē-iddin, the head of the Egibi family in the second generation, officiated, as has been mentioned, for 12 years, until his death, as a judge under Nabonidus. Committees of royal judges consisted of three to eight judges, presided over by the governor in charge (*šākin-ṭēmi*) or a supreme judge (*sartennu*, *sukkallu*) and assisted by usually several legal clerks. They were recruited from a very limited circle of persons, and never were two members of the same family represented in a single committee. Their family names are also well documented in business records of this period which proves what was to be expected at any rate: the well-established and influential circles also had access to the most important offices.

The committees were hierarchically organized and suprisingly stable. Only in a single case did judges change their positions. Newcomers started at the most junior position and acceded to higher positions when someone of superior rank died or left.

The career path proceeded from scribal training and administrative experience. Besides the 'judges of the king' who had a traditional Babylonian education and mastered the cuneiform writing system, there were also officials who wrote on parchments or wax, in alphabetic Aramaic, and were responsible for the legal business and transactions of the non-Babylonian population. We have to assume the 'judges of the king' were appointed by the king in some form or other, presumably from a circle of qualified candidates. The question as to how much freedom of choice the kings had in their selection or whether a recall or suspension of judges for political reasons took place, cannot, so far, be answered. The texts preserved so far show a remarkable continuity of personnel, even across politically turbulent times and changes of dynasties.

It should be underlined that almost all transmitted court documents from the Neo-Babylonian period, apart from those of the temple judiciary, originate from purchases that can be linked to the Egibi archive.[3] Apart from an involvement of the family in the respective legal cases or their direct interest in their subjects (purchase of orchards, fields, slaves), the fact that Nabû-aḫḫē-iddin could have kept copies of such documents in his capacity as judge among his archive could explain why it contains so many court documents, especially from his period in office. The majority of cases concern property, such as the mode of partition on inheritance or the payment of inherited debts. Also, questions of legal status arise, as when a slave maintains that he is thus wrongly described, or when a freed female slave asserts that her child was born after her manumission and could, as such, not be sold as a slave. The royal judges were also responsible for punishing criminals, as in cases of grievous bodily harm. Only a single case documents the presence and the judgment of the king as supreme judge. Tellingly, it is a case of high treason.

CONCLUSION

The example of this family shows just how many interesting details concerning the lives of wealthy Babylonians can be gleaned from the private archives. The economic success and social rise of some families, linking them to the highest circles, contrasts with the financial ruin and human tragedy of others. Terse notes in formalized documents have to be put together like stones in a mosaic to create a vivid image of their protagonists. Even though two and half thousand years separate us from the daily life of the Babylonians, we meet forms of behaviour and traits of character that seem only too familiar.

NOTES

1   Egibi is an abbreviation of Sumerian e.gi-ba-ti.la, a full form used occasionally in the archival records. In a learned text on ancestral names, Babylonian scribes equated it to Babylonian *Sîn-taqîša-libluṭ*, which can be translated as 'O Sin [the moon god], you have given [the child], may he now live and thrive' (see W.G. Lambert, JCS 11 (1957):1–14; 112, comment on col. iii line 53). This follows a well-attested Babylonian name pattern. F.E. Peiser already in 1897 pointed out that it had 'nothing to do' with *Jacob* (MVAeG 2: 307, quoted in Peiser 1890–98:

IV 22[1]). It occurs in Babylonian records since the eighth century BC, long before the time of the Babylonian Captivity. By the sixth century, several different family branches are attested in Babylon and Uruk alone, and more than 200 individuals are known who claim to be descendents of *Egibi* (see Tallqvist 1905: *s.v.*).

2   R. Bogaert's exhaustive 1966 study on early 'banking' shows that the essential characteristic of taking money as a deposit and lending it out at a higher rate cannot be found.

3   See in detail Wunsch 1997–98 and 1999.

BIBLIOGRAPHY

Bogaert, R. 1966 *L'origine antique de la banque de dépôt*. Leiden.

Kohler, J. and F.E. Peiser. 1890–98 *Aus dem Babylonischen Rechtsleben* I–IV. Leipzig.

Lambert, W.G. 1957 'Ancestors, Authors, and Canonicity', *Journal of Cuneiform Studies* 11: 1–14, 112.

Roth, M.T. 1991 'The Women of the Itti-Marduk-balāṭu Family', *Journal of the American Oriental Society* 11: 19–37.

Tallqvist, K.N. 1905 *Neubabylonisches Namenbuch zu den Geschäftsurkunden aus der Zeit Šamaš-šumukîn bis Xerxes* (Acta societatis scientiarum fennicae 32/2), Helsingfors.

van Driel, G. 1985–86 'The Rise of the House of Egibi. Nabû-aḫḫē-iddina', *Jaarbericht van het Voorariatasch-Egytisch Gennootschap 'Ex Oriente Lux'* 29: 50–67.

Wunsch, C. 1993 *Die Urkunden des babylonischen Geschäftsmannes Iddin-Marduk. Zum Handel mit Naturalien im 6. Jahrhundert v.Chr.* (= Cuneiform Monographs 3a und b), Groningen.

—— 1995–96 'Die Frauen der Familie Egibi', *Archiv für Orientforschung* 42/43: 33–63.

—— 1997–98 'Und die Rechter berieten . . . Streitfälle in Babylon aus der Zeit Neriglissars und Nabonids', *Archiv für Orientforschung* 44–45: 59–100.

—— 1999 'The Egibi Family's Real Estate in Babylon (6th Century BC)', in M. Hudson and B. Levine (eds) *Land Tenure and Urbanization in the Ancient Near East*, Cambridge, MA, pp. 391–413.

PART IV

SOCIETY
AND POLITICS

———•◆•———

SOCIAL CONFIGURATIONS IN EARLY DYNASTIC BABYLONIA
(*c*. 2500–2334 BC)

———•❖•———

Petr Charvát

The third segment of the Early Dynastic period (*c.*2500–2334 BC, henceforth ED III) in south-eastern Mesopotamia represents an age when city-state centres competed with each other for power, for glory and the favour of the gods. Numerous cuneiform tablets and archaeological artefacts allow us to sketch a broad outline of the Sumerian society of that age, as it lived its sacred and profane days, months and years.

THE KING

Let us begin by examining the sources of the kings' revenues. First and foremost, they drew on their own personal property, which they inherited from their ancestors. Enmetena of Lagash, for instance, records that he made a pious donation of land which he had presumably inherited from his illustrious forefathers.[1] Second, they could rely on shares in public (landed) property, due to them as citizens of their native community. An example of this is given by texts such as RTC 66, in which a sovereign's official disposes of grain harvested from a 'state' field.[2] In fact, these fields were classified in Sumerian as ni_3-en-na, 'demesne-holding', which refers to a part of the original landed property of a temple. Even the sovereign's consort could have held ni_3-en-na land,[3] theoretically not private, but 'divine' property. The land's first couple could also enjoy possession of kur_6 land,[4] a kind of 'salary' or remuneration to citizens who performed services for the temple. Such land, however, fell to them by the same legal title as it could fall to any Lagash burgers.[5] The arable itself evidently 'belonged' to somebody else, most probably to the gods.

A third source of royal income consisted of any emoluments accruing in consequence of the tenure of their office. We can see an example for this kind of siphoning off of the surplus at Lagash:[6] part of the harvest of a field plot has been 'taken in charge' by the sovereign('s men) and disposed of according to his instructions, while another part went to a storage facility called Ekilamka.[7] However, not all the field plots referred to in Lagash texts belonged solely to the sovereign's family. With whom the rulers shared these lands is not particularly clear, though deities seem to figure

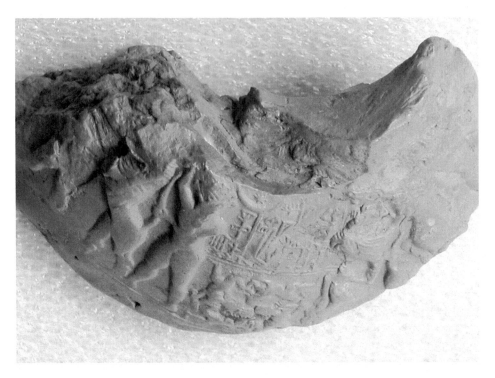

Figure 17.1 Seal impression of king Mesannepada of Ur, 2563–2524 BCE. The triumphal symbolism of the king's seal provided a pictorial emblem of sovereign power for the entire third phase of the Early Dynastic age.

prominently in written sources. At one point, the landed property of the gods Baba and Ningirsu attained incredible proportions: sixty square kilometres for Baba alone.[8] Another category of the rulers' revenue, the extent of which is difficult to specify, were the 'public works', or corvée labour. The sovereigns of Lagash seemed to have felt entitled to impose this on their own subjects,[9] and the Shuruppak texts refer to mustering a large labour- or military force from the subservient population.[10]

Revenues from occasional and irregular sources, such as the greeting gifts by newly appointed officials, came in handy as a fourth kind of income.[11] We do possess lists of such 'gifts'.[12] When Lugalanda's consort Barnamtara gave birth to a daughter, for instance, she received gifts including livestock and beer.[13]

Finally, let us also list the fifth kind of resources available to kings, which were the result of their own 'entrepreneurial' activities, mainly the outcome of publicly sponsored works such as canal building or the reclamation of waste land. Urnanshe of Lagash, for example, initiated the digging of an irrigation channel. The fields and gardens thus fertilized, however, did not belong to the sovereign but to the goddess Baba.[14] This case shows that in carrying out projects of common good, the sovereigns of Early Dynastic Sumer were acting as public figures, putting the results of their managerial skills at the disposal of the community which they directed. It goes without saying that in many cases, the princes of early Sumerian cities drew profit from leasing their own lands.[15]

There was also an income deriving from military pursuits, booty amassed in war, as well as revenues supplied by the subjugated populations. We have the well-known inventory of the ravages caused by Lugalzagesi's campaign against Uru'inimgina.[16] In addition, an inscription on a clay pot, presumably from contemporary Lagash, describes how the invader loaded 'their precious metal and lapis lazuli, their timber and treasure' on to ships.[17] But let us notice the fact that at least some commanders of victorious armies took care to dedicate a part of the booty to the gods in order to give thanks for their protection. Thus, Enshakushanna of Uruk dedicated a share in items looted from Kish to Enlil at Nippur.[18]

In return for the revenues, the rulers were supposed to discharge their duties, the foremost among which was undoubtedly the administration of royal property: the central management of the sovereigns' holdings might have been the E_2-sa_3, referred to in an inscription of Enannatum of Lagash,[19] an institution which disposed of its own personnel, including scribes.[20] Alternatively, this function could have been carried out by the E_2-mi_2, the 'wifely house', for which I suggest an interpretation of a 'state provisioning centre', operated by the sovereign's consort in her function of mistress and manager of the land's first household. Attributes such as a spindle and whorl of precious materials defined high-status women, at least in burials.[21] The Lagash texts point to a third structure apparently employed by the sovereigns' administration. This is the E_2-ni_2-ga, presumably a type of magazine, which may have served the needs of the present ruler or his consort,[22] and received chiefly comestible products.[23] It is unclear to what extent any of these institutions could be seen in the enigmatic 'Area C' building, excavated by the US team at Lagash.[24]

The kings took care, at least according to their own words, for those deprived of ordinary means of subsistence: in addition to a declaration of Uru'inimgina,[25] let it suffice here to cite Gudea's Statue B, viii: 42–46, where he speaks in favour of orphans, widows and heirless 'houses'.[26] Of course, we need not fall prey to illusions: in ED III Lagash, male and female orphans constituted a welcome source of labour force of the sovereigns' workshops ('*ergasteria*').[27]

The rulers were also responsible for the maintenance of public order. This involved, among other measures, debt cancellations, clearly a periodically repeated procedure in favour of restoration of an economic balance of sorts, alleviating the lot of the heavily indebted social strata.[28] The practice is first attested to under Enmetena of Lagash.[29]

The appointment of public officials belonged to royal duties; Urnanshe of Lagash had a 'spouse' of the goddess Nanshe appointed by an omen.[30]

Dispensation of justice constituted another claim of the kings: this function of the ruler may be alluded to by the name of a shrine 'Bagar Provides Justice', built by Urnanshe of Lagash.[31] Mesalim's surveying of the Lagash–Umma border and its promulgation by means of a public monument constitutes another case of this kind.[32] The provision for just and publicly approved weights and measures belongs here as well.[33]

The sovereigns represented their communities in international relations. Thus, Eannatum of Lagash concluded a 'treaty' with the anonymous sovereign of Umma after the victory of the Lagash military forces, complete with supernatural sanctions for any transgressor.[34] The 'brotherhood' between Enmetena of Lagash and Lugalkiginedudu of Uruk falls also under this heading.[35]

In warfare the rulers commanded their armies. Urnanshe of Lagash personally 'went to war against the leader of Ur and the leader of Umma', and won.[36] The famous 'Stele of Vultures' shows Eannatum leading his troops.[37]

The Fara (Shuruppak) texts (*c*.2500 BC, ED IIIa) have preserved for us a unique testimony of the efficiency of a Sumerian realm with respect to the logistical support of its 'State Department' (E_2-gal). Its four sections – transport and communication (gal-nimgir), external economic relations (gal-damgar), religious matters (gala-mah) and, finally, of provisions and supplies to this centre (e_2-geme$_2$) – represented a body well-suited for the execution of tasks of nationwide importance.[38] The unidentified sovereign who steered this social machine, most probably one of the early kings of Kish,[39] entrusted the tasks of provisioning his 'State Department' to another large organization, the E_2-uru, of a similar administrative complexity.[40]

Sumerian kings understood well the 'giving unto gods what belongeth to gods'. In fact, sometimes the 'support' started with the very building of the temples concerned: Uru'inimgina gave bread rations to employees of the brick-making establishment of Nanshe.[41] Gifts and donations of every kind are known from sovereigns' inscriptions of ED III Lagash and other Sumerian cities.[42] In Gudea's Statue B, we hear of the complex arrangements made for the ritually appropriate inauguration of a temple.[43] Generous sponsoring of public institutions dedicated to divine cults, especially in the form of jewellery, donated presumably to embellish statues of gods and goddesses, took place during religious festivals, such as that of the goddess Nanshe.[44] Of course, this form of piety worked both ways; in times of war, it made the temples welcome targets for marauding troops.[45] Some sovereigns of early Sumer would have kept personal 'chaplains' at their courts, such as Urnanshe's 'snake charmer'.[46] In some instances, the sovereigns' progeny served as priests and priestesses in temples. In addition to the well-known EN office holders, a measure of continuity may be presumed to have existed between the lyre-players of the 'Royal graves' of Ur, and princesses of blood royal dedicated to this art under the Akkadian kings.[47] At ED III Lagash, an institution called 'Harp' received regular offerings of oil and dates.[48] We may also ask whether the 'music conservatory' at Akkadian Eshnunna[49] was established with funds provided by the king.

Early Dynastic rulers were chief officiants of divine cults, one of their most important functions. It has been observed, for instance, that the ideational structure underlying the early state of Lagash, including the choice of the deities venerated, the ceremonies held for this purpose, as well as the city's cultic calendar, are inconceivable without the activities undertaken by its founder Urnanshe.[50] In Shuruppak, the chief role of the king's (lugal) office seems to have fallen within the religious sphere.[51] Sovereigns could perform religious ceremonies in person. Mesalim of Kish, for instance, carried out the bur-gi$_4$ rite in the temple of Adab.[52] Another example of such activities is represented by the ceremonial offerings on behalf of the rulers' ancestors, known from ED III Lagash.[53] Let us, however, notice that even public-benefit measures took on a garb of serving the great gods.[54]

Finally, kings provided for their own families. In addition to material upkeep, this meant perpetuating the dynastic line through genealogies and various forms of ancestor cults, clearly visible at ED III Lagash.[55] The oft-cited Urnanshe, for instance, took particular care to leave for posterity many sculptures of himself and his family.[56] A most curious Tello (Lagash) statue of a kneeling nude male, holding a pair of snakes

Figure 17.2 A Sumerian temple of early third millennium BCE. The chief role of the temples was the activation and distribution of fertility throughout the world of plants, animals and people.

which, much as a couple of fish hovering before his chest, lay their heads on his beard, might depict a 'totemic ancestor'.[57] Sovereigns of Early Dynastic Sumer undoubtedly considered it their duty to carry out the rites of family coherence with appropriate grandeur. When Lugalanda and Barnamtara were marrying off a son, they honoured the young couple with exquisite gifts, especially textiles.[58] Successive members of the ruling dynasties apparently displayed a degree of 'sovereign solidarity' which is sometimes reflected in art: one of Uru'inimgina's seals visibly copies an earlier signet of Lugalanda.[59]

THE ELITE STRATA

First and foremost, the Sumerian elites toiled to build foundations of family wealth by all means accessible. Among various branches of enterprise, extensive trade of this period brought much coveted precious materials. Let us notice that, for example, as early as the Fara (Shuruppak) age, merchants brought in quantities of lapis lazuli measured in gu_2, 'talents' (= 30 kg, or over 60 lb).[60] At the same time, it helped introduce into the land humbler products. Such are the foreign pottery imports, Syrian[61] and Iranian,[62] being a corollary to the staples of the trade. Functions of an 'internal market' may be seen in the sealings of goods mentioning Uremush, the 'chief commercial agent' of Lagash, from Girsu (Lagash) and Kish.[63] A relatively high accessibility of silver, and thus at least the possibility of a certain 'monetization' of

Early Dynastic economy, may be surmised from the fact that silver, unlike other precious metals, remained a stable component of grave goods deposited throughout the third millennium in the Ur cemetery.[64]

The strengthening of internal ties of the individual elite groups was imperative in order to prevent fragmentation of great holdings. This is one of the topics shining through the otherwise rather murky literary work known as 'Instructions of Shuruppak'.[65] The author of the composition takes particular care of instructing his audience 'not to manage their houses with discord', to consider their 'elder brothers as fathers and elder sisters as mothers', and especially tries to inculcate in them his most famous dictum, that a 'loving heart builds houses, and a hateful heart tears them down'. The author does not forget to admonish his readers to bow to authority, but also not to repudiate one's wife and not to rebel against the authority of parents.

The solidification of family structures meant that power was concentrated in the hands of chiefs of elite groups,[66] and it also entailed the diminution of the social significance of certain of their members, such as women: the elite engagement in public affairs is reflected by the observation that the group of personages appearing in various transactions recorded by the Fara texts is, in fact, rather limited.[67] Women seem to participate actively in real-estate transactions less frequently than men there.[68] The less prominent status of women in the later Early Dynastic period is also borne out by art historical record. Out of some ninety inscribed intercessor statuettes of this age, women commissioned no more than six.[69]

On the public side, the elites participated intensely in the exercise of public charges. Hundreds of men and thousands of track animals fulfilled the orders of the Shuruppak managers,[70] toiling on arable lands measured in hundreds of hectares. Bondsmen from all over Sumer set out towards Fara to discharge their obligations.[71] Two Fara texts feature a breathtaking number of more than 160,000 labour hands.[72] Supplies for these masses of workers might have been deposited in the local baked-brick silos, built sometime in the ED III period.[73]

The elites did not fail to engage in public cults. Elite sponsorship of religious establishments did take place at Lagash,[74] and in other Sumerian cities, examples being known from as far as Mari.[75] Possible traces of 'chiefly rituals' were discovered at the Abu-Salabikh ash tip.[76] Human and animal figures, including model chariots, however crudely done, might have served in temple rituals pertaining to high-status males. Comparable finds clearly turned up at Ur. Perhaps we can imagine them being used for something of the nature of the Egyptian 'execration rituals' which sought a magical victory over a feared adversary.

Members of influential families took up the development of the land's spiritual heritage. As early as the first segment of the Early Dynastic period, inhabitants of elite households such as, for instance, the West Mound of Abu Salabikh, did appropriate – and even use for purely domestic purposes – such inventions as the cuneiform writing and cylinder seals.[77] It was the exercise of their creativity that brought forth the burgeoning of the late Early Dynastic literary tradition. All of a sudden, such original and unique creations as the very first incantations of Sumerian literature,[78] or the 'Instructions of Suruppak',[79] make their appearance. The Early Dynastic Geographical List[80] was another innovation. Pietro Mander (1986) treated at great depth the Early Dynastic lists of divinities, taking note of the adjustments and developments of the earlier, Late Uruk tradition. The integration of the first Semitic deities into the Sumerian pantheon was also an achievement of the scribes attached to Early Dynastic elite households.[81]

THE COMMONERS

What of the average Sumerians? We still know very little about the Sumerian countryside of the period. The common cereal varieties were apparently cultivated, with the predominance of barley (*Hordeum vulgare*) and emmer (*Triticum dicoccum*) over other grain varieties and over such garden produce as lentils or dates.[82] The Tell Brak evidence includes chiefly two-rowed hulled barley, einkorn and emmer wheat, 'bread/macaroni wheat' (*Triticum aestivum ssp. durum*), lentils and common peas.[83] The rural hinterlands of Sumerian settlement sites still await detailed mapping of the worn-sherd clusters likely to have resulted from manuring tilled land by domestic refuse containing such admixtures, and thus to visualize the extent of ancient arable land.[84] However, large-scale deforestation of Near Eastern landscapes had very likely not set in until about 2000 BC.[85] Cereals seem to have been harvested close to the soil, as low-growing weed taxa are present among the surviving grain samples from Brak.[86] Straw obviously represented an article of common utility, for instance, as a tempering agent for mud-bricks. The post-harvest procedures included threshing, winnowing, coarse-sieving and fine-sieving.[87] Only then was the product passed on to the millers.

The rising predominance of oxen, together with increasing representation of donkey and horse, give evidence of employment of domestic animals as a source of traction power.[88] For the inhabitants of late Early Dynastic Abu Salabikh, pigs supplied pork for the table, and sheep and goats were likely sources of milk and wool.[89] The Brak donkeys enjoyed reasonably good care, were stabled, though ridden and probably also used as pack animals, and obeyed orders transmitted by bits.[90]

At least some villages could have assumed the dispersed settlement pattern, consisting presumably of individual households or farmsteads, as appears to be the case at Tell Yelkhi.[91]

The arts and crafts now. Complex and sophisticated technologies, such as bronze casting, apparently became widely accessible.[92] Surprisingly enough, both stone-working production waste and copper slag turned up at the Jebel-Hamrin site of Tell Yelkhi, indicating that rural settlements also practised some craft production.[93] Traditional manufacturing procedures continued, side by side with more advanced ones, as is indicated by the persistence of chipped-flint sickle blades throughout the Early Dynastic and Akkadian levels at the same site.[94] Trade in food staples must have enriched many a table in early Mesopotamia, as is indicated by the presence of marine fish species in Early Dynastic and Akkadian inland sites. A few turned up as far as Tell Brak, some 2,000 kilometres from the Persian Gulf they came from.[95] The import of wine from abroad, though primarily aimed at the needs of the elite, gives evidence of the logistical capability of Sumerian transporters.[96]

Some new social developments are visible. At Shuruppak, the im-ru-a communities (re?)emerged. The term for such groupings denotes both 'land segment, rural district' and 'a structured and coherent group of people'. Such im-ru-a seem to refer to independent social bodies which might have accepted obedience to an external power such as the royal palace, which would then send a 'liaison officer' (ugula), to see that their obligations towards the overlord are fulfilled.[97] The linkage of such communities into higher groupings and the build-up of conical clans has been documented by Charles Maisels.[98]

Commoners could have access to the political arena through various means. First, as passive participants in ventures proposed by the elites,[99] and then as 'customers' of enterprises initiated and carried out by elites (e.g. peasants profit from land-reclamation projects such as those initiated by Urnanshe or Lugalzagesi).

In contemporary written documents, these peasants assumed most likely the garb of the 'sovereign's bondsmen (shub-lugal)',[100] or 'ration-takers' (lu_2-kur_6-dab_5-ba),[101] sharecroppers who received rations for a part of the agricultural year. Profit could be made by those who chose to serve the sovereigns: a number of persons on all-year rations under Enentarzi rose to the lu_2-kur_6-dab_5-ba status under his successor Lugalanda. They must thus have received arable land, which they tilled themselves.[102]

There was also the possibility that commoners formed politically active groups. The legitimizing claims of both the Enmetena[103] and Uru'inimgina[104] point to the conclusion that the Early Dynastic Lagash polity was perceived as a collective entity, composed of a given number of essentially equal subjects. When the ruling dynasty changed, the Lagash public enforced a written record of activities deemed as being of common good. Agenda of the Bau temple at Lagash had been put in writing since

Figure 17.3   Fragment of a storage jar from Tepe Gawra, layer VI, twenty-fourth century BCE. A snake is depicted on the jar's rim.

the time of Enentarzi, while large temple projects initiated earlier by Eannatum functioned perfectly well without a single word having been written.

In spiritual matters, the survival of traditional symbols in such common everyday articles as pottery shows that traditional beliefs, rooted in the countryside from time immemorial, were as vivacious as ever. Let it suffice here to point to decoration of pottery vessels of Tepe Gawra VI.[105] Storage vessels bear images of such denizens of the earthly and subterranean kingdom as snakes or scorpions, invoking presumably the sphere of fertility.[106]

THE UNDERPRIVILEGED

The written sources document two categories of underprivileged persons: 'serfs' and prisoners of war. Male serfs (igi-nu-du$_8$ in Uru'inimgina's texts) constituted service personnel and performed what was presumably the heaviest menial work, digging wells and irrigation channels.[107] Women ground grain.[108] As an example of the conditions under which these 'corn-grinders' (geme$_2$-kikken)[109] worked, we have the milling room at Ebla in which sixteen sets of grinding stones were set into the clay banks of the palace.[110] In economic texts, people identified as igi-nu-du$_8$ worked as auxiliary personnel and received food rations all year long.[111] At least some of them ended up in this situation through 'voluntary' enslavement as a consequence of heavy debts.[112] Others may have been purchased already as slaves or slave girls.[113] Their low status is indicated by the prices some of them fetched: Dim$_3$-tur, consort of Enenetarzi, bought a gala slave(?) for one-third of a mina of silver (= twenty shekels), while a 'serf' cost fourteen shekels.[114] The igi-nu-du$_8$ found employment not only in gardening, but also assisted craftspeople.[115] In texts, they were distinguished according to their geographical origin.[116] It is possible that one of the aims of the so-called edicts of Uru'inimgina may have been to determine something like their 'minimum wage'.[117]

Prisoners-of-war (nam-ra) seem to be depicted on art monuments in which naked prisoners with bound hands, or set into stocks, are shown. A Girsu (Lagash) text of possibly ED III age refers to binding the arms of personnel abandoned by their superiors, presumably by the invader.[118]

CONCLUSIONS

In general character, this era of Sumerian history was not unlike our own times. The old aristocratic order of firmly rooted customs, usages and obligations sanctioned by long-term social practices gave way and the political arena was now free for anyone who felt the urge to assume a position of importance. The commoners looked up to people whom they trusted and respected to provide examples of righteous conduct. The elites, being only human, did whatever they could, bringing their subject here to jubilation, there to despair. The overall performance of the foremost women and men of ED III Sumer may be measured by language: for the first time in recorded human history, notions such as 'liberty' and 'justice', but also of 'sin' and 'guilt', turn up in public parlance.

NOTES

1 Cooper 1986, 63–64, No. La 5.17, col. v on p. 63.
2 Chiodi 1997, 82 n. 138; Chiodi 1997, II, 168–170.
3 Barnamtarra: Rosengarten 1960, 38–39.
4 Rosengarten 1960, 41–42, n. 4.
5 Rosengarten 1960, pp. 40–42 n. 4, on p. 41.
6 Text Riftin 1: Rosengarten 1960, 49 and 373.
7 Rosengarten 1960, 50–55.
8 Selz 1995, 40–47.
9 Rosengarten 1960, 348 n. 6.
10 Visicato 1995, 144.
11 The term *mašdaria* probably means a sort of a 'gift', presented to the sovereign by the high dignitaries of his realm (Rosengarten 1960, 111–112; Rosengarten 1960a; Chiodi 1997, 51 n. 94, with ref.
12 For instance, DP 42: Chiodi 1997, II, 41–43, DP 59: ibid., 83–90; Nik 159, ibid. 145, and many others.
13 Nik 157, Nik 209, TSA 45, Rosengarten 1960, 160–161; ibid., pp. 336–342.
14 Selz 1995, 187–188; ibid. 269, # 2, n. 1314.
15 As we know from ED III Lagash (investment of grain paid by a holder of an apin-la$_2$ lease, Fö 11: Rosengarten 1960, 57–58.
16 E.g. Selz 1995, 235.
17 Cooper 1986, 85, No. La 10.2.
18 Cooper 1986, 105, Nos. Uk 4.1, 4.2.
19 Cooper 1986, 53, No. La 4.17, n. 1.
20 HAR-tud, lu$_2$: Rosengarten 1960, 160–168.
21 Grave 21 at the 'A' cemetery of Kish: Mackay 1925, table between the pp. 20 and 21, and pp. 43, 52, 61, Pls. III: 5, IV: 24, VI: 13 and XVIII: 17.
22 Uru'inimgina's Enigga in DP 163: Rosengarten 1960, 236–238, on p. 237, on the Enigga of the E$_2$-mi$_2$ cf. ibid. 237 n. 1.
23 Rosengarten 1960, 365 n. 4.
24 Bahrani 1989; also, for instance, Hansen 1987.
25 Selz 1995, 235.
26 Chiodi 1997, 168–169.
27 Selz 1995, 59–60.
28 For instance, Gudea's Statue B: Chiodi 1997, 167–169, esp. p. 168.
29 Cooper 1986, 58–59, No. La 5.4, col. iv; ibid. 66–67, No. La 5.26, col. iii; Selz 1995, 186, n. 853.
30 Cooper 1986, 28, No. La 1.17, col. i; Selz 1995, 182 n. 829.
31 Cooper 1986, 24–25, No. La 1.6, col. i.
32 Cooper 1986, 39–40, No. La 3.2; ibid. 54–57, No. La 5.1.
33 Uru'inimgina: Cooper 1986, 82, No. La 9.13.
34 Cooper 1986, 33–39, No. La 3.1.
35 Cooper 1986, 58, No. La 5.3.
36 Cooper 1986, 24–25, N. La 1.6 on p. 25, rev. col. i.
37 Cooper 1986, 33–39, No. La 3.1.
38 Visicato 1995, 91–112.
39 Pomponio and Visicato 1994, 10–21; Visicato 1995, 140–148.
40 Visicato 1995, 113–133, cf. also his Table 1 on p. 138.
41 Selz 1995, 202 # 69.
42 Cf. Cooper 1986, as well as Chiodi 1997, 176–178.
43 Chiodi 1997, 164–172.
44 Selz 1995, 199–200.
45 E.g. Selz 1995, 235–236, Lagash.
46 Cooper 1986, 22–23, No. La 1.2, n p. 23, and on pp. 23–24, No. La 1.4, p. 24.

47 E.g. Lippusš-ia'um, granddaughter of Naramsin: Parrot 1948, 134, fig. 32: g, cf. also Westenholz 1999, 72 n. 344, and possibly p. 73, fig. 8: c.
48 Rosengarten 1960, 245 n. 6; Selz 1995, 103–105.
49 Westenholz 1999, 72 n. 344.
50 Selz 1995, 298.
51 Visicato 1995, 129 n. 99.
52 Cooper 1986, 19, No. Ki 3.2.
53 Chiodi 1997, 47–51, 78–80, 98–99.
54 'Justice of Nanshe and Ningirsu', in Gudea's Statue B, ll. viii: 38–40: Chiodi 1997, 168.
55 Cf. Chiodi 1997.
56 E.g. Parrot 1948, 69–124, esp. pp. 77–95.
57 Parrot 1948, Pl. III and p. 74.
58 Rosengarten 1960, 93; Selz 1995, 178 n. 802 with ref.
59 Parrot 1948, 120.
60 Steible and Yyldyz 2000, 986.
61 Martin 1988, 52; Reade 2001, 24–26.
62 For Early Dynastic commerce with Elam cf. Selz 1991, 37–42.
63 Cooper 1986, 70. No. La 8.5.
64 Rehm 2003, 74.
65 Alster 1974.
66 Inscribed cylinder seals: Charvát 1996.
67 Visicato and Westenholz 2000, 1127–1128; Martin *et al.* 2001, p. xxvii, and pp. 118–119 with ref.
68 Martin *et al.* 2001, 118 sub a.
69 Boese 1996, 29–31, n. 32.
70 Martin 1988, 89.
71 Martin 1988, 98–99.
72 Insofar, of course, as this is not a mathematical exercise (Martin 1988, 128).
73 Martin 1988, 42–47, 110–112.
74 For instance, Dudu for Ningirsu: Cooper 1986, 68–69, No. La 5.28 on p. 68.
75 Cooper 1986, *passim*, esp. 86–89, Nos. Ma 1.2 to Ma 5.3.
76 McAdam 1993, esp. p. 91.
77 Postgate 1983, 85, inscribed miniature jar No. 2GS: 190 with Fig. 289, and Pl. VIII: c; Postgate 1983, 103 N. 2GS: 94, and Pl. X: e.
78 Krebernik 1984.
79 Alster 1974; on Fara literary texts cf. also Martin 1988, 89.
80 Steinkeller 1993, 119–120, n. 30 and 31 with ref.
81 Though the data base is woefully inadequate: Selz 1995, 303–304.
82 For the evidence of the Hamrin sites, Bergamini *et al.* 1985, 58–60.
83 Charles and Bogaard 2001, 309, 323.
84 For instance, Wilkinson and Tucker 1995; Wilkinson 1997, 121 Fig. 2 for Sweyhat, or Bernbeck 1997/1998, 462.
85 Miller 1998, 205.
86 Charles and Bogaard 2001, 322.
87 Charles and Bogaard 2001, 313.
88 Fedele 1985, table on p. 68.
89 Clark 1993, 181.
90 Clutton-Brock *et al.* 2001.
91 Bergamini *et al.* 1985, ill. on p. 43.
92 Rehm 2003, passim, esp. pp. 71–75 on the frequency of cast-bronze axes in graves, as against the later part of the third millennium, when they were replaced by cold-hammered ones.
93 Bergamini *et al.* 1985, 44.
94 Bergamini *et al.* 1985, 44–45.
95 Clutton-Brock *et al.* 2001, 339–345.
96 Selz 1995, 233 # 65, Uru'inimgina.

97 On them cf. now Visicato 1995, 17, 25–26; Martin *et al.* 2001, 121 n. 40.
98 1999, 156–159 with ref.
99 Cf. above, corvée work enforced by the Fara chiefs.
100 Selz 1995, 56, reads RU-lugal.
101 Maekawa 1973–1974, esp. p. 110; Selz 1995, 50–51.
102 Maekawa 1973–1974, 113–114.
103 Selz 1995, 231 # 55.
104 Cooper 1986, 70–74, N, La 9.1, col. v and following on p. 71; Selz 1995, 235.
105 Dating to the close of the ED III/Agade transition (Cross 1935, 49–56).
106 Cross 1935, Pl. LXXVI: 7, 11, 12, for snake depictions at the Abu Salabikh ED-III Ash Tip cf. Moon 1993, 149, fig. 10: 3, No. 794; on contemporary snake symbolism cf. Muller 1998, 188.
107 Cooper 1986, 70–74, No. La 9.1, col. v and following on p. 71.
108 At ED III Lagash: HAR-tu-mi$_2$, Maekawa 1973–1974, 104 n. 36.
109 Selz 1995, 61 # 122.
110 Hopkins 1997, fig. on p. 25.
111 Maekawa 1973–1974, 92.
112 Cooper 1986, 70–74, No. La 9.1, p. 74 n. 26.
113 Rosengarten 1960, 56 n. 1; Maekawa 1973–1974, 92 n. 21; ibid. 93 n. 23; Selz 1995, 60, sag-sa$_{10}$.
114 Rosengarten 1960, 173 n. 5.
115 Giš-kin-ti (Rosengarten 1960, 56 n. 1; also Selz 1995, 58).
116 Igi-nu-du$_8$ of the city Az: Rosengarten 1960, 197 n. 5.
117 Cooper 1986, 74–76, No. La 9.2, col. v and following on p. 75.
118 Cooper 1986, 85, No. La 10.2.

BIBLIOGRAPHY

Alster, Bendt 1974 *The Instructions of Šuruppak – A Sumerian Proverb Collection.* (Mesopotamia, Copenhagen Studies in Assyriology volume 2), Copenhagen: Akademisk Forlag.

Bahrani, Zainab 1989 *The Administrative Building at Tell Al Hiba, Lagash I-II.* Dissertation in the Department of Fine Arts, New York University, UMI Dissertation Services, Ann Arbor, Michigan 1996.

Bergamini, Giovanni, *et al.* 1985 'Tell Yelkhi', in Quarantelli (ed.) 1985, 41–61.

Bernbeck, Reinhard 1997/1998 Review of Wilkinson and Tucker 1995, *Archiv für Orientforschung* 44–45, 457–467.

Boese, Johannes 1996 'Zu einigen frühdynastischen Figuren aus Mari', in U. Magen, M. Rashad (eds), *Vom Halys zum Euphrat, Thomas Beran zu Ehren, Mit Beiträgen von Freunden und Schülern.* Münster: Ugarit-Verlag, 25–49.

Charles, Mike and Bogaard, Amy 2001 'Third-millennium BC Charred Plant Remains from Tell Brak', in Oates *et al.* 2001, 301–326.

Charvát, Petr 1996 'On sealings and officials: Sumerian DUB and SANGA, c. 3500–2500 BC', in: P. Zemánek (ed.), *Studies in Near Eastern Languages and Literatures – Memorial Volume of Karel Petráček.* Prague: Academy of Sciences of the Czech Republic, Oriental Institute, 181–192.

Chiodi, Silvia Maria 1997 *Offerte 'funebri' nella Lagaš presargonica I-II.* Materiali per il vocabolario sumerico 5/1, Rome: Università degli Studi di Roma 'La Sapienza'.

Clark, Gillian 1993 'Faunal Remains', in Green (ed.) 1993, 177–201.

Clutton-Brock, Juliet, Roselló, Eufrasia Izquierdo, Muñiz, Arturo Morales, Weber, Jill A. and Molleson, Theya 2001 'Faunal Evidence', in Oates *et al.* 2001, 327–338.

Cooper, Jerrold S. 1986 *Sumerian and Akkadian Royal Inscriptions, I: Presargonic Inscriptions.* New Haven, CT: The American Oriental Society.

Cross, Dorothy 1935 'Pottery', in Speiser 1935, 38–61.

Fedele, Francesco 1985 'Mesopotamian Zooarchaelogy', in Quarantelli (ed.) 1985, 66–68.

Graziani, Simonetta (ed.) 2000 *Studi sul Vicino Oriente Antico dedicati alla memoria di Luigi Cagni I–IV*, Naples: Istituto Universitario Orientale.

Green, Anthony (ed.) 1993 *Abu Salabikh Excavations vol. 4: The 6G Ash-Tip and its Contents: cultic and administrative discard from the temple?* London: British School of Archaeology in Iraq.

Hansen, Donald P. 1987 'The Fantastic World of Sumerian Art; Seal Impressions from Ancient Lagash', in A. E. Farkas, P. O. Harper and E. B. Harrison (eds), *Monsters and Demons in the Ancient and Medieval Worlds, Papers Presented in Honor of Edith Porada*, Mainz on Rhine: Philipp von Zabern, 53–63.

Hopkins, John 1997 'Agriculture', in Eric Myers (ed.), *The Oxford Encyclopaedia of Archeology in the Near East*, vols I–IV. New York/Oxford: Oxford University Press, vol. I, pp. 23–28.

Krebernik, Manfred 1984 *Die Beschwörungen aus Fara und Ebla – Untersuchungen zur ältesten keilschriftlichen Beschwörungsliteratur*. Hildesheim, Zürich and New York: Georg Olms Verlag.

Liverani, Mario (ed.) 1993 *Akkad, The First World Empire – Structure, Ideology, Traditions*. Padua: Sargon srl.

Mackay, Ernest 1925 *Report on the Excavation of the 'A' Cemetery at Kish, Mesopotamia, Part I* (Field Museum of Natural History, Anthropology, Memoirs Volume I, No. 1). Chicago, IL: Field Museum of Natural History.

Maekawa, Kazuya 1973–1974 'The development of the É-MÍ in Lagash during Early Dynastic III', *Mesopotamia* 8–9, 77–144.

Maisels, Charles 1999 *Early Civilizations of the Old World – The Formative Histories of Egypt, The Levant, Mesopotamia, India and China*. London and New York: Routledge.

Mander, Pietro 1986 *Il pantheon di Abu-Ṣālabīkh – Contributo allo studio del pantheon sumerico arcaico*. Naples: Istituto Universitario Orientale, Dipartimento di Studi Asiatici, Series Minor, No. XXVI.

Martin, Harriet 1988 *Fara: A Reconstruction of the Ancient Mesopotamian City of Shuruppak*. Birmingham: Chris Martin & Associates.

——, Pomponio, Francesco, Visicato, Giuseppe and Westenholz, Aage 2001 *The Fara Tablets in the University of Pennsylvania Museum of Archaeology and Anthropology*. Bethesda, MD: CDL Press.

McAdam, Ellen 1993 'Clay figurines', in Green (ed.) 1993, 83–109.

Miller, Naomi 1998 'The Macrobotanical Evidence for Vegetation in the Near East, c. 18 000/16 000 BC to 4 000 BC', *Paléorient* 23/2, 197–207.

Moon, Jane 1993 'Pottery', in Green (ed.) 1993, 145–157.

Muller, Béatrice 1998 'Espace réel, espace symbolique: Les "maquettes architecturales" de Syrie', in M. Fortin, O. Aurenche (eds), *Espace naturel, espace habité en Syrie du Nord (10e–2e millénaires av. J.-C.), Actes du colloque tenu à l'Université Laval (Québec) du 5 au 7 mai 1997*. Québec and Lyon: Canadian Society for Mesopotamian Studies, Bulletin 33, Maison de l'Orient Méditerranéen, Travaux de la Maison de l'Orient 28, 179–190.

Oates, David, Oates, Joan, McDonald, Helen (*et al.*) 2001 *Excavations at Tell Brak, vol. 2: Nagar in the third millennium BC*. Cambridge and London: McDonald Institute for Archaeological Research and British School of Archaeology in Iraq.

Parrot, André 1948 *Tello, Vingt campagnes de fouilles (1877–1931)*. Paris: Editions Albin Michel.

Pomponio, Francesco, Visicato, Giuseppe 1994 *Early Dynastic Administrative Tablets of Šuruppak*. Naples: Istituto Universitario Orientale di Napoli, Dipartimento di Studi Asiatici, Series Maior, VI.

Postgate, John Nicolas (ed.) 1983 *Abu Ṣalabikh Excavations vol. 1: The West Mound surface clearances*. London: British School of Archaeology in Iraq.

Quarantelli, Ezio (ed.) 1985 *The Land between Two Rivers – Twenty years of Italian archaeology in the Middle East, The treasures of Mesopotamia*. Turin 1985, Florence 1986, Rome 1986, Torino: Il Quadrante Edizioni.

Reade, Julian 2001 'Assyrian King-Lists, the Royal Tombs of Ur, and Indus origins', *Journal of Near Eastern Studies*, 60/1, 1–29.

Rehm, Ellen 2003 *Waffengräber im Alten Orient – Zum Problem der Wertung von Waffen in Gräbern des 3. und frühen 2. Jahrtausend v. Chr. in Mesopotamien und Syrien.* BAR International Series 1191, Oxford: Archaeopress.

Rosengarten, Yvonne 1960 *Le concept sumérien de consommation dans la vie économique et religieuse – Etude linguistique et sociale d'après les texts présargoniques de Lagaš.* Paris: Editions E. de Boccard.

—— 1960a *Le régime des offrandes dans la société sumérienne d'après les textes présargoniques de Lagaš.* Paris: Editions E. de Boccard.

Selz, Gebhard 1991 '"Elam" und "Sumer" – Skizze einer Nachbarschaft nach inschriftlichen Quellen der vorsargonischen Zeit', in L. De Meyer and H. Gasche (eds), *Mésopotamie et Elam – Actes de la XXXVIème Rencontre Assyriologique Internationale, Gand, 10–14 juillet 1989* .(Mesopotamian History and Environment, Occasional Publications I), Ghent: The University of Ghent, 27–43.

—— 1995 *Untersuchungen zur Götterwelt des altsumerischen Stadtstaates von Lagaš.* Philadelphia: Occasional Publications of the Samuel Noah Kramer Fund, 13.

Speiser, Ephraim Avigdor (ed.) 1935 *Excavations at Tepe Gawra I – Levels I-VIII.* Philadelphia: American Schools of Oriental Research – University of Pennsylvania Press.

Steible, Horst, Yyldyz, Fatma 2000 'Lapislazuli-Zuteilungen an die "Prominenz" von Šuruppak', in Graziani (ed.) 2000, 985–1031.

Steinkeller, Piotr 1993 'Early Political Development in Mesopotamia and the Origins of the Sargonic Empire', in Liverani (ed.) 1993, 107–129.

Tallon, Philippe, Van Lerberghe, Karel 1997 *En Syrie, Aux Origines de l'Écriture. Catalogue d'une Exposition.* Turnhout: Brepols.

Visicato, Giuseppe 1995 *The Bureaucracy of Šuruppak – Administrative Centres, Central Offices, Intermediate Structures and Hierarchies in the Economic Documentation of Fara.* Münster: Ugarit-Verlag.

—— and Westenholz, Aage 2000 'Some unpublished sale contracts from Fara', in Graziani (ed.) 2000, 1107–1133.

Westenholz, Aage 1999 'The Old Akkadian Period: History and Culture', in W. Sallaberger and A. Westenholz, *Mesopotamien – Akkade-Zeit und Ur III-Zeit, Annäherungen.* hrsg. von P. Attinger – M. Wäfler (Orbis Biblicus et Orientalis 160/3), Freiburg and Göttingen: Universitätsverlag and Vandenhoeck & Ruprecht, 17–117.

Wilkinson, Tony 1997 'Le paysage archéologique de la Djézireh syrienne', in Tallon-Van Lerberghe 1997, 119–121.

——, Tucker, David 1995 *Settlement Development in the North Jezira, Iraq – A Study of the Archaeological Landscape.* Baghdad: British School of Archaeology in Iraq and Department of Antiquities and Heritage.

CHAPTER EIGHTEEN

THE PALACE AND THE TEMPLE IN BABYLONIA

——— ·◆· ———

Walther Sallaberger

Two institutions dominated Babylonia, the palace and the temple, representing the political power and the religious centre, respectively. As seat of the political power, the palace housed the king and his court. In the temples the dozens, even hundreds, of gods of Babylonia were venerated, the main city god or minor gods in smaller sanctuaries.

Both palace and temple can be regarded as oversized houses, since one of their functions was to serve as living place: for the king or for the deity. Therefore, the simple layout of a Babylonian house may also be seen in the gigantic dimensions of a palace or of a temple: the rooms placed around a central courtyard with one main reception room opposite the entrance. The master of the house lived in his fitting abode: the king with his family, including a large section of women, the wives, daughters, wet-nurses, their attendants, along with all the servants and officials in charge; and the god with his divine consort, the main point of reference for all women of the town, their children and their divine staff.

THE TEMPLE IN THE CITY

In a larger Babylonian city one would find many temples, but only one palace. The latter was not necessarily restricted to the royal capital of a state, but the king disposed of palaces at several places and also provincial governors could build their palace.

The different roles of palace and temple in society become immediately clear after a look at the map of any Babylonian town (see Figure 18.1). As an example we take the city of Babylon in the first century, the time of its largest extension, which boasts the main palaces of the Chaldean kings, of Nebuchadrezzar and his dynasty. The palaces occupied a prominent position in the north-western corner of the town at the bank of the river Euphrates and at both sides of the main street. The living quarters were separated from the palace, which was itself surrounded by massive walls. This is a fitting expression of the distance and separation of royal power.

Marduk, Babylon's god and, by the first millennium, the divine ruler called Bel, 'Lord', venerated highly all over the country, occupied the centre of the town: the large temple precinct occupied a remarkable portion of the whole inhabited area of

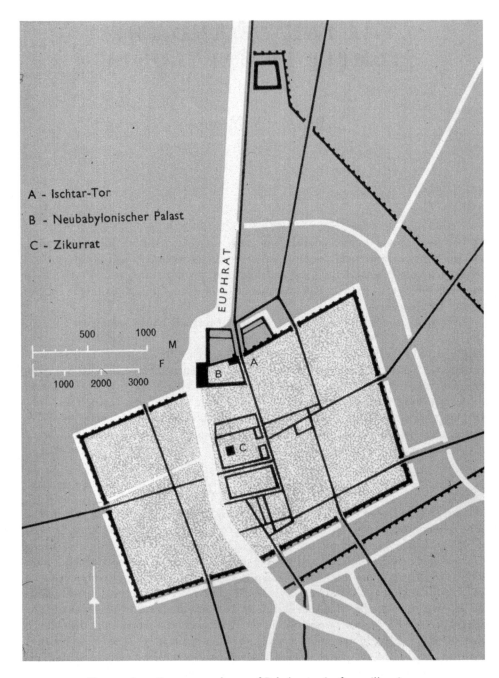

A - Ischtar-Tor

B - Neubabylonischer Palast

C - Zikurrat

Figure 18.1   Reconstructed map of Babylon in the first millennium.

Figure 18.2 Model of the Marduk sanctuaries in Babylon (above); the Processional Way and the Ishtar Gate (below) (H. Schmökel, *Ur, Assur und Babylon* Tf. 114).

Babylon. A temple was bound to its traditional place and it was mandatory to keep the right spot of the cella at every rebuilding of the temple. The huge temple of a city's main deity is the main public building of any town, situated at its centre and providing the largest open space, perhaps even the only large open space. The stepped temple tower of Babylon, the ziggurat, extending over a square of ninety metres on the ground, rose in seven large steps to a height of probably sixty-six metres as an artificial massive mountain built of bricks and decorated at the outside (Allinger-Csollich 1998). The temple towers of the main Babylonian cities became thus the most prominent landmarks in the flat alluvial plain.

The position of the temple is an apt expression of its function as a focus of the city's identity. The main deity of a town together with his wife, his son and his divine staff could constantly protect the citizens, and the people would easily reach the gods. Everybody enjoyed the annual festival when the god left the temple in a procession and beer and food were generously distributed.

The city god's presence was felt in everyday life, too. Oaths were sworn by the city god, and not only lawsuits, but any simple legal transaction such as marriage, adoption or sale demanded an oath. The presence of the deity in legal cases could be guaranteed by bringing a symbol of the god such as a standard or a weapon (Veenhof 2003). The city god was often addressed in greetings, which are known to us only in a written version from private and business letters. A standard Babylonian letter to a colleague or a family member usually opened with good wishes, such as 'May god Marduk keep you in good health!' (Old Babylonian) or 'May Marduk and Nabû [i.e. Marduk's son] bless my father!' (Neo-Babylonian). Finally, any larger group of persons from a town would reveal the name of their city god by simply telling their names (Edzard 1998). Babylonian names most often included a divine name, and many citizens gave their children names that venerated the care and help of the city god; thus Babylonian names consisted of little phrases such as Marduk-apla-iddina 'Marduk has given me an heir', Ina-Esagil-shuma-ibni 'In Esagil [i. e. Marduk's temple] he created the name [i.e. offspring]', or Nabû-balata-iqbi 'Nabû pronounced life'.

The close connection between a god in his temple and his town remained basically constant through millennia, and so god and city could almost become synonymous. There is no doubt that the city god and his temple became the true symbols of a city for all its inhabitants. This connection between a god and his city in Babylonia can sometimes be detected in the cuneiform signs used to express a town or a god. So the sun god's city, Larsa, is written with a combination of the sign for 'sun(god)' and for 'abode'; if this sign for 'abode' or 'place' is combined with the standard of Inana, one gets the name of Inana's town Zabalam, or with the standard of the moon-god Nanna, the resulting ideogram is the one of the moon-god's city, Ur (Michalowski 1993). On the other hand, a main god could be just called 'Lord' of his city, like Ningirsu, that is 'Lord of (the city) Girsu' or Nin-Nibru 'Lady of (the city) Nippur'. These examples indicate that the close connection between city and its deity evolved at least in the first stage in the development of writing around 3000 BC or in the early third millennium.

A considerable number of persons, especially of the 'better' families took part in the daily provisioning of the temple (Jursa 1995; Bongenaar 1997). The deity literally lived in the temple and, therefore, had to be served beverages and food several times a day. These daily offerings were prepared by citizens who held the respective rights and who were entitled to use the left-overs of the divine meal. Such prebends, income from the daily services, could be inherited or even sold (van Driel 2005). Also the temple personnel received regular food rations from the temple's income. A temple housed craftsmen, such as carpenters or basket weavers, for its upkeep and eventual repair, millers, bakers or brewers in the food production, guards, gate keepers and courtyard sweepers for the care of the temple. The temple's fields were cultivated by ploughmen and their attendants. Furthermore, a temple cared for orphans, blind or elderly people; apparently, by sustaining the temples, the ruler fulfilled his promise to care for the poor and neglected and for the widows and orphans of his country (cf. Zettler 1992). All these persons linked to a temple who did not perform priestly duties lived on the temple's resources.

Temples employed singers and musicians, and they must have sung regularly the hymns and prayers praising the gods. The priests served the food to the gods and assisted in the rites which were performed by the high priest and purification priests (Sallaberger and Huber-Vulliet 2005). In approaching the temple from the perspective of the persons living on the temple's holdings and income of food, it becomes obvious that a Babylonian temple was much more than a home of the deity. The temple as an important employer is certainly only one aspect of its social relevance, but it is not the least one which can be added to the points addressed above.

RELIGION AT THE PALACE

As we have seen, a Babylonian temple was much more than a religious institution. On the other hand, as we are going to discuss presently, religion was not at all restricted to the temple. Religion may be seen as a salient feature of Babylonian culture, which could not exist independently of the culture: being a Babylonian meant believing in the Babylonian gods. So the so-called political centre of the country, the palace, was always a centre of religion, too. The king acted for his land and his people before the gods, and the immortals bestowed well-being and fertility to the king as representative of his country. In this role the king participated in the state festivals at the temple, first and foremost the New Year's festival at Babylon. Every year the king returned his insignia to the god and, after swearing that he had not done any harm to Babylon, he was set in office again. The divine ruler Marduk and the earthly ruler left the cella hand in hand for the festival's procession, and at the 'socle of destinies' in the central courtyard of Marduk's monumental sanctuary at Babylon, the god pronounced the destiny of the king for the coming year. So in the annual festival at Babylon the king was presented as the one crowned and protected by the divine ruler (Black 1981; Pongratz-Leisten 1994).

The king as sole representative of his people needed special protection, and so religious specialists were present at the palace to explore the will of the gods and to dispel evil. Religious life at the royal court is best known for the Assyrian palace of the seventh century BC, but since the rituals of the diviner and the exorcist were, as a rule, of Babylonian origin, we may safely assume a similar religious life at the palace of Babylon, too. This is confirmed by inscriptions of Babylonian kings or by incidental references in various kinds of texts. The diviner had to disclose the decisions of the gods, be it past or future events. The usual way to obtain this knowledge was by means of extispicy, that is the observation of a lamb's liver and other intestines

(Maul 2003 and this volume). In this technique of future-telling, the formation and wrinkles of the fresh liver were regarded as a message of the gods which could only be deciphered by highly trained specialists, the 'seers'. And they had to work quickly since after a very short period the uneven surface of the liver became smooth and so the 'writing' disappeared. The diviner was consulted before important decisions such as a military expedition or the appointment of an official. In the case of any evil that had befallen the king, an illness or even a malicious ominous sign, the exorcist or incantation priest was called to perform the appropriate rituals to dispel the evil and to let the king's personal god return. These religious specialists were not affiliated to a temple and they performed their services for every person who could afford it. The most able specialists, however, were employed by the palace.

Private habitations could include small shrines in the early periods of Babylonia and, in the same way, a palace could house sanctuaries for the protective deities of the royal family. In Babylonia, this seems to be restricted to the early periods until the early second millennium. Also the cult of the ancestors of the family was a religious duty performed in the palace as in any other house: the forefathers of the master of the household were venerated and their names were called and thus preserved from oblivion, as every person would hope for his own future (Radner 2006).

In summary, the palace was an important centre of Babylonian religion. This religious role, however, differed mainly in scale but less in substance from the private houses and their inhabitants. The uniqueness of the figure of the king in Babylonian society, however, implies a unique importance of the king as religious person.

THE PALACE IN THE LIFE OF THE BABYLONIANS

In Babylonia, 'the palace' was not only a building but also an institution that could, for example, 'sell' goods or 'write tablets' to testify the ownership of a field. The palace as seat of the ruler controlled law and order in Babylonia, and the king himself was the highest juridical authority. So the palace issued various regulations to the country, but it served also as the highest law court (Westbrook 2003). In this regard, the royal palace of Babylon was very much respected by the inhabitants: it was hoped that a legal dispute would not end up in Babylon. The private letters of the Old Babylonian period allude to this function at various occasions, and one may find threatening phrases such as 'if this is not the case, I will write to the palace' or 'you will not be able to meet the claims' of the palace at Babylon (Sallaberger 1999: 251).

The respect paid to the palace by the Babylonians is not only based on its juridical role. Because of its concentration of economic means, the palace employed the most able and most influential persons of the state. So it seems to have been the Babylonian dream to 'go up' to Babylon to enter the palace, and whoever had managed this was accompanied by the good wishes of his relatives and his clients. This is expressed in the greetings of an Old Babylonian letter: 'The protective deities of my daddy may grant you, my father, a long life (still) as old man and with a good name in the palace where you are walking about!' (Kraus 1964: no. 15).

Also in an economic sense the palace was central in the life of the Babylonians: the ultimate owner of the land was the king who gave it to his subjects who were obliged, in exchange, to perform corvée work. The palace collected taxes from various brands. In the Old Babylonian period, various economic sectors were not directly controlled by the palace, but entrusted to entrepreneurs. These entrepreneurs had to deliver either the products of agriculture, cattle-breeding, cultivation of dates or fishing directly, or an equivalent in silver (Renger 2004). Thus, the surplus of the economy of the country was collected by the palace. Only a part of the incoming goods was stored, since they had to be used to meet the state's expenses.

THE TREASURES OF THE PALACE

The cuneiform archives of administrative texts found in palaces are primarily concerned with a specific category of goods that one may term prestige or luxury goods. This shows clearly that the administration of goods, such as the storable textiles and precious stones, well as delicacies, formed a central task of the palace. This can be observed in the whole ancient Near East in impressive continuity and constancy.

These prestige goods, of course, did not serve the basic needs of food, clothing and tools of everyday use, but they stand out both for their 'uselessness' and their immense value. The least obvious case is, perhaps, the character of meat as a luxury good; we should not forget that meat was usually not offered at the ordinary man's table. Of the delicacies served at the palace, one should also mention that wine was served instead of the more ordinary beer. Objects of silver and gold were of high value because of the material used. Precious metals had to be imported, but silver was the standard currency in Babylonia, only interrupted by a short phase of gold prices. Textiles are more difficult to evaluate, but here the enormous amount of labour spent to produce more valuable textiles has to be accounted. Also precious metals were transformed into masterpieces of handicraft, such as vessels or jewellery, and the texts abound in references to figurative decoration, inlays or granulation. The female weavers or the goldsmiths working at the palace had to be sustained by the income of the country, too, and the amount of labour spent added to the high value of the goods of the palace's treasury. Although only the palace could acquire and produce these luxury goods at a high level, the production involved many more craftsmen and specialized workers and in this way segments of the population participated in the economy of the palace.

The precious goods were not only kept in inaccessible treasure chambers of the palace. This would contradict the character of prestige goods, which have to be shown in order to have an effect of excessive splendour and thereby power. This principle of the conspicuous consumption, the multiple presentation of the acquired goods, is dealt with in the brilliant analysis by Thorstein Veblen in his 'Theory of the Leisure Class' (1899). As a matter of principle, prestige goods are always diametrically opposed to the useful and productive. This concerns not only the character of the goods but also their users. Veblen points in his contemporaneous world to women, serving for prestigious purposes and relieved of the ordinary duties; to the army of liveried servants; the members of an elite class who are not occupied with productive work.

It is important to note that only the palace was able to distribute such treasures. Of course, the court followed the common social norms and conventions, and thus presents can be found at other levels of society, too. But only at the palace did the expenditure of goods take place on such a scale that it was regularly documented in administrative texts. And, here, only the palace was able to distribute such treasures, not the other institutions of Mesopotamia, including the temple. Temples managed the agriculture, they received rich donations by the ruler, including gold and silver, and thus served as a kind of treasure-chamber, but temples could not pass on these goods.

Not all the treasures delivered to the palace were stored there, but a part of them was distributed. Interestingly, not only the materials treated by the administrative texts from palace archives, but also the recipients of the goods, were strikingly similar throughout the history of Babylonia.

A large amount of goods were delivered to the gods in the temples: meat or other delicacies for offerings, or silver and gold as dedications. This meets our expectations, since the ruler owed his office, the stability of his rule and the welfare of the country to the gods. Therefore, the gods received a fitting share of the precious goods that had been produced by the combined forces of the whole population.

The palace also spent some of its treasures for 'purchases'. But, perhaps contrary to our expectations, the palace did not only invest the silver to buy necessary goods and materials, especially tin to produce bronze, but spent it for luxury goods such as lapis lazuli, expensive riding animals or textiles. The Mesopotamian merchants acquired the materials that could not be found in the alluvial plain, namely wood and resins, stones and metals, in the Eastern mountain ranges. A large part of trade was thus linked to the prestige economy of the palace.

Textiles or jewels could be presented as gifts to persons. In large part, the presents left the country and were given to other rulers and their courts, or they were presented to messengers and representatives from abroad who came to visit the royal court. The scribes of the pertinent administrative texts sometimes noted that these presents were sent at birth, marriage, illness and death in the family. Of course, after an appropriate time, the recipients of the gifts repaid their debt with a counter-gift according to the habit and expectations; and these gifts were noted in the administrative documents as incoming goods. Seen in a strictly economic perspective, this might look like an exchange without any profit or loss, but at least products typical for their provenience were exchanged. To mention just one example: in the Later Bronze Age, the fourteenth century BC, some documents shed light on the exchange between the courts of Babylon and of Egypt. Here, Babylon sent lapis lazuli, which it acquired from the East, and horses, which were especially used for battle-chariots, to Egypt, and the Egyptian pharaohs returned the much desired gold to Babylon. The letters exchanged between the courts give a vivid description of the exchange. The Babylonian king complains:

> But now when I sent a messenger to you, you have detained him for six years, and you have sent me as my greeting-gift, the only thing in six years, 30 minas of gold of the quality of silver . . . When you celebrated a great festival, you did not send your messenger to me, saying, 'Come to eat and drink'. Nor did you send my greeting-gift in connection with the festival. It was just 30 minas of gold that you sent me.

And he ended the letter: 'for 10 wooden chariots and 10 teams of horses I send to you as your greeting gift' (Moran 1992: EA 3). The letters make no secret of the purpose of the gift exchange: it is for the good 'brotherly' relations that are maintained by the constant exchange of gifts. So the given away riches prove to be clever investments in the political future of the own state.

Another group of recipients mentioned in the administrative texts are persons from the ruler's own country. To understand these presents, we have to be aware of the ambivalent character of the gift. The material benefit is always connected with the obligation to repay the debt. This debt need not be repaid materially as by the equal, but the status of debt can be kept forever and thus it implies a permanent obligation. The ruler generously distributing gifts by this means obliged his people, thereby acquiring a symbolic capital which only enabled his exertion of power. Who received the precious presents of textiles and jewellery from the royal court? First, there was the family of the ruler, his wife and the queen-mother, sons and daughters, and the wet-nurses. Birth, marriage, festivals, illness and death offered the occasions for presents to other courts as well as to members of the family or the highest dignitaries of the palace. Personal occasions, not political deeds, provided the background for gifts; but the close relations within the family and with the highest officials was the firm fundament of any exertion of power.

The study of administrative archives leads to the recognition of the important role of the army: generals are among the most important recipients of gifts; military success is the occasion for festivals where gifts are distributed, and even the messenger bringing good news is rewarded. Large quantities of the best food, especially of meat, are given to the army when 'invited' by the palace. The 'meal of the king' in the palace of Mari was an opportunity to show off the wealth of the palace, through the richness of the food that was offered. It was also a chance to display the elite of the country, who were invited to the banquets with generals of the army and foreign messengers.

The administrative personnel of the palace received such goods only occasionally and priests are rarely mentioned among the recipients. Without doubt, the cultic personnel received its share of the offerings brought to the temple, but apparently the king was not interested in obliging the highest priests with the bribe of precious goods.

And finally, one group also appears regularly among the recipients of prestige goods, namely performing artists such as singers, musicians, dancers and acrobats. Art is linked to the palace, and the artistic decoration of metal vessels and, probably, of textiles is another instance of this connection.

Even if the prestige goods are concentrated at a restricted upper class, they determine the economy and society of the whole country. Their acquisition by ways of trade and gift exchange, and their production require all available resources. These goods could be distributed to more persons than just a small group in the centre of power, if one considers recipients such as messengers or the army. And, furthermore, festivals offered occasions to distribute the precious goods of the palace to all the people. These goods served a more important purpose than the economic one, because the gifts of the ruler consolidated and strengthened the society.

THE RULER AND THE TEMPLE

The palace was the home and the governmental centre of the king and so his treasures were used to erect buildings of the largest dimensions and to embellish them with the best works of art or to assemble collections of rare plants and animals there. Interestingly, the building of a palace is hardly a main topic in inscriptions of Babylonian kings, a fact that distinguishes them from the Assyrians. Babylonian kings dedicated more efforts to the large and venerated temples of the gods and to their equipment, with cultic objects such as a throne or a harp for the deity. This programme concurs with the self-presentation of Babylonian kings in their texts as being protected and guided by the gods and whose deeds are considered a more or less cogent consequence of their status and power, but not historical deeds. Royal inscriptions are mostly written on durable materials such as stone, metal or baked clay objects, so that the name of the ruler may be preserved forever in the context of his dedication to the eternal gods.

The care of the ruler for the gods was based on ideology but was not restricted to that. Ideology always determines the distribution of resources, and so the dominant role of the gods in the world view of Babylonian rulers led to the most impressive royal building programmes being the erection and equipment of temples. Furthermore, the sacred furniture was donated by the king, and, at various occasions precious objects such as vases of gold and silver or jewels were dedicated to the temples. Together with dedications of new buildings or of cultic objects, the king usually funded the temple with grants of land or other sources of income so that continuous offerings were ensured. In this way the temple was enabled to care for its dependants as outlined above.

On the preceding pages, various aspects of the main institutions of Babylonia, temple and palace have been discussed. One could easily add other related topics, outline the personnel of each institution, the rules to be obeyed within the palace or the regulations to become a priest. Instead the focus has been laid on the basic functions as they emerge from a contrastive discussion of the two realms: for example, the restricted religious role of the palace and the economic supremacy of the palace deriving from its control of prestige goods.

The two institutions can hardly be imagined independent of each other for most of Mesopotamian history. But Babylonia experienced a major change in 539 when the rule of the last Chaldean king Nabonidus was ended by Cyrus the Great of the Persian Achaemenids. From then on, no indigenous Babylonian king ruled over Babylonia, and the fact that hardly any building inscriptions of the Achaemenids exist reveals that the close relationship between palace and temple had changed. It is surely no coincidence that, after the end of a Babylonian royal palace, the temples gained a larger importance in the tradition of knowledge in Babylonia, and that all scholarly experts were linked to the temple. Only now priests controlled the Babylonian literary and scholarly texts written in cuneiform, and our sources document their scribal productivity until the first century BC. The learned priests of the temples, furthermore, became experts in astronomy-astrology, which included both mathematical calculations and the omens to predict the impact of the celestial bodies. This science was the foundation of the later fame of Babylonia in the West (see Brown in this volume). So after a long tradition of coexistence between temple and palace, the Babylonian temple outlived the latter by half a millennium, thereby preserving and developing the culture and scholarship which was once prominent at the palace.

BIBLIOGRAPHY

Allinger-Csollich, W. 1998: 'Birs Nimrud II. "Tieftempel" – "Hochtempel". Vergleichende Studien Borsippa – Babylon', *Baghdader Mitteilungen* 29, 95–330.

Black, J. A. 1981: 'The New Year Ceremonies in Ancient Babylon: "Taking Bel by the Hand" and a Cultic Picnis', *Religion* 11, 39–59.

Bongenaar, A. C. V. M. 1997: *The Neo-Babylonian Ebabbar Temple at Sippar* (Leiden/Istanbul: Nederlans Instituut voor het Nabije Oosten).

Edzard, D. O. 1998: 'Name, Namengebung (Onomastik). A. Sumerisch, B. Akkadisch', *Reallexikon der Assyriologie* 9, 94–116.

George, A. R. 1992: *Babylonian Topographical Texts*. Orientalia Lovaniensia Analecta 40 (Leuven: Peeters).

—— 1993: *House Most High. The Temples of Ancient Mesopotamia*. Mesopotamian Civilizations 5 (Winona Lake: Eisenbrauns).

Jursa, M. 1995: *Die Landwirtschaft in Sippar in neubabylonischer Zeit*. Archiv für Orientforschung Beih. 25 (Wien: Universität, Institut für Orientalistik).

Kraus, F. R. 1964: *Briefe aus dem British Museum (CT 43 und 44). Altbabylonische Briefe in Umschrift und Übersetzung 1* (Leiden: Brill).

Maul, S. M. 2003: 'Omina und Orakel', *Reallexikon der Assyriologie* 10, 45–88.

Michalowski, P. 1993: 'On the Early Toponymy of Sumer: A Contribution to the Study of Early Mesopotamian Writing', in: A. F. Rainey *et al.* (eds), *kinattûtu ša darâti. Raphael Kutscher Memorial Volume* (Tel Aviv: University, Institute of Archaeology) 119–135.

Moran, W. L. 1992: *The Amarna Letters* (Baltimore, MD and London: Johns Hopkins University Press).

Pongratz-Leisten, B. 1994: *Ina šulmi īrub. Die kulttopographische und ideologische Programmatik der akītu–Prozession in Babylonien und Assyrien im I. Jahrtausend v. Chr.* Baghdader Forschungen 16 (Mainz: Zabern).

Postgate, J. N. 1992: *Early Mesopotamia. Society and Economy at the Dawn of History* (London and New York: Routledge).

—— *et al.* 2004: 'Palast', *Reallexikon der Assyriologie* 10, 195–276.

Radner, K. (2006): *Die Macht des Namens. Altorientalische Strategien zur Selbsterhaltung* (Wiesbaden: Harrassowitz).

Renger, J. 2004: 'Palastwirtschaft', *Reallexikon der Assyriologie* 10, 276–280.

Sallaberger, W. 1999: *'Wenn Du mein Bruder bist, . . .'. Interaktion und Textgestaltung in altbabylonischen Alltagsbriefen*. Cuneiform Monographs 16 (Groningen: Styx).

—— 2004: 'Pantheon', *Reallexikon der Assyriologie* 10, 294–308.

—— and F. Huber-Vulliet 2005: 'Priester', *Reallexikon der Assyriologie* 10 (in print).

van Driel, G. 2005: 'Pfründe', *Reallexikon der Assyriologie* 10.

Veenhof, K. R. 2003: 'Fatherhood is a Matter of Opinion. An Old Babylonian Trial on Filiation and Service Duties', in: W. Sallaberger *et al.* (eds), *Literatur, Politik und Recht in Mesopotamien. Festschrift für Claus Wilcke* (Wiesbaden: Harrassowitz) 313–332.

Westbrook, R. (ed.) 2003: *History of Ancient Near Eastern Law*. Handbook of Oriental Studies 72 (Leiden: Brill).

Zettler, R. L. 1992: *The Ur III Temple of Inanna at Nippur*. Berliner Beiträge zum Vorderen Orient 11 (Berlin: Reimer).

CHAPTER NINETEEN

POWER, ECONOMY
AND SOCIAL ORGANISATION
IN BABYLONIA

————•◆•————

Gebhard J. Selz

POWER AND IDEOLOGY

Power derives from many sources: physical strength, personal charisma, economic and social influence, or from legal or conventional traditions, such as inheritance. In the Babylonian world view, natural causes were not clearly distinguished from supra-natural influences and so the different sources of power remained intertwined despite the development of a legal system based on writing, and the mythical roots of power were never neglected. The ruler's main task was to mediate between different social groups as well as between deities and human beings. The proof for the divine mandate of the ruler was the efficiency of his government, the welfare of the people being its outward sign (Selz 2004). Economical and social organisations, therefore, had to be at the centre of Babylonia's royal ideology. No legitimate or lasting power could permanently ignore the welfare of its subjects or of a substantial group that supported the government. Therefore, different interests had to be taken into account and antagonistic forces had to be restricted and controlled. Adversaries from within society were as dangerous as enemies from the outside. Not surprisingly though, official inscriptions deal primarily with the latter and information about conflicts within Babylonian society remains scarce. As a result of this unbalance in the original sources, modern historiographers often tend to reiterate the official ancient Mesopotamian account of historical events. It focuses on the various kings and their deeds, and often attempts to ascribe dramatic historical changes, and even the decline of a whole dynasty, to one major outside cause. Our picture of Mesopotamian history is formed by a number of outstanding rulers, some being examples of efficient, some of unsuccessful governments. However, their reigns cover only a limited period of time. There are many examples where the influence of a dynastic family or a single ruler resulted just in a rather short-lived period of stability. Even the dynasty of the famous Hammurabi was already in decline during the reign of his successor and son Samsu-iluna. The stability of a government did not result from the efficient management of the different groups of the society alone, but also depended on the rulers' or the ruling elite's ability to generate support in the society by conjuring a vision of an ideal society. Such images were not simply 'created' by the kings and their administration but had strong roots in a centuries old tradition, and were normally just modified and adapted to the needs of the day. Such images were spread by various forms of what we would term propaganda – and the bulk of our so-called 'historical' sources are in fact that: propaganda. Therefore, when we read ancient sources and look at the surviving pictures, we need to question their historical value. Letters, administrative texts, legal decisions, as well as remnants of the material culture, help to balance our historical account. However, the factor of propaganda and ideological distortion of social reality is important in itself: every ruler and every ruling class is bound to the images they propagate or create.

IMAGES OF THE RULER

Sure enough, every Babylonian king had to adhere to his own proclamations, at least to some degree; otherwise he would soon have lost any credibility. Among Hammurabi's lengthy and flowery self-description as a king we find the following words:

> I am Hammurabi, noble king, I have not been careless or negligent toward human-kind, granted to my care by the god Enlil with whose shepherding the god Marduk charged me . . . I removed serious difficulties, I spread light over them.

As the king was commissioned by the gods to 'direct the land along the course of truth and the correct way of life', he published a collection of regulations, the so-called 'Laws of Hammurabi', stating as their purpose:

> In order that the mighty not wrong the weak, to provide just ways for the waif and the widow, I have inscribed my precious words upon my stele and set it up before the statue of me, the king of justice, in the city of Babylon.
>
> (Roth 1995: 133)

The main metaphor for the ruler in the epilogue of Hammurabi's laws is that of the 'Righteous Shepherd', which is central to the Babylonian concept of kingship and has survived well into the Christian era. In the prologue of his laws, Hammurabi focuses on another equally important image, that of the ruler as builder of temples, cities and palaces (cp. Z. Bahrani's contribution in this volume). In this function he is receiving the measuring rope and the rod from his god, as depicted on the sculptured top of Hammurabi's stele. Three centuries earlier, the founder of the so-called Ur III-Dynasty, Ur-Nammu, had been portrayed in much the same way (Figure 19.1). Indeed, the rod and the measuring rope, *regula* and *norma*, are the royal insignia that connect the ruler's building activities – and perhaps the surveying of land – with the realm of law and order, as it is still reflected in the modern usage of these terms.

All Babylonian kings stress their piety towards the deities, and in this respect they depict themselves as humble servants. Since all building activities involved the movement of huge amounts of material, especially earth and bricks, the number of basket carriers needed was very high and this heavy work earned little respect. Already from the third millennium onwards there are many figurines depicting the king as basket carrier. In Babylonia this tradition was so strong that the Assyrian king Ashurbanipal, as well as his brother Shamash-shumu-ukin, who reigned in Babylon, was depicted in this manner (see Bahrani's contribution and Figure 10.1 in this volume).

Figure 19.1   Detail of the Code of Ur-Nammu, showing the measuring rope.

This concept of an ordered society and the king's responsibility govern centuries of Babylonian ideology, down to Nabonidus (555–539 BC), and it was already ancient when Hammurabi drafted his famous Laws. The Laws themselves are embedded within a larger pro- and epilogue. From the viewpoint of a literary historian, the whole text is basically an elaborated example of a typical Mesopotamian 'votive inscription'. This is much in the third-millennium (Sumerian) tradition, where neither Gudea of Lagash nor the kings of the subsequent Third Dynasty of Ur had paid special attention to their military campaigns. In their often very lengthy inscriptions, they had focused instead, almost exclusively, on the metaphor of the shepherd and the builder. The Babylonians, too, in sharp contrast to the Akkadian and, later, the Assyrian kings, did not consider either military achievements or inheritable kingship as the dominant source of legitimisation. At least on ideological grounds, the most important concerns of the Babylonian government were peaceful deeds and the maintenance of social equilibrium.

CONSCRIPTED LABOUR AND MILITARY PERSONNEL – THE SOCIAL EQUILIBRIUM

Any government needs a solid economic basis, and welfare can only be upheld by a controlled equilibrium between the different sectors of society. In Babylonia, as compared to the Akkadian or the Assyrian kingdoms, conquest and booty played a minor role. Only in the Late Babylonian period did this situation change when the Babylonian empire followed the model of the Assyrian expansion. By this time, Babylonia had adjusted its political doctrine to those of other competing powers. At that time colonies, booty and the resulting influx of wealth became central for its economic performance. The militia, however, played an important role during all of Mesopotamian history. Originally, their duties were manifold: in times of conflict they had to fight against the enemy, in periods of peace they were used in various public activities – such as building canals, temples or palaces. Military personnel devoted almost exclusively to warfare – what we might term a 'standing army' – was probably a relatively new achievement. Conscripted labour of the younger male population was likely to have existed early in Mesopotamian history, and we might assume that this was linked to the formation of complex and hierarchic societies. This sort of compulsory labour cannot have been popular. Already in late Early Dynastic times, in the mid-third millennium, king Enmetena from the state of Lagash stated that he had sent home the 'children' of those cities he had drafted for the building of a temple in the city of Badtibira. Such freeing of drafted personnel was later incorporated in most of ancient Mesopotamian 'laws', from Iri-KA-gina (also read Uru-inimgina) down to Hammurabi of Babylon. In fact, it was soon understood as a measurement to establish or to uphold the social equilibrium. This was generally supplemented by provision for the weak and the poor.

THE EMERGENCE OF BABYLONIAN SOCIETY

We have already alluded to the fact that the written documentation – on which modern historiography primarily depends – comes from a limited segment and is therefore biased. More mundane matters are generally neglected which hampers our understanding of the administrative records. There is ample evidence that, during all periods of Mesopotamian history, two larger groups of population inhabited the area. One was permanently settled in cities and towns, another was formed by semi-nomadic people in the hinterlands, among the Akkadian, Hanaean and Amorite tribes, as well as non-Semitic people (Stol 2004: 645–650). They arrived first in western and northern parts of Mesopotamia but after the end of the Third Dynasty of Ur, Elamite intruders from the east also played a major role in Mesopotamian politics. Though it is difficult to evaluate their impact, society clearly changed due to the influence of these different groups. From the Old Akkadian period onwards, land in the open country was given as fief in return for 'feudal' duties and military service. In doing so, the state attempted to generate loyalties and to create strongholds outside the main cities with their discontented and rebellious populace. Their resistance was often led by religious or administrative personnel contesting the king's central power.

It was not until the beginning of the second millennium that the city of Babylon slowly started to play a role in greater Mesopotamian politics. The end of the third millennium was marked by the destruction of the royal capital of Ur. The victor Ishbi-Erra and the kings of the subsequent competing dynasties from Isin and Larsa all came from an Amorite (and Elamite) background – as did Hammurabi of Babylon, roughly 200 years later. It is probably due to this Amorite influence that we can detect several changes within these societies: the role of private property increased, the 'palace' became the undisputed seat of governance. An important factor in the Babylonian economy, down to the Neo-Babylonian period, was patrimonial estates. Tribes and families, organised along a patrilinear descent, gained considerable influence in all social organisations (for a more detailed account of this process, see Goddeeris in this volume). This coincides with the observation that commemorative inscriptions from the Larsa dynasty show greater interest in filiation and family ties (Frayne 1990: 107–322). Judging from the extant sources, the concept of inheritable rulership began to play a major role, beginning with the Larsa dynasty. In the inscriptions from Babylon the situation was similar, but it was by no means compulsory for a ruler to mention his patronymics since the concept of divine son-ship was still maintained. Generally speaking, all rulers saw themselves as heirs of the old Mesopotamian traditions, and their native Amorite idiom was nearly abandoned. The kings usually just kept their Amorite names. In the religious sphere there was one especially remarkable change: whereas the kings of Isin followed the custom of the kings of Ur III to add to their names the cuneiform sign AN, marking them as living deities, the kings of Larsa (as other Old Babylonian rulers) broke with this tradition (cf. Frayne 1990: 5–106 (Isin) and 107–322 (Larsa)). However, the concept of the ruler's responsibility for welfare and economic equilibrium remained important. In the tradition of his forerunners, Ishme-Dagan proclaimed:

> (Ishme-Dagan) relieved the citizens of (the city of) Nippur from military service, removed (obligations) from the temples of the gods Enlil, Ninlil, and Ninurta, [ca]nce[lled] the tithe of the land of Sumer (and) [Akkad, (and) made the nation content].
>
> (Frayne 1990: 33)

Several copies of the laws of his successor Lipit-Eshtar come from this city, Nippur: they clearly follow the laws of Ur-Nammu in structure if not in size and, although written in Sumerian, they are a predecessor of the laws of Hammurabi. Of special interest here are the regulations Lipit-Eshtar made concerning family matters, especially inheritance, and concerning the obligations of households to perform public service:

> I imposed service (equally) on the household of a living father and on the undivided household [of brothers]. I, Lipit-Eshtar, son of the god Enlil, obligated those in a household of a living father and in an undivided household of brothers to service

for seventy (days per year), I obligated those in a household of dependent workers to service for ten days per month.

(Roth 1995: 25f.)

An earlier contemporary of Hammurabi of Babylon, king Dadusha of Eshnuna, dismisses any religious framework for his legal stipulations, known to us as the 'Laws of Eshnuna'. There is no prologue and no epilogue, and only a slight hint of the religious sphere is given in the date formula at the beginning of the text. This formula, unlike the rest of the text, is written in Sumerian. The main body of the text shows us – quite similarly to the laws of Hammurabi – which matters were considered important for the functioning of the social order, but the text was never intended to be a law 'code' in the modern sense. Its first concern is the standardisation of prices for various commodities, of wages and of certain exchange rates, an old royal prerogative and duty. Other entries deal with different topics from the civil or criminal law, among them such issues as rents and loans, pledges and deposits, theft and debt servitude, various injuries, as well as property rights. In sum, these Laws of Eshnuna may be considered a predecessor of the 'edicts of justice' of later Old Babylonian kings (Roth 1995: 57–70).

SOCIAL GROUPS AND SOCIAL ORGANISATION IN MESOPOTAMIA

Scholars have correctly remarked (see Sallaberger's contribution in this volume) that the well-known antagonism between the 'palace' and the 'temple' often conceals the fact that both institutions display a similar organisational type, usually termed as 'households'. Even if this is a rather rough characterisation, it points to their common origin. In fact, there is good evidence to support the hypothesis that this antagonism originated as a result of Old Akkadian policies, when the rulers formed an empire chiefly based on family ties and personal loyalties. In doing so they restricted the power and influence of other big institutions, especially of the large temple-households in the 'Sumerian' south of Mesopotamia. Whereas the Dynasty of Ur III attempted to reconcile the differing organisational principles, the increasing Amorite and Elamite influence (Charpin 2004: esp. 213–227) changed the situation slowly but persistently. The patrimonial estates, continuing a chiefly northern Babylonian tradition (see Goddeeris in this volume), now achieved the significance they kept for the rest of Babylonian history (Jursa 2004: 58–65). As already remarked, we observe an accompanying change in the royal ideology from the more traditional stress on function towards the concept of heritable kingship. The role of tribes and families increased and the 'house of the father' became an important term in the matters of law. The duty to pay reverence to the spirits of the deceased was widely observed. Not all of this was new: a state cult for the ancestors existed already in Old Sumerian times, as can be demonstrated by the documents from the state of Lagash. Already, then, the role of the family had started to increase. Slightly later, the Old Akkadian kings in their curse formulas used to threaten the trespasser with the extinction of his 'seed' (Selz 2004: 168–173, 182f.).

By the end of the third millennium the major economic player was the state. It organised the big institutions, e.g. the former 'temple households' from Southern

Mesopotamia, in a predominantly planned economy, encompassing the whole empire of the Third Dynasty of Ur. In this 'global' economy, Van De Mieroop (1992) named three different sectors: palace, temple and private. However, the economic role of private property and private landholdings or that of the merchants is still disputed (see Renger 1995, van Driel 1995, 1998 and compare Steinkeller 2002: 115). Partially this is certainly due to the laconic nature of our sources; they do not explain what appeared obvious to the contemporaries. However, the concept had existed already for a longer period. In passing we mention the outstanding role of the Old Assyrian entrepreneurs in the overland trade to Anatolia at the turn from the third to the second millennium who apparently enjoyed a greater autonomy than their Old Babylonian counterparts (cf. Goddeeris in this volume).

In the second half of the third millennium, the planned economy of the big institutions followed the principle of redistribution (see Charvát in this volume). A larger part of the population depended on a big institution for their subsistence, usually a temple. The majority must be considered as a kind of temple-slaves. They were the property of these institutions, temples or palaces. They were sometimes bought in exchange for goods, or came into the cities as prisoners of war. They worked the fields or found their occupation in a variety of professions. The documents make a clear distinction between this mass of workers and the so-called house-born slaves, e.g. those people with lesser rights depending on the master of a specific house, the patron of an extended family. Higher in the social ranking stood a group that partly depended on fiefs: during part of the year they sustained themselves by their own harvest, but in return for the use of land they had to fulfil certain obligations towards the institutions and the state. They were drafted for military and other public work, especially for building activities. It is this group of people the ruler addresses when he orders the 'freedom of obligations', mentioned so often in the royal inscriptions from Early Dynastic to Old Babylonian times. Administrative and state officials in temples and palace certainly formed the upper stratum of the society, although threatened in their precarious position by the increasing and continuing accumulation of property in private hands.

ECONOMY, SOCIAL GROUPS AND SOCIAL ORDER IN BABYLONIA

The general framework of this type of social organisation, characteristic for the third millennium, was still the basis of the social order in Old Babylonian times. However, the private sector of economy had drastically grown by then, and temples and palace had to cope with the power resulting from a sizeable portion of the economic resources in private hands. By this time prebends were still connected to certain official duties or payments, now chiefly under the control of the palace, but they had become hereditary, and, as a part of the 'house of the father', they were passed on from the father to the son(s) (see Goddeeris in this volume). The land of the paternal estate must not be sold to others, albeit this was not formally forbidden (Stol 2004: 698). Attached to these family estates were a relatively small number of slaves who were occasionally sold. An average family possessed one to four slaves, very rich ones up to ten. Slaves were physically marked, but they were not under the absolute authority of their master – as compared to classical antiquity – and not without any rights.

These so-called 'house-born' slaves could advance sometimes in their social position, and stipulations in the Old Babylonian laws concern their duties and their rights. In the case of people taken as prisoners of war and enslaved thereafter, a considerable number of them were transferred to the big institutions to serve as agricultural workers or in the army. In accordance with older customs, the females were often assigned to textile manufactures, at least in Old Babylonian Mari.

Buying and selling slaves was a common practice in Mesopotamia. According to some authors chattel slavery is considered a precondition for the use of the term slave. However, the citizens from Babylon and of certain other cities enjoyed some protection against entering into chattel slavery (Stol 2004: 915). At least in theory, all slaves came from outside of Babylonia proper.

The citizens at the upper end of the social ladder had various obligations towards the state. In return for their services, they received either prebend fields or rations. They were termed *awīlum*, the Akkadian word for the '(male) human being', and in the law texts the term is often translated as 'free man', 'gentleman', or the like, ignoring thus the obligatory ties this class of people had towards the state. The members of this class possessed full rights and the state was responsible for their welfare. They formed the backbone of the Babylonian society. They often transferred their duties to other persons; then their so-called *ilku*-service was often performed by a class of people of lower social status, called *muškēnum*, roughly translated as 'commoner'. They received various payments from the citizens for their services, such as subsistence fields (Stol 2004: 761). In later periods silver became the standard for such compensations (Stol 2004: 741f.). The commoners had no formal obligations towards the state, but they had also to look after themselves and possessed lesser rights. Especially in times of an economic crisis, these people suffered greatly. Whereas institutions provide a social net to 'catch' people under such circumstances, the *muškēnum* fell through the cracks (Stol 2004: 732f.). Even belonging to the class of slaves may sometimes have been better.

It may, nevertheless, come as a surprise that such a social safety net existed at all. Old Babylonian documents give good evidence that the institutions provided for their members in case of need, rather in the sense of a social security. There are records of silver expenditures or extra rations in cases of illness, such as a broken leg, or in times of hardship, e.g. following the death of a member of the family. Such expenditures are listed among other, 'normal' or regular expenditures that did not require any extra explanation (Breckwoldt 1995).

ECONOMIC CRISIS

Already in the planned economy of the third millennium, certain groups of people received their share of the profits made through their work. However, the amount of produce they had to deliver to the big institutions was fixed in advance and temporarily adjusted according to changing expectations and the needs of an always-demanding state. If, for one reason or another, a group of people could not meet the demands of the institution, the shortfall was entered in the institution's accounts as a kind of debt, to be met in one of the following years. In the course of several 'bad' years the debts could accumulate to a considerable amount. With this concept of institutional debt and credit, it was just a small step further to introduce the concepts of interest and loan. Naturally, these ideas spread to the private sector (Steinkeller 2002) – some scholars assume that it even originated in this sphere – and the interest-bearing debt became, more than other forms of lending, an important economic issue (Postgate 1992: 168f.). Interest rates were high but varied greatly; the figures usually given in our history books are 33⅓ per cent on barley and 20 per cent on silver loans, but for all such estimations the running time of the loan needs to be taken into account (Stol 2004: 863). Van De Mieroop's observation demonstrates how profitable the loan business had become: 'the overseers of the merchants sometimes preferred to invest their capital in loans rather than in new trade expeditions' (Van De Mieroop 1992: 206). Consequently, some people were able to amass great wealth, and they began to make use of their new economic power. The resulting problems that the central power had to deal with were twofold: on the one hand, the *nouveaux riches* were contesting the existing social order and could eventually even threaten the position of the king and the ruling elite, although this could be lessened by involving such groups in public affairs and by entrusting them with higher positions in the state. On the other hand, the impoverishment of a larger part of populations endangered the political stability at the lower end of the social hierarchy.

While some interest-bearing loans may have had purely speculative character, the mass of debtors were people in dire need. If a citizen was repeatedly unable to meet his debts, he could be forced to hand members of his family over to the creditor to work on the creditor's behalf in order to make up for outstanding payments. This kind of debt slavery was not uncommon, and a considerable number of the population lost any chance to improve their economic situation. To counter the possible permanent enslavement of large parts of the population, Hammurabi restricted in his laws the period of debt service to a maximum of three years, 'their release shall be secured in the fourth year' (§ 117). Nevertheless, debt obligations and the resulting impoverishment seriously tilted the balance of the social order. In fact often a kind of vicious circle was started, which Van De Mieroop describes as follows:

> The borrowers were placed in a very bad economic situation by loans whose interest rates seem to have been exorbitant. When a loan defaulted and a field was mortgaged the creditor obtained the usufruct of the property, and usually rented the field out again to the debtor for a rental fee. When the debtor was unable to pay the rental fee with the products he grew, he had to borrow more silver and so became more indebted to the creditor.
>
> (Van De Mieroop 1992: 208)

In order to avoid the imminent collapse of the entire Old Babylonian economy, the rulers promulgated 'edicts of justice', edited and studied by F.R. Kraus in his groundbreaking work of 1984 (cp. Charpin 2004: 307–310, 370–371).

THE OLD BABYLONIAN ROYAL EDICTS AND THE CRISIS MANAGEMENT

Already the cancellation of service obligations by the Early Dynastic ruler Enmetena, the remission of debts, and protection of the poor proclaimed by Uru-inim-gina, were royal measures aimed at the stabilisation of the social balance and the social order within the state. When, at the beginning of the Old Babylonian period, private property rights gained increasing significance, the need for such balancing measurements grew also. Already Ishme-Dagan exempted the citizens of Nippur from their tax-payments and military service. In the Laws of Lipit-Eshtar many stipulations aimed at stabilising the social order, and in a royal inscription he mentions halving barley taxes and reducing the periods of compulsory service. Slightly later, in the archives from the city of Larsa, we have good evidence that king Rim-Sin issued several royal decrees. One is concerned with the annulment of property transfers, apparently an attempt to secure the subsistence of the selling families. In Babylon, the first kings of the dynasty mention either that they had (re-)established 'just social order' or that they cancelled existing debts. Similar stipulations are well attested later. After Hammurabi, every Old Babylonian king apparently issued such edicts in the year of his inauguration (Selz 1999/2000; Renger 2002). This was clearly an attempt to obtain the support of the people.

The main concern of Hammurabi's laws was, as we have seen above, to establish 'just order' in his kingdom. Of particular interest in this context are the edicts of his successors Samsu-iluna and Ammisaduqa. These edicts deal with the following topics (Kraus 1984: 291ff. and 315ff.):

The proper act of oblivion with:

> cancellation of outstanding payments;
> cancellation of private debts;
> remission from debt servitude;
> remission of the rent for prebend land;
> regulations concerning additional income of certain tenants.

Additional stipulations in the edict of Ammisaduqa concerning:

> prohibition of forcible collection of small debts;
> business relations between government and merchants;
> punishment for certain criminal offences.

The first group of these measures are evidently a royal intervention in valid contracts and somehow challenging the existing legal system (Kraus 1984: 118; Bouzon 1995: 21). Of special interest here is the fact that the king has ordered the 'destruction of the tablets concerning debts' which was evidently understood as a measurement to establish 'just order'. Kraus had already linked the popularity of these edicts in Old Babylonian times to the development of private land holdings. Division of inherited estates reduced the sizes of the subsistence fields, and people were forced to borrow money in order to survive. Ultimately, even the income of the palace was at risk, and such edicts became a necessity for the survival of the entire economic and social system. Seen from another perspective, the edicts themselves threatened the society as a whole. The royal intervention in the existing legal order and the annulment of valid contracts must have provoked legal insecurity among certain circles, and must have shaken any trust in the binding force of the existing legal regulations. But distrust in the law does finally open the path to arbitrary actions. Indeed, this may have contributed to a development where these edicts finally lost their economic and political significance. To avoid any possible misunderstandings, there always was a propaganda side of such edicts (Kraus 1984: 122), but later, in the Neo-Assyrian period, the stipulations degenerated to sheer propaganda statements (Otto 1997).

This outline of the role of 'Power, Economy and the Social Organisation in Babylonia' is based chiefly on Old Babylonian evidence, in an attempt to understand the concepts that formed Babylonian society for more than a millennium thereafter. Of course, there were several and even important changes in these concepts, but the general framework remained astonishingly stable. Major changes can be observed due to the imperial strategy of the Neo-Babylonian Empire, but this belongs to a different chapter of history.

LITERATURE

For the history of the Old Babylonian period, Charpin, Edzard and Stol 2004 survey the state of research; for later periods this may be supplemented by Jursa's sketch from 2004.

Breckwoldt, T. (1995) *Economic Mechanisms in Old Babylonian Larsa*. Ph.D. diss., Cambridge, UK.
Charpin, D. (2004) 'Histoire Politique du Proche-Orient Amorrite (2002–1595)', in Charpin, Edzard and Stol 2004: 23–403.
——, Edzard, D.O. and Stol, M. (2004) *Mesopotamien. Die altbabylonische Zeit. Annäherungen* 4 (P. Attinger, W. Sallaberger, M. Wäfler (eds)). *Orbis Biblicus et Orientalis* 160/4, Fribourg and Göttingen.
Frayne, Douglas R. (1990) *The Royal Inscription of Mesopotamia, Early Periods vol. 4, Old Babylonian Period (2003–1595 BC)*. Toronto: University of Toronto Press.
Haring, B. and de Maaijer, R. (eds) (1998) *Landless and Hungry? Access to Land in Early and Traditional Societies*. Leiden: Research School CNWS.
Hudson, M. and Levine, B.A. (eds) (1996) *Privatization in the Ancient Near East and the Classical World. International Scholars Conference on Ancient Near Eastern Economics, Vol. 1*. Cambridge, MA: Peabody Museum of Archaeology and Anthropology, Harvard University.
—— and Van De Mieroop, M. (eds) (2002) *Debt and Economic Renewal in the Ancient Near East. International Scholars Conference on Ancient Near Eastern Economics, Vol. 3*. Bethesda, MD: CDL Press.
Jursa, M. (2004) *Die Babylonier. Geschichte – Gesellschaft – Kultur*. Munich: C.H. Beck Verlag.
Kraus, F.R. (1984) *Königliche Verfügungen in altbabylonischer Zeit. Studia et Documenta ad iura Orientis Antiqui pertinentia XI*. Leiden: E.J. Brill.
Olivier, J.P.J. (1997) '"Restitution as Economic Redress". The Fine Print of the Old Babylonian *mēšarum*-Edict of Ammiṣaduqa'. *Zeitschrift für Altorientalische und Biblische Rechtsgeschichte* 2: 12–25.
Otto, E. (1997) 'Programme der sozialen Gerechtigkeit. Die neuassyrische *(an-)duraru*-Institution sozialen Ausgleichs und das deuteronomische Erlaßjahr in Dtn 15. *Zeitschrift für Altorientalische und Biblische Rechtsgeschichte* 3: 26–63.
Postgate, J.N. (1992) *Early Mesopotamia. Society and economy at the dawn of history*. London and New York: Routledge.
Renger, J. (1995) 'Institutional, Communal, and Individual Ownership or Possession of Arable Land in Ancient Mesopotamia from the End of the Fourth to the End of the First Millennium BC'. *Chicago Kent-Law Review* 71/1: 269–319.

—— (2002) 'Royal Edicts of the Old Babylonian Period – Structural Background', in Hudson and Van De Mieroop (eds) 2002: 139–161.

Roth, M.T. (1994) 'Mesopotamian Legal Transactions and the Laws of Hammurabi', *Chicago Kent-Law Review* 71: 13–39.

—— (1995) *Law Collections from Mesopotamia and Asia Minor. Writings of the Ancient World. Society of Biblical Literature, vol. 6*, Atlanta, GA: Scholars Press.

Selz, G.J. (1999/2000) '"Wirtschaftskrise – Legitimationskrise – Staatskrise". Zur Genese mesopotamischer Rechtsvorstellungen zwischen Planwirtschaft und Eigentumsverfassung'. *Archiv für Orientforschung* 46/47: 1–44.

—— (2001) '"Guter Hirte, Weiser Fürst" – Zur Vorstellung von Macht und zur Macht der Vorstellung im altmesopotamischen Herrschaftsparadigma'. *Altorientalische Forschungen* 28: 8–3. Berlin: Akademie-Verlag.

—— (2004) '"Wer sah je eine königliche Dynastie (für immer) in Führung!" Thronwechsel und gesellschaftlicher Wandel im frühen Mesopotamien als Nahtstelle von *microstoria* und *longue durée*', in Sigrist, Ch. (ed.) *Macht und Herrschaft, Alter Orient und Altes Testament* 316. Münster: Ugarit-Verlag.

Steinkeller, P. (2002) 'Money-Lending Practices in Ur III Babylonia', in Hudson and Van De Mieroop (eds) 2002: 109–137.

Stol, M. (2004) 'Wirtschaft und Gesellschaft in altbabylonischer Zeit', in Charpin, Edzard and Stol 2004: 641–1027.

Van De Mieroop, M. (1992) *Society and Enterprise in Old Babylonian Nippur, Berliner Beiträge zum Vorderen Orient 12*. Berlin: Reimer Verlag.

van Driel, G. (1995) 'Private or not so Private?' in *Cinquante-deux reflections sur le Proche-Orient Ancien – Festschrift Leon de Meyer, Mesopotamian History and Environment II*: 181–191. Leuven: Peeters.

—— (1998) 'Land in Ancient Mesopotamia: "That which remains undocumented does not exist"', in Haring and de Maaijer (eds) 1998: 19–49.

Westbrook, R. (1995) 'Social Justice in the Ancient Near East', in Irani and Silver (eds), *Social Justice in the Ancient World*, Westport, CT: Greenwood Press, pp. 149–163.

—— (2003) 'Old Babylonian Period', in Westbrook (ed.), *A History of the Ancient Near Eastern Law, vol. 1*, pp. 361–430. *Handbook of Oriental Studies, Section One: The Middle and the Ancient Near East, Vol. 72/1*. Leiden: Brill Academic Publishers.

CHAPTER TWENTY

ARAMEANS
AND CHALDEANS
Environment and society

———•◆•———

Frederick Mario Fales

At that time, the road of yore for going to Babylon, the cult-center of (Marduk), the Enlil of the gods, was not open; and the track was impassable. The country was a desert, where passage had long since become very arduous. The way was choked and without paths; where thorns, thistles, and scrub brush had taken over, it was impossible to go through. Lions and jackals roamed there in packs and frisked about like lambs . . . In that desert terrain, Aramean and Suteans – tent-dwellers, fugitives, thieves, and robbers – had come to dwell and made its road desolate. Long since, the settlements had fallen into ruin; on their (once) watered land, there were neither irrigation dikes nor furrows, and spiders spun their webs. Their flourishing meadows had lapsed from cultivation, their (formerly) irrigated land had been deprived of the sweet harvest song, and grain was cut off.

Royal inscription of Sargon II, first edited by
C. J. Gadd, *Iraq* 18 [1954], 192: vii 45–68

INTRODUCTION: THE SOURCES AND THE
GENERAL HISTORICAL BACKGROUND

Territorial divisions and their wider implications – i.e. in which areas people live, what economic resources they have at their disposal, and how their territorial particularities affect their society and culture in general – still play a fundamental role in the history of Iraq at present, as may be deduced from the daily chronicles of war and peace of the last few years. It thus seems particularly fitting, within the framework of an overall investigation on ancient Babylonia, to draw attention to a specific case-study in environmental and social history together, such as is represented by the tribally based Arameans and Chaldeans of the first half of the first millennium BC.

Historical information on these two population groups, which inhabited adjacent areas of the alluvial plain between the lower reaches of the Tigris and Euphrates, is available from two specific sets of sources in cuneiform discovered in the Assyrian capital cities Nineveh and Kalḫu. The first set is represented by official sources of historiographic scope (chronicles and royal inscriptions). Specifically, the Assyrian royal inscriptions, which were couched in a literary language with epical overtones, provide us with a basic chronological framework on Assyrian conquests from one ruler to the next (Fales 1999–2001); and are particularly precious for us – despite a high degree of rhetorical exaggerations and ideological–propagandistic biases in the narration – for the indication of peoples and places involved in the kings' repeated attempts to subjugate and rule the Babylonian region. The second source group, on the contrary, was not intended for public presentation and judgement: it is constituted by 'everyday' written materials of the Assyrian court, from administrative or legal documents to letters sent by the officials to the royal palace, which present casual and random, but decidedly more trustworthy, information on people and places marking the Assyrian military and political thrusts in Babylonia (Fales 2001). Such 'everyday' information finds also copious and useful parallels in the similar documents that were written down in the Babylonian cities themselves, albeit in the local (Neo-Babylonian) dialect (Cole 1996a, b).

The historical origins of the Arameans and Chaldeans on the lower Tigris and Euphrates alluvium are still relatively unclear (Brinkman 1968, 1984; Lipinski 2000). Aramean tribal groups are most prominently attested from the eleventh century BC onward as new occupants of strategic areas (and perhaps of pre-existing fortified settlements) throughout the northern Mesopotamian and Syrian steppe – the so-called Jezirah – from where they would oppose until *c*.850 BC the Assyrian military thrust towards the Euphrates fords and thence westward into the Transeuphratene and the Levant. In parallel, official Babylonian texts indicate that tribal groups variously labelled as 'Arameans' or 'Suteans' (a traditional designation for West Semitic nomads) carried out the looting of Sippar and other cities in the northern alluvial plain in different moments of the eleventh and tenth centuries. At roughly the same time, even the Assyrian main cities on the upper and middle Tigris had been menaced by Aramean marauders; the strong Assyrian armed reaction which ensued during the late tenth–early ninth centuries could have forced the tribal groups to migrate down-stream (Lipinski 2000), where they occupied land from the Tigris riverbank to the nearby Euphrates near Sippar, and especially in the vast south-eastern plain between the Tigris and Elam. There are, however, other theoretical reconstructions of this scenario, e.g. linking the Aramean takeover of the lower Tigris reaches directly to the plundering actions of the eleventh century (Brinkman 1968: 281–283). And even long-term connections between these southern Arameans and the middle Euphrates area cannot be ruled out entirely, as in the case of the Ḫaṭallu tribe, which is mentioned in the annals of the philo-Babylonian rulers of Suḫu around 770/760 BC, and reappears, with some of its sub-groups, in the long list (Tadmor 1994: 158–161) summarizing the names of the Aramean tribes defeated by Tiglath-pileser III (745–722 BC).

In any case, for the mid-to-late eighth century, when the Arameans in the lower Tigris catchment area are most clearly attested as objects of intense Assyrian military pressure, we may recognize almost 40 distinct names of medium- to small-sized tribal entities, some of which were further fragmented under the leadership of different 'sheikhs' (*nasiku*). Since the late eighth century also witnessed an unexpected but short-lived occupation of the Assyrian-ruled territory of the Central Mesopotamia steppe by camel-raising tribes of 'Arabs' (*Arubu*), as described in anxious terms by Assyrian officials to king Sargon II in a series of letters (Fales 1989), it is not to be entirely ruled out – following older theories – that some intermingling of these Arabs with the southern Arameans could have taken place: certainly a few traits in the tribal and clanic onomastics of the Arameans do present a Southern Semitic flavour (Lipinski 2000: 422–424).

Now for the Chaldeans (*Kaldu*), not attested in the written sources before 878 BC. Their place names, and especially those of their vast territorial and political enclaves, were characterized by the noun *Bît*, 'household', followed by the linguistically West Semitic personal name of an eponymic ancestor figure, exactly as in the case of the contemporary Aramean states of the Jezirah and Transeuphratene. This feature allows us to postulate a connection of the Chaldeans with the northern and western Arameans in the general perspective of a shared heritage of ethnicity; while some slight hints in the texts might more specifically point to political affiliations of long standing with the Aramean tribes of the Middle Euphrates area. On the other hand, no direct similarities between the two large and important allogenous groupings interspersed in the Babylonian area may be traced. The Chaldeans, quite differently from their Aramean neighbours, seem to have embraced Babylonian ways from virtually all points of view quite soon after their arrival. Both Chaldean leaders and commoners mentioned in the texts bore fully Babylonian personal names, with devotional reference to the traditional Sumero–Akkadian pantheon of the region; and although they nominally retained a social and political structure based on kinship ties, they appear to have taken on a basically sedentary way of life in their southern Euphrates enclaves, with occupations in agriculture, stock raising, and intra-regional trade (Brinkman 1984; Cole 1996a). The natural development of this situation, that of entering into the arena of outright territorial-military appropriation and political supremacy in the local context, would not have been long in coming, under the specific stimulus provided by continuous Assyrian interference in Babylonian affairs.

THE NATURAL AND HUMAN 'LANDSCAPE'

The southern Mesopotamian alluvium represents an extremely complex territory from an ecological viewpoint; a reconstruction of ancient living conditions here must therefore take into account a variety of interconnected factors, with alternatively positive or negative implications as regards anthropic settlement and the ensuing opportunities for the development of plant and animal husbandry. As is well known, the overall ecological 'profile' of this area, per se geographically and climatically arid (between 100 and 200 mm of yearly rainfall), and yet potentially open to intensive and wealth-producing primary production like no other in Western Asia (due to the combined action of the Twin Rivers which formed it and traverse it with yearly floodings of silt- and salt-ridden discharge), has been modelled and modified over time by a series of natural and man-made dynamics involving the interaction of water and soil.

This is especially true for the course of the Euphrates, which may be proved to have significantly shifted during history, with the natural or man-aided formation of 'dead' meanders, swampy niches, new channels, and offshoots toward the more stable bed of the Tigris; and such shifts, in their turn, have influenced in the short or the long run the human settlement patterns in the adjacent catchment areas. This is demonstrated not only by the stratigraphically recorded history of occupation within the archaeological sites themselves, but also by the criss-cross pattern of the canals for irrigation, navigation and military-strategic purposes, which – as aerial and satellite photography has shown in the last decades of research – scars the southern Mesopotamian countryside in a factually inextricable network: thus revealing pluri-millennial mutations in the presence, size, and direction of these man-made water-courses, together with their accompanying earthworks (embankments, barrages, levees, weirs, sluices, etc.).

Other alterations in human occupation of the alluvium during history resulted from structural conditions, i.e. the quantity and localization of the silt and salt deposits borne by the watercourses to specific areas during the yearly flooding process. It is demonstrated that river levees, although more difficult to irrigate, retain through adequate drainage the best deposits and allow for a variety of crops, from cereals to small fruit trees, legumes, and the date palm. Beyond the levees, the river overflow may concentrate in low-lying basin areas, which are more at risk of inadequate drainage, waterlogging and consequent salinization; however, irrigation is easier here and, through crop-fallow alternation, these lands are adequate for crops of winter cereals, flax and vegetables. As is obvious, excessive silting in the river beds or un-controlled overflows in the surrounding territory have been constant risks, to which Mesopotamian man has been exposed and has variously responded – with vast protective earthworks and excavations or, alternatively, with the abandonment of the tracts which had become either too salinized or boggy or fully dry. In a nutshell, the Tigris and Euphrates prove to have literally created the overall profile of the surrounding countryside over time (Potts 1997).

In their final tracts, the Twin Rivers prove to have accumulated such a vast mass of sediments year after year, as to have altered the ancient coastline of Mesopotamia on the Arabian (or Persian) Gulf. There is as yet no consensus on the exact range of this phenomenon throughout history (cf. Lees and Falcon 1952; Larsen 1975), and in fact the presence of two fully oppositional forces is nowadays recognized, that of the progradation of the delta (due to constant river siltation) and that of tectonic subsidence (with an ensuing rise of sea-level and progressive erosion of the shoreline). It is, however, clear that the impact of both these natural dynamics (with the occasional aid of man-made modifications of the environment) is to be viewed behind the particular 'mosaic-like' appearance of southernmost Mesopotamia, with its unique interspersal of marshland, steppeland, orchards and fields, and where – proceeding southward toward the Gulf – enclosed sweet-water swamps progressively gave way to more open and salty lagoons (Adams and Nissen 1972).

All the above factors represent the essential environmental backdrop on which a reconstruction of the socio-economic and political-geographical 'landscape' of the alluvium during the first half of the first millennium BC should be projected: as scenario for the multifaceted interactions of the traditional 'Akkadian' population of the Babylonian region with the allogenous and recently intrusive groupings of the Arameans and Chaldeans. During the last half-century, the characteristics of anthropic presence in southern Mesopotamia have been the object of a number of regional or local surveys and analyses in an anthropological–archaeological perspective (Adams 1965, 1981; Adams and Nissen 1972; Gibson 1972; Cole and Gasche 1999). From the combined data, an overall long-term trend for the period between the twelfth and the late eighth centuries BC in the lower Euphrates region and in that of the Diyala (an affluent reaching the Tigris in the area of present-day Baghdad) may be presumed (Brinkman 1984: 8–11): it appears marked by a general decline in population levels and by a diminution of urbanism, with a corresponding increase of economic and social ruralization. Another feature that characterizes this phase is that of extensive abandonment of settlements in both surveyed areas, with limited compensation in the foundation of new sites; but it is difficult to state whether, and to what extent, this trend should be viewed in connection with the shifting away and drying up of specific watercourses – which, in its turn, according to some, represented the outcome of a perceptible climatic change towards aridity (Neumann and Parpola 1987) – or rather due to social and political disruptions for internal/external causes. In any case, a large part of the surveyed area (and especially the Nippur-Uruk hinterland) is known from the texts to have been inhabited by partially mobile Aramean groups, essentially devoted to pastoral activities; and the low level of urbanization of these peoples may be partly responsible for the scarce traces of settlements detectable through extensive regional survey techniques.

In general, while the named surveys have provided a reasonably valid and detailed picture of human occupation for the specifically observed areas, they cannot claim to be fully representative for the entire southern Mesopotamian environment, in its extraordinary ecological intricacy. And it is thus not surprising to note that other – even not particularly distant – areas in the alluvium seem to have enjoyed quite different living conditions from the ones described above, in relation to their closeness to the main – and active – watercourses or secondary channels thereof: e.g. Sennacherib's claim (cf. below) of widespread destructions of walled cities belonging to the Chaldeans points clearly to a solid economic prosperity in these tribal enclaves around 700 BC. For greater precision on this count, however, it would be necessary to have an in-depth reconstruction of the hydrological status of the main sectors of the alluvium at hand; unfortunately, such a reconstruction is at present still in progress, and is marked by particular complexities, arising from the need to reconcile the status of the watercourses as observable from archaeology with their many alternative denominations to be found in the ancient texts.

In any case, it has at present been convincingly shown that, in the early part of the first millennium, some changes had affected a previously attested bifurcation of the Euphrates north of Sippar, with a western branch (the Araḫtu/Purattu) proceeding southwards to Babylon, and the other (main branch) turning to the south-east in the direction of the Tigris; only the former still remained viable as a waterway, while the latter had dried out and required artificial rejuvenation in the seventh century as the 'King's Channel'. Also, the easternly Kutha and Kish branches of the Araḫtu/Purattu were now dry, and the two areas in the alluvium had to be fed by man-made canals (Cole and Gasche 2000). Finally, Pallukkatu – a name deriving from Abgal/Apkallatu, that of an inner branch of the Araḫtu/Purattu since the third millennium – was now the designation of a westernmost arm of the river, possibly also of artificial origin, which should have branched out from present-day Fallujah (as the correspondence in names through time might show), and thereupon flowing on the desert terrace to the west of Babylon and through Borsippa before rejoining the Araḫtu. In a nutshell, all the main branchings of the 'Euphrates' had shifted westward, and an abundance of water characterized the entire western sector of the alluvium from the eighth to the seventh centuries BC onward, with Borsippa finding itself progressively surrounded by marshes and crossed by a 'swollen' river, as a Neo-Assyrian letter states (Fales 1995: 209); whereas the eastern cities, such as Nippur, were plagued by a serious lack of water (Brinkman 1995). Thus, the fact that the territories of the three main Chaldean tribes (Bit-Dakkuri, Bit-Amukkani, Bit-Yakin) extended in a sort of arc, along the 'living' Euphrates branches from the Borsippa region to the Uruk countryside to the southernmost reaches of the Euphrates around Ur and into the marshlands to the east, does not seem irrelevant for an evaluation of the prosperity and ever-growing power of these kinship-based polities; whereas the more economically 'modest' profile of the Aramean tribes might be correlated to some extent with the progressive aridification which occurred in various territories of their chosen residence. Not surprisingly, for example, documents from Babylon and Borsippa of the eighth and seventh centuries indicate that the local 'Akkadian' population sometimes had to fight to remove Aramean squatters from their richly watered fields (Brinkman 1995: 24).

SOCIAL MODELS

As implied above, the Arameans of south-eastern Babylonia retained their basic West Semitic ethnolinguistic traditions (both in personal and group onomastics), and held fast to their kinship-based social structure with only minimal yield to the pressures of adjacent sedentary states. Thus, the Utu' or Itu' tribe, which occupied the west bank of the Tigris around present-day Samarra, would seem to have had mixed living quarters, perhaps in relation to seasonal transhumance, comprising 'encampments' (*maškanate*) made of tents as well as actual (agricultural) 'villages', when Tukulti-Ninurta II first attacked them in 885 BC.

The Arameans, in the main, also prove to have resisted the power of attraction of indigenous Babylonian culture with its prestigious network of beliefs and lore, ennobled by a great antiquity. This social and cultural 'separateness' is all the more noteworthy in that many of the Aramean tribes were in close contact with the Babylonian settlements for everyday matters: thus, for example, the vast group of the Puqudu was active for a time in the area surrounding the ages-old cultural and political centre of Nippur, to the extent of frequenting the city *en masse* to participate in a festival (*isinnu*) during the month of Ululu (Cole 1996b: 27, 9–13). Other textual attestations for this tribe point, on the other hand, to a variety of non-urban settings for its predominant economic activities; some of its main grazing grounds were in the general area of Lahiru, eastwards of the Tigris between the Diyala and Der; while a number of reports place the Puqudu in the marshy areas further south, along the Babylonian–Elamite border. It is in an even more southerly location, along the lower reaches of the Tigris and of its inner branches, that we find the Puqudu in league with the Chaldean chieftain Marduk-apla-iddina (Merodach-baladan) II of Bit-Yakin (see Figure 20.1) against the Assyrians during the years 712–709 BC. In later phases, this tribe will be again associated with anti-Assyrian activities, but now operating from the southernmost sector of the alluvium, from where it sometimes reached out westward to constitute a menace for the philo-Assyrian governors of Uruk and Ur.

A further characteristic of the Arameans lies in their permanent rejection of an ideology of unified leadership encompassing wider complexes than the individual kinship-based groups. On the contrary, in fact, as the case of the geographically ubiquitous Puqudu might show, it is the kinship-based group itself that seems to have split up in various inner ramifications, albeit retaining its common tribal

Figure 20.1   Kudurru of Marduk-apla-iddina II (Berlin) Vorderasiatisches Museum, SMB/Jürgen Liepe. The king, on the left, receives the greetings of a governor to whom he granted land.

denomination. The social (and, when necessary, military/political) leadership of each ramification or clanic unit went back to a specific *nasiku*, 'sheikh', as indicated by Assyrian and Babylonian texts from the reign of Sargon II onward. On the other hand, it has been noted that *nasikus* are attested in the written records in connection with a multiplicity of institutional or even purely geographical entities: i.e. not only tribes, but also lands, cities, even rivers (Brinkman 1968: 274–275). Leaving aside the possibility for specific inaccuracies on the part of the scribes, this very feature would seem to point to a high degree of ongoing segmentation within the tribal units themselves. Somewhat similarly, it may be observed that Tiglath-pileser III's list of 'unsubmissive Arameans' comprised, alongside many indisputably tribal groupings, some entities elsewhere known only as toponyms (Rapiqu, Hiranu, Rabilu, Radê, Karma', etc.); this aspect might not point so much to an 'Assyrian fabrication or simplification' (Brinkman 1968: 271) as to the reality of a process of social and territorial subdivision which was under way among the groups themselves.

In sum, the Arameans of the eighth–seventh centuries BC provide – even through the distorted lens of the Assyrian and Babylonian chroniclers – the overall picture of a kinship-based society in which various procedures of segmentation and renewed identification were in progress. Some tribal units had attained an ideal balance between their demographical dimensions, their specific territorial quarters, and their distinctive ethnicity: such as the Utu'/Itu', who would, after their subjugation by Tiglath-pileser III, be integrated into the ranks of the Assyrian administration as a corps of 'military police' characterized by their original ethnonym (cf. the Pope's 'Swiss guards', present in the Vatican for the last five centuries). Other units are captured by the contemporary texts as being still in the process of internal accretion, as in the case of the Rupu' who had incorporated the smaller group of Q/Gamu according to a letter from Nippur (Cole 1996b: 83, 5–7). Finally, the vaster and geographically more dispersed tribal complexes, such as the Puqudu and the Gambulu, while still retaining their distinctive self-identification, had developed a number of inner clanic subdivisions with reference to different 'sheikhs', who united their military and political efforts or took individual courses of action, according to the circumstances. In this case, the possibility that (periodical or random) comprehensive 'conventions' could have dictated the tribal policies to be undertaken, is realistic, but has not hitherto surfaced as a specific occurrence in the textual record.

As hinted above, the Chaldeans' settlement patterns in Babylonian territory differed greatly from that of the neighbouring (and partially interspersed) Arameans; and the same may be said for their general socio-economic profile. Despite the preservation of their tribal ethnonyms, we may observe the Chaldeans in the Assyrian record (texts and palace reliefs) tending permanently to large tracts of land within their well-watered enclaves, where they practised agriculture (including date-palm cultivation) and breeding of horses and cattle. The structures for communal living within these enclaves comprised not only rural villages and small townships, but also a fair percentage of walled cities. Thus, Sennacherib, describing his first campaign into

Figure 20.2   Assyrian palace relief showing Chaldean captives in a date palm grove (courtesy of the Trustees of the British Museum).

Babylonia (703 BC), boasts of having besieged and conquered 33 walled cities and 250 townships of Bit-Dakkuri; 8 walled cities and 120 townships of Bit-Ša'alli; 39 walled cities and 350 townships of Bit-Amukkani; 8 walled cities and 100 townships of Bit-Yakin – a grand total of 88 major urban sites with defensive structures and 820 smaller settlements of mainly rural character in their environs (Luckenbill 1924: 54–56, 36–50; Frahm 1997: 9). That, all rhetoric aside, some of these Chaldean fortified cities represented a challenge for even the best Assyrian armies, with all their sophisticated siege-technologies, may be demonstrated by a letter to Tiglath-pileser III, in which the writer – a high-ranking Assyrian military officer – describes at some length to a slightly incredulous ruler how he had to fight tooth and nail to overcome the resistance opposed by the besieged population of Šapi'a, where the Chaldean rebel (Nabû)-mukin-zeri and his son had taken refuge (Saggs 2001: 45–46; Fales 2005).

But the strategic position of the main Chaldean enclaves along the westernmost and southern axes of the alluvium also had important implications for commerce. The lists of precious goods offered already in the ninth century, and then again under Tiglath-pileser III, by the Chaldean chiefs as tribute to the Assyrians, which included elephant hides and tusks, ebony and sissoo-wood, prove that the Chaldean tribes had gained full control of the trade routes cutting through the Babylonian region (Brinkman 1968: 198–199; Frame 1992: 37), and were thus on the receiving end of a vast commercial network which reached Mesopotamia from the Levant, Northern Arabia and Egypt by land, and from the Gulf area and points east by sea. The random but increasing presence of Arab kinship-based groups in the southernmost alluvium, a permanent relationship of cooperation between the Chaldean tribes and the adjacent Elamite state, and evidence for direct contacts with the Levant – all these pieces of information point to the progressive constitution of a 'southern Mesopotamian axis' of trade, based on seamanship and the recently introduced large-scale exploitation of the camel as pack-animal, which tended to antagonize, and eventually would replace, the northern Mesopotamian routes dominated by the Assyrian empire.

The social structure of the Chaldeans was rigidly centred upon the tribal unit (*Bit*+ name of the eponymic ancestor) of which all subjects were jointly 'members' (*mār*, literally, 'son' of the eponymic ancestor); but it would be more precise to state that such tribal units, in fact, represented tribal confederations, which must have undergone – similarly to the Aramean tribal 'households' of the northern Jezirah and Inner Syria – a relatively long process of social coalescence, although no trace of the latter is preserved in the written record. The leader of each tribal confederation was indicated in the Assyrian texts as *ra'su*, 'chieftain'. The fact that all such chieftains mutually recognized their status within a wider territorial-political complex, which ideally united the different Chaldean confederations, is made clear by a letter from Nimrud/ Kalkhu from the time of Tiglath-pileser III (Saggs 2001: 25–26, 5'–6'), in which the young Merodach-baladan is described as 'one of the chieftains of the land of Chaldea' (*ina libbi re'asāni ša māt Kaldi*).

POLITICAL REFLEXES

This status of the Chaldean leaders as 'chieftains' of vast kinship-tied confederations, which were moreover rooted in specific territorial enclaves and perceived as parts of a vast ethnically based political structure, was to become one of the 'prime movers' in the tormented situation of Babylonian politics during the ninth and eighth centuries BC, from an ideological and practical point of view. The Chaldeans, although nominally subjects of the kings of Babylonia, who had ruled over the entire alluvium for a thousand years, seem to have enjoyed *de facto* independence virtually since the time of their formation and first settlement (Brinkman 1968: 261); and their status was considered that of tribal troops allied (like the Arameans) to Babylonia by the Assyrian scribes describing the defeat of the Babylonian ruler Marduk-balassu-iqbi at the hands of Shamshi-Adad V in 814 BC. (Grayson 1996: 188; IV 37–45). But during the period of Assyrian political weakness, which began with the reign of Adad-nirari III (810–783 BC), the Chaldeans began their rise to power, seizing the dynastically unstable throne of Babylon; first with Marduk-apla-uṣur, at an uncertain date, then with Eriba-Marduk, around 769, possibly followed by others. The extensive campaigns of Tiglath-pileser III against both Arameans and Chaldeans did not prevent (Nabû)-mukīn-zēri of Bit-Amukkani from seizing the throne and staging a vast anti-Assyrian revolt, which however ended in defeat, also due to the lack of a united military-political front among the Chaldeans themselves.

With the rise of Merodach-baladan of Bit-Yakin, who seized the Babylonian throne in 722 after two successive Assyrian kings had split their rulership between the northern and southern parts of Mesopotamia, an entire new chapter opened. This brilliant Chaldean chieftain managed to join all of his peers to the cause of a liberation of the alluvium from Assyrian intrusion, and secured the friendship of the Elamites by utilizing his vast wealth; claiming royal descent from Eriba-Marduk, he portrayed himself as the 'saviour' of his country, with specific reference to repair works in the cult places of the main cities of the alluvium (Brinkman 1964).

While this is not the place to go into an extensive analysis of Chaldean political history, suffice it to say that Merodach-baladan, with his ten-year rule of Babylon, opened decidedly the way to the notion that the overall political destiny of the southern alluvium as a region independent from Assyrian interference and rule was henceforth to be tied to the Chaldeans' political choices, military power, and capacity for inner and external alliances. While, on many an occasion during the next century, the older 'Akkadian' populations of the main Babylonian cities wavered heavily in their allegiances, and often gave a show of full subjection to their Assyrian overlords, the Chaldeans retained a staunch 'resistance-type' approach towards the objective of territorial and economic self-government, despite numerous military setbacks, vast destructions of land and staples, and extensive deportations at the hands of the Assyrians. Their capacity to muster armies and mobilize the economic resources within their tribes proved to be a major asset during the various phases of revolt, and their adroit use of the natural environment created many a difficulty for the Assyrians in their repeated punitive campaigns (Frame 1992: 43).

The Arameans – once again – present a less clear-cut profile to the historian. With the onslaughts of Tiglath-pileser III and Sargon II against the Aramean tribes in the lower Tigris area, and the ensuing mass deportations to other areas of the empire, many of the smaller gentilic formations must have ceased to exist as such (cf. above for the Utu'/Itu'), or possibly took on sedentary habits, thus blending silently into the general population in or around the major cities. Only the major tribes of the Gambulu and the Puqudu – both placed by now in specific enclaves of the marshy region between south-eastern Babylonia and Elam – may be still clearly identified in the written sources of the seventh century BC, engaged at times in alliances with the Chaldeans or the Elamites, at other times paying political homage to the Assyrians. Certainly their most memorable heritage is represented by their native West Semitic language, which, due to the 'confusion of tongues' which must have characterized the constant forced removal of non-Akkadian-speaking peoples from one corner of the empire to the other, had become – in the southern alluvium as well as in the major cities and agricultural regions of Northern Mesopotamia – the most viable instrument for interpersonal, business, and to some extent institutional, relationships; and would remain as such even long after the Assyrians and, in their wake, the Chaldeans no longer ruled over the land of the Twin Rivers.

BIBLIOGRAPHY

Adams, R. McC., 1965 *Land Behind Baghdad*, Chicago, IL and London.

—— 1981 *Heartland of Cities*, Chicago, IL and London.

—— and Nissen, H.-J., 1972 *The Uruk Countryside*, Chicago, IL and London.

Brinkman, J.A., 1964 *Merodach-baladan II*. In: *Studies presented to A. Leo Oppenheim*, Chicago, IL: 6–53.

—— 1968 *A Political History of Post-Kassite Babylonia*, 1158–722 BC, Rome.

—— 1984 *Prelude to Empire. Babylonian Society and Politics, 747–626 BC*, Philadelphia.

—— 1995 *Reflections on the Geography of Babylonia*. In: M. Liverani (Ed.), *Neo-Assyrian Geography*, Rome: 19–29.

Cole, S.W., 1996a *Nippur in Late Assyrian Times, c.755–612 BC*, Helsinki.

—— 1996b *The Early Neo-Babylonian Governor's Archive from Nippur*, Chicago, IL and London.

—— and Gasche, H., 1999 *Levees, Floods, and the River Network of Northern Babylonia: 2000–1500 and 1000–500 BC – A preliminary report*. In: J. Renger (Ed.), *Babylon: Focus mesopotamischer Geschichte*, Berlin: 87–110.

Fales, F.M., 1989 *Pastorizia e politica: nuovi dati sugli Arabi nelle fonti di età neo-assira*. In: A. Avanzini (Ed.), *Problemi di onomastica semitica meridionale*, Pisa: 119–134.

—— 1995 *Rivers in Neo-Assyrian Geography*. In: M. Liverani (Ed.), *Neo-Assyrian Geography*, Rome: 203–215.

—— 1999–2001 *Assyrian Royal Inscriptions: Newer Horizons*, State Archives of Assyria Bulletin 13: 115–144.

—— 2001 *L'impero assiro. Storia e amministrazione (IX-VII sec. a.C.)*, Roma-Bari.

—— 2005 *Tiglat-Pileser III tra annalistica reale ed epistolografia quotidiana*. In: F. Pecchioli Daddi and M. C. Guidotti (Eds), *Narrare gli Eventi*, Rome: 163–191.

Frahm, E., 1997 *Einleitung in die Sanherib-Inschriften*, Wien.

Frame, G., 1992 *Babylonia 689–627 BC: A Political History*, Leiden.

Gibson, McG., 1972 *The City and Area of Kish*, Coconut Grove.

Grayson, A.K., 1996 *Assyrian Rulers of the Early First Millennium BC, II (858–745 BC)*, Toronto.

Larsen, C.E., 1975 'The Mesopotamian Delta Region: A Reconsideration of Lees and Falcon', *Journal of the American Oriental Society* 95: 43–57.

Lees, G.M. and Falcon, N.L., 1952 'The Geographical History of the Mesopotamian Plain', *Geographical Journal* 118: 24–39.

Lipinski, E., 2000 *The Aramaeans. Their Ancient History, Culture, Religion*, Leuven.

Luckenbill, D.D., 1924 *The Annals of Sennacherib*, Chicago.

Neumann, J. and Parpola, S., 1987 'Climatic Change and the Eleventh-Tenth Century Eclipse of Assyria and Babylonia', *Journal of Near Eastern Studies* 46: 161–182.

Potts, D., 1997 *Mesopotamian Civilization: The Material Foundations*, London.

Saggs, H.W.F., 2001 *The Nimrud Letters, 1952*, London.

Tadmor, H., 1994 *The Inscriptions of Tiglath-pileser III, King of Assyria*, Jerusalem.

CHAPTER TWENTY-ONE

WOMEN AND GENDER
IN BABYLONIA

———.◆.———

Laura D. Steele

In the Old Babylonian version of the Epic of Gilgamesh, Siduri the barmaid encourages the hero to return to his household and to enjoy the good things in life:

> You, Gilgamesh, let your stomach be full;
> Day and night enjoy yourself.
> Each day, sustain happiness;
> Day and night dance and play.
> Let your clothes be immaculate;
> Let your head be washed, may you bathe in water.
> Consider the child who clutches your hand;
> Let your wife enjoy herself in your lap.
>
> (Gilg. Me. iii, 6–14; Tigay 1982: 168; Dalley 1998: 150)

Thus are wives introduced as the domestic pleasure *par excellence*. The next line of the text is broken, but it likely reads "For this is the work [of women]" (Tigay 1982: 168 n. 17). If so, the passage explicitly defines the ideal life of a woman as well as that of a man, and the wife (*marhitum*) becomes the crux of the daily life extolled by Siduri (Abusch 1993: 4). The broken line 14 refers most immediately to the sexual task of procreation adduced by lines 12–13 (Assante 1998: n. 15), but the "work of women" is implied throughout the passage: *someone* must launder clothes, prepare food, heat water, and bear children so that Gilgamesh might live up to the male ideal (Harris 1990). Ultimately, the androcentric language of this passage spares Gilgamesh from the labors associated with the "good life."[1]

Other such glimpses of what Babylonians might have considered to be the ideal domestic life are rare. Lines 64–65 of a Late Babylonian hymn to Gula describe the lifecycle of a typical free woman: "I am daughter, I am bride, I am spouse, I, indeed, manage the household" (Lambert 1967; translation in Foster 1993: 496; cited in Stol 1995a). Lest we think of Gula as a quotidian household goddess, she goes on to claim prowess as a physician (ll. 79–87, 146, 177–187), as a warrior (l. 101), and as a diviner (ll. 182–184). Omen apodoses of all periods also give a sense of some women's experiences, especially in cases – such as childbirth and adultery – that appear frequently because of their significance to a male audience (Koch-Westenholz 2002; Guinan 1997). Babylonian mythological and wisdom texts do not provide much information regarding the actual lives of (mortal) women, whereas we may glean a number of details regarding the activities and perspectives of men, to whom the literature is primarily directed.[2]

For a social history of women and gender, we must therefore rely principally upon the law codes, individual legal documents, and personal letters, which can be most revealing (Oppenheim 1967: 64). Taken together, the documentary sources allow us to elaborate the characteristics of various gendered categories (Roth 1998: 174; Asher-Greve 2002b: 16). The best-documented category comprises free women whose lives conformed more or less to the ideals expressed above and whose lives and choices customarily revolved around and were circumscribed by male relatives – father, husband, brother, or son – before, during, and after their marriages. Most free women did, however, retain a legal and social status allowing them to do business, to own property, and to participate in court proceedings. In addition to this category, we may distinguish other gendered groups that deviated, to varying degrees, from the norm represented by free, adult, married, domestic women. Indeed, the study of "minority" groups is essential to an understanding of the role of women and of gender in Babylonian society, for the legal and literary texts adduce each group selectively in order to define the ideal. I will focus on the Old and Neo-Babylonian periods, from which most of our documentation comes; and I will devote more attention to slave women than is usually accorded them by general surveys of women in Mesopotamia.

FREE, MARRIED OR MARRIAGEABLE WOMEN IN UPPER-MIDDLE-CLASS HOUSEHOLDS

We know very little about the early lives of Babylonian women, regardless of class, in part because the high rate of infant mortality precluded the legal and economic documentation of most girls until they had reached marriageable age.[3] As with members of the "minority" groups we shall consider below, the fate of an individual girl in Mesopotamia would have been documented only if it had attracted the attention of a third party who required a contract or a court decision, an unlikely circumstance given the institution of male inheritance. Rare glimpses of Babylonian girlhood are provided, however, by a few abstract texts: a late incantation against phantoms (Landsberger 1968: 45ff., cited in Cooper 2002: 92), for example, describes the unfortunate soul of a girl who died before marriage: she is "the girl who was never impregnated like a woman, the girl who never lost her virginity like a woman" (SBTU II 6, pp. 38–49); "the girl who made her cheek ugly through unhappiness, who did not enjoy herself with (other) girls, who never appeared at her city's festival" (SBTU II 7, pp. 4–7; trans. Foster 1991: 871).[4] Texts such as this one suggest that Mesopotamians did not value premarital virginity inherently if a girl were unable to experience the closure provided by wife- and motherhood (Leick 1994: 228). Virginity was, rather, a social and financial asset that attracted appropriate husbands and that promoted patriarchal control over the family (Cooper 2002: 101–105). It is interesting to note that the corresponding male phantom-demon, Etel-lilî, is not explicitly described as a virgin, though he is unmarried (Cooper 2002: 103); thus, in accordance with Mesopotamian sexual convention more generally, young men appear to have been less scrutinized than young women in this respect.

Marriages between free men and women were, in cases involving the propertied class or manumitted slaves, enforced by legal contracts made between the groom (and his family) and those who were responsible for the bride, usually her male relatives (Roth 1989: 26). The mother of the bride, however, could exercise considerable control over her daughters' marriages (Westenholz 1990: 517–518), particularly in fatherless households (Roth 1988b: 132). Brides clearly are objects rather than agents of most transactions, though independent women, e.g. divorcées and widows, could make contracts on their own behalf (Westbrook 1988: 61–62; Roth 1989: 20).[5] There has been a great deal of debate regarding the nature of the marriage contract and of the *terhatum* (often translated as "bride-price"): the primary legal issue in marriage certainly was one of transfer of responsibility for, and control of, the bride, but it has been argued that marriage was formulated quite differently from the sale of property (Westbrook 1988: 58–60; but see Leemans 1991: 140). The following outline of the legal and social framework of marriage is based largely upon the general legal codes (Roth 1997) and upon records of individual contracts and court cases.

In the Old Babylonian period, the act of marriage – in the usual case of a young woman leaving her parents' house for the first time – appears to have involved several stages: a groom (or, if he were still a minor, his parents) first would make an oral, promissory contract with the bride's representative(s) and then would offer a *terhatum* payment that would confirm his intent and accord him certain rights (Westbrook 1988: 59–60). At this point, the couple were protected to a certain extent in an institution that scholars term "inchoate marriage," in which the inchoate wife was responsible for her sexual behavior. A prospective groom accuses his inchoate wife of infidelity in a legal deposition from the time of Hammurabi (FLP 1340), demanding both that his *terhatum* payment be returned and that the authorities "tie her up and throw her into the river!" (Owen and Westbrook 1992). This case may be associated with one of the laws of Hammurabi (hereafter LH) §143, which stipulates that an unfaithful (inchoate?) wife who refuses her husband should be punished by drowning (see Malul 1991: 282 *contra* Westbrook 1988: 45–47). Because the bride-to-be sometimes moved into her father-in-law's house before completion of the marriage, however, the groom's father might have sexual access to her in some cases before the consummation of the marriage (Westbrook 1988: 36–39).[6]

Eventually, an Old Babylonian inchoate marriage would be finalized when the groom "took" the bride (*ahazum*). There is much debate regarding the mechanism(s) used to "seal the deal" of marriage; the sources suggest some combination of official vows (*verba solemnia*), the bride's habitation in the groom's home (*in domum deductio*), and sexual consummation (*copula carnalis*) (Westbrook 1988: 48–53).[7] The latter is occasionally described as "opening the pin of virginity" (Malul 1991–1992; see also Cooper 2002). In any event, upon the completion of the marriage, the bride's familial dowry (*nudunnûm, šeriktum* in LH) was transferred to her new husband, who would safeguard it for his wife and future children, and who might add to it some gifts of his own (Westbrook 1991). In the Neo-Babylonian period, private documents dealing with marriage focus almost exclusively on the substance of the dowry and therefore can be said to be "dowry agreements" rather than marriage agreements in the Old

Babylonian tradition (Roth 1989: 26–28).[8] In all periods, the bride appears to have had full control over some property, including parts of the dowry and other gifts from her family (including, in some cases, the *terhatum* itself; Malul 1991: 280) and/or husband; in the Old Babylonian period, the bride's discretionary funds might be bound "in her hem" (Westbrook 1991, 1988), while in the Neo-Babylonian period, they were said to be kept in her "basket" (Roth 1989–1990, cited in Stol 1995b).

The not infrequent dissolution of marriages is illuminated by divorce and adultery clauses of marriage agreements, as well as by contracts and legal cases involving extramarital affairs and polygamy. Old Babylonian divorce was usually effected rather simply, either when one party voiced the *verba solemnia* "you are not my husband/wife" or when a husband formally "cut his wife's hem" (Westbrook 1988: 69ff.). Throughout Mesopotamian history, however, "clauses in the private contracts tried to curb [the wife's right to divorce] by imposing formidable penalties, thus rendering it virtually impossible . . . [whereas] no such penalties were imposed upon the husband's right to divorce" (Malul 1991: 282).[9] Significantly, a number of Neo-Babylonian marriage contracts foresee the explicit possibility that a wife might be caught with another man, but only one anticipates that a wife might initiate divorce (Roth 1989: 14–15); the Old Babylonian agreements, on the other hand, often envisage a wife's repudiation of her husband, while remaining silent on the issue of adultery in particular (cf. Westbrook 1988: 83). Thus, we may consider whether the general legal category of repudiation subsumes uxorial adultery in the Old Babylonian sources – hence, perhaps, the severity of the consequences for the former – whereas the Neo-Babylonian sources generally consider that a woman could cause the dissolution of her marriage only by reason of her infidelity, because women rarely had the legal right to divorce for any other reason.[10]

The evidence suggests that most husbands who sought new wives had been frustrated in their efforts to secure an heir, either because their first wives did not bear sons at all, or because their wives' potentially adulterous behavior cast doubt on the paternity of their children. In the first instance, childless wives of the Old Babylonian period could be "released" and compensated by their husbands (Westbrook 1988: 71–75), leaving both parties free to remarry. By the Neo-Babylonian period, many divorce clauses anticipate the possibility that the husband might take another wife; in these cases, the first marriage either ended in divorce with compensation or continued concurrently with the second (Roth 1989: 13–14). A comparable legal (double) standard applied to cases of adultery. Men could take on secondary wives and/or concubines in addition to their primary wives, and could solicit intercourse from men or women, prostitutes or non-professionals, outside the marriage (cf. Bottéro 1992: 186). Women, on the other hand, faced harsh penalties for adultery, including death by drowning in Old Babylonia (Westbrook 1991) or "by the iron dagger" in Late Babylonia (Roth 1988a, 1989: 15). Even so, the accusation of adultery must have been difficult to prove unless a wife was caught *in flagrante delicto* (cf. Westbrook 1988: 75–76); according to an oral proverb cited in a Neo-Assyrian letter, "in court the word of a sinful woman prevails over her husband's" (ABL 403; Lambert 1960: 281).[11] Indeed, legal and other texts demonstrate that women persistently engaged in extramarital sex despite the prohibitions against it.[12]

Female sexuality, both within and outside marital relationships, comes to the fore in a number of Babylonian sources. Middle- and Neo-Babylonian women who are not explicitly identified as wives evidently recited sexual potency incantations in order to obtain sexual pleasure from male partners, and these texts often express jealousy of other women (Biggs 1967, 2002); thus "it is clear that [the incantations'] use was not limited to married couples" (Bottéro 1992: 190). Likewise, women appear as the initiators in a variety of sexual situations envisioned by tablets 103 and 104 of the first-millennium *šumma alu* divinatory series (CT 39). One omen predicts that "if a man is with a woman (and) while facing him she repeatedly stares at his penis, whatever he finds will not be secure in his house" (Guinan 1997: 5; Guinan 2002: 188), while another more succinctly warns that "if a man, a woman mounts him, he will lose his vigor." Ultimately, however, both the omens and incantations focus on *male* sexuality and ability (cf. Biggs 2002: 72): as A. Guinan (2002: 199) observes,

> the omens oppose male public persona and male/female eroticism in such a way that the denial of one is the assertion of the other. When a woman directs sexual action toward a man, it is inauspicious. . . . Issues of desire and behavior become questions of masculine agency.

The value of the omen texts for social history is limited as well by their preoccupation with "sexual acts that . . . stand out from the non-signifying background of everyday life [insofar as] they deviate in some way from the norm" (Guinan 2002: 196).[13] An equally complicated view of female sexuality is provided both by literary texts, such as the "steamy" Inanna-Dumuzi texts of the Old Babylonian period (Assante 2002: 39) and the famous epics compiled in the first millennium (cf. Leick 1994), and by the visual arts (cf. Bahrani 2001). Among the most intriguing examples of the latter are a number of Old Babylonian terracotta plaques representing couples lying in bed or copulating while standing; Assante (2002) has interpreted these as representing Inanna and Dumuzi, though she stresses as well their magico-apotropaic significance in a domestic setting.

Not surprisingly, most middle-class married women in Babylonia were occupied with the bearing and raising of children, with the organization of the household, with the maintenance of the domestic religious practices (van der Toorn 1994), and with some organization of family business and production of goods for use or sale outside the home.[14] Regarding the latter, we have some evidence from contracts and letters, especially in the Neo-Babylonian period, that women were at least well acquainted with their family's financial business (cf. Beaulieu 1993). The role of women in the production and trade of textiles is most clearly demonstrated, however, by a number of Old Assyrian letters discovered at the entrepôt (*karum*) of Kanish in present-day Turkey. In regular correspondence with their distant husbands, wives in Ashur discussed the quantity and/or quality of textiles that apparently were to be produced by the women of their households – aided, perhaps, by paid employees in some cases – and delivered to Kanish (Larsen 1976; Dercksen 1996). During their husbands' absences, Old Assyrian wives took on the responsibility of running the household and of managing many of the family affairs; thus, "if financial disaster struck – as it did occasionally as a result of bad deals or unwise investments – it seems that women bore the brunt of the consequences" (Larsen 2001: 285). It appears as well that women of the Old Babylonian and later periods were no longer able to take up certain professions practiced by at least some women in earlier times; indeed,

Figure 21.1   Old Babylonian terracotta relief of couple making love, while the woman is drinking beer through a long straw (Musée du Louvre).

"not a single woman appears among the thousands of scribes, scholars, diviners, [and] astronomers . . . mentioned by name in Neo- and Late Babylonian documents" (Beaulieu 1993: 13; cited in Assante 1998).

A woman named Esirtum appears both as financial associate and as expectant mother in a representative Neo-Babylonian letter (CT 22, 40) from her brother, who gets right down to business after congratulating her: "Why do I never hear any news from all of you? My heart rejoiced about your being pregnant. The things I heard are bad indeed. Give me that mina of silver, but . . . get refined silver!"[15] Pregnancy was of course fraught with the risks common to non-industrial societies, and women used amulets, plants, and incantations to ward off sorcery, demons, and other causes of miscarriage and of difficulty in labor (Stol 2000; Wiggermann 2000). A woman in labor (*harištu*) customarily delivered on the "brick of birth," assisted by a midwife and perhaps by others,[16] and in the presence of a mother goddess. The fact that all these precautions did not always guarantee a safe delivery is lamented in a famous dialogue:

> On the day I bore fruit, how happy I was, . . . [but] on the day I gave birth, my eyes became cloudy. . . . [In] those days I was with my husband, I was living with him who was my lover, When death crept stealthily into my bedroom.
>
> (translation in Stol 2000: 140–141)

When the outcome was successful, infants would breast-feed for roughly three years; in the Old Babylonian period in particular, upper-class women frequently relied on slave women or employed wet-nurses to nurture their children (Gruber 1989). See generally M. Stol's comprehensive monograph (2000) for very detailed discussions of pregnancy, birth, infancy, contraception, and infertility.

This portrait of married life is most relevant for women who were in the free-citizen (*awīlu*) class described, for example, in the LH. Somewhat different rights and responsibilities likely applied to women of the free commoner (*muškenu*) class in the Old Babylonian period; and the living conditions of queens and of the elite are of course to be distinguished from those of the working classes. Letters from Mari that are contemporary with the Old Babylonian reign of Hammurabi demonstrate that Shiptu, wife of Zimri-Lim, played a key role in public policy and diplomacy, in addition to her duties as supervisor of the palace household and workshops (cf. Harris 1989: 146–147). We lack comparable documentation from the Neo-Babylonian period: in a "fictional autobiography" commissioned by Nabonidus for the funeral monument of his mother, Adad-Guppi, the king's rise to power is attributed to her influence (Longman 1991); but we have no other record of her status in the royal household (Beaulieu 1993: 9). As I noted above, elite women in the Neo-Babylonian period often owned property and conducted business in their own legal right, even though it appears that they were unable to act as full witnesses to contracts, and there is no evidence of literacy among women (Greenfield 1987; Beaulieu 1993).

OTHER UNMARRIED FREE WOMEN: "PROSTITUTES," WIDOWS, AND PRIESTESSES

Several texts suggest that the antithesis of traditional marriage for a free woman was *harimūtu*, traditionally understood to mean "prostitution." This understanding recently has been called into question by J. Assante (1998), who argues at length and with a great deal of evidence that the term refers instead to a social class comprised of "single" women who had left their ancestral household, not all of whom were paid prostitutes. In none of the extant texts is a *harimtu* demonstrably subject to the authority of any head of household, e.g. father, husband, brother, husband's family, or *almattu*-widow, and in only two literary texts is a *harimtu* explicitly identified as a sex professional. Indeed, it is not surprising that *harimtu* status might have been a social rather than a professional designation, because only a few female professions are recorded from the Old Babylonian period onward (cf. Assante 1998: 63). The next scholarly challenge will be to determine what exactly *harimātu* did for a living, if not sex work.[17] Certainly, *harimātu* are often mentioned together with practitioners of witchcraft and with other marginal members of society, and they were considered to be poorly trained for

Figure 21.2 Old Babylonian terracotta bust of a woman
(courtesy of the Trustees of the British Museum).

domestic life and wifehood (cf. Bottéro 1992: 194–197). Regarding sorceresses, we know relatively little; Old Babylonian sources associate the performance of black magic almost exclusively with women, and though male sorcerers appear in later periods, the sorceress remained a popular motif in ritual texts (Sefati and Klein 2002). I will note simply that none of the many recent studies on the subject of cultic prostitution has found clear evidence that it existed in Mesopotamia (cf. Assante 1998), and scholars have instead focused on critiquing the passage in Herodotus that describes routine prostitution in Babylonian temples (cf. Budin 2003: 153).

Widows, like *harimātu* and other "women in transition" who were at least temporarily without a clear household affiliation, appear frequently in the legal texts, suggesting "that the status of each was carefully negotiated" (Assante 1998: 34). The studies by M. Roth (1988b, 1991–1993) of widows in the Neo-Babylonian period suggest that widowhood was fairly common and that most widows were dependent upon the goodwill of their husband's family and heirs. If their husbands did not "make explicit provisions allowing their wives the lifetime right of habitation" (Roth 1991–1993: 26) in the conjugal home, they might be required to leave; and in a number of cases, property disputes between the widow and the rest of the family had to be adjudicated. In an Old Babylonian letter from Tell Asmar (AS 22, 12, in Whiting 1987), a woman named Battum, who is likely a widow, admonishes her son-in-law: "My slaves are not your slaves. . . . If you are my son-in-law and I am your mother, I should be in your thoughts. Do not make me unhappy."[18] Widows appear to have been differentiated by class: the often powerful *almattu* was head of her own household; older widows might have continued living with their adult children; young widows might have been remarried by their paternal agents or been given *harimtu* status; and destitute women might devote themselves to a temple, despite harsh living conditions, or enter a *bīt mār banî*. The latter institution is described only obliquely but appears to have been a Neo-Babylonian recourse for "women in transition" more generally to seek physical or social protection within the household of a free citizen such as a temple official (Roth 1987).

There were several classes of priestesses in the Old Babylonian period, some (but not all) of whom were to remain celibate and/or unmarried, and some of whom lived in a common, cloister-like community (Harris 1989: 150ff.) The best-known of these priestesses were the *nadītu*, whose records have been found in great quantities at the *gagû* (cloister) in Sippar (Harris 1975), and – in fewer numbers – in private neighborhoods of Nippur as well (Stone 1982). Several laws of Hammurabi pertain to these women, who could marry so long as they remained childless; if they did marry, they could either adopt children or provide their husbands with slave concubines who could bear children (LH §146). *Nadītu*-priestesses often owned substantial property, including their own individual houses within the cloister and taverns (Roth 1999) and engaged in the business of money-lending. Many of them came from elite households, and the ownership of their property returned to their father's heirs (typically their brothers) after their deaths. For this reason, it has been argued that elite families welcomed the opportunity to devote a daughter to the cloister in order to limit the dispersal of the family estate, and *nadītu*-women appear have been able to broker deals outside the family circle more easily than could the men of their paternal household (see discussion in Harris 1989); but it is clear as well that to become a *nadītu* was an honor and an opportunity for the exercise of piety. See Assante (1998) for a re-assessment of some of the other classes of religious women who were thought to have engaged in cultic prostitution; instead, they seem to have had a variety of roles, from wet-nurse (*qadištu*) to (theoretically) celibate high-priestess (*entu*).

SLAVE WOMEN IN DOMESTIC HOUSEHOLDS

A Middle Babylonian contract from Nippur (BE 14 40) nicely outlines the three options available to young free women from poor households (cf. Assante 1997: 16): a girl's biological father gives her up for adoption under the conditions that she may marry or enter into *harimūtu*, but she may not be sold into slavery. By the Neo-Babylonian period, "within the class of free citizens there was enormous variation in economic circumstances, from the land-owning entrepreneurial families . . . to the tenant farmers and hired labourers" (Baker 2001: 20); and the poorest women seemed to be quite aware of the possibility of enslavement, either as a punishment for transgressions or as a means of income for their families. It evidently was not uncommon for even persons of moderate means to own three to five slaves in the NB period (Dandamaev 1984: 216), whereas the wealthy Egibi family owned over 100 slaves, most of whom presumably were born in the household (Baker 2001). Thus slaves comprised a significant sector of Neo-Babylonian society, though it was not nearly as large as the population of private slaves in the Roman Empire. I will focus on slave women in private households; much more could be said about institutionally owned slave women, who likely had very different rights, responsibilities, and experiences than their domestic counterparts (cf. Kuhrt 1989).

A few Babylonian texts reveal the usual duties of slave women in domestic households, and, for the most part, their duties parallel those of free wives: in a Sumerian love song preserved in Old Babylonian copies dating to 2000–1600 BCE, (Ni2377 = DI C$_1$; translation in Sefati 1998), Dumuzi assures his new wife Inanna that she need not perform household duties – i.e., weaving cloth, spinning flax, carding wool, and baking bread – as if she were a slave woman. The association of slave women with household textile production appears in two Old Babylonian letters as well: in the first (AbB VAS 2, 12, p. 14), the author instructs his associate to purchase a slave woman "if [she] is house-born and knows how to weave" (cf. Diakonoff 1974: n. 63); and the author of the second (VAS 188, 6) mentions an apparently anomalous "slave girl who is not a weaver" (cf. CAD, A/II, 81). Though Babylonian law generally treated slaves as though they were not legal persons (Finkelstein 1966: 359; Westbrook 1998), both male and female slaves were able to testify in courts of law and often served as witnesses of their owners' business transactions in the Neo-Babylonian period (Dandamaev 1984: 308ff.), even though free women could not do so (see above). Indeed, a Neo-Babylonian slave woman ran a tavern on behalf of the Egibi family, which supplied her with the necessary materials (Baker 2001: 23).

Mesopotamian sources of all periods embrace the stereotype of rivalry between free and slave women, and they seem to single out female slaves as more inattentive than their mistresses, who themselves are not portrayed as overly vindictive or "hysterical." Mesopotamian literary texts might have insisted upon this distinction precisely because slave women who bore their master's children threatened the cultural and economic status of free women in several tangible ways. The legal distinction between wives and slave women was not entirely clear in the first place: according to LH §141, for example, if a wife decides to leave her husband and "appropriates goods, squanders her household possessions, or disparages her husband" (translation in Roth 1997: 108) a man may marry another woman and keep his first wife "like a slave," even if she is not legally a slave (cf. Westbrook 1988: 66). Thus, we find a number of texts that reinforce the authority of the free woman who owns or supervises slaves, such as an Old Babylonian bilingual proverb text (UET 6/2: 386–387; translation in Alster 1997) that states, "I, a slave girl, have no authority over my lady. Let me go!"

Two specific documents of the Old Babylonian period describe cases in which the treatment of a slave attracted the attention of a third party: the author of an Old Babylonian letter (AbB 1, 18) questions whether a man who hired a slave woman can beat her with a stick to "make her talk" when she has said something slanderous, presumably because this punishment has already been meted out, and a slave woman named Shala-ummi is said in another letter (AbB 1, 27) to have been "thrashed" by the slave-trader Awil-Adad, though she was apparently able to defend herself by finding protectors (cf. Diakanoff 1974; see further below). It is possible that fugitive slave women were punished particularly harshly by their owners, but few texts discuss such treatment.[19]

Several sale documents (cited in Mendelsohn 1949: 52–53) record the purchase of slaves for the express purpose of "marriage" to other slaves, much like the slave "breeding" practiced in other slaveholding societies. As in LH §175–176, slaves (usually male) also married non-slaves (usually female; cf. Westbrook 1998). There has been much debate regarding the legal status of their offspring, even though LH §171 and §175 clearly imply that legal marriages between a free person and a slave, regardless of the slave's sex, produce free children (cf. Mendelsohn 1949: 56 *contra* Diakonoff 1974: 73).

Slave owners occasionally gave or sold sexual access to their slave women to men outside their household as well: some female slaves worked as prostitutes, particularly in the Neo-Babylonian period, when brothels were sometimes called "the place where they know slave women" (Dandamaev 1984: 132ff.); but some women may also have engaged in non-commercial relationships with men who did not own them. A unique Old Babylonian legal document from Ur (UET 5, 191, cited in Diakonoff 1974) describes an interesting family dynamic stemming from the sexual relationship between a slave woman and her master's brother. Their son was legally recognized by his half-brothers after their father's (i.e., the slave owner's brother's) death, implying that it was difficult for free men to legitimize their children by slave women who were owned by someone else (Diakonoff 1974: 74). An even more complex case is revealed by several engaging Old Babylonian letters (AbB 1, 27 and 28), in which an occasional slave trader named Awil-Adad describes his difficulties with Shala-ummi, a slave woman whom he inherited from his mother. Shala-ummi herself, however, insists that she rightfully belonged to another man named Belshunu. Here is Diakonoff's (1974: n. 70) synopsis of the letters, which contain many classic elements of Graeco-Roman farce:

> Withdrawing into a room of the upper story of the house, Shala-ummi yelled incessantly and when Awil-Adad went out of the house, she went down, locked the outer door and for five days did not let anybody into the house. At last, Awil-Adad penetrated into the house by force, tied Shala-ummi hand and foot and thrashed her. However, she found protectors. They ran after Awil-Adad, but in the scuffle they were defeated.

Diakonoff (1974: n. 70) argues that Shala-ummi was likely the concubine of Belsunu; hence her insistence that her late mistress had willed her to him and not to Awil-Adad.[20]

Not surprisingly, slave women often were bought expressly for concubinage. A well-known Old Babylonian contract (CT 8, 22b = UAZP 77), records the sale of a slave woman named Shamash-nuri to a free couple: "to Bunene-abi [the husband] she is a wife, to Belshunu [the wife] she is a slave. On the day to Belshunu her mistress, 'you are not my mistress' [Shamash-nuri shall] say, she shall cut her hair and sell her for money" (Mendelsohn 1949: 9, 51). Several such contracts employ language that suggests that the slave will act as the second wife to the husband, while she simultaneously fulfills her obligations as the legal slave of the primary wife (see references in Westbrook 1998). Slave owners often paid above-average prices for female slaves (Mendelsohn 1949: 142, n. 93), indicating that they had concubinage in mind. Indeed, several Neo-Babylonian sale documents go out of their way to describe certain slave women as "beautiful" (*babbanitu*) (Dandamaev 1984: 204–205).

Babylonian wisdom literature disparages sexual relationships between free men and both female and male slaves, even though the legal texts often anticipate these relationships, which must have been quite common in practice. In the Kassite or Late Babylonian *Counsels of Wisdom*, for example, a father advises his son not to "honor a slave woman [*amtu*] in your house, . . . The house which a slave woman rules, she disrupts" (translation in Lambert 1960: 103).[21] A more sympathetic portrayal of slave–master relationships is given in a Standard Babylonian extispicy text: "If the *sibtu* [of the liver] is as big as the lobe, a slave will be as important as his master, or a slave girl [*amtu*], (since) her master loves her, will be as important as her mistress" (CT 20, 39: 10).[22] Slave women thus were considered to be capable of supplanting free wives within the household. The development of overly close relationships between owners and slaves therefore jeopardized the cosmological ideal – namely the nuclear patriarchal family – that is often reflected in literary texts (cf. Bottéro 1992: 196–197). In common practice, of course, most house-born slaves appear to have been treated very much as members of the household, if low-status ones.

Several Babylonian laws (e.g., LH §119, §146, NB §6) imply that it was in the master's interest to retain slave women who bore him children, whether or not he acknowledged them legally. LH §170–171 stipulate that a master may legitimize his slave woman's children, so that they might divide his estate with his free-born children, but the woman and her children are to be released even if the children remain illegitimate. The ideal manumission of slave mothers and their children was, however, probably an unusual occurrence in reality.[23] Old Babylonian wives were specifically prohibited from selling slave women who had borne children to their masters (LH §146); but the sale contract of Shamash-nuri cited above (CT 8, 22b) demonstrates that a wife might negotiate this right in individual cases. Alternatively, this text and two laws of Hammurabi (CT 8, 22b; LH §146; LH §144) jointly indicate that some non-childbearing wives viewed concubinage as a more favorable alternative to polygamy or divorce. In fact, wives such as the one described in the Old Babylonian sale contract (CT 8, 22b) sometimes fulfilled their marital obligations by providing slave women who could bear surrogate children, and these children were therefore not subject to the usual rules of legitimation (Westgate 1998; cf. Postgate 1992: 105).

As in most ancient slaveholding societies, specific sources rarely describe the relationship between a male owner and a slave woman in clear terms or from the woman's perspective. The most notable exception is an extraordinary NB court decision (YOS 7, 66) in which the slave woman Nubtâ testifies in the first person: she reports that she had been dedicated to a temple by her first master, but upon his death, his brother Shamash-zer-ushabshi took Nubtâ to his own house, where she bore three sons. Though she does not say so explicitly, the clear implication is that the children were fathered by her new master. The court confirms, based upon a mark on her hand, that Nubtâ has been dedicated to the temple; but it places Nubtâ and her sons in the care of Shamash-zer-ushabshi until he passes away, at which time Nubtâ will belong exclusively to the temple.[24] The most interesting clause of the document is one outlining the mutual responsibilities of Nubtâ and of Shamash-zer-ushabshi during the time that she remains in his household: "While Shamash-zer-ushabshi is alive, she is to serve him, and he is not to desire (her), and Shamash-zer-ushabshi is not to sell (her) for silver or marry (her) to a slave" (trans. Dandamaev 1982: 478–9).

The text suggests that the prohibition of Hammurabi against selling a slave woman who had borne her master's children (LH §146) no longer was observed in sixth-century Babylonia, if indeed it ever had been;[25] Shamash-zer-ushabshi is legally prevented from selling Nubtâ only because she ultimately belongs to the temple rather than to him (Dandamaev 1984: 410).

NOTES

1 Cf. Assante 1998: 59. In addition to the fact that the passage is directed to Gilgamesh (though ostensibly delivered by the woman Siduri), it is difficult to imagine that a Babylonian mother would likewise be enjoined to "consider the child who clutches your hand" (*ṣubbi ṣihram ṣabitu qātika*). The verb *šakanu* used in line 8 connotes authority (cf. CAD Š), as if to suggest that a man must "establish the institution of happiness" in his household. Indeed, the perspective of this passage is strongly reminiscent of the similarly male-oriented wisdom literature (see n. 2 below).

2 We learn, for instance, a great deal about male politics, relationships, entertainment, hygiene, clothing, and modes of travel in the Standard Babylonian epic of Gilgamesh. The wisdom literature in particular is explicitly for and about men; the Late Babylonian Counsels of Wisdom, for example, define the ideal wife only by contrast to undesirable candidates for marriage (lines 66–80; Lambert 1960: 103). G. Leick rightly observes that:

> [in] Sumerian, the most suitable medium for the articulation of physical love was lyric poetry, and we found that the woman's voice was its most vociferous exponent. In Akkadian, the tone of poetry is more solemn and official, . . . which makes the intimate revelation of feeling more difficult. However, the Old Babylonian dialogues do betray a new delicacy and sensitivity. But as we have so few love-songs in Akkadian, we have to beware of jumping to conclusions.
>
> (Leick 1994: 78)

3 That we have so little information about Babylonian girlhood is somewhat surprising, since several pre-adult stages – i.e., nursing child, weaned child, child, and adolescent – are identified in Neo-Babylonian sources (cf. Stol 1995a: 487).

4 See also the Neo-Babylonian version of *Nergal and Ereshkigal*, in which the queen of the netherworld complains that "since I was a young girl, I have not known the play of maidens, nor have I known the frolic of little girls" (Foster 1993: 424). Sumerian texts, many of which were copied in later periods, more frequently extol the pleasures of girlhood (e.g., Sefati 1998: 187).

5 Roth (1998: 82) speculates that the typical bride lacked legal independence, unlike the autonomous groom, primarily because of a difference in *age* rather than in gender per se, given the fact that most husbands were at least a decade older than their wives (cf. Roth 1987).

6 Westbrook (1988: 42–43) notes that this sort of *kallūtum* arrangement merely prevented third parties from committing adultery with, or raping, the inchoate bride, who was still considered a virgin at the time of her completed marriage. Because fathers-in-law in these arrangements had themselves offered the *terhatum* payment on behalf of their (presumably minor) sons, they were party to the contract and were not considered to be outsiders. Similarly, the friends with whom the groom delivered his marriage gifts might attempt to gain access to the bride, but these friends would forfeit their claim to the bride in case they managed to convince the groom's father-in-law of the groom's unworthiness (Malul 1991: 282).

7 Roth 1989: 26–28 for the Neo-Babylonian period; see Westbrook, 1988 for further discussion of the role of the *terhatum*.

8 In these documents, the payment by the groom to the bride's agents is known as *biblum* rather than *terhatum* and possibly is even more clearly conceived as a counter-dowry (Roth 1989: 12). Like the OB *terhatum*, however, the financial value of the NB *biblum* was often less than that of the dowry (cf. Westbrook 1988: 55 and Roth 1989: 1–12); Stol (1995b: 126) raises the

novel but largely unsupported possibility that the *terhatum* was paid in installments, eventually equaling the amount of the dowry, and thus qualifying as a true bride-price. The term *biblum* occurs in the Old Babylonian period as well but "does not appear in any of the marriage contracts which so carefully record payment of the *terhatum*" (Westbrook 1988: 42, 101–102 and references therein).

9 The penalties for divorce attempts were pecuniary and capital, respectively, in southern and northern Mesopotamia in the Old Babylonian period (Westbrook 1988: 83; Malul 1991: 282). Among the latter, some marriage contracts from Sippar stipulate that the repudiating wife shall be "bound and cast in the water" or "cast from the tower" (Westbrook 1988: 83).

10 Cf. Stol (1995b: 131–132), who contends as well that "the primary meaning of the divorce clause is to determine the degree of (in)dependence of both people." This interpretation does not exclude the one suggested here.

11 Cf. Roth 1988a: 195, cited in Foster 1993: 349.

12 There is also some evidence for healthy marital sexuality, and spouses occasionally forgave one another for sexual or legal faults (cf. references in Bottéro 1992: 186–187).

13 Men clearly exercised their extramarital prerogative to solicit other men as well. The *Shumma alu* apodoses contemplate several same-sex situations (e.g., a man's intercourse with an *assinnu*, with a male slave, and with a social peer; Guinan 1997), and the Late Babylonian "Almanac of Incantations" (BRM 4, 20) contains a prayer which appeals to the gods for the success of "the love of a man for a woman, of woman for a man, and of a man for a man" (translation in Bottéro and Petschow 1975: 468). Bottéro (1992: 192) asserts that

> the omission of the expected parallel of *a woman for a woman* does not indicate that female homosexuality was condemned or unknown. We have at least one record of it [a divinatory text in which women are said to "come together" (TCS 4, 194: XXIII 33?)] and I have been told that there is a still more explicit one in the Berlin Museum that remains unpublished.

Asher-Greve (2002b) considers the evidence for a "third gender" in Mesopotamian society, perhaps made up of intersexed, transgendered, and/or androgynous people, such as the effeminate or sexless (*sinnisânu*) dedicants to Ishtar known as *assinnu*, *kurgarru*, and *kala'um* (cf. Bottéro 1992: 191). Gender ambiguity was considered to be related to the powers of magic and of healing (Maul 1992), and some literary texts associate it with liminal places such as the boundary of the netherworld (Leick 1994).

14 See below for a discussion of a Sumerian text preserved in Old Babylonian copies that offers a sense of the domestic duties of both free wives and their female slaves: "Dumuzi's Wedding" (Ni2377=DI C$_1$, cited in Sefati 1998). A number of other texts mention women grinding flour and weaving textiles.

15 Translation in Oppenheim 1967: 194, n. 147; cf. Campbell Thompson 1906: xxxi.

16 Other assistants include conjurers, cloistered priestesses acting as midwives, and family members, such as the Old Babylonian grandmother who closely watched a delivery and who swore to the baby's parentage in a legal case (PBS 5, 100; cf. Stol 2000: 173–174).

17 Assante's (1998) analysis is far-ranging and not always convincing: her discussion of the legal rights of slave women vis-à-vis marriage, for example, is unclear (pp. 32–33; cf. Westbrook 1998; 1988). But her central point is well-argued and merits further study.

18 Both men and women frequently used comparable rhetoric in their personal correspondence; in an Old Assyrian letter found at the *karum* at Kaniš, for example, a male trader responds to a woman as follows: "why have you thus changed your mind and acted to belittle me, (claiming that) I have loved only money and have not loved our father's house, you or my brother?" (KTK 18; translation in Larsen 2001: n. 24). Thus, the pleading tone adopted by some women – e.g., widows (Roth 1991–1993) and the *nadītu* women of Sippar (Harris 1989: 155–9) – is not patently gendered. See Van De Mieroop 1999 for an argument that scholars have been too quick to attribute certain activities and conditions to Mesopotamian women alone without reference to male parallels.

19 For the treatment of fugitive slaves in general, see Snell 2001: 46–62, 74–86; Mendelsohn 1949: 66; Postgate 1992: 107.

20 Legal texts clearly treat the unapproved rape of slave women outside the household as a violation of their owner's rights: one of the Babylonian laws of Ešnuna considers the same legal situation in the context of economic deprivation, not of sexual offense. The latter case resembles those involving the rape of free women except insofar as the slave's consent is not an issue, probably because "the slave girl is not a legal person" (Finkelstein 1966: 360).

21 This passage is followed by an even longer section on the unsuitability of *harimtu* as wives, implying both that they were grouped together with slave women in a sexually liminal class, just as they were in the Middle Assyrian laws (MALA §40), and that this class threatened the social order.

22 Cf. CAD A/II 84A; M/I 346A; Langdon 1906.

23 The passive language of §171 leaves open the question of whether the owner is expected to release his slave-concubine during his lifetime, and because responsibility for such a manumission is not placed on any particular agent, the law is unlikely ever to have been enforced.

24 Nothing is said about Nubtâ's sons, whose status as either free men or as slaves apparently went without saying (Dandamaev 1984: 409–410), despite the contradictory Mesopotamian legal precedents.

25 The clause prohibiting Shamash-zer-ushabshi from "desiring" Nubtâ also suggests that Neo-Babylonian courts were willing to involve themselves in domestic affairs, at least insofar as Shamash-zer-ushabshi did not have the right to maintain a sexual relationship with a slave woman who did not legally belong to him. This stricture may have been related to rules governing the treatment of women who were pledged as collateral for debt, although we know relatively little regarding the latter.

BIBLIOGRAPHY

Abusch, T. (1993) Gilgamesh's request and Siduri's denial: Part I. In Cohen, M. *et al.* (eds) *The Tablet and the Scroll: Near Eastern Studies in Honor of William H. Hallo.* Bethesda, Maryland: CDL Press, pp. 1–14.

Alster, B. (1997) *Proverbs of Ancient Sumer: The World's Earliest Proverb Collections.* Bethesda, Maryland: CDL Press.

Asher-Greve, J. (2002a) Decisive sex, essential gender. In Parpola, S. and Whiting, R.M. (eds) 2002, pp. 11ff.

—— (2002b) Women and gender in ancient Near Eastern cultures: bibliography 1885 to 2001 AD. *NIN: Journal of Gender Studies in Antiquity* 3: 33–114.

Assante, J. (1998) The kar.kid/*harimtu*: prostitute or single woman? A reconsideration of the evidence. *Ugarit-Forschungen* 30: 5–96.

—— (2002) Sex, magic and the liminal body in the erotic art and texts of the Old Babylonian period. In Parpola, S. and Whiting, R.M. (eds) 2002, pp. 27–52.

Bahrani, Z. (2001) *Women of Babylon: Gender and Representation in Mesopotamia.* London: Routledge.

Baker, H.D. (2001) Degrees of freedom: slavery in mid-first millennium Babylonia. *World Archaeology* 33(1): 18–26.

Batto, B.F. (1974) *Studies on Women at Mari.* Baltimore, Maryland: Johns Hopkins University Press.

Beaulieu, P.-A. (1993) Women in Neo-Babylonian society. *Bulletin of the Canadian Society for Mesopotamian Studies* 26: 7–14.

Bottéro, J. (1992) "Free love" and its disadvantages. In *Mesopotamia: Writing, reasoning, and the gods.* Translated by Z. Bahrani and M. Van De Mieroop. Chicago, Illinois: University of Chicago Press.

—— and Petschow, H. (1975) Homosexualität. *Reallexikon der Assyriologie*, Volume 4. New York: Walter de Gruyter, pp. 459–468.

Budin, S.L. (2003) *Pallakai*, prostitutes, and prophetesses. *Classical Philology* 98: 48–159.

Campbell-Thompson, R. (1906) *Late Babylonian Letters.* London: Luzac & Co.

Cooper, J.S. (2002) Virginity in Ancient Mesopotamia. In Parpola, S. and Whiting, R.M. (eds) 2002, pp. 91–112.

Dandamaev, M. (1984) *Slavery in Babylonia from Nabopolassar to Alexander the Great (626–331 BC)*. Rev. edn. Translated by Victoria A. Powell; M. Powell and D.Weisberg (eds). DeKalb, Illinois: Northern Illinois University Press.

—— (1997) The composition of the citizens in first millennium Babylonia. *Altorientalische Forschungen* 24: 135–147.

Dercksen, J.G. (1996) *The Old Assyrian Copper Trade in Anatolia*. Istanbul: Nederlands Historisch-Archaeologisch Instituut te Istanbul.

Diakonoff, I. (1974) Slaves, helots, and serfs in early antiquity. *Acta Antiqua* 22: 45–78.

—— (1985) Extended families in Old Babylonian Ur. *Zeittschrift für Assyriologie* 75: 47–65.

Finkelstein, J.J. (1966) Sex offenses in Sumerian law. *Journal of the American Oriental Society* 86(4): 355–372.

Foster, B. (1993) *Before the Muses: an Anthology of Akkadian Literature*. Bethesda, Maryland: CDL Press.

Gelb, I. (1982) Terms for slaves in ancient Mesopotamia. In Postgate, N. (ed.) *Societies and Languages of the Ancient Near East: Studies in Honor of I.M. Diakonoff*. Warminster, England: Aris and Phillips Ltd, pp. 81–98.

Geller, M.J. (1990) Taboo in Mesopotamia: A review article. *Journal of Cuneiform Studies* 42(1): 105–117.

Greenfield, J.C. (1987) Some Neo-Babylonian women. In Durand, J.-M. (ed.) *La femme dans le Proche-Orient antique. Compte rendu de la XXXIIIe Rencontre Assyriologique Internationale (Paris, 7–10 Juillet 1986)*. Paris: Editions Recherche sur les Civilisations, pp. 75–80.

Grosz, K. (1989) Some aspects of the position of women in Nuzi. In Lesko, B. (ed.) 1989, pp. 167–189.

Guinan, A. (1989) The perils of high living: Divinatory rhetoric in *Šumma Alu*. In Behrens, H. *et al.* (eds) *DUMU-E2-DUB-BA-A: Studies in honor of Åke W. Sjöberg*. Occasional Publications of the Samuel Noah Kramer Fund, 11. Philadelphia, pp. 227–235.

—— (1990) The human behavioral omens: On the threshold of psychological inquiry. *Bulletin of the Canadian Society for Mesopotamian Studies* 19: 9–14.

—— (1997) Auguries of hegemony: The sex omens of Mesopotamia. *Gender and History* 9(3): 462–479.

—— (2002) Eratomancy: Scripting the erotic. In Parpola S. and Whiting, R.M. 2002, pp. 185–201.

Harris, R. (1975) *Ancient Sippar: A Demographic Study of an Old Babylonian City 1894–1595 BC*. Istanbul: Nederlands Historisch-Archaeologisch Instituut te Istanbul.

—— (1989) Independent women in ancient Mesopotamia? In Lesko (ed.) 1989, pp. 141–166.

—— (1990) Images of women in the *Gilgamesh Epic*. In Abusch T. *et al.* (eds) *Lingering Over Words: Studies Presented in Honor of William C. Moran*. Atlanta, Georgia: Scholars Press, pp. 219–230.

Koch-Westenholz, U. (2002) Everyday life of women according to first millennium omen apodoses. In Parpola, S. and Whiting, R.M. (eds) 2002, pp. 301–309.

Kuhrt, A. (1989) Non-royal women in the Late Babylonian period: A survey. In Lesko (ed.) 1989, pp. 215–243.

Lambert, W.G. (1960) *Babylonian Wisdom Literature*. Oxford: Clarendon Press.

—— (1967) The Gula hymn of Bullutsa-rabi. *Orientalia* 36: 121–165.

Landsberger, B. (1968) Jungfräulichkeit. In Ankum, J. *et al.* (eds) *Symbolae iuridicae et historiae Martino David dedicatae*, pp. 41–105.

Langdon, S. (1906) An Assyrian grammatical treatise on an omen tablet; CT 20, pp. 39–42. *Journal of the American Oriental Society* 27: 88–102.

Larsen, M.T. (1976) *The Old Assyrian City-state and its Colonies*. Copenhagen: Akademisk Forlag.

—— (2001) Affect and emotion. In Van Soldt, W.H. *et al.* (eds) *Veenhof Anniversary Volume: Studies Presented to Klaas R. Veenhof on the Occasion of his Sixty-fifth Birthday*. Leiden: Nederlands Instituut voor het Nabije Oosten, pp. 275–286.

Leick, G. (1994) *Sex and Eroticism in Mesopotamian Literature*. London: Routledge.

Lesko, B. (ed.) (1989) *Women's Earliest Records from Ancient Egypt and Western Asia. Proceedings of the Conference on Women in the Ancient Near East, Brown University, Providence, Rhode Island, November 5–7, 1987.* Atlanta, Georgia: Scholars Press.

Longman, T. (1991) *Fictional Akkadian Autobiography.* Winona Lake, Indiana: Eisenbrauns.

Malul, M. (1991) Review of *Old Babylonian Marriage Law* by Raymond Westbrook. *Orientalia* 60(3): 278–284.

—— (1991–1992) *Sillâm patārum* "to unfasten the cloth-pin": *Copula carnalis* and the formation of marriage in ancient Mesopotamia. *Ex Oriente Lux* 32: 66–86.

Matthews, V. *et al.* (eds) (1998) *Gender and Law in the Hebrew Bible and the Ancient Near East.* Sheffield: Sheffield Academic Press.

—— (2003) Marriage and family in the ancient Near East. In Campbell, K. (ed.) *Marriage and Family in the Biblical World.* Downers Grove, Illinois: InterVarsity Press, pp. 1–32.

Maul, S.M. (1992) *Kurgarrû* und *assinu* und ihr Stand in der babylonischen Gesellschaft. In Haas, V. (ed.) *Aussenseiter und Randgruppen: Beiträge zu einer Sozialgeschichte des Alten Orients. Xenia* 32: 159–172.

Mendelsohn, I. (1978) *Slavery in the Ancient Near East: a Comparative Study of Slavery in Babylonia, Assyria, Syria, and Palestine from the Middle of the Third Millennium to the End of the First Millennium.* 3rd edition. Westport, Connecticut: Greenwood Press.

Nemet-Nejat, K. (1998) *Daily Life in Ancient Mesopotamia.* Westport, Connecticut: Greenwood Press.

Oppenheim, A.L. (1967) *Letters from Mesopotamia.* Chicago, Illinois: University of Chicago Press.

Owen, D.I. and Westbrook, R. (1992) Tie her up and throw her into the river! An Old Babylonian inchoate marriage on the rocks. *Zeitschrift für Assyriologie* 82: 202–207.

Parpola, S. and Whiting, R.M. (eds) (2002) *Sex and Gender in the Ancient Near East. Proceedings of the 47th Rencontre Assyriologique Internationale, Helsinki, July 2–6, 2001.* Helsinki: Neo-Assyrian Text Corpus Project.

Postgate, J.N. (1992) *Early Mesopotamia: Society and Economy at the Dawn of History.* New York: Routledge.

Roth, M.T. (1987) Age at marriage and the household: A study of the Neo-Babylonian and Neo-Assyrian forms. *Comparative Studies in Society and History* 29: 715–747.

—— (1988a) "She will die by the iron dagger." Adultery and Neo-Babylonian marriage. *Journal of the Economic and Social History of the Orient* 31: 186–206.

—— (1988b) Women in transition and the *bīt mār banî. Revue d'Assyriologie* 82: 131–138.

—— (1989) *Babylonian Marriage Agreements: 7th-3rd Centuries BC.* Verlag Butzon & Bercker Kevelaer: Neukirchener Verlag Neukirchen-Vluyn.

—— (1989–1990) The material composition of the Neo-Babylonian dowry. *Archiv für Orientforschung* 36–37: 1–55.

—— (1991–1993) The Neo-Babylonian widow. *Journal of Cuneiform Studies* 43–45: 1–26.

—— (1997) *Law Collections from Mesopotamia and Asia Minor.* SBL Writings from the Ancient World, Vol. 6. Second Edition. Atlanta, Georgia: Scholars Press.

—— (1998) Gender and law: A case study from ancient Mesopotamia. In Matthews *et al.* (eds) 1998, pp. 173–184.

—— (1999) The priestess and the tavern: LH §110. In Böck, B. *et al.* (eds) *Munuscula Mesopotamica: Festschrift für Johannes Renger.* Münster: Ugarit-Verlag, pp. 445–464.

Sauren, H. (1990) á-ás, ás, as, "concubine". *Revue d'Assyriologie* 84: 41–43.

Sefati, Y. (1998) *Love Songs in Sumerian literature.* Jerusalem: Bar-Ilan University Press.

—— and Klein, J. (2002) The role of women in Mesopotamian witchcraft. In Parpola, S. and Whiting, R.M. (eds) 2002, pp. 569–597.

Snell, D. (2001) *Flight and Freedom in the Ancient Near East.* Leiden: Brill.

Stol, M. (1995a) Private life in ancient Mesopotamia. In Sasson, J. (ed.) *Civilizations of the Ancient Near East.* New York: Scribner, pp. 485–501.

—— (1995b) Women in Mesopotamia. *Journal of the Economic and Social History of the Orient* 38(2): 123–144.

—— (2000) *Birth in Babylonia and the Bible: Its Mediterranean Setting*. Gröningen: Styx.

Stol, M. and Vleeming, S.P. (eds) (1998) *Care of the Elderly in the Ancient Near East*. Studies in the history and the culture of the ancient Near East, vol. 14. Leiden: E.J. Brill.

Stone, E. (1982) The social role of the *nadītu* women of Nippur. *Journal of the Economic and Social History of the Orient* 25: 50–70.

—— (1987) *Nippur Neighborhoods*. Chicago, Illinois: The Oriental Institute of the University of Chicago.

—— (1996) Houses, households and neighborhoods in the Old Babylonian period. In Veenhof, K.R. (ed.) *Houses and Households in Ancient Mesopotamia. Papers read at the 40e Rencontre Assyriologique Internationale, Leiden, July 5–8, 1993*. Istanbul: Nederlands Historisch-Archaeologisch Instituut, pp. 229–235.

Sturlock, J.A. (1989/90) Was there a "love-hungry" *entu*-priestess named Etirtum? *Archiv für Orientforschung* 36/37: 107–112.

Tigay, J.F. (1982) *The Evolution of the Gilgamesh Epic*. Philadelphia: University of Pennsylvania Press.

Van De Mieroop, M. (1999) *Cuneiform Texts and the Writing of History*. London: Routledge.

Van der Toorn, K. (1994) *From her Cradle to her Grave: The Role of Religion in the Life of the Israelite and the Babylonian Woman*. Sheffield: Sheffield Academic Press.

Westbrook, R. (1988) Old Babylonian Marriage Law. *Archiv für Orientforschung* Beiheft 23.

—— (1998) The female slave. In Matthews et al. (eds) 1998, pp. 214–238.

Westenholz, J.G. (1990) Towards a new conceptualization of the female role in Mesopotamian society. *Journal of the American Oriental Society* 110(3): 510–521.

Whiting, R.M. (1987) *Old Babylonian Letters from Tell Asmar*. Assyriological Studies No. 22. Chicago, Illinois: The Oriental Institute of the University of Chicago.

Wiggerman, F.A.M. (2000) Lamaštu, daughter of Anu: A profile. In Stol, M. *Birth in Babylonia and the Bible: Its Mediterranean Setting*. Gröningen: Styx, pp. 217–252.

PART V

RELIGION

—·◆·—

CHAPTER TWENTY-TWO

THE ROLE AND FUNCTION OF GODDESSES IN MESOPOTAMIA

———•·•———

Brigitte Groneberg

When looking at some Mesopotamian goddesses, for example at the mightiest, Inanna-Ishtar, or the healing goddesses, Gula and her 'sisters', one is impressed by the power they exercised. Often they are symbolic leaders of towns and cities, the so-called city-deities. They may accompany kings into war but, on other occasions, they may function as their symbolic sexual partners, in both ways sustaining royalty. They can lead sick people out of the underworld, back to good health towards a new and successful life. They have their own rituals in many of the main Babylonian cities and enormous wealth is kept in their names, including real estate, animals, buildings, treasure of gold and silver. They also have their personnel, such as administrators and slaves. In all these respects the chief goddesses are equal to their male counterparts.

The religious imagination of a particular people reflects the conditions of their society, their norms and values. Therefore, when we notice the might of goddesses, the wealth of their property and the importance of their roles, how female deities are important members of an imaginary elite of a city's pantheon, we may conclude that this mirrors conditions in the real, human world of the people who ascribed to these beliefs. Societies and their ideologies are in constant flux, however, and only by examining a local pantheon in a particular space of time can we attempt to correlate the reconstruction of a concrete historical situation with the imagined conditions of a pantheon. I have chosen the time of the kings of the Third Dynasty of Ur (Ur III) (2100–2000 BC), which preceded the Old Babylonian period, and, in addition, I concentrate upon evidence from the city of Nippur. The chief reason for choosing this time and place lies in the relatively large body of written evidence that is available. Furthermore, Ur III Nippur has been the subject of several useful studies (Sallaberger 1993, 2003 and Such-Gutiérrez 2003) which form a backgound to the present examination of the role and function of Mesopotamian goddesses.

Geographically Nippur is situated in Babylonia but during the Ur III period cultural life was not yet dominated by Babylonian inhabitants. The extension of Babylonian influence over the southern Mesopotamian alluvial region can be dated to the beginning of the second millenium. But even during the first hundred years of their rule they accepted classical Sumerian as their main written language, studied mainly Sumerian literature and practised some of the old local religious rites and traditions.

We could say that the Sumerian cities of Nippur and Ur were the role models for the emergent Old Babylonian culture (Van De Mieroop 1999: 222–225). Nippur during Ur III may be seen as the forerunner of the later concept of 'Sumer and Akkad' which provided the ideological frame that connected the early Babylonian city-states.

The god Enlil, for instance, not only kept his most important dwelling place and that of his ancestors in his temple in Nippur, but he remained for centuries the highest god of this ideological entity. To mention another example, during a later phase of Babylonian rule the city god of Nippur, Ninurta-Ningirsu, was the one on which Marduk, the highest god of the Babylonian pantheon, was modelled. Only after centuries, at the time of Hammurabi's dynasty, did the old Sumerian traditions become less important.

Having asserted that both society and their ideology are subject to change, this should not blind us to the fact that some values appear rather persistent. Thus, the wealth of written documents and the art of writing was always held in high esteem as a valuable skill of divine inspiration, as were the various arts and crafts. The dominant position and the institution of the priest-king (ensi) or of the king was never questioned. Only when a king acted immorally were such deeds criticised, but not the office itself (George 2003: Vol. I 543: Gilgamesh I: 67–93; Vol. II 786: 67 ff. and 84ff.).

From the early historical period onwards we know that the institution of the 'family' formed the social order. The size of families, with its head, his wife, concubines, children and slaves varied over time, but, as can be seen from the Codex Hammurabi, they were perceived as the essential unit of organisation in towns and cities. They were presided over by the householder. The terminus bītum ('house') is meant in a strict, material sense but also in the meaning of 'family' or 'clan'. It is also a key concept on all levels of society and social structures which are couched in kinship terms.

During all historical periods, the relationships between various gods and goddesses were a reflection of the hierarchical, refined civic society and its traditional values. The gods were divided into males and females and they were presided over by a figure not unlike a paterfamilias, who is often referred to in royal terms, *lugal* 'king' with his *šarratum* 'queen' next to him in importance. Gods also have servants, sometimes given the rank of 'children', or assigned the position of *sukkallu*, 'messenger god', just as at the human level a *sukkallu* occupied a high office at the court. A divine hierarchy can be seen in the relationships of various city gods but also in lists of divine names. The origin of these lists lies in the school-curriculum; they were conceived for teaching cuneiform writing and the Sumerian and/or Akkadian language(s) (see Jon Taylor in this volume). The first god lists date from the early third millennium when cuneiform literature also developed. They refer to some extent to the organisation of the divine world but not in an overtly theological way, as these lists emerged from within a widespread literary tradition. The gods are arranged in an order that reflects the mainstream religious thinking and cults. In the older periods, lists of gods were clearly confined to local traditions, for on the local level deities could be assigned cult-symbols which could be treated like deities themselves, and thus become included in the lists among the gods.

Deities were assigned roles that stabilised the social fabric and the central power. The king asked for their opinions, they accompanied him when he went to war. They guaranteed justice and they regulated human life from the cradle to the grave and beyond. The gods determined the *šimtu* 'fate' of a human, but at the same time their own fate was determined. The principle that determined the force of destiny in Meso-potamia did not have a special name and thus was not personified, but it may be seen as having been administered via the social hierarchical order. In the world of the gods the 'Tablets of Destiny' were kept by the highest deity: it was symbolic of his leading position. These Tablets of Destiny represent power: a popular mytho-logical theme was the scenario of an evil force getting hold of these tablets which the deity had to fight off in order to regain custody. The Tablets of Destiny imply that the fate of gods was also variable and that the holder of these tablets represented the function of upholding order (Dalley 2000: 254ff.: *Enuma elish*-myth v–vii; 218: Anzû-myth iii).

The struggle for the top position among the gods was typically limited to those of male sex, but goddesses could also rise in the hierarchy, mainly by becoming the beloved wife of a chief god, as happened to Ishtar in literary tradition (Lambert 1967; Hruška 1969). Myths that stress the acquisition of ultimate power of the chief deity – see the case of Ninurta/Marduk in the beginning of the first millennium (cf. Oshima in this volume) – are probably the reflection of a parallel change in the human world, such as the absorption of the religious traditions of a neighbouring people or a reorgan-isation after a period of political chaos.

The structure of the divine world is based upon the human world, and the gods also act not unlike humans. Gods can have offspring, goddesses can and do give birth as we learn in the myth of creation *Enuma Elish*. But although the world of the gods was conceived of in analogy to that of the humans, it was a much better world. Thus, the gods were healthy through the consumption of food that they received in the form of offerings. Food suitable for offerings had to be luxurious: meat, flour, cakes and beer, although it was also possible to donate symbolic food, such as an incense offering. Usually gods were thought of as being handsome, healthy, vigorous adults. The only exceptions were some deities that lived in the underworld, such as Ereshkigal and Nergal, that were said to be unattractive or bald and limping (Hutter 1995: 29, 38). Only one deity suffered a temporary death, namely the goddess Inanna-Ishtar in her visit to the underworld (Hutter 1995: 123–124 and *passim*; Katz 1993: 261, 169–172 and *passim*). Gods were, in principle, immortal.

In their exulted realm the gods live in a manner that reflects an ideal version of the human world. Here reside the deities who are honoured on earth with temples, personnel and a regular cult to keep them happy. The realm of demons and hybrid creatures on the other hand may be seen as a negative imprint of life on earth. Those are confined to the underworld, but are mutating between both worlds, mostly frightening people out of their wits.

The ideal world of the gods who were honoured and fed in Mesopotamian temple complexes is also characterised by its division into the male and female gender. This dual aspect can be seen throughout the divine hierarchy: at the top we find the oldest or supreme divine couple, followed by lesser figures or offspring and their dependants.

While the hierarchical aspect may be seen as a reflection of the political relations between the central authority and the chief urban centres, the gender roles of gods and goddesses also present clues as to ideological principles that govern the relations between the sexes and the social position of women on earth. In as far as the divine world is an idealised representation of life on earth we may recognise, in the goddesses at least, aspects of the life of some of the more privileged women that actually lived.

Let us now take a closer look at the city of Nippur during the UR III period (between 2100–2000 BC). In the written sources of that time we find the names of many goddesses. Most of them had a long tradition and were also worshipped in places other than Nippur. When we look at the manner in which they are addressed, the questions asked from them in prayers, and note what kind of goods accumulated in their temples in Nippur, we see that these goddesses had only a limited number of distinct roles and functions. Some goddesses are particularly important in a political sense, in that they support the king and the realm, some are only connected with the underworld, some specialise in medical matters and the interpretation of dreams, and others are responsible for the harvest of wheat or grapes. Each of these categories will be noted in some detail.

SUPPORTING THE KING AND THE REALM

This cluster is related to the maintenance of royal power. This aspect has a long tradition in the figure of the Goddess Ninsun, 'mistress of the wild cows', the wife of Lugalbanda and mother of the legendary King Gilgamesh (Wilcke 2001: 501–504). Ninsun is addressed and revered in temples of the highest divine couple but also in the royal palace (Such-Gutiérrez 2003: 358–361). Her inclusion in the royal cult may have had a political motivation in that the king wished to link himself to the legendary predecessors. Ninsun was closely connected to the cult of the ancient legendary king Lugalbanda, predecessor of Ur III kings in the 'cult of ancestors' but she remained a goddess of minor importance.

In the period of the Third Ur Dynasty Nippur was – next to Ur – the religious centre of a political-ideological entity known as 'Sumer' but it has never been the seat of a king (Sallaberger 1997: 148). It gained importance by being the main dwelling of Enlil, the chief deity in Sumer, in his temple E-kur, 'House, Mountain'. His wife was Ninlil, the main goddess of grain. In Nippur, Enlil was served by the messenger god Nuska. Apart from the temple of the chief gods of the realm, Nippur also had its own city god, Ninurta, whose wife was the goddess Nin-Nibru, 'Mistress of Nippur'. Even a thousand years later these chief gods of Nippur, Enlil and Ninurta, are still mentioned in their function as maintaining the state (Dalley 2000: Myth of Anzû; Groneberg 2004: 78ff.). In this later period we also still find Nin-Nibru mentioned as 'Mistress of Nippur' in hymns of praise to goddesses, such as Inanna and Gula (Lambert 1969, 1976; Biggs 2001: 476f.).

Most prominent among the group of goddesses that played a special role in royal ceremonies was Inanna-Ishtar, at the same time goddess of war and goddess of love and fertility (cf. Westenholz in this volume). Her significance for the royal cult can hardly be overstated. It is she who bestowed sovereignty. This goddess not only controlled the fertility of plants and animals, as well as humans, and thus was ultimately responsible for all wealth and offspring, but, in addition, she stabilised the king's power, allowing him to protect his realm also by destroying his enemies. The latter function is clearly visible since the Akkade Period (from 2300 BC) when she was known as Anunitum, 'the fighting one'. It ought to be noted, however, that she did not possess a separate temple in Nippur related to the latter aspect.

She is also known by the name Nanaya, which probably means 'little Inanna', when her aspect as loving goddess is being stressed (Selz 2000). Nanaya's cult suddenly emerged in the city of Uruk during the Old Babylonian period and was maintained there until the end of the first millennium BC. But her cult flourished also in other towns, such as the ancient cities of Ur, Babylon and Kazallu and in the more recent Borsippa, Assur and Usbassu (George 1993: Nos. 540, 1147, 1195, 1015, 1361). Only in the cities of Babylon and Uruk are the names Inanna-Ishtar and Nanaya found next to one another, indicating that her Nanaya-aspect must have been rather special there. In Ur III-Nippur we have the earliest attestations of some offerings to her in Ninlil's sanctuary Tummal, and she is once mentioned journeying (from Uruk?) to Nippur. Although there is no indication of a distinctive cult of Nanaya (or of Anunitum, or of Ninsiana) in Ur III-Nippur it is remarkable that her statue was placed in the local temple of the chief god Enlil when she was carried to Nippur (Such-Gutiérrez 2003: 344–345).

The name Ninsiana, 'Dilbat-star', evokes her astral aspect as the planet Venus and in Old Babylonian times she was at the centre of some very important royal ceremonies (Römer 1965: 128ff.; Heimpel 2001: 487–488). Yet as Ninsiana the great goddess Inanna-Ishtar is still missing in Ur III-Nippur. However, it is suspected that the goddess with the epithet Nin-é-gal, 'Mistress of the Palace', was none other than Ishtar, as well as the later Belet-ekallim, 'Lady of the Palace', in the towns of Qatna, Dilbat and Assur (George 1993: Nos. 949, 604, 1031, 1119). In Nippur there was also the cult of Ningirgilum, 'Mistress of Girgilum', which relates to a particular image of Ishtar that originated from the town Girgilum near Nippur (Cavigneaux and Krebernik 2003: 362).

Much property in Nippur was assigned to Inanna-Ishtar. She had her own temple Eduranki 'Place of the Link between Heaven and Earth' with an Apsû 'water-cleansing-basin' and also owned cattle and store houses outside this temple complex. In her temple there was a room for the symbol of royal power: the tiara. In addition there was a room for her musical instruments, a special room for her own image, a bathroom, a 'clean room' (its purpose not clear to us), a room for the gate-keeper, a living room, storerooms, as well as storehouses for various types of grain, a cattlepen, a sheepfold, looms, a room for the women working at the mills and one for the men. In addition there is mention of a special 'sheepfold of the king'. Her servants include an administrator, a supervisor, a *lumahhu*-purification priest who has two servants and a cook of his own, someone who looked after the harps, a gala-lamentation priest, a snake charmer, various male and female singers (among them one especially trained to accompany the harp), musicians playing wind instruments and drums (Such-Gutiérrez 2003: 191–213, 213–221 and 221–224). The goddess Inanna apparently was at least as well endowed with property as the chief god Enlil.

Interestingly some new Ishtar temples were integrated in the empire's regions. The persons who introduced this cult were high-ranking local women from the outer borders of the empire who had become wives of the king of Ur. Thus was born the cult of Belet-Daraban 'Lady of Daraban', Belet-Shunir 'Lady of Shunir', Inanna-Haburitum 'Haburitic Inanna', and the worship of Ishhara (Sallaberger 1993: 18–20). This movement of cults from the periphery to the centre must have been closely linked with the person of the king's wife, for the cult comes to an end when they die (Weiershäuser 2004: unpubl. diss.). This phenomenon is not only of interest in the political history of the region, it also has important implications for understanding the religious system. The sponsoring of a cult was apparently directly linked with the successful career of powerful individuals. The activities in the temple ensure that the person who organised the cult would continue to receive divine assistance. It also seems relevant to note that successful women invested in the cult of a goddess, which strengthens the case of those who argue that in Mesopotamia there existed a separate religious sphere for men and women.

The great goddess Inanna-Ishtar is, in some traditions, depicted as the spouse of the deity Anu, who played a central role during the enthronement of a new king but otherwise remains a rather vague figure. In other legends she was married to the shepherd god Dumuzi, a character who at the beginning of the second millennium BC was closely associated with the role of the king.

There are some goddesses whose task it was to act like a protective mother to the king. These are, for example, called Nin-tu 'Mistress of Birth' or 'Mistress of the Womb' (Cavigneaux and Krebernik 2001: 507f.), Ninhursaga 'Mistress of the Mountains' and Dingirmah 'Sublime One'. Ninhursaga is described as wet-nurse of the king, she feeds him while he sits on her divine lap (Selz 1995: 253). This provides him with a 'milk' brotherhood to some of the gods, and links the human king genealogically with immortal gods, a procedure which is part of the ruler's legitimation. In Nippur of the Ur III period, this type of goddess was mostly venerated as Ninhursaga, but Dingirmah also received some offerings (Such-Gutiérrez 2003: 235). Ninhursaga played an important role and was well endowed. She had an altar in the palace of the king, but also her own temple, as well as an offering place in Ninlil's temple and another one even in Enlil's temple. A special *lumahhu*-purification priest directed her ceremonies. On the list of those working for her are guards, some to tow her ships, as well as other workers (Such-Gutiérrez 2003: 274–279).

GODDESSES OF THE UNDERWORLD

A separate category of goddesses are those connected with the underworld. In Nippur these were, in particular, Ereshkigal, 'Mistress of the large earth', and Allatum. Their main function was the supervision of the realm of the dead. After dying, all humans, whether king or ordinary citizen, had to enter the underworld. Allatum had been imported from far, she comes from a region in the Eastern Tigris, but in Nippur she was still honoured with the offering of a ram (Sallaberger 1993: 46; Such-Gutiérrez 2003: 311–312).

Another deity having a task in maintaining order in the underworld was Nungal 'Great Princess' (Cavigneaux and Krebernik 2001: 615–618). In the regular division of agricultural produce in Nippur she is mentioned in a prominent place, directly after the king. She also received offerings at the 'place of offering water', the place where the living performed ceremonies for their dead. In Nippur she seems to be connected with the chief deity Enlil (Such-Gutiérrez 2003: 364), so that it would seem that locally she merged with the Goddess Ninlil, his wife, adding another dimension to the latter's activities.

MEDICINE AND THE INTERPRETATION
OF DREAMS

There are several names of goddesses who are connected with the care and healing of the sick and possibly also with the interpretation of dreams. In the Ur III period, the main healing goddesses were known as Gula, Nintinugga (Edzard 2001: 506) and Ninisinna (Edzard 2001) and, specifically in Nippur, the Goddess Ningagia may be added to this group (Cavigneaux and Krebernik 2001: 351f.) All three have certainly been venerated as one type of goddess with the same tasks to fulfil and probably as one goddess. The differentiation in names should then be understood as different cultic representations of the same goddess in local styles of hair-dressing, clothes, other cultic paraphernalia, other physiognomy. The name Gula means 'Greater one' or 'the Greatest' (Groneberg 2000b). Like Nun-gal, 'Great Princess', such appellations indicate reverence and contain no clear indication as to a deity's function.

In Mesopotamian thinking the concepts of healing and death are closely related. Each serious illness was a likely precursor of an imminent death and subsequent voyage to the underworld. This may help explain the name of the healing goddess Nintinugga, 'Mistress who revives the dead'. The name Nin-gagia, 'Mistress of the Monastery', seems to be a mis-reading as indicated by an alternative spelling of her name, Nin-egia, 'Mistress young lady'. This title, which is often applied to Gula, suggests the possibility that here we have yet another name for Gula (Cavigneaux and Krebernik 2001: 351f.). The fact that Nin-gagia (or Nin-egia) received offerings from rich people, that she possessed a special storehouse, that she had an altar in Enlil's main temple, and that she probably had her own messenger-god (Such-Gutiérrez 2003: 270–273) strengthens the hypothesis that, indeed, she is no other than Gula.

Outside the city of Nippur the most important therapeutic goddess is called Gula (Such-Gutiérrez 2003: 246–248; ibid. to gú-lá). Within the city itself, this healing deity was worshipped under a specific local name as Gula-Umma, 'Gula of (the city) Umma' (Such-Gutiérrez 2003: 330). She was the owner of a harp, which was placed in the royal palace. This instrument is perceived as her symbol, it carries the name Ninegalesi and was worshipped as if it were the deity herself. In literary traditions Inanna-Ishtar and Gula seem to get rather close to each other: they seem to merge. Both are called Nin-Nibru. The goddess Gula was still worshipped in temples of her own during the last centuries of the second millennium (George 1993: Nos. 544, 812, 946). Judging by the number of her cult-places she seems to have become a rather important goddess at the time of some Neo-Babylonian and later kings.

The main healing goddess in the city of Nippur was, however, Nintinugga, who possessed a temple complex complete with stables (Such-Gutiérrez 2003: 289–296) certainly in Tummal, sanctuary of the goddess Ninlil, but apparently also in Nippur itself. This may be interpreted as a sign that large offerings were made from her own livestock, and that her clientele was of high social status. In addition there is mention of an Apsû 'water-cleansing-basin' and we know that the king and one of his daughters attended one of the cleansing ceremonies. Nintinugga was also served by her own gala lamentation-singer. In her temple we find also the king's personal protective deity, the Goddess Lama-lugal (Such-Gutiérrez 2003: 295). This may be interpreted as a sign that Nintinugga herself guarded the king's health and well-being. The king's personal deity represented the well-being of the state. In times of great hardship this personal deity could disappear and thus leave the populace to their fate (Lambert 1960: 33: 45–46; 38: 4–5). The importance of Nintinugga is confirmed by the fact that she also received extra offerings in the temple of the Goddess Ninlil, wife of Nippur's chief deity, where we may expect the queen to make her offerings, in order to care for her husband's welfare.

The third important healing deity in Nippur during Ur III was called Ninisinna 'Mistress of Isin'. In Isin, where the centre of her cult was located, about which we still know too little, she was the city goddess (Edzard 2000: 287f.; Groneberg 2000b; Such-Gutiérrez 2003: 353).

The differentiated, richly endowed cult of the healing goddesses in Nippur may be taken as an indication of the importance of these deities, both for the well-being of the ruler and for the other inhabitants. The citizens of Nippur apparently had a choice of therapeutic goddesses, some of whom had their cult centre in a far away region. Whether this implies the presence of a clientele that had migrated to Nippur from that region and who had brought their own goddess with them, or whether this means that the cult of a regional deity had gained such a reputation that she could successfully compete with Nintinugga, has not yet been determined.

Another prominent therapeutic deity with a long history is the goddess Baba. She interpreted dreams and had a healing function from Ur III right up to the second half of the first millennium BC. Later, her name was synonymous with the meaning 'guardian angel'. Her husband from earlier times is known as Nin-Girsu 'Leader of (the city) Girsu'. But already in Ur III times Nin-Girsu had merged with Ninurta, the city god of Nippur (Streck 2001: 512–522). In the palace of Nippur, Baba received offerings, whereby it is remarkable that she is referred to before her husband and received more sacrificial offerings. In her temple administration sixty workers were employed and many individuals had chosen her name as part of their names, and even a street in Nippur was named after her (Such-Gutiérrez 2003: 321–322).

FERTILITY

Nippur was surrounded by an agricultural belt and the city depended for its prosperity on its produce. One of the central tasks of the city was the regular cult of those deities that made the land fertile and safeguarded the crops. Prominent were goddesses who had been assigned the responsibility for agricultural matters such as the yield of the fields, the grain harvest, the ripening of fruit on the trees and grapes on the vines. Besides Ninlil, the highest city-goddess, who owned the temple district Tummal outside the city, we found in the first place Nisaba (Michalowski 2001: 575–579), but also the names Kusu, Ashnan, Ninkasi (Cavigneaux and Krebernik 2001: 442–445) and Ninkirsigga may be found` in the texts (Such-Gutiérrez 2003: 141–142; 335–337; 354–356). The logogram of the name Nisaba shows a plant, sometimes interpreted as 'an ear of barley'. Kusu means 'ripe stalk' and Ashnan means 'grain', so that we are here dealing with three names of the same goddess. Ninkasi is 'Mistress who pours wine and beer', an important task, for beer in Mesopotamia was staple food. Ninkirsigga 'Mistress of gentle lambs' cared for cattle. These evocative names are only applied to goddesses and clearly indicate their function. To these we may add Ninegunu 'Mistress of the many-coloured house' who also is addressed as Geshtinanna, 'vine of heaven' (Cavigneaux and Krebernik 2000: 347f.). She looked after all cultivated plants.

Nisaba's duties were probably, at first, the maintenance of the grain crops. Already from the earliest texts in the third millennium they extended to the protection of the art of writing (Michalowski 2001: 577–578). It is notable that this important intellectual skill was at first connected with a goddess; she consequently also became the transmitter of wisdom. The reason must have lain with the idea that writing was a precise manual craft which at that time was honoured as an intellectual skill. During the second millennium the god Nabû gradually took over as the god of scribes. Nevertheless, Nisaba's functions, as well as those of the therapeutic goddesses, and, as we shall see below, the various powerful aspects of Ishtar, give rise to the assumption that, prior to the middle of the second millennium BC, women were respected for accomplishments that go beyond their roles as mothers or housekeepers. The Middle-Assyrian legal texts that depict women as being completely subjugated to their husbands and which relegate women to their role in the household do not paint the full picture (Groneberg 2000a: 10–14) or reflect a situation that differed markedly from the Ur III period.

GODDESSES IDENTIFIED THROUGH THEIR SPOUSES

Another group of goddesses that had cult status in Nippur had a clearly circumscribed practical function but their main role was being the wife of an important god. At the same time it is clear that they were being worshipped in their own honour. Queen Shulgi-simti seemed to prefer to worship goddesses rather than gods. But as a queen, she addressed herself to the more important goddesses – Inanna, for example – whose role was to support royalty. But also other women of higher standing are known to have had their own festivities (Sallaberger 1993: 189, 217ff., 307). This, in itself, is of interest, for it indicates that women of the elite had the opportunity, the ability and the means to practise religion and that they did so sometimes without men. Women's religion was characterised by its own calendar and they sacrificed their own animals. This we find not just in old Nippur, but in the whole of the Ur III empire. We do not know enough, however, to extend the cult of women from the upper class to the religious habits of ordinary women during the Ur III period. In general it seems that especially those goddesses who functioned as partners of gods were chosen by women to fulfil their own religious needs.

Among this group of goddesses we must count Ninlil. Her name was already known in analogy to Enlil, her husband's name (Krebernik 2000–2001: 452–461). During the third millennium she occupied the high office of spouse of Sumer's chief god Enlil. In this role she received an excellent endowment. In her role as mistress of the state and chief grain-goddess (Such-Gutiérrez 2003: 113) she obtained at least as many grain-offerings as Enlil. Her temples in Nippur, 'Levelled place' and 'Exalted palace', comprised a warehouse, a grain store, a brewery, at least one large kitchen, weaving mills and a treasury. Among her property we find a building 'for the plough' and one 'for the footstool', various unspecified cult rooms and an Apsû water-cleansing-basin. In addition there were rooms for Enlil's and Ninlil's lyres, symbols that may have served as deities in their own right, as their representatives. The lyres had their own administrator, a Nindingir-priestess (the highest priestess in the land), a gate-keeper and a herald (Such-Gutiérrez 2003: 131–138). Her temple shared the administrative personnel with that of Enlil's temple, so she was not completely independent from him. Ninlil had major functions; in particular she gave judgement.

While Ninlil was the spouse of Sumer's chief god Enlil, there were also two concubines, Shuzianna and Enzikalama, the first being the more important, as indicated by her extensive possessions. Shuzianna seems to have been Enlil's 'travelling spouse'. She possessed a ship on which she accompanied him when he went visiting. The institution of a travelling spouse also existed in the human world, it was found in the royal court (Grégoire 1979). Shuzianna 'The just hand of heaven' was well looked after. She was worshipped not only in Nippur but also in Umma. Her temple possessed some cattle, arable land, gardens (among them possibly date palm gardens) and reeds. She had her own administrator, workers and servants (Such-Gutierrez 2003: 299–302).

The goddess Nin-Nibru 'Mistress of Nippur', was, like Ninlil, in the first place identified by her position as spouse, in Nin-Nibru's case of the city god Ninurta. Her role and identity remain rather vague, because it is questionable whether she had her own temple in Nippur in this period (Such-Gutiérrez 2003: 170, but Biggs 2001: 476). In contrast to Enlil's wives she had two male children: the god Igalima 'Bison-gate' and Shulshagana 'Beloved youth'. These two divine children had been mentioned two hundred years earlier as offspring of Ningirsu and Baba, the couple worshipped by earlier kings who served as paradigms for the Ur III kings (Selz 1995: 144–146, 277–279). This raises some questions about Nin-Nibru's identity. Such-Gutiérrez offers the hypothesis that she was a hypostasis of Baba (parallel to the change from Ningirsu to Ninurta). The other possibility could be that she had become identical with Ninlil, the leading goddess of Nippur. All this is related to the question when exactly the god Ninurta blended with Enlil, the chief god. In later times her name was used as an epithet for Ishtar and also for Gula.

Then there is Damgalnuna 'Great prince's spouse', the wife of the creator-god Enki. She had a shrine in the royal palace and a temple, but we have no record of a particular cult surrounding her, except some offerings, always as Enki's spouse (Sallaberger 1993: 99, 102, 140). The wife of Nuska (Enlil's mesenger god) is Sadirnuna, probably 'Prominent prince's net'. She possessed just as many cattle as her husband Nuska (Such-Gutiérrez 2003: 183).

A final goddess who is identified through her husband is Ningirida, the wife of the underworld-god Ninazu. Little is known about her but she might be connected to the gods in charge of the underworld where also her husband Ninazu was at home (Krebernik 2000: 362f.).

Hitherto we have divided the goddesses as to their chief functions. However, sometimes these overlap. Thus, Nungal is chiefly a healing goddess but in the lists of gods she is placed quite near the gods of the underworld. In mythology, Dingirmah and Ninhursaga are very active as creator-goddesses modelling proto-humans in assistance to the chief creator Enki. Also we have seen that under the general name Inanna-Ishtar many different functions are described, and in specific functions she is then known to us under a special name.

All these important goddesses and still some more received offerings in the city of Nippur near the end of the third millennium BC. There were, however, great differences in the degree of support and the amount of goods that were assigned to them. The volume of goods, the type of location as well as the nature of their possessions stand in direct relation to their importance and role in the social and ideological network of the city. Those goddesses who boasted of a cult-place in the king's palace were apparently linked to royalty. Those who displayed, in their own temple, the lama-god, were directly connected with the king's well-being and those who guarded his symbols of power were in charge of the exercising of his power. Those who possessed their own administrative buildings or farms seem to have been economically independent. All of them fulfilled functions for sections of the population other than the ruling one.

When looking at the personnel engaged in the various temples, it is noteworthy that we see a division of men and women. For example, in Nippur's Inanna-Ishtar temple, men and women working in the mills had separate rooms. When men and women had clearly separate religious activities, this would indicate that such a division would also have been practised in secular life. We may, however, not jump to the conclusion that in Mesopotamia a discrimination against women was accepted. It is particularly notable that some of the goddesses had a very powerful position. It is true that some major gods had rather insignificant spouses, but also the opposite is true. The husband of the healing goddess Ninisinna is usually taken to be Pabilsag, who already in early times replaced Ningirsu and later Ninurta as her husband. During the second millennium BC he is encountered as husband to other healing goddesses. The husband of Ninhursaga (the king's wet-nurse) is the rather pale Shulpa'e whose role is difficult to reconstruct in myths and hymns. In addition, the equal division of power between Enlil and Ninlil does not support the idea of a society with widespread discrimination against women – at least not in the upper class.

A shining example of of women's power is Inanna-Ishtar. Her personality is so sparkling and many-sided that a male companion automatically shrinks in her shadow. Her function in the king's legitimation is proof of the perceived necessity to grant power to a female deity. Inanna-Ishtar's legendary adventures and her control of the fertility of the whole country are indications that the female principle at times occupied centre stage.

It can also be noted that when gods and goddesses are depicted as being wedded to one another, very rarely are we confronted with divine children. The kinship terms father, mother, brother, sister and child are frequently used in legends and hymns, but it would be misleading to interpret such terms in a strict genealogical sense. It is to be assumed that these kinship terms are used metaphorically, indicating a certain hierarchy among the gods.

CONCLUSION

In this chapter we have begun with the assumption that the realms beyond our physical world are a reflection of the total of human experiences. During the third, second and first millennia BC, Mesopotamia had a complex society, bound together through an intricate net of relationships. Cities could only exist by virtue of an administrative apparatus that was hierarchically maintained. That is why the world of the deities was also hierarchical and complex.

We have also noted that the gods do not present an exact mirror image of human beings: they live in an ideal world, they do not toil. Indeed, it is clearly stated in their myths, that the burden of working is delegated from the gods to mankind (Lambert 1969). In this ideal realm of gods we have traced the feminine element by concentrating on a particular case, that of the religious institutions of the city of Nippur. We have seen that feminine deities were being revered in many localities, that their roles and functions ranged widely, that in some cases their resources were spectacular. This could mean that in the human world of Mesopotamia there were also women who were highly respected and honoured, that they could also play many roles and that in the large cities they must have had chances to develop.

BIBLIOGRAPHY

Biggs, R.D. 2001. 'Nin-Nibru', *Reallexikon der Assyriologie* 9: 476.

Cavigneaux, F. and M. Krebernik 2000. 'Nin-eguna', *Reallexikon der Assyriologie* 9: 347f.

—— and —— 2001. 'Nin-gagia', *Reallexikon der Assyriologie* 9: 351f.; 'Ninkasi', ibid. 442–445; 'Nin-tur', ibid. 507f.; 'Nungal', ibid. 615–618.

—— and —— 2003. 'Nin-girgilu', *Reallexikon der Assyriologie* 9: 62.

Dalley, S. 2000. *Myths from Mesopotamia. Creation, the Flood, Gilgamesh, and Others.* Revised Edition. Oxford.

Edzard, D.O. 2000. 'Nin-Isina', *Reallexikon der Assyriologie* 9: 287f.

—— 2001. 'Nin-tin-uga', 'Nin-tila-uga', *Reallexikon der Assyriologie* 9: o6.

George, A.R. 1993. *House Most High. The Temples of Ancient Mesopotamia.* Mesopotamian Civilizations 5. Winona Lake, Indiana.

—— 2003. *The Babylonian Gilgamesh Epic. Introduction, Critical Edition and Cuneiform Texts,* Vol. I. II. Oxford.

Grégoire, J.P. 1979. 'Le Sceau d'Ea-nisha', *Révue d'Assyriologie et Archéologie* 73: 191.

Groneberg, B. 2000a. 'Haus und Schleier in Mesopotamien'. In T. Späth and B. Wagner-Hasel (eds) *Frauenwelten in der Antike. Geschlechterordnung und weibliche Lebenspraxis.* Stuttgart, Weimar, 1–16.

—— 2000b. *Tiere als Symbole von Göttern,* TOPOI, Orient–Occident, Suppl. 2. S. 283–320. Lyon.

—— 2004. *Die Götter des Zweistromlandes.Kulte, Mythen, Epen.* Düsseldorf and Zürich.

Heimpel, W. 2001. 'Ninsiana', *Reallexikon der Assyriologie* 9: 487f.

Hruška, B. 1969. Das spätbabylonische Lehrgedicht 'Inannas Erhöhung', *Archiv Orientalni* 37: 473–522.

Hutter, M. 1985. *Altorientalische Vorstellungen von der Unterwelt. Literatur- und religionsgeschichtliche Überlegungen zu "Nergal und Ereshkigal".* Orientalia Biblica et Orientalis Band 63. Freiburg, Schweiz, Göttingen.

Katz, Dina 2003. *The Image of the Nether World in the Sumerian Sources.* Bethesda, Maryland.

Krebernik, M. 2000. 'Nin-girida', *Reallexikon der Assyriologie* 9: 362f.

—— 2000–2001. 'Ninlil', *Reallexikon der Assyriologie* 9: 452–462.

Lambert, W.G. 1960. *Babylonian Wisdom Literature.* Oxford.

—— 1967. 'The Gula Hymn of Bullutsa-rabi (Tafel VIII–XXIII)', *Orientalia* 36: 105–132.

—— 1982. 'The Hymn to the Queen of Nippur', in G. van Driel *et al.* 1982. *Zikir Shumim. Assyriological Studies Presented to F.R. Kraus on the Occasion of his Seventieth Birthday.* Nederlands Instituut voor het Nabije Oosten. Studia Francisci Scholten Memoriae Dicata Vol. Quintum. Leiden, 173–218.

—— and A.R. Millard 1969. *Atra-hasis. The Babylonian Story of the Flood. With the Sumerian Flood Story by M. Civil.* Oxford.

Michalowski, P. 2000. 'Nisaba', *Reallexikon der Assyriologie* 9: 575–579.

Römer, W.H.Ph. 1965. *Sumerische 'Königshymnen' der Isin-Zeit.* Documenta et Monumenta Orientis Antiqui Volume 13. Leiden.

Sallaberger, W. 1993. *Der kultische Kalender der Ur III – Zeit*. Teil 1. Untersuchungen zur Assyriologie und Vorderasiatischen Archäologie Band 7/1. Berlin, New York.

—— 1997. 'Nippur als religiöses Zentrum Mesopotamiens im Historischen Wandel', in Wilhelm, G. *Die Orientalische Stadt: Kontinuität, Wandel, Bruch*. Internationales Colloquium der Deutschen Orient Gesellschaft 9–10 May 1996 in Halle/Saale. Saarbrücken, pp. 147–169.

—— 2003. *Literatur, Politik und Recht in Mesopotamien. Festschrift für Claus Wilcke*. Walther Sallaberger, Konrad Volk and Annette Zgoll (eds). Orientalia Biblica et Christiana. Band 14. Wiesbaden.

Selz, G. 1995. *Untersuchungen zur Götterwelt des altsumerischen Stadtstaates von Lagasch*. Occasional Publications of the Samuel Noah Kramer Fund 13. Philadelphia.

—— 2000. 'Five Divine Ladies: Thoughts on Inana(k), Ischtar, In(n)in(a), Annunitum, and Anat, and the Origin of the title "Queen of Heaven"', in J. Asher-Greve (ed.) *NiN,. Journal of Gender Studies in Antiquity*. Vol. 1. Groningen, pp. 29–62.

Sommerfeld, W. 2002. 'Der Stadtgott von Eshnunna und der Prozess des frühen sumerisch-akkadischen Synkretismus', in O. Loretz *et al.* (eds) *Ex Mesopotamia et Syria Lux. Festschrift für Manfried Dietrich zu seinem 65. Geburtstag*. Alter Orient und Altes Testament 28, pp. 699–706.

Streck, M. 2001. 'Ninurta/Ningirsu', *Reallexikon der Assyriologie* 9: 512–522.

Such-Gutiérrez, M. 2003. *Beiträge zum Pantheon von Nippur im 3. Jahrtausend, Teil I. Materiali per il Vocabolario Sumerico-9/I, 9/II*. Rome.

Van De Mieroop, M. 1999. *The Ancient Mesopotamian City*. Oxford: Oxford University Press, New York.

Weiershäuser, F. 2004. *Die königlichen Frauen der Mesopotamischen Kulturen des 3. Jahrtausends v. Chr.: Ebla, Akkadzeit, Ur III-Zeit* (Diss., Göttingen unpubl.)

Wilcke, C. 2001. 'Ninsun', *Reallexikon der Assyriologie* 9: 501–504.

CHAPTER TWENTY-THREE

INANNA AND ISHTAR –
THE DIMORPHIC VENUS
GODDESSES

——— •◆• ———

Joan Goodnick Westenholz

Inanna (in Sumerian) and Ishtar (in Akkadian) were the most revered and popular goddesses of ancient Mesopotamia. As it says in the Great Prayer to Ishtar: 'Where is not your name, where are not your daises, where are not your powers?' (Boghazköy version lls. 17'–18', Zgoll 2003: 57). Despite their notoriety, these goddesses present an enigma. Controversy surrounds the figures of Inanna and Ishtar both in scholarly and popular literature. Although there is consensus concerning the factual evidence, scholars differ greatly on the interpretation of that evidence. The etymology of their names,[1] their genealogy, consorts, children, and manifestations are all unsettled and debatable topics.

When looking at Inanna/Ishtar's variety of contradictory traits, it seems as if one is peering through a kaleidoscope which sees diffused and shifting patterns of the goddess' manifestations. Each turn of the kaleidoscope comes from a different type of literature, from a different time, and reveals different patterns. Gazing at Inanna/Ishtar through the pattern of *mythology*, one beholds the young maiden Inanna, a beautiful young girl self-absorbed and materialistic, who holds out the promise of sweet delight to her beloved. She is also the rebellious teenager that can break all bonds. She confronts various father figures: she contends with An, the god of the heavens, in *The Capture of Eanna* (ETCSL 1.3.5)[2] and competes with Enki the god of the depths in *Inanna and Enki* (ETCSL No. 1.3.1). Her rivalling her elder sister, the Queen of the Netherworld, is narrated in *The Descent of Inanna* (ETCSL No. 1.4.1).

Examining Inanna/Ishtar through the pattern of *theology*, one discerns her shifting importance according to the religious scholars trying to arrange the divine world. The ancient theologians were concerned with systemising the constellations of gods in god lists by devising hierarchical and genealogical relationships. While one hierarchical roster lists Inanna after the high god of the heaven, An, and the executive head of the pantheon Enlil and before the mother goddess, a genealogical catalogue places Inanna in sixth place after her father, the moon-god Nanna.

Looking at Inanna/Ishtar through the pattern of *royal rhetoric*, one sees her relationship to the body politic of Sumer, Akkad and Babylonia in general and to the holders of political power in particular. The essential role of Inanna in the legitimation myth of kingship was expressed through the Sumerian doctrine of 'king by love of Inanna' which was attained through the divine consecration manifested in the rite of 'sacred marriage' that sanctioned the authority of the ruler. The concomitant royal sobriquet 'spouse of Inanna' and the love songs replete with amatory attributes of the divine bride are the hallmark of Sumerian kingship.

Perceiving Inanna/Ishtar through the pattern of the *devotional literature*, one descries a compassionate goddess of celestial judgement or an angry goddess who inflicts sufferings on humankind. The righteous sufferer who falls ill and is given up for lost is certain that his travails are due to the goddess' withdrawal of favour.

Observing Inanna/Ishtar through the pattern of *ritual observance*, one notes the variant celebrations of the goddess involving transgendered and transvestite cultic personnel. The carnivalesque festivals of the goddess were occasions when reversals in age, species, status, and sex all came into play, when social rules were in abeyance, and were possibly times of institutionalised license (Harris 1991: 273).

Viewing Inanna/Ishtar from a pattern of *sexual orientation*, one focuses on her sexual identity. She could be viewed as a beautiful goddess of love who rules the day and as a bearded god(dess) of war who rules the night.[3] This apparent androgyny of Inanna/Ishtar provided a powerful symbol of the ambiguities of pure sexuality, which is said to be reflected in her cult and in the transvestism of her cultic personnel (Groneberg 1986).

HISTORICAL OUTLINE

Inanna/Ishtar is the one and only deity whose worship is known from the dawn of Babylonian civilisation. Over the millennia, her identity underwent a continual process of reinterpretation and syncretism, mutation and fossilisation, fusion and fission which generated a goddess who was a complex multi-layered conglomerate.

Fourth millennium

Inanna first appears in the late fourth millennium as the patron deity of Uruk, the first urban centre on the Mesopotamian alluvium (Szarzyńska 2000). The sign with which her name was written goes back to an archaic pictograph representing a gatepost with a volute finial. This decorative post, which originally stood outside the gate to her temple or shrine, developed into her earliest cult symbol (see Figure 23.1). Next to the volute-like symbol of Inanna appears also a rosette/star, the icon that became the major symbol of Inanna/Ishtar throughout ancient Mesopotamian history down to the Neo-Babylonian period. From this period, we have not only images of her cult symbols, but also representations of the goddess. A one metre-high vase reveals the goddess receiving a procession headed by the *en*, priest-ruler of the city of Uruk, as he leads a procession bearing the produce of the land, perhaps on the occasion of the New Year (Figure 23.2). This vase is said to illustrate Inanna's relationship with vegetable and animal fertility (Selz 2000: 40 note 12) and to render the 'sacred marriage' of Inanna and the king (ibid. 30–32).

In the written sources, Inanna appears in various manifestations, each of which, in different measure, seems to possess a separate cult, temples with cultic functionaries, and the right to receive offerings. The manifestations are: NUN 'prince', **húd** 'morning', **sig** 'evening' and **kur** 'mountain'. It is important to review these manifestations in

Figure 23.1 Green calcite cylinder seal and impression depicting a cultic scene (sacred marriage?), flanked by the reed gatepost, symbol of the goddess Inanna, Uruk III period, *c.*3100–2900 BCE (BLMJ Seal 204). David Harris, Courtesy of the Bible Lands Museum Jerusalem.

relation to her later epiphanies in order to determine their significance as regards her origin, character and function.

The earliest epithet, NUN, may be related to NUN, the sign with which the god Enki and the city Eridu were written. Thus, instead of Inanna 'the princely', Inanna-NUN could be interpreted as Inanna of the city of Eridu. Such an interpretation would give some support to the genealogy of Inanna as daughter of the god Enki, or to an early diffusion of the worship of Inanna and her establishment outside Uruk. It may also relate to her stealing the **me**-principles from 'her father' Enki. The **me**-principles are the cultural norms that are the basis of Sumerian civilisation and comprise all aspects of human life, including the insignia of kingship as well as the proprieties of sexuality, and are particularly associated with Inanna (Glassner 1992). This epithet NUN also appears in the name of her archaic temple the É.NUN, possibly to be read agrun, 'cella'. In general, the name é-agrun-na refers to the cella of a sanctuary and judging from the occurrences of the word in contexts dealing with night and resting, it was conceived as the bedchamber.

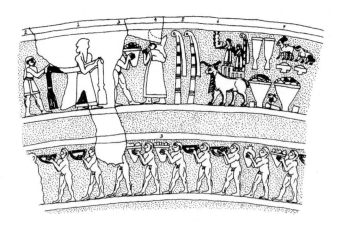

Figure 23.2 Drawing of the top two registers of the cultic vase from Uruk depicting scene of offerings being presented to the goddess Inanna, found in the temple treasury hoard of level III, *c.*3000 BCE or earlier (F. A. M. Wiggermann).

The two epithets **húd** 'morning' and **sig** 'evening' describe the goddess as two manifestations of the planet Venus, one shining in the morning and one in the evening sky. Although only a temple to the evening aspect of Venus is mentioned in the administrative records, each manifestation of Venus was honoured with its own festival, and different sets of offerings were presented to each of them (Szarzyńska 2000). This veneration of Inanna reflects the cycle of the planet Venus during which the planet is visible twice for a period of about eight months. During one period, Venus rises and sets in the east as the morning star and during the other, Venus rises and sets in the west as the evening star. Between these two periods, when it is closer to the Earth (inferior conjunction), the planet is invisible for about three days during the winter and about two weeks in the summer and at its furthest point from Earth (superior conjunction), the planet is invisible for two months and some days. Her astral symbol is the rosette/star.

The myth, which we know from later sources, that explains the periodic invisibility of Venus is named by modern scholars as *Inanna's Descent to the Netherworld* (Katz 1996, 2003: 93–98). It tells of her journey to the realm of the dead, situated in the **kur**, literally 'mountain' (rather than netherworld),[4] her attempt at usurpation and arrest there and her release through Enki's contrivance. It is based on the periodic disappearance of Venus from sight and her reappearance. According to the phrase 'descending/ascending to/from the kur'[5] in the list of Inanna's **mes**, she descended to and ascended from the realm of the dead repeatedly. In the myth, she is portrayed as entering the realm of the dead from the Mountain in the west; she gives the excuse for her passage to the gatekeeper that she is passing through going to the east. The myth is based on the speculations of the Sumerians on her course behind the mountain ridges outside the north-eastern borders of Sumer.

The last aspect of Inanna of Uruk, but one for which no offering texts have been found, is Inanna-kur, literally 'Inanna, the mountain' for which various interpretations have been offered such as Inanna, (from) the 'mountain' in which **kur** may indicate the mountainous place of her birth and appearance (Szarzyńska 2000). Moreover, Inanna frequently travels to the **kur**, the mountain lands around the Mesopotamian plane, not only to enter the realm of the dead but also for other reasons. For instance, 'the young woman went up into the mountains, holy Inanna went up into the mountains. To detect falsehood and justice, to inspect the Land closely, to identify the criminal against the just, she went up into the mountains' (*Inanna and Shukaletuda* lls. 4–8, ETSCL No. 1. 3. 3). Further, it might be possible to understand the epithet Inanna-kur as the well-known epithet of Inanna which appears more fully as nin-kur-kur-ra 'Mistress of (all) the lands', Inanna in her aspect of political mastery over the inhabited world.

Among the proto-cuneiform texts from various cities at the turn of the fourth millennium, there is a distinctive group of tablets each of which bears a sealing on which the names of several cities are recorded and each of which concludes with lines tallying offerings sent to Inanna in Uruk. What this evidence seems to indicate is that, in the earliest period, there existed a pan-Mesopotamian religious league centred on Uruk and its chief deity, Inanna.

Third millennium

In this period, there were many local forms of Inanna as shown by the god lists and offering lists as well as the literary texts. These local manifestations were distinguished from each other by epithets or honorific titles. In Kish, she was thus known as Inanna-GAR, in Zabalam, as Inanna-Zabalam. This phenomenon may have resulted from the universal veneration of Inanna during the Uruk expansion and the possible identification of Inanna with local female deities. Did this influence or change the distinctive identity of the underlying deity, and was there any reciprocal influence upon Inanna? Perhaps her contradictory and multifaceted character can be traced to these early syncretisms, in addition to her various manifestations.

The most common epithet given to her by the Old Sumerian kings was nin-kur-kur-ra 'Mistress of (all) the lands', extolling her authoritarian power on earth as well as nu-gig(-an-na), a title of uncertain meaning but characterising her astral presence in the heavens (Zgoll 1997). Although we cannot read with any certainty the early literary texts, we do find descriptions that can be understood to mean 'flashing' or 'radiant', which point to Inanna's manifestation as the Venus star and the designation of 50 **me** in association with Inanna. While Old Sumerian personal names, such as Inanna-ur-sag 'Inanna is a warrior' indicate Inanna's martial nature, there is no dedication addressed to Inanna of Uruk as 'Lady of Battle' until the end of the third millennium in the Neo-Sumerian period.

'Semitic' Ishtar vis-à-vis 'Sumerian' Inanna

The supposed history of the syncretism and fusion of the Sumerian Inanna with the Akkadian Ishtar is a complex problem. It has been suggested that the warlike character of Ishtar (Figure 23.3) that appears for the first time on the seals of the Old Akkadian period was a specifically Akkadian trait. However, while it is true that Ishtar as the city goddess of Akkade – Ashtar Annunitum – is indeed the Lady of Battle, the Akkadian Ishtar in general was already by the third millennium more than any one characteristic. For instance, our earliest love incantation invoking Ishtar is Akkadian rather than Sumerian. On the other hand, a warlike inclination is not entirely excluded as one of the character traits of the Sumerian Inanna. To complicate matters further, these two cultures Sumerian and Akkadian lived side-by-side, mutually influencing each other.[6] Further, just as there was a plethora of Inanna goddesses of local pantheons, there were such Ishtar figures.

Pietistic Akkadian names borne by ordinary persons find her described as 'mother' of the name-bearer. Even though the exact meaning of such a statement is not clear, it does seem that the early Akkadians could see Ishtar as a motherly figure, a trait that presumably was unknown in Inanna. However, she is so addressed occasionally in Sumerian hymns.

Literary texts are now produced that can be understood and the hymns that were sung in her praise give us an insight into the character of Inanna. Although most of her work is known from later editions, the daughter of Sargon, Enheduanna composed hymns extolling Inanna. In one, she chronicles Inanna's responsibility for all aspects of human affairs – positive and negative, beneficial and harmful, sexual and ethical – all are enumerated as her possessions:

Figure 23.3 Impression of Old Babylonian cylinder seal depicting suppliant goddess and king facing Ishtar in her guise as warrior goddess with her right foot resting on a lion's neck and beneath a six-pointed star-disc (her symbol) and crescent (symbol of her father, Sin, the moon-god). In her left arm, she holds a *harpe*-sword and in her right hand, the double lion-headed mace. She wears two quivers on her back which may contain maces as well as arrows. *c.*1850–1720 BCE (BM 130694) (courtesy of the Trustees of the British Museum).

114	Without you no destiny at all is determined, ...
115	To run, to escape, to quiet and to pacify are yours, Inanna.
117	To open up roads and paths, a place of peace for the journey, a companion for the weak, are yours, Inanna.
118	To keep paths and ways in good order, to shatter earth and to make it firm are yours, Inanna.
119	To destroy, to build up, to tear out and to settle are yours, Inanna.
120	To turn a man into a woman and a woman into a man are yours, Inanna.
121	Desirability and arousal, goods and property are yours, Inanna.
123	Gaining wealth and having success in wealth, financial loss and reduced wealth are yours, Inanna.
125	Assigning virility, dignity, guardian angels, protective deities and cult centres are yours, Inanna.

132   ... mercy and pity are yours, Inanna.

134   To cause the ... heart to tremble, ... illnesses are yours,
       Inanna.

135   To have a wife, ..., to love ... are yours, Inanna.

138   To build a house, to create a woman's chamber, to possess
       implements, to kiss a child's lips are yours, Inanna.

140   To interchange the brute and the strong and the weak and the
       powerless is yours, Inanna.

142   To interchange the heights and valleys ... is yours, Inanna.

143   To give the crown, the throne and the royal sceptre is yours,
       Inanna.

156–157 To bestow the divine and royal rites, to carry out the
         appropriate instructions, slander, untruthful words, abuse, to
         speak inimically and to overstate are yours, Inanna.

164–168 strife, chaos, opposition, fighting and speeding carnage, ..., to
         know everything, ... to instill fear ... and to hate ... are
         yours, Inanna.

         (*Inninshagurra,* ETCSL No. 4. 07. 3)

This litany of Inanna's antithetical attributes contains polar notions that reflect the dimorphism of Venus and, at the same time, indicate the whole by defining the limits.

Among the courtly tales told in the court of the Neo-Sumerian kings, the epic poems of the heroic cycle of Uruk were recounted. One poem narrates the conflict between Enmerkar of Uruk and Ensuhkeshdanna of Aratta, over whom would be the most beloved of Inanna. Enmerkar won more favour in her eyes and Ensuhkeshdanna submits in these words:

> You are the beloved lord of Inanna, you alone are exalted. Inanna has truly chosen you for her holy lap, you are her beloved. From the south to the highlands, you are the great lord, and I am only second to you.
>
> (lls. 276–278, ETCSL No. 1. 8. 2. 4)

In like manner, the Neo-Sumerian kings considered themselves the spouses of Inanna.

It is difficult to evaluate when Inanna was first linked with sexuality; certainly by the Sargonic period she was invoked in Akkadian love incantations. This aspect became pre-eminent in the Sumerian corpus of love lyrics from the Neo-Sumerian period onwards. The theme of this corpus is the love between the goddess, the young maiden Inanna, and the shepherd god Dumuzi, as the archetypical bride and groom. The cycle of texts includes various stories of Dumuzi's courtship of Inanna, preparations for the wedding and the wedding itself. These songs portray Inanna as a young woman, with her teenage enthusiasms, her passionate love and sexual yearnings for her beloved. The temporal setting of the poetry is at sunset or later when day has passed and night has come, the time of lovers and Inanna's appearance in the night sky.

As all young love, it ends in tragedy with the death of Dumuzi at the hands of bandits. Inanna and his sister search unceasingly for him. Among the rituals mentioned in connection with Inanna in the Neo-Sumerian period, there are wailing ceremonies of Inanna performed at full moon, month's end, and possibly also at its beginning. At some point in time, the death of Dumuzi becomes linked to his relationship to Inanna. It is only at a later stage that the myths of Inanna's victory over death (*The Descent of Inanna*) and of her erotic relationship with Dumuzi found in the love songs were combined to make Inanna responsible for the death of Dumuzi at the hand of the underworld demons who claim a substitute for her to remain in the underworld when she departs their realm. In later millennia, the tale of Inanna's ill-fated descent to the netherworld, resulting in the demons seizing her husband Dumuzi as her substitute, was a fertile source for new compositions not only in Sumerian but also in Akkadian which retold, elaborated upon, and alluded to, this story. It is the only Inanna myth that survived as an Ishtar myth.

Dumuzi was not only a god but also an antediluvian legendary king, a shepherd who was the king of the city of Bad-tibira. Some of the love poems praise the reigning king as Dumuzi. The Sumerian divine love poetry in which the king takes the role of Dumuzi probably had its cultic context in 'sacred marriage' rituals as well as its entertainment setting in courtly love poetry.

Mesopotamian theologians structured the expanding pantheon by creating additional kinship ties between individual gods. Previously, Inanna was placed after her father, the moon-god Nanna, and before her spouse, Dumuzi, now she is followed by a daughter Nanaya and sons Lulal, Latarak and Shara. Thus, from the theological and perhaps political angle, came the image of Inanna as a mother goddess although her maternity is of no consequence. The father of the children is not Dumuzi and her sons play no role in her mythology or worship.

Second millennium

The multiplication of manifestations of the goddess Inanna/Ishtar reaches its zenith in the second millennium – a cult of Inanna and/or Ishtar is performed in most major cities – before the reaction sets in and syncretism begins its sway in the first millennium. Characteristic also is the worship of different forms of Ishtar in the same city. In this period Ishtar became the generic name for goddess and *ištaratu*, a plural form of her name, the term for goddesses: 'Ishtar holds in her hand the nose-rope of the people, Their goddesses (*ištaratašin*) attend to her word' (Agushaya A ii 12, Groneberg 1997: 75).

Ishtar has become the most prominent goddess among goddesses; the Babylonian mindset is gender oriented in their social constructions and this is reflected in their view of the divine world. One Old Babylonian god list arranged the deities according to their gender. Not only does Inanna appear now after her spouse Dumuzi, but all various Inanna manifestations and other female deities are grouped together. Even the consort of Marduk, Zarpanitum, is listed among these Inanna goddesses. Another list, which becomes the basis of the standard Babylonian god list, placed all Inanna manifestations together after the various courts of the male gods.

Royal rhetoric shifts its focus. Only through Enlil, the executive leader of the Sumerian pantheon, could other gods partake of political power:

He placed the heavens on my head as a crown.
He put the earth at my feet as sandals.
He wrapped the holy *ba* garment around my body.
He put the holy sceptre in my hand.

(Inanna Hymn F 10–13, ETCSL No. 4. 07. 6)

Consequently, one royal hymn praises the bestowal of powers by Enlil and his spouse Ninlil on the goddess Inanna who is thereby relegated to a subordinate position, though her powers still include the dominion over the four quarters of the earth. Rather than choosing her spouse, Inanna is presented with her husband the king Ishme-Dagan by Enlil and Ninlil. The symbolisation of the close union between the divine goddess and the mortal king in the 'sacred marriage' ceremony continues for the first centuries of the millennium as do the concomitant royal sobriquet 'spouse of Inanna' and the love songs until the demise of Sumerian kingship. Yet, even in Babylonian tradition, Ishtar's love for her king remains a productive mythologeme – the royal insignia remain hers to bestow on her favourite king. However, the second-millennium paradigm found in the Akkadian royal hymns, is the petitioning of Ishtar to persuade her spouse to bless the king.

The emphasis shifts away from the loving relationship between Ishtar and the king to a protective one, to Ishtar 'mistress of battle and warfare' who stands at the sides of kings and smashes their enemies. Her frenzy in battle is constantly mentioned in hymns, both Sumerian and Akkadian: 'Great fierce storm, . . . Inanna, emitting fearsomeness and radiance in battle!' (Inanna Hymn A 1–2, ETCSL No. 4. 07. 1) and 'Let me praise the greatest one, the warrior among the gods' (Akkadian hymn, *Agušaya* A i 1–2, Groneberg 1997: 75). Images of Ishtar were carried into battle at the head of the armies.

Her fondness for violence also colours her relationship with the people. Seeking the aid of the goddess Inanna to relieve the sufferings of her daughter, the wife of the ruler of the city of Larsa dedicated a stone basin: 'For the goddess Inanna, the angry goddess' (Frayne RIME 4. 2. 14. 23: 1–2). In an Akkadian prayer to Ishtar, the petitioner describes his anguish: 'Who can approach me because of the anger of your heart?' ('Ishtar Baghdad' 22, Groneberg 1997: 110), and misery: 'you scattered my nest in your anger' ('Ishtar Baghdad' 38, Groneberg 1997: 110). Ishtar thus becomes the address for persons suffering various ills, one of which is later called the 'touch of Ishtar'. A narrative hymn to Ishtar tells how a substitute being is created to protect humankind against the more capricious and destructive of Ishtar's tendencies – to control her violence.

Her anger can be pacified and she can be merciful and compassionate. 'Merciful is the daughter of Nanna, she hears my speech' ('Ishtar Baghdad' 6, Groneberg 1997: 110). Appealing to her for clemency, the petitioner addresses her as 'mother': 'mother, look on my troubles' ('Ishtar Baghdad' 76, Groneberg 1997: 112). Personal names reflecting this pious wish also employ the epithet *ummi* 'my mother' *Ištar-ummi* 'Ishtar-is-my-mother' and *Ištar-ummi-eništim* 'Ishtar-is-a-mother-of-the-weak (female)'.[7]

Ishtar first appears as *mater dolerosa* in liturgical compositions of this period, in particular, the lamentations over destroyed cities. In these lamentations which are mainly outpourings of grief and despair, the goddess weeps over her destroyed temple and city, while in others she is overcome with grief over the death of Dumuzi.

In this period, the character of the goddess shifts from Inanna, the Sumerian troublesome young woman, to Ishtar, the queen of heaven as well as the queen of the people. Underlying her queenly image is her command of the **mes** (also termed **garza** in Sumerian and translated as *parṣu* in Akkadian) and her control of all the negative and positive aspects of human society.

Among the **me** and **garza** which Inanna/Ishtar controls are those of sexuality – sexual attraction and intercourse, and its outcome, conception and even childbirth. We learn about the concerns of the people in these areas of life from love spells and potency charms, prayers and petitions for help, many invoking the love of Inanna and Dumuzi.

Inanna/Ishtar becomes the manifestation of sex and eroticism – patron of brides, married women and prostitutes. Concomitant with her shift to queen is her shift to prostitute. One hymn puts these words into the mouth of Inanna:

> When I sit in the alehouse, I am a woman, and I am an exuberant young man.
> When I am present at a place of quarrelling, I am a woman, a perfect figure.
> When I sit by the gate of the tavern, I am a prostitute familiar with the penis;
> the friend of a man, the girlfriend of a woman.
>
> (Inanna Hymn I 16–22, ETCSL No. 4. 07. 9)

In a Sumerian love incantation, the prostitute is named the daughter of Inanna (Falkenstein 1964: 114 line 2).

The cult of Inanna/Ishtar focuses on sexual identity and gender roles. From this period come two royal rituals, one encased in a Sumerian hymn and the other in an Akkadian prescriptive ritual text. The first describes a 'sacred marriage' ritual between the King of Isin and the goddess Inanna. It takes place at the New Year, beginning at sunset with the rising of the evening star, climaxing in a dawn ceremony and concluding with a joyous morning celebration. The hymn opens with an invocation to the goddess as the evening star followed by a description of a carnival-like procession. Not only do the people parade playing musical instruments but also costumed asexual or hermaphrodite personnel, transvestites, wearing male attire on their right side and female on their left and **kurgarras** wielding swords in ecstatic frenzy and shedding blood, to the resounding beat of the drums. As night falls, the focus shifts to Inanna who is pictured as looking down from the heavens on all the creatures of the earth and passing judgement on the sleepers. At the dawning of the new day, the celebration of the 'sacred marriage', with Inanna as the bride and the king as the bridegroom, begins. The preparations for the wedding ceremony are described, the setting up of the wedding bed, the bride's pre-nuptial bath, the consummation of the marriage, and the magnificent wedding banquet. The diurnal celebrations conclude with a public holiday for the people.

The second royal ritual is another description of a 'sacred marriage' between the king (probably Samsi-Addu of Upper Mesopotamia) and the goddess Ishtar which takes place inside the temple of Ishtar in the city of Mari. The participants include the king, the goddess Inanna, other deities, various types of priests, courtiers, singers, ecstatics and even craftsmen. Games and sports are performed by various entertainers, the 'eaters', jugglers, wrestlers and acrobats.

Other ritual information is fragmentary but provides some interesting insights. The night-until-morn bellowing shrieks mixed with a great wailing seem to indicate a mourning ceremony connected with the Venus cycle in the period between her heliacal setting at night in the east and her heliacal rising in the morning in the west. Ishtar's astral manifestation in Akkadian is Ishtar-*kakkabum* ('Ishtar-the-Star') which is found in the early second millennium but changes by the end of the millennium into Ishtar-*kakkabi* ('Ishtar-of-the-Stars'). A fragmentary bilingual *Exaltation of Ishtar* known from first millennium manuscripts (Hruška 1969), but probably composed in the late second millennium, dealt with the elevation of Ishtar by the high gods: the god of heavens, Anu; the god of the inhabited world, Enlil; and the god of the deep, Ea, in turn. Anu accepts the young maiden as his equal and spouse under the name Antu, endows her with the all me/*parṣu* in his possession and exalts her in the sky as Venus (Sumerian Dilbat, Akkadian 'Ishtar-the-Star') to be on the same level as the sun (her brother) and the moon (her father). As Anu gave her the heavens, Enlil gives her the earth, martial powers and war games, assigns her the name Queen of Nippur and surrenders to her the me/*parṣu* in his possession. Unfortunately, Ea's blessing is totally lost but it also probably concerned the mes in his possession. Thus, an explanation was given as to how Ishtar obtained the mes.

First millennium

In the first millennium, a levelling theological homogeneity can be observed among the local pantheons of Babylonia. Two major goddesses were known as the lady (*beltu*) and the queen (*šarratu*) of their home city and such appellations occur both as names of these goddesses and as epithets. Ishtar commonly took one of these roles. At Nippur, Ishtar presided as the Queen-of-Nippur while Gula was accorded the title 'lady of Nippur' (see Groneberg in this volume). At Uruk, Nanaya was 'queen of Uruk' while Ishtar was worshipped as the Lady-of-Uruk. Ishtar was further venerated as the Queen-of-Sippar and Queen-of-Larsa. In Babylon, there seems to be intentional confusion among the titles and epithets. Whereas Ishtar was known as Ishtar-of-Babylon or Lady-of-Babylon and even Queen of Babylon', Zarpanitu was worshipped as 'lady of Babylon' or 'Queen of the Esagil (temple of Marduk)'. The apparent purpose of this confusion was probably to express the notion that Ishtar-of-Babylon and Zarpanitu were not only syncretised theologically, but also thought to be absolutely identical with one another. Further steps were taken in the eighth–seventh centuries to identify Zarpanitu with Ishtar-of-Uruk and to pair her with Marduk as Beltiya. Marduk and his symbol were introduced into the temple of Eanna, the temple of Ishtar-of-Uruk, so that Marduk became consort of the goddess. This symbolised her subordination to an ideology centred politically on Babylon and theologically on the status of Marduk as ruler of the pantheon (Beaulieu 2003: 75–79).

In Babylon, the theologians created a ménage-à-trois between the central deities of the city: the national god Marduk, his consort Zarpanitum, and his paramour Ishtar-of-Babylon. This relationship is reflected in the first-millennium rituals of her cult, the so-called 'Love Lyrics', a ritual of divine adultery or jealousy, which provide short notes for movements of actors around the city of Babylon and for recitations at various locations. The main actors are Marduk playing the role of the lover, Zarpanitum playing the role of the wronged wife who reviles her rival in the most offensive language, and Ishtar-of-Babylon playing the role of the seductive woman flaunting her sexual attraction. Leick (1994: 246) has suggested that these rites might be understood as travesties of the traditional *haddašutu*-marriage rituals celebrating the harmonious conjugal love of Marduk and Zarpanitum.

While Ishtar of the Eturkalamma (her primary temple in Babylon) was the Lady-of-Babylon, there were several other temples dedicated to various Ishtar figures in the city of Babylon. Of these temples, only the Emashdari, dedicated by the Neo-Babylonian king Nabonidus to the third-millennium goddess Ishtar of Akkade, has been excavated:

> To Ishtar, the supreme, beloved of the gods, the valiant,
> Innin, goddess of battle, maker of melee,
> Radiant, lady of creation, exalted among the Igigi,
> Great among the Anunnakki, bearing awe,
> Lady whose aura covers the heavens,
> Whose rays overwhelm the wide earth,
> Ishtar of Akkade, lady of battle, she who incites fighting,
> She who dwells in the Emashdari
> Which is in the midst of Babylon, my Lady;
>
> (Ehelolf 1926: i 1–15)

The worship of Ishtar-of-Uruk waxed and waned in popularity during the first millennium in her city Uruk. First, the image of Ishtar-of-Uruk was twice abducted from the Eanna temple and, during her absence, alterations of her cult took place. In the eighth century, a representation of an 'inappropriate goddess' was installed in the Eanna temple and in seventh-century texts the name Beltiya occurs in place of Ishtar-of-Uruk pointing to the theological agenda which aimed at assimilating Ishtar-of-Uruk to Zarpanitu, and consequently to Ishtar-of-Babylon as well and suggests that the 'inappropriate goddess' may have been her Babylonian counterpart. With the return of the 'original' Ishtar-of-Uruk to Uruk under Nebuchadnezzar II, further theological reform was undertaken (Beaulieu 2003: 129–138). Finally, local theologians again reorganised the pantheon of Uruk during the Achaemenid and Seleucid periods reinstating Anu and Antu as sole patron gods of the city and demoting Ishtar to a secondary position (see Beaulieu 1992). However, rather than a ménage-à-trois of Anu-Antu-Ishtar in late Uruk, a syncretism was created between Antu and Ishtar, with Antu absorbing the attributes of Ishtar (Beaulieu 1995). Nevertheless, not only do we have many copies of the poem *The Exaltation of Ishtar* from Hellenistic Uruk, but also a description of one celebration in her honour – a procession in which Ishtar promenades together with a retinue of goddesses and her costumed cult personnel, the *kurgarru* and *assinnu*, from her temple to the *akitu*-temple on the outskirts of the city. The importance of this ritual is its royal character – the participation of the king and the Sceptre of Kingship in the procession and the action of the king who takes the hand of Ishtar and leads her into her sanctuary and seats her on her throne (Lackenbacher 1977). This royal ritual echoes that of earlier millennia in which the king was legitimised only through his relationship with the tutelary goddess of Uruk, Inanna.

Royal hymns and personal prayers directed to Ishtar for assistance are plentiful in the first millennium. In liturgical compositions, Ishtar features as *mater dolerosa* and appears as revengeful yet broken-hearted over the demise of Dumuzi/Tammuz. Her angry and capricious nature continues to need calming: 'May (various gods) pacify your heart, calm your liver'. Prayers contain entreaties for alleviation of physical and mental ills and its sources – witchcraft and sorcery – as well as social and economic problems understood as punishment for sins and iniquities, known and unknown. To regain the goddess' favour, the sufferer stresses in his/her supplication the merciful and protective nature of Ishtar while, in his/her invocation of the goddess, he/she lauds her astral manifestation Ishtar-*kakkabi*, in particular that of the morning star, *ilat šerti*, and her control of destinies, her military mien, her possession of the *parṣu* and her exaltation among the gods:

> I implore you, Lady of ladies, Goddess of goddesses
> Ishtar, queen of all the inhabited world, who governs the people . . .
> You are the luminary of heaven and earth, the valiant daughter of Sin
> (the moon-god),
> Who brandishes weapons, who prepares for battle,
> Who gathers to herself all *parṣu*, who dons the lordly tiara.
> O Mistress, splendid is your greatness, exalted over all the gods.
> Planet for the war cry, who can make harmonious brothers set at one
> another, . . .
> You render final judgement and decision, the ordinances of earth and
> heaven, . . .
> You look upon the oppressed and abused and always set them right.
> Have mercy, mistress of heaven and earth, shepherdess of the human race!
> . . .
> I myself call upon you, your exhausted, desperate, most stricken servant,
> Look upon me, mistress, accept my entreaty.
>
> (Great Prayer to Ishtar 1–9, 13, 26–27, 42–3;
> Zgoll 2003: 42–54)

In addition to these themes seen above, two prayers petition her to safeguard offspring and perhaps for conception. Ishtar thus derived her widespread popularity through her intense involvement in human affairs.

As we have seen above, Ishtar could bless and curse with equal measure. Consequently, she was invoked not only in prayers but also in mantic texts during the first millennium. Love magic and potency incantations are addressed to Ishtar for her intervention for the afflicted or frustrated lover and even to secure brisk trade at a tavern. In addition to their story retold in the liturgy, the tragic relationship of Inanna and Dumuzi is enshrined in a series of incantation rituals related to rites for the month of Tammuz, the month when Dumuzi's death was mourned:

> In the month of Tammuz, when Ishtar causes the people of the land to weep for her lover Dumuzi, (and when every) man's family is assembled at an appropriate place, Ishtar appears and deals with the affairs of people. She takes away disease

and she causes disease. On the 28th, the day of the byre, you dedicate to Ishtar a vulva of lapis lazuli with a little gold star. You pronounce the name of the sick person.

(Farber 1977: 140–141 AII a 3–10)

Among the incantations to be recited are those addressed to Ishtar to plead on behalf of the sufferer to Dumuzi, and among the rituals to be performed is the symbolic offering of a stylised vulva, which illustrates the connection between sexuality and Ishtar, and a star which highlights the astral aspect of Ishtar.

THE GODDESS

We have traced the development of the conception of Sumerian Inanna and her Akkadian counterpart Ishtar from their first appearance in the cuneiform records and have examined the diverse elements of the personality of the goddess. We have seen that her most archaic and basic aspect of astral dimorphism is the source of the ambiguities and contradictions in her character including her apparent androgyny. In like manner, she held dominion over all polarity of behaviours from capricious to caring, and represented both order and disorder, structure and antistructure. Her bi-polarity was founded on a natural phenomenon: the planet Venus appears twice in its course, once in the east, once in the west, as morning and as evening star. Her very mutability may have intrigued the ancient Mesopotamians and led to the conception of Inanna/Ishtar as the one and only divine entity able to embody such opposing aspects.

NOTES

1 The etymology of both Inanna's and Ishtar's names is uncertain. The name Inanna was explained by ancient as well as modern scholars as deriving from nin-an-na 'lady of Heaven' [(n)in 'lady' + an 'heaven' + a(k) genitive] (Hallo 1995:768) while Ishtar (originally 'Ashtar, a form with no gender marking) has been derived from the root 'ṯr, 'to be rich' (Krebernik 1983: 31, no. 805). Note the litany of her names in the Ishtar (Queen of Nippur) hymn beginning with Ninanna 'Queen of Heaven' (Lambert 1982: 198f., iii 52ff. and see comment to line 211). For a discussion on the original form of her name in Sumerian as Innin, see Beaulieu 2003: 116, 122f. Note, however, the suggestion by Selz (2000: 29, 33f.), basing himself on the third millennium material that In(n)in(a) is of Semitic origin, most probably a deity of war.

2 For this and other Sumerian litarary compositions, see Black, J. A., Cunningham, G., Ebeling, J., Flückiger-Hawker, E., Robson, E., Taylor, J. and Zólyomi, G. *The Electronic Text Corpus of Sumerian Literature* (http:/etcsl.orinst.ox.ac.uk, Oxford 1998–2006 (abbreviated ETCSL).

3 Even in her male role, she never becomes fully male, but seems to be a female with male gender characteristics. For a possible visual image of a bearded Inanna/Ishtar in the third millennium and the written descriptions of a bearded Ishtar in first millennium astrological sources, see Reiner 1995: 5, fig. 2 and 6 with notes 14–16. See further Beaulieu 2003: 136f. and note his references to possible two-faced male-female images.

4 It should be also noted that the mountains at the end of the earth and the netherworld were a continuum in Mesopotamian thought. The realms of the dead were probably at the foothills of the mountain lands rather than under the ground.

5 Verb e_{11} describes vertical movement.

6 Another conundrum comes from the cuneiform writing system. The fact is that the names of the Akkadian goddess, Ashtar, is written syllabically consistently *aš-dar* in personal names and just as consistently as a logogram INANNA in all other contexts. Only from the second

345

millennium onwards do the two writings alternate in such a way as to prove that the cuneiform sign INANNA should be read *Ishtar* in Akkadian context.

7 Similar names expressing this relationship between a male god and a man also occur as *Abi-enšim-Urash* 'Urash is a father of the weak (male)'.

BIBLIOGRAPHY

Selected bibliography on Inanna/Ishtar in general

Abusch, T., 1995, 'Ishtar', in van der Toorn, K., Becking, B. and van der Horst, P.W. (eds), *Dictionary of Deities and Demons in the Bible* (Leiden, New York, Köln): 848–852; reprinted in *NIN, Journal of Near Eastern Gender Studies*, 1 (2000): 23–27.

Bahrani, Z., 2000, 'The Whore of Babylon', *NIN, Journal of Near Eastern Gender Studies*, 1: 95–106.

Beaulieu, P.-A., 2003, *The Pantheon of Uruk during the Neo-Babylonian Period* (Leiden, Boston).

Bruschweiler, F., 1987, *Inanna: La déesse triomphante et vaincue dans la cosmologie sumérienne* (Leuven, Geneva).

Colbow, G., 1991, *Die kriegerische Ištar – Zu den Erscheinungsformen bewaffneter Gottheiten zwwischen der Mitte des 3. und der Mitte des 2. Jahrtausends* (Munich).

Farber, W., 1977, *Beschwörungsrituale an Ištar und Dumuzi* (Wiesbaden).

Frymer-Kensky, T., 2000, 'Lolita-Inanna', *NIN, Journal of Near Eastern Gender Studies* 1: 91–94.

Glassner, J.-J., 1992, 'Inanna et les me', in de J. Ellis, M. (ed.), *Nippur at the Centennial* (Philadelphia): 55–86.

Groneberg, B., 1986, 'Die sumerisch-akkadische Inanna/Ištar: Hermaphrodotos?', *Welt des Orients* 17: 25–46.

——, 1997, *Lob der Ištar, Gebet und Ritual an die altbabylonische Venusgöttin* (Groningen).

Hallo, W. W. and van Dijk, J. J. A., 1968, *The Exaltation of Inanna* (New Haven).

Hansen, D. P., 2002, 'Through the Love of Ishtar', in Al-Gailani Werr, L., Curtis, J., Martin, H., McMahon, A., Oates, J. and Reade, J. (eds), *Of Pots and Plans: Papers on the Archaeology and History of Mesopotamia and Syria presented to David Oates in Honour of his 75th Birthday* (London): 91–112.

Harris, R., 1991, 'Inanna-Ishtar as Paradox and a Coincidence of Opposites', *History of Religions* 30: 261–278.

Heimpel, W., 1982, 'A Catalog of Near Eastern Venus Deities', *Syro-Mesopotamian Studies* 4: 59–72.

Hruška, B., 1969, 'Das spätbabylonische Lehrgedicht "Inannas Erhöhung"', *Archiv Orientalní* 37: 473–522.

Lackenbacher, S., 1977, 'Un nouveau fragment de la "Fête d'Ištar"', *RA* 71: 39–50.

Lambert, W. G., 1975, 'The Cult of Ishtar of Babylon', in *Le temple et le culte* (CRRAI XXXVII, Leiden): 104–106.

——, 1982, 'The Hymn to the Queen of Nippur', in van Driel, G., Krispijn, T. J. H. *et al.* (eds), *Zikir Šumim: Assyriological Studies presented to F.R. Kraus* (Leiden): 173–218.

Leick, G., 1994, *Sex and Eroticism in Mesopotamian Literature* (London).

Selz, G. J., 2000, 'Five Divine Ladies: Thoughts on Inanna(k), Ištar, In(n)in(a), Annunītum, and Anat, and the Origin of the Title "Queen of Heaven"', *NIN* 1: 29–62.

Steinkeller, P., 1998, 'Inanna's Archaic Symbol', in Braun, J. *et al.* (eds), *Written on Clay and Stone. Ancient Near Eastern Studies Presented to Krystyna Szarzyńska on the Occasion of her 80th Birthday* (Warsaw): 87–100.

Szarzyńska, K., 1993, 'Offerings for the Goddess Inanna in Archaic Uruk', *RA* 87: 7–28.

——, 2000, 'Cult of the Goddess Inanna in Archaic Uruk', *NIN, Journal of Near Eastern Gender Studies* 1: 63–74.

Vanstiphout, H. L. H., 1984, 'Inanna/Ishtar as a Figure of Controversy', in Kippenberg, H. G. *et al.* (eds), *Struggles of Gods* (Berlin, New York and Amsterdam): 225–238.

Westenholz, J. G., 2000, 'King by Love of Inanna – an image of female empowerment?', *NIN, Journal of Near Eastern Gender Studies* 1: 75–89.

Wilcke, C., 1976, 'Inanna/Ištar (Mesopotamien), A. Philologisch', *Reallexikon der Assyriologie* 5: 74–87.

Zgoll, A., 1997, 'Inana als nugig', *ZA* 87: 181–95.

——, 2003, *Die Kunst des Betens, Form und Funktion, Theologie und Psychagogik in babylonisch-assyrischen Handerhebungsgebeten an Ištar* (AOAT 308, Münster).

Bibliographic references in article

Beaulieu, P.-A., 1992, 'Antiquarian Theology in Seleucid Uruk', *ASJ* 14: 47–75.

——, 1995, 'Theological and Philological Speculations on the Names of the Goddess Antu', *Orientalia* 64: 187–213.

Ehelolf, H., 1926, 'Die Bauurkunde des Königs Nabonid, Umschrift und Übersetzung', *WVDOG* 47: 136–137.

Falkenstein, A., 1964, 'Sumerische religiöse Texte, 6. Ein sumerischer Liebeszauber', *ZA* 56: 113–129.

George, A. R., 2000, 'Four Temple Rituals from Babylon', in George, A. R. and Finkel, I. L. (eds), *Wisdom, Gods and Literature, Studies in Assyriology in Honour of W. G. Lambert* (Winona Lake, Indiana): 259–299.

Hallo, W. W., 1995, 'Scurrilous Etymologies', in Wright, D. P., Freedman, D. N. and Hurvitz, A. (eds), *Pomegranates and Golden Bells, Studies in Biblical, Jewish and Near Eastern Ritual, Law, and Literature in Honor of Jacob Milgrom* (Winona Lake): 767–776.

Katz, D., 1996, 'How Dumuzi Became Inanna's Victim: On the Formation of "Inanna's Descent"', *ASJ* 18: 93–102.

——, 2003, *The Image of the Netherworld in the Sumerian Sources* (Bethesda, MD).

Krebernik, M., 1983, 'Zu Syllabar und Orthographie der lexikalischen Texte aus Ebla', *ZA* 73: 178–236.

Reiner, E., 1995, *Astral Magic in Babylonia* (Philadelphia).

CHAPTER TWENTY-FOUR

THE BABYLONIAN
GOD MARDUK

——— ·◆· ———

Takayoshi Oshima

This chapter will be discussing Marduk's rise to supremacy in the Mesopotamian pantheon, various aspects of this deity through an analysis of ancient literature, and the history of Marduk's cult centre. The god Marduk was important not just because he was a god of high status in Babylonia, but also because his multiple responsibilities were deeply related to the daily life of the ancient Mesopotamians. He was the king of the gods, the architect of the heavens and the earth, and the creator of the life. Furthermore, different ancient texts suggest that Marduk was also the supplier of water, the god of abundance, and the saviour of people.

MARDUK'S RISE TO SUPREMACY

The god Marduk was the patron deity of the city of Babylon, and therefore the history of Marduk is intimately related to the history of Babylon. Just as political power of Babylon grew, so did the position of its national god, Marduk, who was also gradually elevated within the polytheistic religious system of Babylonia. By the end of the second millennium he had become the Babylonian god *par excellence* and was simply called *bēl*, 'the Lord'.[1]

Marduk had not always been the god of supremacy. Although it is likely that he was worshipped already in the Early Dynastic period, documentation about him before the Old Babylonian period is scarce and not conclusive.[2] This fact perhaps reflects the relatively insignificant position of Marduk and his city Babylon in the early history of Mesopotamia.

Marduk's rise began when Hammurabi of the First Dynasty of Babylon (1792–1750) put wide areas of Mesopotamia under his control by conquering Eshnunna, part of Elam, Larsa, Assur, and Mari.[3] The rise of the political power of the Babylonian king prompted a new theological view – Marduk as sovereign as manifested in the prologue of the *Codex Hammurabi* i 1–26:

> When the august god Anu, king of the Anunnaku deities, and the god Enlil, lord of heaven and earth, who determines the destinies of the land, allotted supreme power over all peoples to the god Marduk, the firstborn son of the god

Ea, exalted him among the Igigu deities, named the city of Babylon with its august name and made it supreme within the regions of the world, and established for him within it eternal kingship whose foundations are fixed as heaven and earth.

(Roth 1995: 76)

The god gradually absorbed the identities of a number of different deities as he gained importance. One of the first gods to lose his identity to Marduk was Asalluhi, the god of incantation, the divine exorcist, and the local deity of Ku'ar a village near Eridu. Asalluhi was the son of Enki/Ea, the god of the underground waters, wisdom, and magic and third in rank after An/Anu and Enlil in the Mesopotamian pantheon.[4] Although the process of the Marduk = Asalluhi syncretism may have started already in the early second millennium, it was probably only fully established late in the reign of Hammurabi. Through the syncretism with Asalluhi, Marduk gained the position as the son of Enki/Ea in the Mesopotamian pantheon. By the end of the Middle Babylonian period, Marduk assumed 50 names, such as Tutu, Shazu, and Enbilulu in addition to Asalluhi.[5] Like Asalluhi, they were originally the names of different deities, but after the syncretism with Marduk, each name presented different aspects of Marduk, such as the god of water, the god of fertility, and the saviour.

From the late Old-Babylonian period onwards, Marduk gained popularity among the populace. For instance, the personal names containing the divine name Marduk came to form the second largest group after the god Sin in the theophoric names known from the late Old-Babylonian period.[6] He is also featured in Kassite private cylinder seals, with short prayers to different deities seeking personal benefit, welfare, and salvation. More than 60 out of around 150 available prayers of this kind are addressed to Marduk.[7] It is remarkable too that 15 such cylinder seals from the Kassite period Nippur, the city of Enlil, bear prayers to Marduk while only one cylinder seal contains a prayer to Enlil.[8] Incidentally, although Enlil at that time still occupied the highest position in the Babylonian pantheon Marduk is often invoked as the 'creator' or 'chief of the heavens and the earth' in these short prayers. This fact suggests that the notion of Marduk as the god of supremacy first started at the level of personal belief during the Kassite period[9] and became the official view of the Babylonian court later, probably in the twelfth century.

After the relatively long and stable period under the Kassite kings, Babylonia suffered foreign aggressions of two other great powers – the Assyrians and the Elamites. Tukulti-Ninurta I (1244–1208) was the first to attack Babylon. He destroyed the city wall of Babylon, captured the statue of Marduk, and controlled Babylon for three decades.[10] The series of raids launched by the Elamite kings were even more traumatic. They brought chaos and destruction to the cities of Babylonia. The Elamites under Shutruk-Nahhunte I (1185–1155) and his son, Kudur-Nahhunte (1155–1150), plundered the great cities of Mesopotamia and carried away ancient monuments such as Hammurabi's Law Code and the statues of the gods from the sanctuaries of Mesopotamia including Marduk and his consort Zarpanitu as booty.[11] Kudur-Nahhunte also put an end to the Kassite dynasty by taking the last king, Enlil-nadin-ahi, into captivity.

After some decades of political chaos, Nebuchadrezzar I (1124–1103), from the Second Dynasty of Isin, ascended the Babylonian throne. Although the historical fact

Figure 24.1   Drawing based on a cylinder seal of Marduk dedicated by the Babylonian king, Marduk-zakir-shumi. Drawing by Takayoshi Oshima. (The object is in the Staatlisches Museum zu Berlin.)

is that Marduk's statue had been captured by the Elamites, Nebuchadrezzar claims in an ancient text that Marduk had ordered his own departure to Elam because during the reign of his predecessor, Enlil-nadin-ahi, 'good had departed and evil was regular, the Lord [Marduk] became angry and got furious'.[12] Another ancient text, 'The Marduk Prophecy', probably also composed during the reign of Nebuchadrezzar I, states that the people suffered famine and political unrest after Marduk and other gods had left Babylonia for Elam.[13] The Babylonians must have faced a serious loss of morale.

One of the priorities of Nebuchadrezzar I was, not surprisingly, reconciliation with Marduk, i.e., the recovery of Marduk from Elam. Despite the failure in his first attempt, Nebuchadrezzar led his army, surprising the Elamites by attacking in summer, and successfully retrieved the statue of Marduk.[14] Although his victory over Elam did not bring long-lasting peace to the Babylonians, it must have boosted their confidence. Various literary works were produced to commemorate this act of bravery and the return of Marduk to Babylon.[15] It is commonly accepted that the creation epic, known as *Enuma Elish*, which canonises Marduk's supreme position in the Mesopotamian pantheon, was also composed during Nebuchadrezzar I's reign. With his exaltation during this period, Marduk assumed the name *bēl*, 'the Lord', as his proper name.

LITERATURE

In addition to a large number of religious texts (hymns, prayers, incantations, and lamentations), there are two major long literary works of Marduk – *Enuma Elish*, 'When Above', and *Ludul Bel Nemeqi*, 'Let Me Praise the Lord of Wisdom'.[16] Each composition presents a completely different image of Marduk. *Enuma Elish* speaks of Marduk's bravery in the battle against Tiamat ('the Sea'), the creation of the universe, and Marduk's accession to divine kingship, while *Ludlul Bel Nemeqi* is a poetic monologue telling the sufferings of a man and his salvation by Marduk.

ENUMA ELISH[17] – MARDUK AS THE KING OF THE GODS

The epilogue of *Enuma Elish* describes the composition as a 'song of Marduk [who] defeated Tiamat and took the kingship' (VII 161–162). In other words the *Enuma Elish* tells how Marduk gained the supremacy in the Mesopotamian pantheon and how his city, Babylon, became the 'capital' of the world. It is commonly accepted that *Enuma Elish* was composed after the victory of Nebuchadrezzar I over Elam and the return of Marduk from the exile,[18] but an Old-Babylonian[19] and a Kassite period date[20] have also been suggested. The latest possible date of composition is no later than the tenth century BC as some manuscripts found in Assur are written in Middle-Assyrian script.

We now know from Late Babylonian ritual instructions that *Enuma Elish* was chanted in front of Marduk's statue on the fourth day of the month Nisannu (Month I, March–April)[21] and the month Kislimu (Month IX, November–December), during the *Akitu*-festivals.[22] Although *Enuma Elish* was not the climax of the *Akitu* festivals of Babylon, the festivals served to affirm the position of Marduk as the king of the gods, and that of Babylon as the centre of the universe by including recitation of *Enuma Elish*.

The plot of the story is as follows: Apsu, 'the Deep Water', and Tiamat, 'the Sea', are the first gods, and the father and the mother of the gods. After the gods of the younger generation become numerous, they start making too much noise and disturb Apsu. Following the advice of Mummu, his vizier, Apsu decides to exterminate his children. However, Ea, of the fourth generation from Apsu and Tiamat, learns their plan and kills Apsu by means of an incantation. Ea builds Apsu, his temple, using the corpse of the god Apsu, wherein, Marduk is born as the son of Ea.

After having been accused for coolly allowing the death of Apsu, Tiamat decides to wage war against her children. She creates 11 creatures as her army, chooses Kingu as her consort and the military commander. Tiamat also grants the Tablet of Destiny to Kingu.[23] None of the younger gods, not even Ea, dare to confront Tiamat. When asked, Marduk agrees to wage battle against Tiamat, but he demands the kingship in return. The gods can do nothing but accept his request. Marduk fights against Tiamat and her army, and defeats her. Marduk, then, fashions the world by using the corpse of Tiamat, and builds Babylon as its centre.

After the creation of the universe, Marduk assumes the kingship and the gods recite his Fifty Names. The last name, *bēl mātāti*, 'the Lord of the Lands', was originally an epithet of Enlil, the god of the ancient city of Nippur and the traditional Mesopotamian supreme deity. This name marks the canonization of Marduk's status as the 'King of the Gods' and his take-over of Enlil's authority.[24] *Enuma Elish* also acted as theo-political propaganda affirming the position of Babylon as the new political and/or spiritual centre instead of the ancient Sumerian city of Nippur.

In certain Mesopotamian traditions, the water of the Sea (Akk. *tâmtu*/(*tiāmtu*) was also identified with the underground water.[25] In *Atra-hasis*, the Babylonian Flood Story, Enlil attempts, among other measures, to wipe out the noisy human beings by bringing famine, he blocks the rains and the seasonal floods from emerging from the deep. Enki/Ea finds a way to save the people. Although he was supposed to guard it, Enki/Ea allowed the Bolt – The Snare of the Sea – to be broken in half, letting the water and agricultural products escape, and thus end the drought.[26] A similar concept of the Sea as the source of underground water is attested in *Enuma Elish*. Tiamat was initially the mother-goddess, the gods are her children. But after her death, Marduk creates the deep springs by drilling into Tiamat's head, and the Tigris and the Euphrates by opening her eyes. This means that the water running on the surface of the earth was considered ultimately to be the water of the Sea. If so, the choice of Tiamat as the opponent of Marduk might not be just coincidence or a reflection of a historical event. The motif – Marduk subduing the chaotic waters (Tiamat) and turning them instead into a source of fertility (springs and rivers) – is a reflection of his aspects as the god of watercourses and fertility.[27]

LUDLUL BEL NEMEQI[28] – MARDUK AS THE DIVINE SAVIOUR

While *Enuma Elish* speaks of the victory of Marduk over Tiamat and his rise to the supremacy, *Ludlul Bel Nemeqi* presents Marduk as the ultimate divine saviour of human beings. The theological base of this composition is the Babylonian belief in protective spirits and especially of a personal god who, like a guardian angel, protects his protégé and keeps away attacks of evil spirits which were thought to cause illness.

They were also responsible for teaching ethical behaviour to their human wards. In earlier periods the ancient Mesopotamians worshipped their personal gods as their sole saviours from sufferings.[29] However, it seems that a new belief – Marduk surpassing the personal gods in the punishment and the salvation of people – was formed, probably in the Old Babylonian period. It is likely that *Ludlul Bel Nemeqi* is the manifestation of this new belief. In *Ludlul Bel Nemeqi*, the personal gods and protective spirits act according to the wishes of Marduk, in other words, they are somehow extensions of Marduk's power. The date of composition of this work is probably the Kassite period.[30]

Ludlul Bel Nemeqi is written in the first person with the narrator, Shubshi-meshre-Shakkan, presenting himself as a rich man of high rank. He claims that he never neglected his prayers or forgot to make offerings.[31] One day, however, hardship strikes him. The narrator claims that his misery started when Marduk decided to punish him and caused his protective spirits and his personal gods to leave him. He lost all – his property, friends, family, physical strength, and health. Illness takes him prisoner. He turns to his personal gods and protective spirits, but they do not come to rescue him. He attempts an exorcism to expel evil-demons. He asks diviners to find out what his sin was. But no one can help him. His family was already conducting his funeral before his death. He saw his grave open, he heard the funeral laments.

Drifting between consciousness and unconsciousness, the narrator sees men and a woman of outstanding appearance in a series of dreams. He says that each one took part in cleansing and absolution. At the end, Urnindinlugga, an incantation priest, announces that he had been sent by Marduk to show the sign of salvation. He is then delivered from his suffering.

The climax opens with the testimony of Shubshi-meshre-Shakkan on the power of Marduk. He says that it was Marduk who saved him from this most difficult condition. Marduk imposed all the sufferings to Shubshi-meshre-Shakkan, but when his anger was calmed and he took the prayers, he absolved his sins. Shubshi-meshre-Shakkan then goes to Esagila, the temple of Marduk, and meets (the images of) Marduk and his consort Zarpanitu. He offers prayers and offerings as tokens of his gratitude. The Babylonians who saw him also proclaimed the greatness of Marduk's mercy and salvation.

Due to the similarity of motif, this poem is often compared with the Book of Job and even referred to as 'The Babylonian Job' or 'The Poem of the Righteous Sufferer' by modern scholars. These are, however, misnomers as there is a fundamental difference between the Babylonian and biblical worlds. Job in the Bible does not doubt his righteousness and says that all misery brought upon him was a trial for his faith. On the other hand, although Shubshi-meshre-Shakkan claims that he did not forget prayers to the gods, he is sorry and asks forgiveness for his unknown crimes. Hence, he was delivered not because he spoke the right words about Marduk, but due to Marduk's mercy.

Ludlul Bel Nemeqi teaches that mankind could never know exactly what the gods wished of them, i.e., that there was no human way of knowing absolute right and wrong. Thus mankind was destined to sin, often unintentionally. For instance, Shubshi-meshre-Shakkan says:

I wish I knew that these things were pleasing to one's god!
What is proper to oneself is an offence to one's god.

What seems bad in one's own heart is proper to one's god.
Who knows the will of the gods in the heavens?
Who understands the plans of the underworld gods?
Where have people learnt the way of a god?

(II 33–38)

A similar concept is also attested in a prayer to Marduk of Old Babylonian period origin[32] which was recited for the sake of an individual who was also suffering from deadly diseases, just like Shubshi-meshre-Shakkan:

Who was not negligent? Who has not bo[rn any guilt]?
Who was so on his guard so as not to make a mistake?
Where is the one who was so careful has not born any guilt?
They did not know their invisible [*sin*(?)],
The god is the one who reveals what is Good and what is [B]ad.
The one who has his god, his sins are [se]nt away,
The one who does not have his god, his crimes are many.
When you, his god, are at his side,
His speech is well chosen, his word is honest.

(Prayer to Marduk, no. 1, lines 104–112)

These passages clearly suggest that no man can be 'righteous' without the guidance of gods, since only divine beings understand what is 'Good' and 'Bad', i.e., no one mortal can comprehend absolute ethics.

If the righteousness of a man is not the issue, what is the main subject of *Ludlul Bel Nemeqi*? The hint to this question is found in the hymnic introduction of this work – the first 40 lines of *Ludlul Bel Nemeqi*. Each couplet of this section repeatedly offers praises to Marduk as the one whose anger is devastating although he is merciful enough to save all. In fact, this is what happened to Shubshi-meshre-Shakkan. It is Marduk who punishes Shubshi-meshre-Shakkan, but it also Marduk who saves Shubshi-meshre-Shakkan after he is appeased by repentance and prayer. In other words, the main theme of this story is that, although one may experience severe hardship due to crimes committed, Marduk is merciful enough to absolve the sins and deliver the repentant from any misery. Hence, the above discussed prayer to Marduk from the Old Babylonian period compares his compassion with that of a father: 'Your benevolent attention is pleasant, your mercy is like that of a father' (Prayer to Marduk no. 1, lines 10/12).

The ancient Babylonians sought Marduk's mercy as they knew that his forgiveness was unfailing and unconditional, like a father's to his son. *Ludlul Bel Nemeqi* is a testimony to this ultimate forgiveness and compassion of Marduk.

Marduk kept this aspect of the saviour of people, even after his rise to the supremacy in the Mesopotamian pantheon. There are a large number of so-called *Shuila*-prayers to Marduk attested.[33] These prayers were used in the rituals for absolution of sins and salvation from hardship and in the anti-witchcraft rituals. Some of the prayers to Marduk offer praises to him as the king of the gods or the creator of the universe but at the same time they also seek Marduk's mercy and forgiveness in order to escape hardship or to be redeemed. Enlil, the traditional Mesopotamian supreme deity, on the other hand, was hardly invoked when one sought absolution of his sins and redemption in prayers of this kind.[34] This fact suggests that the ancient people turned to Marduk in hardship probably not because of his power or supreme authority but because of Marduk's unfailing compassion as witnessed by Shubshi-meshre-Shakkan in addition to his role as the divine exorcist under the name Asalluhi.

CULT CENTRE OF MARDUK

Marduk's main cult centre in Babylon was the temple Esagila ('House whose Top is High'), with its ziggurat Etemenanki ('House, the Foundation Platform of Heavens and Underworld').[35] We do not know how early the origin of this temple is. However, with countless rebuilding and restorations, Esagila served not only as the core of worship of Marduk but also as the centre of intellectual and economic activities over two millennia until it finally fell into disuse in the third century AD.[36]

The German archaeological team headed by R. Koldewey unearthed, although not entirely, the huge building complex of Esagila which measured about 170 m × 110 m when complete.[37] The massive structure of Esagila, in addition to other monumental buildings, such as the ziggurat Etemenanki and the Ishtar-gate, is a manifestation of the wealth and the importance of Babylon as the capital of Babylonia.

Herodotus (183) records 'a great golden image of Zeus (Belus) sitting at a great golden table', and the footstool and the chair of gold. According to the Chaldeans, Herodotus continues, the total amount of the gold was 'eight hundred talents' weight'. This account of Marduk's temple is not entirely accurate but not far from the truth either. The ancient temple that dated from the times of Hammurabi had been destroyed by the Assyrian king Sennacherib (704–681) in 698 BC. Although Esarhadon (680–669), the successor of Sennacherib, had started rebuilding the temple early in his reign, it seems that the glory of Esagila was fully restored only in the time of the Chaldean king Nebuchadrezzar II (604–562). In the account of the refurbishment of Eumusha ('House of Command'), Marduk's cella in Esagila,[38] Nebuchadrezzar claims that 'I overlaid the furnishings of Esagila with red gold, and the processional boats with yellow gold and (precious) stones like the stars of the heavens'.[39]

The images of the gods played central roles in official cults as well as in private worship by being involved in different daily rituals, annual ceremonies and festivals, and occasional religious practices such as exorcism or absolution rituals. The ancients understood that the cult statues were manifestation of the divine presence. In other words, in the case of Marduk, the ancients saw his cult statue as the living image of Marduk himself wherein he was present. Hence, his statue also received the appropriate treatment – for example, it was clothed with expensive garments and presented with large food and drinks on a daily basis.[40]

Despite Herodotus' reference to a solid gold statue of 'Zeus Belus', (meaning Marduk), the main cult statue of Marduk was made of a wood overlaid with gold and inlaid with various precious/semi-precious stones. The Erra Epic[41] refers to the *mesu*-tree as the main material of Marduk's image:

> Where is the *mesu*-tree, the flesh of gods, appropriate to the king of a[ll],
> The holly tree, magnificent young man, which is suitable for the
>   lordship . . .?

Some statues of Marduk were made of this type of wood, but other materials were also used.[42]

The *Akitu*-festivals, particularly that of the month of Nisannu (the first month in the Babylonian calendar, corresponding to March/April in our calender), which was also known as the New Year Festival, occupied the most important position in the official cult activities in Babylon. The statues of other deities including Nabu, the god of Borsippa and the son of Marduk, Anu, Enlil, and Ea also participated in the *Akitu*-festival of the first month of Babylon. Most of the rituals of this festival were conducted by the priests in Esagila where very few people had access, but the citizens of Babylon also had the chance to see Marduk. On the eighth day of Nisannu, his statue left Esagila escorted by the king of Babylon and was carried in the Great Procession through the Procession Road of Marduk and the Ishtar-gate to the *Akitu*-temple located outside of the city.[43] This procession was the climax of the *Akitu*-festival of Nisannu[44] and was also the moment when Marduk revealed the omen of the year to the people of Babylon.[45] This procession was important for the rulers of Babylon too. Escorting Marduk by holding his hand demonstrated to its citizens the monarch's 'good' relation with the patron deity of Babylon.[46] On the tenth day, the people brought offerings, tributes, and booty of war to the presence of Marduk in the *Akitu*-temple.[47] These offerings brought to Marduk during the festival were the source of wealth of Esagila and sustained its activity even after the loss of Babylonian independence in 539 BC.[48]

It seems that the cult centre of Marduk in Babylon survived about 800 years after the fall of the Neo-Babylonian empire. Although the surrounding city was no longer inhabited already in the mid-first century AD,[49] a Jewish rabbi Rav from the early third century AD refers to the temple of Bel in Babylon and the temple of Nabo in Borsippa as the 'permanent temples of idolatry', explaining that these temples were 'still standing, and people pray there all year around'.[50] Although Esagila was not taken seriously by foreign kings probably since the mid-first century AD,[51] the passages from the Babylonian Talmud denote that the worship of Marduk was still conducted in the early third century AD.

NOTES

1 Non-cuneiform texts, such as the Bible, the Babylonian Talmud, Herodotus, Pliny, etc. also refer to Marduk by this name.

2 A votive inscription of unknown provenance, YOS 9, no. 2, refers to a builder of the temple of ^dAMAR.UTU, the most common writing of the divine name Marduk. For a recent edition of the text, see Gelb and Kienast 1990: 34–35. Further, a fragment of a god list from Abu Salabikh mentions ^dUD-AMAR which could be an early writing for the later ^dAMAR.UTU. Biggs 1974: pl. 48, no. 89, col. i', 2'. For the further discussion, see Sommerfeld 1982: 19–21 and Alberti 1985: 13, 276.

3 Kuhrt 1995: 109.

4 For a general discussion of Enki/Ea, see E. Weidner, 'Enki (Ea)', *Reallexikon der Assyriologie* 2: 374–381; Black and Green 1992: 75–76.

5 There are two lists of the Fifty Names of Marduk attested: (1) *Enuma Elish*, VI 121–VII 144 (see Foster 2005: 473–484); and (2) An=*Anum* II, 185–235 (see Litke 1998: 89–95). Although the names listed are similar there are some minor differences between the two.

6 Sommerfeld 1979–1981: 97–100.

7 Sommerfeld 1979–1981: 100. For the reference of the cylinder seals from the Kassite period, see Sommerfeld 1982: 156–157, n. 1.

8 W.G. Lambert, in Matthews 1992, *passim*.

9 Lambert 1984: 3.

10 Kuhrt 1995: 355–358. See also Brinkman 1968: 86–87.

11 Kuhrt 1995: 372–373. See also Brinkman 1968: 86–90.

12 Lambert 1967: 128–130, 15–16.

13 The Marduk Prophecy, i 18′–ii 11. For an English translation and references of the Marduk Prophecy, see Foster 2005: 388–391. Cf. also Lambert 1967: 128–130, 19–21. Like another text of Nebuchadrezzar quoted above, the Marduk Prophecy also demonstrates a notion or opinion of the past event from the point of view of Nebuchadrezzar's court.

14 See Foster 2005: 383–384.

15 See Foster 2005: 376–391.

16 Both texts are very often referred to by their ancient titles *Enuma Elish* and *Ludlul Bel Nemeqi*, rather than modern titles. The ancient intellectuals generally used the incipits of different texts as the titles of the works just like the Hebrew Bible.

17 For a recent English translation and reference, see Foster 2005: 436–486.

18 Lambert 1984: 4–6.

19 Dalley 1991: 228–230. See also Dalley 1997: 163–171, esp. 171.

20 Jacobsen 1976: 165–191, esp. 189–190; Sommerfeld 1982: 175.

21 Thureau-Dangin 1921: 136, 282.

22 Çagirgan and Lambert 1991–1993: 96, 62–63. The *Akitu*-festival was also carried out in Tashritu (Month VII, September–October) in Babylon. See Cohen 1993: 451. It seems that the *Akitu*-festival was originally an agricultural fertility festival that took place for different gods in ancient Mesopotamian cities throughout history. Each city had its own dates and rituals for this festival. See Cohen 1993: 401. For more recent studies of the *Akitu* Festival, see Bidmead 2002 and Linssen 2004.

23 For the Tablet of Destinies, see Black and Green 1992: 173.

24 Lambert 1964: 9ff.

25 Note that the Akkadian word *tâmtu* also indicates 'lake', in other words, water being salty or not was not the criteria of the definition of 'sea' in the ancient Mesopotamian world. Note also the Hebrew cognate *yam* that also indicates 'sea' as well as 'lake'.

26 Lambert and Millard 1969: 118–121 x rev. ii 9′–23′, and *passim*.

27 Note that under the name Neberu, following pleas are offered in *Enuma Elish*, VII 132–134:

> May he (= Marduk under the name Neberu) overcome Tiamat, he shall keep
>   the days of her life short,
>   in the future time of mankind, with the passing of times,
> May she be away always, May she be distant forever.

These appear to allude to the destructive power of earthly water, i.e., flood, rather than the sea or the goddess Tiamat. Marduk as the god of the watercourse, cf. Abusch 1995, 'Marduk', 1015–1016.)

28 For a recent translation see Foster 2005: 392–409.

29 *The Sumerian Man and His God*, see Klein 2003: 573–575, and for a recent translation and references of *the Babylonian Man and his God*, see Foster 2005: 148–150. For further discussion on the belief in the personal god and *Ludlul Bel Nemeqi* see Moran 2002: 182–200.

30 Lambert 1960: 21.

31 An ancient text known as 'The Counsels of Wisdom' instructs to offer sacrifice and prayers to the (personal) gods in order to secure a prosperous and long life. See Lambert 1960: 104–105, lines 135–147.

32 W.G. Lambert titled this prayer 'Prayer to Marduk, no. 1', and published in *Archiv für Orientforschung* 19: 55–60. His edition serves as the most recent comprehensive edition of this text, and so is used as the base of our discussion here. For a recent English translation and references, see Foster 2005: 611–616.

33 Mayer 1976: 394–400.

34 Only two so-called *Shuila* prayers to Enlil are known so far, see Mayer 1976: 384–385. Note also that only one short prayer to Enlil, engraved on a cylinder seal, is attested so far. See above.

35 Cf. Herodotus, I 183.

36 The earliest documentation of Esagila is the date formula of the year 10 of Sabium, Horsnell 1999: 70–71. For a short discussion of restoration and rebuilding of Esagila, see George 1993: 139–140, no. 967.

37 They also found a wall ten metres high.

38 George 1993: 156, no. 1176.

39 Langdon 1912: 126–127, col. iii, 8–10.

40 For the attitude of the ancient Babylonians to the statues of the deities, see Oppenheim 1977: 183–198. For the removal of the statue of Marduk, see above. A god also could leave his statue when the statue lost his divine glory or was totally destroyed. In such cases, the statue was repaired or remade if it was substantially damaged through a series of careful rituals. See Walker and Dick 2001: 6.

41 For a recent translation and references, see Foster 2005: 880–911.

42 See W.G. Lambert, 'Processions to the Akitu House', *Révue d'Assyriologie* 91 (1997), pp. 75–77, lines 1–7.

43 Cohen 1993: 439. See also Linssen 2004: 83–86.

44 For instance, The *Akitu Chronicle* records the interruptions of the *Akitu* festival by solely repeating the sentence 'Nabu did not come from Borsippa for the procession of Bel (and) Bel did not come out'. See Grayson 1975: 35–36 and *passim*. Note that The *Nabonidus Chronicle* also records the interruptions of the *Akitu* festival by the same sentence, see Grayson, ibid., p. 21 and *passim*. Interestingly, ther is no reference to the recitation of *Enuma Elish* in attested chronicles. Commonly the phraseology 'He (the Babylonian king) took the hand of Bel' marked the observance of the *Akitu* festival throughout the *Chronicles*, see Grayson 1970: 169.

45 Pongratz-Leisten 1994: 258–259, 14–35.

46 Grayson 1970: 169.

47 Cf. George 1992: 390.

48 Herodotus reports a yearly festival of Babylon wherein the Chaldeans offer 'a thousand talents' weight of frankincense', Herodotus, 183.

49 Pliny from the mid-first century wrote, 'The temple of Jupiter Belus in Babylon is still standing . . . but in all other respects the place has gone back to a desert' (Pliny, *Natural History*, VI 121).

50 *Babylonian Talmud, Abodah Zarah*, 11b. See, S. Dalley, 'Bel at Palmyra and Elsewhere in the Parthian Period', *ARAM* 7 (1995), p. 143.

51 For instance, in 115 AD, when Trajan entered Babylon during the campaign against the Parthians, he found nothing but ruins in the former glorious city. He did not offer a sacrifice to Marduk like other kings who had entered Babylon, but to Alexander the Great who died in Babylon 400 years earlier. Dio Cassius 30.1).

BIBLIOGRAPHY

Abusch,T. 1995 'Marduk', in K. van der Troon, B. Becking, and P.W. van der Horst (eds), *Dictionary of Deities and Demons in the Bible*, 2nd edn, Brill, Leiden, Boston, and Cologne, 1014–1026.

Alberti, A. 1985 'A Reconstruction of the Abū Šabīkh God-List', *Studi epigrafici e linguistici*, 2, pp. 3–23.

Bidmead, J. 2002 *The Akītu Festival: Religious Continuity and Royal Legitimation in Mesopotamia*, Gorgias Press, Piscataway.

Biggs, R.D. 1974 *Inscriptions from Tell Abū Ṣalabīkh* (OIP 99), The University of Chicago Press, Chicago.

Black, J. and A. Green 1992 *Gods, Demons and Symbols of Ancient Mesopotamia: An Illustrated Dictionary*, British Museum Press, London.

Brinkman, J.A. 1968 *A Political History of Post-Kassite Babylonia: 1158–722 BC* (An Or 43), Pontificium Institutum Biblicum, Rome.

Çagirgan, G. and W.G. Lambert 1991–93 The Late Babylonian Kislīmu Ritual For Esagil', *Journal of Cuneiform Studies* 43–45.

Cohen, M.E. 1993 *The Cultic Calendars of the Ancient Near East*, CDL Press, Bethesda.

Dalley, S. 1991 *Myths from Mesopotamia: Creation, The Flood, Gilgamesh, and Others*, Oxford University Press, Oxford·and New York.

—— 1997 'Statues of Marduk and the Date of *Enūma Eliš*', *Altorientalische Forschungen* 24: 163–171.

Foster, B. 2005 *Before the Muses*, CDL Press Bethesda, Maryland.

Gelb, I.J. and B. Kienast 1990 *Die altakkadischen Königsinschriften des dritten Jahrtausends v.Chr.* (Freiburger altorientalischen Studien 7), Franz Steiner Verlag, Stuttgart.

George, A.R. 1992 *Babylonian Topographical Texts* (OLA 40), Department Oriëntalistiek/Uitgeverij Peeters, Leuven.

—— 1993 *House Most High: The Temples of Ancient Mesopotamia*, Eisenbrauns, Winona Lake.

Grayson, A.K. 1970 'Chronicles and the Akītu Festival', *Comptes rendu, Rencontre Assyriologique Internationale*, 17: 160–170.

—— 1975 *Assyrian and Babylonian Chronicles*, J. J. Augustin, Locust Valley and Glückstadt.

Horowitz, W. 1998 *Mesopotamian Cosmic Geography*, Eisenbrauns, Winona Lake.

Horsnell, M.J.A. 1999 *The Year-Names of the First Dynasty of Babylon*, vol. II, McMaster University Press, Ontario.

Jacobsen, Th. 1976 *The Treasure of the Darkness. A History of Mesopotamian Religion*, Yale University Press, New Haven and London.

Klein, J. 2003 'Man and His God', in W.W. Hallo (ed.), *The Context of Scripture*. vol. I, Brill, Leiden and Boston, pp. 573–575.

Kuhrt, A. 1995 *The Ancient Near East*, Routledge, London.

Lambert, W.G. 1960 *Babylonian Wisdom Literature*, Oxford University Press, Oxford.

—— 1964 'The Reign of Nebuchadnezzar I: A Turning Point in the History of Ancient Mesopotamian Religion', in W.S. McCullough (ed.), *The Seed of Wisdom: Essays in Honour of T. J. Meek*, University of Toronto Press, Toronto, pp. 3–13.

—— 1967 'Enmeduranki and Related Matters', *Journal of Cuneiform Studies* 21: 128–130.

—— 1984 'Studies in Marduk', *Bulletin of the School of Oriental and African Studies* 47: 1–9.

—— and A.R. Millard 1969 *Atra-ḫasīs: the Babylonian Story of the Flood*, Oxford University Press, Oxford.

Langdon, S. 1912 *Die neubabylonischen Königsinschriften* (VAB 4), J.C. Hinrischs'sche Buchhandlung, Leipzig.

Linssen, M.J.H. 2004 *The Cults of Uruk and Babylon: The Temple Ritual Texts as Evidence for Hellenistic Cult Practice*, Brill/Styx, Leiden/Boston.

Litke, R.L. 1998 *A Reconstruction of the Assyro-Babylonian God-Lists*, AN: ^{d}A-NU-UM *and* AN: ANU ŠA AMĒLI, Yale Babylonian Collection, New Haven.

Matthews, D.M. 1992 *The Kassite Glyptic of Nippur*, Universitätsverlag, Freiburg Schweiz, Vandenhoeck & Ruprecht, Göttingen.

Mayer, W. 1976 *Untersuchgen zur Formensprache der babylonischem 'Gebetsbeschwörungen'*, Biblical Institute Press, Rome.

Moran, W.L. 2002 *The Most Magic Word: Essays on Babylonian and Biblical Literature*, The Catholic Biblical Association of America, Washington DC.

Oppenheim, A.L. 1977 *Ancient Mesopotamia: Portrait of a Dead Civilization*, The University of Chicago Press, Chicago.

Pongratz-Leisten, B. 1994 INA ŠULMI ĪRUB: *Die kulttopographische und ideologische Programmatik der* akītu-*Prozession in Babylonien und Assyrien im I. Jahrtausend v. Chr.*, Verlag Philipp von Zabern, Mainz am Rhein.

Sommerfeld, W. 1979 and 1981 'The Rise of Marduk – Some Aspects of Divine Exaltation', *Sumer* 41: 97–100.

—— 1982 *Der Aufstieg Marduks: Die Stellung Marduks in der babylonischen Religion des zweiten Jahrtausends v. Chr.* (AOAT 213), Verlag Butzon & Bercker, Kevelaer, Neukirchener Verlag, Neukirchen-Vluyn.

Thureau-Dangin, F. 1921 *Rituels Accadiens*, Éditions Ernest Leroux, Paris.

Walker, C. and M. Dick 2001 *The Induction of the Cult Image in Ancient Mesopotamia: The Mesopotamian Mīs Pî Ritual*, The Neo-Assyrian Text Corpus Project, Helsinki.

CHAPTER TWENTY-FIVE

DIVINATION CULTURE AND THE HANDLING OF THE FUTURE

——— .◆. ———

Stefan M. Maul

An omen is a clearly defined perception understood as a sign pointing to future events whenever it manifests itself under identical circumstances. The classification of a perception as ominous is based on an epistemological development which establishes a normative relationship between the perceived and the future. This classification process is preceded by a period of detailed examination and is thus initially built on empirical knowledge. Omina only cease to be detected empirically when a firm conceptual link has been established between the observed and the future which then allows omina to be construed by the application of regularities. In the Mesopotamian written sources from the first and second millennia BC, omina based on regularities far exceed those based on empirical data. Mesopotamian scholars generally collected data without formally expressing the fundamental principles behind their method. It was the composition of non-empirical omina as such which allowed students to detect the regularities on which they were based without this formulated orally or in writing. Modern attempts at a systematic investigation of such principles however, are still outstanding.

It is interesting that there is no Sumerian or Akkadian equivalent for the terms 'oracle' or 'omen'. Assyriologists use the term omen for the sentence construction 'if x then y' which consists of a main clause beginning with *šumma* ('if') describing the ominous occurence, and a second clause which spells out the predicted outcome. The former is called protasis (Greek for 'cause, question'), the latter apodosis (Greek for 'rendition', 'renumeration'), following the Graeco-Roman divination system. Such sentence constructions are also common in the so-called legal codes (such as the Code of Hammurabi) and in medical diagnostic texts without being classified as omina by Assyriologists, a distinction which probably did not occur to ancient scholars. The most important form of the oracle was the examination of entrails of sacrificial animals (extispicy). Like the spontaneous signs and other oracles, extispicy and various other forms of oracles (see below) had to be performed and interpreted by schooled specialists. Since the meaning of these signs was codified in the sentence structure of 'if x then y', Assyriologists classify them as oil omina, smoke omina, liver omina, etc. even though the associated practices are really oracles.

The relationship between empirical observation and the systematic study of regularities has parallels to the working methods of modern science and there are also structural similarities in the form of presentation ('scientific' systematization). The notion that the world is full of signs does not have to imply a belief in the existence of gods, in contrast to the system of oracles. However, at least during the historical periods in Mesopotamia, ominous signs were indeed interpreted as divine revelations and insights into the intentions of the gods. The future outcome revealed by the sign was hardly ever considered as irrevocable. Human beings could resort to prayer, sacrifice and incantations in order to soothe the angry gods and to make them revise divine intentions in their favour.

We can see that the future as crystallized in the present was not considered by the Babylonians as created solely by the gods but as the result of a dialogue between man and god, an act of communication that could be initiated by gods or men. Deities could speak directly through the medium of a prophet or ecstatic, or appear in dreams, in order to convey their wishes and directives. They also announced their will by a plethora of signs that had to be read like a written text. Such unsolicited signs, which appeared spontaneously in the sky, on earth, and even on people, were not immediately intelligible by themselves but needed to be read by a trained interpreter of signs who had spent many years learning the highly sophisticated art of divination.

Often there was no time to wait for such spontaneous manifestations of the gods' will, as when decisions about important undertakings had to be made which needed divine approval. The human beings could take the initiative and seek for divine guidance in a variety of ways. The different procedures used to ellicit the will of the gods are generally called oracles. Rituals, complete with sacrifices and prayers, prepared the way for communication with the deities. An oracle was always tied to a concrete enquiry about a future event or whether a planned activity would be sanctioned or not. It was also possible to provoke the divine word directly or indirectly through a priestly medium. A consciously evoked dream within the framework of the incubation ritual could also lead to a response. If the dream was not unequivocal, it had to be interpreted. In legal practice the divine will was revealed by the ordeal which was considered proof.

THE WORLD AS A SYSTEM OF SIGNS

The careful and detailed observation of nature and environment convinced the Babylonians, long before omina were first written down, that there were connections between apparently discrete natural phenomena which, in their entirety, could allow conclusions as to what could be expected. Since the theistic world view of the ancient Orient did not allow for chance or hazard, this meant that everything was an expression of the divine, creative will which manifested itself in the world again and again. This form of thinking made it possible to draw conclusions about the divine plans for the future on the basis of exact observations of the ever changing material world. The future as envisaged by the gods could only come into being within and through the material world and the constituents of the material world were united by the common desire to become their will. That is why the different procedures of divination not only led to identical conclusions but furnished complementary insights. Hence it was obvious that conclusions based on astral observations could be refined through extispicy, for instance, or that stellar signs always had to be examined together with terrestrial ones. It was taken as evident that the different sign systems of sky, the earth or the complex surface of a sacrificial animal's liver were all 'saying the same thing'. Such a concept must have been deeply influenced by the Mesopotamian scholars' long-established habit of bilingualism.

The Babylonian interpreters of signs did not only collect signs to predict the future but considered a future that had become present by looking for related signs, or those that may have been overlooked, among events of the past. One product of such a search is a document know as the 'Babylonian Book of Prodigies', which brings together 47 signs of different provenance which collectively led to the 'downfall of the land Akkad' (Kessler-Guinan 2002). The collection known as 'Astronomical Diaries, assembled over centuries, can also be seen as a daring long-term project to record the signs of the world in greater detail (Hunger and Sachs 1988–1996). These 'diaries' were produced in the form of annual reports which record not only astral signs and meteorological data, but also the price of staples, the water levels, ominous terrestrial events, as well as significant historical happenings. The aim must have been to register regularities in world events in order to make such knowledge useful for the political activities of the (royal) client.

THE IMPORTANCE OF OMINA AND ORACLES IN BABYLONIAN SOCIETY

The extraordinary amount of writing concerned with the 'science of portents' and oracles in the second and first millennia BC reveal that the future was ultimately considered as a threat, something that had to be reified in time in order to deal with it.

Mesopotamian omina can be seen as a sort of warning of what was to come rather than an attempt to predict the future. They made it possible to act before the foreseen could actually happen. Divination was, therefore, not an expression of fatalism or a listless resignation. Instead, it allowed shape to be given to an amorphous, in many situations threatening, future. This deprives the at first unfathomable future of some of its dread. After all, the perspective towards the future as revealed by the omen marshalls a human response, a directive that was needed especially when the portents were bad. Omina concretized the future which could then be furthered or prevented by specific actions. In this way, the omen lore fulfilled the purpose of modern trend predications or statistics. A vital difference, however, was the fact that Babylonians considered the appearance of negative signs as the manifestation of an essentially benign divine will. The various oracular procedures made it possible to consider important, or even controversial decisions as not having been made by a possibly errant individual but by the will of the gods. Since the oracles and omina must have enhanced the decisiveness and self-confidence of the rulers who utilized them, they were politically highly important and effective. To what extent the knowledge of diviners was considered to be of hegemonic impact (Pongratz-Leisten 1999) can be seen in the wording of oaths taken by omen interpreters (Durand 1988: 13–15), as well as in the fact that the specialist tablet collections were plundered on royal command (Lambert 1957/58: 44). Nor is it surprising that everything to do with omina was seen as 'classified' by large sectors of the population.

After the fall of the Neo-Babylonian empire, the Greeks and Romans used the title 'Chaldean' (a synonym for 'Babylonian') to designate the much appreciated Babylonian soothsayers, astrologers, diviners, incantation priests and scholars.

This also shows how much the science of omina and oracles were considered the most characteristic trait of Mesopotamian culture during classical antiquity.

THE AREAS OF COMPETENCE OF THE VARIOUS DIVINATORY PRACTICES

Increasingly complex political structures forced the kings to submit their relationship to the gods to a form of permanent scrutiny. Such a practice would be able to diagnose and soothe any enflamed divine wrath before it could unleash its destructive potential to destabilize a dynasty and the whole kingdom. Astrology was almost ideally suited to this purpose because the night sky could be observed and 'deciphered' at professionally staffed observation posts. In Mesopotamian cosmology, the sky above the earth was seen as its mirror image and its signs concerned 'all four corners of the world'. According to literary sources from the first millennium BC, the movements of the stars in all their complexity were considered as a stellar script which gave initiates permanent access to the evolving divine intentions, to which other methods of divination could only have momentary access. This universal applicability of astrology contributed greatly to its popularity during the second and first millennia BC. Political leaders with imperial intentions beyond the Mesopotamian heartland found it an invaluable source of information on a universal scale.

In contrast to astral signs, terrestrial signs were perceived within a much more circumscribed radius and hardly observed systematically. Unless they were visible across larger distances or of such momentous nature that they caused a great stir, such as really weird birth defects, they were generally not considered relevant for political or social contexts on a large scale and only achieved local interest. Terrestrial omina obtained the status of royal or national importance only if they occurred in places visited by the king. Although royal ordinances decreed that terrestrial omina should be painstakingly recorded, they were only collected systematically if other omina, for instance an impending lunar eclipse, had indicated a grave danger for the king. Then more detailed guidance was sought to obtain more precise indications in order to counteract the potential ill fortune by magical means.

We have seen that Babylonian diviners did not rely solely on spontaneous signs of nature but solicited provoked responses. Oracles which delivered divine verdicts were particularly popular because they made it possible to check whether a planned activity had the gods' approval or not. Especially extispicy became an important royal device to legitimize decisions and thus it had a great political importance, although it could also be used for private purposes. Other, less costly and time-consuming forms of divination were also available, for all levels of Babylonian society.

THE LIMITATIONS OF OMINA AND ORACLES

Although the achievements of diviners were highly respected and inspired great confidence, cuneiform sources known as Wisdom Literature also document the conviction that diviners were unable to deal with all contingences of life within their hermeneutic framework. On the other hand, although literary sources refer to circumstances where people have disregarded divine 'signs', there is not a single document which challenges the fundamental efficacy of divination. Doubts about the competence and reliability of individual diviners, however, are amply documented in literary and non-literary sources.

SIGNS OF THE SKY: ASTROLOGICAL OMINA

An exact observation of the sky was needed for agricultural and calendric purposes, especially in order to calibrate lunar months with the solar year. The experience that conditions of the sky, the stars, wind and weather could furnish useful information must have had a very long history in Mesopotamia. Since highly evolved omen compendia were available and transmitted in the Old Babylonian period, the beginnings of astral divination must go back to the third millennium BC.

Towards the end of the second millennium, astral omina (lunar, solar, weather, earthquake, planets and star omina) were collected in an all encompassing series called *enuma Anu Enlil* after its mythological introductory line (Koch-Westenholz 1995: 77; Hunger and Pingree 1999: 14). The apodoses of the astrological work all concern the wellbeing of the collective and the king. It contains not only information about military matters, harvest yields and the fate of the kingdom but prognoses about other parts of the world. Catalogues, as well as a short version, allowed some overview over this text which comprises several thousand entries. Furthermore, there were excerpts under different headings, as well as commentaries, for the purposes of studying and teaching, as well as for divinatory practice.

Astronomically trained experts called themselves 'scribes of *enuma Anu Enlil*'. Together with the incantation specialists (*ašipu*) they were responsible for the interpretation of stellar signs, which always had to be considered in connection with terrestrial signs, never in isolation, as the Manual for Divination expressively records. The danger predicted in an astral event could be averted by the appropriate rituals. The death of the king, for instance, presaged by a lunar eclipse or an earthquake, could be prevented by the ritual of the 'substitute king'. The idea that the power of the stars influences the lives of individuals (Parpola 1983: xxii–xxxii; Bottéro 1992: 138–155) has great antiquity (already documented in the Hittite omen collections) but the earliest cuneiform protocols concerning the position of stars at the birth of a child date only from the the fifth century BC. The century-long activities of Babylonian astrologers exerted considerable influence on Egyptian, Indian and Greek astrology and led to calculated astronomy during the Seleucid-Parthian period.

SIGNS OF TIME

The theory of generally favourable or unfavourable days, as well as days and months that were favourable or unfavourable for particular activities, is documented in the Akkadian hemerologies and menologies known from the middle of the second millennium until the end of cuneiform writing. The insight that there was a connection between the fundamental meaning of a sign and the timing of its manifestation led to the formulation of rules which considered certain times to be ominous for certain activities. A mainly menologically ordered calendar, dating from the last third of the second millennium and known as *iqqur ipuš* ('he demolished, he built up') provides information in the form of lists and tables as to when activities such as building works or certain rituals, were auspicious or unauspicious. Since the text was presented in omen form ('If he builds a house in the months x, then . . .') it allowed quick access as to the future significance of daily events that were considered ominous, or of certain diseases, fires, or important astral signs for each month of the year.

SIGNS OF THE EARTH

Terrestrial omina and the collection *šumma alu*

The unusual behaviour of animals, extraordinary happenings in and around the house, peculiarities of plants, were all considered to point towards forces that may compromise the safety of human existence. Unbidden signs of this nature were probably observed, collected and pondered as early as the prehistorical period. Knowledge of the hidden connections between terrestrial signs and their effects on human beings were considered of such importance that omen compendia listing such signs and their outcomes were already written down in the Old Babylonian period. They can be seen as precursors of the very comprehensive collection of terrestrial omina that are first documented for the eleventh century BC (Freedman 1998: 13) but fully represented by the much later texts in the library of the Neo-Assyrian king Ashurbanipal. This series, comprising at least 120 thematically defined tablets and more than 10,000 entries, was called after its initial line *šumma alu ina mele šakin* ('when a city is built on high ground'). The majority of signs in this collection were gathered from the natural urban and rural environment of the Mesopotamian populace and not the royal court. Apart from signs originating from the immediate surroundings of the human home (within the house, in animals, and in other various manifestations of and around the house, tablets 1–53), the series is dedicated to ominous signs within the city, the fields and gardens (tablets 54–60), in rivers and watercourses (tablets 61–63), and the birds of the sky (tablets 64–79). Other sections are devoted to the behaviour of humans and animals (tablets 80–87, 103–104). The original kernel of the composition must have been house and city omina, hence the justified name of the whole collection as 'If a city' (tablets 1–88). Other sections of work that enumerate interpretative rules for oracular procedures and are therefore not unprovoked omina, must be later additions. It also noteworthy that the majority of the apodoses of house and city omina concern the well-being and health of the persons in whose household they were observed, rather than royal or public concerns. Terrestrial signs did not refer to an unalterable future since the diviners were trained to avert the potential misfortune before it could happen, which is why almost all the main thematic sections contain redemption rituals (Maul 1994).

Despite the enormous scope of the terrestrial omen series, the user was able to navigate it with the help of catalogues and thematically ordered short versions. Numerous excerpts and commentaries prove the extent of its usefulness to scribes and scholars.

Terrestrial signs, quite unlike the heavenly signs could not be observed systematically. Therefore, extraordinary occurences had to be reported to the king if they were suspected to concern the public welfare. Written reports about such signs are known from the Old Babylonian, as well as the first millennium BC. They were interpreted, at least during the latter period, by the incantation specialist, the *ašipu*. The hermeneutic principles of interpretation which cannot be reduced to simple folk rules remain to be investigated. Various 'handbooks' warn practioners not to consider terrestrial signs without correlating them to astral ones.

Birth omina

Teratomancy (from Greek *téras* 'monster' and *manteía* 'prediction'), the procedure of deriving insights into the future from the malformations of newborn humans and animals, was one of the most important Babylonian divination methods. The appearance and formation of birth defects (*izbu*) were regarded as concerning primarily the future of the whole country and hence the kingship. Teratomantic compendia were already written in the Old Babylonian period but the first comprehensive collection, consisting of 24 tablets, comes from the library of Ashurbanipal and was called *šumma izbu* ('if a birth defect') (Leichty 1970). The protases deal with all the varieties of possible congenital malformations. As mentioned, the majority of the apodoses concern the king. The few exceptions which document private usage mainly refer to the person in whose household the malformation occured. An *izbu* was examined by a *baru* 'seer', a specialist in the interpretation of extispicy. Sometimes, an *izbu* observed in the country was pickled and sent to the city for a more detailed examination. There are texts from the first millennium which concern the purification rituals that had to be performed in the house where the birth defect had happened.

SIGNS ON HUMAN BEINGS: OMEN COLLECTIONS AS AIDS IN THE EXAMINATION OF HUMAN BODIES

Babylonian healers could also make use of a comprehensive collection of so-called diagnostic and prognostic omina which were compiled in the eleventh century BC and transmitted into the Seleucid period. They contained thousands of entries describing symptoms (in the protasis) with comments about the chances of recovery and the nature of the disease concerned (in the apodsis) (Heeßel 2000). As soon as the deity who had sent the affliction was identified by means of the omen collection, the incantation specialist could proceed with the therapy. This consisted as much of a reconciliation with the gods achieved by magic-religious means as medical treatment in the modern sense. Numerous medical-therapeutic cuneiform texts show clearly that the Babylonians considered both treatments as a single, homogeneous discipline. Various compendia of physiognomic omina and others which are concerned with human behaviour provided prognoses about possible life expectancy, the general state of health, the character and the social standing of the investigated person. Omina concerning women refer to fertility as well as prognoses for her future husband and his household. The physiognomic omen collection served diviners as a teaching and reference work for the scrutiny of human beings. It was thus much in demand at court, on occasions when people were about to be admitted to the inner circle around the king, achieve high office, or get married to a high status person.

SIGNS DURING SLEEP: DREAM OMINA

Procedures concerning dream interpretation are mentioned in the oldest comprehensible cuneiform text from Mari, dating from the mid-third millennium BC (Bonechi and Durand 1992). A mantically important dream which was not immediately clear, say through a divine message, had to be interpreted regardless of whether the dream had been solicited through the incubation ritual or appeared spontaneously. This was done by the *barum* 'seer', as well as by male and female 'questioners' (Sum. ensi, Akkad. *ša'ilu(m)*, *šailtum*) who clarified the relationship between the dream content and future happenings, not least to allow counter measures to be taken in time.

Despite the great antiquity of Mesopotamian dream omina, there are few tablets outside Ashurbanipal's library which put together images and events seen in dreams, and their meaning. Ashurbanipal's edition, known to us as the 'The Assyrian Dream Book', was called *iškar Za/iqiqu* after the dream-god Zaqiqu/Ziqiqu and comprised 11 tablets (edition: Oppenheim 1956). Many of the described dream motives do not occur in real life or transgress against existing moral and ethical standards. The interpretations contained in the apodoses always concern private matters as well as prognoses about success, health and life expectancy. A separate chapter concerned the dreams of the king and their meaning.

Dreams by third persons that were considered important had to be reported to the king and then interpreted (see, for instance, Durand 1988: 455–482). A prognosis supplied by a dream interpretation could be made more precise by additional divinatory procedures. There were numerous rituals to procure dream omina, as well as those meant to avert the predicted misfortune.

INVESTIGATION OF SACRIFICIAL ANIMALS, OF THEIR ENTRAILS (EXTISPICY), THEIR LIVERS (HEPATOSCOPY)

The observation of a sacrificial animal (generally a sheep) during and after the sacrifice, the inspection of its carcass and inner organs, was first documented in Mesopotamia in the third millennium and then spread throughout the Ancient Near East and the classical Mediterranean (though not to Egypt). It promised insights into future happenings as well as divine approval or disapproval for important decisions.

It was held in highest esteem during all periods of Mesopotamian history because it provided for the rulers the ultimate legitimation for decisions concerning political, military, personal and religious matters. The examination of the sacrificial sheep, which established a direct line of communication between man and god, had sacramental character and was performed as a ritual by a professional diviner. The sacrifice was directly related to the intention of the sacrificer.

Almost innumerable numbers of cuneiform tablets document the various forms of sacrificial divination, from the Old Babylonian period onward. Apart from the tablets that constituted a sort of 'handbook' which diviners and their students copied again and again for reference and teaching purposes and which were collected into sometimes very large series of omen collections and omen commentaries, there were incantations for the ritual context of such divination (Starr 1983; Lambert 1995), as well as detailed instructions for such rituals (Zimmern 1901, Nr. 1–25 and Nr. 71–101).

Protocols about specific oracular rituals and the letters exchanged between rulers and their advisers, dating from the second and first millennia BC, allow a deep insight into the practice of sacrificial divination. The ritual instruction tablets for the diviner (*barum*), trace the origin of extispicy to Enmeduranki, the first prediluvian (mythical) king of Sippar. He had been granted access to the 'secret of heaven and earth' by the gods Shamash and Adad, to pass it on to 'the sons of Nippur, Sippar and Babylon' (Lambert 1998).

Around the turn from the second to the first millennium BC, the written sources about sacrificial divination underwent a process of large-scale systematization, most likely in response to the increasingly powerful role of Mesopotamian kings, who demanded a comprehensive and reliable system of divination. This process culminated with the edition of a work called *iškar barūti* (Koch-Westenholz 2000: 27–31), which brings together thousands of sacrificial omina on some 100 tablets, sub-divided into ten series. King Ashurbanipal, who declares in a colophon that he made copies with his own hand 'in the assembly of scholars', had the first-known examples of the massive compendium in his library (Jeyes 1997). The series describes in great detail the outer appearance of the sacrificial sheep, the shape of its entrails, and particularly the 'topography' of the liver, gall bladder and the lungs. It was made easy to use by the list form of the individual tablets and by catalogues. For the purposes of further studies and for practical purposes, there were numerous excerpts (Koch-Westenholz 2000: 437–473).

The apodoses of the omina almost exclusively address the concerns of the king and the state: the well-being of the royal family, catastrophes and good harvest, wealth of the kingdom, epidemics and, last but not least, success in warfare. The huge importance of the omen collection for the exercise of kingship can be seen by the fact that Tukulti-Ninurta I ordered the confiscation of extispicy tablets on the occasion of his Babylonian campaign (Lambert 1957/58: 44) and by the efforts made by Ashurbanipal to assemble all relevant texts in his library.

Oracle questions from the Old Babylonian period (Durand 1988: 24–34, 44–46 and passim) and the first millennium (Starr 1990) also document the enormous political importance of sacrificial divination at Mesopotamian courts. They also show that strict secrecy surrounded not only the object of enquiry but the knowledge of the discipline as such, which constituted vital 'hegemonic knowledge'. A considerable proportion of royal enquiries concerned decisions of a military and strategic nature and many must have been made during campaigns. Others were meant to clarify the success of a war, the development of threatening situations in the provinces and occupied territories.

Private queries generally concern the health and well-being of the person consulting the oracle but there are also some about the likely outcome of business ventures. Occasionally there are questions concerning the fidelity of a wife.

Prayers and rituals frequently refer to the inner organs of the sacrificial sheep as a 'tablet' inscribed by the gods which reflects the hermeneutic basis of extispicy. The richly structured surface of the liver was seen as a text, rather like the night sky, which described the human world in an initially incomprehensible but ultimately accessible manner. The various observed individual phenomena were like the ideograms of the cuneiform script which have more than one reading (and meaning), the correct one of which is made clear only through context. An oracular result could be classified

Figure 25.1 Old Babylonian clay model of a sheep's liver, *c.*1700 BC. The text refers to the ominous implications of any mark in that place (courtesy of The Trustees of the British Museum).

as auspicious (positive), unclear, or unauspicious (negative). In the worst case, as in the absence of a certain sign on the liver (Leiderer 1990: 24), it meant that the deity was absent and refused to enter into communication with the person commissioning the oracle. Some of the more unusual results were considered to be highly dangerous and the negative effects had to be averted by specially constructed rituals.

The Mesopotamian practice of sacrificial divination had a widespread influence. Collections of omina from Mesopotamia were found at the courts of Anatolia, Syria and Iran as early as the second millennium BC and they were translated into different languages (Hittite, Hurrian, Ugaritic). Ancient Israel practised it under Mesopotamian influence, as did the Greeks, Etruscans and Romans.

OTHER ORACLES

The inspection of (sacrificial) birds ('ornithoscopy') involved the appearance of the body of a dead and plucked but unopened bird where spots on the skin were given particular attention. Existing omen compendia from the Old Babylonian period show that this form of divination was also used by kings and generals since not a few refer to future wars or warn of enemies (edition: Durand 1997).

The patterns made by oil poured into a bowl of water (lecanomancy, from Greek *lekáne* 'bowl') was also considered as an ancient divinely sanctioned practice. It appears that the plant oil used for the oracle was seen as a sacrifice to the gods, and thus a vehicle of divine communication in itself. The diviner poured oil on the water filling the basin and then more water on top of the oil. The oracular result was derived from the colour, the direction and form of movement the oil made. Oil and water were seen as opposing forces and their collision triggered movements understood as a fight between two principles. The inherent hermeneutic principle of the oil omina can also be revealed by the fact that one could elicit information about the relationship between two people by pouring out a few drops of oil 'for' these persons and then examining how they behave towards each other (edition: Pettinato 1966).

Libanomancy (from Greek *líbanos* 'incense'), the method of using incense to gain insights into the future, is first known from the third millennium BC and omen collections are, so far, only documented in four Old Babylonian tablets (Finkel 1983/84). Here, too, incense was seen as an offering to the gods who then communicated their will by means of its substance. The diviner sprinkled flour or incense into a container with glowing coals and observed the shape of the resulting fire or smoke. While some of the apodoses provide answers for private queries, the majority show clearly that military leaders consulted this oracle on royal command. They were technically easy enough to perform even in the midst of battle.

Aleuromancy, divining by means of scattered flour (from Greek *áleuron* 'flour') is, so far, only known from a single late Babylonian omen tablet (Nougayrol 1963).

There is little evidence that oracles concerning birds in flight played an important role in Mesopotamia, unlike in Anatolia. Unsolicited signs concerning flying birds, however, were carefully observed.

Popular forms of folk divination which everybody could undertake were doubtlessly important during all periods of Mesopotamian history but because they were easily accessible they rarely entered the written evidence.

BIBLIOGRAPHY

Bonechi, M. and J.-M. Durand 1992 'Oniromancie et magie à Mari à l'époque d'Ébla', in: Franzaroli, P. (ed.) *Literature and Literary Language at Ebla*, Quaderni di Semitistica . Universita di Firenze, Florence 18, 151–159 and Pl. I–II.

Bottéro, J. 1992 *Mesopotamia. Writing, Reasoning, and the Gods.* Chicago: University of Chicago Press.

Durand, J. M. 1988 *Archives Royales de Mari*, Vol. 26/I. Paris: Editions recherches sur les civilisations

—— 1997 'La divination par les oiseaux', *Mari: Annales de Recherches Interdisciplinaires* 8, 273–282.

Ebeling, E. and F. Köcher 1953 *Literarische Keilschrifttexte aus Assur*. Berlin: Akademie-Verlag.

Falkenstein, A. 1966 '"Wahrsagung" in der sumerischen Überlieferung', in: CRRA 14, 45–68.

Finkel, I. L. 1983/84 'A New Piece of Libanomancy.' *Archiv für Orientforschung* 29/30, 50–55.

Freedman, S. M. 1998 *If a City Is Set on a Height. The Akkadian Omen Series Šumma Alu ina Mālê šakin*. Volume 1: Tablets 1–21, Philadelphia: Samuel Noah Kramer Fund.

Heeßel, N. P. 2000 *Babylonisch-assyrische Diagnostik*. Alter Orient und Altes Testament 43, Münster: Ugarit Verlag.

Heintz, J.-G. (ed.) 1997 Oracles et Prophéties dans l'antiquité. Actes du Colloque des Strasbourg 15–17 juin 1995. Paris: Boccard.

Hunger, H. and D. Pingree 1999 *Astral Sciences in Mesopotamia.* Handbuch der Orientalistik, 1. Abteilung 44. Band, Boston: Brill.

—— and A. Sachs 1988–1996 *Astronomical Diaries and Related Texts from Babylonia.* Vienna: Österreichische Akademie der Wissenschaften.

Jeyes, U. 1997 *Assurbanipal's bārûtu*, in: CRRA 39, 61–65.

Kessler-Guinan, A. 2002 'A Severed Head Laughed: Stories of Divinatory Interpretation', in: Leda Ciraolo, Jonathan Seidel (eds), *Magic and Divination in the Ancient World, Ancient Magic and Divination* II, Leiden: Brill, Styx, 7–40.

Koch-Westenholz, U. 1995 *Mesopotamian Astrology. An Introduction to Babylonian and Assyrian Celestial Divination.* Copenhagen: Carsten Niebuhr Institute of Near Eastern Studies: Museum Tusculanum Press, University of Copenhagen.

—— 2000 *Babylonian Liver Omens.* Copenhagen: Carsten Niebuhr Institute of Near Eastern Studies: Museum Tusculanum Press, University of Copenhagen.

Labat, R. 1965 *Un calendrier babylonien des travaux des signes et des mois* (series iqqur ipuš), Paris: Librairie Honoré Champion.

Lambert, W. G. 1957/58 'Three Unpublished Fragments of the Tukulti-Ninurta Epic'. *Archiv für Orientforschung* 18, 38–51.

—— 1995 'Questions Addressed to the Babylonian Oracle. The *tamītu*-texts', in: J.-G. Heintz (ed.) *Oracles et prophéties dans l'antiquité*, 85–98.

—— 1998 'The Qualifications of Babylonian Diviners', in: S.M. Maul (ed.), *Fs. R. Borger*, CM 10, 141–158.

Leichty, E. 1970 *The Omen Series šumma izbu*, TCS 4.

Leiderer, R. 1990 *Anatomie der Schafsleber im babylonischen Leberorakel.* München/Bern/Wien/San Francisco: Zuckschwerdt Verlag.

Maul, S. M. 1994 *Zukunftsbewältigung. Eine Untersuchung altorientalischen Denkens anhand der babylonisch-assyrischen Löserituale (Namburbi).* Baghdader Forschungen 18. Mainz: Verlag Philipp von Zabern.

Nougayrol, J. 1963 'Aleuromancie babylonienne', *Orientalia Nova Seria* 32, 381–386.

Oppenheim, A. L. 1956 *The Interpretation of Dreams in the Ancient Near East.* Transactions of the American Philosophical Society 46/3, Philadelphia: The American Philosophical Society.

—— 1974 'A Babylonian Diviner's Manual', *Journal of Near Eastern Studies* 33, 197–220.

Parpola, S. 1983 *Letters from Assyrian Scholars to the Kings Esarhaddon and Assurbanipal, Part II: Commentary and Appendices.* Alter Orient und Altes Testament 5/2 Neukirchener-Vluyn: Neukirchener Verlag.

Pettinato, G. 1966 *Die Ölwahrsagung bei den Babyloniern.* Rome: Istituto di Studi del Vicino Oriente, Università di Roma.

Pongratz-Leisten, B. 1999 *Herrschaftswissen in Mesopotamien.* Helsinki: the Neo-Assyrian Text Corpus Project.

Reiner, E. 1995 *Astral Magic in Babylonia.* Philadelphia: Transactions of the American Philosophical Society 85/4. Philadelphia: The American Philosophical Society.

Rochberg-Halton, F. 1998 *Babylonian Horoscopes.* Transactions of the American Philosophical Society 88/1. Philadelphia: American Philosophical Society.

Starr, I. 1983 'The Rituals of the Diviner', *Bibliotheca Mesopotamica* 12.

—— 1990 *Queries to the Sungod.* State Archives of Assyria 4. Helsinki: Helsinki University Press.

Zimmern, H. 1901 'Beiträge zur Kenntnis der babylonischen Religion', Assyriologische Bibliothek 12, Hinrichs'sche Buchhandlung Leipzig (Reprint: Zentralantiquariat der Deutschen Demokratischen Republik, Leipzig 1975).

CHAPTER TWENTY-SIX

WITCHCRAFT LITERATURE
IN MESOPOTAMIA

————·◆·————

Tzvi Abusch

Let us begin with simple definitions of magic and witchcraft in Mesopotamia. We classify as magical those rites that address the needs, crises, and desires of the individual. In contrast to some later western societies, magic in Mesopotamia was regarded as legitimate and as part of the established religion. Therefore, in a Mesopotamian context, witchcraft refers not to magical behavior as such, but to inimical behavior, that is, to the practice of magic for anti-social and destructive purposes (though, as we shall note later, not all behavior so labeled was, in fact, motivated by evil intentions).

Over the course of some 2,500 years (*c.*2600–100 BCE), numerous cuneiform texts written in both the Sumerian and Akkadian languages refer to personal crisis and individual suffering (e.g., letters, curses, and literary compositions that treat the problem of theodicy); but, by and large, the most important sources detailing ways to cope with illness, danger, and personal difficulties are the various types of texts that describe symptoms, provide etiological or descriptive diagnoses, and prescribe ways to deal with evil and suffering. These treatments include medical therapies, ritual prescriptions, and oral rites (prayers and incantations). Among the rituals, we find several long and complex ceremonies.

The principal agencies in the religio-magical world view were gods, demons, personal gods, ghosts, witches, evil omens, curses, and sins. Frequently Mesopotamian traditional texts treated personal distress or illness as the result of the action or inaction of supernatural powers. In this view, the universe was understood to be hierarchically structured and to be centered on divine powers. This approach seems, however, to have emerged from, or to have drawn upon, an earlier approach that viewed the world holistically.

The changing explanations of suffering and the changing configurations of causal agents and chains of causation probably reflect different social situations and can be explained in historical terms. The earlier mechanistic magical universe reflected the social context of traditional society: the village and pre-urban settlement. A traditional world view probably continued to remain operative for the mass of rural and urban dwellers. But alongside this world view and based upon it, a new world view that reflected the values and interests of the emerging urban elite arose; in this new view, the gods increasingly gained more control over the world. With the decrease in viewing society primarily in corporate terms, a relationship was developed between the citizen and his national god(s); the individual human might now be punished by the god for his own sins. A further development in this human–divine relationship took place with the subsequent emergence of the imperial state, in which powers were further centralized and integrated. Centralization and integration caused various changes in religious outlook, including the emergence of the witch as a major force able to control personal gods, demons, and mortals.

In the later periods, man suffered not only because of sin, but also because of outside forces such as witchcraft. As an explanation for misfortune, witchcraft had the advantage of shifting much of the responsibility for one's suffering away from oneself and onto other human beings. This way of seeing oneself and others surely fits the conditions of a new and more complex urban world in which heightened social interdependence was experienced as a source of danger by an individual placed in relationship with others with whom he did not have close or traditional ties, and in which the extended family played less of a defining and supporting role and the individual was confronted by more extended, impersonal, and hostile social forces and felt weak, helpless, and anxious.

WITCHCRAFT AND THE WITCH: HISTORICAL SPECULATION

Actually, the case of witchcraft may serve as a useful illustration of a form of evil that seems to have changed over time. One possible reconstruction suggests the existence originally of a popular village and/or domestic witch, and the subsequent transformation of this personage or image into an evil form, first as an opponent of the emerging exorcist, and, then, as an enemy and threat to society as a whole.

Thus, several stages can be identified in the development of Mesopotamian witchcraft. The development begins with an early stage of "popular" witchcraft that may have taken an archaic shamanistic form. In this early popular form, the witch probably belonged to a rural, non-urban world. S/he was not, of necessity, an evil being and took the form of both a "white" and "black" witch. Not infrequently, she helped her fellows by means of magical abilities and medical knowledge; in this popular form, she occasionally exhibited behavior otherwise associated with ecstatic types of practitioners.

Originally, then, the witch was not primarily a doer of evil. Perhaps because the witch was often a woman who possessed knowledge and power, the female witch eventually became a focus of interest and even a threat to the prerogatives of the male exorcist; for this and other reasons, she was made into the evil counterpart of the exorcist. The village witch was, thus, turned into an anti-social, malicious, evil force that was the polar opposite of the benevolent and helpful *āšipu*. The development went even further, for the witch was even transformed into an alien and/or demonic force that threatened society as a whole; she came to represent an enemy of the state, even sometimes a foreign force that could threaten the late Assyrian empire. In the first-millennium *Maqlû* ceremony, she was a representation not only of internal, but also of external, danger; as such her image could be used as an instrument of state propaganda.

The late stage during which the witch became a major force able to control the personal god represents a resurgence of a late Mesopotamian urban world and an imposition of that world upon a tribal one. Looking backward over the materials that describe the evils that beset the individual, we note that they would seem to reflect different social contexts (town/city and family) and/or evolutionary stages. Demonic attacks on the individual and the ability of the demons to chase away the personal god reflect the world of the general Mesopotamian urban (Sumerian) community of the third millennium. The centrality and power of the personal god who punishes the individual because of infractions that he has committed is a Semitic feature: it reflects the life of the Semitic (Akkadian or Amorite) tribal/rural family or clan and should probably be understood in the context of the patriarchal/tribal family culture in Old Babylonian times; as such, it is a conceptual intrusion into the Mesopotamian urban landscape. Finally, the emergence of the witch as a major force represented the re-ascendancy of an urban world in which women had a public role over a tribal one where the role of women was more circumscribed.

Let us pursue this analysis from an even more explicit gender point of view. We notice, first, that the witch overpowered the personal god, a representation, specifically, of maleness and, more generally, of male parenthood, and second, that she was able to make the demons, the representatives of chaos and the destructive aspect of nature, subservient to her and even took their place as the primary malevolent magical force of destruction. The independent woman was a threat and may have been regarded as uncontrollable and malicious. This female was, then, seen as the source of chaos, destruction, and evil in the world. In the new urban world, where the individual had fewer family and traditional supports, this woman – the female witch – overpowered the male gods who represented the tribe and obedience to the family and replaced demons as the power of destruction and chaos. She threatened and overpowered family rule; and in place of natural violence, she set social violence, a violence that both symbolized, and was symbolized by, her nature as a female who was both powerful as well as isolated and marginal. Not unlike Tiamat in the *Enuma Elish* and biblical *təhôm*, this female now came to represent and to create chaos and destruction.

WITCHCRAFT AND THE WITCH: NORMATIVE DESCRIPTION

Witchcraft in Mesopotamian sources normally refers to malevolent destructive magic performed usually, though not exclusively, by a witch, *kaššāpu* (m.)/*kaššaptu* (f.). In the main, witches are illegitimate practitioners of magic. Normally, they are regarded as antisocial and as motivated by malice and evil intent. Although lists of witches include both male and female forms, the witch is usually depicted as a woman. She is normally presented as one who uses forms of destructive magic to harm other human beings and whose purpose is essentially malevolent. She is able to control or harm her victim by means of indirect contact: she steals objects that have been in contact with and represent her victim; she makes an image in the likeness of her victim and then twists its limbs so that they suffer agony and debilitating disease; she prepares figurines and buries them in holes in the wall or in the ground; she feeds statues to animals. The witch may even open up a grave and place the representation of her victim in the lap of a dead person, thus effecting a marriage of her victim and a corpse. Contact is still indirect when she sends evil omens that augur doom; that is, the witch is also able to harm her victim by sending against him emissaries in the form of experiences, living beings, and objects. Such confrontations are perceived as bringing about harm and are interpreted as signs that result in misfortune.

There need not always be a lack of proximity between victim and witch. Somewhat closer relations seem to be implied by the claim that she causes her victim to incorporate witchcraft by means of food, drink, washing, and ointment. The witch is even described as one who can directly seize and harm the various parts of the victim's body, can even push, press, and strike his chest and back. In addition to such manipulations and activities, the witch may even form an evil word in her heart and utter an incantation.

Personal distress ascribed to witchcraft includes the individual's experience of physical, psychological, and/or social difficulties. Texts may focus on specific symptoms, such as gastrointestinal, respiratory, sexual, or psychological difficulties, on life-threatening circumstances such as childbirth and infancy, on more generalized illnesses involving systemic physical and/or psychological breakdown, or on situations involving socio-economic loss of wealth and status as well as social isolation.

WITCHCRAFT LITERATURE

The Mesopotamian witchcraft corpus (or, rather, anti-witchcraft corpus, since we have no texts composed by witches) comprises hundreds of magical and medical texts that contain many different elements. These traditional texts come from the early second millennium through the late first millennium BCE. A few texts are Old Babylonian; a somewhat larger number come from late second-millennium collections, mainly those of Boghazkoi and Assur. But by far the largest number come from first-millennium collections. Pride of place goes to the royal collections of seventh-century Nineveh; but, in addition, major groups derive both from the Assyrian sites of Assur, Kalhu (Nimrud), Harran (Sultantepe) and from the Babylonian ones of Uruk, Ur, Nippur, Babylon, and Sippar.

The constituent parts of traditional anti-witchcraft documents include: oral rites (prayers, incantations, utterances), symbolic rituals (e.g., the burning of statues), medical treatments (e.g., preparation of potions), descriptions of symptoms, diagnoses, and prognoses.

Prayers and incantations may occasionally appear alone. Originally, incantations were recorded only in part as an aide-memoire, but eventually the entire incantation was committed to writing, and instructions regarding the time, place, and manner of ritual performance as well as other types of information (particularly, an objective description of the problem, a diagnosis, and a statement of purpose) were subsequently added. Incantations are found in various written contexts: as part of short rituals; in short collections of incantations (with some ritual instructions); and in standardized scribal series – some of which were collections, while others represented complex lengthy ceremonies, such as *Maqlû*.

The texts were composed as guides to practicing magicians and physicians; hence, the texts usually present in varying combinations the crucial elements that constitute the actual ritual activity or performance (oral and manual rites and preparation or applications of ceremonial/medical materials) as well as a statement describing the circumstance and purpose of the activity. Two typical text forms are: the text of an incantation followed by a rubric (an ancient classificatory label) and ritual instructions; and a description of the patient's symptoms followed by a diagnosis (e.g., "that man suffers from bewitchment"), ritual or medical instructions (e.g., instructions to create a sacred space such as a reed hut or altar, to prepare salves or potions, and/or to recite an oral rite as well as the text of the oral rite itself), and finally, a prognosis (e.g., "the man will live").

Introductory and concluding scribal statements (symptoms, diagnoses, purposes, prognoses) and the oral and manual rites of the various anti-witchcraft compositions may be classified, for example, as follows:

- descriptions of symptoms: physical, psychological, and/or social;
- diagnoses: etiological or descriptive;
- oral rites: prayers addressed to gods (especially the sun god, Shamash) or to ritual objects;
- oral rites: incantations: addressed to witches or to materials;
- rituals: introductory acts – preparation of a sacred space (e.g., the erection of reed huts or altars);
- rituals: central acts – destruction of the witch by burning, burying, or drowning her representation;
- rituals: acts that counteract witchcraft (through the elimination of forms of miasma) by means of washing or wiping-off the patient;
- rituals: the employment of apotropaic devices such as plants or amulets;
- medical preparations and treatments: the preparation and administration of salves, potions, or lotions.

The basic textual unit prescribes the performance of a discrete ritual; these independent rites are the fundamental units of scribal composition. In the course of time, scribes attempted to organize the vast body of magical and medical literature, generally, and the witchcraft materials, specifically, into coherent groups and collections. Scribes differed in the way they organized these materials. Tablets often contain more than one ritual-unit; moreover, the same ritual-unit may appear in different religious, literary, or scribal contexts. These larger literary-editorial constructs may be either canonical or ad hoc compositions and may contain either a series of units that share some commonality (e.g., the evil addressed) or the text of a complex ritual.

ANTI-WITCHCRAFT RITUALS

In almost all instances, the patients on whose behalf witchcraft rituals were performed were members of the elite. The bewitched person, normally a man, is described in the third person in the symptomologies and diagnoses, and addresses the gods or the witch in the first person in the prayers and incantations. A few rituals serve the needs of women: a woman who blames the estrangement of her husband on a witch, or a woman who is pregnant and fears that bewitchment will cause her to miscarry. Sometimes when the witch is said to disrupt public activities or places, the public is described as comprising young men and young women. But overall, in our texts, the bewitched is male, though I have no doubt that women, too, felt themselves to be victims of witchcraft, but their cases usually did not enter the written record of the exorcist.

Procedural texts prescribe the treatment of witchcraft-induced illness either by means of various ritual or ceremonial therapies or by means of traditional herbal therapy. The traditional scribal literature contains and occasionally juxtaposes both forms of treatment.

In the witchcraft texts that preserve the lore of the herbalist (*asû*), descriptions of symptoms are followed by instructions for preparing and administering medications. For example:

> If a man has repeated headaches, sleep . . ., his dreams are terrifying, he is repeat-edly frightened in his sleep, his knees are bound, his chest . . . paralysis, he is constantly sweating; that man is bewitched. You crush tamarisk, soapwort, and leaves of the *ḫaluppu*-tree together. You wash him with water, you rub him with cedar oil. Afterwards you put tamarisk, soapwort and potash in . . ., you heat it in the oven, you wash him with it; he will then recover.
>
> (Thompson, *AMT* 86/1)

Turning to the ritual practitioner (*āšipu*), we note that he used both oral and manual rites in his attempt to combat witchcraft. Many different kinds of incantations were recited by the *āšipu*; in the main, they address evil forces such as the witch as well as beneficent forces that are meant to aid in the fight against evil forces. A subgroup of these incantations are in the form of a prayer; more specifically, the prayers used in rituals against witchcraft often take the form of *Gebetsbeschwörungen*, incantation-prayers, (*šuilla*) and are designated by modern scholars as "special" *Gebetsbeschwörungen*, for they have the form of a *šuilla* but do not carry that designation and are often directed against a specific type of evil and are recited as part of a magical ritual.

The ritual of the *āšipu* might range from a relatively simple one to an extensively elaborated performance, and could last a few hours or continue for a day or more. The ceremony often centered on an operation directed toward significant objects or symbols (e.g., the destruction of figurines, the use of substitutes).

Ebeling, *KAR*, no. 80 and duplicates may serve as an example of a relatively short ritual against witchcraft performed by the *āšipu* and may be summarized as follows:

> After a description of a patient's symptoms, a diagnosis of witchcraft, and a statement that the release of witchcraft is the purpose of the ritual, the ritual instructions prescribe the setting out of offerings to Šamaš the sun god, the preparation of statues of a warlock and witch, the raising up of these statues, and the recitation of an incantation to Šamaš. In this incantation, the statues are designated as representing the evildoers who have harmed the victim and their destruction by fire is described. Subsequent to the threefold recitation of this incantation, the statues are placed in a container, sprinkled with fish oil, and set on fire. Then, a second incantation, "I lift up the torch, I burn your statues," invoking the aid of Ea, Asalluḫi, and Girra (gods of magic and burning) and addressing the burning statues, is recited, and the burned statues are trampled

in water and their remains buried. The ritual is performed either at sunrise or at sunset. In sum, statues of the witch are raised to Šamaš and burned; the burned statues are then drowned and buried.

As an example of a complex ritual against witchcraft that was performed by the *āšipu*, special mention should be made of the Akkadian magical series *Maqlû*, "Burning." This composition is the longest and most important Mesopotamian text concerned with combating witchcraft.

Maqlû comprises eight tablets of incantations and a ritual tablet. The incantation tablets record the text of almost one hundred incantations; in the ritual tablet, these incantations are cited by incipit, and alongside each citation appropriate ritual directions are prescribed. The present form of *Maqlû* seems to be a creation of the early first millennium BCE, the standard lengthy text having developed from an earlier short form by means of a series of sequential changes. In the main, the incantations and rituals of *Maqlû* are directed against witches and witchcraft. The ceremony was intended to counteract and dispel evil magic and its effects, to protect the patient, and to punish and render ineffectual those responsible for the evil.

The ceremony was performed during a single night and into the following morning at the end of the month Abu (July/August), a time when spirits were thought to move back and forth between the netherworld and this world. The primary participants were the exorcist and his patient (who on occasion would be the king). The series (and ceremony) was composed of three major subdivisions. The first two divisions (Tablets I–V, VI–VII 57) were performed during the night, the third (VII 58–VIII) during the early morning hours of the following day.

The ceremony itself centered on the recitation of incantations and the performance of such rites as burning of figurines, fumigation, salving, washing, disposal, and protection against future attack. Each division centered on a different set of rites: division one, burning and dousing figurines of the witch; division two, fumigation and protection of the patient's house and massaging the patient; division three, washing the patient over representations of the witch. The incantations of each division have common themes; they thus develop a set of ideas that parallel or derive from the rites of the division, thereby reiterating the central idea and ritual activity of the section. The bulk of the material of each incantation division is set out in blocks of "similar" incantations, each block reiterating a theme linked to a standard ritual act, and these blocks in turn follow one another in accordance with standard ritual patterns. The work as a whole has introductory, connecting, and concluding sections, as do the individual subdivisions. Thus, the work has both a ritual and ideational structure as well as a narrative progression that impart a distinctive character and tone to the ceremony.

Instead of presenting a detailed analysis of the ceremony and its ideology, let us sample some of the more characteristic incantations of each of the three divisions.

Division one

This division opens with the patient's invocation of the gods of the cosmos – the powers of the night sky, of the netherworld, and of nature – to assist him in his struggle against the witch. It then turns to its main concern – the judgment, execution, and expulsion of the witch. The witch is destroyed by fire and water; these symbolic acts of burning and drowning are performed ritually on representations.

The fire-god Girra is a primary actor in this division. The incantation II 76–102 is addressed to the fire-god and is recited alongside the ritual burning of images of the witch:

> O blazing Girra, firstborn of Anu,
> It is you who renders judgment, the secret speech,
> You illumine darkness,
> You set straight confusion and disorder.
> You grant decisions for the great gods,
> Without you, no god delivers a verdict,
> It is you who gives instruction and direction.
> It is you who speedily captures the evildoer,
> And who speedily overcomes the wicked (and the) enemy.
> I, your servant, So-and-so, the son of So-and-so, whose god is
> So-and-so, whose goddess is So-and-so –
> I have been attacked by witchcraft, and so I stand before you,
> I have been made detestable before god, king noble and lord, and so
> I come before you,
> I have been made sickening in the sight of anyone who beholds me,
> and so I bow down before you.
> O most great Girra, pure god,
> Now in the presence of your great godhead
> Two images of the warlock and witch (made) of bronze I have
> fashioned with your power.
> In your presence I have crossed them and to you I have given
> them.
> May they die but I live,
> May they be driven away (or perhaps bound) but I be acquitted
> (lit., be/go straight),
> May they come to an end but I increase,
> May they weaken but I become strong.
> O stately Girra, most eminent one of the gods,
> Vanquisher of the wicked and the enemy, vanquish them so I not
> be wronged.
> May I, your servant, live and be well so that I may serve you
> (lit., stand before you).
> You alone are my god, you alone are my lord,
> You alone are my judge, you alone are my aid,
> You alone are my avenger!

The request to the fire-god to destroy the evildoer is continued in the next incantation (II 104–125), the first part of which (II 104–115) is here quoted:

> O blazing Girra, warlike son of Anu,
> It is you, the fiercest among your brothers,

Who decides lawsuits like (= in the stead of) Sin and Šamaš –
Judge my case, hand down my verdict.
Burn my warlock and my witch;
O Girra, burn my warlock and my witch;
O Girra, scorch my warlock and my witch;
O Girra, burn them;
O Girra, scorch them;
O Girra, vanquish them;
O Girra, consume them;
O Girra, consume them completely (lit. mix them together completely).

The witch against whom the ritual is directed is a powerful and destructive creature, as we learn from III 1–16, the opening of the first incantation in Tablet III:

The sorceress, she who roams the streets,
Who continually intrudes into houses,
Who prowls in alleys,
Who spies about the broad ways –
She keeps looking (lit. turning) around in front and in back,
Standing in the street she turns (her) foot (movement) around,
And in the square blocks (commercial) traffic.
She robbed the fine young man of his virility,
She carried off the attractiveness of the fine young woman,
With her malignant stare she took away her charms,
She looked at the young man and (thereby) took away his vitality,
She looked at the young woman and (thereby) carried off her
    attractiveness!
The witch saw me and came after me,
With her venom, she cut off (commercial) traffic,
With her spittle, she cut off my trading,
She drove away my god and goddess from my person.

Again, the fire-god is asked to destroy the agency of evil in III 158–183:

Hand, Hand,
Strong hand of humankind,
Which, like a lion, seized a man,
Like a bird trap, clamped down on a young man,
Like a net, overwhelmed the warrior,
Like a battle net, caught the leader,
Like a trap, covered the strong one.
O warlock and witch, may Girra burn your hand,
May Girra consume, may Girra drink, may Girra wholly consume
    (lit. mix together completely),
May Girra roar at your strong hand,
You whose hand bewitched, may he burn your body,

May the son of Ea, the exorcist, scatter your cohort.
May the smoke of Girra cover your face,
Like an oven through your cracks,
Like a pot through your mud,
May fierce Girra scatter you.
May your witchcraft and evil spells not approach me.
I rise up like fish in my water,
Like a pig from my mud,
Like a soap plant at the edge of the (inundated) meadow,
Like *sassatu*-grass at the canal bank,
Like seed of an ebony tree at the seashore.
By pure Ishtar (Venus), who illumines fate,
I have been designated for the design of life (i.e., "inscribed for life").
By the command pronounced by awesome Girra
And blazing Girra, son of valiant Anu.

Subsequent to burning, the smoldering remains of the effigies are doused with water; in V 139–148, we hear how the evil beings are thereby deprived of the power to perform evil:

Fierce, raging, powerful, furious,
Overbearing, tough, hostile, wicked are you!
Who but Ea can dampen you?
Who but Asalluḫi can cool you?
May Ea dampen you,
May Asalluḫi cool you.
My mouth is water, your mouth is fire:
May my mouth extinguish your mouth,
May the curse of my mouth extinguish the curse of your mouth,
May the plots of my heart extinguish the plots of your heart!

Finally, in V 166–184, the dead witches are expelled and commanded never to return:

Be off, be off, begone, begone,
Depart, depart, flee, flee!
Go off, go away, be off, and begone!
May your wickedness like smoke rise ever heavenward!
From my body be off!
From my body begone!
From my body depart!
From my body flee!
From my body go off!
From my body go away!
To my body turn back not!
To my body approach not!

To my body near not!
On my body abut not!
By the life of Šamaš, the honorable, be adjured!
By the life of Ea, lord of the deep, be adjured!
By the life of Asalluḫi, the magus of the gods, be adjured!
By the life of Girra, your executioner, be adjured!
From my body you shall indeed be separated!

Division two

In this division, fumigation is performed to counteract and disperse attacks of witchcraft. Following fumigation, objects are set up for protection, and the patient, himself, is then massaged with oil.

Salt figures prominently among the materials burned. In VI 111–119, it is addressed as if it were a god:

O you Salt, who was created in a pure place,
For food of the great gods did Enlil destine you.
Without you no meal is set out in Ekur,
Without you god, king, noble, and prince do not smell incense.
I am so-and-so, the son of so-and-so, whom witchcraft holds captive,
Whom bewitchment holds in (the form of a skin) disease.
O Salt, release my witchcraft, release my spell,
Receive from me the bewitchment so that, as the god my Creator,
I may constantly praise you.

And in VII 31–49 the oil used for salving is also addressed:

Pure oil, clear oil, bright oil,
Oil that purifies the body of the gods,
Oil that soothes the sinews of mankind,
Oil of the incantation of Ea, oil of the incantation of Asalluḫi.
I have coated you with soothing oil
That Ea has granted for soothing,
I have anointed you with the oil of healing,
I have cast upon you the incantation of Ea, lord of Eridu, Ninshiku,
I have expelled *asakku*, jaundice, chills of your body,
I have removed stupor, apathy, and misery of your body,
I have soothed the sick sinews of your limbs.
By the command of Ea, lord of the deep,
By the incantation of Ea, by the incantation of Asalluḫi,
By the gentle bandaging of Gula,
By the soothing hands of Nintinugga
And Ningirima, mistress of incantation.
On So-and-So, Ea cast the incantation of the word of healing
That the seven *apkallu*s of Eridu soothe his body.

Division three

With the coming of morning the patient washes himself repeatedly; this is the primary rite in this division. Subsequently, representations of the witch in an edible form are thrown to dogs, protective amulets are then prepared, and concluding rites are performed.

The patient welcomes the day and repeatedly washes himself over representations (frequently of flour) of the witch; this washing serves the dual purposes of cleansing the patient of evil and causing the witchcraft to return to and seize the witch (reversion), as we learn in the three incantations VII 153–160, 161–169, and 170–177:

Dawn has broken; doors are now open;
The traveler has passed through the gate;
[The messenger] has taken to the road.
Ha! witch: you labored in vain to (lit. you shall not) bewitch me!
Ha! enchantress: you tried for nought to (lit. you shall not)
      enchant me!
For I am (now) cleansed by the rising sun;
May [the sorceries] that you performed or had performed (against me
      during the night)
Turn back and seize you yourself!

It is morning, yea, morning.
This is (the morning) of my warlock and witch;
They arose, playing their *n'iu* instrument like musicians.
At my door stands Pālil;
At the head of my bed stands Lugaledina,
I am sending against you the one at my door, Pālil (and)
The one at the head of my bed, Lugaledina.
Over one whole mile your speech (extends), over the whole road your
      word (extends) –
I turn back your witchcraft and your spells, they will seize you
      yourself!

At dawn my hands are washed.
May a propitious beginning begin (the new day) for me,
May happiness and good health ever accompany me,
Whatever I seek may I attain,
May the dream I dreamt be made favorable for me,
May anything evil, anything untoward,
The spells of warlock and witch,
Not approach me, not touch me.
By the command of Ea, Šamaš, Marduk, and the princess Bēlet-ilī.

In conclusion, I should emphasize that the study of Mesopotamian witchcraft beliefs and rituals is more than just an exposition of esoterica. It is important not least because the relevant texts address physical, psychological, existential, and social difficulties that not infrequently formed the center of concern of Mesopotamian life;

the beliefs and accusations, moreover, are barometers of personal and societal tensions and indicators of problems and conflicts in that ancient society that are often not revealed as clearly, and sometimes not at all, by our more standard and official texts. But in addition to shedding light on problems that the Mesopotamians shared with general humanity, Mesopotamian witchcraft beliefs and rituals are an integral part of the larger system of religious belief and of the broader cultural cosmology of that civilization and, thus, a source of information regarding its history and culture.

BIBLIOGRAPHY

In studying Mesopotamian witchcraft, I have found it very useful to consult anthropological literature on witchcraft as well as studies of European witchcraft. I list here a few general studies and collections. In addition to the classic works by Kluckhohn on the Navaho and Evans-Pritchard on the Azande, see, e.g., the essays in *Witchcraft and Sorcery: Selected Readings*, ed. M. Marwick (Baltimore: Penguin Books, 1970), and in *Anthropological Studies of Witchcraft, Magic, and Religion* (= vol. 1 of *Articles on Witchcraft, Magic, and Demonology: A Twelve-Volume Anthology of Scholarly Articles*), ed. B. P. Levack (New York: Garland, 1992); see also A. F. C. Wallace, *Religion: An Anthropological View* (New York: Random House, 1966), esp. pp. 113–116 and 177–187; D. L. O'Keefe, *Stolen Magic: The Social History of Magic* (New York: Random House, 1983), esp. pp. 414–457. For European witchcraft, see, e.g., the essays in *Early Modern European Witchcraft: Centres and Peripheries*, ed. B. Ankarloo and G. Henningsen (Oxford: Clarendon Press, 1990), and such studies as R. Kieckhefer, *European Witch Trials: Their Foundations in Popular and Learned Culture, 1300–1500* (Berkeley: University of California, 1976); R. Briggs, *Witches and Neighbors: The Social and Cultural Context of European Witchcraft* (New York: Viking, 1996).

For the nature of magic in Mesopotamia, see W. van Binsbergen and F. A. M. Wiggermann, "A Theoretical Perspective, and its Application to Ancient Mesopotamia," in *Mesopotamian Magic: Textual, Historical, and Interpretative Perspectives*, ed. T. Abusch and K. van der Toorn (Groningen: Styx, 1999), pp. 3–34. For recent discussions of therapy and oral rites in Mesopotamia and bibliographies on these subjects, see my "Mesopotamian Prayers and Incantations," and "Illness and Healing in Ancient Mesopotamia," in *Religions of the Ancient World: A Guide*, ed. S. I. Johnston (Cambridge: Belknap Press of Harvard University Press, 2004), pp. 353–355 and 456–459.

The present chapter on witchcraft summarizes and repeats some of the positions that I have taken in years past on this topic. See especially the essays collected in Abusch, *Mesopotamian Witchcraft: Toward a History and Understanding of Babylonian Witchcraft Beliefs and Literature*, AMD 5 (Leiden: Brill/Styx, 2002); and *Babylonian Witchcraft Literature: Case Studies*, Brown Judaic Studies 132 (Atlanta: Scholars Press, 1987); for a recent discussion of the *Kultmittelbeschwörung*, see my "Blessing and Praise in Ancient Mesopotamian Incantations," in *Literatur, Politik und Recht in Mesopotamien*, ed. W. Sallaberger *et al.* (Wiesbaden: Harrassowitz, 2003), pp. 1–14. For other discussions of Mesopotamian witchcraft, see S. Rollin, "Women and Witchcraft in Ancient Assyria," in *Images of Women in Antiquity*, ed. A. Cameron and A. Kuhrt (Detroit: Wayne State University Press, 1983), pp. 34–45; M.-L. Thomsen, *Zauberdiagnose und schwarze Magie in Mesopotamien* (Copenhagen: CNI Publications 2, 1987).

The translation of *Maqlû* is based on my synoptic edition of the text; however, for the sake of convenience, I have followed the line-count in G. Meier, *Die assyrische Beschwörungssammlung Maqlû*, AfO Beiheft 2 (Berlin, 1937). An English translation of *Maqlû* will appear in the series, *Writings from the Ancient World*; a German translation (with D. Schwemer) will appear in the series, *Texte aus der Umwelt des Alten Testaments*.

PART VI

INTELLECTUAL LIFE
Cuneiform writing and learning

——·◆·——

CHAPTER TWENTY-SEVEN

INCANTATIONS WITHIN AKKADIAN MEDICAL TEXTS

——— ·◆· ———

M. J. Geller

The use of magical incantations within Akkadian medicine has long been recognised as a characteristic feature of healing therapy in Babylonia, although often with the wrong inferences being made. Historians of medicine have seen Babylonian medicine as influenced by magic and less rational than its Greek counterpart (Sigerist: 1955: I, 477ff.). This misconception about Babylonian medicine stems from a period when relatively few Babylonian medical texts (and medical incantations) had been published, although significant progress had been made in publishing major Sumerian and Akkadian magical texts, such as *Utukku Lemnūtu* (Thompson 1903), *Shurpu* (Reiner 1970) and *Maqlû* (Meier 1967). Recent publications on Babylonian medicine (Stol 1993 and 2000; Heeßel 2000) allow for a more balanced view of Babylonian magic and medicine, and we can assess how incantations within the medical corpus affect our attitudes towards the rational nature of Babylonian medicine.

The usual supposition is that magic and medicine, although at times complementary, represent different points on the scale of rational 'science'. Hence, the oldest Sumerian medical text known, from the end of the third millennium (Civil 1960), contains recipes but not a single incantation. This text serves as the paradigm example of 'medicine' versus magic. Already by the Old Babylonian period, however, single incantations appear with 'medical' themes, referring to illnesses of the eye, internal organs, etc., and similar incantations with these same themes appear within medical texts. It seems probable that the medical incantations, referring to physical symptoms of an illness, were likely to have circulated in three phases: (1) orally transmitted and recited incantations which (2) were committed to writing in the form of single-column tablets containing one incantation and, finally, (3) medical incantations were incorporated into longer tablets containing medical recipes or medical omens.

The question is how to distinguish a 'medical' incantation from any other type of incantation. Medical incantations appear in both Sumerian and Akkadian, or occasionally as Sumerian–Akkadian bilinguals, or as mixtures of both Sumerian and Akkadian. In some ways, the distinction between a 'medical' incantation and other types is not difficult to ascertain, since the main criterion refers to incantations that have been incorporated into medical texts. Incantations on related themes referring to health matters, such as snakebite, dogbite, scorpion bite, could be excluded on these formal grounds, although we will include them in this survey because they are thematically related to the subject matter.

There are many different kinds of Sumerian and Akkadian incantations from Mesopotamia, although they fall within certain patterns. The Sumerian incantation prototypes were already studied by Adam Falkenstein in his Leipzig dissertation (Falkenstein 1931), and this work is still useful, despite new studies along the same lines (Cunningham 1997). Within formal Sumerian incantations, certain features are nearly always present. The incantations usually begin with a 'problem', described as the attack of a particular demon or perhaps an angry god, whom the patient has offended. Within these texts, an illness such as 'headache' may be indistinguishable from a demon of the same name. The problem is then discussed by Enki, god of healing, with his son Asalluhi, and the Akkadian gods Ea and Marduk assume the same roles. During the course of a polite dialogue, Enki (Ea) advises his son Asalluhi (Marduk) about the appropriate ritual to be performed to 'resolve' the magical problem. Other major incantation compendia address themselves to specific problems, such as witchcraft (*Maqlû*) or guilt and unwitting sin (*Shurpu*), while the earlier *Udug-hul/ Utukkū Lemnūtu* incantations appear to be an encyclopedia of incantations without any particular goal or target in mind. Like *Utukkū Lemnūtu*, some of the longer incantation collections appear in Sumerian or in Sumerian–Akkadian bilingual forms, particularly those addressed to 'migraine' or the Asag demon (not yet edited in a modern edition), or the Ban (Schramm 2001), or comprise parts of *Shurpu*. Others, such as *Maqlu*, are in Akkadian, although many anti-witchcraft incantations in Akkadian also appear within the medical corpus (Abusch 1984). Incantations in Sumerian only or in bilingual Sumerian–Akkadian versions were employed for the 'mouth-washing' ceremony of cult idols, or for rituals dealing with the building of a temple or cultic building (Ambose 2004) or for ceremonies inaugurating a new idol (Walker and Dick 2001). These formal incantations, usually found within the great libraries of Nineveh and Assur, differ considerably from 'medical' incantations which appear within the medical corpus.

So what is so special about 'medical' incantations?

The medical incantations have most recently been studied in an unpublished University of Chicago doctoral dissertation (Collins 1999), in which the author forcefully argues for thematic distinctions between medical incantations and the rest of Mesopotamian magic. The central thesis revolves around 'causes' of illness, with the point being that medical incantations focus on medical problems for which a 'natural' cause can be attributed, such as a kernel of grain flying into the eye, or flatulence causing pain within the patient's body. Such 'natural' causes can be imaginary, such as a serpent within the patient's body disrupting internal organs, or a gnawing worm within a painful tooth. In other cases, the causes of illness can be seen as analogies from the natural world, such as menstrual bleeding being analogous to a river overflowing its banks, or simply 'fire' as an analogy for fever. Such causes are contrasted with other genres of incantations in which demons or angry gods are the declared causes of illness or misfortune, with the incantation being aimed at preventing demons from approaching, or ridding the patient of them ex facto. Collins takes his argument a step further by suggesting (virtually without recourse to evidence) that diseases or ailments considered to be 'normal' would have been attributed to natural causes, such as those above, while 'abnormal' cases of illness would, conversely, have

Figure 27.1 Seal impression showing an incantation priest at work on a patient (Teisser, B. *Ancient Near Eastern Cylinder Seals from the Marcopli Collection* 231) (courtesy of the Trustees of the British Museum).

been attributed to supernatural causes, such as demonic attack ultimately resulting from the patient's guilt of sin.

There is much to be said in favour of such a scenario, although some refinements are required to make this scheme workable. First, it is generally agreed that, within Mesopotamian cosmology, disease can be caused both by immediate and more remote (or higher) factors; the patient can be ill because he was bitten by a rabid dog and because he angered the gods, who control all aspects of human destiny (see Stol). The question, then, is one of focus. Medical incantations tend to be addressed to the more immediate causes of illness, such as a draught or bile, while more formal magical texts concern themselves with the ultimate causes of demonic attack and divine disfavour. All incantations, however, can be assumed to have a psychological dimension (Stol 1999; Geller 1999), and hence the question is how these incantations were designed to be effective within the contexts in which they were used.

One immediate question which arises in medical incantations is why they were used at all. With other types of incantations, rituals accompanied the incantation to reinforce the magic, such as the peeling of an onion to symbolise breaking the spell, as in *Shurpu* incantations. Other rituals might include the burning of incense, etc. Medical incantations occurring within a medical text obviously serve some ancillary function, to increase the effectiveness of the recipes themselves, added for good measure. On the other hand, the great majority of medical texts have no incantations, nor is it easy to determine the reason why a spell would appear within one medical text and not within another. From a modern perspective, we might think that although a spell may or may not help, it would not do much harm either, although such a sceptical approach to magic or medicine is unlikely to be found in our ancient sources. Another possibility is that the healer may have thought that an appeal to Gula, the goddess of healing, or even a meaningless mumbo-jumbo Sumerian charm, may have had a desirable psychological impact on the patient, to enhance the placebo effect of the drugs, although again there is not a single Mesopotamian text which recognises drugs as placebos. Unfortunately, we have no manuals of medicine or instruction manuals explaining when such incantations were to be used by healers, and when not.

The use of medical incantations can be viewed from the perspective of the ancient physician or patient as a means of altering certain realities. The belief was that similar causes can stimulate similar effects, which is the essential principle behind sympathetic magic. Hence, diarrhoea is seen in one incantation as analogous to an overflowing canal. If damming the canal solves one problem, then medications acting in the same way will staunch the flow of diarrhoea. The incantation draws the patient's attention to the sympathetic power of the analogy, with the psychological by-product of creating greater confidence in the herbal remedies and prescriptions.

One thing, however, is clear, and that is that the medical incantations are not useful as diagnostic statements about the medical state of the patient or the perceived or real cause of his disease (*pace* Collins). The analogies within medical incantations are intended to portray the disease to the patient in a graphic way, but not as actual explanations of 'cause'. A few examples will illustrate the point.

Painful toothache is depicted in an incantation within medical prescriptions as the work of a tooth-worm (*tultu*) who gnaws away at the patient's teeth and jaws. The incantation explains that the tooth-worm was one of the primordial creatures of creation, who complained before the gods Shamash and Ea that he had nothing to eat, i.e. no raison d'être. When offered fruit as his host, the worm declined and replied, 'what are a ripe fig and an apple to me? Set me to dwell between teeth and jaw, that I may suck the blood of the jaw, that I may chew on the bits (of food) stuck in the jaw' (Foster 1993: II 878; Collins 1999: 262f.). The incantation is hardly a diagnosis, but a way for the patient to visualise his toothache in a non-abstract form. In addition to medical remedies applied to the tooth and jaw, the incantation serves to help the patient cope with the pain by imagining the incantation's power forcing the worm out of the tooth. No such illustration is offered by the medical prescription itself. A similar ontological myth accompanies the 'ergot' incantation, which describes a tiny ergot (*mirhu*) entering a lad's eye, at the very beginning of creation when the gods Shamash and Sin first learned to reap and harvest (Foster 1993: II 854; Collins 1999: 95f.). The incantation offers a way of explaining a sty in the eye as by-product of the natural order of things, rather than as a demonic invasion.

In some cases, the medical incantation incorporates a simple ritual, in addition to the complex prescriptions which are applied to the patient to alleviate the symptoms of disease. In another 'eye-disease' incantation, the spell opens with a statement that:

> the lad's eye is sick, the maiden's eye is sick. Who will heal the eye of the lad and maiden? You send (for ones who) take for you the pure heart of the date palm. You break it up in your mouth and roll it in your hand, you bind it on the foreheads of the lad and maiden and the eye of the lad and maiden will get better.

This leads us to the central difference between 'classical' incantations, best attested in either Sumerian or as Sumerian–Akkadian bilinguals, and medical incantations (usually in Akkadian) which appear within the medical corpus. One assumption is that, since these different types of incantations refer to different gods, they originate from different professional atelier. *Utukku Lemnūtu* incantations, for instance, which have a long and complex history, usually invoke the gods Enki (Ea) and Asalluhi (Marduk), in contrast to medical incantations which usually invoke the healing gods Gula or Damu. It seems likely, therefore, that classical incantations belong to *ašipūtu* or the craft of the exorcist, while medical incantations belong to *asūtu*, the physician's handiwork. The respective roles of the *āšipu* and *asû* have been reconsidered recently, and the clear-cut distinctions between their activities are no longer seen as definitive (Scurlock 1999). It now seems that the *āšipu* was required to have considerable knowledge of medicine, usually thought of as *asūtu*, and many medical texts have been found in the private archives of the *āšipu* of Assur. It might seem logical to assume, therefore, that medical incantations were composed by the *asû*, at the same time as he compiled his recipes, while incantation tablets were composed by the *āšipu*.

In fact, no such assumption can be proven. We do not know who composed any of the incantations in the various compendia, including medical incantations, nor can we be sure that some incantations were composed specifically for use in medical texts, by an *asû*. It could easily be the case that some incantations were quoted in medical texts because they seemed to be contextually appropriate, but these could have been composed by an *āšipu* as well as an *asû*. We must look elsewhere for the essential differences between medical incantations and other genres of magical texts.

In only a few cases are incantations recommended for use within the corpus of medical literature known as the Diagnostic Handbook (Heeßel 2000: 323: 84′), and in the few cases when reciting an incantation is recommended, it is usually associated with symptoms of chronic or serious disease, such as *bennu*, for which little could be done to help the patient. Although the Diagnostic Handbook technically should belong to the physician, nevertheless according to colophons and rubrics, the text originates from the workshops of exorcism (Heeßel 2000: 17f., 107–109). Relatively few instances, however, of incantations are recommended within the context of prognosis.

The idea of hierarchy is a cardinal feature of magic. In terms of causes of disease or misfortune, the ultimate causes are cosmic in nature, since it is gods who personally decide the fate of every individual. An offended or angry god, therefore, needs to be appeased through the most powerful forms of incantation, prayer, and ritual. Demons are part of this cosmic process, since they are often sent directly by the gods or are sent from the Netherworld specifically to bring chaos, disease, and destruction. The incantations and prayers and rituals assigned to deal with these causes are, by their very nature, cosmic as well, being addressed to the highest powers within the pantheon to intercede on behalf of the patient or sufferer in order to appease anger or alter an evil decree or fate. Much of the work of the *āšipu* was therefore directed towards this aim.

The hierarchy comprised lower levels as well, however, although the relative weights of these levels may be disputed. The attack of ghosts was feared as much as that of demons, but for different reasons, not always related to the sin of the patient or victim. A ghost of an ancestor could cause harm to a victim because he brought a complaint against his human victim in the court of the Netherworld (Alster 1991: 85; Geller 1995: 104–107), or because the ghost's funerary *kispu* offerings may have been neglected by his living progeny. On the other hand, a ghost could revisit someone simply because of casual contact, such as eating and drinking together. Incantations to rid victims of such ghosts often involved ritual weddings, as well as incantations (Farber 2004: 128–131).

Witchcraft forms another level of magic, although usually caused by human rather than divine agents. Evil eye (envy) and evil tongue (gossip and slander) would qualify under this category, as well as love incantations which compel someone to fall in love. The nature of the incantations is generally more focused on earthly rather than cosmic themes, enumerating the dangers and potential harm of witchcraft and spells (Abusch 2002 and this volume). The moral stature of the victim may not be relevant to the fact that he is the one being attacked by black magic, for which various counter-incantations and rituals are prescribed. A similar category of incantations is known under the rubric of Egalkurra, in which the victim faces slander and rivalry at court.

Finally, incantations against dogbite, snakebite, and scorpion bite, as well as incantations to deal with crying babies (Farber 1989), are probably on a similar level to *Namburbi* incantations and rituals, which are intended to ward off evil portents and omens (Maul 1994). *Namburbi* incantations, although seeking divine help, are essentially concerned with the nature of the evil portent and how to avoid it, with incantations appealing for help combined with rituals to rid the victim of the danger.

There is a pattern which emerges from these data which is relevant to medical incantations. The higher the level within the hierarchy of incantations, the more cosmic are the incantation themes and the less reliance is placed upon rituals and ritual acts. The incantations themselves are sufficiently powerful to move the gods to action, without much in the way of elaborate ritual to help things along. The lower orders of the incantation hierarchy depend increasingly upon sympathetic rituals and rituals to avoid or counteract evil.

Medical incantations form part of this same hierarchy, despite the fact that these other incantations formally belong to the art of 'exorcism' (*āšipūtu*). Once incorporated into medical texts, medical incantations were no longer independent compositions but part of the elaborate system of healing which could include rituals, such as fumigation, but also comprised prescriptions of drugs to be applied internally and externally, as potions, suppositories, and bandages. The focus of medical incantations, therefore, was not 'cosmic' in the sense of being concerned with the ultimate causes of disease; little mention is made of the patient's guild, angry gods, or even demons. The themes expressed by medical incantations were more immediate, and hence 'natural', causes of disease, such as the ergot or tooth-worm, for which prescriptions were to be employed. In the same way that classical incantations focused on the ultimate causes (guilt, negligence, sin), medical texts focused on symptoms (pain, fever, swelling), and the incantations associated with medicine were aimed at elucidating the causes of symptoms, through various kinds of analogies.

Examples of medical incantations will illustrate how this works. Marten Stol has translated a number of Sumerian and Akkadian incantations dealing with all aspects of childbirth (Stol 2000: 59–70, 129–131). On one hand, these incantations appear to be high on the scale of hierarchy, since they include the dialogue between Enki (Ea) and Asalluhi (Marduk), discussing the woman's plight and condition, and the woman is said to have been impregnated by the Moon God himself. However, the subject matters expressed in these incantations do not refer to demons or ghosts, but to practical matters of childbirth. Once these incantations have been incorporated into the medical corpus, the main focus shifts to childbirth, in which the mother is portrayed as a foundering boat with cargo which cannot be unloaded. The associated ritual consists mostly of rubbing the woman's body with a combination of oil and dust from rain gutters.

Potency incantations are a unique genre of magical texts from Mesopotamia, in which the incantations and rituals are closely associated with each other. In this case, the aphrodisiac or even erotic nature of the incantation coordinates with ritual instructions for the man and woman to rub their respective genitals with oils (Biggs 1967: 33, 40, 42) while reciting lurid incantations, comparing the man to a wild stag, bull, or onager having an erection. The incantations focus on the problem to hand, rather than on divine interference to any great extent. Other incantations in a related magical (rather than medical) genre are intended to induce a woman to have intercourse with a man, through a combination of incantations addressed to certain stars or to Ishtar and rituals which include making figurines or having the woman suck the juices of an apple or pomegranate (Biggs 1967: 70ff.; see Foster 1993: II 884).

Samana incantations represent another case of a genre with a long history, culminating in these incantations being incorporated into the medical corpus (Finkel 1998: 85–106). Athough *Samana* may be some form of symptom, it is portrayed in these incantations as a fierce animal, either dog or lion, coming from the distant mountains or across the river (i.e. from abroad). *Samana* incantations seem to argue against the hierarchy discussed above, but they are also exceptional. The popularity of *Samana* incantations in late third-millennium Ur III incantations determined their 'cosmic' character in the upper levels of the hierarchy, but by the time they were incorporated into the late medical corpus, the emphasis was somewhat altered; the concern appears to be with *Samana* now as a disease or with symptoms associated with disease.

Not all incantations are thematically related to medicine or healing, but some incantations (usually in Akkadian) simply function as prayers inserted into the text, ostensibly to make the rituals more efficacious. Such prayers may be 'cosmic' in theme, referring back to creation or primordial deities, but otherwise have no specific role within the ritual. Good examples occur within building rituals and incantations designed to sanctify the building of a temple or cultic building, during which offerings are made to various deities. A typical incantation recited with such offerings invokes Enmešarra, the lord of the Netherworld, one of the earliest divinities in the pantheon (Ambose 2004: 120).

Within medical texts, however, the Sumerian and Akkadian incantations tend to be relatively short and simple, lacking much of the literary sophistication of the incantation corpus. Within the series referring to fever, a few incantations occur that are repetitive in nature and difficult to relate to the theme of the medical texts. One incantation reads:

> The *locust*, the *locust*, a red *locust*[1] has arisen and covered a red cloud, red rain has arisen and inseminated red earth, the flood water has arisen and filled a red river. The red farmer has taken up the red shovel and red basket in order to dam up the red waters. As for the red door and red night-bolt: with each case (i.e. patient)

which opens their 'gate' for you, it has *planted offspring*, it has *planted offspring*.
Incantation-spell.

(Worthington 2005: 13 198'–201'; see Collins 1999: 277f.
(unpub.); Foster 1993: 875; Finkel, 1998: 81)[2]

The incantation rubric refers to something not being retained in the patient's body or head, presumably body fluids. The imagery of the red worm, rainwaters, and even the red farmer with his red implements is not easy to comprehend. The implication seems to be that nature is corrupted in several ways, since the colour red in medical contexts is usually dangerous, associated with *samanû*-disease, with symptoms of fever or bleeding, or inflammation (see, for example, Fincke 2000: 153). The last line of the incantation is difficult, suggesting some 'solution' to the problem. Anyone who opens the orifices (lit. gates) and hence relieves the excess fluid which is trapped, at the same time will somehow 'perpetuate' the remedy (if the translation is correct).

A Sumerian incantation in the same text is hardly more informative, but is more relevant: 'the hair is shorn, the hair is strong, the hair grows, the hair which remains grows; incantation for the hair left on the head to grow' (Worthington 2005: 159'–161'). The relevance to the medical passage is found in the previous context which refers to the patient's hair falling out as a result of his illness, with the medical recipe being designed to retain what remains of the patient's hair. The Sumerian incantation itself, however, offers little in the way of explanation or even an invocation to gods, but simply reiterates the wish that the hair should grow (back). Another incantation in the same passage is mumbo-jumbo, or possibly a phonetic Sumerian incantation in an unusual orthography which makes it difficult to decipher (Worthington 2005: 13: 175'–177'). A similar pattern occurs in incantations within eye-disease texts, which contain incantations showing an 'abracadabra' pattern (Fincke 2000: 302), as well as incantations which describe some cause for eye disease, either 'wind' or else a foreign body in the eye (ibid. 302f.). Potency incantations also include a number of abracadabra incantations (see Biggs 1967: 46f.).

The leitmotif of colour associated with disease in a medical incantation, similar to the one cited above, occurs within a medical text against cough, and the particular incantation is directed against bile (*martu*); (see Collins 1999: 231f. and Cadelli 2000: 198, 215). It is sufficient to cite the opening line of the incantation: 'the goat is green, its young is green, its shepherd is green, its herdsman is green'. The incantation explains that the goat eats green grass from a green field and drinks green water from a green canal, and the goat was not fazed by having a staff or clod thrown at it, and only when a mixture of thyme and salt was thrown at the goat did the bile dissolve like a cloud.[3]

The nursery-rhyme character of the two incantations treated here has not been considered by those who have commented on these texts. The simplicity and even humour of 'medical' incantations distinguishes these brief compositions from the more formal (and usually longer) incantations from the magical corpus. This nursery-rhyme quality occurs in another 'bile' incantation, in which the bile addresses those eating food and drinking beer and says, 'when you eat food and drink beer, I will pounce upon you and you will belch like an ox!' (Cadelli 2000: 215; Collins 1999: 230). A similar example of a simple nursery-rhyme type of incantation occurs within the same genre of incantations against 'cough', in a two-line incantation against 'wind' (flatulence) (Foster 1993: II 858; Cadelli 2000: 84), which is addressed to flatulence: 'O wind, wind, you are the hot wind of the gods, the wind (situated) between the turds and urine! You have exited and your stool is placed among the gods (or spirits), your brothers!' The jocular tone of the incantation seems clear.

The difference in tone between 'medical' incantations and those found within traditional magical texts may be explained by context and purpose of the compositions themselves. Although incantations as separate compositions were intended to solve certain kinds of problems, usually primarily addressed to the patient's anxieties or fears, medical texts existed for entirely different reasons. The medical corpus was intended for the alleviation of symptoms through prescriptions and uses of drugs, with the incantations only serving an ancillary function. Hence, the incantations did not have to define the patient's problems in the same way, nor did they actually have to treat the problems, but the incantations within the medical corpus were used to illustrate the problems in some way easily understandable to the patient, without being too technical or complex. Hence the use of simple analogy, often in a nursery-rhyme style, was adopted, since the real work of the medical text was performed by the diagnosis and prescription, combined with the application of the drugs.

Finally, not all medical incantations are either simple or humorous, since occasionally we encounter spells of more literary value, which also serve some sort of therapeutic purpose. One good example are incantations against *maškadu*-illness, which refer to the goddess Gula – patron goddess of healing – and her role within the process of therapy. The following examples of incantations to Gula within the medical corpus speak for themselves in encouraging the patient to accept his treatment and hope for a cure.

> I, [Gula's] servant, have called on you in the midst of the remote heavens.
> Alone [. . .] I stand before you, I am speaking, listen to me!
> Because I am ill, I stood before you, woe is me!
> Great one who knows illness, I am alone, woe is me!.
> You are the august queen who grants good life and good health.
> My lady, be calmed and have pity.
> O she who saves lives help me (lit. take my hand) with this unknown sickness,
> (and) to my dying day let me praise you.
> May the onlooker praise your divinity,
> (and) as long as I am alive let me praise you.
> [I], your servant [the] incantation-priest, will praise you.

> Incantation. I beheld your face, [O Gula], august healer,
> [. . .], you are supreme and pre-eminent,
> together . . . this drug which I hold up before you.
> In these days, there exists *pardannu* or *šaḫḫiḫu*-diseases,
> discharge or stricture or rectal-disease or incontinence, or one bleeds like a
>   woman or whatever illness that I am sick with,
> and you know what I do not know: am I to drink this drug?
> With these drugs (or days?) let me be healthy, let me be well, let me be
>   happy,
> so that I may praise your great divinity!

In every corner let them bless Gula,
who is supreme in spells and healing,
great is her medicine, Gula heals those who revere her.
By the command of (the goddess) Baba I will praise and call her name to
    everyone,
when I go before her. Three times you will make him (the patient) recite it
    (the incantation) and he (the patient) will bow down,
will drink this drug and bow down, and recite thusly:
'I drank this healing drug of my goddess, and I
. . . am cured'. He says this three times and bows down.
. . . have him drink this drug (repeatedly) and he will get better.

(Geller 2004: 607)

NOTES

1   Interpreting *urbatu* in this context as a swarm or grasshopper, forming a cloud (*urpatu*), which is the same play on words as the more standard word for locust, namely *erbu* (locust) and *erpetu* (cloud).
2   Note lots of variant translations, some (Collins and Foster) treating *irišmara* as abracadabra, while Finkel attempts to translate 'he irrigated the . . .'.
3   See also Foster 1993: 847 and Küchler 1904: 52f.; and Michel 2004: 398.

BIBLIOGRAPHY

Abusch, T. 1984 'Magical and Medical Texts: Further Joins and Duplicates', *Revue d'Assyriologie* 78, 93–94.
—— 2002 *Mesopotamian Witchcraft, toward a History and Understanding of Babylonian Witchcraft Beliefs and Literature* (Leiden).
Alster, B. 1991 'Incantation to Utu', *Acta Sumerologica* 13, 27–96.
Ambose, C. 2004 *Mesopotamische Baurituale aus dem 1. Jahrtausend v. Chr.* (Dresden).
Biggs, R. 1967 *Ancient Mesopotamian Potency Incantations* (Locust Valley).
Cadelli, D.S. 2000 *Recherche sur la Médecine Mésopotamienne* (unpub. Ph.D., University of Geneva).
Collins, T.J. 1999 *Natural Illness in Babylonian Medical Incantations* (unpub. Ph.D., University of Chicago).
Cunningham, G. 1997 *'Deliver Me from Evil'* (Rome).
Farber, W. 1989 *Schlaf, Kindchen, Schlaf! Mesopotamische Baby-Beschwörungen and -Rituale* (Winona Lake).
—— 2004 = Idem., 'How to Marry a Disease', *Magic and Rationality in Ancient Near Eastern and Graeco-Roman Medicine*, ed. H.F.J. Horstmanshoff and M. Stol (Leiden), 69–132.
Fincke, J. 2000 *Augenleiden nach Keilschriftlichen Quellen* (Wurzburg).
Finke, I.L. 1998 'A Study in Scarlet', *Festschrift für Rykle Borger zu Seinem 65. Geburtstag am 24. Mai 1994*. ed. S. Maul (Groningen), 85–106.
Foster, B. 1993 *Before the Muses* (Bethesda).
Geller, M.J. 1995 'Very Different Utu Incantations', *Acta Sumerologica* 16: 101–126.
—— 1999 'Freud and Mesopotamian Magic', *Mesopotamian Magic: Textual, Historical, and Interpretative Perspectives*, ed. K. van der Toorn and T. Abusch (Groningen), 49–55.
—— 2004 'Ancient Medicine: the Patient's Perspective', *Journal of Nephrology* 17: 605–610.
Heeßel, N. 2000 *Babylonisch-assyrische Diagnostik* (Münster).
Küchler, F. 1904 *Beiträge zur Kenntnis der Assyrisch-Babylonischen Medizin* (Leipzig).

Maul, S.M. 1994 *Zukunftsbewältigung, Eine Untersuchung altorientalischen Denkens anhand der babylonisch-assyrischen Löserituale (Namburbi)* (Mainz am Rhein).

Michel, C. 2004 'Deux incantations paléo-Assyriennes', *Assyria and Beyond. Studies Presented to Mogens Trolk Larsen*, ed. J. Dercksen (Leiden).

Scurlock, J. 1999 'Physician, Exorcist, Conjurer, Magician: a Tale of Two Healing Professionals', *Mesopotamian Magic: Textual, Historical, and Interpretative Perspectives*, ed. T. Abusch and K. van der Toorn (Groningen), 69–79.

Stol, M. 1993 *Epilepsy in Babylonia* (Groningen).

—— 1999 'Psychosomatic Suffering in Ancient Mesopotamia', *Mesopotamian Magic: Textual, Historical, and Interpretative Perspectives*, ed. K. van der Toorn and T. Abusch (Groningen), 57–68.

—— 2000 *Birth in Babylonia and the Bible, its Mediterranean Setting* (Groningen).

Thompson, R.C. 1903 *The Devils and Evil Spirits of Ancient Babylonia*.

Worthington, M. 2005 *Le Journal des médecines cunéiformes* 5, 6–43.

CHAPTER TWENTY-EIGHT

THE WRITING, SENDING AND READING OF LETTERS IN THE AMORITE WORLD*

———•◆•———

Dominique Charpin

The archives left in the palace of Mari by the Babylonians when they destroyed it in 1759 BC cover a period of some twenty-five years, during which the throne was occupied first by Yasmah-Addu and then by Zimri-Lim.[2] Alongside the very numerous administrative documents they contain several thousand letters, of which some 2,500 have been published in their entirety. Many studies have been devoted to their content but not to the way in which the letters were actually written by, or on behalf of, the sender, conveyed to the addressee, and then read by or to the latter. Yet this is something that historians need to know if they are to properly understand the correspondence. The well-known advantage of the Mari archives is that they offer documentation on a number of different kingdoms, some even outside the Middle Euphrates region. This chapter will be essentially concerned with the writing and reading of royal correspondence, that is to say, with letters sent or received by kings, but I shall on occasion also consider letters that do not form part of the royal correspondence so defined.[2]

THE WRITING OF LETTERS

Letters seem to have been written in one of two ways, being either dictated, or drafted by a scribe. Once the tablet was inscribed, the scribe would read it over to his master, making corrections as necessary, and then enclose it in an envelope, which he would seal with the sender's cylinder-seal. The letter was then ready to be sent to its addressee.

Letters written in Akkadian

It has to be said first of all that with the exception of only one (written in Hurrian), all the letters discovered in the Mari archives are in the Akkadian language. None are written in Amorite, a language known to us only from proper names and a number of technical terms.[3] The question arises, then, whether Akkadian was the language spoken in the kingdom of Mari and its neighbours, or whether we are faced with a case of bilingualism, with Akkadian serving as the language of written culture and

Amorite as the language of speech. Opinions vary greatly, but it is likely that the elite spoke both Amorite and Akkadian (Durand 1992: 123–126), a situation that would account for the possibility of dictation.

Dictation or drafting from notes?

In some cases the scribe would appear to have written directly from dictation. Several letters of the king Samsi-Addu in which he rages against his son Yasmah-Addu were clearly dictated in anger; some sentences remain unfinished, some have long incisions, while in others the verb is not in the final position where it ought to be, and so on. An explicit mention of dictation comes from the city of Andarig, south of Jebel Sinjar, where a prophet of the god Šamaš asks the Mari representative to provide a scribe so that he may dictate to him a letter from his god to the king Zimri-Lim.[4]

Most often, however, the king would simply provide his secretary with the gist of the message to be communicated; a number of tablets contain notes taken on such occasions (Joannès 1983, 1985 and 1987). These served as a skeleton for the definitive text composed by the scribe, who was actually responsible for the drafting. The style of the letters is furthermore characterised by a relatively rigid rhetoric – a fact that allows us today to reconstruct gaps in the text. Writing not from dictation but from instructions provided had a number of advantages, such as avoiding the need to write quickly[5] and allowing the selection of a tablet of a size appropriate to the length of the message. Certain unsent letters may well represent such first drafts.

The quality of scribal drafting was variable[6] as was the clarity of a dictated message. Išme-Dagan on one occasion complains to his brother Yasmah-Addu that the meaning of one of his letters is unclear,[7] a reproach also addressed to him by Samsi-Addu.[8] Given this, it may be supposed that the drafting of royal letters was not work for any scribe, being a confidential role that could only be fulfilled by someone close to the king. Proof of this is offered by Išme-Dagan, who not having sent news to Yasmah-Addu for some time, explains this by the absence of a certain Limi-Addu, who clearly acted as his secretary:[9] 'Earlier you sent me a letter, but I had just returned from an expedition and had sent Limi-Addu to organise his estate. There was no-one to write a full message; so I sent no reply to your letter.' It is unlikely that Išme-Dagan had no other scribes in his entourage, but what he needed was a scribe who could write him a 'full message' (*ṭêmum gamrum*), which here we may understand as 'a detailed letter'.

Certain letters make explicit allusion to the fact that the text could be longer, but that there was no point in spending more time on the subject. The minister Habdu-malik even justifies brevity by the need not to exceed the limits of a tablet:[10]

> I went to Karana and I conveyed to Asqur-Addu all the instructions that my lord gave me. Why should I delay any longer in writing to my lord? So that the information should not be so abundant as to be incapable of being written on one tablet I have summed up the gist of the matter and have written to my lord.

It used to be thought that only professional scribes were able to write, but there is much evidence, especially in the Mari archives, to indicate that this was not the case. Some administrators but also generals were able to read, and, if necessary, to

Figure 28.1   Example of a memorandum which shows signs of carelessness. The scribe has divided different topics into paragraphs separated by a double line. (A.3209: 23–25; published by F. Joannès, *Mél. Birot*: 108–109.

write.[11] Certain letters of poor quality may have been written by their senders without the mediation of a scribe.[12]

When thinking of sending a letter, a king might ask the advice of a counsellor or of someone close to him, who would make suggestions. One thus sees Zimri-Lim ask Sammetar to join him to draw up a reply to a letter received from Hammu-rabi:[13] 'A tablet has come to me from Babylon; come, so that we may hear this tablet, discuss it and reply.'

There is also another letter, in which, inversely, Sammetar submits to Zimri-Lim the draft of a letter to be sent to the king of Aleppo.[14]

Scribal conventions of letter writing

Within the class of 'practical documents' a distinction is traditionally drawn between legal and economic texts on the one hand and letters on the other, the former being essentially formulaic while the latter are much more lively. Yet letters, too, represent a literary genre with its own rules, even though they seem less constraining. We know, too, that the scribal apprenticeship included the copying of letters (Sallaberger 1999: 149–154). Rather than a specific format, there are scribal conventions or formulae, particularly for the address and the conclusion, as well as a number of recurrent rhetorical figures.

The opening formula of an Old-Babylonian letter betrays the oral origins of the transmission of messages; the first lines always consist of two parts:[15] 'To X, say: thus speaks Y.' Who is addressed by the imperative 'speak'? It is generally thought that the formula retains the memory of its oral origins, and that it is the messenger who is addressed (Kraus 1973: 40). Two examples confirm this as they demonstrate how messengers communicated orally their master's message. This is how Išme-Dagan's envoys to Hammu-rabi accomplished their mission:[16] 'They were asked for news. They therefore delivered their report: "Thus [speaks] your servant Išme-Dagan (. . .)".'

In the same way, when one of king Šarraya's ministers passes on his message to a neighbouring king he says:[17] 'Thus [speaks] Šarraya.'

These examples clearly show that the first part of the address is directed to the messenger. The addressee is identified at the beginning, by his name or title or both. In general, letters from a subject to his king begin with the formula 'To my lord'. When this is followed by the name of the king ('To my lord Zimri-Lim'), the sender is a foreigner.

The second part of the address identifies the sender: he may be identified by title rather than by name, or the name may be followed by an epithet that situates him in relation to the addressee. Very often a subject addressing his sovereign is described as 'your servant'. As the rest of the letter is written in the third person, the employment of the second person here indicates that the second part of the address is speech put into the mouth of the messenger who speaks to the addressee. It is only then that one finds the words the sender intends directly for his correspondent. The wording adopted is by no means a matter of chance: the manner in which a king addressed another in a letter was governed by a strict code of etiquette. Certain texts show that there were clear rules which the ancients took care to observe: according to his hierarchical position, a king would address another as his father, brother, son or servant. One thus sees the nomad chief Ašmad advising king Zimri-Lim at the beginning of his reign, concerning his relations with Aduna-Addu, the powerful king of Hanzat:[18]

> Aduna-Addu had a tablet brought to me, saying: 'Why does your lord write to me as a father?' This tablet was brought to me by Yattu-Lim. Let my lord question Yattu-Lim. My lord must gain the goodwill of Aduna-Addu, because of the Benjaminites. Aduna-Addu, continually . . . [gap] . . . 'Why does Zimri-Lim not address me as a brother?' Now, tone down your address. When you have a tablet taken to Aduna-Addu, write to him as a brother, if you wish him to reject an alliance with the Benjaminites. My lord must gain the goodwill of Aduna-Addu.

One notices that blessings appear only in private correspondence and never in letters addressed to kings or written by them (Dalley 1973). It was common, however, to reassure the addressee regarding matters of concern to them. Governors and other local officials thus generally write that 'all is well with the district'. Generals on campaign, on the other hand, report that 'all is well with the troops; my lord need not be concerned'. These formulae often appear immediately after the address, and are sometimes used to conclude the letter. Very often, the sender closes by indicating that he requires a reply, sometimes urgently.

Unlike our own, these letters generally bear neither a date nor an indication of geographical origin. It may be that the bearer of the message would provide this information, whose absence is such a problem for us today. When letters are dated, they show the day of the month, and never the year, proving that such dating owed nothing to the requirements of archiving – unlike the case of administrative and legal texts.

Re-reading

Whether dictated or otherwise, once the tablet was inscribed the scribe had to read it back to his master before placing it in its envelope. This confirms the point made earlier regarding the use of the Akkadian language, for such re-reading would make no sense if the sender were incapable of understanding what was read out by the scribe. During re-reading, the sender would sometimes indicate changes to be made in the text: this, likely, is how we must understand those occasions when words, or even entire lines, have been erased and rewritten. That a certain number of mistakes (signs omitted, etc.) remain in the letters despite this re-reading is probably an inescapable consequence of 'global reading' (word read without sign-by-sign decipherment), practised by the scribes as it is by us. One episode shows how in the absence of re-reading, a scribe mixed up one place name with another, resulting in the king receiving false information about the capture of a town by the enemy.[19]

Scribes did not generally keep copies of the letters they wrote. What survive in the way of letters written by the kings of Mari to persons outside the capital[20] are either first drafts[21] or letters that were for some reason not sent. The absence of copies explains a constant feature of the letters: an opening reference to the burden of the letter earlier received from the person to whom the reply is addressed.

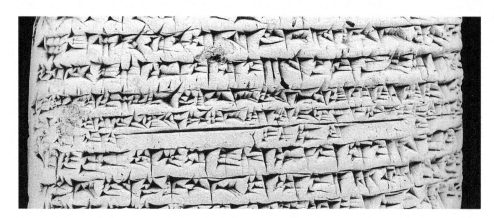

Figure 28.2 Passage of a letter which shows a change of mind by the scribe who has erased two lines in order to fit in three, using smaller characters. (A.486+, published by P. Villard, *FM* [I]: 141).

Figure 28.3   Envelope of a letter by Zimri-Lim to Tiš-ulme. On the surface we can read 'To Tiš-ulme'. Also visible is the imprint of the sender's cylinder seal on the obverse and the reverse (the edge of the seal has left a rather deep groove), as well as on the edge. (Museum of Dêr ez-Zor, photo: Archives royales de Mari). The seal shows a classic scene ('warrior with mace' facing a protective goddess) and a six-line inscription.

Figure 28.4 Label of a tablet-basket in the shape of an olive; on the left is a trace of the string used to tie up the contents. The inscription indicates that four letters used to be kept there before they were sent (M.8762, published in D. Charpin 2001: 21).

Envelope and seal

Once the letter had been written and read back, it was put in its envelope. Inevitably this envelope would be destroyed by the addressee in gaining access to the letter within, which explains the scarcity of envelopes that have survived entire or in part. The imprint of the seal of Zimri-Lim has been found on fragments of letter envelopes in the palace of Mari,[22] and also at that of Qaṭṭarâ.[23] The impression of the sender's seal both ensured the confidentiality of the message and guaranteed its provenance. Once the tablet was in its envelope, it was too late to add anything at all, and if further information had to be sent to the king, a new letter would have to be written. This is explicitly mentioned by Buqâqum:[24] 'My tablet had just been put in its envelope when the couriers, four men of Asqur-Addu's, arrived, saying; . . .'.

A very particular document shows how the royal chancellery stored letters awaiting dispatch: this is a label from a tablet-basket, bearing the inscription:[25] 'Four [tablets] to be read to [*Iddiyatum*], Yasim-El, Menirum and Belšunu; they are ready.'

It would appear that these were letters to persons in official positions in the region of Djebel Sinjar: clearly they were intended to travel in the same bag. Either one messenger would have taken each to its addressee, doing a 'round' passing through Andarig and Karana, or they would have travelled by relay, and the tablets at the end forwarded to their addressees.

CARRYING THE MAIL

The ways in which letters were conveyed to their addressees varied considerably (Lafont 1997). We shall look first at the rich vocabulary that describes 'messengers' and then see that there were, side by side, letter-carriers invested with a personal mission and a postal service that transported the letters by using a system of relays. We will consider, finally, the dangers these messengers might encounter, especially in time of war.

A very rich vocabulary

The vocabulary designating persons responsible for carrying letters is very diverse, and the nuances implied by the different terms are not yet entirely understood. A first distinction, however, is clear: there were on the one hand messengers proper (*mâr šiprim*) and on the other mere 'tablet-carriers' (*wâbil ṭuppim*), who were generally expected to return immediately after making delivery. Unpublished text M.5696, recording the enrolment (*piqittum*) of soldiers in the gardens of Saggaratum on 8/xii/ZL 9, is in this respect doubly important. First, because one finds in it the distinction evoked above, expressed in another terminology that distinguishes between 'those to whom messages are confided' (*ša šipirâtim*) and 'runners' (*lâsimum*). And second, because this document gives us the number of men mobilised when Zimri-Lim departed with all his army to help the king of Aleppo: he was accompanied by no less than 100 *ša šipirâtim* and 64 *lâsimum*. These figures are unexpected: never has it been thought that the kingdom of Mari had such a number of messengers. They find confirmation, however, in a document covering the district of Saggaratum alone, which testifies to the existence there of 19 *ša šipirâtim* and 22 *lâsimum*. M.5696 is thus by no means the result of exceptional circumstances attending the preparation of a military campaign: use was made of those who were normally responsible for the transport of mail.

Personal letter-carriers and relay systems

In the context of diplomatic relations, messengers were often given a tablet which they carried to the king to whom the letter was addressed. However, once the messages were first set down in writing, there was no need to entrust them to a single messenger to travel the whole distance between sender and addressee. There is, in fact, evidence for established relay systems, which allowed mail to be conveyed more rapidly, in that they used a sequence of couriers one after the other, and not one single messenger who would necessarily have to rest from time to time.[26]

Officials were expected to reply to the king by return of post: they often stated the time at which they received the letter to which they were replying (Lafont 1997: 331–332), which in certain cases was offered as an excuse for delay. Thus Mukannišum added at the end of one of his letters:[27]

> My lord should not say: 'Mukannišum has been negligent about these spears.' When my lord's tablet arrived, it was night: the bars of the palace had been set and I was not able to send out these spears.

In addition, mention is sometimes made of abnormal delays in the conveyance of mail.[28]

The dangers of the journey

Like every important undertaking, the dispatch of messengers was preceded by the consultation of omens, more especially in time of war. Thus Asqudum declared:[29] 'I took the omens for the safety of the messengers: they were not good. I will take them again for them. When the omens are favourable, I shall send them.'

If the omens were bad and there was need for haste, one could send the messengers under escort, as is suggested by Išme-Dagan:[30]

> When you have this letter brought to me, give strict orders for [its] protection during the journey. Take omens for the safety of the carriers of the letter, or have thirty of your servants escort them to the river and [then] return to you.

Despite these precautions, it happened that messengers were stopped by the enemy and the letters they carried intercepted: this accounts for those letters in the palace of Mari addressed 'to my lord' which were not intended for the Mari king.[31] Recourse was sometimes achieved with merchants, who would carry messages in secret through the lands of the enemy.

THE READING OF LETTERS

There were different ways in which letters were read to the king, depending on the nature of the correspondence, domestic or diplomatic. Letters were also sometimes forwarded to a third party who was not an intended addressee, or they might be copied in part or in whole. We will see later how a good many of the messages sent in antiquity remain unknown because for various reasons they were not sent in writing.

The reading of royal correspondence

The way in which the king had letters read to him could vary with the sender, depending on whether this was an official or another king. In the case of administrative correspondence, letter-carriers would not normally be admitted to the royal presence but left their letters 'at the door of the palace'. It was only in case of urgency that they would have direct access to the sovereign. Hence the great importance of the royal secretary who read the correspondence to his master. Among such officials the best known is Šu-nuhra-Halu, secretary to Zimri-Lim (Sasson 1988). Correspondents would often attach to their letter to the king another addressed to Šu-nuhra-Halu, in which they copied or summarised the first. In this way the royal secretary would know in advance the content of the message he was to read and could draw the king's attention to specific points; the letter he received would often conclude with the announcement that a gift was on its way. A letter to Šu-nuhra-Halu from Ibal-Addu shows that messages sent to Zimri-Lim had first to be heard by his secretary, even when delivered orally and not in tablet form:[32] 'Behold, I have sent you a complete report by Ladin-Addu. Pay close attention to his report and bring him before the king.'

It is notable that certain correspondents implicitly accuse Šu-nuhra-Halu of having 'censored' parts of certain letters they had sent to the sovereign. The general Yasim-Dagan, for example, threatened to come and read his letter to the king in person.[33] Others would flatter the powerful royal secretary:[34] 'When I found myself at Mari, with my lord, and you were my friend and you fought by my side, I saw your power. Everything you said before my lord was agreed; nothing happened without your consent.'

In the case of letters between kings, the process was nearly always the same: the king gave his instructions (*têmam wu'urum*) to those whom we call 'messengers' (*mâr šiprî*), but who were in fact diplomats (Lafont 1992). The latter, having arrived at the court of the addressee, repeated this *têmum*, whether by reading a tablet or reciting on oral message committed to memory. In most cases the foreign 'messengers' were brought before the king in the course of an audience, during which they would themselves read the tablet they had brought. Certain messengers insisted that their message be heard with due attention:[35]

> [While Yan]ṣib-Addu delivered my lord's message, Hammu-rabi [. . .] all the while as he delivered the message [did not cease to lis]ten and opened not his mouth; he remained [very] attentive until he had finished his message. [When the message was finish]ed he addressed us in these terms.

In a number of cases, messages were read not in open audience but in secret. Thus Iddiyatum, Zimri-Lim's envoy to Asqur-Addu in Karana, informs him that messengers have come from Kurda but that he was unable to attend the meeting at which they gave their message.[36] One knows too of the complaints of Yamṣum, who was no longer admitted to the secret council of Haya-sumu and so no longer heard the news

Figure 28.5 Example of a copy of a letter within a letter. After the address (lines 1–2: 'Say to my Lord, thus speaks Itûr-Asdû your servant') the sender announced (l.3–4): 'Here is a copy of the letter which I had made to be carried, may my Lord take note (literally 'hear')'. After a double line, we read (5–6): 'Tell Turib-adal, thus speaks Itûr-Asdû, your brother (the rest is broken).'
(J.-M. Durand, *Mél. Garelli*: 25 and 29).

brought by foreign messengers.[37] Yamṣum even explains that Haya-sumu refuses to have letters from Zimri-Lim read in his presence:[38]

> My lord had a tablet brought to Haya-sumu. My lord wrote me this: 'Let the tablet be opened before you, and listen to it.' He (= Haya-sumu) has received the tablet, but I was not (able) to hear the contents of the tablet.

Many other such examples could be given.

When the king travelled, his secretary stored in a chest the tablets received, and deposited them in the palace archives on his return. This explains why many of the letters at Mari were, in fact, addressed to the king while he was away from the palace: this was the case for the letters from queens, from the palace steward Mukanništum, and so on. It could happen that one has both the letter to the king and the reply to it.[39]

Letters forwarded or copied

Certain letters were read several times. So it was when Samsi-Addu forwarded to one of his sons a letter that had been addressed to himself, as in this example:[40] 'Behold, I send you the tablet that Ṣuprerah sent me: listen to it.'

410

Certain functionaries saw fit to forward to the king, together with a covering letter, correspondence they had received themselves. This is an example from La'um:[41] 'Behold, I have put under seal the tablet of Yašub-El which he had brought to me, relating to the inhabitants, and which I have just had sent to my lord. May my lord take note of it (lit. "hear it").'

This was done more particularly when the governor of a province received a letter from a foreign king (Durand 1991: 28–29). He would take note of the letter and then send it on to the king, having placed it in an envelope under his own seal. A letter from Zakira-Hammu, governor of Qaṭṭunan, is a good example. Having reproduced the content of a letter he had received from Qarni-Lim, king of Andarig, he adds:[42] 'I have just sent the messenger of Qarni-Lim to my lord. Furthermore, I have sealed the tablet from Qarni-Lim that came to me, and I have had it taken to my lord.'

In a case like this, the tablet would have travelled from Andarig to Qaṭṭunan under the seal of its sender, Qarni-Lim; then from Qaṭṭunan to Mari, under the seal of its addressee, Zakira-Hammu, who forwarded the letter to a third person, in this case the king of Mari, together with a covering letter.

Sometimes the original was retained and its contents copied in whole or in part:[43] a substantial proportion of the correspondence that has not come down to us directly may thus be reconstituted, at least in part. The most extraordinary case I know of is represented by *FM* II 116. Turum-natki, king of Apum, sent a letter to Zimri-Lim. The latter wrote to Sumu-hadu, attaching to his own letter the letter from Turum-natki. Writing to the Benjaminites, Sumu-hadu quoted in his letter what Turum-natki had said. And finally, Sumu-hadu reported to Zimri-Lim on his mission in a letter in which he copied the letter he sent to the Benjaminites. The only letter we have is this last, but through it we know of three others.

Written letters and oral messages

In certain cases, to counter the risk of interception, messages were not set down in writing. Zimri-Lim's sister, the princess Atrakatum, revealed to her brother the existence of a plot at the court of her husband Sumu-dabi, the Benjaminite king of Samanum, which she hoped to recount in detail at a meeting with Zimri-Lim in person:[44]

> Another thing: the Bedouin, the sheikh whom my lord once sent to Sumu-dabi and to whom he (the latter) had accorded a ration of textiles, one day, in the middle of the night, came here and told all sorts of things to Sumu-dabi. When I have a meeting with my lord, I will repeat to him all the man's words. If that should not happen and the affair is urgent, he should write to me what should be done; I will have written on a tablet the details of what this man said, and I will have it taken to my lord.

The notion that certain things cannot be set down in writing occurs repeatedly. Samsi-Addu thus writes to Yasmah-Addu:[45]

> On the subject of what Samsi-Dagan told you, this is what you wrote to me: 'It is not appropriate to write such things on a tablet.' Why is this? Do it and send

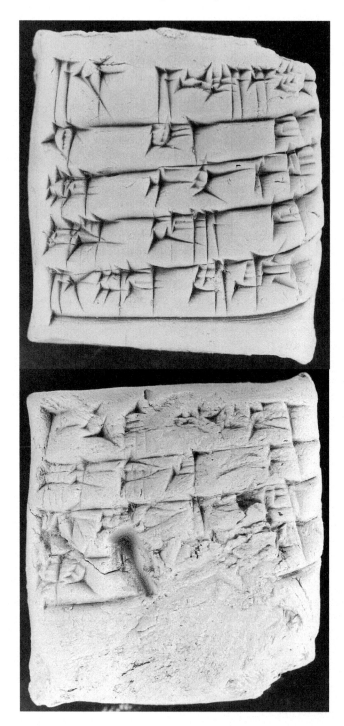

Figure 28.6 A short letter of accreditation. 'Say to my father Zimri-Lim, thus (speaks) Iškur-andullî, your son. That I have given instructions to Yašûb-Addu, in response to your message and that I have just sent him to my father' (unpublished A.2746).

412

it to me! If not [there must be] a trusted man who can bring an oral message (lit. who can take the words in his mouth). Give him your instructions and send him to me so that he may set out these things before me.

Messengers who brought a purely oral message had to offer proof of their status, as is shown by this letter of accreditation sent to Zimri-Lim by Haya-Sumu:[46]

Behold, I have given full instructions to Aqbu-Abum, my servant, and I have sent him to you. Give great attention to the instructions I have given him. Give him [your] instructions promptly and send him back to me. Apart from him there is no-one in my service suitable for a mission.

The danger of purely oral communication was on one occasion explicitly underlined by Samsi-Addu: was what he had been told by a messenger of the Gutis resident in Šikšabbum, with regard to the instructions he had purportedly received from their leader Indušše, true or not? Samsi-Addu explains the different tests that allowed him to trust the message the envoy brought:[47]

He gave me as evidence a *hullum*-ring I had given to the messenger Mutušu. Furthermore, Etellini, a colleague of Mutušu's, was ill at Arrapha: he spoke of this man's illness. He gave me these two proofs and so I had trust in his words.

To send envoys without a written tablet could cause problems. Hence, the messengers sent to Babylon by Išme-Dagan were embarrassed by the presence at the audience of envoys from Zimri-Lim, against whom their master wished to make complaints. Hammu-rabi, sensing that they were withholding part of their report, tried in vain to make them speak. He therefore had brought to him the Babylonian who had accompanied Išme-Dagan's messengers from Ekallatum:[48] 'After he had repeated the report which Išme-Dagan's messengers had given, he completed it in these terms.'

One sees that all had had to learn by heart the message that Išme-Dagan intended for Hammu-rabi, as the Babylonian has to begin by repeating the same thing as the messengers from Ekallatum.

A very interesting case, in which the oral message was deliberately misleading while the truth was put in writing, is provided by a letter from the nomad chief Ibal-El:[49]

When my lord sends me a messenger, let my lord send orally this message: 'Let your people be gathered together. Assuredly, I shall be going to Der' (or wherever my lord wishes). Let him send me this message orally, but on the tablet inform me of the true route that my lord will follow.

The passage makes no sense unless, on the arrival of a messenger, Ibal-El had to listen, in the presence of a number of people, to the message delivered orally; the ruse he proposes to the king suggests furthermore that he would afterwards read or have read to him the true content of the tablet that had been brought to him. It appears, then, that the messenger, in this case, would have completed in person the whole journey from the king to Ibal-El, having received special instructions on his departure.

It might happen that a royal order was communicated only orally. The official to whom it was addressed would not fail to note the fact, in case of future problems, as here Ašak-magir:[50] 'Iṣi-Ahu, the courier, Zibnatum's man, came to me, bringing no tablet from my lord. He said: "By my lord's command, place seals on the house of Bannum and Zakura-Abum."'

Often, too, written confirmation might be asked for news that had been heard only by rumour. Hence this letter from a governor of Qaṭṭunan:[51] 'I have heard only by public rumour of my lord's visit to Qaṭṭunan. If my lord is coming, a tablet should be sent to me quickly so that I can be ready for his arrival.'

Sometimes an official explicitly expressed his desire for a written order from the king before complying. So it was that queen Šibtu wrote to Zimri-Lim:[52]

> Mukanniŝum came and said to me: 'This gold, it was to me that it was assigned.' I replied: 'So long as no tablet has come from my lord, I shall not hand over the gold.' Was the gold assigned to Mukanniŝum? Let a tablet be sent by my lord if I ought to hand over (this) gold.

CONCLUSION

We have seen the degree of sophistication attained by the correspondence of the Amorite Near East and the importance attached to written communication in this period. It must be emphasised, however, that it was not only the most powerful kings who sent their messages in written form: nomad chiefs did the same, affording us for once an opportunity to know something of them other than through the distorting lens of the writings of sedentary populations. Women, too, had recourse to writing. The evidence that survives, of course, relates primarily to queens and princesses, but these left behind them a considerable body of letters. And finally, it is because certain prophets were unable to pass on their god's messages directly to the king that several dozen of their prophecies are known to us from their letters (Charpin 2002). It is easy for us to understand a woman of the time of Samsi-Addu when she writes that, thanks to the post, distance is in a way abolished:[53] 'At present, I fear that Akatiya will say: "Mari is far." It is not far at all: the city of Mari is, in relation to Aššur, like the suburbs of Aššur. And the City is near for the post.'

And to conclude, one cannot do better than cite from a letter of Šadum-Labua, king of Ašnakkum, who writes *cum grano salis*:[54] 'My servants are tired from going to the nomad chief (*merhûm*) and I have exhausted the clay of Ašnakkum for the letters that I endlessly send out.'

NOTES

* This chapter summarises my forthcoming book entitled *Lire et écrire en Babylonie ancienne. Ecriture, acheminement et lecture des lettres d'après les archives de Mari*, in which the unedited texts quoted here will be published.

1 For a summary of the period's political history, see Charpin and Ziegler 2003, with a list of sources pp. 1–27; bibliography in Charpin 2004a: 453–475.
2 For the correspondence between private individuals, see especially Sallaberger 1999.
3 See Streck 2000.

4 *ARM* XXVI/2 414: 30–33: 'Send me a discrete scribe, that I make (him) write the message which Šamaš has sent through my intermediary for the king.' We do have this message: see *ARM* XXVI/1 194.

5 Which may entail a greater literary quality, highlighted by Finet 1986.

6 One could cite the extreme case of some petitions where the style is particularly refined. At Mari, there is the example of a bilingual letter (Sumerian and Akkadian), sent by a scribe who wished to curry favour with Zimri-Lim soon after the latter's accession to the throne (*LAPO* 16 22). One could also consider the letter *OBTR* 150 (see Foster 1993).

7 *ARM* IV 86 (= *LAPO* 17 772).

8 *ARM* I 18 (= *LAPO* 16 43).

9 Unpublished A.3611+ (to appear in *ARM* XXIX).

10 *ARM* XXVI/2 394: 3–8.

11 See Charpin 2004b.

12 This is particularly the case in some of the correspondence of Yamṣum, captain of the Mari garrison at Ilan-ṣura, see Charpin 1989.

13 *ARM* XXVI/1 276: 6–10.

14 A.1101 (= *LAPO* 16 230); see Sasson 1988, esp. p. 462.

15 *Ana* X *qibi-ma umma* Y.

16 *ARM* XXVI/2 384: 18'–19'.

17 *ARM* XXVI/1 127: 18.

18 Unpublished: A.861: 7–13 and 1'–8'.

19 See A.427, published in Charpin 1995a; see the detailed commentary in Sasson 2002.

20 I am not talking here about the letters sent by the king to a palace official or a family member during a journey.

21 As is the case, for example, of the 'plaidoyer *pro domo*' of Yasmah-Addu (see J.-M. Durand, MARI 5, p. 175) or *ARM* I 109, after J.-M. Durand, *LAPO* 16 70.

22 One might recall the existence of a particular seal in the 'foreign office' of Mari that was used exclusively to seal letters sent by Zimri-Lim, different from the one used to seal administrative documents: see Charpin 1992, esp. pp. 70–71, § 3.2.3.

23 *OBTR*, p. 250 no. 5.

24 *ARM* XXVI/2 490: 4–7.

25 M.8762, published in Charpin 2001: 21.

26 See *ARM* XXVI/1 29: 4–9.

27 *ARM* XIII 8 (= *LAPO* 16 104).

28 The nicest example comes in the letter *ARM* III 59 [= *LAPO* 16 329] (see the commentary by Lafont 1997: 326).

29 *ARM* XXVI/1 87.

30 *FM* III 14: 18–25.

31 See especially *ARM* XXVI/1 168–172.

32 *ARM* XXVIII 75: 4–9.

33 A.4215 (= *LAPO* 16 65).

34 *ARM* XXVIII 109: 5–8.

35 *ARM* XXVI/2 449: 7–12.

36 *ARM* XXVI/2 521: 42–44.

37 *ARM* XXVI/2 307, 308 and 309.

38 *ARM* XXVI/2 315: 4–7.

39 For example: *ARM* X 16 and X 136 (= *LAPO* 18 1158 and 1157); X 131 (= *LAPO* 18 1154) and XXVI/1 242. See also the case of A.1285 and *ARM* XIII 10 (= *LAPO* 16 136 and 134).

40 *ARM* I 16 (= *LAPO* 16 301): 5–8.

41 *ARM* V 78 (= *LAPO* 17 631): 5–11.

42 See *ARM* II 79 = XXVII 69: 29–33.

43 See, for example, *ARM* I 24+ (= *LAPO* 16 no. 330): 3–8 or *ARM* XXVI/1 25.

44 *ARM* X 91 (= *LAPO* 18 1186): 3'–15'.

45 *ARM* I 76 (= *LAPO* 16 58): 20–29.

46 *ARM* XXVIII 85: 5–12 and 15–20.

47 ShA 1 11: 25–34.
48 *ARM* XXVI/2 384: 52′–53′.
49 Unpublished A.836.
50 *FM* II 49: 5–10.
51 *FM* II 47: 4–11.
52 *ARM* X 18 (= *LAPO* 18 1132): 5′–14′.
53 A.1248: 29–34 (unpublished, quoted by J.-M. Durand, MARI 4, p. 410, n. 155).
54 *ARM* XXVIII 105: 9–10.

ABBREVIATIONS

ARM   =   Archives royales de Mari
FM II   =   Charpin et Durand 1994
FM III   =   Charpin et Durand 1997
LAPO 16, 17 and 18   =   Durand 1997, 1998 and 2000
MARI   =   MARI, *Annales de Recherches Interdisciplinaires*
OBTR   =   Dalley, Walker and Hawkins 1976
ShA 1   =   Eidem and Laessoe 2001

BIBLIOGRAPHY

Charpin, D. 1989 'L'akkadien des lettres d'Ilân-ṣurâ', in M. Lebeau and P. Talon (eds), *Reflets des deux fleuves, volume de mélanges offerts à André Finet*. Leuven: 31–40.

—— 1992 'Les légendes de sceaux de Mari: nouvelles données', in G. Young (ed.), *Mari in Retrospect*. Winona Lake: 59–76.

—— 1995a '"Lies natürlich. . ." A propos des erreurs de scribes dans les lettres de Mari', in M. Dietrich and O. Loretz (eds), *Vom Alten Orient zum Alten Testament, Festschrift für Wolfram Freiherrn von Soden zum 85. Geburtstag am 19. Juni 1993*. Neukirchen-Vluyn: 43–56.

—— 1995b 'La fin des archives dans le palais de Mari'. *Revue d'Assyriologie* 89: 29–40.

—— 2001 'L'archivage des tablettes dans le palais de Mari: nouvelles données', in W.H. van Soldt *et al.* (eds), *Veenhof Anniversary Volume. Studies Presented to Klaas R. Veenhof on the Occasion of his Sixty-fifth Birthday*. Leiden: 13–30.

—— 2002 'Prophètes et rois dans le Proche-Orient amorrite: nouvelles données, nouvelles perspectives', in D. Charpin and J.-M. Durand (eds), *Recueil d'études à la mémoire d'André Parrot, Florilegium marianum VI*. Paris: 7–38.

—— 2004a 'Histoire politique du Proche-Orient amorrite (2002–1595)', in D. Charpin, D. O. Edzard and M. Stol, *Mesopotamien: Die altbabylonische Zeit*. = P. Attinger, W. Sallaberger and M. Wäfler (eds), *Annäherungen 4*. OBO 160/4, Freiburg and Göttingen: 25–480.

—— 2004b 'Lire et écrire en Mésopotamie: une affaire de spécialistes?', *Comptes rendus de l'Académie des Inscriptions et Belles Lettres*: 481–508.

—— and Durand, J.-M. (eds) 1994 *Recueil d'études à la mémoire de Maurice Birot, Florilegium marianum II*. Paris.

—— and —— 1997 *Recueil d'études à la mémoire de Marie-Thérèse Barrelet, Florilegium marianum III*. Paris.

—— and Joannès, F. (eds) 1992 *La circulation des biens, des personnes et des idées dans le Proche-Orient ancien. Actes de la XXXVIIIe Rencontre assyriologique Internationnale (Paris, 8–10 juillet 1991)*. Paris.

—— and Ziegler, N. 2003 *Mari et le Proche-Orient à l'époque amorrite: essai d'histoire politique, Florilegium marianum V*. Paris.

Dalley, S. 1973 'Old Babylonian Greeting Formulae and the Iltani's Archive from Rimah.' *Journal of Cuneiform Studies* 25: 79–88.

——, Walker, C. B. F. and Hawkins D. J. 1976 *The Old Babylonian Tablets from Tell al Rimah.* London.

Durand, J. -M. 1991 'Précurseurs syriens aux protocoles néo-assyriens: considérations sur la vie politique aux Bords-de-l'Euphrate', in D. Charpin and F. Joannès (eds), *Marchands, diplomates et empereurs. Etudes sur la civilisation mésopotamienne offertes à Paul Garelli.* Paris: 13–72.

—— 1992 'Unité et diversités au Proche-Orient à l'époque amorrite', in Charpin and Joannès 1992, Paris: 97–128.

—— 1997 *Les Documents épistolaires du palais de Mari.* Vol. I, *LAPO* 16, Paris.

—— 1998 *Les Documents épistolaires du palais de Mari.* Vol. II, *LAPO* 17, Paris.

—— 2000 *Les Documents épistolaires du palais de Mari.* Vol. III, *LAPO* 18, Paris.

Eidem, J. and Laessoe, J. 2001 *The Shemshara Archives Vol. 1 The Letters.* Historisk-filosofiske Skrifter 23, Copenhagen.

Finet, A. 1986 'Allusions et Réminiscences comme source d'Information sur la Diffusion de la Littérature', in K. Hecker and W. Sommerfeld (eds), *Keilschriftliche Literaturen. Ausgewählte Vorträge der XXXII. Rencontre Assyriologique Internationale.* Berlin: 13–17.

Foster, B. R. 1993 'Letters and Literature: a Ghost's Entreaty', in M. E. Cohen *et al.* (eds), *The Tablet and the Scroll. Near Eastern Studies in Honor of William W. Hallo.* Bethesda: 98–102.

Joannès, F. 1983 *ARM* XXIII: 87–104 (copies in *MARI* 5, 1987: 345–380).

—— 1985 'Nouveaux mémorandums', in J.-M. Durand and J.-R. Kupper (eds), *Miscellanea Babylonica. Mélanges offerts à Maurice Birot.* Paris: 97–113.

—— 1987 'Un nouveau mémorandum de Mari', *NABU* 1987/29.

Kraus, F. R. 1973 *Vom mesopotamischen Menschen der altbabylonischen Zeit und seiner Welt.* Amsterdam and London.

Lafont, B. 1992 'Messagers et ambassadeurs dans les archives de Mari', in Charpin and Joannès 1992, Paris: 167–183.

—— 1997 'Le fonctionnement de la poste et le métier de facteur d'après les textes de Mari', in G. D. Young *et al.* (eds), *Crossing Boundaries and Linking Horizons, Studies in Honor of Michael C. Astour on His 80th Birthday.* Bethesda: 315–334.

Sallaberger, W. 1999 *'Wenn Du mein Bruder bist, . . .': Interaktion und Textgestaltung in altbabylonischen Alltagsbriefen.* Groningen.

Sasson, J. M. 1988 'Shunukhra-Khalu', in E. Leichty *et al.* (eds), *A Scientific Humanist: Studies in Memory of Abraham Sachs.* Philadelphia: 329–351.

—— 1998 'The King and I. A Mari King in Changing Perception.' *Journal of the American Oriental Society* 118: 453–470.

—— 2002 'The Burden of Scribes', in T. Abusch (ed.), *Riches Hidden in Secret Places. Ancient Near Eastern Studies in Memory of Thorkild Jacobsen.* Winona Lake: 211–228.

Streck, M. 2000 *Das Amurritische Onomastikon der altbabylonischen Zeit. Band 1: Die Amurriter. Die onomastische Forschung. Orthographie und Phonologie. Nominalmorphologie.* Münster.

CHAPTER TWENTY-NINE

MATHEMATICS, METROLOGY, AND PROFESSIONAL NUMERACY

———•◆•———

Eleanor Robson

INTRODUCTION

Since the great decipherments of the 1930s and 1940s (Neugebauer 1935–37; Thureau-Dangin 1938; Neugebauer and Sachs 1945) Babylonia has had a well-deserved reputation as the home of the world's first 'true' mathematics, in which abstract ideas and techniques were explored and developed with no immediate practical end in mind. It is commonly understood that the base 60 systems of time measurement and angular degrees have their ultimate origins in Babylonia, and that 'Pythagoras' theorem' was known there a millennium before Pythagoras himself was supposed to have lived.

Most accounts of Babylonian mathematics describe the internal workings of the mathematics in great detail (e.g., Friberg 1990; Høyrup and Damerow 2001) but tell little of the reasons for its development, or anything about the people who wrote or thought about it and their reasons for doing so. However, internal textual and physical evidence from the tablets themselves, as well as museological and archaeological data, are increasingly enabling Babylonian mathematics to be understood as both a social and an intellectual activity, in relation to other scholarly pursuits and to professional scribal activity. It is important to distinguish between mathematics as an intellectual, supra-utilitarian end in itself, and professional numeracy as the routine application of mathematical skills by working scribes.

This chapter is a brief attempt at a social history of Babylonian mathematics and numeracy (see Robson 2008). After a short survey of their origins in early Mesopotamia, it examines the evidence for metrology and mathematics in Old Babylonian scribal schooling and for professional numeracy in second-millennium scribal culture. Very little evidence survives for the period 1600–750 BCE, but there is a wealth of material for mid-first-millennium Babylonia, typically neglected in the standard accounts of the subject. This chapter is doubtless flawed and incomplete, and may even be misguided, but I hope that at the very least it re-emphasises the 'Babylonian' in 'Babylonian mathematics'.

ORIGINS: NUMERACY AND MATHEMATICS
IN EARLY MESOPOTAMIA

Professional numeracy predates literacy by several centuries in Babylonia. From at least the early fourth millennium, bureaucrats and accountants at economic centres such as Uruk used tiny counters made of unbaked clay, shell, or river pebbles, along with other bureaucratic apparatus such as clay sealings and bevel-rim bowls. Over the course of the fourth millennium, the scribes began to mark the external surface of the rough clay envelopes (*bullae*) in which they were stored with impressions of the counters contained inside them, before abandoning the storage process all together in favour of impressions alone. Some of the earliest tablets, then, are simply tallies of unknown objects, with no marking of what was being accounted for (Schmandt-Besserat 1992).

This need to identify the objects of accounting was, arguably, a prime motivation behind the invention of incised proto-cuneiform script. By the end of the Uruk period complex calculations were carried out: estimates were made of the different kinds of grain needed for brewing beer and making bread; harvest yields were recorded and summed over many years (Nissen *et al.* 1993). Several different number systems and metrologies were used, depending on the commodity accounted for. Trainee scribes practised area calculations and manipulating very large and very small numbers (Friberg 1997–8).

Over the course of the third millennium the visual distinction between impressed numbers and incised words was eroded as writing became increasingly cuneiform. But, as in almost all ancient and pre-modern societies, in early Mesopotamia writing was used to record numbers, not to manipulate them. Fingers and clay counters remained the main means of calculation long after the development of literacy.

Handfuls of school mathematical exercises and diagrams survive from ED III Shuruppag (Melville 2002) and from the Sargonic period, poorly executed in Sumerian on roughly made tablets (Foster and Robson 2004). Most concern the relationship between the sides and areas of squares, rectangles, and irregular quadrilaterals of conspicuously imaginary dimensions. They take the form of word problems, in which a question is posed and then either assigned to a named student or provided with a numerical answer (which is often erroneous).

Successive bureaucratic reforms gradually harmonised the separate metrologies, so that all discrete objects came to be counted in tens and sixties, all grains and liquids in one capacity system, etc., although there were always local variations both in relationships between metrological units and in their absolute values. The weight system, developed relatively late in the Early Dynastic period, is the only metrology to be fully sexagesimal; the others all retain elements of the proto-historic mixed-base systems of the Uruk period (Powell 1990).

However, the different metrological units – say length and area – were still not very well integrated. The scribes' solution was to convert all measures into sexagesimal multiples and fractions of a basic unit, and to use those numbers as a means of calculating, just as today one might convert length measurements in yards, feet and inches into multiples and fractions of metres in order to calculate an area from them. Clues in the structure of Sargonic school mathematics problems show the sexagesimal system already in use (Whiting 1984), while tiny informal calculations on the edge of Ur III institutional accounts show its adoption by professional scribes (Powell 1976).

Figure 29.1 The obverse of a mathematical tablet. Ashmolean 1922.277 (OECT 15: 7). An inspection of estimated yields (*šukunnû*) of fields in the towns of Nirda and Kurhianu, it was written in Hammurabi's thirty-fifth year. It has an introductory paragraph, headings, three levels of calculation (subtotals and totals), and interlinear notes. (Ashmolean Museum).

The earliest extant tables of reciprocals, which list pairs of numbers whose product is 60 – e.g., 2 and 30, 3 and 20, 4 and 15 – also date from the Ur III empire or early Old Babylonian period (Oelsner 2001). They are essential tools for sexagesimal arithmetic, as they neatly convert division by one number into multiplication by its reciprocal.

OLD BABYLONIAN MATHEMATICS AND NUMERACY

Metrology

By the beginning of the second millennium all the essential building blocks of Old Babylonian mathematics were already in place: the textual genres – tables, word problems, rough work and diagrams – and the arithmetical tools – the sexagesimal place value system, reciprocals, and standardised constants for calculations and metrological conversions. However, the changes that had taken place in mathematics by the eighteenth century BCE were both quantitative and qualitative. In line with other products of scribal training, the sheer volume of surviving tablets is overwhelming: many thousands of highly standardised arithmetical and metrological tables and hundreds of word problems, mostly in Akkadian, testing increasingly abstract and complex mathematical knowledge. The majority of the published sources are unprovenanced, having reached museum collections through uncontrolled excavation or the antiquities market in the late nineteenth and early twentieth centuries. However, archaeologically contextualised finds from Ur, Nippur, and Sippar have recently enabled close descriptions of the role of mathematics in the scribal curricula of particular schools (Friberg 2000; Robson 2001b; Tanret 2002).

House F in Nippur has produced by far the most detailed evidence, if only because of the vast number of tablets excavated there (Robson 2002). This tiny house, about 100 metres south-east of Enlil's temple complex E-kur, was used as a school early in the reign of Samsu-iluna, after which some 1,400 fragments of tablets were used as building material to repair the walls and floor of the building. Three tablet recycling boxes (Sumerian pú-im-ma) containing a mixture of fresh clay and mashed up old tablets show that the tablets had not been brought in from elsewhere. Half were elementary school exercises, and half extracts from Sumerian literary works. Both sets of tablets yield important information on mathematical pedagogy.

Mathematical learning began for the handful of students in House F in the second phase of the curriculum, once they had mastered the basic cuneiform syllabary. The six-tablet series of thematically grouped nouns – known anachronistically as OB Ur₅-ra, but more correctly as ᵍᶦˢtaskarin, 'tamarisk', after its first line – contains sequences listing wooden boats and measuring vats of different capacities, as well as the names of the different parts of weighing scales. Later in the same series come the stone weights themselves and measuring-reeds of different lengths. Thus students were first introduced to weights and measures and their notation in the context of metrological equipment, not as an abstract system (albeit always in descending order of size).

In House F, systematic learning of metrological facts took place in phase three, along with the rote memorisation of other exercises on the more complex features of cuneiform writing. This time the metrological units were written out in ascending order: first the capacities from ⅓ sila to 3,600 gur (ca. 0.3–65,000,000 litres); then weights from ½ grain to 60 talents (0.05 g–1,800 kg); then areas and volumes from ½ sar to 7,200 bur (12 m²–47,000 ha), and finally lengths from one finger to 60 leagues (17 mm–650 km). The entire series, fully written, contained several hundred entries, although certain sections could be omitted or abbreviated. It could be formatted as a list, with each entry containing the standard notation for the measures only, or as a table, where the standard writings were equated with values in the sexagesimal system. Further practice in writing metrological units, particularly areas, capacities, and weights, came in the fourth curricular phase, when students learned how to write legal contracts for sales, loans, and inheritances.

Arithmetic

Arithmetic itself was concentrated in the third phase of the House F curriculum, alongside the metrology. Again the students memorised a long sequence of facts, this time through copying and writing standard tables of reciprocals and multiplications. There were about 40 tables in the sequence after the reciprocals, in descending order from 50 to 1;15.[1] Each table had entries for multiplicands 1–20, 30, 40, and 50. When the students first learned and copied each table they tended to write them in whole sentences: 25 a-rá 1 25 / a-rá 2 50 ('25 steps of 1 is 25, <25> steps of 2 is 50'), but when recalling longer sequences of tables in descending order abbreviated the entries to just the essential numbers: 1 25 / 2 50. Enough tablets of both kinds survive to demonstrate that although the House F teacher presented students with the entire series of multiplication tables to learn, in fact the students tended to rehearse only the first quarter of it in their longer writing exercises.

Active engagement with mathematics came only on entering the advanced phase of learning, which focused heavily on Sumerian literature. About 24 literary works were copied frequently in House F. Some, such as *The Farmer's Instructions*, have some sort of mathematical content; others convey strong messages about the role of mathematics in the scribal profession. Competent scribes use their numeracy and literacy in order to uphold justice, as Girini-isag spells out in criticising his junior colleague Enki-manshum:

> You wrote a tablet, but you cannot grasp its meaning. You wrote a letter, but that is the limit for you! Go to divide a plot, and you are not able to divide the plot; go to apportion a field, and you cannot even hold the tape and rod properly; the field pegs you are unable to place; you cannot figure out its shape, so that when wronged men have a quarrel you are not able to bring peace but you allow brother to attack brother. Among the scribes you (alone) are unfit for the clay. What are you fit for? Can anybody tell us?[2]

Girini-isag's point is that accurate land surveys are needed for legal reasons – inheritance, sales, harvest contracts, for instance. If the scribe cannot provide his services effectively he will unwittingly cause disputes or prevent them from being settled peacefully. Thus mathematical skills are at the heart of upholding justice. This point is also made in the curricular hymns to kings such as Ishme-Dagan and Lipit-Eshtar, who attribute their skills in numerate justice to the goddess Nisaba, patron of scribes, who 'generously bestowed upon [them] the measuring rod, the surveyor's gleaming line, the yardstick, and the tablets which confer wisdom'.[3]

On one or two literary tablets from House F students also carried out arithmetical calculations, showing all the intermediate steps as well as the final answer. At Ur students made calculations on the same tablets as Sumerian proverbs (Robson 1999: 245–72). Many of them can be linked to known types of word problems – most of which, unfortunately, have no known archaeological context. We must therefore leave House F behind to explore the more sophisticated aspects of Old Babylonian mathematics.

Mathematical word problems

The OB corpus of mathematical problems splits into two roughly equal halves: on the one hand, what might loosely be called concrete algebra (Høyrup 2002); and on the other, a sort of quantity surveying (Robson 1999; Friberg 2001). It is too crude and anachronistic to label these halves 'pure' and 'applied'; there are also significant overlaps between them.

Old Babylonian 'algebra' was for many years translated unproblematically into modern symbols, so that a question such as 'A reciprocal exceeds its reciprocal by 7. What are the reciprocal and its reciprocal?' could be represented as $x - 60/x = 7$ and the prose instructions for solving it understood as manipulations of that equation to yield $x = 12$ (YBC 6967: Neugebauer and Sachs 1945: text Ua). However, Jens Høyrup's pioneering discourse analysis (Høyrup 1990; 2002) made it clear that all 'algebraic' procedures should be understood as the manipulation of lines and areas. In this case, by visualising the unknown reciprocals as the sides of rectangle of area 60, the rectangle can be turned into an L-shaped figure, and the original lengths found by completing the square:

> A reciprocal exceeds its reciprocal by 7 [Figure 29.2a]. What are the reciprocal and its reciprocal? You: break in two the 7 by which the reciprocal exceeds its reciprocal so that 3;30 (will come up) [Figure 29.2b]. Combine 3;30 and 3;30 so that 12;15 (will come up). Add 1 00, the area, to the 12;15 which came up for you so that 1 12;15 (will come up) [Figure 29.2c]. What squares 1 12;15? 8;30. Draw 8;30 and 8;30, its counterpart, and then take away 3;30, the holding-square, from one; add to one. One is 12, the other is 5 [Figure 29.2d]. The reciprocal is 12, its reciprocal is 5.

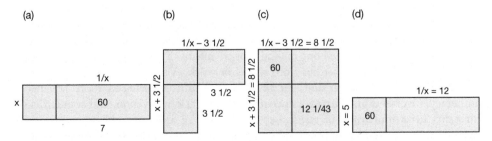

Figure 29.2 The geometrical manipulations implicit in YBC 6967.

No diagrams such as those shown in Figure 29.2 actually survive. Either they were ephemera drawn in the dust or instantly recycled clay, or they were simply imaginative, conceptual tools that never took written form. Nevertheless, their real or imagined existence fits features of the mathematical text that could not be comfortably explained by interpretation through symbolic algebra.

Fully half the known corpus of Old Babylonian mathematical problems uses the management of building work and agricultural labour as a pretext for setting exercises in line geometry or geometric algebra. Carrying bricks, building earthen walls, and repairing canals and associated earth works are among the commonest problem-setting scenarios. Some are illustrated with diagrams of plane or three-dimensional figures. Although many use terminology and technical constants that are also known from earlier administrative practice the majority of the problems are highly unrealistic, both in the measurements of the objects described and in the nature of the questions posed. Quantity surveying could also be used as a pretext for developing complex problems on geometrical algebra. For instance, problem 19 of YBC 4657 (Neugebauer and Sachs 1945: text G) asks, 'A trench has an area of 7½ sar; the volume is 45. Add the length and width and (it is) 6½ rods. What are the length, width, and its depth?' A professional surveyor would never find himself knowing the parameters given in the question without also knowing the measurements that the question asks for.

YBC 6967 is a single tablet; YBC 4657 is one of a series of four, of which three survive. Most collections of mathematical problems are more or less thematic, and their structuration is often explicitly pedagogical, with problems getting progressively harder. The numerical values in the collections tend to stay constant, though; teachers kept separate lists of different parameters that could be given to students in their actual exercises. Plimpton 322, the famous table of 'Pythagorean' numbers, is one such parameter list (Robson 2001a). Some of the calculations from OB Ur are witnesses to a single problem assigned with different numerical values to six pupils – or to the same student six times.

Professional numeracy

Although scribal students sometimes signed their names at the bottom of their tablets, it has not yet been possible to trace any individual's career from the school house to life as a working scribe; nor has anyone attempted to chart the relationship between school mathematics and the needs of the professionally numerate. OB school mathematics went way beyond practical necessity; rather, it – like the messages of curricular Sumerian literature – instilled confidence, pride, and a sense of professional identity into the young scribes.

Institutional accountants needed, at the most basic level, only to be able to count, add and subtract, and to record numbers, weights and capacities accurately. Additions and subtractions were carried out mentally or by means of counters; such calculations are never found on tablets, either from school or work. A scribe writing daily records of commodities coming in and out of storage might never need more advanced numeracy. Overseers and surveyors needed multiplication, division, and standardised constants for a multitude of tasks such as calculating areas of fields or volumes of canal excavations, and for estimating harvest yields or the number of labourers needed. I have never seen an institutional account that called for any more complex arithmetical method, such as finding non-standard reciprocals or square roots (both favourite school exercises).

That said, the complexity of some OB accounts is astonishing. Ur III documents were all formatted as rather cumbersome lists in which qualitative and quantitative data are mixed in sentence-like entries. During the early OB period, scribes developed the tabular account, as an efficient way of recording, storing, and sorting data. Tabulation enabled the horizontal separation of different categories of quantitative information and the easy addition of quantitative data, along a vertical axis (see Figure 29.1). At the same time, data could be sorted by criteria such as responsible officials, destination, or date of transaction. Headings obviated the necessity to repeat descriptive information. Columns of derived data – additions, subtractions, multiplications – enabled calculations to be performed along both horizontal and vertical axes for the purposes of double-checking. At the same time, the columnar format could be ignored where necessary to provide note-like explanatory interpolations. Tables were truly powerful information-processing tools, cognitively distinct from well-organised lists, but they remained a minority preference for Old Babylonian scribes. It was in Kassite Nippur that tabular accounts had their greatest heyday (Robson 2004a).

FIRST-MILLENNIUM MATHEMATICS AND NUMERACY

Metrology in scribal schools

There are currently very few sources for mathematics, or for any other scholarly activity, in Babylonia between around 1600 and 750 BCE. For the succeeding five centuries there is a rich variety of evidence, much of it archaeologically contextualised, for the learning, teaching, and practical use of mathematical skills.

All metrologies had changed drastically since Old Babylonian times, but it was the areal system that had been most radically overhauled. In 'reed measure', the standard unit of area was no longer the sar, or square rod (ca. 36 m^2), but the square reed, 7 × 7 cubits (ca. 12.25 m^2). It was subdivided into the areal cubit = 7 × 1 linear cubits, and the areal finger = 7 cubits × 1 finger). Alternatively, in 'seed measure', areas were considered to be proportional to one of several fixed capacity measures and thus expressed in terms of the capacity of seed needed to sow them.

In Neo-Babylonian times, a formal elementary curriculum that seems to have varied little from city to city is attested at Ur and the cities of northern Babylonia (Gesche 2000). It had changed significantly since Old Babylonian times: metrological lists occupied a marginal position in this curriculum, being found on around five per cent of published school tablets. These particular tablets all have the same format: there is a long extract from one of half a dozen standard lexical lists on the front, and many shorter pieces from a variety of texts on the back. Lists of capacities, weights, and lengths are attested in roughly equal numbers. Most are long extracts or entire lists, but some consist of two or three lines repeated over and over again. There are no tables, either giving sexagesimal values of metrological units, as in the Old Babylonian period, or describing relations between metrological systems, as in other first-millennium contexts. Lists of squares of integers are the only other type of mathematical exercise attested in the first-millennium school curriculum (Robson 2004b).

Metrological lists were found among school tablets excavated by an Iraqi team in Babylon in the late 1970s. They had been reused as packing materials under the floors of two temples near the north-east corner of the precinct of Etemenanki, Marduk's ziggurat in Babylon. The larger temple was dedicated to Nabû of *harû* (a name of his primary temple in Borsippa); the smaller temple belonged to the minor goddess Ashratum 'Lady of the steppe'. Almost all the tablets originally bore colophons naming their student authors and dedicating them to the god Nabû, either in his primary aspect or as 'Nabû of accounts'. They may well have been brought to the temple as votive offerings, having been written somewhere else (Cavigneaux 1981).

On present evidence, the mathematical elements of formal elementary scribal education in the mid-first millennium BCE consisted *only* of metrological lists – lengths, capacities, areas – and tables of squares. For more sophisticated mathematical activities we must look to professional scholars in Babylon and Uruk.

Mathematics for *āšipus*

The Shangu-Ninurta family of *āšipus* (exorcists, or incantation priests) occupied a courtyard house in eastern Uruk in the fifth century BCE. Three rooms and a courtyard have survived. Before the family left, they had carefully buried much of their household library – about 180 tablets – and whatever archival tablets they did not want to take with them, in clay jars within the house. The approximate proportions of the library's scholarly contents were:

- 30 per cent medical (physiognomic and diagnostic omens; medical prescriptions and incantations);
- 20 per cent other incantations, rituals, and magic;
- 19 per cent hymns, literature, and lexical lists;
- 12 per cent observed and induced omens (*Enuma Anu Ellil*, terrestrial omens, extispicy, etc.);
- 12 per cent astronomy, astrology, and mathematics; and
- 7 per cent unidentified (Hunger 1976; von Weiher 1983–98).[4]

Fifty tablets have colophons on, recording information such as the owner and scribe of the tablet, its source, and its place within a scholarly series. Seven of the family's tablets are mathematical, written or owned by one Shamash-iddin, and his son Rimut-Anu. Their mathematics is predominantly concerned with reciprocals, lengths, and areas, with a secondary interest in time-keeping.

Two large tablets, one of which appears to be a continuation of the other, contain a sequence of about 50 mathematical rules and problems about the 'seed' and 'reed' measures of area (Friberg *et al.* 1990; Friberg 1997). The second one has a catch-line before the colophon, '*Seed and reeds*. Finished', which suggests that they comprised a standard series. The colophon itself, which states that the tablet is a 'copy of a wooden writing board, written and checked against its original', is a salutary reminder that much first-millennium scholarship was written on perishable media. The very last problem of this second tablet is about finding the square area that can be paved with standard square baked bricks ⅔ cubit (ca. 35 cm) long:

9 hundred baked bricks of ⅔ cubits each. I enlarged an animal yard. What is the square side of the animal yard? You go 0;40 steps for each brick. You take 30 each of 15 00. You go 30 steps of 0;40: 20. The square side of the animal yard is 20 cubits.

The solution is simply to find the number of bricks that would make up the edge of the square area, by finding the square root of the total number (happily a square integer), then to multiply by the length of each brick. Although the problem itself is reminiscent of OB mathematics, the technical terminology and method of solution are both radically different.

Three tablets from Shamash-iddin's house bear metrological tables and reciprocal tables. Two contain various tables relating length and both systems of area measure to each other and to the sexagesimal system, and to various time-keeping schemes. One begins with a list of numerical writings for the major gods. The third tablet is a common first-millennium table of many-place reciprocal pairs from 1 to 4. It appears to have been calculated, at least in part, not simply copied from another exemplar, as witnessed by two rough tablets with nine calculations of regular reciprocals taken from near the beginning of the table. The original number is multiplied repeatedly by simple factors of 60 until it is reduced to 1; then 1 is multiplied up again by those same simple factors in reverse: once more, a favourite OB school problem is solved using a new method (Friberg 1999).

Mathematics for *kalûs*

The latest dateable mathematical cuneiform tablets were written by members of the Sîn-leqi-unninni family in Seleucid Uruk. The Sîn-leqi-unninnis are the best known of all the scribal families of Late Babylonian Uruk, partly because their eponymous ancestor was considered to be the author of the famous Epic of Gilgamesh, and partly because they have left a vast amount of documentary evidence (Beaulieu 2000). While most of their tablets come from uncontrolled excavation (Thureau-Dangin 1922), several were found in the Resh temple of Anu in the city centre (van Dijk and Mayer 1980). Anu-belshunu and his son Anu-aba-uter, who worked there as *kalûs*, or lamentation priests, wrote and owned a large number of mathematical astronomical tablets, mostly ephemeredes, or tables of predictions. Unlike other scribal families, they put their name to very few copies of the standard series of omens or medical compilations, but concentrated instead on the *kalûtu*, the standard series of incantations and rituals associated with their profession as lamentation priests working for Anu's temple Resh in Uruk city centre. Their scholarly tablets almost all reflect their professional concerns: the mathematical prediction of ominous celestial events, and the correct performance of ritual reactions to them (Pearce and Doty 2000).

Anu-belshunu made a copy of the 'Esangila tablet', for a member of another scribal family, in the 220s BCE. This text, known also from the vicinity of Babylon, uses the measurements of the great courts and the ziggurat Etemenanki near Marduk's temple Esangila as a pretext for some simple metrological exercises in seed and reeds, the different kinds of area measure (AO 6555: George 1993: 109–19, 414–34).

Anu-aba-uter's compilation of mathematical problems, which must have been written in the 180s BCE, is the latest datable mathematical cuneiform tablet known.

Few of its 17 problems, allowing for changes in writing habits, would look out of place within the OB mathematical corpus. Problems 1–2, for instance, concern the sum of arithmetical series, 9–13 the capacity of a cube whose sides are known, and 14–17 regular reciprocal pairs whose sums are known, solved by a standard OB cut-and-paste method. The only innovatory methods of solution are for problems 3–8, about triangles, squares, and the diagonals of rectangles – which are not exactly innovatory mathematical subjects in themselves. Problem 6 – to find the area of a rectangle given the length, width and diagonal – is not attested at all in the OB corpus but is found in a contemporary mathematical compilation from Babylon (AO 6484: Neugebauer 1935–37: I 96–107).

ADMINISTRATIVE METROLOGY AND NUMERACY

The mathematical obsession with 'seed and reeds' suggests that much pedagogical effort was expended in teaching conversion between the two area systems, but in fact numerate professionals seem to have had entirely separate uses for them. For instance, some 70 house plans and agricultural land surveys survive from the reign of Darius I, perhaps drawn up for taxation purposes. They seem to have been housed in a central archive with agricultural land surveys, although their original archaeological context is now lost (Nemet-Nejat 1982).

The field plans are typically not drawn to scale, as the dimensions of the boundaries are recorded textually, along with the area in seed measure. This was calculated by the traditional 'surveyors' formula', by which the lengths of opposite sides were averaged and then those averages multiplied together and converted from square reeds to seed. The cardinal directions of the field boundaries are written on the edges of the tablet, along with damaged details of the neighbouring properties. Calculations were still carried out in the sexagesimal place value system, even when the preferred recording format used partly decimalised absolute value.

Contemporary house plans, also drawn up by professional surveyors, look very similar, but use the 'reed measure' system of area metrology. The dependence of the reed measure on the number 7, which is not a factor of 60, may even have been a deliberate move to professionalise and restrict access to urban land measurement. Yet analysis of the actual calculations involved in house mensuration shows that the surveyors used several simple strategies to lessen the burden of calculation and conversion between sexagesimal and metrological systems. Nevertheless, it was an arithmetically fiddly operation which must have been learned on the job: as we have seen, institutionalised schooling would have prepared surveyors only to measure and write the numerals and metrological systems, not to convert between, and multiply with them.

In the Hellenistic period, legal documents recording the sale of prebends, or rights to shares in temple income, show a fascinating move away from sexagesimal numeration towards the Greco-Egyptian notation of fractions as sums of unit fractions ($1/n$) (Cocquerillat 1965). For instance, in 190 BCE the *kalû* Anu-belshunu bought a Temple Enterer's prebend of 'one-sixth plus one-ninth of a day [on the 1st] day, 24th day, and 30th day – a total of one-sixth plus one-ninth of one day on those days – and one-third of a day on the 27th day' (HSM 913.2.181: Wallenfels 1998). The scribe, one Shamash-etir, could easily have expressed the first fraction sexagesimally as 0;16 40 [= ⅜] of a day if he wanted: he was the chief priest of the Resh temple and was later to tutor Anu-belshunu's son Anu-aba-uter extensively in mathematical astronomy. But in this context he – and all other scribes of prebendary contracts – made a contextual, social choice against the sexagesimal system and in favour of Greek-style expression. Shamash-etir's notation hints that his priestly circle's legal contracts and scholarly writing were now a tiny cuneiform island in a sea of alphabetic Greek and Aramaic; it is no wonder that his protégé Anu-aba-uter is the last Babylonian mathematician known to us.

CONCLUSIONS

Babylonian mathematics underwent many changes in the millennia of its history, but those changes cannot be fully understood – or sometimes even identified – if viewed from a mathematical standpoint alone. Terminology, methods, metrologies, notations all adapted to changing social needs and interests as well as intellectual ones, while shaping and challenging the ideas of the individuals and groups who created and used them. It is often assumed that Otto Neugebauer left nothing more to be said about Babylonian mathematics. On the contrary: its very Babylonian-ness is only now beginning to be explored.

NOTES

1   Sexagesimal numbers are transcribed with spaces separating the sexagesimal places and a semicolon marking the boundary between integers and fractions. For example, 1 12;15 represents 1 × 60 + 12 + 15/60, or 72¼.
2   *Eduba* dialogue 3, lines 19–27: Vanstiphout (1997: 589).
3   Lipit-Eshtar hymn B, lines 23–24: Black *et al.* (1998–2006: 2.5.5.2).
4   The other tablets from the house belonged to later inhabitants, most notably Iqisha of the Ekur-zakir family (later fourth century BCE).

BIBLIOGRAPHY

Beaulieu, P.-A. 2000. 'The descendants of Sîn-leqi-unninni', in J. Marzahn and H. Neumann (eds), *Assyriologica et Semitica: Festschrift für Joachim Oelsner*. (Alter Orient und Altes Testament, 252), Münster: Ugarit-Verlag, 1–16.

Black, J.A. *et al.* 1998–2006. *The Electronic Text Corpus of Sumerian Literature*. University of Oxford. http://etcsl.orinst.ox.ac.uk.

Cavigneaux, A., 1981. *Textes scolaires du temple de Nabû ša Harê* (Texts from Babylon, 1), Baghdad: State Organization of Antiquities and Heritage.

Cocquerillat, D. 1965. 'Les calculs practiques sur les fractions à l'époque séleucide', *Bibliotheca Orientalis* 22, 239–42.

Foster, B.R. and E. Robson 2004. 'A new look at the Sargonic mathematical corpus', *Zeitschrift für Assyriologie* 94, 1–15.

Friberg, J. 1990. 'Mathematik', in D.O. Edzard (ed.), *Reallexikon der Assyriologie und vorderasiatischen Archäologie*, vol. 7. Berlin/New York: de Gruyter, 531–585.

—— 1997. 'Seed and reeds continued: another metro-mathematical topic text from Late Babylonian Uruk', *Baghdader Mitteilungen* 28, 251–365.

—— 1997–98, 'Round and almost round numbers in proto-literate metro-mathematical field texts', *Archiv für Orientforschung* 44–45, 1–58.

—— 1999. 'A Late Babylonian factorisation algorithm for the computation of reciprocals of many-place regular sexagesimal numbers', *Baghdader Mitteilungen* 30, 139–161.

—— 2000. 'Mathematics at Ur in the Old Babylonian period', *Revue d'Assyriologie* 94, 97–188.

—— 2001. 'Bricks and mud in metro-mathematical cuneiform texts', in J. Høyrup and P. Damerow (eds), *Changing views on ancient Near Eastern mathematics* (Berliner Beiträge zum Vorderen Orient, 19), Berlin: Dietrich Reimer, 61–154.

—— *et al.* 1990. 'Seed and reeds: a metro-mathematical topic text from Late Babylonian Uruk', *Baghdader Mitteilungen* 21, 483–557.

George, A.R. 1993. *Babylonian topographical texts* (Orientalia Lovaniensia Analecta, 40), Leuven: Peeters.

Gesche, P.D. 2000. *Schulunterricht in Babylonien im ersten Jahrtausend v. Chr.* (Alter Orient und Altes Testament, 275), Münster: Ugarit-Verlag.

Høyrup, J. 1990. 'Algebra and naive geometry. An investigation of some basic aspects of Old Babylonian mathematical thought', *Altorientalische Forschungen* 17, 27–69, 262–354.

—— 2002. *Lengths, widths, surfaces: a portrait of Old Babylonian algebra and its kin*, Berlin and New York: Springer.

—— and P. Damerow (eds) 2001. *Changing views on ancient Near Eastern mathematics* (Berliner Beiträge zum Vorderen Orient, 19), Berlin.

Hunger, H. 1976. *Spätbabylonische Texte aus Uruk*, I (Ausgrabungen der Deutschen Forschungsgemeinschaft in Uruk-Warka. Endberichte, 9), Berlin: Mann.

Melville, D. 2002. 'Ration computations at Fara: multiplication or repeated addition', in J.M. Steele and A. Imhausen (eds), *Under one sky: mathematics and astronomy in the ancient Near East* (Alter Orient und Altes Testament, 297), Münster: Ugarit-Verlag, 237–252.

Nemet-Nejat, K. 1982. *Late Babylonian field plans in the British Museum* (Studia Pohl Series Maior, 11), Rome: Pontifical Biblical Institute.

Neugebauer, O. 1935–37. *Mathematische Keilschrift-Texte*, I–III (Quellen und Studien zur Geschichte der Mathematik, Astronomie und Physik, A3), Berlin: Springer.

—— 1948. *The exact sciences in antiquity*, Princeton: Princeton University Press.

—— and A.J. Sachs 1945. *Mathematical cuneiform texts* (American Oriental Series, 29), New Haven: American Oriental Society.

Nissen, H., P. Damerow, and R.K. Englund 1993. *Archaic bookkeeping: early writing and techniques of administration in the Ancient Near East*. Chicago: Chicago University Press.

Oelsner, J. 2001. 'HS 201 – eine Reziprokentabelle der Ur III-Zeit', in J. Høyrup and P. Damerow (eds), *Changing views on ancient Near Eastern mathematics* (Berliner Beiträge zum Vorderen Orient, 19), Berlin: Dietrich Reimer, 53–59.

Pearce, L.E. and L.T. Doty 2000. 'The activities of Anu-bēlšunu, Seleucid scribe', in J. Marzahn and H. Neumann (eds), *Assyriologica et Semitica: Festschrift für Joachim Oelsner* (Alter Orient und Altes Testament, 252), Münster: Ugarit-Verlag, 331–342.

Powell, M.A. 1976. 'The antecedents of Old Babylonian place notation and the early history of Babylonian mathematics', *Historia Mathematica* 3, 417–439.

—— 1990. 'Maße und Gewichte', in D.O. Edzard (ed.), *Reallexikon der Assyriologie und vorderasiatischen Archäologie* 7, Berlin and New York: Walter de Gruyter, 457–530.

Robson, E. 1999. *Mesopotamian mathematics, 2100–1600 BC: technical constants in bureaucracy and education* (Oxford Editions of Cuneiform Texts, 14), Oxford: Clarendon Press.

—— 2001a. 'Neither Sherlock Holmes nor Babylon: a reassessment of Plimpton 322', *Historia Mathematica* 28, 167–206.

—— 2001b, 'The tablet house: a scribal school in Old Babylonian Nippur', *Revue d'Assyriologie* 95, 39–67.

—— 2002. 'More than metrology: mathematics education in an Old Babylonian scribal school', in J.M. Steele and A. Imhausen (eds), *Under one sky: mathematics and astronomy in the ancient Near East* (Alter Orient und Altes Testament, 297), Münster: Ugarit-Verlag, 325–365.

—— 2004a. 'Accounting for change: the development of tabular bookkeeping in early Meso-potamia', in M. Hudson and C. Wunsch (eds), *Creating economic order: record-keeping, standardization, and the development of accounting in the Ancient Near East* (International Scholars Conference on Ancient Near Eastern Economies, 4), Bethesda: CDL Press, 2004, 107–144.

—— 2004b. 'Mathematical cuneiform tablets in the Ashmolean Museum, Oxford', *SCIAMVS – Sources and Commentaries in Exact Sciences* 5, 3–65.

—— 2008. *Mathematics in ancient Iraq: a social history*, Princeton: Princeton University Press.

Schmandt-Besserat, D. 1992, *Before writing: from counting to cuneiform*, Austin: University of Texas Press.

Tanret, M. 2002. *Per aspera ad astra* (Mesopotamian History and Environment, Series III: Texts, 3), Ghent: University of Ghent.

Thureau-Dangin, F. 1922. *Tablettes d'Uruk à l'usage des prêtres du temple d'Anu au temps des Séleucides*. (Textes cuneiforms du Louvre, 6), Paris: Geuthner.

—— 1938. *Textes mathématiques babyloniennes* (Ex Oriente Lux, 1), Leiden: Brill.

Van Dijk, J. and W. Mayer 1980. *Texte aus dem Rēš-Heiligtum in Uruk-Warka* (Baghdader Mitteilungen Beiheft, 2), Berlin: Mann.

Vanstiphout, H.L.J. 1997. 'Sumerian canonical compositions. C. Individual focus. 6. School dialogues', in W.W. Hallo (ed.), *The context of scripture, I: Canonical compositions from the Biblical world*, London/New York/Köln: Brill, 588–593.

von Weiher, E. 1983–98. *Spätbabylonische Texte aus Uruk,* (Ausgrabungen der Deutschen Forschungs-gemeinschaft in Uruk-Warka. Endberichte, 10–13), Berlin: Mann.

Wallenfels, R. 1998. *Seleucid archival texts in the Harvard Semitic Museum: text editions and catalogue raisonné of the seal impressions* (Cuneiform Monographs, 12). Groningen: Styx.

Whiting, R.M. 1984. 'More evidence for sexagesimal calculations in the third millennium BC', *Zeitschrift für Assyriologie und vorderasiatische Archäologie* 74, 59–66.

CHAPTER THIRTY

BABYLONIAN LISTS OF WORDS AND SIGNS[1]

———·◆·———

Jon Taylor

The Babylonians are famous for their habit of making lists of things. Scribes wrote lists of names, lists of places, lists of sheep and other animals, lists of stars, lists of gods, lists of objects made from wood and metals, lists of professions and many other lists besides. Lists were also used to store other kinds of information. For example, the Babylonians were renowned for their skills as astronomers, doctors and fortune-tellers; knowledge derived from each of these fields was also committed to writing in lists. We also find collections of proverbs written in a similar style. So why did the Babylonians expend so much effort compiling lists, and what can the lists tell us about the Babylonians themselves?

A tremendous quantity of information was stored in the lists. One of the constant concerns was how to order that information in a useful and meaningful way.[2] The early word lists contained words belonging to a particular theme. During the third millennium the system of grouping together words whose spelling shares a particular character of the script developed; to an extent this is a natural extension of the thematic system, since many items within a theme will share a common sign in their writing. Signs and words could also be grouped by some kind of 'natural' order, such as moving from head to foot in the body. In the case of sign lists, the signs could be arranged according to similarity of form. Within a list, individual entries may be grouped according to various other considerations, such as similarity of sound or word shape, or in terms of synonyms/antonyms or paradigms such as positive/negative or colour terms. Indeed, within any one list, one may find many of the techniques used.

THE ORIGINS OF LISTS

To understand the Babylonian lists, we must first explore their origin and history. The earliest known writing in the Near East comes from the city of Uruk (in what is now southern Iraq) around the end of the fourth millennium BC. Most of these documents are economic records, tracking the movements of commodities through the temple household of the goddess Inanna. A few of the documents are lists of words, however. So the humble list is present right from the beginning. The kind of list that was written was a simple catalogue of types of pots, metals, domesticated animals etc. In other words, the types of item being recorded were those found in the contemporary economic documents. There are no lists for wild animals, although we see them depicted in art, no lists of gods, although there are temples to them, nor of stars, although we can be confident that the inhabitants of Uruk observed them. It seems likely that the list began as a practical tool to help administrators learn the new accounting device that we now know as writing. But the lists soon gained an aspect to their character that was to stay with them throughout their life in the Ancient Near East. It is the case both that there are items found in the economic texts that are not in the lists, and, more tellingly, that there are many items in the lists which cannot be found in the economic texts. Lists always contain a more theoretical, sometimes academic, element.

THE PRE-BABYLONIAN HISTORY OF LISTS

The very earliest lists from Uruk did not have a fixed form. The terms they contained and the order in which those terms were listed differed from one document to the next. They began to stabilise, however, and by the beginning of the third millennium BC there was a high degree of consistency. New material was generally not added to the lists; they remained frozen. These lists spread with writing across Mesopotamia; we have quite large numbers of such texts from Fara and Abu Salabikh in Mesopotamia and Ebla in Syria. This was to become a second feature of lists throughout Mesopotamian history. As the technology of writing spread, the lists travelled with it. During this time, however, both society and the system of writing were developing. The lists were still copied but became ever further detached from the reality of what was written in economic documents. Through their antiquity and unchangeable form they had acquired prestige status. Most copies from the third millennium are beautiful, well written texts by accomplished scribes. They would continue to be treasured, and copied faithfully, for many more centuries to come. We shall resume their story shortly. In the meantime, in the middle of the third millennium, new lists were composed. They were in a similar style to the early lists, containing many names of birds, fish, trees or the like. These words were again closer to what could be found in the texts of daily life. But they, too, were fixed and over time would become obsolete. They, too, would live on to be revered by the scribes of the Old Babylonian period.

THE EDUCATIONAL REVOLUTION OF THE
OLD BABYLONIAN PERIOD

As always in the study of the ancient world, we are at the mercy of our sources. For the last few centuries of the third millennium we possess only a few texts of the school type. By this we mean those texts dedicated to scribal training and education as opposed to those of direct administrative, legal or economic function, for example. From what little we have, it seems that there was a large degree of continuity with earlier practice. Scribes were still copying the old lists. The picture at the beginning of the second millennium, at the start of what we call the Old Babylonian period, was radically different. For while the Old Babylonian educational institution may have had its roots in this earlier period, a whole new set of lists had been developed. These were very different to the earlier lists and were used in a very different way.

433

Before looking more closely at these new lists, it is useful to look at the context in which they were produced. Fortunately, we are relatively well informed about Old Babylonian schools.

LITERACY AND THE OLD BABYLONIAN SCHOOL

Nowadays 'school' conjures up a picture of large numbers of children sitting in massed ranks at desks, with separate teachers for each subject. Old Babylonian schools were not like this at all. Literacy in Babylonia was always somewhat restricted. Unlike us today, the average Babylonian was not surrounded by writing and could go about daily life without having to read or write anything. Large households would use writing to keep track of goods and employees. Members of the administration would write letters to each other to give or respond to orders or otherwise conduct business. But the average citizen had little or no use for writing. They did not have books to read or forms to fill in, nor would they write their own personal letters or diaries, or perform any of the other literate activities that are such a major part of modern daily life. This is not to say that they might not possess a few documents. For example, they might own the deeds to their house or contracts stipulating the terms of a marriage or adoption. These would have been written by professional scribes, however. They would be needed only in the event of a dispute and even then would have been handed over to the authorities to be read. Written documents did not list all terms and conditions and were not considered as having the final say in a dispute. Greater trust was placed on testimony and oaths. It was not necessary even to be able to sign one's name. This was done using a cylinder seal (for the better off) or by impressing into the clay the hem of one's garment or a fingernail. There was no general education; writing was a specialised craft. Most daily business was conducted orally. The number of scribes was always low, and they would be employed (for one-off jobs or for the longer term) whenever required, mostly by the administration. There were no school buildings as such in the Old Babylonian period. Education took place in the courtyard of ordinary houses. There individual teachers (probably in many cases the owner of the house) taught small numbers of children, including their own sons; literacy seems largely to have been a male preserve.

LISTS IN THE SCRIBAL CURRICULUM

The first thing apprentice scribes would learn to do was to make the clay tablets upon which writing was inscribed. Next would come practice in strokes of the stylus, forming 'wedges' in the clay (such as ↑, ⊢, ◁). Having mastered the basic technique, the next step was to put wedges together to make the various characters (known as 'signs') of the cuneiform script,[3] starting with simple ones such as 𐏑 and ⊢. At this point the student learned the sounds represented by the signs. The next step involved putting the signs together in meaningful combinations, first people's names then various words. This is where the lists come in. Lists taught the students to read and produce signs and words. After this came training in mathematics, drafting contracts and letters and the study of proverbs and literary texts. Thus lists occupy a position within a greater system. That system taught them primarily about writing and its uses. This fact is crucial to understanding what the lists represent.

THE OLD BABYLONIAN LISTS

There are actually many different kinds of list. Already when students practised making single wedges this was done in list format. The same was true for the combinations of wedges into signs, such as the ones contained in a list called Syllable Alphabet A.[4] This list provided instruction in common, simple signs in various combinations. Next, the student learned sets of related syllables, still without real meaning, through a list called Tu-ta-ti. That list begins: tu ta ti, nu na ni and continues in this way, listing sets of three signs combining a consonant with a standard sequence of three vowels.

The first meaningful list encountered was that of personal names. Learning how to write names is a very natural way to start learning how to write, being relatively easy, interesting and also useful. Here the student would come across features of the cuneiform writing system that he would learn more systematically later.

The next stage was to learn the series of lists known today as Urra. The series comprised six lists, each containing many words on various themes: (1) trees and wooden objects; (2) reed, vessels, clay, hides, metals; (3) domestic and wild animals and meats; (4) stones, plants, birds, fish, clothing; (5) geographical terms, stars; (6) foods. The first tablet begins:

^{giš}taskarin	'boxwood'
^{giš}esi	'ebony'
^{giš}nu$_{11}$	(type of tree)
^{giš}ha-lu-ub$_2$	'oak'

There was also a list of professions, known as Proto-Lu,[5] but this was not part of Urra; it was taught later in the curriculum.

Next came what we refer to as Proto-Ea, a sign list teaching the various possible readings of individual cuneiform signs (it is a feature of the cuneiform writing system that a sign may be read in several different ways). The first section deals with the A-sign:

reading	*sign*	*meaning*
a$_2$	A	(an anguished expression)
ia	A	(reading derived from context)
du-ru	A	'moist'
e	A	(reading derived from context)
a	A	'water'
	A.A	'father'
	A.A.A	'grandfather'
sa-ah	HA.A	'runaway'

| am | A.AN | '(s)he/it is' |
| še-em₃ | A.AN | 'rain' |

The signs in this list are grouped according to similarity of shape. Signs progress by the addition or removal of wedges.[6] After the readings of a single sign have been covered, the text proceeds to list repetitions of the sign, modifications of it, and then sometimes combinations of the sign with others to form new signs. Students would already previously have encountered the use of signs with different readings but here they learned these in a systematic fashion. A more comprehensive version of this list, known as Proto-Aa, is also found.

There was also a list for other, more complex, signs; these were combinations of the simple signs. The list is known as Proto-Diri, and such compounds are named 'Diri-compounds' after it. Proto-Diri taught the student how to read combinations of signs where the reading was not predictable from the component parts. For example:

reading	*sign*	*translation*	*meaning*
si₂-is-kur	AMARxŠE.AMARxŠE	*niqû*	'offering, sacrifice'
		karābum	'to praise, pray'
		ikribum	'blessing, prayer'

Another important list was Proto-Izi, which contained miscellaneous groups of vocabulary that did not fit easily into Urra or Proto-Lu. It made extensive use of a technique called acrography, whereby each entry in a group contains a sign in common with the others. This principle is applied more strictly as the list advances. The list begins with the NE-sign, for which izi, ne and bi₂ are all readings:

izi	'fire'
NE	'brazier'
NE	'embers'
NE	'flame'
NE	'ashes'
izi-gar	'furnace'
i-bi₂	'smoke'
ne-mur	'glowing ashes'
sag-izi	'torch'

The list continues with related terms, including ganzer₂ (written with the signs NE.SI.A) 'flame' and an-bar₇ (bar₇ is another reading of the NE-sign) 'midday', before moving on to terms including the AN-sign, and so on through the list. There were further, less commonly used lists employing this technique more systematically; these are known as Kagal, Nigga and the SAG-tablet. Kagal, for example, begins with terms related to gates and buildings, before moving onto terms beginning with the A-sign, then those beginning with the GIŠ-sign.

One great innovation of the Old Babylonian period was the bilingual format of the lists. Until then, all lists in Mesopotamia had been in just one language, namely Sumerian.[7] Now a second column of text (in Akkadian) was added to some lists. This raises the sophistication of the list to a new level, as scribes had to learn how the two columns of data interacted with each other. Not all lists contained the Akkadian column but it can be shown that the Akkadian equivalents of the Sumerian terms were implicitly part of the composition, despite not being put into writing. By this time Sumerian was a dead language, retained in learned and religious circles, rather like Latin in post-Roman Europe.

Several other lists were also used in Old Babylonian schools, although less commonly so than the others. They included another list of professions (called Azlag = *ashlaku* 'fuller'; known in several different versions), a list of diseases and a list known as Ugumu ('my cranium'). The latter listed human body parts ordered from head to foot. This system of ordering is a natural one, and can be found elsewhere in Mesopotamian texts, such as in medical texts, as well as in the later list Nabnitu (discussed below).

The student would continue to meet other types of list, such as mathematical and metrological tables and proverbs. One further category of list was also copied by a few students. These were the old third-millennium lists discussed above. The Old Babylonian scribes were conscious of their great heritage and copied these lists as a matter of academic, antiquarian interest. They are found only in small numbers and did not form a standard part of the scribal training system.

THE MIDDLE BABYLONIAN LISTS

In the latter half of the second millennium BC, we again suffer from a scarcity of sources. Most of our knowledge about the Middle Babylonian period comes from outside of Babylonia. During this period, Akkadian had become the *lingua franca* of the Ancient Near East, and knowledge of cuneiform spread across the region. With it went the lists. Thus we have versions of many of the lists from sites such as Hattusa (capital of the Hittite empire) in Anatolia, Emar and Ugarit in Syria, and El-Amarna, which, for a brief period in the fourteenth century, was capital of Egypt. We are also aided by Babylonia's great rival, Assyria. The Assyrians looked to the south for much of their scholarship, and following Tiglath-pileser I's conquest of Babylon at the turn of the eleventh century, many tablets travelled north to Assyria. These, plus the few sources known from Babylonia itself, taken together with the first-millennium sources, give us a reasonable idea of what was happening to the lists in Babylonia during what was clearly a pivotal period in their history.

We know that some of the Old Babylonian lists (and all of the third-millennium lists) fell out of use during this period, along with much of the Sumerian literature known from Old Babylonian schools. Some lists (particularly Aa, Ea, Urra, Lu, Izi and Diri) survived, however. Many sources remained in monolingual Sumerian format, although significant numbers of bilingual sources are also known, often in use alongside the monolingual versions.

Two great innovations can be attributed to the Middle Babylonian period. The first is the creation of yet another type of list. In the Old Babylonian period, bilingual Sumerian–Akkadian lists had appeared in Babylonia. The peripheral sites of the

Middle Babylonian period yield some trilingual versions, as scribes translated the foreign Sumerian and Akkadian languages into something more familiar to them. From Hattusa come Sumerian–Akkadian–Hittite texts, from Syria Sumerian–Akkadian–Hurrian and sometimes even quadrilingual Sumerian–Akkadian–Hurrian–Ugaritic texts. Exceptionally other languages are known: there is one fragment of Kassite–Akkadian and another of Egyptian–Akkadian text.[8] With the trivial exception of these two fragments, all lists had the Sumerian column on the left, with the Akkadian column to the right. And until now all lists had been organised according to the text of the Sumerian column. While tradition dictated that the Sumerian column remain on the left, lists could now be organised (in part or in whole) according to the text of the right hand, Akkadian column.[9] Sumerian was by now long since dead, but it still retained great prestige and new texts were even composed in that language. The new lists of this period were designed to help with that process, and act as a kind of index to the older lists.

The new lists include Nabnitu, Erimhush and perhaps already Antagal. Nabnitu is ordered according to two major principles. It is thematic, containing terms for body parts and activities relating to them in head-to-foot order. These are then grouped etymologically (according to the Akkadian column[10]), with individual entries then arranged according to phonological shape. It begins:

Sumerian	Akkadian	meaning
SIG$_7$.ALAN	*nabnītu*	'appearance'
ALAN$^{a\text{-}lam}$.ALAN	*bunnannû*	'appearance'
$^{na\text{-}ab}$nab$_4$	DITTO	
$^{sa\text{-}a}$sa$_7$	DITTO	
igi	*būnu*	'features, face'
i-bi$_2$	DITTO EME.SAL	'same, in the Emesal dialect'
igi-KA	DITTO	
i-bi$_2$-KA	DITTO EME.SAL	
muš$_3$-me	DITTO	
sag-ki	DITTO	
muš$_3$-me-sag-ki	DITTO	

Erimhush collects small groups of related words. It begins:

Sumerian	Akkadian	meaning
erim-huš	*anantu*	'battle'
LU$_2$. LU$_2$	*ippiru*	'struggle'
zag-nu-sa$_2$-a	*adammû*	'onslaught'

Antagal is one of the most intriguing of Babylonian lists. Although familiar to us mostly from Neo-Assyrian sources, one Neo-Babylonian source is known and scribal colophons inform us that these are copies of ancient clay and wooden tablets from

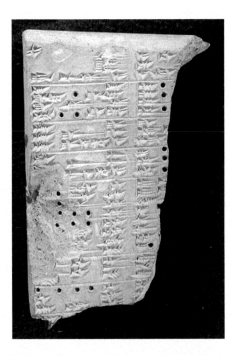

Figure 30.1 K 214: a fragment of the first tablet of Erimhush from Nineveh, seventh century BC. The division of the text into ruled sections can be seen clearly. (Courtesy of The Trustees of the British Museum.)

both Assyria and Babylonia. No overall principle of structure is visible either within or between its many tablets, but several principles are evident for ordering the entries within the groups. For example, one finds synonyms and antonyms listed together, as in this example:

Sumerian	Akkadian	meaning
dul	*mūlû*	'high ground'
tul$_2$-la$_2$	*mušpalu*	'pit'
$^{bu-ur}$bur$_3$	*šuplu*	'low place'
a-su$_3$-ra	*asurrakku*	'deep waters'

One finds also words derived from the same (or similar) Akkadian root, or different words that happen to share a common form, as in this example:

Sumerian	Akkadian	meaning
^{giš}suhur-la$_2$	*kaparru*	'tree top'
^{giš}kak-uš	DITTO *ša ziqti*	'same, as in barb' (= barbed whip)
sipa-tur	DITTO *ša amēli*	'same, as in the man' (= shepherd)

Another new addition to the lexical corpus came about by the regular addition of a further column to Syllable Alphabet A mentioned above, yielding what is known as

Syllable Vocabulary A. The Akkadian words in the new column were an attempt at interpretation of the signs, which previously had been practised here purely for their visual form rather than for any underlying meaning. Some of the interpretations are sober (since some signs can be used to represent whole words) but others seem more speculative and fanciful. We also see lists of deities become a standard part of the curriculum; they were to remain so in the Neo-Babylonian period. Such lists had been known already from the middle of the third millennium but only now did they become standard.

The second great innovation of the Middle Babylonian period is the canonisation of the lists. It is evident that the flexibility of the lists so characteristic for the Old Babylonian period was sacrificed in favour of a common, fixed form. Clearly there were still different versions of the compositions in circulation, since not every source known agrees with every other. But from both Babylonia and Assyria we find a significant number of sources containing text in a form familiar to us from the first millennium version of the compositions.

The Middle Babylonian versions of lists are much longer than the corresponding Old Babylonian versions. This is a result of several factors. Knowledge of Sumerian was steadily declining, and while Old Babylonian lists could be in somewhat abbreviated form, Middle Babylonian lists were far more explicit and also comprehensive. As scribes struggled with interpreting existing Sumerian texts and composing new ones, less could be taken for granted than before. Also, as the lists were used as an aid to translation, and Akkadian translation technique tended towards word-for-word transposition, we see the appearance of entries where a translation has been attached to only part of its original equivalent.

From the Middle Babylonian period we also see the emergence of a practice largely unknown from the Old Babylonian period but much better known from the Neo-Babylonian period. Whereas the transmission of texts had previously been predominantly oral, now the direct copying of tablets from manuscript examples becomes more commonplace. Concern is also shown for the quality of sources. Tablets contain colophons at the end, stating the origin and antiquity of the original being copied, plus various notes bearing on the copying process, including such information as the name of the copier and whether or not the copy has been checked against the original.

THE NEO-BABYLONIAN AND LATE BABYLONIAN LISTS

From the first millennium we possess texts from several sites in Babylonia, but again we are in debt to the Assyrians. Many lists are best known from the famous library of Ashurbanipal at Nineveh. As mentioned above, the Middle Babylonian period saw the lists assume a stable form. This is the form we see in Neo-Babylonian sources. All the major lists from the Middle Babylonian period survived, and so did the concern for the source and quality of the manuscripts from which the lists were copied. By this point, the lists had grown to huge proportions. The sign list Ea had grown to eight 'tablets',[11] containing altogether approximately 2,400 entries. The more comprehensive Aa was 42 tablets long, containing 14,400 entries. Diri held 2,100 entries on seven tablets, Urra over 9,700 entries on 24 tablets and Nabnitu

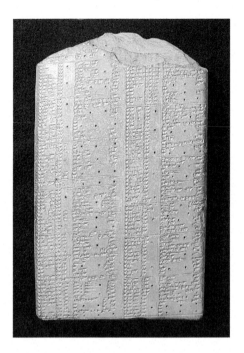

Figure 30.2 BM 108862: an example of the first tablet of Ea, from Assur, *c*.eleventh century BC. (Courtesy of the Trustees of the British Museum.)

Figure 30.3 BM 92693: an example of the second tablet of Aa, from Sippar, fifth century BC. (Courtesy of the Trustees of the British Museum.)

10,500 on 32 tablets. In addition there are also seven tablets of Erimhush, more than ten of Antagal, more than 30 of Izi and yet more besides. The canonical lists preserved a truly vast corpus of learning.

Not all lists were treated in the same way. Some of the older ones seem to have been treated mostly as scholarly reference works, useful for the interpretation of other ancient texts. Other lists formed the corpus of standard scribal training texts. For example, among the lists of signs, Aa was used as a scholarly reference work, and the related but much simpler Syllabary A (known already in the late Old Babylonian period) and Syllabary B were used as elementary practice texts. The Neo-Babylonian scribes were also heir to several traditions. During the Old Babylonian period, compositions existed in slightly different versions in each of the various scribal centres. More than one of these versions might survive, but they might be treated now in very different ways to each other; the one as a reference work, the other as a practice text. Among the school texts, some lists had fixed forms (the 'canonical' forms that had taken shape during the Middle Babylonian period), while others – such as the new professions list ummia = *ummianu* 'scholar' – did not (these are known as 'non-canonical'). The scribes respected the bank of knowledge accumulated by their forebears but they did not behave as automata, reliant upon and slavishly reproducing a fossilised body of texts. They actively preserved their traditions, differentiating and categorising them according to source and quality. The scribes also reflected upon and utilised their inheritance and remained free to innovate.

Yet more new lists were created. Reciprocal Ea is an interesting example. It can be seen as a kind of reverse index to Ea. It gathers together signs with homophonous readings, with groups ordered according to the u-a-i vowel sequence seen above in the Old Babylonian exercise Tu-ta-ti. By way of illustration, here is the section of the list dealing with the /tu/ sound:

reading	sign	translation	meaning
tu-u	KU 𒆪 (= tu_9)	*ṣubātum*	'garment'
DITTO	KAxLI(𒆬 = tu_6)	*šiptum*	'incantation'
DITTO	KAM(𒄭 = tu_7)	*ummarum*	'soup'
DITTO	ŠU.NAGA(𒋗𒉀 = tu_5)	*ramāku*	'to bathe'
DITTO	HUB₂(𒄷 = tu_{11})	*ḫatû*	'to smite'
DITTO	HUB(𒄷 = tu_{10})	DITTO: *kamārum*	'same: to heap up'
DITTO	ŠID(𒋭 = tu_{14})	*maḫāṣu ša ṣubāti*	'to hit, said of cloth' (i.e. to weave)

The list is neither complete nor fully systematic, and some common signs are omitted.

The great innovation of the Neo-Babylonian period is the creation of the commentaries. The Old Babylonian lists were never intended as a self-teaching device. They were a kind of summary. A teacher with expert knowledge was always required to provide an oral commentary. While the Middle Babylonian versions became more explicit, the need for expert assistance cannot have gone away. By the Neo-Babylonian period, help was needed more than ever. For now not only was the Sumerian difficult but also some of the Akkadian had become obscure. Hence, we see the creation of written commentaries and synonym lists.[12] It is clear from commentaries on other genres of text that lexical lists could act as sources of authority in the interpretation of difficult passages in those other types of text.

Commentaries do not treat the entirety of a text, but only selected portions. They typically offer synonyms to explain a word, or sometimes give the infinitive of a verbal form or a better-known writing of the word in question. Less often a general explanation such as 'a disease' will be given. Quotations from classic texts may be given by way of illustration. Some commentaries draw on more esoteric knowledge; these can be particularly difficult for us to understand. Sometimes alternative explanations are offered, marked as 'secondly' or 'thirdly'.

The standard Neo-Babylonian commentary retains a columnar format, simply adding an extra column as required. An example is HARGUD, a commentary to Urra. Its first line runs: mur-gud = *imrû* = *ballu* (each word meaning 'fodder'). Here a Sumerian term (mur-gud) and its Akkadian equivalent (*imrû*) taken from the first tablet of the list Urra are explained by adding, in a third column, another Akkadian term (*ballu*), a synonym better understood by scribes of the time. The Late Babylonian format of commentary is slightly different. There we find running text, with elements separated by special textual marks (known as '*Glossenkeile*').

Related to the commentaries are the synonym lists, such as *Malku* = *šarru*. Here difficult Akkadian (or foreign) words were explained by other Akkadian words. For example, in the first line of the text the word *malku* is explained by *šarru*, meaning 'king'.

Perhaps the last significant development in the Babylonian list tradition was the creation of a type of text known to us as 'Graeco-Babyloniaca'. Here Sumerian and Akkadian words are transcribed into Greek letters (but note that the text is not translated into Greek). Their text is that of the canonical version. This small but interesting group of texts dates from very late in Babylonian history, perhaps even as late as the early centuries AD.

THE USE AND SIGNIFICANCE OF THE LISTS

We are very fortunate indeed to have so many sources for the lists. Apart from their interest for the history of ideas, they have played a central role in modern attempts to penetrate the complexities of reading cuneiform, and have provided an invaluable source for the reconstruction of the lexicons of Sumerian and Akkadian. They have been particularly useful in the case of Sumerian, for which no related language is known. Akkadian is a Semitic language, so we can draw on other Semitic languages to help us understand it. Our knowledge of Akkadian makes bilingual texts very helpful. In fact, we see Sumerian largely through the eyes of the Babylonians.

In the early days of Assyriology, a theory was developed whereby the thematic lists were explained as primitive steps towards science. According to that theory, the ancients tried to list everything around them in an attempt to understand the universe, assigning everything a place within it. Much work has been done on the lists since then and such ideas are no longer tenable. We now know much more about the people who wrote the lists, the circumstances in which they were studied, and particularly about the lists themselves and the individual clay tablets upon which they were written. The thematic lists cannot be separated from the other lists. And there is no strict ordering of items into a particular place within a particular list. It should be remembered that ordering by meaning, shape or sound are the only options open when using a non-alphabetic writing system such as cuneiform. The Babylonian lists cannot meaningfully be compared to Greek scientific writings because they were not intended as science. Rather, the lists form one part of a wider system, one aimed at initiating new scribes into the intricacies of cuneiform writing and enculturating them via the accumulated ancient tradition of learning. The transmission of lists over the centuries and the different uses to which they were put are complex stories. Attempts to interpret the different appearance of the lists over time simply as cognitive development – as has occasionally happened in the past – are mistaken.

There are a number of difficulties involved in the interpretation of the lists. These stem from the fact that they were never intended as self-teaching resources; a skilled teacher was always required. The written text that remains for us to study represents only part of the original text and none of its explanation. This is a particular problem with the Old Babylonian lists, but applies also to the later lists. For the lists do not function in the same way as modern dictionaries. They do not provide definitions, but rather equivalents. These are often only single word equivalents; of course, there is no simple one-to-one correspondence in the use and meaning of words in Sumerian and Akkadian. Interpretation of the lists requires knowledge of the context (semantic, phonological or otherwise) in which the correspondence was valid; such information was not usually committed to writing. What the Akkadian equivalents provide is, therefore, a partial correspondence; in some circumstances, Sumerian word *a* could be used where Akkadian would use word *x*, or vice versa. In other circumstances, other words would have to be used. Occasionally the later texts may add a comment such as 'as in *x*'. But we are not told whether this means 'as for example in *x*' or 'only in *x*'.

The situation is further complicated by the concise formulation of the lists, especially in earlier periods. The relationship between the Sumerian and Akkadian columns is not always a simple one-to-one pairing. For example, text written in the format:

Sumerian term 1	Akkadian term 1
Sumerian term 2	Akkadian term 2

might indicate that there are two different words, each with a different translation, or might conceal something more complicated. For instance, one of the words may be a valid translation of either of the opposing terms and the other not, or both sets may be interchangeable. Added to this is the problem of partial equations mentioned above.

The nature of our sources is also a significant factor. Most are school texts, the by-products of inexperienced scribes learning their trade. Thus the sources can contain mistakes or poorly written signs, and often can be in very poor physical condition, making them difficult to read. They survive only accidentally. They were produced during a learning process which focused on internalisation of knowledge. Once written (and presumably checked), they no longer served a purpose and would be disposed of. Usually they would be returned to the store of clay found in the bins of the courtyards that served as scribal schools, there to be recycled into new practice tablets. Occasionally tablets could be used as building rubble,[13] as is well exemplified by the famous House F in Nippur. There, hundreds of tablets were found in the floors and walls, and yet more were found made into a bench. In the case of sudden disruption, tablets could survive. An example of this is the house of Ur-Utu in Tell ed-Der, which caught fire and was abandoned. In and around the recycling bin were found a small number of school exercises.

To modern eyes, lists of words or signs can seem rather primitive and mundane, and certainly not very interesting. To the Babylonian scribe, lists were held in high esteem. They served as a vehicle for much of the vast cultural–intellectual heritage of the Ancient Near Eastern world. There were many different kinds of list, with a variety of uses. They were highly flexible devices, capable of holding large quantities of information in a very concise form. They could also be highly complex devices. Part of the meaning could be contained in the ordering and grouping of entries and in the interaction between the parallel columns of information. The simple appearance of the Babylonian lists hides a sophistication that we are only gradually beginning to appreciate. They are neither an unthinking aggregation of material nor a hopelessly complicated store into which data were put with little hope of retrieval. While the lists do contain some schoolboy errors and errors of transmission, it is becoming clear that many of the apparent flaws are due to modern ignorance of scribal conventions, gaps in the recovery of cuneiform material and, particularly, the absence for us of the guiding hand that helped the ancient scribal trainees. The breadth and depth of coverage of material present in the lists, their remarkable longevity and the overall fidelity of transmission are eloquent testimony the significant achievement that the Babylonian lists represent.

NOTES

1 Ancient texts are quoted here in a simplified form, for clarity's sake.
2 Alphabetic order was not an option for the Babylonians because of the nature of the cuneiform writing system.
3 The term 'cuneiform' comes from the Latin word *cuneus*, meaning wedge.
4 A different version, known as Syllable Alphabet B was in use in Nippur. The use of the word 'alphabet' is potentially misleading. Cuneiform script is non-alphabetic. It uses characters variously to represent words, syllables or the semantic set to which something belonged, such as 'wood', 'deity' or 'place'. These compositions seem to have acquired the label 'alphabetic' as part of their modern title because they drill the student in the forms of the individual signs, much like children today practise their a, b, c.
5 In antiquity, compositions were known by their first line of text. This practice is usually kept in the modern study of those compositions. The term 'proto' has historically been attached to compositions known also in a 'canonical' first-millennium version. This term erroneously implies that the Old Babylonian versions are imperfect first steps towards the later version. In reality, the Old Babylonian versions are fully evolved for the system within which they functioned. The term is retained as a useful way to distinguish between earlier and later versions.
6 A rough equivalent would be to start with 'o', add a stroke to make 'a', then extend it to make 'd'.
7 Bilingual lists dating to the third millennium are known from the Syrian site of Ebla. There, the scribes copied Mesopotamian lists, adding translations in the local language.
8 Kassite was the native language of the dynasty ruling Babylonia during the Middle Babylonian period. Only rarely was Kassite committed to writing.
9 Tradition kept the Sumerian column as the ordering column in all the older lists.
10 The Akkadian words here are all derived from the same 'root' (three letters carrying a general meaning, around which other elements were added to specify more specific meaning), in this case *b n y*.
11 Long lists are divided into parts called 'tablets', corresponding to how many standard-sized clay tablets were required to contain the full text of the composition.
12 Commentaries also existed for other list-type genres, such as medical texts or the omens; commentaries to the omens are, in fact, much more common than those to the lexical lists. Commentaries were not restricted to list-like genres, however. Literary texts were also subject to commentaries. These other types of text had also begun to assume a fixed, standardised form and their interpretation required assistance.
13 Mesopotamian architecture is mud-brick based.

BIBLIOGRAPHY

Cavigneaux, A. (1983) 'Lexikalische Listen', in *Reallexikon der Assyriologie und vorderasiatischen Archäologie* 6 (Berlin/New York: W. de Gruyter) pp. 609–641.

Civil, M. (1975) 'Lexicography', in *Sumerological Studies in Honor of Thorkild Jacobsen on His Seventieth Birthday, June 7, 1974* (Assyriological Studies 20. Chicago/London: University of Chicago Press) pp. 123–157.

—— (1995) 'Ancient Mesopotamian Lexicography', in J. Sasson (ed.), *Civilizations of the Ancient Near East* IV (New York: Scribner) pp. 2305–2314.

Frahm, E. (2005) 'Royal Hermeneutics: Observations on the commentaries from Ashurbanipal's libraries at Nineveh', in *Iraq* 66, pp. 45–50.

Gesche, P. (2001) *Schulunterricht in Babylonien im erstern Jahrtausend v. Chr.* (Alter Orient und Altes Testament 275. Münster: Ugarit-Verlag).

Krecher, J. (1983) 'Kommentare', in *Reallexikon der Assyriologie und vorderasiatischen Archäologie* 6 (Berlin/New York: W. de Gruyter) pp. 188–191.

Landsberger *et al.* (1937–) *Materials for the Sumerian Lexicon* (Rome: Pontifical Biblical Institute). Vols 14, 16–17, Supplementary Series 1.

Leick, G. (1983) 'Über Tradition und Bedeutung thematischer Listenwerke', in I. Seybold (ed.) *Meqor hajjim. Festschrift für Georg Molin zu seinem 75. Geburtstag* (Graz: Akademische Druck- u. Verlagsanstalt) pp. 221–239.

Robson, E. (2001) 'The Tablet House: a scribal school in Old Babylonian Nippur', in *Revue d'assyriologie et d'archéologie orientale* 95, pp. 39–66.

Tanret, M. (2002) *Per aspera ad astra: l'apprentissage du cunéiforme à Sippar-Amnanum pendant la période paléobabylonienne tardive* (Mesopotamian history and environment. Series 3, Texts 1/2. Ghent: University of Ghent).

Veldhuis, N. (1999) 'Continuity and Change in Mesopotamian Lexical Tradition', in B. Roest and H. Vanstiphout (eds) *Aspects of Genre and Type in Pre-modern Literary Cultures* (COMERS/ICOG communications 1. Groningen: Styx) pp. 101–118.

—— (2000) 'Kassite Exercises: literary and lexical extracts', in *Journal of Cuneiform Studies* 52, pp. 67–94.

Digital Corpus of Cuneiform Lexical Texts (University of California, Berkeley): http://cuneiform.ucla.edu/dcclt//dcclt.html.

CHAPTER THIRTY-ONE

GILGAMESH AND THE LITERARY TRADITIONS OF ANCIENT MESOPOTAMIA

———•◆•———

A. R. George

The Epic of Gilgamesh is usually cited as the masterpiece of Babylonian literature. This poem is only one of several literary texts about the legendary hero, King Gilgamesh of Uruk. In many respects the evolution of these texts over more than two thousand years can serve as a paradigm for the history of ancient Mesopotamian literature. This chapter sketches this history, with special reference to Gilgamesh and other narrative poems, focusing on key moments by introducing individual scholars (real and fictitious) from five points in time.

The literature of Mesopotamia in the pre-Christian era was composed mainly in Sumerian, Akkadian and Aramaic (largely lost). By literature is meant here writings that bear the imprint of creative imagination, i.e. belles-lettres; excluded are the corpora of professional texts, such as the huge compendia of divination, astrology and exorcism that accounted for a large proportion of the Babylonian scribal tradition. Modern scholars have evolved a refined typology of this literature, dividing it into categories such as mythological narratives, epic poetry, hymns, wisdom literature and folk tales. In most cases this typology has no counterpart in the ancient world. There were no Sumerian or Akkadian words for myth or for heroic narrative, and no ancient recognition of narrative poetry as a genre.

For present purposes we can identify as narrative poetry a group of long or longish poems that share many features of form and style with the Gilgamesh texts and are representatives of the same literary traditions. Some of these are mythological narratives that relate the exploits of the gods. Others have as their subject matter the adventures of mortals. In Sumerian these are the tales of Lugalbanda, Enmerkar and Bilgames (Akkadian Gilgamesh). In Akkadian we can include, alongside the great poem about Gilgamesh, two shorter heroic tales named after their protagonists: Adapa and Etana. These poems about legendary heroes were probably all rooted in entertainment but became, over the course of the centuries, pedagogical tools.

Our understanding of the history of ancient Mesopotamian literature relies on random finds and chance survival: what emerges is a succession of periods when we know something of written traditions, punctuated by longer intervals of which we know very little. When literary texts are first encountered in the mid-third millennium, two literary traditions are witnessed by roughly contemporaneous Sumerian and Akkadian compositions. Old Sumerian texts of the period far outnumber those in Akkadian. Neither body of material is yet fully intelligible. Old Sumerian literature comes chiefly from Tell Abu Salabikh (ancient name uncertain), Shuruppak and Adab in Sumer. Slightly later copies of some of these compositions have been found in Syria, at Mari on the middle Euphrates and at Ebla south of Aleppo. An archaic Akkadian hymn to the sun god first encountered at Abu Salabikh was also known at Ebla. The surviving texts bear witness to an early spread of ancient Mesopotamian literature, in both its traditions, well beyond the southern alluvial plain where cuneiform writing was developed late in the fourth millennium. While no text relating stories of Gilgamesh has been identified in this early material, we do have an Old Sumerian composition that clearly features King Lugalbanda of Uruk and the goddess Ninsun. These two occur in the later epic traditions as Gilgamesh's parents. Already at this early time, the legendary dynasty of Uruk which, according to the Sumerian King List, included three great Mesopotamian heroes, Enmerkar, Lugalbanda and Gilgamesh, was the inspiration for mytho-poetic narrative.

Little literature, either Sumerian or Akkadian, survives from the latter part of the third millennium, though there have been isolated discoveries of important texts. The very last century of this millennium, however, certainly witnessed a great activity in the redaction and recording of Sumerian literature, especially under the direction of King Shulgi of Ur, who set up academies of Sumerian learning at Nippur and Ur, respectively the religious and political centres of his empire. A few scraps of this Neo-Sumerian literature are extant, including some pieces of narrative poems about Lugalbanda and Gilgamesh.

Some of the courtly Sumerian literature that was written under Shulgi and his successors was adopted into the curriculum of Old Babylonian scribal schools. Large numbers of eighteenth-century tablets, discovered in scholars' houses at Nippur and Ur, provide us with a set of more-or-less standardized texts, which we may treat as a canon of classical Sumerian literature. This corpus is currently under reconstruction from tablets and fragments scattered around the world. Because the corpus was quite limited, and many texts are extant in dozens of exemplars, there is a real prospect of a complete reconstruction of this literature; however, much Sumerian literature no doubt was excluded from the school curricula, and is gone forever. A small proportion of the extant corpus is representative of the Sumerian tradition of narrative poems about legendary kings: a pair of compositions about Lugalbanda, two about Enmerkar, and five about Gilgamesh.

By the eighteenth century, Sumerian had died out as a living language in Babylonia. The vernacular tongue in cities was an Old Babylonian dialect of Akkadian. The language of literary expression remained Sumerian in the scribal schools, but few new Sumerian texts were added to the traditional corpus. At court Akkadian had overtaken Sumerian as the preferred medium, not only in administration but also in the formal literature of courtly piety, such as royal hymns and lyrics of divine marriage. It seems very likely that court entertainment had also made the transition from Sumerian to Old Babylonian.

During the Old Babylonian period we find written traces of a vibrant Old Babylonian literature, including the oldest fragments of the Babylonian Gilgamesh epic and pieces of other well-known narrative poems in the Akkadian language (Anzû, Etana, Atrahasis, the Naram-Sîn legend). Some of these fragments come from the scribal schools, where they form a tiny minority of Babylonian texts among the huge mass of Sumerian compositions. But this is an opportunity to indulge in a little fantasy, and introduce the first of our five scholars.

Sîn-iddinam (*c.*1760 BC); Nippur, Central Babylonia

Let us imagine: Sîn-iddinam, son of Ili-iddinam, sits on the ground on the shady side of the courtyard of his father's house, shaping in his hands a writing tablet out of moist clay got from the bin nearby. He is sixteen years old and has been learning to write for five years. His mother tongue is the local Babylonian dialect of Akkadian but he long since learned Sumerian.

Today he is tired from the night before. His father, a priest of Ekur, the great temple of the god Enlil, had let him attend a banquet in honour of Hammurapi, king of Babylon, who was visiting Nippur to pay homage to Enlil and his cult. Now his assignment is to inscribe a clay tablet with the first sixty lines of the Sumerian poem entitled 'The Lord to the Living One's Land', one of the old compositions about the legendary king and hero, Gilgamesh. Instead the boy's mind keeps returning to the evening before, to the sights and sounds of the great royal banquet, and especially to the words of the epic poem that the old king's minstrel had sung. It was in the living language, Akkadian, and it stuck in his mind. One day, he thinks, he would try to set it all down in writing. But for now, he writes out on his clay tablet what he could remember of its beginning.

> Surpassing all other kings, heroic in stature,
>   brave scion of Uruk, wild bull on the rampage!
> Going at the fore he was the vanguard,
>   going at the rear, one his comrades could trust!
>
> A mighty bank, protecting his warriors,
>   a violent flood-wave, smashing a stone wall!
> Wild bull of Lugalbanda, Gilgamesh, the perfect in strength,
>   suckling of the august Wild Cow, the goddess Ninsun!
>
> Gilgamesh the tall, magnificent and terrible,
>   who opened passes in the mountains,
> who dug wells on the slopes of the uplands,
>   and crossed the ocean, the wide sea to the sunrise.
>
> (Gilgamesh I 29–40, translated
>   by George 1999: 2)

This is the prologue of the Old Babylonian epic. It does not survive on any Old Babylonian tablet yet known, but comes down to us embedded in the later version. However, other parts of the Old Babylonian poem are extant on tablets written by scribal apprentices in the eighteenth century, so that, while Sîn-iddinam is the product of my imagination, the scenario presented above is not pure fantasy. An oral origin for the poem of Gilgamesh is to be expected, though it cannot be proved. The existence alongside the school tablets of larger, library tablets inscribed with parts of the Old

Babylonian epic demonstrates that several attempts were made at this time to commit longer sections of the poem to writing. They give a glimpse of the poem that may well have been very close to the oral tradition from which it sprang. This oral tradition must have continued to evolve but naturally we know only of the development of the written tradition.

Towards the end of the eighteenth century, in the reign of King Samsuiluna of Babylon, the urban centres of southern Babylonia experienced a catastrophe that shows both in the archaeological record and in the documentary evidence. Large tracts of cities such as Nippur were abandoned as the populace fled; a sharp decline in economic activity is witnessed by the sudden termination of archives. Though Nippur, at least, enjoyed a short recovery, the city was quickly lost to invaders from the southern marshes (the Sealand) and did not recover until the fourteenth century. This disruption brought with it the closure of the scribal schools at Nippur, Isin, Uruk and Ur, and heralded the end of the southern scribal curriculum that had kept the traditions of Sumerian literature alive for three centuries.

We do not yet know exactly when the curriculum underwent the transition that saw most of the old Sumerian compositions discarded and the adoption in their place of literature in Akkadian, for evidence for scribal education in the succeeding four centuries is scarce. It is likely, though, that the collapse of economic and intellectual life in the south played a large part in what happened. A shift of wealth and power to the north can already be observed in the early eighteenth century, under King Hammurapi. The events that ushered in a long interval in the Babylonian domination of the south reinforced that shift. Small discoveries of school texts from northern towns show that, already in the early eighteenth century, the curriculum there included rather more Akkadian than was the case further south. Therein lay the roots of the later scribal tradition.

Two bodies of material give us a glimpse of ancient Mesopotamian literature in the last third of the second millennium BC. First there are tablets written in Mesopotamia proper. A small number of Middle Babylonian scribal exercises and library tablets from such old Mesopotamian centres as Babylon, Nippur and Ur date roughly to the twelfth century. A larger corpus of Babylonian literary texts in Middle Assyrian script derives from the city of Ashur, on the middle Tigris, and dates roughly to the period between kings Tukulti-Ninurta I (1243–1207) and Tiglath-pileser I (1114–1076). Already the Babylonian scribal tradition has become thoroughly Akkadianized: many of the great works of Babylonian narrative poetry are present, including Gilgamesh, Atrahasis, Ishtar's Descent to the Netherworld, and Etana. Only a few Sumerian compositions survive, and almost all are equipped with Akkadian translations in bilingual format.

The second body of material is the tablets from Syria, Palestine, Anatolia and Egypt. These tablets mostly stem from scribal education. Here again we see an Akkadianized corpus of traditional Mesopotamian literature, including Gilgamesh, Adapa, Nergal and Ereshkigal, Atrahasis, and legends of Sargon. Some of these traditional Middle Babylonian texts were subject to local adaptations, being retold in paraphrase and even translated into vernacular languages such as Hurrian and Hittite.

As manuscripts proliferated, variant recensions grew up. At the same time new compositions were introduced, many of them of an explicitly scholarly nature or the work of learned scholar poets. Newly prominent were the Poem of the Righteous Sufferer (*Ludlul bel nemeqi*) and other 'wisdom' poems that dealt with questions of morality and the perceived unjustness of human life. It was probably towards the end of this era that the Babylonian Gilgamesh poem was reshaped into the form in which it remained for the rest of its history: a second opportunity to fantasize.

Sîn-leqi-unninni (*c.*1200 BC); Uruk, Southern Babylonia

Just suppose: Sîn-leqi-unninni is a scholar of thirty-five or forty years, still young enough to be able to read cuneiform script on clay but highly learned and respected. By profession he is an expert in medicine and prophylactic-apotropaic rituals (Akkadian *ashipu* 'exorcist'), supported by the great temple of Uruk since graduating from scribal school about fifteen years earlier. There he mastered the Sumerian language, studied the antique classics of Babylonian literature and committed to memory the written lore of his profession. He has maintained his interest in the intellectual legacy of his forbears and is now a scholar of high reputation for learning. He has the task of establishing the definitive text of a fine old traditional poem that exists in many variant versions. It is the poem 'Surpassing All Other Kings', an epic narrative that sings the glory of Gilgamesh. Sîn-leqi-unninni finds the poem very old-fashioned in language and style. And although his colleagues have managed to assemble before him dozens of different clay tablets from far afield to help him establish a reliable text, it is clear that parts of the poem are missing entirely. He knows it by heart anyway, but has long thought that it needs equipping with a greater sophistication of narrative and language, filling out with fashionable diversions and embellishing with a more modern, less naively heroic mood. He sets aside the dusty old tablets that have been collected for him and begins to write:

> He who saw the Deep, the country's foundation,
>   who knew the proper ways, was wise in all matters!
> Gilgamesh, who saw the Deep, the country's foundation,
>   who knew the proper ways, was wise in all matters!
>
> He explored everywhere the seats of power,
>   and learnt of everything the sum of wisdom.
> He saw what was secret, discovered what was hidden,
>   he brought back a tale of before the Deluge.
>
> He came a far road, was weary, found peace,
>   and set all his labours on a tablet of stone . . .
>
> See the tablet-box of cedar,
>   release its clasps of bronze!
> Lift the lid of its secret,
>   pick up the tablet of lapis lazuli and read out
> the travails of Gilgamesh, all that he went through.
>
>   (Gilgamesh I 1–28, lightly restored,
>   after George 1999: 1–2)

According to Babylonian tradition the exorcist Sîn-leqi-unninni of Uruk was the author of the poem 'He who saw the Deep', the ancient title of the late or Standard Babylonian version of the Gilgamesh epic. An extended family of Late Babylonian cult-singers from Uruk considered him their ancestor, and he was falsely reckoned by native scholarship to have lived in the reign of Gilgamesh himself. Nothing more is known of him. It is improbable that he was the first to set the poem down on clay. More likely he was responsible for establishing, as envisaged above, the standard written text that circulated in first-millennium Assyria and Babylonia. In this case he lived some time towards the end of the second millennium BC, a time when exactly this kind of activity was being carried out by learned Babylonian scholars.

Comparison of the very fragmentary Old Babylonian and Middle Babylonian versions of Gilgamesh with the much better-preserved Standard Babylonian poem suggests that the modernizing of the epic wrought profound changes on it. The poem that celebrated the glorious heroism of the most famous king and mightiest hero of Babylonian legend gained the new prologue quoted above, a prologue that established a mood and emphasis very different from the Old Babylonian poem. Large and small alterations occurred throughout the text. The result is a poem of greater sophistication in terms of plot development and literary effect, though one less vibrant in its language. Most of all, the epic is recast as a sombre meditation on death, its hero a man who endured terrible hardship for no ultimate gain. Other literary compositions, chiefly the philosophical and didactic texts known as 'wisdom' literature, reveal that a greater profundity of thought, coupled with a bleakness of expectation by the individual in the face of the great unseen powers that govern the universe, are motifs characteristic of the late second millennium.

The next large body of extant material is the royal library of the late Assyrian kings, comprising tablets written in possibly the ninth century, certainly the eighth century and especially the seventh century. This library, discovered in the 1850s, remains the paramount source of later ancient Mesopotamian literature; contemporaneous tablets from private Assyrian libraries add to our knowledge of the corpus, as do a growing number of later tablets from Babylonia. The masterpieces of Babylonian poetry are all present in seventh-century Assyria and later Babylonia, including parts of all the well-known narrative poems: Gilgamesh, Adapa, Etana, the legend of Naram-Sîn, Anzû, Atrahasis, the Creation Epic (*Enuma elish*), Erra, Ishtar's Descent to the Netherworld, and Nergal and Ereshkigal. Most of these compositions clearly survive in standard versions deriving ultimately from Old or Middle Babylonian recensions, and are the result of what seem to have been deliberate attempts to establish received texts. However, a few traces survive of variant versions that remained extant in imperial Assyria alongside the more commonly attested standard versions.

Among ancient Mesopotamian libraries, the Assyrian royal library of Nineveh constitutes a very valuable exception. Its holdings were the result of a deliberate attempt by King Ashurbanipal (668–627) to bring together in one place the sum of traditional learning, which he considered a resource essential for good governance. For this reason the library, buried in the palaces of the citadel when the Medes and Babylonians sacked Nineveh in 612 BC, had a comprehensive collection of texts of the Babylonian scribal tradition, some in multiple copies. Other first-millennium libraries, Babylonian as well as Assyrian, are random accumulations of samples of the traditional texts. Typically they are found in private houses belonging to families of the literate professional classes, and such collections appear mostly to be the result of scribal teaching and learning spread over two or more generations. Other collections come from temple contexts, but again a close connection with pedagogy is suspected.

Traditional learning in this period still depended on a mastery of cuneiform writing and a thorough knowledge of the Sumerian and Akkadian languages. In a world where Aramaic was the vernacular and increasingly the language of officialdom, and where the predominant technology of writing was more and more the West Semitic alphabet penned on ostraca, parchment and papyrus, the old, traditional learning began to become obsolete. Traces of a court literature in Aramaic suggest that the language of living literature was no longer Babylonian. A third vignette offers a glimpse of the place of Babylonian literature in this time of cultural transition.

Ashur-ra'im-napishti (*c.*725 BC); Ashur, Assyria

The Assyrian empire is at its peak as a political and military superpower. Ashur-ra'im-napishti is fourteen years old. His family, rich and privileged, has produced generations of singers at the royal court. As natives of Ashur, they speak the Assyrian dialect of Akkadian at home, but use Aramaic when ordering the servants about and haggling for luxury goods in the market place. As long as his voice stays good when it breaks, Ashur-ra'im-napishti will also be a royal singer, performing courtly songs in Assyrian and Aramaic. But like his father and grandfather before him, he is undergoing the traditional education of the literate professional classes. In order to write cuneiform, Ashur-ra'im-napishti has learned primeval Sumerian and an antiquated literary dialect of Babylonian, and is now what is called a junior apprentice. Let us watch him starting an important assignment. He has to make a perfect copy of Tablet VI of 'He who Saw the Deep'. It is the bit when the goddess Ishtar tries to seduce the hero, Gilgamesh is rude back to her, and he and Enkidu save the city of Uruk from the Bull of Heaven. It is a classic of the old literature, no longer a living text, but his father says it is a key component of a proper education.

Suppressing a yawn, Ashur-ra'im-napishti takes up his new stylus, the one exquisitely decorated with lapis lazuli and carnelian, and sits himself down on his mother's best woollen carpet amid a scatter of silky cushions. Reaching out a plump hand, he pulls nearer an ivory-inlaid tablet stand on which some unseen servant has placed a beautifully prepared clay tablet already ruled off neatly in three columns on each side. In a clear and practised hand of precocious elegance Ashur-ra'im-napishti begins to write:

> He washed his matted hair, he cleaned his equipment,
>> he shook his hair down over his back.
> Casting aside his dirty gear he clad himself in clean,
>> wrapped cloaks round him, tied on a sash.
> Then did Gilgamesh put on his crown.
>
> On the beauty of Gilgamesh Lady Ishtar looked with longing:
>> 'Come, Gilgamesh, be you my bridegroom!
> Grant me your fruits, O grant me!
>> Be you my husband and I your wife!
>>> (Gilgamesh VI 1–9, translated by George 1999: 48)

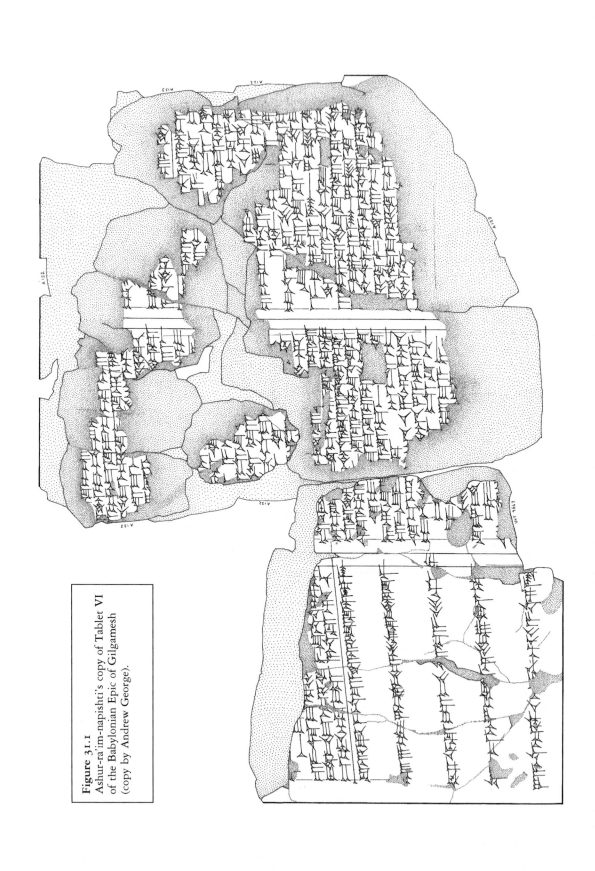

Figure 31.1
Ashur-ra'im-napishti's copy of Tablet VI of the Babylonian Epic of Gilgamesh (copy by Andrew George).

A young apprentice scribe called Ashur-ra'im-napishti really did write a beautiful copy of Gilgamesh VI on a three-column tablet, for it was excavated at Ashur in the ruins of his family's house, complete with a colophon reporting his name and title (Figure 31.1). The family was certainly well off, but the picture of privileged adolescent ennui is fantasy.

The final and most glorious century of the Assyrian empire was a time when both Assyrian and Babylonian were rapidly losing ground as vernacular languages to Aramaic. Increasingly their use was confined to those areas of human activity that had long demanded literacy in cuneiform: the guidance of the king, the administration of the law and the old institutions, and the scribal education that was the vehicle for training the professional elite that serviced them. Against this background it is unlikely that a written work of the old tradition such as the Standard Babylonian Gilgamesh epic had any life as literature outside pedagogy, where it was studied for its Old Babylonian quality as a good story and for its veneer of Middle Babylonian profundity.

The very last literary texts written in cuneiform come from Babylon in the last two centuries BC, when a residue of professional families connected with the temple of the god Marduk (Bel) – astrologers and cult-singers – still passed on the old scribal tradition in teaching cuneiform writing to their offspring. Eventually, however, this activity came to an end, and with it passed from human memory whatever of the written intellectual legacy of ancient Mesopotamia was no longer of use in the Helleno-Parthian east. Near the end of the long centuries of cuneiform writing, a fourth scholar grappled with Gilgamesh.

Bel-ahhe-usur (15 Kislimu, *c.*130 BC); Babylon

It is a bright day late in autumn. Bel-ahhe-usur squats in a corner of the courtyard of his family's large but dilapidated house in the centre of Babylon. The city is slowly becoming a vast ruin. Power moved elsewhere years ago, when the royal court decamped to Seleucia, and most of the population went with it. All that remains of the city is Esangil, the ancient temple of the god Marduk built by Kings Esarhaddon and Ashurbanipal 550 years before, the families that work for it and a few Greek colonists.

Bel-ahhe-usur's family are astrologers and members of the assembly of Esangil. He himself is seventeen and has been learning the old cuneiform traditions for years from his father, Itti-Marduk-balatu, an astrologer who holds a senior bureaucratic office in Babylon. At home Bel-ahhe-usur speaks Aramaic, but as an apprentice astrologer he has had to learn Sumerian and Babylonian Akkadian. Working under his father has also exposed him to a little Greek. Today is the day of an important examination. He is making a perfect copy of an old tablet inscribed with Tablet X of the Epic of Gilgamesh. He knows the poem well. It is a distillation of ancient wisdom but not of any practical use. The same can be said for most of the classic works of the old literature. Bel-ahhe-usur will pass on the cuneiform tradition to his sons, if he has any, but he is not confident that they in turn will do the same for their sons. He can see that one day soon the tradition of writing in cuneiform on clay will die out.

We can imagine the boy shivering in the cooling afternoon. He pulls an old woollen blanket over his shoulders. With a sigh he picks up his well-worn stylus, a family heirloom bequeathed to him by his grandfather, Iddin-Bel, and proceeds to finish his tablet. It is the passage where the wise Uta-napishti, immortal survivor of the flood, instructs the hero Gilgamesh on the fragility of human existence and on the inevitability and unpredictability of death:

> Man is snapped off like a reed in a canebrake!
> The comely young man, the pretty young woman –
> *all* [*too soon in*] their [*prime*] Death abducts them!

> No one at all sees Death,
> no one at all sees the face of Death,
> no one at all hears the voice of Death,
> Death so savage, who hacks men down ...

> The Anunnaki, the great gods, held an assembly,
> Mammitum, maker of destiny, fixed fates with them:
> both Death and Life they have established,
> but the day of Death they do not disclose.
> (Gilgamesh X 297–322, translated
> by George 1999: 86–7)

A lad called Bel-ahhe-usur did indeed write out a copy of Gilgamesh X in Babylon on the fifteenth day of the month Kislimu in a year reckoned in the Parthian era, for such is reported in a colophon appended to one of the latest surviving copies of Gilgamesh. Assuming his identity with the astrologer of the same name and ancestry known from other dated tablets from Babylon, he would have been a scribal apprentice in the 130s BC.

This was a time of great political upheaval, in which Babylonia stood on the battlefield between the Seleucid kingdom of Syria and the Parthian Arsacid kingdom of Iran. Bel-ahhe-usur may have been old enough to remember the conquest of Babylonia by the Parthians under Mithridates I in 141 BC. He would certainly have witnessed the brief restoration of Seleucid power in 130–129 and also the rapid return of Arsacid hegemony under the vice-regent Himeros. By 127, when Babylon was briefly ruled by Hyspaosines of Characene, Bel-ahhe-usur and his brother Nabû-mushetiq-uddi were already taking over some of their father's duties as astrologers in the temple Esangil. We last hear of Bel-ahhe-usur twelve years later, when he would have been in his middle thirties and Babylon was firmly under the control of the great Mithridates II.

Bel-ahhe-usur's lifetime bridged the transition of Babylonia from a province ruled by the Macedonian heirs of Alexander the Great to a dominion of an Iranian empire. Hellenism survived the departure of the Seleucids, but so did the much older native traditions of Babylonia. Writing in cuneiform survived at Babylon well into the first century AD. The old cults continued for maybe hundreds of years more. And Babylonian practical expertise found its way into Greek, Aramaic and other intellectual traditions. At the turn of the eras, however, the written Epic of Gilgamesh was not a text with any obvious or identifiable use beyond the part it played in training the dwindling number of scribes who wrote in cuneiform. Its death knell was sounding.

But the cuneiform tradition was not the only tradition of literature in Mesopotamia in the first millennium BC. Important elements in Mesopotamia's legacy to its neighbours and successors must have been the vital indigenous literature in Aramaic, which survives only in a few traces, and the equally vital oral literature of market-place entertainers, by the mid-first millennium BC also in Aramaic. It is from these lost literatures and from later adaptations of them in Judaized and Christianized forms, that one must suppose to have arisen many elements of later literatures which invite a Mesopotamian derivation. One story ostensibly of Babylonian origin is that handed down by the last of our five scholars.

Claudius Aelianus (*c.*AD 200); Italy

The Roman rhetorician Aelian was writing his treatise on the 'Nature of Animals' (*De natura animalium*) and wanted to illustrate a point about the occasional kindness of animals to human beings. He recalled an old story about a king of Babylon. It was the tale of the king's birth that interested him. Summarizing it in his best Greek (which some unkind people considered bad Greek), he wrote out the episode as follows:

> A love of man is another characteristic of animals . . . When Seuechoros was king of Babylon the Chaldeans foretold that the son born of his daughter would wrest the kingdom from his grandfather. This made him afraid and . . . he put the strictest of watches upon her. For all that, since fate was cleverer than the king of Babylon, the girl became a mother, being pregnant by some obscure man. So the guards from fear of the king hurled the infant from the citadel, for that was where the aforesaid girl was imprisoned. Now an eagle which saw with its piercing eye the child while still falling, before it was dashed to the earth, flew beneath it, flung its back under it, and conveyed it to some garden and set it down with the utmost care. But when the keeper of the place saw the pretty baby he fell in love with it and nursed it; and it was called Gilgamos and became king of Babylon.
>
> (*De natura animalium* xii 21, transl.
> Scholfield 1958–9: III 39–41)

Aelian's story of Gilgamos has some connections with Babylonian traditions about Gilgamesh, essentially that he was a grandson of Enmerkar (of which Seuechoros is a corruption), of uncertain paternity, and a king of lower Mesopotamia; but beyond the tenure of kingship the account holds nothing in common with the written epic that we know. Where, then, did it come from? As Aelian knew, the story of the princess imprisoned because of a prediction of the king's overthrow by his grandson, but impregnated nevertheless, also occurs in the well-known myth of the birth of Perseus. Mid-air rescue by an eagle and the king raised by a gardener are motifs that occur in Mesopotamian literature, in the poem of Etana and the legend of Sargon of Akkade. The saving by wild animals of national heroes as babies is a more international topos, for it informs famous legends about the founders of Persia and Rome. Probably it was a favourite motif of storytellers in the second half of the first millennium BC.

Aelian's story of Gilgamos is thus a composite of narrative elements drawn eclectically from the mythology of the east Mediterranean and Near East. It is unlikely that it was his own invention, for Gilgamesh was a figure alien to the Greek and Roman world. More probably he had encountered a tale of Gilgamesh translated into Greek from Aramaic or Phoenician. Such a story would have stemmed from an oral tradition of the poem of Gilgamesh that in its accretion of detail bore the imprint of non-Mesopotamian traditions but was ultimately descended from the oral poem of the Old Babylonian period. With the passing of two thousand years, it need not surprise us if the Babylonian poem is unrecognizable in Aelian's account of Gilgamos. What else could we expect after a succession of some sixty generations of tellers of tales?

It is obvious that written traditions are likely to be more stable than oral ones. The Mesopotamian evidence, as interpreted here, corroborates this. Many efforts have been made in recent years to bridge the gap between ancient Mesopotamian literature and other contemporaneous and later literatures. In doing this, too much emphasis has been placed upon the cuneiform tradition. This is unsurprising, for most literature written on media other than clay has perished and the ancient oral traditions are of course lost and unknowable. But, by the late first millennium BC, the cuneiform tradition was the jealously guarded property of a tiny scribal elite. The contemporaneous oral traditions of literature no doubt had a wider currency, as well as a greater influence on the cultural traditions of the new civilizations that occupied the Near East in the Hellenistic and Christian eras.

FURTHER READING

Essays that describe ancient Mesopotamian literature appear in Jack Sasson's encyclopedic *Civilizations of the Ancient Near East* (Sasson 1995): for literature in Sumerian see Michalowski 1995; for that in Akkadian see Bottéro 1995. Narrative poems about legendary heroes ('epics') are treated by Alster 1995 and Renger 1978; the history of the Gilgamesh traditions is given by George 2003, alongside a critical edition and facsimiles of the cuneiform texts. For the standardized Babylonian literary traditions of the first millennium see especially Reiner 1991.

Useful anthologies of Sumerian literature are Jacobsen 1987 and Black *et al.* 2004; the fullest source is the Electronic Text Corpus of Sumerian Literature (www.etcsl. orient.ox.ac.uk). Outside this on-line resource, the most complete translations of the Sumerian Gilgamesh poems are those of George 1999: 141–208 and of Douglas Frayne in Foster 2001: 99–155. For printed translations of the poems about Lugalbanda and Enmarkar see Vanstiphout 2003.

The best collection of English translations of literature in Akkadian is Benjamin Foster's monumental anthology (Foster 2005). For paperback translations of the Babylonian Gilgamesh see George 1999 and Foster 2001. Translations of all the other narrative poems are given in Foster 2005; less complete is Dalley 1989.

REFERENCES

Alster, Bendt 1995. Epic tales from ancient Sumer. Pp. 2315–26 in Sasson 1995.
Black, Jeremy, Graham Cunningham, Eleanor Robson and Gábor Zólyomi 2004. *The Literature of Ancient Sumer*. Oxford: Oxford University Press.
Bottéro, Jean 1995. Akkadian literature: An overview. Pp. 2293–303 in Sasson 1995.

Dalley, Stephanie 1989. *Myths from Mesopotamia*. Oxford: Oxford University Press.

Foster, Benjamin R. (ed.) 2001. *The Epic of Gilgamesh*. New York: Norton.

—— 2005. *Before the Muses. An Anthology of Akkadian Literature*. 3rd edn. Bethesda, Md.

George, Andrew 1999. *The Epic of Gilgamesh*. Harmondsworth: Penguin Books.

—— 2003. *The Babylonian Gilgamesh Epic: Introduction, Critical Edition and Cuneiform Texts*. 2 vols. Oxford: Oxford University Press.

Jacobsen, Thorkild 1987. *The Harps that Once . . . Sumerian Poetry in Translation*. New Haven: Yale University Press.

Michalowski, Piotr 1995. Sumerian literature: An overview. Pp. 2279–91 in Sasson 1995.

Reiner, Erica 1991. First-millennium Babylonian literature. Pp. 293–321 in J. Boardman, I. E. S. Edwards, N. G. L. Hammond and E. Sollberger (eds), *The Cambridge Ancient History*. 2nd edn, Vol. III Part 2. Cambridge: Cambridge University Press.

Renger, Johannes M. 1978. Mesopotamian epic literature. Pp. 27–48 in Felix J. Oinas (ed.), *Heroic Epic and Saga. An Introduction to the Word's Great Folk Epics*. Bloomington and London: Indiana University Press.

Sasson, Jack M. (ed.) 1995. *Civilizations of the Ancient Near East*. 4 vols. New York: Scribner.

Scholfield, A. F. 1958–9. Translation of Aelian's *On the Characteristics of Animals*. 3 vols. Loeb Classical Library. London: Heinemann.

Vanstiphout, Herman 2003. Epics of Sumerian Kings: The Matter of Aratta. Atlanta: Society of Biblical Literature.

CHAPTER THIRTY-TWO

MESOPOTAMIAN ASTRAL SCIENCE

———.◆.———

David Brown

CELESTIAL DIVINATION

The Sun, Moon, and Venus are identified as gods in our very earliest written sources (Brown 2000: 246, §1). Various stars, or star groups, and the next two brightest planets,[1] Jupiter and Mars, are alluded to as gods in Sumerian literary sources, which broadly speaking reflect the intellectual achievements of the end of the third millennium BC at the latest, even if attested in younger copies.[2] The stars were used in a practical way by farmers,[3] and are referred to in the earliest incantations.[4] Mercury and Saturn were likely to have been discovered after the bulk of the constellations had been named (Brown 2000: 75–6). There are no celestial omens attested from the third millennium, although it is clear that a form of divination from the heavens was widely accepted in scribal circles.[5] Further study of this material is desirable. It is from the Old Babylonian period (*c.*1700 BC) that our earliest celestial omens appear, for example: 'An eclipse in its middle part; it became dark all over and cleared all over: The king will die, destruction of Elam (a foreign land to the East).'[6]

Examples, describing eclipses on days of the month upon which eclipses cannot happen, indicate that from the earliest times astral omens were not collections of observations, correlated with simultaneous happenings on earth, but were the literate creations of certain scholars who embellished them with historical allusions, internal cross-referencing, word-play, and a raft of cultural prejudices. (An analysis is offered in Brown 2000: Ch. 3.) The simple associations between a planet, Mars say, and the portending of ill, show that the linkage between celestial event and earthly prognostication bore little or no relationship to observation. The planets, the constellations, and certain phenomena had long since been categorised and assigned benefic or malefic values. Eclipses, for example, tended to predict ill for the monarch. Indeed, virtually all celestial phenomena were believed to provide information on the future of the monarchy or the land. Other forms of divination catered to the needs of the private individual. In common with all forms of divination, the prognostications were not real predictions as to what would happen, but rather of what might happen if the appropriate counter measures were not enacted, and a system of apotropaic rituals ran parallel to the omen-interpreting industry.

Why celestial omens appear first in Old Babylonian sources may be a consequence only of selective survival of our sources. Brown (2000: 151) showed, however, that the vast majority of cuneiform celestial omina can all be reduced to a simple prognostication of good or bad, accompanied by a statement as to which of four countries the prediction applied to. Clearly, such a simple code would have been well suited to an oral environment. Perhaps celestial divination was simply not written down in the third millennium, but was deemed to be of sufficient importance that it came to be included in the rich scribal repertoire of the Old Babylonian period, resulting in its elaborate embellishment. Certainly, later generations of scribes assigned third-millennium roots to celestial divination.[7]

Although, as yet, evidence for the creation of a major series of celestial omens in the Old Babylonian period is wanting, a proto-form of the compilation known by its incipit (in Akkadian) as *Enūma Anu Ellil* 'When the gods Anu and Ellil' appears to have existed then.[8] This omen series was seemingly redacted into a fairly stable form during the Middle Babylonian period (*c.*1200 BC), in common with many other compositions, but is best known to us through many copies dating to the late Neo-Assyrian period (*c.*700 BC) and thereafter, when it was regarded as a composition of divine authorship. Although wider in extent, there is little to distinguish the later *c.*70-tablet *Enūma Anu Ellil* from its Old Babylonian forerunner in terms of the underlying principles used to determine prognostications from the heavens.[9]

One tablet included among the 5,000 or so omens that make up the classical version of *Enūma Anu Ellil* deserves special mention. Tablet 14[10] offers arithmetic schemes (in one case with a geometric appendage) pertaining to the duration of lunar visibility and the length of the night. They are of Old Babylonian origin or earlier (Brown 2000: 114; Brown and Zólyomi 2001). Although at first glance 'astronomical', the schemes are in fact numerical elaborations based on a set of very simple assumptions, namely that the year lasts 360 days, that the longest night is twice the length of the shortest, that months are 30 days long, and that mid-month occurs on the fifteenth, during which time the Moon is visible from sunset to sunrise, and finally that change is linear. These numerical elaborations mirror the word-based elaborations that formed the celestial omens. The assumptions made, however, do not permit one to predict, even remotely accurately,[11] the length of lunar visibility on any given day. What, then, was the purpose of such schemes? Brown (2000: §3.1.2) argued that the numerical elaborations described the ideal behaviour of the universe and its constituents. The assumptions behind tablet 14 correspond exactly to the parameters of the year and month as laid down by Marduk when he formed the universe according to the *Epic of Creation* V i f. (Brown 2000: 235), for example. When the universe was seen to run according to the pattern of its ideal, original construction, that boded well, when not, it boded ill. For example, 30-day months boded well, whereas months of any other length boded ill. Many other examples are adduced (Brown 2000: 146–51). Far from being an early attempt to calculate the phenomena of the heavens beforehand, tablet 14 offered a way of permitting the diviner to make interpretations on any day of the year, by comparing the length of observed lunar visibility with the ideal value.

Tablet 14 of *Enūma Anu Ellil* is 'astrological' in purpose, and its placement within a series of omens is entirely appropriate. The two-tablet series known by its incipit as Mul.Apin 'the Plough Star' (this is not Ursa Maior, incidentally) outlines many similar schemes, but also includes star lists and omens.[12] It is known from texts dating no earlier than the Neo-Assyrian period, but contains much material that is undoubtedly older. It has long been thought of as an early astronomical text, but again contains nothing that would have permitted the scribes to know in advance when an astronomical phenomenon would occur to even a moderate degree of accuracy. Its schemes are still no more then elaborations based on fundamental ideal periods, such as 30 days for the Moon, and 360 days for the Sun, idealisations that were common currency from the beginning of the third millennium at least (Brown 2000a: 106).

The symbol of an eight-pointed star is known from pre-historic times, and its association with the goddess Inanna and thus Venus is assured from the mid-third millennium onwards (Black and Green 1992: 169–70). It can hardly be coincidence that the shortest period in years after which Venus repeats one of its characteristic phenomena is approximately eight. I would add, then, the eight-year synodic period of Venus to the list of ideal periods known throughout the third millennium BC. A related ideal pattern of Venus's behaviour is attested in the second section of the sixty-third tablet of *Enūma Anu Ellil*, the first part of which records phenomena dating to the reign of an Old Babylonian king (Brown 2000: 249 §9).

Attuned as we are to seeking antecedents to modern thinking, we tend to regard the awareness on the part of the Mesopotamian scholars of the periodicity of the heavens, their assignment to those periods of round and ideal numbers, and the numerical elaboration therefrom, as in someway antecedent to our own exact science of astronomy. We confuse, though, the potential of such ideal periods to make accurate predictions with their intention, which, I argue, was instead to make the date and or time of an observation interpretable (Brown 2001). The ideal periods served the same purpose as the broad categories into which the visible phenomena of the heavens were divided – the constellations of the ecliptic, the four colours, the four cardinal directions, above and below, brightness and faintness, and so forth. Both reduced what would otherwise have been an infinite number of variables in any observation to a manageable few, all of which could be encoded with a particular value, and thereby made the heavens interpretable: 'If Nergal [meaning Mars] stands in [the constellation] Scorpius; a strong enemy will carry off the land [an ill-boding prognostication for the land, expressed as an enemy attack, since Nergal is associated with "the enemy"]' (Hunger 1992: no. 502: 11).

Intrinsic to this approach to the phenomena of the heavens, one that prevailed from the earliest times to the end of the cuneiform tradition, was that the gods were the sign-givers. This view is made explicit in many contexts, and is widely accepted by modern scholars[13] and need not be justified here. I emphasise only that the particular configurations of the heavens, whether the month was 29 or 30 days long, whether lunar 'opposition' occurred on the fourteenth or not, whether Venus rose in month X or Y, was bright or dim, when Mars entered Scorpius, and so forth, were treated as expressions of the arbitrary will of the god in question, and were understood to be indicative of his or her displeasure at mundane events. Being able to predict the length of the next few lunations, for example, would thus instantly remove any sense that the Moon god had decided, on the basis of current events, to leave a sign indicating his approval or otherwise. Accurate prediction was, in essence, antithetical to the theological basis underpinning Mesopotamian celestial divination.

PREDICTIVE ASTRONOMY

It is, thus, all the more remarkable that accurate predictions of ominous phenomena were eventually made, and by scholars whose livelihoods depended upon royal support for celestial divination. We have been fortunate enough to have recovered many hundreds of the letters (Parpola 1993) and reports (Hunger 1992) the Neo-Assyrian scholars working in the entourages of the kings sent to their masters. Many included extracts from *Enūma Anu Ellil* that best applied to the current state of the heavens, some accompanied these with comments which show that the scholars were beginning to make accurate astronomical predictions.[14] Still, as the scholar Balasî writes in a letter to his king: 'The god has (only) wanted to open the king's ears. He should pray to the god, perform the apotropaic ritual, and be on his guard' (Parpola 1993: no. 56: r.18f) revealing that celestial phenomena continued to be regarded in the highest circles as the manifestations of the arbitrary will of the gods (or at least that is what the astrologer wanted the king, who was after all financing him, to believe). We should not be surprised, however, if, for some, accurate prediction could not sit easily with celestial divination, and Brown has traced the evidence for this point of view in Mesopotamian sources (Brown forthcoming a). In 2000 (239–43), Brown concluded that the reason for the appearance of accurate prediction at this time was due to the particular circumstances under which the Neo-Assyrian scholars worked, where being able to know in advance when an ominously dangerous phenomenon would occur gave them a competitive advantage over their colleagues in their dealings with the king.

Thus far, our evidence for Mesopotamian predictive astronomy derives from the ca. 1,500 astronomical cuneiform texts recovered from Babylonia that date from *c.*750 BC to AD 75, and the occasional references to accurate astronomical calculation made in the Neo-Assyrian letters and reports almost entirely from Nineveh. Our sources for Assyria end around 612 BC, and those for Babylonia are scant in this regard until the Hellenistic period. We have reason to suspect that the Neo-Babylonian kings employed celestial diviners, as perhaps did the Persians after they conquered Babylonia in 539 BC, though direct evidence is lacking. Nevertheless, enough has been recovered from the temples to indicate that calculations of the dates and locations of planetary phases based on an initial observation and a characteristic interval were being made from the seventh century BC onwards.[15] In 568 BC, an interval between Moonrise and Sunrise, known as 'kur', was calculated according to the Diary preserved for that year. It seems likely that this interval, summed with other similar luni-solar intervals, was used in conjunction with a characteristic interval, after which their sum repeats, to calculate the length of lunations, as elucidated by Brack-Bernsen (1997). The use of characteristic intervals and initial observations to make astronomical predictions continued until the very end of the cuneiform tradition. We refer to texts recording predictions made on this basis as 'non-mathematical astronomical texts' and these include the Diaries,[16] Goal-Year Texts, and two types of Almanac. The Goal-Year Texts present, for a given year, data for the phases of the planets and their passing by of certain stars that occurred a characteristic number of years earlier. For example, after 59 years, Saturn repeats a given phase, say heliacal rising, at the same point in the ecliptic. A Goal-Year Text thus includes 59-year-old data on Saturn. The Almanacs contain computations for the size of the various luni-solar phenomena, the dates of the phases of the planets, the dates upon which the planets cross the boundaries from one zodiacal sign to the next, and various other phenomena, all for a given forthcoming year. Although the attested examples date to the Hellenistic period, and the computations they contain could have derived from the ephemerides (discussed below), it is far likelier that they also were based on characteristic intervals and a record of initial observations (Hunger and Pingree 1999: 167).

Concomitant with the non-mathematical astronomical texts of the last five[17] centuries BC are the so-called astronomical cuneiform texts (ACTs). These represent the high-point of Babylonian astronomical endeavour. Some 300 texts are known, most of which are termed (rather incongruously) 'ephemerides', some procedure texts which outline how one might construct an ephemeris, and some unusual, but important, often earlier, texts which describe other ways in which an entire *set* of astronomical phenomena might be predicted using only one initial observation of position and location and a series of parameters describing the mean motion of a body and the variation about that mean. That variation was modelled using piece-wise linear functions, which we thus term 'arithmetic', in contrast to the trigonometric functions of Greek kinematic astronomy (described below). A good command of the basic mathematical operations with large numbers is shown in these texts, though the difficulties of non-terminating fractions often determine the particular parameters chosen. There is little evidence of a consistent treatment of approximations, or of systematic error. Calculations are peppered with redundant accuracy. The highly accurate mean values were determined from the shorter characteristic intervals used in the non-mathematical astronomical texts, and estimates as to the respective observational errors in the latter. Mars' accurate mean value for the interval after which it returns to its initial longitude and exhibits the same phase is 284 years, for example, derived from a combination of its shorter characteristic intervals of 79 and 47 years, and an estimate that the error in the former is a third of that of the latter, and of opposite sign. Thus $3(79) + 47 = 284$.

A prediction of where Mars next might rise and when, based on its characteristic interval of 79 years and a record of that planet's behaviour 79 years earlier, does not require either that the luni-solar calendar be regulated, or that locations in the sky be assigned relative longitudes. The ACTs and related texts did, however, for they predicted, for example, the date and location of Mars' rising on each occasion over the following years, given one initial starting point. Successive risings do not occur after whole numbers of years, nor at the same point in the ecliptic, the path on which the planets travel. Using the parameter of 284 years and the fact that during that interval Mars performs 133 phenomena of one type, it follows that the mean temporal and spatial intervals between successive phenomena of that type can be calculated. Variations about that mean can then be added according to some scheme depending either on location in the ecliptic (described by a step function), or on which number in the cycle of 133 has been reached (described by a zig-zag function). In order to *express* the temporal variation in terms of dates, however, some fixed value giving the number of months in a year was required, given that 12 lunations fall short of a year, and periodically a thirteenth was needed. Furthermore, it needed to be determined when best to intercalate these additional months. The ratio 235 months = 19 years was known at least by 500 BC, and a particular scheme placed the intercalary months either after the twelfth month or after the sixth in particular years of the 19-year cycle. Later ephemerides used still more accurate relationships.[18] In order to be able to plot spatial intervals that are less than whole returns, some means of dividing up the great circle of the ecliptic was also needed. Sometime after 500 BC this resulted in the invention of the zodiac, whereby 30 UŠ of arc were each assigned to 12 signs, whose names were taken from nearby constellations, in a circle of 360 UŠ. We translate these UŠ as 'degrees', though they should not be confused with degrees describing angles subtended from a point (Brown 2000a: 106). They are fractions of a great circle.

The 'regulation' of the luni-solar calendar and the invention of the zodiac were primarily effected in order to assist in the further development of astronomy in Babylonia from a non-mathematical variety to a fully mathematised one. Both found far wider uses. The 19-year scheme was adopted by Meton of Athens in the late fifth century, and remains the basis of the Hebrew calendar to this day. The zodiac, of course, went on to become the dominant tool of divination, particularly through the spread of personal astrology, especially horoscopes. The division of the great circle into 360 units became the standard means of dividing any circle.

We have ca. 80 full planetary ephemerides, several templates giving just longitudes and no dates, and about 30 procedure texts. We also have a few texts of a mathematical nature which deal with various aspects of planetary behaviour – variation in latitude, errors in characteristic periods, subdivisions of the arc between successive phenomena of the same type (the synodic arc). The earliest of these (BM 36301) dates back to the fifth century BC, but the most advanced stage was reached during the third to first centuries BC. While most attested planetary ephemerides calculate the location and dates of the phases, ones for Jupiter and Mercury offered schemes giving the location of the planet on a day-by-day basis, essentially fulfilling the same aim as Greek kinematic astronomy (Neugebauer 1975: 452). No doubt similar tables once existed for all the planets (see further Steele 2000 on text A 3405). We must, therefore, entertain the notion that one of the most important aims of the planetary ephemerides was to provide data that would have been of use to those writing horoscopes, for which the location of the planets at any given moment was crucial. Much as we might wish to imagine that the most advanced Babylonian astronomy was undertaken by scholars who were interested in planetary behaviour for its own sake (e.g. Neugebauer 1975: 412; *contra* Brown 2000: 220), that view does appear to be little more than the projection of modern sensibilities.

The aim of non-mathematical astronomy may also have increasingly become devoted to providing data useful to those doing zodiacal astrology, and away from providing data on the ominous phases of the planets, which would have been useful to those divining with omens. The Almanacs, for example, from early in the Hellenistic period and perhaps as early as the invention of the zodiac itself, give, among other things, calculated data on when planets entered zodiacal signs for a given year. At the moment of any birth, the horoscoper could easily have read from the Almanacs the sign in which each planet was located.

The masterpieces of cuneiform astronomy are the lunar ephemerides. These determined the moments of luni-solar conjunction and opposition (the so-called syzygies), the lengths of lunar first and last visibilities, and the details of eclipses. The intervals between syzygies depend on the varying velocity of both Moon and Sun, the latter having the dominant effect. The authors of the lunar ephemerides successfully modelled both, and how they managed this remains a topic of some

Figure 32.1 Copy of part of a Babylonian treatise on astronomy and astrology which was used as a reference source for students at Borsippa. The copy was made by Bel-ahhe-iddina in the year 138 BC. (Courtesy of the Trustees of the British Museum.)

controversy. The periods of visibility at conjunction or opposition also depend on the varying length of day, the latitude of the Moon, and the angle of the ecliptic. All five effects were successfully handled. Most striking is that ephemerides belonging to what is known as 'System A'[19] are all connectable. They form one ephemeris with predictions dating from 476 BC to 42 AD (Britton and Walker 1996: 61). The lunar ephemerides do provide calendrically useful information, but their prime purpose was astrological. The length of the month, the date of opposition, the lengths of first and last visibility,[20] and eclipses were all viewed as ominous signs. The early date for the invention of the system A mathematical-astronomical lunar model also suggests that its aim was unconnected to the demands of zodiacal astrology. We should thus assume that it was invented to assist astrologers undertaking omen divination. In due course, the data produced by the lunar ephemerides would have proved useful to those writing horoscopes, for whom the location of the Moon at birth was also significant. It would appear, though, that eclipse prediction continued to provide the main motivation for the further development of the lunar models. System B (see note 19), attested from the mid-third century BC, employed rather more ad hoc methods, but more accurate parameters than System A (Britton and Walker 1996: 62; Britton 2003), which we presume derived from a close scrutiny of the existing database of cuneiform Diaries and similar materials (Britton 2002: 53). Why a change was considered necessary is hard to fathom. Aaboe's suggestion of 'a delight in mathematical complexity' (quoted in Britton 2003: 46), seems improbable. Dissatisfaction with existing parameters seems far likelier, and we can only assume that that dissatisfaction emerged through a comparison of what was predicted with what was seen.

CONCLUSION

In Babylonia during the Hellenistic period, scholarly activity was particularly vibrant when it came to the astral sciences. More than half of all surviving texts written in cuneiform dating to the period after the fall of Persian Babylonia to Alexander were astronomical-astrological in content. So important to the scholars of Hellenistic Babylonia was the significance of the motions of the heavenly bodies that they continued to use cuneiform for far longer than might otherwise have been expected (Brown forthcoming b). The youngest of the most sophisticated sort of astronomical texts stopped being written in cuneiform around 30 BC (though the data predicted applied to still younger times), simultaneously with the last datable literary texts. Less sophisticated astronomical texts, however, continued to be written in that script for at least another century, the very latest of them showing signs that their authors no longer mastered cuneiform as their predecessors once had.

The period from the first century BC onwards saw the rapid increase in the popularity of personal astrology, such as horoscopy, in areas exposed to Hellenistic thinking. While Babylonian astronomy-astrology had influenced scholars writing in foreign languages and scripts in earlier times, it would appear that, during the century and a half before the birth of Christ and the century after, the methods, parameters, and insights that had once been known virtually exclusively only to those well-versed in cuneiform came to be understood by those writing in cursive scripts – Greek, Demotic and Aramaic in particular. Cuneiform's last niche market was lost to competitors, and the script slipped into redundancy.

Thereafter, the awareness of Babylonia's legacy in both astronomy and astrology was gradually lost. The Egyptians, for example, were often falsely credited with an astrological tradition that was essentially Babylonian. The Indians adopted zodiacal astrology and Babylonian parameters in their *siddhāntas* written in the centuries after Christ, but credited only the *Yavana*, or 'Ionian' Greeks. Ptolemy the astronomer, writing in Alexandria during the second century AD, recorded Babylonian observations in his *Syntaxis*,[21] and this, combined with an awareness that some parameters were 'Babylonian' and a confused record of 'Chaldaean' astrology preserved in some Greco-Roman literature and in the Bible,[22] constituted pretty much all that posterity had passed down to the nineteenth century AD of the tremendous legacy of cuneiform astral science.

That changed, however, with the decipherment of cuneiform. From the 1880s onwards discoveries have been made that Swerdlow (1998: 2) has characterised as 'the most important, the most revolutionary, in the entire study of science in antiquity, perhaps in the entire study of the history of science', and they continue to this day.

So far as astrological thinking is concerned, it first became clear the extent to which the Greek zodiac descended from the cuneiform one, as well as many other aspects of classical astrological theory. This study was then revolutionised by the recognition that some already published 'astronomical notes' were in fact Babylonian 'horoscopes', now known to date from 410 to 69 BC (Sachs 1952; Rochberg 1998). These texts do not use the ascendant (*horoscopos* in Greek) as a signifier, but are nevertheless records of a snapshot of the heavens at birth designed to provide data that can be interpreted for the benefit of the client in question.

Celestial divination was *democratised* first in Babylonia.[23] A system that once provided prognostications for a king was transmuted into one that could be used by everyone, and what made that possible was the invention of accurate prediction, giving the location of all significant heavenly bodies at any given moment – i.e. the time of birth. This was the change that turned the interpretation of the heavens into a system that could spread all over the world, and it occurred on the back of the earlier invention of predictive astronomy, and, in its turn, served to motivate the development of still more accurate techniques in that field.

As to astronomy, the decipherment of the cuneiform sources revealed that, while the achievements of those Greeks who devised kinematic astronomy was great, it nevertheless depended on the adoption of certain key Babylonian parameters.[24] In the kinematic model, it is assumed that the heavenly bodies move in a way that is the sum of certain circular motions. Circular motion is a premise, derivable from particular assumptions in respect of the nature of the matter which makes up the universe, and, while patently wrong so far as the heavenly bodies are concerned, was much admired until the later Middle Ages. The kinematic model was, and often still is, seen as a great leap forward in terms of mankind's thinking about the universe, based as it was on a physical and not merely numerical model of heavenly behaviour. Its premises were, however, ideological, and the best fit with observed reality, when finally achieved, was done so on an ad hoc numerical basis, using parameters that could not themselves be derived from considerations as to the material of the universe. Only with Newton does a true physics of the universe, in this sense, commence.

Most recently it has become clear that specific Babylonian astronomical methods spread along with Babylonian astrology. Even after Greek kinematic astronomy had developed to a level whereby it was capable of making all the calculations astrology required, many astrologers continued to favour Babylonian and Babylonian-style arithmetic astronomy for centuries to come. Recent discoveries in the papyri from Oxyrhynchus in Egypt have shown that Babylonian astronomy did not simply provide Greek astronomers with observational data and parameters that they could 'cherry-pick' to serve their own ends, it also had a profound, direct influence on great swathes of Greek society, particularly that of Ptolemaic Egypt (see now Jones 1999).

We have over-estimated the importance of the kinematic astronomy of Hipparchus (see note 24) and Ptolemy vis-à-vis its arithmetic uncle, simply because knowledge of the former was never lost. The discoveries in the cuneiform texts from Mesopotamia have revealed the sophistications of arithmetic astronomy, and evidence from Roman Egypt means that it is now no longer clear if, when, and to what extent Greeks and Romans themselves favoured kinematic astronomy over arithmetic. It is no longer clear that the adherence of the former to a materialistic explanation of the nature or *physis* of the heavens added to its appeal. The cuneiform ephemerides, in particular, reveal that highly accurate astronomical systems had been devised in Babylonia that could be both logically consistent (e.g. the System A lunar ephemerides), and be adapted in an ad hoc manner as a (probable) consequence of empirical feedback (e.g. System B of the lunar ephemerides). The schemes adhered to accepted notions as to the manner in which the year should be divided (i.e. the 360 degrees in the zodiac recall the 360 days in the ideal year), months should be divided (in the planetary ephemerides, a thirtieth-of-a-month unit was employed, which mirrors the ideal month), and the way change could be modelled using piece-wise linear techniques (Brown 2000: 239). Even in the most sophisticated of mathematical astronomical texts, many links with the ancient, highly esteemed art of celestial divination were preserved. A lack of physical underpinning does not seem to have dented their appeal in antiquity. Nor should it now.

FURTHER READING

Britton and Walker 1996 offer a superb, concise summary of Mesopotamian astral science. Koch-Westenholz's 1995 slim book on astrology is excellent and accessible. Neugabauer 1975 devoted Book II to a detailed elucidation of cuneiform astronomy, though data on the long-lasting utility of Babylonian astronomical methods can be found scattered throughout that *magnum opus*. Hunger and Pingree 1999 is a thorough, accurate survey of all publications on cuneiform astronomy, as defined by them, at times strictly for the specialist. Brown 2000 attempts to place the development of predictive astronomy, as opposed to the mere ordering of the heavens, or calendrics, within the context of cuneiform celestial divination and Mesopotamian history. Rochberg 2005 is devoted (mainly) to contextualising the rise of personal predictive astrology in Babylonia after *c.*450 BC and to placing cuneiform astronomy-astrology within the context of the history and philosophy of science. The above does provide an overview of the sources from ancient Iraq that pertain to astral concerns, but is concerned rather more with those aspects of this field that strike me as the most interesting, the least written about, and the hardest for the non-specialist to appreciate.

NOTES

1 I use the term in the literal sense, as 'wanderers', corresponding to the Sumerian ^{mul}udu.idim and Akkadian *bibbu*, or 'wild sheep' (Horowitz 1998: 153).

2 According to ETCSL 4.15.2 (*Nergal B*): 16, Nergal 'travels through heaven', suggestive of Mars, with whom Nergal is later closely associated. In ETCSL 4.31.1 (*Hymn to Šul-pa-e*): 1, Šulpae 'shines forth like moonlight', a probable reference to Jupiter.

3 The Sumerian text ETCSL 5.6.3 9 (*The Farmer's Instructions*): 38 ud mul-an-na šu im-ma-ab-du$_7$-a-ta (39) 10-am$_3$ a$_2$ gud a-šag$_4$ zi-zi-da-še$_3$ igi-zu nam-ba-e-gid$_2$-I 'When the constellations in the sky are right, do not be reluctant to take the oxen force to the field many times.' Cf. also ETCSL 5.5.5 (*The Song of the Ploughing Oxen*).

4 *Šamaš,* the Sungod, *Sîn,* the Moongod and *Kakkabu* 'star' appear in the earliest Semitic incantations from Ebla, in Syria (Cunningham 1997: 18).

5 Brown 2000: 246–7, §3. Additionally, Inana is a 'celestial sign' according to the translation of ETCSL 4.07.04 (*Hymn Inana D*): 6. She is also referred to as dilibat in ETCSL 2.5.3.1 (*Iddin-Dagan A*): 135. Dilibat is specifically the name for the celestial body we know as Venus, and is typically used in omens. It is noteworthy that this name first appears in the Isin-Larsa period. Nisaba's association with the stars is explicit in ETCSL 1.6.2 (*The Exploits of Ninurta*): 712f.

and indirect in ETCSL 2.1.7 (*Gudea Cylinders A and B*) 134f., and in ETCSL 4.16.1 (*Hymn Nisaba A*), and is perhaps very ancient. Enlil is also a star according to ETCSL 2.4.2.07 *Šulgi G*): 1–8.

6 BM 22696: 6, cited in Rochberg 2005: 68. ETCSL 5.3.6 (*The debate between Silver and Copper*) refers to tablets of the stars.

7 As made clear by the many references within the omen corpus to kings of the Old Akkadian and Ur III periods. Bibliography in Brown 2000: 246 §2.

8 In a catalogue of incipits from Ur, dating to the Old Babylonian period, the title *Enūma Anu Ellil* appears in both Akkadian and Sumerian (Brown 2000: 248 §7). Cf. now Rochberg 2005: 69 on the small series of eclipse omens from Old Babylonian times.

9 Approximately half of *Enūma Anu Ellil* has been edited to date (Brown 2006, n.23).

10 Al-Rawi and George 1991–2.

11 The reader may justifiably ask what is meant by 'remotely' here. As he or she reads on, it will become clear that the accuracy of the ideal schemes of *Enūma Anu Ellil* 14 and the like were such as to ensure that the actual date, or time, of the phenomenon could still be understood to have been the consequence of the arbitrary will of the god in question. Later, the higher levels of accuracy achieved would of necessity have made that understanding questionable.

12 Hunger and Pingree 1988.

13 See most recently Rochberg 2005: Ch. 2.

14 Brown 2000: 189–207 summarises the relevant data. The evidence that these scholars were capable of producing some accurate observations and predictions, and were aware of some characteristic periods for the planets is unequivocal. The limits of their abilities can also be determined from the Letters and Reports, showing that this science was still in its infancy in the seventh century BC.

15 The clearest evidence is in text DT 72+, last treated in Brown (2000: 193). There is also a hint that a particular interval of 6,585 days and ca. 8.5 hours, used to determine not only the date of an eclipse but its time, the so-called Saros, was in use in the seventh century BC and perhaps even the mid-eighth (Brown 2000: 205; Steele 2002).

16 The surviving 'Astronomical Diaries' come almost entirely from Babylon and represent a small part of a database that in its complete form dated from the mid-eighth century BC until perhaps as late as the first century AD. Most are published in Sachs and Hunger 1988–96. The Diaries record not only observations of astral phenomena such as planetary phases, but weather phenomena, the level of the Euphrates, and some historical data. Many of the astronomical data were calculated, apparently when the phenomena in question could not be seen. On the purpose of the Diaries see Hunger and Pingree 1999: 140, *contra* Brown 2000: 97–103; 2001. Data pertaining to eclipses that occurred as early as the mid-eighth century BC are listed separately on cuneiform tablets, as are data pertaining to the location of the planets and their phenomena, the earliest of which date to the Neo-Assyrian period. See now Hunger 2001 and Huber and de Meis 2004.

17 See Hunger and Pingree 1999: 189 for a possible seventh-century scheme comparable to one particular column of the lunar ephemerides.

18 There is no definitive evidence that a distinction was ever made in Babylonian sources between the equinoctial or sidereal years, a prerequisite to discovering precession (in some form). Hipparchus is credited with this discovery. It was theorised that the Babylonians had indeed discovered it first, but Neugebauer refuted this idea in the 1950s (references in Hunger and Pingree 1999: 201). The fact that cuneiform texts linked the phases of a star (Sirius) with seasonal phenomena does seem to support this (Neugebauer 1975: 543), but Britton 2002: 51–2 has raised the possibility that values of the sidereal and equinoctial years were indeed differentiated in late cuneiform sources.

19 Meaning that the longitude of the syzygy is determined using a step function which has longitude as its argument. System B lunar ephemerides describe the longitude of syzygy with a zig-zag function with month number as an argument. This is less consistent than system A.

20 Proposed in Brown 2000: 166, and now attested directly in BM 47494: rev. 16, edited by Hunger 2004.

21 Barton 1994: 23–31, and for details on the cultural interactions in the astral sciences between Mesopotamia, India, Greece, Iran, the West Semitic areas, and Egypt, see Brown (forthcoming c).

22 E.g. Isaiah 47: 12–14.

23 While Hellenistic astrology was a far more complicated beast than its Babylonian counterpart, Neugebauer is wrong to argue (1975: 613) that 'with the exception of some typical Mesopotamian relics the doctrine [of astrology] was changed in Greek hands to a universal system in which form alone it could spread all over the world'. That many Babylonian astrological techniques spread to Greece, Egypt, India, and elsewhere gives the lie to this.

24 Hipparchus (fl. *c.*125 BC) was probably the first Greek astronomer who managed to devise a workable kinematic model. His debt to cuneifom astronomy was first revealed by F. X. Kugler 1900: 21, 24, 40, 46, 108. Toomer 1988: 361 writes that Hipparchus' 'originality and inventiveness are beyond question', but that his achievement 'would not have been possible without the resources of Babylonian astronomy' to which he adds that 'the idea of astronomy as a practical predictive science was another debt of his to the Babylonians', and finally that Hipparchus 'both directly as an advocate of astrology, and indirectly as a developer of astronomical methods which became an essential part of it, was pivotal' to the spread of Babylonian astrology to the Greek world.

BIBLIOGRAPHY

Al-Rawi F. N. H. and George, A. R. (1991–2) '*Enūma Anu Enlil* XIV and Other Early Astronomical Tables', *Archiv für Orientforschung* 38/39, 52–73.

Barton, T. (1994) *Ancient Astrology*. London, New York: Routledge.

Black, J. A. and Green, A. (1992) *Gods, Demons and Symbols of Ancient Mesopotamia*.London: British Museum Press.

Brack-Bernsen, L. (1997) *Zur Entstehung der babylonischen Mondtheorie: Beobachtung und theoretische Berechnung von Mondphasen*.Boethius 40, Stuttgart: F. Steiner.

Britton, J. P. (2002) 'Treatments of Annual Phenomena in Cuneiform Sources', in J. M. Steele and A. Imhausen (eds), *Under One Sky: Astronomy and Mathematics in the Ancient Near East*. AOAT 297, Münster: Ugarit-Verlag, 21–78.

—— and Walker, C. B. F. W. (1996) 'Astronomy and Astrology in Mesopotamia', in C. Walker (ed.), *Astronomy before the Telescope*. London: British Museum Press, 42–67.

Brown, D. R. (2000) *Mesopotamian Planetary Astronomy-Astrology*. Cuneiform Monographs 18, Groningen: Styx.

—— (2000a) 'The Cuneiform Conception of Celestial Space and Time', *Cambridge Archaeological Journal* 10:1, 103–21.

—— (2001) 'Astronomy-Astrology in Mesopotamia', *Bibl. Or.* 58, 41–59.

—— (2006) 'Astral Divination in the Context of Mesopotamian Divination, Medicine, Religion, Magic, Society, and Scholarship', in Hans Ulrich Vogel (ed.), *East Asian Science, Technology, and Medicine* 25, Tübingen: University of Tübingen. Volumes 24 and 25 constitute a Festschrift for Ho Peng Yoke.

—— (forthcoming a) 'Disenchanted with the gods? The advent of accurate prediction and its influence on scholarly attitudes towards the supernatural in ancient Mesopotamia and ancient Greece', in G. Zólyomi, E. Robson and H. Baker (eds), *Gs. Jeremy Black*.

—— (forthcoming b) 'Increasingly Redundant – the growing obsolescence of the cuneiform script in Babylonia from 539 BC on', in J. Baines, J. Bennet, and S. Houston (eds), *Last Writing*. London: Equinox.

—— (forthcoming c) *The Interactions of Ancient Astral Science*. Vergleichende Studien zu Antike und Orient X, Bremen: Hempen.

—— and Zólyomi, G. (2001) '"Daylight converts to Nighttime" An astrological-astronomical reference in Sumerian literary context' *Iraq* 53, 149–54.

Cunningham, G. (1997) *'Deliver Me From Evil', Mesopotamian Incantations 2500–1500 BC. Studia Pohl: Series Maior 17*, Rome: Pontifical Biblical Institute.

ETCSL = Black, J. A., Cunningham, G., Ebeling, J., Fluckiger-Hawker, E., Robson, E., Taylor, J. and Zólyomi, G.(1998–) *The Electronic Text Corpus of Sumerian Literature* (http://etcsl.orinst.ox.ac.uk/), Oxford.

Horowitz, W. (1998) *Mesopotamian Cosmic Geography*. Mesopotamian Civilizations 8, Winona Lake, I: Eisenbrauns.

Huber, P. J. and de Meis, S. (2004) *Babylonian Eclipse Observations from 750 BC to 1 BC*. Milan: Mimesis.

Hunger, H. (1992) *Astrological Reports to Assyrian Kings*. State Archives of Assyria 8, Helsinki: Helsinki University Press.

—— (2001) *Astronomical Diaries and Related Texts from Babylonia. Volume V. Lunar and Planetary Texts*. Vienna: Verlag der Österreichischen Akademie der Wissenschaften.

—— (2004) 'Stars, Cities, and Predictions', in C. Burnett, J. P. Hogendijk, K. Plofker and M. Yano (eds), *Studies in the History of the Exact Sciences in Honour of David Pingree*. Islamic Philosophy, Theology, and Science, Texts and Studies vol. LIV, Leiden and Boston: Brill, 16–32.

—— and Pingree, D. (1989) *MUL.APIN: An Astronomical Compendium in Cuneiform, Archiv für Orientforschung* Bh. 24, Horn, Austria: Ferdinand Berger & Söhne.

—— and —— (1999) *Astral Sciences in Mesopotamia*, Leiden, Boston, Köln: Brill.

Jones, A. (1999) *Astronomical Papyri from Oxyrhynchus*. Vols 1, 2, Memoirs 233 Philadelphia: American Philosophical Society.

Koch-Westenholz, U. (1995) *Mesopotamian Astrology: An Introduction to Babylonian and Assyrian Celestial Divination*. Copenhagen: Carsten Niebuhr Institute of Near Eastern Studies, Museum Tusculanum Press.

Kugler, F. X. (1900) *Die babylonische Mondrechnung. Zwei Systeme der Chaldäer über den Lauf des Mondes und der Sonn*. Freiburg im Breisgau: Herder.

Neugebauer, O. (1975) *A History of Ancient Mathematical Astronomy*. Berlin: Springer.

Parpola, S. (1993) *Letters from Assyrian and Babylonian Scholars*. State Archives of Assyria 10, Helsinki: Helsinki University Press.

Rochberg, F. (1998) *Babylonian Horoscopes*. Transactions 88/1 Philadelphia: American Philosophical Society.

—— (2005) *The Heavenly Writing – Divination, Horoscopy, and Astronomy in Mesopotamian Culture*. Cambridge: Cambridge University Press.

Sachs, A.(1952) 'Babylonian Horoscopes', *Journal of Cuneiform Studies* 6, 49–74.

—— and Hunger, H. (1988–96) *Astronomical Diaries and Related Texts from Babylonia. Volumes I-III*. Vienna: Verlag der Österriechischen Akademie der Wissenschaften.

Steele, J. M. (2000) 'A 3405: An Unusual Astronomical Text from Uruk', *Archive for the History of the Exact Sciences* 55, 103–35.

—— (2002) 'A Simple Function for the Length of the Saros in Babylonian Astronomy', in J. M. Steele and A. Imhausen (eds), *Under One Sky: Astronomy and Mathematics in the Ancient Near East*. AOAT 297, Münster: Ugarit-Verlag, 405–20.

Swerdlow, N. M. (1998) *The Babylonian Theory of the Planets*. Princeton, NJ: Princeton University Press.

Toomer, G. J. (1988) 'Hipparchus and Babylonian Astronomy', in E. Leichty *et al.* (eds), *A Scientific Humanist: Studies in Memory of Abraham Sachs*. Occasional Publications of the Samual Noah Kramer Fund 9, Philadelphia: Babylonian Section, University Museum, 353–62.

CHAPTER THIRTY-THREE

LATE BABYLONIAN
INTELLECTUAL LIFE

——•✦•——

Paul-Alain Beaulieu

Late Babylonian intellectual life is known from thousands of cuneiform texts dating between the eighth and first centuries BC and unearthed in the libraries of palaces, temples and private houses. Most of the sources from the eighth and seventh centuries originate in Assyria, especially in the libraries collected by king Ashurbanipal in Nineveh. Although Assyria exerted its hegemony over the entire Near East during that period, Babylonia remained culturally dominant and Babylonian texts of every kind were avidly collected for the royal libraries (Parpola 1983b). Even scholarly texts in the Assyrian script were as a rule composed in the Standard Babylonian dialect of Akkadian and largely recorded knowledge compiled in Babylonia. Therefore it is not surprising that after the fall of Assyria at the end of the seventh century the cuneiform tradition retreated to Babylonia, where it had begun nearly three millennia earlier, and continued its existence in temples and the private houses of scholars until the Hellenistic and Parthian periods. While Babylon and Uruk stand out as the two most important intellectual centers of the late Babylonian period, important finds were made at other sites, notably Sippar, Borsippa and Nippur. Our sources consist largely of texts belonging to the so-called "stream of tradition." This is the generally accepted term to designate the corpus of authoritative editions of texts which stood at the core of ancient cuneiform scholarship. Another very important source is the correspondence between the Assyrian kings of the Sargonid dynasty (721–610 BC) and the scholars who advised them. Many of them were Babylonian and their correspondence helps us understand how they interpreted the knowledge recorded in scholarly texts.

Cuneiform writing was the preserve of a small caste of professionals. In a letter to his employer the Assyrian king Esarhaddon, the Babylonian scholar Ašarēdu the Younger alludes to the restricted diffusion of writing with a touch of wit when he warns him that "the scribal craft is not heard about in the market place" (SAA 8: 339). Even kings were rarely literate beyond limited training in reading and writing. Among late Mesopotamian rulers, only the Assyrian king Ashurbanipal and the Babylonian king Nabonidus laid claim to advanced literacy and learning. Yet, in spite of limited dissemination, writing occupied a prominent symbolic place in the Babylonian world. Marduk, the demiurge and patron god of Babylon, regulated cosmic order through his possession of the Tablets of Destinies. His son Nabû, who even surpassed him in popularity to become the most important god of the pantheon during the time of the Neo-Babylonian empire (626–539 BC), was the god of the scribal craft. Scribes endowed the written word with great power. Even texts that may appear straightforward on the surface were made to convey deeper meanings through a complicated exegesis which fully exploited the resources of Sumero–Akkadian bilingualism (Maul 1997) and the infinite possibilities of the cuneiform script for phonetic and logographic permutations (Bottéro 1977). More important, after the political demise of Babylon with the Persian conquest of 539 BC, traditional education in cuneiform became a badge of cultural identity for the Babylonians, now threatened by the imposition of foreign rule and the rise of new official vernaculars such as Aramaic. Such factors even increased the symbolic importance of cuneiform writing as the civilization that had supported it for three thousand years entered its twilight.

However, our complete dependence on the textual record to study ancient intellectual life should not obscure the fact that the Babylonians lived largely in an oral world. Only a small part of the body of knowledge was ever committed to writing. Entire fields of technical learning were transmitted exclusively by oral tradition, and a number of significant intellectual activities, such as the production of art, were almost never discussed in the written record. Our knowledge of Babylonian intellectual life is also impeded by the fact that the writings themselves tend to be succinct and non-discursive. Even in the late periods, Babylonian scholarly literature still adhered to the basic format of lists, whether they were lists of words, of omens, or of scientific observations. This trait has often and erroneously been invoked in the past to argue that the Babylonians lacked analytical skills. Yet this peculiarity simply stems from the fact that writing in the Ancient Near East was essentially an aid to memory. If lists were explained, analyzed, and provided with a theoretical foundation, this was done orally. At any rate, the existence of analytical thinking leading to the formation of theoretical statements is proven by such clues as, for instance, the appearance of grammatical terms in the late lists of Sumerian verbal forms known as the Neo-Babylonian Grammatical Texts (Civil 1994: 84–85). Canonical or authoritative editions of texts were mostly organized into series (*iškāru*), such as the series *Šumma izbu* (teratological omens) and *Enūma Anu Enlil* (astrological omens). Together with a corpus of supplemental texts which were extraneous (*ahû*) to the series, they formed the backbone of Babylonian learning (Rochberg 1984: 137–144). The textual record often refers to the tradition handed down by the masters as *ša pî ummâni*, which means literally "that of the mouth of a master." It is debatable whether this expression refers specifically and always to the oral tradition. Nevertheless, it seems certain that ongoing discussions and exegeses of the texts by the scholars were the main element bringing cuneiform learning to life, its flesh and blood.

The oral tradition occupied such a prominent place that in order to attain the rank of scholar, basic training in the scribal craft and the ability to read texts were insufficient. One must learn personally from the masters. This, however, began after a period of initial schooling. The curriculum of late Babylonian education has been reconstructed from hundreds of fragmentary school exercises (Gesche 2001). Two options were available to students. Those students whose goal was to serve in the royal administration learned the fundamentals of the cuneiform script, the basic corpus of lexical and metrological texts, lists of personal names, and how to write legal and administrative documents. They also studied a selection of traditional texts and works of literature promoting the royal ideology, such as the *Epic of Gilgamesh*, the *Legend of Sargon*, the *Cuthean Legend of Narām-Sîn*, and the *Weidner Chronicle*. Students with higher intellectual ambitions started with the same basic education, but soon branched out to an enriched curriculum which was very heavily oriented towards the craft of the exorcist (*āšipūtu*). They copied incantations, such as the series *Utukkū Lemnūtu*, magical and exorcistic series (*Šurpu* and *Maqlû*), literary hymns and prayers, and the advanced corpus of lexical lists, including the encyclopedia *Har-ra = ḫubullu*. They also studied the fundamental theological texts that promoted the vision of Babylon as cosmic center and of its god Marduk as demiurge, namely the Babylonian *Epic of Creation* (*Enūma eliš*) and the topographical series *Tin.tir = Babilu*. Here the focus was not on the king, but on the gods.

Specialized training did not take place in schools. After completing the basic curriculum, students who found employment in the administration presumably perfected their skills under the guidance of senior colleagues. As for students oriented towards the intellectual sphere, they could specialize in one of the three recognized disciplines of scholarship: the *āšipūtu* "craft of the exorcist," the *kalûtu* "craft of the lamentation singer," and the *bārûtu* "craft of the diviner." At this point they continued training under the guidance of master scholars who often happened to be older members of their family. Indeed, if we rely on the colophons of library manuscripts and the information gleaned from private and temple archives, it appears that young aspiring scholars usually embraced the profession of their fathers. Writing in the first century BC, the Greek historian Diodorus of Sicily confirms the cuneiform evidence on this point. He gives us a vivid portrait of Chaldean scholarship, insisting particularly on its hereditary nature:

> For among the Chaldeans the scientific study of these subjects is passed down in the family, and son takes it over from father, being relieved of all other services in the state. Since, therefore, they have their parents for teachers, they not only are taught everything ungrudgingly but also at the same time they give heed to the precepts of their teachers with a more unwavering trust.
>
> (Library of History II.29.4; Oldfather 1968: 447)

Families of scholars congregated into larger clans claiming descent from a common ancestor. Some clans maintained a virtual monopoly on a particular discipline. In Seleucid Uruk, for instance, all the lamentation singers (*kalûs*) descended from Sîn-lēqi-unninni (Beaulieu 2000). The exorcists (*āšipus*), on the other hand, were divided among several clans, such as the descendants of Ekur-zākir, Ḫunzû, and Šangû-Ninurta, and we find astronomers (*ṭupšar Enūma Anu Enlil*) among the descendants of both Sîn-lēqi-unninni and Ekur-zākir. Some families can be traced over several generations through the colophons of library texts copied by junior scribes, and the history of the Sîn-lēqi-unninnis can be followed, albeit with some gaps, from the sixth until the second century. A number of colophons contain additional notations on the purpose of the scribe in copying a particular text (Pearce 1993). Often texts were copied "for perusing" (*ana tāmarti*), "for learning" (*ana aḫāzi*), or "for recitation, reading" (*ana šitassi*). This last term is based on the root *šasû*, whose primary meaning is "to shout, call." It indicates that reading in Babylonia, as in many ancient cultures, was not internalized (silent), but performed by reciting the text *sotto voce*. The expressions *liqinnû qabû* "to learn" and *liginnû šuqbû* "to teach" convey the same idea. They mean literally "to recite excerpt tablets" and "to cause to recite excerpt tablets," the basic meaning of the root *qabû* being "to speak" (Beaulieu 1992). That reading, learning, and teaching were conducted by recitation and repetition of the texts orally is also suggested by mistakes in manuscripts that can be attributed only to poor hearing. Higher education involved years of reciting and copying scholarly series and supplemental texts, and above all discussing them with the teachers who initiated their students into the oral tradition of the masters.

Thus, higher education and scholarship were private and often secretive, and only a small number of individuals ever became proficient in cuneiform learning. These two factors eventually gave rise to the notion that knowledge had been preserved since the beginning of time through a long line of sages and masters who had transmitted it to a select number of pupils. This tradition culminated in the lists of antediluvian sages (*apkallu*s) and postdiluvian masters (*ummânu*s) who were ascribed the authorship of works of literature and scholarship and remembered as advisors to real and legendary kings. The first *apkallu* according to the late tradition was U'anna, identified with the mythical sage Adapa and sometimes appearing under the name U'anna-Adapa. He is better known as Oannes from the writings of Berossus, who wrote his *Babyloniaca* in Greek at the beginning of the third century BC. Berossus tells us that Oannes was half fish and half man, came out of the sea in the First Year to teach humans all they needed to know in order to lead a civilized life, and that after him nothing more had been discovered (Verbrugghe and Wickersham 1996: 44). Other *apkallu*s came later but only explained in greater detail what Oannes had revealed. This tradition is nothing but a projection back into mythical time of the conservative and incremental nature of late Babylonian scholarship. The role of the learned was essentially to preserve, explain, and transmit an immutable body of knowledge revealed once and for all in primeval time. Such refusal to entertain the possibility of progress is very typical not only of the Babylonian world view, but pervades the thinking of all ancient civilizations.

Progress, however, did take place. In the Achaemenid and Hellenistic periods, for instance, the Babylonians invented mathematical astronomy, which ranks as the first exact science in history. The possibility of progress was denied mainly because of the belief that knowledge ultimately resided with the gods. This hierarchy is very apparent in the *Catalogue of Texts and Authors* found in the library of Ashurbanipal (Lambert 1962). The *Catalogue* ranks second the works attributed to the culture bringer U'anna-Adapa, giving first place only to those attributed to Ea, the god of wisdom. Ea is thus attributed authorship of the entire corpora of the exorcist and lamentation singer. He is also given paternity of a number of other series. These include *Enūma Anu Enlil* and *Sagigga* (medical diagnoses and prognoses), and even *Lugale* and *Angim-dimma*, the ancient Sumerian epics of the god Ninurta that had been provided with intralinear Akkadian translations in the course of the second millennium. Other sources trace the craft of the diviner to the gods Šamaš and Adad, who had entrusted it at the beginning of time to Enmeduranki, the antediluvian king of Sippar (Lambert 1967). He, in turn, taught it to the men of Sippar, Babylon, and Nippur and thus became the spiritual ancestor of all diviners. The goddess Gula and her consort Ninurta were credited with the art of medicine (*asûtu*). A number of minor gods were given the patronage of various crafts. Kulla was the god of brickmaking, and Guškinbanda was the god of goldsmiths, but here we leave the world of intellectuals *stricto sensu* to enter the world of craftsmanship, although there was no rigid separation between the two in the Babylonian world. Indeed, the word *ummânu* refers to both expert craftsmen and master scholars. Intellectual disciplines were, in their essence, crafts revealed by the gods.

The most prominent intellectual discipline was the craft of the exorcist. A compendium known from several manuscripts dating between the seventh and third centuries includes titles of series and procedures belonging to it (Geller 2000: 242–258). No fewer than a hundred titles are listed there, including omen series, incantations, purification rituals, and medical treatises. The compendium also includes a smaller, alternative list detailing the corpus of the exorcist according to a certain Esagil-kīn-apli. There we find a higher concentration of medical texts and esoteric learning than in the main list. This Esagil-kīn-apli was also known as compiler of the medical treatise *Sagigga* and allegedly lived during the reign of the Babylonian king Adad-apla-iddina (1068–1047 BC) (Finkel 1988). Since the *Catalogue of Texts and Authors* attributes authorship of *Sagigga* and the entire corpus of the exorcist to the god Ea, it ensues that, in the native view, Esagil-kīn-apli did not accomplish a creative act but only put into writing knowledge imparted to him by the god. "This is not my incantation, this is the incantation of Ea and Asalluhi," routinely pronounced the exorcist after performing his duty. This must have been understood literally, in that the exorcist acted merely as medium, almost as divine impersonator. Indeed, another text claims that "the incantation is the incantation of Marduk, the exorcist is the very image of Marduk." The intervention of the exorcist was efficacious only if the gods allowed it to be so, because only the gods possessed all knowledge. The same was true of the other two disciplines, the crafts of the lamentation singer and diviner, which were also defined by a textual corpus. The corpus of the former can be appraised from the libraries of families of lamentation singers living in Babylon in the late second century BC, principally the descendants of Nanna'utu. They included mainly hymns and laments in the Emesal dialect of Sumerian, and indeed some of the colophons indicate that these texts were copied "for chanting" (*ana zamāri*). The corpus of the diviner was more precisely and narrowly defined and consisted essentially of texts dealing with extispicy and devoted mainly to various configurations of the liver of the sacrificial sheep. These texts were known collectively as the "series of the diviner's craft" (*iškār bārûti*).

The fact that these disciplines were defined by corpora of texts and involved years of studying with the masters means that their practitioners can truly be called intellectuals. This label appears all the more justified when we take into consideration that in the native view, exorcists and lamentation singers were responsible for most of the literary and scientific output of late Babylonian civilization. For instance, the *Catalogue of Texts and Authors* attributes the Exaltation of Ištar to the lamentation singer Taqīš-Gula, and the Babylonian *Theodicy* to the exorcist Saggil-kīna-ubbib, an attribution also embedded in that composition in the form of an acrostic (Lambert 1960: 63). The same catalogue attributes the Epic of Gilgamesh to the exorcist Sîn-lēqi-unninni; the Series (Fable) of the Poplar to the exorcist Ur-Nanna; and the Series (Fable) of the Spider to the lamentation singer Šumu-libši. We find exorcists and lamentation singers at the forefront of science, especially mathematical astronomy. Although breakthroughs in astronomy were accomplished by individuals bearing the title of *ṭupšar Enūma Anu Enlil* "scribes of the (astrological series) *Enūma Anu Enlil*," evidence from Babylon and Uruk clearly indicates that most, if not all astronomers were also exorcists or lamentation singers (Rochberg 2000).

Even between the three main disciplines there must have been considerable overlap. In a letter addressed to an unknown Assyrian king of the seventh century, the Babylonian scholar Marduk-šāpik-zēri, seeking employment for himself and his colleagues, thus proclaims his mastery of his own discipline, the craft of the lamentation singer: "I fully master my father's profession, the discipline of lamentation (*kalûtu*); I have studied and chanted the (appropriate) series." He quickly moves on, however, to advertise his knowledge of the series, rituals, and medical procedures belonging to the craft of the exorcist in order to increase his chances of employment:

> I am competent in . . ., the mouth-washing ritual, the purification of the palace rituals . . ., I have examined healthy and sick flesh, I have read (the astrological series) *Enūma-Anu-Enlil* . . . and observed the stars, I have read (the teratological series) *Šumma izbu*, (the physiognomic series) [*Kataduggû, Alandi*]*mmû*, and *Nigdimdimmû*, [and the (terrestrial omen) series *Šumma Alu*] *ina mēlê šakin*.
>
> (SAA 10: 160)

In another letter, an unnamed sender complains to the Assyrian king that a goldsmith named Parruṭu bought a Babylonian slave to teach portions of the corpora of the exorcist and of the diviner to his son, as well as excerpts from *Enūma Anu Enlil* (SAA 16: 65). The evidence from late Babylonian colophons and libraries also provides clear evidence that scholars often collected and copied texts from all disciplines, irrespective of their own specialization. In general, however, late libraries still reflect the practice of one particular discipline. For instance, the libraries of Achaemenid and Hellenistic Uruk reflect the crafts of the exorcist and lamentation singer. The sixth-century library found in the 1980s in the Ebabbar temple of Sippar contain mostly texts which, not surprisingly, reflect the craft of the diviner, an art reputedly revealed to humans in antediluvian times by the local gods Šamaš and Adad. The only exceptions seem to have been the very large encyclopedic libraries such as those of Ashurbanipal at Nineveh and of the Esagil temple in Babylon. The latter is less well known than the former but seems to have fulfilled the role of general reference library in Babylon until the end of the Hellenistic period (Clancier 2005: 193–335).

What is the significance of this division of knowledge between *āšipūtu*, *kalûtu*, and *bārûtu*? Does it tell us anything about the nature of the Babylonian intellectual quest? In a colophon from his library, king Ashurbanipal lays the following claim:

> I wrote on tablets, according to copies from Assyria and Babylonia, the wisdom of the god Ea, the series of the lamentation singer, the secret knowledge of the sages, which is suited to quiet the heart of the great gods.
>
> (Hunger 1968: 102)

In a fictitious letter of the Old Babylonian king Samsu-iluna, copied in late Babylonian schools, the king states that:

> after the great lord Marduk, supreme king of the gods, *prince* of his brethren, had created gods and humankind and allotted them their destiny, he [*set up*] the

purifying exorcist to heal the [*numerous*] people, and the lamentation [singer, for] appeasing the *heart*, [for] prognostication, rites of intercession, and lamentations.

(Al-Rawi and George 1994: 138)

These statements clearly define the role and purpose of the craft of lamentation, which was to appease the hearts of the angry gods with chanting and performing rites of intercession. As for the exorcist, his role was not only to heal and purify. He was also a magical practitioner who reconciled the ailing worshiper to his deity. This was the purpose of a widespread form of ritual accompanied by incantations and prayers known as *šu'illa*. Prevention and cure, spiritual as well as physical, were both placed under the care of the exorcist, who thus occupied a paramount place in a culture where diseases were often explained as the strike of a deity or demon, or attributed to the abandonment of the worshiper by his personal god. Thus, it seems fair to say that the general purpose of the craft of the exorcist was to prevent and conjure up the punishments sent by the gods. Finally, in a culture where omens were viewed as warning signs sent by the gods to humans, the goal of the diviner's craft, the science of omens and, above all, of extispicy was to interpret these signs and foresee the will of the gods and their intentions towards humans.

If we follow this line of reasoning, we come to the inescapable conclusion that the foundations of Babylonian intellectual life were theological. Indeed, the exorcist, lamentation singer, and diviner were essentially clerics in the employment of the temple. They played an important role in the cult, and their offices were remunerated by the temple, sometimes with a prebendal income. It is important to keep in mind that in the intellectual history of the ancient world, the Babylonians stand at the very polar opposite of the Epicurean school. Epicurus espoused the goal of liberating his fellow humans from the fear of nature and of the gods. Epicurean gods lived in a state of bliss analogous to ataraxia, never interfering in the lives of humans. The Babylonians, on the contrary, were hopelessly and unremittingly dependent upon the gods. Their scholars acted as mediators between them and the supernatural world, trying to alleviate the effects of that abject dependence. The entire corpora and disciplines of the exorcist, lamentation singer, and diviner make perfect sense as a vast intellectual construction celebrating the absolute power of the gods and alleviating human subjection to their unfathomable will. When seen in this light, the ancient view that attributed most of these crafts to the god Ea seems perfectly comprehensible. In Mesopotamian myths of the deluge it is Ea who issues a warning about the impending flood, thereby saving humans from the ire of the god Enlil, who had decreed their destruction. Ea's revelation of the crafts of the exorcist and lamentation singer completed his friendly deed toward humans, as it provided them with the knowledge necessary to prevent and cure the destructive effects of divine anger.

Of course, we must not lose sight of the fact that our sources stem largely from individuals who operated within the context of the temple, its cult and rituals, and whose sole *raison d'être* was worshiping the gods. Therefore, the assessment of Babylonian knowledge exclusively as a theology may distort a reality which was far more complex. Indeed, there is little doubt that certain fields and traditions of knowledge operated relatively free of religious assumptions. Medicine and astronomy are cases in point. The main branch of medicine was known as the *asûtu*. The *asû* was a physician, surgeon and herbalist, and during the earlier periods of Mesopotamian history he was in fact the main, if not sole, practitioner of medicine. However, the rise of the *āšipūtu* in the late periods favored a division of medicine into two branches. The *asûtu* became confined to the more practical aspects of medicine, as the physician's practice was based essentially on empirical knowledge. The *āšipūtu*, on the other hand, considered both the spiritual and physical components of the disease, the exorcist being as much a doctor of the soul as one of the body, and it included a significant part of speculative knowledge, chiefly divination and magic. Yet there is evidence that the two disciplines frequently overlapped, especially as the exorcist often integrated the *asûtu* into his own practice. In other terms, the *āšipūtu* represented a form of medicine that was primarily oriented towards a theological goal, while the *asûtu* was an empirical pursuit, potentially independent from religious considerations. Astronomy presents another case of duality. There is no doubt that the tasks carried out by the astronomers in late Babylonia can be defined as exact science, with regular compiling and sifting of data and the demonstrable existence of revisionary processes in the elaboration and application of theories. There is also compelling evidence that these tasks were performed mainly by the *ṭupšar Enūma Anu Enlil*. In the past three decades, scholars have stressed the integrated nature of late Babylonian knowledge and science and the undeniable fact that most, if not all astronomers were also practitioners of the crafts of the exorcist and lamentation singer. The discipline of *ṭupšar Enūma Anu Enlil* constituted only a further specialization of their art. Far from being secularized scientists in rebellion against the irrational doctrines propagated by Babylonian clerics, they probably saw no contradiction between their scientific pursuits and the religious and theological foundations of their scholarship. It seems fair to assume that their scientific activities were conducted independently of all other considerations.

Thus far this survey has focused on men, but what about the role of women? Goddesses played a significant role as providers of knowledge. Physicians and exorcists praised Gula as *azugallatu* "great healer" and patron of the medical arts of the *asûtu*. Earlier, the goddess Nisaba was worshiped as mentor of the scribes, before Nabû gradually replaced her in that role during the second millennium. In spite of this, late Babylonian intellectual life appears to have been essentially a world of men. Indeed, one can hardly find a single mention of a woman as cuneiform scribe in that period, although there were inevitably exceptions. The letter SAA 16, 28 shows that, in the seventh century for instance, princesses at the Assyrian court were expected to reach a certain level of scribal proficiency. This was surely not limited to Assyria, and comparable training was probably bestowed upon Babylonian princesses of the sixth century. Nabonidus' daughter, who was elevated to the status of high priestess of the moon-god at Ur under the name En-nigaldi-Nanna, may well have been literate like her father. Babylonian women of patrician background were sometimes encouraged to embrace intellectual disciplines. This is suggested by the late document CT 49, 140, which records the admission of a woman and her daughter to the profession of exorcist by the assembly of that profession (Boiy 2004: 271). Yet it should be stressed again that these were exceptional cases in a world where men monopolized learning and official positions. The only areas where women must have played a significant and sometimes even central role are traditional medicine and midwifery, but knowledge of these disciplines was largely transmitted orally and is therefore lost to us.

Another important aspect of late Babylonian intellectual life is the corporate insistence on secrecy, manifested mainly in colophons discouraging the user from disseminating its content beyond a narrow circle of initiates. The standard formula reads: "The initiate may show the initiate; the uninitiated must not see; taboo of (such and such) god" (Beaulieu 1992). It seems a priori difficult to ascribe any significance to such formulas beyond the fact that they point to a certain *esprit de corps* among scholars, especially in a world where higher learning had become the preserve of restrictive clans claiming an old patrician lineage. In fact, each of the three great disciplines is, in one way or another, characterized as secret knowledge in our sources. However, it is undeniable that a significant portion of the texts that are labeled as restricted belong to a particularly difficult type of scholarship which explored the interrelations between various branches of knowledge, mainly divination. This probably signals the emergence of a native tradition of esotericism in Mesopotamia. Increased complexity and sophistication of Babylonian scholarship is also evidenced by the appearance of a new genre of text in the early part of the first millennium: the commentary (Krecher 1980–1983). Commentaries provided traditional works of scholarship with philological explanations. In this respect they essentially adhered to the format of word lists. Most of the surviving commentaries pertain to divinatory series such as *Šumma izbu* and *Enūma Anu Enlil*, others to medical texts, but even some works of literature such as the Poem of the Righteous Sufferer (*Ludlul bēl nēmeqi*) and the Babylonian *Theodicy* were provided with commentaries. The best example is undoubtedly the commentary to the exegesis of the fifty names of the god Marduk which conclude *Enūma eliš*, the Babylonian Epic of Creation. Although the purpose of commentaries was often to clarify other texts, it would be erroneous to see them exclusively as works of scholarship on textual material that had become too old and arcane to be understood by scribes. In fact, no commentary is known for a text predating the latter part of the second millennium. It is possible that a number of commentaries were more or less contemporary with the final edition of the series they sought to explain, and served mainly as teaching tools and companion pieces. Indeed, some commentaries are labeled as *šūt pî maš'altu ša pî ummâni* (literally "oral explanations and questions from a master"), indicating that their purpose was to provide a written compendium of the oral tradition for the advanced levels of teaching and learning. In their most developed form, commentaries became highly sophisticated treatises of hermeneutics (Maul 1999).

In spite of these limited trends towards complexity, the cuneiform writing system did not become intrinsically more contrived and arcane in the same way as hieroglyphics did during the Ptolemaic period. During that time there was a conscious effort on the part of Egyptian priests to make monumental writing completely inaccessible to the uninitiated by multiplying the number of signs and values almost tenfold. In Babylonia, cuneiform had reached the same level of inaccessibility only by the mere fact of its survival as an ancient writing system in a world where a new language written with a simple alphabet, Aramaic, had become the dominant vernacular. Spoken Akkadian in its late Babylonian form probably died out completely during the Achaemenid period and survived in written form mainly for legal documents and administrative memoranda, while Standard Babylonian continued to thrive as the language of scholarly texts. However, transcriptions of Babylonian school texts in Greek letters, the so-called Greco-Babyloniaca, indicate that the pronunciation of traditional texts of Mesopotamian scholarship in the Hellenistic period followed the phonology of the late Babylonian vernacular language, not that of Standard Babylonian.

Figure 33.1 Kudurru of the Babylonian king Marduk-zakir-shumi (left) which shows him handing a document to his scribe (right) (ninth century) (Louvre).

Therefore, even long after its death as a living tool of communication, late Babylonian continued for some time to be transmitted both orally and in writing in the schools alongside Standard Babylonian and Sumerian. Cuneiform civilization remained surprisingly alive in this form until the last decades of Seleucid rule. The large temples, especially the Esagil in Babylon, continued to function as centers of intellectual life and science and as repositories of texts. Babylonian scholars, better known as Chaldeans, even began to spread, with some success, their astronomical science and religious doctrines throughout the Mediterranean world. Only with the installation of Parthian rule at the end of the second century BC can we gather evidence for the disintegration and collapse of Babylonian institutions and the end of cuneiform learning. The last known cuneiform tablet, which is, not surprisingly, an astronomical text, is datable to the year 75 of our era (Sachs 1976).

BIBLIOGRAPHY

Al-Rawi, F.N.H. and George, A.R. (1994), "Tablets from the Sippar Library III. Two Royal Counterfeits," *Iraq* 56, 135–148.

Beaulieu, P.-A. (1992), "New Light on Secret Knowledge in Late Babylonian Culture." *Zeitschrift für Assyriologie und vorderasiatischen Archäologie* 82 (1992) 98–111.

—— (2000), "The Descendants of Sîn-lēqi-unninni," in J. Marzahn and H. Neumann, eds, *Assyriologica et Semitica. Festschrift für Joachim Oelsner anläßlich seines 65. Geburtsages am 18. Februar 1997.* (Alter Orient und Altes Testament 252; Münster: Ugarit Verlag) 1–16.

Boiy, T. (2004), *Late Achaemenid and Hellenistic Babylon* (Orientalia Lovaniensia Analecta 136; Leuven: Peeters).

Bottéro, J. (1977), "Les noms de Marduk, l'écriture, et la logique en Mésopotamie ancienne," in *Ancient Near Eastern Studies in Memory of J.J. Finkelstein.* (Connecticut Academy of Arts and Sciences, Memoir 19) 5–28.

Civil, M. (1994), "Sumerian," in G. Lepschy, ed., *History of Linguistics. Volume 1. The Eastern Traditions of Linguistics.* (London and New York: Longman) 76–87.

Clancier, Ph. (2005), *Les bibliothèques en Babylonie au Ier millénaire av. J.-C.* (Thèse de doctorat, Université Paris 8 Vincennes-Saint-Denis).

Finkel, I.L. (1988), "Adad-apla-iddina, Esagil-kīn-apli, and the Series SA.GIG," in E. Leichty, M. deJ. Ellis, and P. Gerardi, eds, *A Scientific Humanist. Studies in Memory of Abraham Sachs.* (Occasional Publications of the Samuel Noah Kramer Fund 9; Philadelphia: The University Museum) 143–159.

Frahm, E. (2002), "Zwischen Tradition und Neuerung. Babylonische Priestergelehrte im achämenidenzeitlichen Uruk," in R.G. Kratz, ed., *Religion und Religionskontakte im Zeitalter der Achämeniden.* (Veröffentlichungen der Wissenschaftlichen Gesellschaft für Theologie 22; Gütersloh: Chr. Kaiser) 74–108.

Geller, M.J. (1997), "The Last Wedge," *Zeitschrift für Assyriologie und vorderasiatischen Archäologie* 87, 43–95.

—— (2000), "Incipits and Rubrics," in A.R. George and I.L. Finkel, eds, *Wisdom, Gods and Literature. Studies in Assyriology in Honour of W.G. Lambert.* (Winona Lake, IN: Eisenbrauns) 225–258.

Gesche, P.D. (2000), *Schulunterricht in Babylonien im ersten Jahrtausend v. Chr.* (Alter Orient und Altes Testament 275; Münster: Ugarit-Verlag).

Hunger, H. (1968), *Babylonische und assyrische Kolophone.* (Alter Orient und Altes Testament 2; Kevelaer and Neukirchen-Vluyn: Butzon & Becker and Neukirchener Verlag).

Joannès, F. (2000) "De Babylone à Sumer: le parcours intellectuel des lettrés de la Babylonie récente," *Revue historique* 302, 693–717.

Krecher, J. (1980–1983), "Kommentare," *Reallexikon der Assyriologie und vorderasiatischen Archäologie* 6, 188–191.

Lambert, W.G. (1960), *Babylonian Wisdom Literature.* (Oxford: Clarendon Press).

—— (1962), "A Catalogue of Texts and Authors," *Journal of Cuneiform Studies* 16, 59–77.

—— (1967), "Enmeduranki and Related Matters," *Journal of Cuneiform Studies* 21, 126–138.

Lanfranchi, G.B. (1989), "Scholars and Scholarly Tradition in Neo-Assyrian Times: A Case Study," *SAAB* 2, 99–114.

Maul, S.M. (1997), "Küchensumerisch oder hohe Kunst der Exegese? Überlegungen zur Bewertung akkadischer Interlinearübersetzung von Emesal-Texten," in B. Pongratz-Leisten, H. Kühne, and P. Xella, *Ana Šadî Labnani lū allik. Beiträge zu altorientalischen und mittelmeerischen Kulturen. Festschrift für Wolfgang Röllig.* (Alter Orient und Altes Testament 247; Kevelaer and Neukirchen-Vluyn: Butzon & Becker and Neukirchener Verlag) 253–267.

—— (1999), "Das Wort im Worte. Orthographie und Etymologie als hermeneutische Verfahren babylonischer Gelehrter," in G.W. Most, ed., *Commentaries – Kommentare.* (Aporemata. Kritische Studien zur Philologiegeschichte 4; Göttingen: Vandenhoeck & Ruprecht) 1–18.

Oldfather, C.H. (1968), *Diodorus Siculus I, Books I-II, 3.4* (Loeb Classical Library 239; Cambridge, MA: Harvard University Press).

Parpola, S. (1970), *Letters from Assyrian Scholars to the Kings Esarhaddon and Assurbanipal. Part I: Texts* (Alter Orient und Altes Testament 5/1; Kevelaer and Neukirchen-Vluyn: Butzon & Becker and Neukirchener Verlag).

—— (1983a), *Letters from Assyrian Scholars to the Kings Esarhaddon and Assurbanipal. Part II: Commentary and Appendices.* (Alter Orient und Altes Testament 5/2; Kevelaer and Neukirchen-Vluyn: Butzon & Becker and Neukirchener Verlag).

—— (1983b), "Assyrian Library Records," *Journal of Near Eastern Studies* 42, 1–29.

Pearce, L.E. (1993), "Statements of Purpose: Why the Scribes Wrote," in M.E. Cohen, D.C. Snell, and D.B. Weisberg, eds, *The Tablet and the Scroll, Near Eastern Studies in Honor of William W. Hallo.* (Bethesda, MD: CDL Press) 185–193.

Rochberg, F. (1984), "Canonicity in Cuneiform Texts," *Journal of Cuneiform Studies* 36, 127–144.

—— (2000), "Scribes and Scholars: The *tupšar Enūma Anu Enlil*," in J. Marzahn and H. Neumann, eds, *Assyriologica et Semitica. Festschrift für Joachim Oelsner anläßlich seines 65. Geburtsages am 18. Februar 1997.* (Alter Orient und Altes Testament 252; Münster: Ugarit Verlag) 359–375.

SAA 8 = Hunger, H., *Astrological Reports to Assyrian Kings.* (State Archives of Assyria, volume 8; Helsinki: Helsinki University Press, 1992).

SAA 10 = Parpola, S., *Letters from Assyrian and Babylonian Scholars.* (State Archives of Assyria, volume 10; Helsinki: Helsinki University Press, 1993).

SAA 16 = Luukko, M. and Van Buylaere, G., *The Political Correspondence of Esarhaddon.* (State Archives of Assyria, volume 16; Helsinki: Helsinki University Press, 2002).

Sachs, A.J. (1976), "The Latest Datable Cuneiform Tablets," in *Kramer Anniversary Volume.* (Alter Orient und Altes Testament 25; Kevelaer and Neukirchen-Vluyn: Butzon & Becker and Neukirchener Verlag) 379–398.

Verbrugghe, G.P. and Wickersham, J.M. (1996), *Berossos and Manetho, Introduced and Translated. Native Traditions in Ancient Mesopotamia and Egypt.* (Ann Arbor, MI: University of Michigan Press).

PART VII

INTERNATIONAL RELATIONS

Babylonia and the Ancient
Near Eastern world

——•◆•——

CHAPTER THIRTY-FOUR

EGYPT AND MESOPOTAMIA

————•◆•————

David A. Warburton

TWO GREAT LANDS THAT WERE FAR APART

The two greatest civilisations of the Bronze Age Near East were those of southern Mesopotamia and the Nile Valley. In terms of intellectual vibrancy, Mesopotamia must be viewed as the greater of the two. In terms of identity, continuity, monumentality, and power, Egypt had no equals. Although far from enjoying a glorious solitary existence far removed from the hurly burly of daily politics, Egypt was never exposed to constant abrasion by abusive neighbours which was the part assigned to Babylonia. The results are thus expressed in the masterpieces of the two civilisations. Constant challenge forced Babylonia to respond in a fashion at least partially moulded to express the Babylonian identity in a manner recognizable to neighbours. This gave it an enormous advantage, and the result was the development of an intellectual heritage shared by all the civilisations of the Near East. Power and wealth allowed Egypt to impose its will on its own landscape, but it was less concerned about neighbours, and its influence diminished as one left the Nile Valley.

Given the simple geographical distance separating the two civilisations, one could suggest that it is logical that there was very little actual contact between the two, and in fact the two did not come into direct conflict during the Bronze Age, and just barely during the Iron Age. Although the Egyptians moved deep into Nubia, in the south, they never got beyond western Syria in the north, and thus the lack of contact is not surprising. During the second half of the second millennium BC the Babylonians were not very active to the west, and this could likewise be ascribed to geographical distance, or a lack of political ambition. However, neither argument is particularly illuminating, since the Akkadians campaigned in Syria and Anatolia in the third millennium and the Babylonians themselves would return to Syria in the first.

Clearly distance or lack of interest cannot be the sole reason, and the situation was far more complicated, for even in the first millennium BC – when Egypt was overrun by Libyans, Assyrians, Ethiopians, Persians, Greeks and Romans – Egypt was not invaded by the Babylonians. Even the peripheral Hittites were able to invade Babylonia in the Bronze Age, and, under Alexander, the peripheral Greeks were able to subdue both Egypt and Babylonia – quite aside from some more distant lands. Thus, one can hardly argue that simple logistical constraints played a role.

Contact between Babylonia and Egypt was determined by far more than sheer distance: it was a question of the relations each had to its neighbours and their conceptions of their own roles vis-à-vis those neighbours. We will try to explore the situation on two levels.

In an instant, we will take a look at the power politics which dominated the Ancient Near East, and thus appreciate that the relations between Egypt and Babylon were not so much a matter of reciprocal contacts, but, rather, influenced by their respective relations with Greece, Anatolia, Nubia, Syria, Assyria and Iran.

First, however, we will try to see what the sources can tell us about thought patterns, and a letter found at the abandoned capital, Akhetaten (now called Amarna) is among the most valuable sources in this respect. We will begin with this aspect, as the well-known letter from a Babylonian king to an Egyptian Pharaoh bears quoting:

> To Akhenaten/Amenophis IV, Great King of Egypt, my brother: Thus Burnaburiash, Great King of Babylonia, your brother. . . . From the time my brother's ambassador arrived here I have not been well. . . . And I am still not well. Anyway, since I was not well and my brother showed no concern, I for my part became angry with my brother, saying 'Has my brother not heard that I am ill?! Why has he shown no concern?!' . . . My brother's ambassador addressed me, saying, 'It is not so near that your brother can hear about you and send greetings. The country is far away. Who is going to tell your brother so he can immediately send greetings? Would your brother hear that you are ill and still not send an envoy?' I for my part addressed him as follows, saying, 'For my brother, a Great King, are there really distant and close countries?' He addressed me as follows, saying, 'Ask your own envoy.' . . . Now, since I asked my own envoy and he said that the journey was long, I was not angry any longer, and I held my peace.
>
> (EA 7, after Moran 1992: 12–13)

This letter provides a great deal of information.

First, the simple fact that this royal letter from one of the most important rulers of the world at that time was simply abandoned when the capital was moved at the end of the Amarna period shows how important diplomatic correspondence was to the ancient Egyptians. In addition, the fact that the actual correspondence with the great kings (of Hatti, Mitanni, Assyria) makes up only a small proportion of the archive as preserved (perhaps three dozen letters of more than three hundred) may suggest either that most of the important letters were in fact moved away, or alternatively that the greatest part of the Egyptian correspondence was with minor vassals in Palestine and minor kings in Syria. One could speculatively argue both losses and culling, suggesting that the present day composition cannot be used to argue about the composition in antiquity. However, based on the archive itself, it can be argued that the composition of the archive is representative of its original form since the Egyptian ambassador clearly states that messengers were not moving constantly back and forth between the two countries – which contrasts greatly with the speed and volume of the correspondence with the authorities and envoys in Syria-Palestine. Thus we can see that Egyptian priorities lay closer to home, which confirms

Figure 34.1   Letter from Burnaburiash, king of Babylon, to Amenophis IV, king of Egypt, found at Amarna in Egypt. (Courtesy of the Trustees of the British Museum.)

that the attitude of the Babylonian king (to which the letter itself is a testimony to a woeful lack of geographical understanding) was shared by the Egyptians. The two countries were distant from one another in more ways than one.

Second, the fact that the letter (like almost all of the other letters in the archive) was written in cuneiform in a form of Akkadian reveals the intellectual superiority of Mesopotamia, as the origin of writing and the creator of the diplomatic *lingua franca* of the Ancient Near East. The Egyptians apparently saw no reason to impose the use of their language on others; they did not even expect their own vassals in Palestine to use the Egyptian language. Cuneiform Akkadian was a practical medium used throughout the Near East, but no more. The Egyptians certainly did not reveal any great enthusiasm to develop a knowledge of the actual land whence this language and writing originated, nor to pursue a rapid exchange of letters with the kings of that country.

Third, and most important, this letter informs us about the nature of contacts between the 'Great Kings'. In this case, our interest is the relationship between the kings of Egypt and Babylon, but their relationship is illustrative of that prevailing in the Bronze Age. For the most part, the 'Great Kings' of the Bronze Age only had contact via correspondence. There were few, if any, major summit conferences between the cosmic powers.[1] This stands in contrast to the regular contact between these 'Great Kings' and the lesser kings and princes. The 'Great Kings' were themselves celestial and did not intend to share their environment with other celestial beings.

But these 'Great Kings' did regularly meet lesser princes when these came to their land for consultations or instructions, and they also met lesser princes when the 'Great Kings' themselves were campaigning abroad.

THE BALANCE OF POWER IN THE BRONZE AGE

Nevertheless, the archive from the Egyptian capital at Akhetaten (Amarna) does preserve a number of letters exchanged directly between the kings of Egypt and Babylonia. It also includes exchanges with Mitanni, Hatti and Assyria which confirm that the Egyptian foreign ministry had a clear understanding of power relations in Mesopotamia. The Egyptian lack of interest in Babylonia itself is indicative of their consciousness of the balance of power. Within their horizon, the relevant actors were Mitanni and Hatti, and – just barely – Assyria. In Egyptian terms, Babylon had no military role to play, and thus was treated as an observer.

Although the use of writing, the 360-day year, and niched monumental mud-brick architecture are irrefutable traces of Mesopotamian influence in Egypt at the very start of the third millennium BC, there is not much more that one can read in the material. Aside from a couple of stone vessels found in Mesopotamia, there is virtually no trace of any contact with Egypt during the third millennium BC, or indeed through the first part of the second millennium (see, however, Kaelin 2006 for third-millennium influence).

Contact between Egypt and Babylonia only gradually emerged and developed under the impact of the Hittite and Egyptian advances into Syria, from the middle of the second millennium BC. Initially, the Hittite conquest of Babylon (1499 BC),[2] was followed by an interlude during which the Hittites lost all power outside of Anatolia. The resulting power vacuum permitted the Kassites, already on the Euphrates in Syria (Podany 1991–93), to move into Babylonia, the Mitanni empire to spread across northern Mesopotamia, and the Egyptian king Thutmosis I to advance as far as the Euphrates in Syria. At this time, Assyria was basically eclipsed and Kassite Babylonia unconscious of any potential power. The result was that as the Mitanni empire gradually spread further toward the Mediterranean Sea, and the Egyptians cautiously moved northwards, these two powers came into conflict, a conflict which endured until Mitanni was threatened by a revival of Hittite power in the north and Assyrian power in the east.[3]

The period between the Euphrates campaign of Thutmosis I (perhaps *c.*1490 BC) and that of Thutmosis III (perhaps *c.*1446 BC) was marked by the expansion of Mitanni in the north. When Thutmosis I moved, Syria was still suffering from the after effects of the Hittite campaigns which had destroyed the centres of power in northern Syria at Alalakh, Ebla and Aleppo, as well as Babylon itself, whereas Thutmosis III came into direct conflict with Mitanni. Unfortunately for the Egyptians, Mitanni, moving west to the Mediterranean coast and south along the Orontes, proved sufficiently powerful for it to block the Egyptian route north. Mitanni control of the Orontes was secured by treaties with the smaller power centres, such as Alalakh and Tunip, recognising Mitanni sovereignty in northern Syria (Reiner in *ANET*). Therefore, from the final years of the reign of Thutmosis III, and for the duration of that of his son Amenophis II, the Egyptian advances were halted in the region of the Orontes Valley.

At the time that the Egyptian advance into Syria began, Assyria and Babylonia were conscious of the importance of Egyptian activity, and thus they dispatched congratulatory gifts to the Egyptian pharaoh when he crossed the Euphrates (cf. Redford 2003: 250–254). These various hints in the sources must be put together to provide some understanding of events (see Table 34.1).[4]

Although both Assyria and Babylonia were obviously intent on encouraging Thutmosis III to continue with his efforts, their behaviour and motivation were quite different. Throughout the fifteenth and fourteenth centuries, Babylonian attitudes towards Assyria were tempered by a confidence in the power of Babylonia, whereas Assyria was seeking recognition, and viewed itself as being in competition with both Mitanni and Babylon. Thus the Babylonian gifts were no more than cautious greetings, restricted to the year of the Euphrates campaign: interest ceased as it became evident that the Egyptians were unable to maintain the pressure. By contrast, the Assyrian gifts began before the Egyptian advance into Syria, and continued after Thutmosis III had heavy going in the Orontes.

The gifts from Alalakh tell a different story. They began some time after the Euphrates campaign, and ceased in the period thereafter, as Mitanni power was consolidated, and Alalakh accepted that. Gifts from the Hittites reveal a pattern which is a mirror image, as they continue as Hittite concerns with Mitanni grow.

The stalemate begun shortly after the Euphrates campaign of 1446 BC continued for more than a century. Thus, at the beginning of this era, when Thutmosis III reached Carchemish on the Euphrates, Babylon appreciated the Egyptian effort. But after a certain period, disillusionment set in, as the Mitanni hold on northern Syria was consolidated.

It rapidly became evident that the Egyptians were not going to move any further, and the Babylonians had other concerns. Near the early part of the reign of Thutmosis III, Puzur-Assur III had rebuilt the walls of Assur, and forced Burnaburiash, King of Babylonia, to recognise the common border with Assyria. This can only have followed from a conflict between the two, and represented an initial setback, preventing the Babylonians from moving further north. Fortunately for Babylon, the Assyrians would find themselves menaced by Mitanni, and thus Babylonian fears of Assyrian expansion could be put on hold once the boundary was established, and the Assyrians left to face their neighbours to the west.

Not only was Assyria gradually reasserting itself, but it was at precisely this moment that a new era commenced in Elam. Declaring themselves the Kings of Susa and Anshan, the new Elamite rulers represented a major power to the east of Babylon. The appearance of this new power began roughly during the reign of Thutmosis III, and by the reign of Kadashman-Enlil I of Babylon, 'embassies were exchanged between the Babylonian and Elamite court' (Kuhrt 1995: 369).

Assyrian and Babylonian hopes had been raised by the Egyptian campaigns to the Euphrates, but disappointment had ensued as Mitanni consolidated its hold, and the Egyptian advance pushed back and stymied. Their hopes were reawakened, however, when the Hittites began to put pressure on Mitanni. During the reign of Thutmosis IV, Ugarit and some of the principalities in Syria which had recognised Mitanni suzerainty moved towards recognising Egyptian hegemony, evidently as Hittite pressures on Mitanni increased. Without Egyptian campaigns, the Mittani kings themselves initiated openings towards Egypt, and thus the balance of political power moved in Egypt's favour – due to the campaigns of other powers.

Table 34.1 Middle Babylonian period, c. 1600–900

c. BC	Actors	Campaigns to	Gifts to	Bride(s) to	Embassy to	Letter(s) to
1499	Murshili	Babylon				
1490	Thutmosis I	Euphrates				
1454–46	Thutmosis III	Palestine Syria				
1455	Assur		Egypt			
1446	Thutmosis III	Euphrates				
1445	Assur, Babylon, Hatti		Egypt			
1445–35	Thutmosis III	Orontes				
1444–35	Assur, Hatti, Alalakh		Egypt			
1423–18	Amenophis II	Orontes				
1400–1370	Syrian cities, Mitanni					Egypt
1360	Mitanni	Anatolia		Egypt		
1360–20	Babylon			Hatti, Elam, Egypt		Egypt
1340	Assur-Uballit			Babylon	Egypt	
1340–20	Tushratta, Shattiwaza			Egypt	Egypt, Hatti	Egypt
1340–20	Shuppiluliuma	Anatolia, Syria		Mitanni		Egypt
1320–1265	Horemhab, Seti I, Ramesses II	Syria				
1260–20	Hattushili III, Tudkhaliya IV			Egypt		Egypt
1260–1200	Shalmaneser I, Tukulti-Ninurta I	Syria, Babylon, Elam				Egypt, Babylon, Assyria, Myceneans

For Assyria, this meant an opening to foreign recognition which would place it in direct conflict with Babylon. Assur-uballit dispatched envoys to Egypt, and demanded gifts from the Egyptian king with the result that the Babylonian king would demand that Akhenaten send the Assyrian envoys out of his capital immediately and empty-handed. The envoys may well have been overjoyed at the hope since Akhenaten had made them stand out in the sun, worshipping for hours, but the situation reflected a decisive turn in the history of Babylonian power. And the real victims of the political situation were not the sun-burnt Assyrian envoys, but rather the sisters and daughters of the Babylonian Kassite kings, as they were sent off as hostages of political interest to the royal harems of Hatti, Elam and Egypt.

As it was generally the weaker party who sent the bride, these Babylonian beauties were left as signposts of Babylonian frailty. The one case where the Babylonians were able to acquire a bride, from Assyria, became a catastrophe for Babylon when Assur-Uballit invaded after his grandson was murdered and replaced by a 'nobody'. After the Assyrian withdrawal, Kurigalzu II was able to sweep into Elam and take Susa.

In order to understand this reversal of fortune which allowed a brief interlude of Babylonian greatness before Babylon was conquered by successive Assyrian and Elamite kings, we must return to the stand-off in Syria. During the reigns of Thutmosis III and Amenophis II (i.e., the period of *c*.1445, after the Euphrates campaign, until 1397, the death of Amenophis II), the Egyptians had been struggling to maintain their hold in the Orontes valley. However, during the reign of Thutmosis IV, Mitanni had gradually come under Hittite pressure, and the princes of Syria began to align themselves with Egypt, and Mitanni itself continued the overtures towards Egypt begun near the end of the reign of Amenophis II. Thus, there was a change in the balance of power in Syria which did not result from Egyptian advances but, rather, from those of the Hittites.

The beneficiaries of this policy were not merely the Egyptians, but also the Assyrians and the Babylonians. The great Hittite king, Shuppiluliuma I, who was destined to destroy Mitanni during the reign of Akhenaten, benefited from the far-sighted Babylonian policy of sacrificing their daughters, as he – like Amenophis III, and later Ramesses II – had a Babylonian bride. Shuppiluliuma did not necessarily recognise the etiquette as others did since he also sacrificed a daughter to his vassal Shattiwaza, but it may be assumed that the Babylonians understood the rules better. The fact that the Hittite king had a Babylonian Kassite wife reflected the growing threat from the east and thus Shuppiluliuma's wife would be completely unrelated to the power relations between Hatti and Babylon. Instead, through Babylon, the Elamites exercised a direct influence on Hatti. Thus Babylon was pursuing a diplomatic marriage policy to the west and north while maintaining military pressure on Elam. Their opportunity, which allowed the lunge into Elamite territory and the conquest of Susa, followed from the Egyptian conflict with Hatti following the death of Tutankhamun.

Tutankhamun had died while Shuppiluliuma was besieging Carchemish, and his widow had apparently sent a messenger asking Shuppiluliuma to send him one of his sons to make him her husband and king of Egypt. Shuppiluliuma delayed, and when he eventually established that the queen was telling the truth, he dispatched his son – but too late, for the conspirators were able to assure that Shuppiluliuma's son died in Egypt and the widow was married to Aya. What happened to the queen is unknown, for she disappears. However, Shuppiluliuma then attacked Egyptian forces in Syria, and the Assyrians continued the assault on what was left of Mitanni (cf. Hout 1994).

This opened the way for the Babylonian strike at Elam. Babylonia was thus free to act: as long as the Egyptians and the Hittites maintained their fruitless conflict in Syria, and the Assyrians continued their war of attrition against Mitanni. There was a general stand-off, and the next few decades were dominated by diplomatic squabbles related to dynastic intrigue. During his campaigns against Mitanni, Shuppiluliuma had placed Shattiwaza, one of the sons of the murdered Tushratta on the throne of Mitanni. Supporting him through marriage treaties and military support, Shattiwaza had managed to re-establish Mitanni, more or less under Hittite tutelage. This was necessarily a provocation for Assyria, but eventually he was able to free himself from Hittite hegemony and thus Assur-uballit of Assyria seems to have tolerated the state for a while (cf. Wilhelm 1982 for details).

With the exception of a marginal detail, this story would not be relevant to our narrative, but at one point Shattiwaza had turned up in Babylon seeking asylum before securing Shuppiluliuma's aid. Decades later, in Hatti, Hattushili III displaced his nephew Urkhi-teshup as king, and the Hittite usurper achieved a rapprochement with both Kadashman-Turgu of Babylon and Shalmaneser I of Assyria. A minor diplomatic squabble almost became grounds for a major war when the deposed Hittite king Urkhi-Teshup sought to escape from his exile, first seeking aid from Babylon, but finally arriving at the Egyptian court, where he was welcomed by Ramesses II. Being familiar with Shattiwaza's personal history, and confronted with the facts on the ground which had resulted from it (an independent Mitanni allied with Assyria against Hatti), Hattushili demanded that Urkhi-Teshup be extradited. Ramesses II refused and

> Hattusil III prepared to mobilise his forces. When informed of this, Kadashman-Turgu of Babylon promptly severed diplomatic relations with Egypt and offered to send – even to lead – his troops against Egypt alongside Hattusil. This help was courteously refused by the Hittite king . . ., but never had the international storm clouds thickened more darkly in the world of the Ancient Near East.
>
> (Kitchen 1982: 74)

Thus, Babylon and Egypt stood on the verge of a direct conflict aroused by dynastic difficulties in the Hittite royal household. Ironically, a century earlier, Babylon and Egypt had enjoyed excellent relations precisely because there was no real potential for direct conflict, and thus the Babylonian king Burnaburiash had unadvisedly promised continued peace to Amenophis III (Moran 1992: 12). Unadvisedly, because, at that time, the Egyptians apparently permitted Babylonian merchants to be murdered and robbed in their domains (Moran 1992: 16–17). However, in neither case did actual conflict ensue. In the earlier case, it was probably because the root of the problem was not viewed as sufficiently serious, and in the later case because the situation became even more serious.

In the event, Shalmaneser I of Assyria simply eliminated what was left of Mitanni and incorporated it into the Assyrian empire, with the result that Hatti would soon find itself facing the same Tukulti-Ninurta of Assyria who would also menace Babylon. It is no surprise that the changing international situation allowed Ramesses II to pull off a peace treaty with the Hittites despite the defeat at the battle of Qadesh.

A period of peace ensued for the Egyptians, but the eastern Mediterranean was beginning to get restless. The first indications of the Peoples of the Sea can be seen in the sword-bearing Sherden who stood on Ramesses' side at the battle of Kadesh, but they were merely the first hints of the coming waves which would strike at Egypt and the Levantine coast from the reign of Merneptah onwards.

Assyrian operations in northern Syria continued to menace the Hittites, but events in the Levant meant that the Hittites were so weakened that Tukulti-Ninurta I was able to turn his attention back to Babylon. While the Peoples of the Sea kept the Egyptians, the Levantine states and the Hittites occupied, the Elamites were able to pillage Babylon several times. Since Tukulti-Ninurta I was continuously campaigning in both Syria and in areas to the east of the Tigris, this inevitably led to conflict between the Elamites and the Assyrians, both directly, and indirectly through the Assyrian appointed kings in Babylonia.

Thus far we can assert that the direct links between Babylon and Egypt were not the most important aspect of the relationship between the two countries. Instead, it was the regional policies of Egypt in Syria that had an impact on Babylonian activity. The Babylonians and the Egyptians were each conscious of the existence and importance of the other, but the relationship between them was nowhere near as important as the repercussions of Egyptian policy on Babylonian policy.

THE IRON AGE

The situation changed radically in the first millennium BC when Egypt ceased to be an independent power in world affairs. Before the end of the Bronze Age, the Egyptians were retreating out of Nubia and abandoning Palestine. Henceforth, it would be the Egyptians who would be responding to changes in the international environment. For several centuries Egypt would be irrelevant to the constant conflict between Assyria, Babylonia and Elam. The Babylonian respite at the beginning of the Iron Age was due to the power vacuum created by the collapse of Egyptian power. The Aramean and Neo-Hittite states of Syria managed to place the Assyrians on the defensive as well, with the result that, rather than expanding south along the Levantine coast after the reign of Tiglath-Pileser I, the Assyrians were making treaties with the Babylonians and trying to defend their own territory. It would be centuries before the Assyrians would renew their expansion, but this did not benefit the Babylonians since they were under pressure from the Arameans as well.

Once the Assyrians were gradually able to overcome the Arameans and the Neo-Hittites, Babylonia and Elam followed into the Assyrian fold as well – quite aside from Egypt. The two invasions of Egypt were followed by a hasty withdrawal, forced by a conflict with Assurbanipal's brother in Babylon. Paradoxically, Assurbanipal freed himself for expansion against Elam and Urartu when his Saite vassals established their own dynasty. However, by the time that Esarhaddon had conquered Egypt, the Assyrians were overstretching themselves. Although it effectively liberated Egypt from foreign domination, and thus left Assyria a free hand to the East, the Assyrian empire's growth had exposed it to the growing enmity of the Medes.

Making common cause with the Medes, the Babylonians were able to contest Assyrian power. In one of the most bizarre episodes of Egyptian history, this encouraged the Egyptian pharaohs – who had been vassals of the Assyrians after the devastations of Esarhaddon and Assurbanipal – to sweep into Syria. Whereas reaching the Euphrates had been the highpoint of the campaigns of Thutmosis I and Thutmosis III, this venture marked the end of Egypt's history as an independent power, since after the defeat at Carchemish, Egyptian armies would never again sally forth. Ironically therefore, the only time that Egypt and Babylon came into direct conflict can be directly related to Egyptian efforts to defend their former invaders against rivals in Mesopotamia. The situation was, however, far more complicated.

Initially, when Assurbanipal withdrew from Egypt, his vassal Psammetichus I became the glorious ruler who marked the beginning of the final blossoming of Egypt. The 'Late Period' therefore begins with the withdrawal of Assurbanipal, who was compelled to return to Mesopotamia to deal with a civil war. A dozen years after the withdrawal, Shamash-shumu-ukin (Assurbanipal's brother whom he had placed on the throne in 668 BC) called upon the aid of Psammetichus in his conflict with his brother, the king of Assyria. The Egyptians do not appear to have been able to offer any help, and Shamash-shun-ukin lost power and life in 648 BC.

Assurbanipal was thus able to reassert control over most of the Near East, and to rely on Egyptian support, although the Assyrians no longer occupied the country. It was during this period that Assurbanipal's armies were thus able to move against Elam and Urartu, subduing the last enemies in those directions. However, this awakened the opposition of the Medes, who allied with the Babylonians to oppose Assyria. After the defeats in Assyria (614–612 BC), the Assyrian capital was briefly moved to Harran, and the Egyptian army moved up to the Euphrates to support the last Assyrian king, Assur-Uballit. Nabopolassar of Babylon defeated these Egyptian units in 609, but seemingly did not inflict a decisive defeat, since after a second action in 607, he was obliged to abandon the west bank of the Euphrates.

In 605, Nebuchadrezzar II finally managed to defeat the Egyptians at Carchemish and began an advance towards Egypt. Taking Ashqelon in 604, he reached the Egyptian border in 601, but Necho II was prepared and Nebuchadrezzar's assault was followed by a series of defeats culminating in the final action in 599. Henceforth, the Babylonians maintained control of Syria and Palestine, but were unable to approach Egypt.

This stand-off was terminated by the Persian conquest of Babylon itself, rapidly followed by the conquest of Egypt itself by Cambyses. Western interest in the Persians begins with the subsequent unsuccessful efforts to conquer Greece, but Greece also played a role in the Egyptian relationship to the Persians. During the early decades of the fifth century, the Greeks managed to ward off the Persian assaults, but during the final decades of the century, the Persians were able to manipulate Greek politics due to the Peloponnesian War. With the end of that war (404 BC), unemployed Greek mercenaries began to interfere in Persian politics. Although the campaign of the 10,000 described by Xenophon represented a defeat on the ground, the Persians were visibly weakened as Egypt regained its independence at this same point.

The end of the Murashu archive in Babylonia can be related to the end of the various archives at this same time (Waerzeggers 2003/2004), but it can also be related to the fact that the archive was partially related to the activities of the Persian governor of Egypt, who lost his official role with the appearance of Egyptian independence. Thus, one can trace the impact of Egyptian history in Babylonia, but this was not the crucial issue.

Thus Egyptian independence was a by-product of the end of the Peloponnesian War and its maintenance was dependent upon tensions between Greeks and Persians; the Persians were able to recover Egypt after Philip II of Macedonia made peace with the Achaemenids. In effect, during the Iron Age, Egyptian policy and independence were mere relics contingent on Greek politics and bore no relation to Egyptian strength or Persian weakness.

ANCIENT EMPIRES: GEOGRAPHICAL AND INTELLECTUAL

There were historical differences which determined that, in the Bronze Age, Egyptian activity in the Levant had an impact on Babylonian policy whereas, in the Iron Age, Egypt was responding to events abroad. These historical differences reflect the growth and decline of Egyptian power more than anything else.

There is, however, another phenomenon unrelated to Egyptian power which created the fundamental differences between the empires of the Bronze and Iron Ages. This lay in Mesopotamia itself where power structures were subject to constant revision and renegotiation. Egypt was a land with clear boundaries, defined by geography: the cataracts in the south, the Mediterranean Sea in the north, the deserts to the east and west. The lines of the Nile Valley – demarcated by the mountains and the deserts to the east and west – were very much both the highway and the public space of ancient Egypt.

The situation was quite different in Mesopotamia. Whereas Egypt was the Nile, Mesopotamia not only was not the two rivers, but it was not really even the land between the two rivers. It is difficult for a modern observer to understand that the Diyala and the Hamrin were essential arteries of the Mesopotamian world, precisely because they were actually outside of it. Travel between southern and northern Mesopotamia depended upon leaving the rivers and moving along the foothills of the Zagros. And the first part of the trip to the north meant proceeding along the Diyala which thus actually entailed setting off along one of the major international routes. The cities along this route – Eshnunna and the others – were both essential parts of the Babylonian world and also the gateways to the routes leading on to Iran and Central Asia. In the same fashion, following the Euphrates into Syria meant that the river would take one outside of what we consider to be the 'Mesopotamian' world, although strictly speaking more 'Mesopotamian' than the Hamrin and Diyala. Obviously the same types of arguments could be applied to both the Gulf and Assyria, as each of these regions simply lacks any clear boundaries and any clear, easily recognisable regions which developed an identity.

The result of these structures was permeable borders, and thus constant contact. Socially, it meant that the constant exchanges between the rural and urban areas were complemented by the movements of traders and nomads. Above, we noted that the stimulation of this contact contributed to the intellectual development of Babylonia.

The defensive responses necessary when surrounded by neighbours assured that political developments in Mesopotamia differed quite remarkably from the experience in Egypt. Each of the individual states in Mesopotamia was in constant conflict: survival alone depended upon constant defence; expansion was the logical corollary, but such expansion always awakened competition, and thus periods of expansion were short-lived. Neither the Akkadian empire of the third millennium nor the Assyrian empire of the first lasted more than a few centuries. The regions controlled by these empires had very different borders, and both were brought to a swift end – as was also the case for the geographically different, and even shorter-lived, empire of Samsi-Addu of Assyria.

By contrast, the Egyptian state reveals a remarkable continuity. The same borders were repeatedly re-established rapidly after each collapse, and even the periods of decline lasted well over a century each at the end of the Old, Middle and New Kingdoms. By contrast, the Egyptians never managed to penetrate deeply into the lands of their neighbours (with the exception of Nubia, which was not really even a state, let alone an empire).

The Egyptian capacity to expand was limited when the Egyptians came into contact with neighbours, whereas the neighbours were the very source of the resilient defence of identity in Mesopotamia. Constant struggle against neighbours meant that when they were finally overcome, the empires would expand; a development which was not impeded by the absence of easily recognised boundaries. Obviously, the fact that the routes across the mountains and the deserts merged seamlessly into the local communications system of Mesopotamia (as, for example, the Euphrates, the Diyala and the Hamrin) was an essential feature of the Assyrian empire, but on a minor scale this fact played a key role throughout Mesopotamian history. At the same time, it left the borders undefined by geography with the result that a withdrawal to defined limits was likewise excluded.

There are two issues involved in the construction of the empires: one is that of the trade routes which moved materials from the Mediterranean and Anatolia to Meso-potamia; the other is the geographical space of Syria through which the Euphrates flowed. The occupation of Syria was the main issue throughout the Bronze Age, and this geographical issue lay at the centre of the wars of the great Bronze Age warriors (e.g., Naram-Sin, Samsi-Addu, Thutmosis III, Tukulti-Ninurta) who came into conflict with those regions (e.g., Ebla, Aleppo, Mitanni) that were able to create major states in the region.

There were certainly two complementary and related aspects of Bronze Age geo-politics which differed from the situation of the Iron Age. One was the absence of central power in Syria. The other was the balance of power which prevailed because of the simultaneous existence of the other powers. During the early part of the second half of the second millennium, Elam, Babylon, Assyria, Mitanni, Hatti and Egypt were all major powers and all were in competition. A single movement by one power could not destabilise the situation, because the others responded in a flexible fashion, actually taking the other powers into account.

The situation was strikingly different in the Iron Age. Not only was there no major power in Syria, but the major power of the Bronze Age, Egypt, was marginalised, partially by fatigue and partially by internal divisions. The result was a power vacuum in Anatolia and Syria with no major power in the north-eastern corner of Africa able to move forcefully into the gap. The political situation of the Late Bronze Age had been created by the Egyptian kings Thutmosis I, Thutmosis III and Amenophis II, as their efforts had created the basis for the competition between Egypt, Mitanni and Hatti, with repercussions in Babylon and Assyria.

Therefore, the absence of major states in Iron Age Syria and Egypt opened the way for the larger empires. It is thus highly probable that the small states scattered across western Asia at the end of the Bronze Age actually facilitated the growth of the Assyrian empire. Lamprichs (1995) has argued that the Assyrian empire was built on networks which had existed since the dawn of the Bronze Age. Once the Assyrians overcame their initial setbacks, the fragmentary power structures of the scattered states were easily defeated. The adoption of a ruthless policy of expansion meant that the networks served imperial purposes. At this point, the incapacity to resist became the mirror image of the former independence, and the networks allowed Nabopolassar, Darius and Alexander to follow in the tracks of the Assyrians. The same conditions that had facilitated the Assyrian expansion forced other powers to supplant the Assyrians and to expand to similar levels. It was precisely the lack of competing empires that meant that one succeeded the other. The alternative to expansion was defeat; the multitude of conflicts in the Late Bronze Age had given way to the control of empires. Thus the transformation of the system of empire in the Iron Age was historically contingent, related to power structures and trade links rather than technology or iron.

The most ironic event in Mesopotamian history was the establishment of the final capital at Harran, far from the Assyrian homeland. This was only possible because the Assyrian empire had been incorporated into the trade routes and thus Syria (rather than the reverse).

Such a possibility was inconceivable for Egypt. In Egypt, the local identity was sufficient to survive foreign occupation, and also sufficiently arrogant to avoid conflict. Whereas the Hittites simply destroyed Mitanni, the Egyptians accepted it as a kind of limit on their expansion. Whereas the Assyrian and Babylonian empires disappeared without a trace when finally conquered, the Egyptian empire continued to exist as a mind-set which obliged Greek kings and Roman emperors to behave like Egyptians. This mind-set was also transferred into the Roman Empire in the form of such activities as the Isis cult – but here the meaning of the cult was transformed once it was out of the reach of the Egyptians. This was, at least partially, because the means by which the Egyptians expressed their ideas were both ideologically and intellectually quite different from the rest of the world – and again the explanation lies at least partially in those borders.

As noted, the rest of the world adopted the Mesopotamian cuneiform writing system and, indeed, a form of the Semitic Babylonian language – even the Egyptians, and even for some of their own internal correspondence concerning Syria. Real Egyptian thought was expressed in a different language and a different form of writing which were basically inaccessible to the rest of the ancient world, and the Egyptians saw no reason for others to master the system. At the same time, the intellectual experience of verbal discourse, which was the ordinary means of communication in the rest of the ancient world, was not the sole avenue accessible to the Egyptians. Like the other great civilisations of antiquity, they used art and architecture to convey messages, but they relied far more heavily on the principle in general, and even in their written language – and it was thus inevitable that such messages would not be understood by those who were not participants. Thus Egyptian communication was not based upon discourse, but upon understanding by the initiated. Where they cared to dictate, they did; elsewhere they were not concerned. Greek and Semitic communication, by contrast, was based on discourse and communication: even the imagery was intended to convey easily understandable messages. The result is that very few traces of Egyptian thought ever penetrated into other systems of thought whereas traces of Babylonian astronomy survived in Greek science and traces of Babylonian myth survived in the Christian religion (to mention but two examples).

The boundaries of ancient Egypt were not effective at keeping others out (as demonstrated by the invasions of the Hyksos, the Sea Peoples, the Libyans, the Nubians, the Assyrians, the Persians, the Greeks, the Romans, and the Arabs), but they were effective at providing an incubation chamber in which ideas could be nurtured. However, those ideas were not destined for a long life once they slipped across the borders – even if the visual forms remained attractive, the Egyptian content was usually lost.

The frailty of the unprotected Egyptian ideas must be set beside the resilience of Babylonian thought, and placed in the context of the political environments in which these flourished. Nor indeed, however, can the frailty of the Babylonian temples be compared with the durability of the Egyptian tombs. The power and durability of the Egyptian empire differed fundamentally in every way from the power and durability of the Mesopotamian kingdoms.

CONCLUSIONS:
HISTORICAL AND ANALYTICAL

During the Bronze Age several empires shared the stage and none succeeded in the type of hegemony that characterised the enormous empires of the Iron Age. During the Bronze Age, Egypt may have been unsuccessful in a policy of expansion in Western Asia, but it was the greatest power, and Egyptian activity had an influence throughout the Near East. During the Iron Age, by contrast, Egypt was a marginal entity, and the Egyptians were largely reduced to reacting to the movements of others. For Babylon this meant that in the Bronze Age there was little direct activity linking the two powers, while the direct contact between Egypt and Babylonia in the Iron Age was almost peripheral for both.

Until the collapse of the Indus Civilisation in the east, Elam had been exposed to a threat on its eastern flank as well as the Mesopotamian threat on its western flank. With Assyria weakened and the Indus gone, the Elamites posed a threat to Babylon, and thus diminished any potential Babylonian threat to the Hittites. Therefore, although there was no direct connection between Hatti and Elam, Elamite activity did have an influence on Babylonia activity vis-à-vis Mitanni and Assyria.

Certainly, there can be no doubt about the fate of Babylon, which was sacked by the Elamites shortly after Hatti was eliminated: the Elamite sack of Babylon coincided with the period of Assyrian weakness that preceded the expansion under Tukulti-Ninurta I towards the west. Evidently, the forces that eliminated Babylon will have freed the Assyrians to move towards the coast. With the Assyrians occupied at the Mediterranean, the Babylonian renaissance was thus initiated with the conquest of Elam. This era also coincided with the debut of a millennium of conflict during which the Assyrians would repeatedly destroy Babylon.

Although the Mycenean states at Ephesus and Miletus were less important to the other major states of the Near East, they were decisive for the kings of Hatti, and also to Egypt because of the conflict with Hatti. In the same way, the Elamites were relevant to Hatti because of their conflict with Babylon, but they never left the slightest conscious impression on Egypt. Effectively, however, the actions of each of these actors was partially determined by the others, i.e., the Myceneans, the Hittites, the Egyptians, the Mitannians, the Assyrians, the Babylonians and the Elamites.

It is easier to understand the lack of Babylonian interventions in Western Asian politics by referring to Elam, which was threatening Babylon from the East. In this sense, the Babylonian concern with Elam was the mirror image of the Egyptian interest in Nubia. Thus one could not anticipate direct conflict of interest. And yet such did emerge – along the Euphrates in the Iron Age. Strangely enough, however, even the actual direct encounters between the Egyptians and the Babylonians were not actually a reflection of a direct relationship. Although the Egyptians did lose the battles of the Euphrates to the Babylonians, this took place as part of a misguided Egyptian attempt to shore up the Assyrians, and did not reflect a fundamental hostility to Babylon. Thus, one could logically propose that distance imposed some form of perception of interests that permitted logistical issues to determine policy, but it was the perception of interests, not the logistic obstacles, as demonstrated by the campaigns of Naram-Sin and Shuppiluliuma.

Thus, via the Elamites and the Mycenaeans, we return to Egypt. Confronted with the powers of Western Asia, the Egyptians preferred the course of least resistance and pressed deep into Nubia. On the one hand, the lack of serious adversaries left the Egyptians a free hand – and on the other, the Nubian gold was quite useful when it came to satisfying the greed of rulers in Hatti, Mitanni, Assyria and Babylonia. At the same time, the interaction of their adversaries actually made a defensive policy in Western Asia a rational possibility, and thus a cordon of vassals assured a buffer zone against Mitanni and Hatti. For the Egyptians, the policy brought the added advantage of a stream of brides flowing into the royal harem. This necessarily came to an end with the marauding of the Peoples of the Sea, but the immediate results were more devastating for both Hatti and the Assyrians, rather than Egypt. It was only later, as the Assyrian expansion recommenced, that Egypt would experience the changed environment in which it was no longer the leading actor, but merely one more element in a complicated web.

To some extent, the reign of Tiglath-Pileser I can be identified with the birth of the Iron Age, not merely for chronological reasons, but also because the major actors of the Iron Age can all be identified from this stage onwards: Elam, Assyria and Babylonia. Neither Egypt nor the successor states of Hatti would play roles even remotely comparable to those they had played in the Late Bronze Age. By contrast, Egypt had played the decisive role in the Bronze Age.

It is a peculiar paradox of history that, whereas the memory of Egypt never faded when the empires of Asia were effaced from Western history and Egyptian traditions remained as mere monuments in the landscape, the intellectual traditions of the Ancient Near East lived on.

NOTES

1   The only possible encounter of 'Great Kings' in the Bronze Age known to the current author is the postulated visit of a Hittite king to the Egyptian royal court. It is not certain that the Hittite king Hattushili actually went to Egypt, but he was invited, and he may actually have

set off (cf. Kitchen 1982: 90–91). There have been suggestions that Thutmosis III actually met a Babylonian king after his campaign of 1446 BC, but this is based on several misunderstandings and does not correspond to anything in the Egyptian sources. The Egyptian sources merely suggest that a Mitanni king fled before Thutmosis into the interior of his land (which Thutmosis III did not penetrate), and do not suggest a meeting with either that king or any other.

2   For the chronological debate, cf., e.g., Warburton 2000, 2002, 2004.

3   For the historical details, cf., e.g., Redford 1992, 2003; Warburton 2001, 2003; Warburton and Matthews 2003.

4   References can be found in: *ANET*; Bryan 1991; *CANE*; van den Hout 1994; Kuhrt 1995; Manuelian 1987; Moran 1992; Redford 2003; Warburton 2003; Wilhelm 1982.

REFERENCES

Bryan, B. M. 1991. *The Reign of Tuthmose IV*. Baltimore, MD: Johns Hopkins University Press.

Hout, Th. P. J. van den. 1994. 'Der Falke und das Kücken: der neue Pharao und der hethitische Prinz?', *Zeitschrift für Assyriologie* 84: 60–88.

Kaelin, O. 2006. '*Modell Ägypten' Adoption von Innovationen im Mesopotamien des 3. Jahrtausends v. Chr*. Fribourg: Orbis Biblicus et Orientalis Series Archaeologica 26.

Kitchen, K. A. 1982. *Pharaoh Triumphant*. Warminster: Aris & Phillips.

Kuhrt, A. 1995. *The Ancient Near East. Volume 1*. London: Routledge.

Lamprichs, R. 1995. *Die Westexpansion des neuassyrischen Reiches: eine Struktureanalyse*. Neukirchen-Vluyn: Alter Orient und Altes Testament.

Manuelian, P. der 1987. *Studies in the Reign of Amenophis II*. Hildesheim: Hildesheimer Ägyptologische Beiträge 26.

Moran, W. L. 1992. *The Amarna Letters*. Baltimore, MD: Johns Hopkins University Press.

Podany, A. 1991–1993. 'A Middle Babylonian Date for the Hana Kingdom', *Journal of Cuneiform Studies* 43–45: 53–62.

Redford, D. B. 1992. *Egypt, Canaan, and Israel in Ancient Times*. Princeton, NJ: Princeton University Press.

—— 2003. *The Wars in Syria and Palestine of Thutmose III*. Leiden, Brill. Culture and History of the Ancient Near East 16.

Reiner, E. 'Akkadian Treaties from Syria and Assyria', in *ANET* pp. 531–541.

Waerzeggers, C. 2003/2004. 'The Babylonian Revolts Against Xerxes and the "End of Archives"', *Archiv für Orientforschung* 50: 150–173.

Warburton, D. A. 2000. 'Synchronizing the Chronology of Bronze Age Western Asia with Egypt', *Akkadica* 119–120: 33–76.

—— 2001. *Egypt and the Near East*. Neuchatel: Recherches et Publications, Civilisations du Proche-Orient Serie IV. Histoire – Essais 1.

—— 2002. 'Eclipses, Venus-Cycles & Chronology', *Akkadica* 123: 108–114.

—— 2003. 'Love and War in the Late Bronze Age: Egypt & Hatti', in R. Matthews and C. Roemer (eds), *Ancient Perspectives on Egypt* (London: UCL Press), pp. 75–100.

—— 2004. 'Shamshi-Adad & the Eclipses', in J. G. Dercksen (ed.), *Assyria and Beyond* (Leiden: Nederlands Instituut), pp. 583–598.

—— and R. Matthews. 2003. 'Egypt and Mesopotamia in the Late Bronze and Iron Ages', in R. Matthews and C. Roemer (eds), *Ancient Perspectives on Egypt* (London: UCL Press), pp. 101–113.

Wilhelm, G. 1982. *Grundzüge der Geschichte und Kultur der Hurriter*. Darmstadt: Wissenschaftliche Buchgesellschaft.

Wilson, J. A. 'Egyptian Historical Texts', in *ANET* pp. 227–264.

CHAPTER THIRTY-FIVE

A VIEW FROM HATTUSA

———•◆•———

Trevor Bryce

Around 1595 BC,[1] the Hittite king Mursili I, fresh from his conquest of Aleppo in northern Syria, led his troops east to the Euphrates, and then south along the river to the city of Babylon. He attacked, stormed, plundered, and destroyed the city, taking rich spoils from it and many prisoners-of-war. In military terms, this was a momentous achievement for the ruler of the young kingdom of Hatti, which had emerged in central Anatolia but a few decades earlier. Mursili's predecessors had established the kingdom's dominance over much of eastern Anatolia. And his grandfather Hattusili I, to whose throne he succeeded, had carried Hittite arms through northern Syria across the Euphrates into Mesopotamia. Hattusili boasted that his military triumphs exceeded even those of the great Akkadian king Sargon, whose exploits served as a benchmark for all future warrior-kings. Now, by conquering both Aleppo and Babylon, Mursili had matched, indeed surpassed, all that his grandfather had achieved in the field of battle. His conquests were heralded by later kings as two of the greatest triumphs of early Hittite history.[2]

Very likely, a passage inserted in a Babylonian Chronicle of much later date also refers to Mursili's conquest. It states: 'In the time of Samsuditana, the Hittites marched against Akkad' (*Babylonian Chronicle* 20, line 11, ed. Grayson 1975: 156). Samsuditana was the last ruler of the Old Babylonian Empire. If the Hittite campaign mentioned in the Chronicle is, in fact, the same as that which Mursili conducted against Babylon, then Mursili may well be assigned responsibility for bringing the Old Babylonian Empire to an end. Some scholars, however, have doubts about conflating the Hittite and Babylonian sources. They point out that the Hittite record of Mursili's conquest makes no reference to Samsuditana, and that the Babylonian text dates well after the event to which it refers, and does not mention a specific Hittite king or indicate that Babylon actually fell to the Hittites (see Manning 1999: 357, n. 1579). But it is quite clear from Hittite sources that the Hittites never conducted more than one campaign against Babylon, so that there really is no other event in Babylonian–Hittite history to which the Babylonian Chronicle could refer. We can with some confidence attribute to Mursili not only the fall of Babylon, but simultaneously the *coup de grâce* delivered to the once great dynasty of King Hammurabi.

We have no information about what prompted Mursili's expedition to Babylon. There was certainly no prospect of his establishing any lasting form of Hittite authority

Figure 35.1 The restored ramparts of the Hittite capital Hattusa.
(German Institute of Archaeology, Bogazköy-Hattusa Excavations.)

over conquered territory which lay so far to the south-east of his own homeland.
Particularly in this early period of their history, the Hittites had neither the resources
nor the administrative machinery necessary to fulfil such a prospect. We can only
assume that, flushed with his success against Aleppo, Mursili sought both to enhance
his own reputation as a great warlord, and to provide even greater material rewards
for his troops and his kingdom's royal coffers by despoiling and destroying what had
been one of the greatest and wealthiest cities of the Near Eastern world.

Perhaps he had a strategic motive as well. One of the most serious menaces
confronting his kingdom came from the Hurrian peoples who had spread through
much of northern Mesopotamia and northern Syria, and from there westwards into
Anatolia. They had already threatened the Hittite homeland in the reign of Mursili's
grandfather Hattusili. And on their homeward trek after their conquest of Babylon,
Mursili's troops were harassed by Hurrian forces. It has been suggested that Mursili
made some form of agreement with the Kassites, who were to fill the political vacuum
in Babylonia left by the overthrow of Hammurabi's dynasty by creating a new ruling
dynasty there. Perhaps, the suggestion goes, the Kassites had done a deal with Mursili,
promising him a share of the spoils of Babylon, and possibly also a Kassite alliance
to offset the ever-present threat of Hurrian political and military expansion, both in
Syria and Anatolia (see Gurney 1973: 250). This is a very speculative line of reasoning,
and probably assumes too high a degree of sophistication in the field of international

diplomacy for both Hittites and Kassites alike at this stage of their development. Most likely, Mursili's expedition against Babylon was simply a military adventure, very much in the tradition of the campaigns of destruction and plunder which typified his grandfather's reign.[3]

Mursili was assassinated a few years after his return from Babylon, an event which led to serious, ongoing political fragmentation within the kingdom of Hatti, making it highly vulnerable to enemy invasion. The Hurrians, in particular, exploited this period of weakness in Hatti's history, which lasted 60 years or more, by sweeping across the frontiers of the Hittite homeland and plundering its territories. The kingdom was brought to the brink of annihilation. Yet under an enterprising new king, Telipinu (*c.*1525–1500), Hatti recovered many of its lost territories, and by the early fourteenth century had re-emerged as a major international power. Its interest in re-establishing its influence and authority in northern Syria brought it into direct conflict with the Hurrian kingdom of Mitanni. The showdown between the two great powers finally came during the reign of the Hittite king Suppiluliuma I (*c.*1350–1322). In preparation for this showdown, Suppiluliuma sought to bolster his influence and support in the Syria–Euphrates region by a series of diplomatic initiatives. This provided the context for the reappearance of Babylon in Hittite records. A Kassite ruling dynasty was now firmly established in Babylonia. Suppiluliuma sought to establish close links with this dynasty by negotiating a marriage between himself and the daughter of the king of Babylon. At this time Babylon's throne was occupied by Burnaburiash II, who must therefore have been the bride's father.

Apparently by the terms of the marriage agreement, Suppiluliuma had to recognise the Babylonian as his chief wife – which meant disposing of the chief wife he already had. Her name was Henti. She was the mother of all five of her husband's sons. A fragmentary Hittite text *may* indicate that, to make way for his new wife, Suppiluliuma banished her, perhaps to a place of exile in the Aegean world. The Babylonian bride, whose original name has long been assumed to have been Malnigal (see refs in Bryce 2005: 433 n. 24), took on the new name Tawananna as a personal name. It had previously been used as the title of the reigning Hittite queen. Adopting this name, she was associated with her husband on a number of seal impressions, including several which belong within the context of Suppiluliuma's alliance with the king of Ugarit, Niqmaddu II, an alliance which can be dated to Suppiluliuma's 'First' or 'One-year' Syrian war (*c.*1340).[4] The legend in Akkadian cuneiform reads: 'Seal of Suppiluliuma, the Great King, King of the Land of Hatti, beloved of the Storm God; seal of Tawananna, the Great Queen, Daughter of the King of Babylon'.

Strategic considerations almost certainly lay behind Suppiluliuma's marriage alliance with the Babylonian royal family. Very likely, the marriage took place only a year or so before Suppiluliuma launched his comprehensive military operations against the Mitannian king Tushratta and his subjects and allies in Syria. If this sequence of events is correct, it is difficult not to see a connection between the wedding and the war. But Suppiluliuma may have used his marriage link with Babylon's royal family merely as a means of gaining Burnaburiash's benevolent neutrality, rather than his active military support, during the Hittite showdown with Mitanni. Throughout its history, the Kassite dynasty showed little interest in engaging in military campaigns west of the Euphrates. Further, the marriage union would have strengthened any assurances which Suppiluliuma gave to Burnaburiash that Hittite military operations in the region would not extend into Babylonian territory. Kings do not attack the lands of their fathers-in-law! Suppiluliuma clearly realised the importance of anticipating, and eliminating by diplomatic means, any prospect of a Babylonian alliance with Tushratta. Such an alliance might well have eventuated if Burnaburiash had concerns about Hittite aggression against his own kingdom. Conversely, Burnaburiash may have seen his marriage alliance with Suppiluliuma as providing some assurance of Hittite military support in the event of a Mitannian attack on his own kingdom. Marriage links between ruling dynasties almost certainly indicated the existence of political and/or military agreements between the kingdoms ruled by these dynasties.

Like royal offspring throughout the Near Eastern Bronze Age, and indeed in many ages throughout history, the Babylonian princess was a tool of international diplomacy. Yet unlike the foreign princesses who faded into obscurity in Egypt, this princess who assumed the prestigious and time-honoured title Tawananna as a personal name quickly became one of the most powerful figures in the royal court, and the kingdom of Hatti at large. She was a worthy Bronze Age counterpart to Augustus' Livia – if we can so judge from what her stepson Mursili says about her. Mursili was the second youngest of Suppiluliuma's sons from the marriage of the king's first wife Henti, now banished. On the basis of his reports about Tawananna, we might well say that if Suppiluliuma ruled the Hittite world, Tawananna ruled Suppiluliuma. Her high profile on the international scene already very early in her marriage is indicated by the appearance of her name next to her husband's on the document formalising Suppiluliuma's alliance with the Ugaritic king Niqmaddu. And in Suppiluliuma's later years, her influence and power in the kingdom's internal affairs became ever greater, no doubt due in part to her husband's constant absences from the homeland on military campaigns.

Mursili complains of her domineering behaviour and extravagance, and her introduction of undesirable foreign customs into the Hittite kingdom (see Bryce 2005: 207–10). Whether he or his elder brother, the crown prince Arnuwanda, ever expressed concerns to their father about her conduct remains unknown. But if they did, Suppiluliuma may have been too preoccupied with military affairs, or too much under his Babylonian wife's influence, to pay much attention. And after her husband's death of plague, *c.*1322, Tawananna continued as reigning queen, in accordance with Hittite tradition whereby a king's chief wife retained her position throughout her life, even if her husband predeceased her. Her alleged abuse of power continued, according to Mursili. She allegedly stripped the palace of its treasures to lavish on her favourites, or to bribe those whose support she sought. And her office as chief priestess of the realm with its powers of allocating sacrifices, votive offerings, perhaps even temple lands, allowed her to control and exploit in her own interests assets of the state cult.

Mursili and his brother Arnuwanda, whom Mursili succeeded (as Mursili II) when he died after a very brief reign, were apparently powerless, or at least unwilling, to stop her. As Mursili informs us in one of his prayers:

> But when my father became a god, Arnuwanda, my brother, and I did no harm to Tawananna, nor in any way humiliated her. As she governed the house of the king and the Land of Hatti in the lifetime of my father, likewise in the lifetime of my brother she governed them. And when my brother became a god, I did

no evil to Tawananna, nor in any way humiliated her. As she governed the house of the king and the Land of Hatti in the lifetime of my father and of my brother, likewise then she governed them. And the customs which in the lifetime of her husband [were dear to her heart(?)] and the things which in the lifetime of her husband were forbidden to her, [to these I made no changes?][5]

In spite of his complaints and deeply held concerns, Mursili, far from taking action against his stepmother, continued to recognise her status as reigning queen by associating her name with his on royal seals. The final straw came when the young king's wife Gassulawiya fell ill and died. Mursili was grief-stricken. He held his stepmother responsible for the tragedy, convinced that she had brought about Gassulawiya's death through black magic. Perhaps he was right. Tawananna may have begun to suspect that her days as reigning queen were numbered. Gassulawiya's name had begun to appear alongside her husband's in a number of seal impressions – very likely an indication that Mursili was elevating her to the status of reigning queen in place of his stepmother. This may well have been motive enough for Tawananna to eliminate her. Oracular consultation by Mursili allegedly proved Tawananna's guilt, determined that her offence was a capital crime, and sanctioned her execution. But Mursili shrank from inflicting the extreme penalty. Instead, he stripped Tawananna of all her offices, and banished her from the capital, sentencing her to permanent exile in a remote place, but in comfortable conditions.

Personal scruples may have led Mursili to decide not to execute the queen, despite having allegedly received a go-ahead from the gods to do so. Even the justification for her banishment was later questioned by Mursili's son Hattusili. But the decision not to inflict the death penalty may have been influenced primarily by political considerations. Indeed, such considerations may well explain why Tawananna's conduct was tolerated so long after her husband's death. She was, after all, a princess of Babylon. And while foreign kings had no hesitation in using their daughters as chattels on the royal marriage market, they also showed concern on a number of occasions about the welfare of their daughters in the courts of their husbands. Suspected mistreatment of a princess was cause for serious complaint. The execution of a princess would almost certainly have led to a major rift, or even a complete severing of relations, between two kingdoms.

Mursili must have been anxious to maintain good relations with Babylon, especially at this time. For he now faced major problems throughout his kingdom. Among the most serious were the dangers posed to his territories in Syria by a hostile Egypt to the south, and the looming menace, across the Euphrates, of the re-emerging kingdom of Assyria – rapidly filling the power vacuum left by Suppiluliuma's destruction of the kingdom of Mitanni. Babylon, the other Great Kingdom in the region, needed to be kept on side. The sacking and banishment of Tawananna would inevitably have put a strain on Hittite–Babylonian relations. But at least the queen's life had been spared, and a diplomatic mission sent to the Babylonians with the intention of explaining and justifying the action taken against their princess might help limit diplomatic fallout over the affair. That would almost certainly have been impossible if Tawananna had been put to death. If only to maintain a veneer of friendly relations with Babylon, she had to be allowed to live.

But for the remainder of Mursili's reign, and that of his son and successor Muwattalli (II), attention in the Syria-Palestine region focused on the escalating tensions between Hatti and Egypt. These culminated in the battle of Kadesh, fought between Muwattalli and the pharaoh Ramesses II in 1274. Though the battle itself ended in a stalemate, the Hittites subsequently pushed Ramesses' forces back to the region around Damascus, where a frontier was established between Hittite and Egyptian subject territories. Even so, tensions between the two kingdoms continued for the rest of Muwattalli's reign, and probably through the reign of Muwattalli's son and successor Urhi-Teshub. The latter occupied his kingdom's throne for only a few years before he was over-thrown and replaced by his uncle Hattusili (III), *c*.1267. Banished to the Nuhashshi lands in Syria, Urhi-Teshub made approaches to foreign kings for support in his bid to reclaim his throne. Hattusili tells us of his secret plans to travel to Babylon (Karaduniya), perhaps after preliminary negotiations with Babylonian officials in Syria, and presumably to make a direct appeal to the Babylonian king, Kadashman-Turgu at that time. But the exile's plans were discovered, and Hattusili promptly had him removed to another place of exile, whence he escaped and fled to Egypt. Ramesses' alleged refusal to extradite him back to Hatti fanned afresh the still smouldering tensions between Hatti and Egypt.

It is not unlikely that Urhi-Teshub's plans to visit Babylon were made known to Hattusili by Kadashman-Turgu himself. Hattusili claims, in a letter to this king's son and successor Kadashman-Enlil II (transl. Beckman 1999: 138–43), that he enjoyed a warm relationship with the father. His cultivation of this relationship may have been one of the reasons why he distanced himself from his own father's action in sacking and banishing the Babylonian princess Tawananna. Without going so far as to denounce this action, he seriously questioned its legality – by implication endorsing Tawananna's right to continue as the reigning queen during his father's reign. Admittedly, he does this in the context of a prayer to the Sun Goddess (see Singer 2002: 97–9). But Hattusili was above all an astute and opportunistic politician. He would not have hesitated to make his views more widely known if he felt he could derive political capital from them, particularly in the Babylonian court.

Hattusili must have set great store by his warm relations with Kadashman-Turgu, since initially the Babylonian king appears to have been the only foreign ruler to acknowledge Hattusili as Hatti's legitimate monarch. The seizure of the Hittite throne by Hattusili had been blatantly illegal. It had caused major divisions among the king's own subjects, many of whom still supported Urhi-Teshub. Moreover, by granting Urhi-Teshub asylum in his own country, Ramesses too seemed to acknowledge him as the rightful king of Hatti. This infuriated and frightened Hattusili. As long as Urhi-Teshub remained at large, and had the apparent support of the pharaoh, the usurper's position on the Hittite throne would never be secure. Hence the importance Hattusili must have attached to his relationship with Kadashman-Turgu, and to the endorsement which Kadashman-Turgu gave him. Not only did Hattusili succeed in winning acknowledgement from him as Hatti's legitimate king, he apparently also persuaded his Babylonian 'royal brother' to sever relations with Egypt. Indeed, it appears from Hattusili's letter that Kadashman-Turgu had even agreed to give him military support should he decide to march on Egypt in order to get Urhi-Teshub back: '[If your troops] go against Egypt, then I will go with you. [If] you go [against Egypt, I will send you] such infantry and chariotry as I have available to go.' (This and the following excerpts from Hattusili's letter to Kadashman-Enlil are translated by Beckman 1999: 138–43.)

The claims that Hattusili makes about Kadashman-Turgu in his letter seem extraordinary. On the face of it, there is absolutely no reason why Babylon, which had a long history of good relations with Egypt, should now terminate these because the pharaoh had allegedly refused to give up the legitimate king of Hatti to the man who had illegally seized his throne. Also, the promise of sending Babylonian troops across the Euphrates would have been, to the best of our knowledge, totally without precedent in the history of Kassite Babylon's dealings with any of its Late Bronze Age contemporaries. Yet Hattusili could hardly have invented or even exaggerated what he reports Kadashman-Turgu as saying. We cannot check the truth for ourselves since the letter in which Kadashman-Turgu purportedly made the statements attributed to him is now lost to us. But a copy of the letter would certainly have been filed in the royal archives in Babylon, and preserved during at least the early part of Kadashman-Enlil's reign. Its contents could easily have been checked against Hattusili's claims, as Hattusili well knew. In referring to a letter which he wrote to Kadashman-Turgu, Hattusili says to his son: 'Now are none of those scribes still living? Are the tablets not filed? Let them read those tablets to you now.' There was undoubtedly a dossier of Hittite–Babylonian correspondence in the Babylonian as well as in the Hittite capital which could readily be consulted to verify Hattusili's statements.

Almost certainly Kadashman-Turgu did give the undertakings Hattusili attributes to him – within the terms of a treaty drawn up between the two kings. The treaty is referred to early in Hattusili's letter to Kadashman-Enlil. Kadashman-Turgu's willingness to conclude such a treaty may well have been prompted, at least in part, by what we might call the Assyrian factor. Already in the mid-fourteenth century, Burnaburiash II had written to Akhenaten expressing concern about the resurgence of Assyria, under its king Ashur-uballit, in the wake of the destruction of the Mitannian empire. Henceforth, sporadic conflict interspersed with periods of uneasy peace marked the relationship between Babylon and Assyria. In the first half of the thirteenth century, tensions may have abated for a time when the Assyrian king Adad-nirari I (c.1295–1264) reached agreement with his Babylonian counterpart over the boundaries separating the two kingdoms. But the peace remained tenuous. And Kadashman-Turgu may well have seen a new alliance with Hatti, whose eastern frontiers abutted Assyrian subject territory across the Euphrates, as a means of keeping Assyria in check. Hattusili had acquired a formidable military reputation, both in Syria as well as in his own homeland, and had most recently triumphed in the field of battle over his nephew Urhi-Teshub. A calculated decision by Kadashman-Turgu to support his claim to the throne, and to conclude a treaty of alliance with him, could prove to be in Babylon's best interests, particularly in view of the Assyrian factor. Termination of Babylon's friendly relations with Egypt may have been the price that Kadashman-Turgu had to pay for his alliance with Hattusili. But that was part of the calculation. Egypt was nowhere near as well placed as Hatti for providing Babylon with support against Assyrian aggression. Pragmatic considerations favoured giving priority to an alliance with Hatti over ongoing peaceful relations with Egypt – at least in the short term.

But within a year or so of his agreement with Hattusili, Kadashman-Turgu died, and was succeeded by his son Kadashman-Enlil II, who quickly restored diplomatic relations with Egypt. Hattusili was angered and frustrated by the news. There was an acrimonious exchange of correspondence between the Hittite and Babylonian royal courts. The Babylonian vizier Itti-Marduk-balatu accused Hattusili of treating the Babylonians as inferiors: 'You do not write to us like a brother. You pressure us as if we were your subjects.' (Ironically, Hattusili was later to accuse the pharaoh Ramesses of much the same thing.) This accusation is quoted by Hattusili in the still surviving letter which he wrote to Kadashman-Enlil. We have already referred several times to this letter. It is one of the longest and best preserved of all pieces of correspondence to have survived from the archives of the Late Bronze Age Near Eastern world, and provides us with one of our most important sources of information on Babylonian–Hittite relations. In fact what we have is not the actual letter received by the Babylonian king, but a copy of it, perhaps just a draft, which was unearthed in the archives of the Hittite capital Hattusa.

Hattusili refers in his letter to other grievances about which Kadashman-Enlil had written. The latter complained that Babylonian merchants had been murdered while travelling through Hittite subject territory in Syria, and that no attempt had been made to bring their murderers to justice. He also spoke of constant harassment of Babylonian merchants by Benteshina, Hattusili's protégé and vassal ruler of the western Syrian kingdom called Amurru. A further grievance was Hattusili's failure to send back to Babylon a physician who had been sent to the Hittite court on loan. This was in fact the second physician lent to Hattusa in recent times who had failed to return home.

Hattusili's letter is in part a response to these complaints. He also takes his correspondent to task for ending diplomatic communications with Hatti. Kadashman-Enlil had ceased the practice of sending 'messengers', probably meaning diplomatic missions, to the Hittite court. Hattusili contemptuously dismisses Kadashman-Enlil's excuse that the termination of this service is due to attacks on the messengers by hostile Aramean Ahlamu tribesmen, and the refusal by Assyria to allow the messengers permission to travel through Assyrian territory:

> How can this be, that you, my brother, have cut off your messengers on account of the Ahlamu? Is the might of your kingdom small, my brother? . . . What is the King of Assyria who holds back your messenger [while my messengers] cross repeatedly? Does the King of Assyria hold back your messengers so that you, [my brother], cannot cross [to] my [land]?

Hattusili suggests that the real reason for the break in Babylon's diplomatic links with Hatti lies much closer to home: 'Has perhaps Itti-Marduk-balatu spoken unfavourable words before my brother, so that my brother has cut off the messengers?' This was the nub of the matter, to Hattusili's way of thinking: Kadashman-Enlil has been led astray by his evil counsellor, the pro-Assyrian anti-Hittite Itti-Marduk-balatu, an *eminence grise* 'whom the gods have caused to live far too long, and in whose mouth unfavourable words never cease'.

Yet, by and large, the letter is written in a conciliatory tone. Hattusili's main purpose is to renew with the son the close bonds he had enjoyed with the father: 'When your father and I established friendly relations and became loving brothers, we did not become brothers for a single day. Did we not establish brotherhood and friendly relations forever?' In the spirit of reconciliation, Hattusili excuses Kadashman-

Enlil's failure to respond to his earlier declarations of friendship and support: 'But my brother was a child in those days, and they did not read out the tablets in your presence.' And in responding to the young king's complaints, he assures him that the murderers of the Babylonian merchants will be brought to account, in accordance with the Hittite system of justice, and that an investigation of his complaint against Benteshina is already under way. He does, however, mention that Benteshina claims that his action against the Babylonians was prompted by their failure to repay a debt of three talents of silver. Nevertheless:

> If my brother does not believe this, let his servant who heard Benteshina when he continually cursed the land of my brother come here and oppose him in court. And I will put pressure on Benteshina. Benteshina is my subject. If he has cursed my brother, has he not cursed me too?

The matter of the physician who failed to return to Babylon was a cause of some embarrassment to Hattusili, particularly since an earlier Babylonian physician on loan to the Hittite court during Muwattalli's reign had been bribed to remain in the land of his hosts; he had been given a fine house in the Hittite capital and married to a member of the royal family. The second physician sent by Kadashman-Enlil to Hattusili's court had also remained in Hatti. But that was because he had fallen ill and died there. In response to his royal brother's suspicions and protests, Hattusili declared that everything had been done for the physician in his illness; he had, moreover, been held in high regard in the Hittite land for all that he had accomplished there, and been rewarded with lavish gifts in recognition of this. These gifts were all carefully recorded, and the tablet on which they were recorded, along with the gifts themselves, would be sent to Babylon to verify what Hattusili had written.

In spite of the embarrassment over the two physicians, Hattusili showed no hesitation in asking his royal brother for the services of another skilled craftsman: he wanted to have some statues made, to be set up in the royal family's quarters. Could Kadashman-Enlil please send him a sculptor to do the job? The request was accompanied by an assurance that the sculptor would be sent back home as soon as the job was finished.

We do not know what response, if any, Hattusili received from Kadashman-Enlil to his long letter. But henceforth Babylon rates scarcely a mention in texts relating to the Hittite world. With the conclusion of the famous treaty between Hattusili III and Ramesses II in 1259, Hatti's problems with Egypt, referred to in Hattusili's correspondence with both Kadashman-Turgu and Kadashman-Enlil, were considerably diminished. And if Kadashman-Turgu's treaty with Hattusili was ever renewed, either between Hattusili and Kadashman-Enlil, or between later Hittite and Babylonian kings, we have no indication that it was ever put into effect. Certainly the Hittite king Tudhaliya IV, son and successor of Hattusili, made no call on Babylonian support when he clashed with the Assyrians in the battle of Nihriya (c.1230) in northern Mesopotamia – and was resoundingly defeated by them.

Indirectly, however, Babylon may have saved Hittite territories in Syria from the ravages of the Assyrian forces after their triumph at Nihriya. An invasion of these territories by the victorious Assyrian king Tukulti-Ninurta now seemed imminent. Instead, Tukulti-Ninurta turned his attention southwards – against Babylon. Whether or not his decision was prompted by an attack on his own lands by the Babylonian king Kashtiliash IV, Tukulti-Ninurta may have taken the view that he should secure his southern boundaries before venturing upon a major campaign across the Euphrates. Though he won a decisive victory over the Babylonians, and followed it up by incorporating Babylonian territory into his own, his subsequent attempts to hold his expanded empire together severely overtaxed his resources. His armies suffered several defeats, and he himself eventually fell victim to assassination. For the remaining years of its existence, Hatti and its subject territories were no longer threatened by the Assyrian menace, thanks largely to Tukulti-Ninurta's decision to follow up his victory against the Hittites at Nihriya by invading his southern neighbour, the kingdom of Babylon, rather than his western neighbour, the kingdom of Hatti.

While, in a strategic sense, Hatti may have occasionally benefited from its diplomatic links with Babylon, the benefits which it derived from cultural contacts with Babylonian civilisation were far more lasting and pervasive. These contacts extended back to the seventeenth century, the first century of the Hittite kingdom. After literacy in Anatolia disappeared with the Assyrian merchants at the end of the Assyrian Colony period (mid-eighteenth century), the cuneiform script was introduced afresh into the early Hittite kingdom, probably by Babylonian scribes hired or abducted in the course of Hittite campaigns in Syria and western Mesopotamia. These campaigns culminated in the destruction of Babylon by Mursili. Almost certainly, scribes would have been among the booty-people transported back to Hatti in the wake of Mursili's conquest. They, or earlier immigrant scribes from Babylonia, may well have been responsible for establishing a local scribal profession in Hattusa, setting up training institutions along the lines of the Old Babylonian model – though we have no direct evidence of such institutions in the Hittite world.

As part of their training, at least some of the home-grown Hittite scribes would have been required to learn the Akkadian language, the international *lingua franca* of the age, and, to a lesser extent, the Sumerian language. These languages opened up to the Hittites the whole world of Mesopotamian literature. Scribal training provided a means for the introduction of great Mesopotamian literary compositions into the Hittite world, since mastery of the complex cuneiform script involved the trainee scribe in the task of copying and recopying the texts which recorded these compositions. Very likely it was via the scribal schools that the Babylonian epic of Gilgamesh became established in Hittite literary tradition. Fragments of Hittite, Akkadian, and Hurrian versions of the epic have all been found in the archives of the Hittite capital. No doubt Mesopotamian legal traditions were transmitted to the Hittite world in a similar way. The collection of 200 Hittite laws owes much in form, content and expression to a number of its Mesopotamian predecessors. But its most direct model and source of inspiration was undoubtedly the laws of Hammurabi. There are many similarities between Hittite and Hammurabic law. But there are also major differences, reflecting different moral values and concepts of justice. One of the most significant differences is the shift in Hittite law away from blood revenge to a more pragmatically based principle – that of punishing an offender by making him directly responsible for compensating in full, and in a very practical way, the victim of his offence.

Hittite religious belief and practice also drew heavily on Babylonian precedents. The omens of a celestial or astronomical nature which figure prominently in the Hittite collection of omen texts are virtually all of Babylonian origin. Hittite archives contain both oracle texts in the original Akkadian versions and also Hittite versions of such texts. Extispicy was one of a number of oracular practices which the Hittites adopted from Babylonia. As in the Old Babylonian period, Hittite priests kept clay models of livers for consultation purposes. A well-known prayer by Mursili II to the Sun-Goddess of Arinna contains a passage taken directly from a hymn to the Babylonian Sun God Shamash, addressed as 'Sun God, My Lord, Just Lord of Judgment', without even adapting this form of address to make it consistent with an invocation to a female deity (see De Roos 1995: 2002). It is possible that the best known of all Hittite religious sanctuaries, now called Yazılıkaya (just outside the Hittite capital), was the venue for a new year festival not unlike, and perhaps inspired by, the Babylonian *bīt akītu* festival.

We have already referred to the presence of Babylonian doctors at the Hittite royal court. Similarly, Hittite kings sought the services of Egyptian doctors from time to time, particularly to effect cures or to attempt to bring about medical miracles where the king's local physicians had failed (see Bryce 2003: 121–8). In this we see a clear acknowledgement of the more advanced state of medical science in Mesopotamia and Egypt when compared to the study and practice of medicine in the Hittite world. A number of the medical texts in the archives at Hattusa describing symptoms and prognoses and methods of treatments of diseases were based directly or indirectly on original Babylonian texts.

Hittite civilisation was highly eclectic in nature. It readily borrowed and absorbed elements of the civilisations of its contemporaries and predecessors in the Near Eastern world. Babylon provided one of the richest sources for the origins of many aspects of Hittite society and civilisation. And this contributed much to Babylon's lasting cultural contribution to later civilisations, including those of the western world. The kingdom of Hatti provided an important link between east and west. By borrowing, absorbing, and then transmitting further westwards many of the traditions of its eastern neighbours such as Babylon, the Hittites helped ensure the continuation of these traditions and their passage into the civilisations of other worlds in other times.

NOTES

1 Depending on whether one adopts a high, middle, or low chronology, this date could be raised or lowered by 60 years or more. Most recently, Gasche *et al.* (1998) have argued for an ultra-low chronology, thus dating the fall of Babylon a century or so after 1595 BC.
2 For an account of Hattusili's and Mursili's reigns, with references to the relevant Hittite texts, see Bryce (2005: 68–86, 96–100).
3 See also Klengel (1999: 65–6) for references to various possible motives for the Babylonian campaign.
4 See Bryce (2005: 161–3), Freu (2003: 120–38). These accounts differ from each other in a number of respects.
5 For a translation of, and commentary on, the whole text, see Singer (2002: 73–7).

REFERENCES

Beckman, G. (1999) *Hittite Diplomatic Texts*. Atlanta, Scholars Press.
Bryce, T. R. (2003) *Letters of the Great Kings of the Ancient Near East*. Routledge, London.
——— (2005) *The Kingdom of the Hittites*. New edn. Oxford, Oxford University Press.
Freu, J. (2003) *Histoire du Mitanni*. Paris, Association KUBABA.

Gasche, H., Armstrong, J. and Cole, S. W. (1998) *Dating the Fall of Babylon, a Reappraisal of Second-Millennium Chronology*. Chicago.

Grayson, A. K. (1975) *Assyrian and Babylonian Chronicles*. New York, J. J. Augustin.

Gurney, O. R. (1973) 'Anatolia *c.* 1750–1600 BC', in *Cambridge Ancient History*. II. 1, 3rd edn, 228–55.

Klengel, H. (1999) *Geschichte des Hethitischen Reiches.*(Handbuch der Orientalistik, 1, 034), Leiden, Brill.

Manning, S. W. (1999) *A Test of Time*. Oxford, Oxbow Books.

Roos, J. de (1995) 'Hittite Prayers', in J. M. Sasson, *Civilizations of the Ancient Near East*. New York, Charles Scribner's Sons, 1997–2005.

Singer, I. (2002) *Hittite Prayers*. Atlanta, Society of Biblical Literature.

CHAPTER THIRTY-SIX

RELATIONS BETWEEN BABYLONIA AND THE LEVANT DURING THE KASSITE PERIOD

——·◆·——

P. S. Vermaak

INTRODUCTION

The relations between Babylonia and the Levant[1] during the Kassite period have to be understood within the larger cultural context of the Ancient Near East. While this period is richly documented across the whole geographical region,[2] specifically Babylonian texts are in short supply.[3] Therefore the entire scenario in the Ancient Near East should be taken into consideration in order to determine the particular relations between the Levant and Babylonia.

This larger context forms the international playground which fertilised the relations between all these ancient communities. Several terms such as 'cultural interrelations' (Bouzek 1985), 'interconnections' (Davies and Schöfield 1995), 'cultural interaction' (Bunnens 1996) and 'synchronisation of civilisations' (Bietak 2000) have been used in order to characterise the cultural exchange between civilisations living around the Mediterranean, the Near East, Africa, Egypt, Anatolia and the Levant. The relations between Babylonia and Levant, should therefore best be described in the broad terms of cultural exchange. Cultural exchange as an anthropological term (cf. Haviland 1993) includes innovation, discovery, diffusion[4] and acculturation[5] and cultural loss.[6]

The spread of the Akkadian language as *lingua franca* during the Kassite Babylonian period and the presence of Babylonian scribes throughout the Levant provide an excellent indication of an extraordinary cultural exchange that took place over a larger period of time. The major question is how these activities took place and in what way did it occur. We are 'aware of extensive exchange networks, intensive traffic and substantial volumes of goods traversing' the Ancient Near East, 'however, we are largely ignorant of how this operated' (Marfoe 1987: 34).

Many comparative studies in the Ancient Near East have a linear approach to discussing relations between peoples. This is often formulated out of a central market place theory which identifies dominant settlements as the centres of symmetrical compact service areas. These 'central places' (Christaller 1966) and 'isolated states' (Hall 1966) are compact service areas in the shape of circles or hexagons (Hirth 1978: 37). These theoretical models are generally applied in reference to small-scale societies and involve food items, clothing and other necessary commodities, not luxury goods.

In our present context we need to adopt a broader perspective to connect larger regions of the ancient world, such as North Africa, Western Asia, Anatolia and the entire Mediterranean.

GATEWAY COMMUNITIES

Gateway communities emerge along the natural corridors of communication and trade routes at those places that allow the best control over the movement of commodities. They are typically not primary producers but intermediaries between areas of high mineral, agricultural or craft productivity. They may have a high population density with a high demand for scarce resources. They can also be situated at the interfaces of different technologies or levels of socio-political complexity[7] or develop in response to increased trade or sedentarisation in sparsely populated frontier regions.[8] Although the gateway communities may function as the retributive central place within their own physiographic region,[9] it is long-distance trade that creates the dendritic hinterland and their dominant hierarchical position within it. Unlike central places, gateway dendritic networks[10] are based upon the kinds of natural irregularities found in the real world.[11]

Larger gateway communities and their hinterlands serve the inter-regional and international trade and the items exchanged are notably more exotic and luxurious, and very seldom involve ordinary foodstuffs and small animals such as goats and sheep. These communities serve as central points for further extensive trade. This means that these communities needed abundant storage facilities for a certain period until a comprehensive deal has been made with intermediates. These mediators were well trained on the international sea and overland travel routes, knowing their products and what they could be sold for. They could even be compared with the modern-day auctioneers, except that in ancient times the risks incurred were much greater.

Existing gateways were linked to focal places or 'eyes'[12] which concentrated trade activities for a particular period. Research shows that these patterns were constantly changing from one period to another. The search for the 'eye' for each period starts as soon as the available evidence from all areas has been established. Certain elements have to be present in order for a particular gateway to qualify for the 'eye' status of a particular period, such as major or exceptional storage facilities. In searching for the 'eye' of the Kassite Babylonian period there are several possibilities, from the sixteenth to the thirteenth centuries BC. The Babylonians, Hittites and the Egyptians seem to have special gateways, in addition to the peoples from the Levant, where each of them played a tremendous role in enhancing the cultural achievements of the period.

The so-called Kassite period in Babylonia has been roughly divided by scholars into two broad categories, namely the 'Dark Age' and the 'Golden Age' each having further subdivisions. During the so-called Mesopotamian Dark Age[13] of the sixteenth and fifteenth centuries BC the sites and cities in the vicinity of Middle Euphrates, surrounding Carkemish, played crucial roles between the Levant and Babylonia, while the focus of the 'Golden Age'[14] during the fourteenth and thirteenth centuries BC shifted somewhat westwards, to the Eastern Mediterranean coast, where ports such as Ugarit and Byblos increased in strategic stature.

The period of the fourteenth and thirteenth centuries BC in the Levant has been called the 'Golden Age' due to the variety and abundance of available sources, mainly from Ugarit, Amarna, Boghazköy and Nippur. It has to be taken into account that the sites or cities in their heydays did not always overlap. The Mitanni power was the leading power at the beginning of the Amarna period, followed by the Hittites in the fourteenth century BC and the Assyrians during the thirteenth century BC.

LEVANTINE GATEWAY DURING THE KASSITE BABYLONIAN PERIOD

The Levantine region was the melting pot for various ancient cultures over several millennia. While the Hurrians, Mitannis, Egyptians, Hittites and Babylonians had imposed control, with more or less success at different periods, the stability in this strategically located region was of primary importance. The gateway position of the Levant insured that it had a great cultural impact even on the politically dominant states and it explains why various cultural innovations, such as the alphabet, emerged from this region.

Information from Ugarit

The trade of this ancient Syrian port (now Ras Shamra) has been widely discussed.[15] According to the archives discovered there, Babylonian merchants were active in the Canaanite (Brinkman 1972: 275) or Levantine area (Yaron 1969: 70–79). The indirect impact of the Babylonians on the Levant is visible at the scribal processes in Ugarit. This can be seen in the lexical texts discovered which date from the fourteenth and thirteenth centuries BC. The cuneiform tablets found at Ugarit comprise not only bilingual (Sumerian–Akkadian) lexical lists, but trilingual ones (Sumerian–Akkadian–Hittite/Hurrian) and, most importantly, also eight quadrilingual lexical texts (cf. Huehnergard 1989: 6) in Sumerian–Akkadian–Hurrian/Hittite–Ugarit. These multilingual texts provide evidence of the scale of the activities that took place in this small, but influential region. The scribal activity in connection with these multilingual texts had to be enormous in several ways. Scribes had to learn a number of languages and the usages of the cuneiform in different areas of the Ancient Near East. Even the five different scripts which were found at Ugarit (Van Soldt 1986: 196) give an indication of the importance of this city in the international gateway. The syllabary of the Akkadian from Ugarit definitely comes from the Middle Babylonian (or the Kassite) period in Babylonia which means that there had to be direct contact between the two areas, but no documents so far published provide an indication of any special activity between the Ugaritic city and the Babylonian empire. The more than ten thousand unpublished economic and other tablets from Nippur during this period might eventually reveal more. Politically, Egypt, and the Hittites and the Hurrians in the north dominated the Levant at that time (see Warburton in this volume). Babylonia and Egypt had very relaxed relations at the time, as indicated by their diplomatic marriage exchange, so that Babylonia would probably not have tried to interfere in the Levantine region under the domain of the Egyptians. Kassite Babylonia formed the backbone for the Late Bronze period in terms of their influence via the Akkadian language, literature and the cuneiform script, but there are serious gaps in our records as to the actual activities of Babylonians in the Levant.

The spelling of the Ugaritic words in the alphabetic as well as the syllabic cuneiform is a major evidence for the 'realization' of the Akkadian phonemes by the Ugaritic scribes (Van Soldt 1991: xxii). This could in fact only have taken place if Babylonian scribes had been intensely involved in the instruction of Ugaritic scribes. This goes very much beyond gradual diffusion, it is, rather, a major process of acculturation. The Babylonians could even be said to have engaged in a 'decentralised project' in order to enhance their influence in the entire Levant. Van Soldt (1991: xxiii) demonstrated that the Akkadian texts in Ugarit were not written by native speakers of the Akkadian language, 'but by scribes who had to master it as a foreign language' and who also acquired the skill to write the syllabic cuneiform script.

Information from Emar

The indirect relations between Kassite Babylonia and the Levant are also made visible in the cylinder impressions at Emar. Although no actual Mesopotamian cylinder seals were found, more than four hundred cylinder impressions survive on cuneiform tablets from Emar. These impressions illustrate the 'gateway' position of Emar, insofar as they reflect several foreign styles, namely Mitannian, Assyrian, Babylonian, Hittite and Syrian styles (Margueron 1996: 88).

The evidence from Emar on the Middle Euphrates has shown that some cities acted as smaller gateways between the Mediterranean coast and Babylonia during the Late Bronze age. Although Emar played a key role in the region it fell under the broader political supervision of Carkemish (Bruce 1999: 201–203; Pruszinszky 2004: 43–44). Its material culture shows Syrian and Hittite influence, as well as close links with Babylonia and Assyria (Margueron 1996: 90). This hybrid culture of the city of Emar becomes visible with the Hittite palace, Syrian temples and Syro-Anatolian houses (Margueron 1996: 86). The city thus displays the cultural transmission that went through this major gateway during the latter part of the second millennium BC. Close relations with Kassite Babylonia were maintained by the river traffic and caravans along the Euphrates river.

Information from Tell el-Amarna tablets

The Akkadian language used in the Amarna letters found in Egypt and written throughout the Levant, has a hybrid format. Although the majority of the 382 letters resembles the homeland variety of Akkadian usually called Middle Babylonian, the 'bulk of the letters exhibits departures from pure Middle Babylonian' (Gianto 1999: 123). Only letters EA 2–4, 6–11 could be classified as good Babylonian or 'core' or 'focal' Babylonian. However, the actual language of the Amarna letters is basically 'peripheral Akkadian' and has features that reflect also something of the local language. It has been shown that even the word order differed in the northern and southern regions. The southern letters (Beirut, Amqi, Hazor, Megiddo, Shegem, Ashkelon, Lachish, Jerusalem and Gezer) have a sentence structure of verb–subject–object order which is peculiar to the local traditions. By contrast, the northern letters (Ugarit, Qidshu, Siyannu and Ushnatu) show a subject–object–verb word order which is closer to the languages of the Mesopotamian region (Finley 1979: 57–74).

KASSITE BABYLONIAN GATEWAY

The city Dur-Kurigalzu (see below) is generally considered as the main centre of the Kassite kingdom. In addition, several other cities have been identified where the Kassite dynasty made an effort to upgrade (Brinkman 1980: 468–469) regions in order to serve as proper hinterlands or even village communities supporting the overall 'gateway structure'. Eight Kassite sites have been identified in the Babylonian region, three in the Hamrin region, one in the Middle Euphrates, one in Susa, as well as sites in Bahrain and Kuwait. They also restored the temples of Adab, Babylon, Borsippa, Der, Isin, Larsa, Nippur Sippar, Ur and Uruk (Brinkman 1980: 468–469). This means that they had a large decentralised hinterland which qualified as a special gateway at least during the fourteenth and thirteenth centuries BC. Unfortunately we don't have enough published texts in this regard in order to describe the different regions under the control of the governors of the different areas.

Kassite Babylonian archives

Although many Babylonian sites have archaeological levels dating to the Kassite period,[16] they are underneath built up levels of subsequent periods and have therefore not been examined. Olof Pedersén (1998: 103–120) made a major contribution by describing the archives and libraries of some of the sites that can be listed as Kassite cities, namely, Dur-Kurigalzu, Nippur, Babylon, Ur and Tell Imlihiye. The exact function of these communities will eventually become clear when the major bulk of the cuneiform texts from the Kassite period has been published.

Of particular interest is Dur-Kurigalzu[17] (modern 'Aqar Quf, located about 30 km west of Baghdad) which was founded by the Kassite king Kurigalzu I at the end of the fifteenth or the beginning of the fourteenth century BC. It was abandoned during the twelfth century BC and has never been reoccupied. Excavations unearthed two functional areas, namely the 'Aqar Quf tell, the religious district, and the closely related Tell al-Abyad as the palace and administration centre. The ziggurat in the temple area was devoted to Enlil, the main Babylonian god, but references to the war god Ninurta and the goddess Ninlil were also found. The palace complex consisted of several palaces built around inner courtyards with major wall paintings (cf. Tomabechi 1983: 123–131). A treasury area in the eastern section preserved several sculptures, some glass inlays, gold jewellery and gold ornaments and overlays. One archive (Dur-Kurigalzu 1) consists of administrative records conveying gold and other precious materials given to goldsmiths, and another archive (Dur-Kurigalzu 2) has administrative lists of various garments received or distributed.

The city of Babylon (about 100 km west of Baghdad) had been the political capital during the preceding Old Babylonian period. During the Kassite period it became the 'leading cultural centre' (Perdersén 1998: 107). Unfortunately, little excavation has been done on Kassite levels. The few private archives discovered also remain mostly unpublished (cf. Perdersén 1998: 112).[18] Legal documents dating to the early years of the Kassite period were found in a private archive (Babylon 1). Other private archives (Babylon 2–5) contained administrative documents, omens from the inspection of animals offerings, god lists, school texts and others relating to the education and the making of texts, seals and *kudurru*s (cf. Reuther 1926).

Nippur (modern Nuffar – south-east of Babylon on the eastern branch of the Euphrates), with the temple of Enlil, had been an important religious centre since the third millennium BC. During the Old Babylonian period, it was also famous for its scholarly activities, a position it regained during the fourteenth and thirteenth centuries BC. Some 12,000 tablets have been found, mainly of an administrative nature, concerning the delivery and receipt of agricultural products such as grain, goats, sheep, hides and oil. Other texts from the Kassite period comprise of letters, legal texts and lexical lists. This large bulk of the cuneiform tablets gives the impression of Nippur as inter-regional centre serving a much larger community than its own hinterland.[19]

One remote site during the Kassite period is Tell Imlihiye,[20] close to the city of Mê-turran in the lowest part of the Hamrin Basin, produced some agricultural texts. They are business documents dealing with lists of animals, wool and textiles, notes on the delivery of corn, loans of corn, a few payments, a purchase document and a letter (cf. Kessler 1982: 51–116 and 1985: 18–19).

Evidence from Hana

The format and pillow shape of Middle Babylonian cuneiform tablets with a legal content (real estate contracts) from the Hana kingdom discovered at Tell Ashara (Thureau-Dangin and Dorme 1924: 265–293) find some close parallels in the fourteenth-century examples from Emar and Ugarit (Podany 1991–1993: 57). This indicates that cuneiform tablets were subject to similar production and baking processes during this period. This could not be regarded as diffusion, but, rather, acculturation due to the dominance of the scribal processes by Kassite Babylonians.

Lapis lazuli[21]

Lapis lazuli had extraordinary value in Kassite Babylonia. This is shown in the documentary evidence (Röllig 1983: 488–489; 1991: 5–13) and the material remains, especially among prestige and votive objects. The stone had not been in such demand since the mid-third millennium (Moorey 1994: 90). Most of the 'mountain lapis lazuli' mentioned in the Amarna tablets was sent to Egypt or Mitanni from Mesopotamia (Knudzton 1915: 15: 13; 16: 11; 11r24–5; 19: 80–81; 21: 36; 22: 152; 25: i20–21; 25: ii27; 25: iii43). The Hittites also regarded Babylonia as an important trading centre for lapis lazuli (Oppenheim *et al.* 1970: 11). The precious stone did not originate from Mesopotamia, but from the mountains in Afghanistan.[22] The extensive trade of lapis lazuli during the Babylonian Kassite period did not operate on a linear scale but, rather, via an unusual, more complex trading network through the Babylonian gateway system.[23]

The lapis lazuli cylinder seals from this Kassite period found in Greece (Porada 1981: 1–70) could have most likely been transported through the Levant via the eastern Mediterranean ports which were active during that period, such as Ugarit and Byblos. In fact, the lapis lazuli trade in the Levantine region had already been active for several millennia, as can be noticed in the material remains at Ebla during the end of the third millennia BC where at least 13 kg of rough, uncut lapis lazuli were discovered (cf. Pinnock 1986: 221–228).[24]

Horses and chariots

Horses feature prominently in the Kassite texts (Balkan 1954: 11–40). Horses and chariots are among the royal gift-exchanges which were sent from Kassite Babylonia to Egypt according to the Amarna tablets and this led to suggestions that these commodities originated from Babylonia proper. It is now generally believed that they were imported by the Babylonians from the east or north-east of Mesopotamia. In spite of the references to the breeding and training of horses, Babylonia only acted as middlemen and in fact formed only a gateway for these luxurious items (cf. Kuhrt 1995). Mesopotamia also served the Levantine region in a similar way, in that even the Hittites imported their horses and chariots from Babylonia.

Glass

Glass became important during the middle of the second millennium BC and was often used in imitation of lapis lazuli and other precious stones which probably becoming scarce in the Ancient Near East. It is referred to in the cuneiform texts as 'lapis lazuli from the kiln', as opposed to 'the lapis lazuli of the mountain'. In the Egyptian texts a distinction is made between 'stones of casting' and 'stone of the kind that flows' (Nicholson and Shaw 2000: 195). It is believed that glassmaking was introduced to the Egyptians by the Babylonians, but Oppenheim *et al.* (1970) thought that glassmaking started in Syria (in the Levant).

Seals

The seals of the Kassite period seem to be quite peculiar and differ somewhat from its preceding Old Babylonian period and the following Neo-Babylonian period (see Collon in this volume). The materials used in the Kassite period are more exquisite and luxurious, often made from lapis lazuli and carnelian and other imported hard stone items (cf. Matthews 1990, 1992). This leaves the impression of a flourishing period. The layout of the seals is also different in that two-thirds of the surface of the seals consist of inscription and one-third image. One might interpret this as an effort for greater exactness since unwritten or symbolic images do not in themselves reveal sufficient information about the seal's owner. This could even be regarded as a more scientific approach with an impetus from the literary tradition.

CONCLUSION

Babylonia and the Levant formed large separate gateways which consisted each of a few hinterlands as support systems. The relations between these two entities during the Kassite period should be understood within the larger cultural context of the Ancient Near East due to the limited nature of direct sources. The Levantine region was the melting pot of various ancient cultures over several millennia and had been a tremendous impetus for several ancient cultures. It seems that the large Levantine gateway and its hinterlands during the first part of the Kassite Babylonian period were situated on the Middle Euphrates, in the vicinity of Carkemish, as mediators to the east, west and the north. During the latter part of the Kassite period, harbours such as Ugarit and Byblos on the eastern Mediterranean coastline acted as mediators for all four directions.

NOTES

1 The French word Levant defines the eastern Mediterranean region, an alternative term is Syria-Palestine.

2 Major collections of cuneiform tablets were discovered from Amarna (Egypt), Boghazköy (Turkey), Ugarit (Syria), Emar (Syria), Ekallate (Syria) and Hana (Iraq). Cf. Pedersén (1998).

3 Cf. the groundbreaking work by Brinkman (1976). More details will emerge after the full publication of the 2,000 Middle Babylonian cuneiform tablets. See, meanwhile, Sassmanshausen (1995) and Pedersén (1998: 103–120) for the current state of the Middle Babylonian archives of Nippur as well as those from Dur-Kurigulzu, Babylon, Ur and Tell Imlihiye.

4 Diffusion as the transfer of limited or single cultural components from one society to another may occur with or without contact between peoples, which means that certain cultural aspects may have been transmitted via a second people to a third one (cf. Haviland 1993: 402–432). Within the Ancient Near East it is sometimes difficult to establish what the origin of an innovation is and which people is the final recipient thereof. The great variety of Sumerian innovations had a major influence on the Ancient Near East, without direct contact being very widespread.

5 Acculturation as a process of extensive cultural exchange which arises from continuous contact between peoples generates unavoidable change on a large scale to both cultures. Cultures which come into contact (cf. Haviland (1993: 402–432) with one another have a reciprocal influence on each other, but seldom to the same extent such as the cultures on Babylonia and the Levant during the Kassite period.

6 These exchanges took place on various levels, such as individual or social levels, and also appear in various categories of society such as economic, political, religious, social and kinships, etc.

7 Hirth 1978: 37.

8 Hirth 1978: 35–46; Burghardt 1971: 269–285; Flannery 1968: 79–110.

9 Hirth 1978: 35–46; Burghardt 1971: 269–285; Flannery 1968: 79–110.

10 The best possible understanding of the cultural panorama in the Ancient Near East can most probably be found in a 'dendritic structure'. This structure derives from the nervous system in the human body and it has different shapes and several gateways or thoroughfares to serve as intermediates for several places which provide raw material or manmade objects. Cf. the discussions on the dendritic market networks by Hirth (1978: 37–42), Kelley (1976: 219–254), Burghardt (1971: 269–285), Johnson (1970) and Vance (1970).

11 Certain gateway communities can be clearly identified in the Ancient Near East during the third, second and first millennia BC. Even certain very interesting developments can be defined, however, more detailed studies are needed in order to display a more continuous development. Although the entire picture during the second millennium BC cannot at this stage be regarded as fixed, substantial features can be identified which provide more than a test for corroboration in this regard.

12 I am using the word 'eye' which is taken from the dendritic structure of the nervous system and normally used in connection with gateways. The eyes of the nervous system are never at the same place and change without knowing why and how this has occurred. A layout and visual display of the nervous system with the eye at different places in the system can be found in most biological and physiological handbooks.

13 This so-called 'Dark Age' has been discussed at a separate congress in Vienna (2000) and the papers published by Hunger and Pruszinszky (2004).

14 For a summary of the various aspects of trade in Ancient Ugarit, see the discussion and extensive bibliography by Cornelius (1985: 13–31).

15 Gordon (1997: 82–83) described this as the 'Amarna Age' accepting the Mitanni empire as the leading power at the start of the Amarna Age taken over by the Hittites in the fourteenth century BC and followed by the Assyrians during the thirteenth century BC.

16 The sites on the Middle Euphrates reflecting Kassite traces in Babylonia are Terqa, in the Hamrin (Tell Mohammed, Tell Imlihiye, Tell Zubaydi; in Sumer-Babylonia (Ur, Larsa Uruk, Isin, Nippur, Babylon, Dur-Kurigalzu, Sippar); at Susa and on both Failaka (Kuwait) and Bahrain (Qal'atal-Bahrain). The large bulk of these are concerned with the economic life in Babylonia. The large variety of sites economically active during this period substantiates the proposal that a great support system existed, which is required for a gateway status (Brinkman 1980: 468–469).

17 For an introduction to the archaeological site, see Kühne (1997: 156–157); Baqir (1942: 43 and 1946: 73–93) and the texts related to the site, see Pedersén (1998: 104–107), Gurney (1949: 131–149 and 1953: 21–34).

18 Cf. Pedersén (1998: 108–112) for detail on the archaeological discoveries at the site and note 106 for bibliography of excavations.

19 Cf. Pedersén (1998: 112–116) for detail on the archaeological discoveries at the site and note 113 for bibliography of excavations.

20 Cf. Pedersén (1998: 108–112) for detail on the archaeological discoveries at the site and note 121 for bibliography of excavations.

21 It has been accepted (Brown 1991) that lapis lazuli is described in Sumerian as ZA.GIN and in Akkadian as *uqnû*. Different qualities have been identified in antiquity (Cohen 1973: 157ff. and 286ff. and Oppenheim *et* al. (1970: 12) and various types were described as 'multi-coloured', 'wild-donkey coloured' or 'wine-coloured' (Röllig 1983).

22 Cf. other evidence of early lapis lazuli trade in Herrmann 1968: 21–57; Brown 1991: 5–13; Röllig 1983: 488–489; Tosi and Vidale 1990: 89–99; Tosi 1974: 3–33; Tosi and Piperno 1978: 15–23; Reiner 1956: 129–149; Rosen 1990; Wyart 1981: 184–190; and Moorey 1994: 88–92.

23 Evidence provides special contact with Egypt, Anatolia and as far as Greece. Even places such as Hattusa, which could have reached the mountains of Afghanistan without problems, found it economical for them to acquire this from Babylonia, unless Babylonia had a monopoly on the trade of lapis lazuli.

24 The import and export of lapis lazuli was mainly found in an uncut or rough format mostly with the calcite matrix removed. The lumps of raw lapis lazuli were obviously cheaper to import and this already took place in the fourth millennium BC (Tosi and Vidale 1990: 89–99).

BIBLIOGRAPHY

Adams, R.M. (1974). 'Anthropological perspectives on ancient trade', *Current Anthropology*, 15: 239–58.

Balkan, K. (1954). *Kassitenstudien: 1. Die Sprache der Kassiten*. New Haven, CT: American Oriental Series 37.

Barag, D. (1962). 'Mesopotamian vessels of the second millennium BC. *Journal of Glass Studies*, 4: 9–27.

Bietak, M. (ed.) (2000) *The Synchronisation of Civilisations in the Eastern Mediterranean in the Second Millennium BC* (Proceedings of an international symposium at Schloss Haindorf, 15–17 Nov. 1996 and Austrian academy, Vienna, 11–12 May 1998), Wien: Verlag der österreichischen Akademie der Wissenshaften.

Bouzek, J. (1985) *The Aegean, Anatolia, and Europe: cultural interrelations in the second millennium BC*, Praha: Academia.

Brinkman, J.A. (1974). 'The monarchy in the time of the Kassite Dynasty', in P. Garelli (ed.), *Le palais et la royauté*, Compte rendu de la XIXe Rencontre Assyriologique Internationale. Paris: Librairie Orientaliste Paul Geuthner, 395–408.

—— (1976). *A Catalogue of Cuneiform Sources Pertaining to Specific Monarchs of the Kassite Dynasty*. Materials and Studies for Kassite History, vol. 1. Chicago, IL: Oriental Institute of the University of Chicago.

—— (1980) 'Kassiten'. *Reallexikon der Assyriologie* 5: 464–473.

Brown, S. (1991) 'Lapis lazuli and its sources in ancient West/ern Asia', *Bulletin of the Canadian Society for Mesopotamia Studies*, 22: 5–13.

Bruce, T. (1999) *The Kingdom of the Hittites*, Oxford: Oxford University Press.

Bunnens, G. (ed.) (1996) *Cultural Interaction in the Ancient Near East* (Papers read at a symposium held at the University of Melbourne, 29–30 Sept. 1994), Louvain: Peeters Press.

Burghardt, A.F. (1971) 'A hypothesis about gateway cities', *Annals, Association of American Geographers*, 61: 269–285.

Christaller, W. (1966) *Central Places in Southern Germany*, Englewood Cliffs, NJ: Prentice-Hall.

Cornelius, I. (1985). '"A bird's eye" view of trade in ancient Ugarit', *Journal of Northwest Semitic Languages*, 9: 13–31.

Davies, W.V. and Schöfield, L. (eds) (1995) *Egypt, the Aegean and the Levant: interconnections in the second millennium BC*, London: British Museum Press.

Drennan, R.D. (1984) 'Long-distance movement of goods in the Mesoamerican Formative and Classic', *American Antiquity*, 49: 27–43.

Finley, T. (1979) *Word Order in the Clause Structure of Syrian Akkadian*, UCLA: Ph.D. thesis.

Flannery, K.V. (1968) 'The Olmec and the Valley of Oaxaca: a model for inter-regional interaction in formative times', in E.P. Benson, *Dumbarton Oaks Conference on the Olmec*, Washington, DC: Dumbarton Oaks Research Library and Collections, 79–110.

—— (1976) 'The cultural evolution of civilizations', *Annual Review of Ecology and Systematics*, 3: 399–426.

Fossing, P. (1940) *Glass vessels before glass blowing*, Copenhagen.

Gadd, C.J. (1975) 'Assyria and Babylon, *c.*1370–1300 BC', in I.E.S. Edwards, C.J. Gadd, N.G.L. Hammond and E. Sollberger (eds), *Cambridge Ancient History*, vol. 2, pt. 2, 3rd edn, History of the Middle East and the Aegean Region *c.*1380–1000 BC, Cambridge: Cambridge University Press, 21–48.

Gianto, A. (1999) 'Amarna Akkadian as a contact language', in K. van Lerberghe and G. Voet (eds) *Languages and Cultures in Contact: at the crossroads of civilizations in the Syro-Mesopotamian realm*, Leuven: Uitgeverij Peeters, 123–132.

Gordon, C.H. (1997) *The Bible and the Ancient Near East*, New York: W.W. Norton and Company.

Hall, P. (1966) *Von Thunen's Isolated State*, Oxford: Pergamon company.

Harden, D.B. (1968) 'Ancient glass I: pre-Roman', *Archaeological Journal*, 125: 46–72.

Haviland, W.A. (1993) *Cultural Anthropology*, Fort Worth, TX: Harcourt Brace College Publishers.

Herrmann, G. (1968) 'Lapis lazuli: the early phases of its trade', *Iraq*, 30: 21–57.

Hirth, K.G. (1978) 'Interregional trade and the formation of prehistoric gateway communities', *American Antiquity*, 43/1: 35–46.

—— (1987) 'Formative Period Settlement Patterns in the Rio Amatzinac Valley', in D.C. Grove (ed.), *Ancient Chalcatzingo*, Austin, TX: University of Texas Press, 343–367.

—— (ed.) (1984) *Trade and Exchange in Early Mesoamerica*, Albuquerque, NM: University of New Mexico Press.

Huehnergard, J. (1989) *The Akkadian of Ugarit*, Atlanta, GA: Scholars Press.

Hunger, H. and Pruzsinszky, R. (2004) *Mesopotamian Dark Age Revisited* (proceedings of an international conference of SCIEM 2000: Vienna 8–9 November 2000), Wien: Verlag der österreichischen Akademie der Wissenschaften.

Izre'el, Sh. (1990) 'New translation of the Amarna letters', *Bibliotheca Orientalis*, 47: 577–604.

Jaritz, K. (1958) 'Quellen zur Geschichte der Kaššu-Dynastie', *Mitteilungen des Instituts für Orientforschung*, 6: 187.

—— (1960) 'Die Kulturreste der Kassiten', *Anthropos*, 55: 17–84.

Johnson, E.A.J. (1970) *The Organization of Space in Developing Countries*, Cambridge, MA: Harvard University Press.

Johnson, G.A. (1977) 'Aspects of Regional Analysis in Archaeology', *Annual Reviews of Anthropology*, 6: 479–508.

Kelly, K. (1976) 'Dendritic central-place systems and the regional organization of Navajo trading posts', in C. Smith (ed.), *Regional Analysis, volume 1: Economic systems*, New York: Academic Press, 219–254.

Knudtzon, J.A. (1915) *Die El-Amarna-tafeln mit Einleitung und Erläuterungen*, Leipzig: VAB 1, 2 volumes.

Kühne, H. (1997) ''Aqar Quf'', *OEANE*, 1: 156–157.

Kuhrt, A. (1995) *The Ancient Near East ca 3000–330 BC*, London: Routledge.

Marfoe, L.(1987) 'Cedar forest to the silver mountain: social change and the development of long-distance trade in the early Near Eastern societies', M.L. Rowlands, M. Larsen and K. Kristiansen, *Centre and Periphery in the Ancient World*, Cambridge: Cambridge University Press, 25–35.

Margueron, J.-C. (1996) 'Emar: a Syrian city between Anatolia, Assyria and Babylonia', in G. Bunnens, *Cultural Interaction in the Ancient Near East*, Louvain: Peters Press, 77–91.

Matthews, D.M. (1990) *Principles of Composition in Near Eastern Glyptic of the Later Second Millennium BC*, Orbis Biblicus et Orientalis, Series Archaeologica, vol. 8. Freiburg, Switzerland and Göttingen: Universitätsverlag and Vandenhoeck und Ruprecht.

—— (1992) *The Kassite Glyptic of Nippur*. Orbis Biblicus et Orientalis, vol. 116. Freiburg, Switzerland and Göottingen: Universitäätsverlag and Vandenhoeck und Ruprecht.

Moorey, P.R.S. (1994) *Ancient Mesopotamian Materials and Industries: the archaeological evidence*, Oxford: Clarendon Press.

—— (1985) *Materials and Manufacture in Ancient Mesopotamia: the evidence of archaeology and art*, Oxford: Bar International Series 237.

Nicholson, P.T. and Shaw, I. (2000) *Ancient Egyptian Materials and Technology*, Cambridge: Cambridge University Press.

Oppenheim, A.L. *et al.* (1970) *Glass and Glass Making in Ancient Mesopotamia*, Corning, NY: The Corning Museum of Glass.

Pedersén, O. (1998) *Archives and Libraries in the Ancient Near East 1500–300 BC*. Bethesda, MD: CDL Press.

Pinnock, F. (1986) 'The lapis lazuli trade in the third millennium BC and the evidence at the royal palace at Ebla', in Kelly-Buccelati (ed.) *Insight through Images: studies in honour of Edith Porada*, Malibu, CA: Undena Publications, 221–228.

Podany, A.H. (1991–93) 'A Middle Babylonian date for the Hana kingdom', *Journal of Cuneiform Studies*, 43–45: 53–62.

Porada, E. (1981–82) 'The cylinder seals found at Thebes in Boeotia (Greece)', *Archiv für Orientforschung*, 28: 1–70.

Reiner, E. (1956) 'Lipšur litanies', *Journal of Near Eastern Studies*, 15: 129–149.

Röllig, W. (1983) 'Lapis lazuli, A: Philologisch' *Reallexikon der Assyriologie* VI: 488–489.

Rosen, L. (1990) *Lapis Lazuli in Archaeological Contexts*, Partille, Sweden: Pocket-Book 93.

Sassmannshausen, L. (1995) *Beiträge zur Verwaltung und Gesellschaft Babyloniens in der Kassitenzeit*, Tübingen. Ph.D. dissertation, Eberhard-Karls-Universität.

Smith, C.A. (1976) 'Exchange systems and the spatial distribution of elites: the organization of stratification in agrarian societies', in C. Smith (ed.), *Regional Analysis, volume 2: Social systems*, New York: Academic Press, 309–374.

Schortman, E.M. (1989) 'Interregional interaction in prehistory: the need for a new perspective', *American Antiquity*, 54: 52–63.

Sommerfeld, W. (1995) 'The Kassites of Ancient Mesopotamia: origins, politics and culture', in J.A. Sasson (ed.), *Civilisations of the Ancient Near East*, Peabody, MA: Hendrickson Publications, Inc., 917–930.

Thureau-Dangin, F. and Dhorme, E. (1924) 'Cinq jours de fouille à Ashara', *Syria*, 5: 265–293.

Tosi, M. (1974) 'The lapis lazuli trade across Iranian plateau in the third millennium BC', *Gururajamanjarika, Studi in onore di Tucci*, Naples: 3–22.

—— and Piperno, M. (1978) 'Lithic technology behind the ancient Lapis lazuli trade', *Expedition*, 16/1: 15–23.

—— and Vidale, M. (1990) '4th millennium BC lapis lazuli working at Mehrgarh, Pakistan', *Paléorient*, 16/2: 89–99.

Vance, J.E. (1970) *The Merchant's World: geography of wholesaling*, Englewood Cliffs, NJ: Prentice-Hall.

Van Soldt, W.H.(1991) *Studies in the Akkadian of Ugarit: dating and grammar*, Neukirchen-Vluyn: Verlag Butzon & Berker Kevelaer.

Wyart, J. *et al.* (1981) 'Lapis lazuli from Sar-e-Sang, Badakhshan, Afghanistan', *Gems and Gemology*, 184–190.

Yaron, R. (1969) 'Foreign merchants at Ugarit', *Israel Law Review*, 1: 70–79.

CHAPTER THIRTY-SEVEN

LOOKING DOWN THE TIGRIS

The interrelations between Assyria
and Babylonia

———·◆·———

Hannes D. Galter

INTRODUCTION

Assyria and Babylonia – the two parts of Mesopotamia – were different in many
ways: there were different ecological and economical situations, different dialects
of the Akkadian language and different historical developments. Northern Mesopotamia, which comprises the highlands of the Syrian *djezira* as well as the foothills
and hilly flanks of the Taurus and Zagros mountains, has a wetter climate, allowing
for dry-farming. It belongs to the eastern part of the 'Fertile Crescent' that stretches
from Palestine through Syria and Northern Mesopotamia to South-east Iran. It was
here in the north that the first farming villages in Mesopotamia emerged around
8000 BCE. In the flat alluvial plain of Southern Mesopotamia, agriculture needed
artificial irrigation. Settlements occurred later here than in the north. During the
third millennium BCE, the Sumerian culture developed in the south starting from
urban centres such as Uruk or Ur. The population of Southern Mesopotamia consisted
of a mixture of Sumerian- and Akkadian-speaking groups together with peoples from
the east and (later) Amorites from the west. The Sumerian culture was an urban one
based on agriculture and irrigation and with a social structure characterised by
functional stratification and strong institutional ties and loyalties. Over the centuries
the Sumerian political units developed from city states to larger administrative
networks. This development reached its peak in the empire of Ur III towards the
end of the millennium. Under the kings of Ur, most of Mesopotamia was under
Sumerian control.

At the same time in the north the political unit remained the central city with a
number of dry-farming villages in its surrounding. The population was mainly
Akkadian-speaking with substantial Hurrian groups in the west and peoples from
the Zagros Mountains in the east. The economy consisted of rain-fed agriculture,
husbandry and, to a substantial degree, of material exchange, since the political units
in the north remained smaller than those in the south. The society, it seems, was
structured along genealogical lines with strong family ties and clan loyalties. By the
end of the third millennium most of Northern Mesopotamia was part of the Ur III
Empire and under southern control. After the collapse of this Sumerian state around

2000 BCE, the south saw the struggle for supremacy between the various Babylonian cities, which finally led to the rise of Babylon. At the same time, several cities in the north regained their independence. One of them was the city of Ashur.

HISTORY

Babylonia and Assyria were closely linked historically and culturally. The historical relations between Assyria and Babylonia reached from campaigns, conquests and destructions, to border agreements, diplomatic marriages and mutual assistance in times of internal trouble. Unfortunately, the source material relating to the political relations between Assyria and Babylonia is unevenly distributed, especially for the earlier centuries of their history. The German excavations in Babylon seldom reached the levels of the second millennium. Therefore, Babylonian written sources from this period are scarce. We have to rely mostly on accounts written from an Assyrian point of view, such as Assyrian royal inscriptions, administrative texts or letters (cf. Brinkman 1979, 1984 and 1990). In addition we have three literary texts dealing with the Assyro-Babylonian relations in the second millennium BCE:

- The 'Synchronistic History', an Assyrian historical text from the eighth century which enumerates treaties, border agreements and their violations (Figure 37.1: K 4401a + Rm 854) (Grayson 1975: 157–170).
- The so called 'Chronicle P' is a larger fragment of a Late Babylonian tablet that speaks more or less about the same events as the 'Synchronistic History'. We do not know where and when the original of this copy was written (Grayson 1975: 170–177).
- The Tukulti-Ninurta Epic, an Assyrian literary masterpiece from the thirteenth century celebrating the conquest of Babylon by that king (Machinist 1976 and 1978).

Ashur was populated at least since the middle of the third millennium BCE. After the fall of the Ur III kingdom, the city was ruled by a local dynasty which established a network of trading connections with Anatolia, North Syria and the East during the nineteenth century (Larsen 1976). (For the historical development of Assyria compare Mayer 1995 and Cancik-Kirschbaum 2003.) Later on it became part of the 'Kingdom of Upper Mesopotamia' created by Samsi-Addu (*c.*1748–1715), the Amorite ruler of Ekallatum, a city near Ashur. He spent part of his early years in Babylon before he conquered the cities of Ashur, Shechna and Mari, as well as most of Upper Mesopotamia. The empire that Samsi-Addu created lasted for about thirty years, before it fell into various small independent states. Some of them were incorporated in the Babylonian state of Hammurabi. Ashur, it seems, remained independent for a while but was later part of the kingdom of Mitanni that grew out of several Hurrian principalities in the sixteenth century and soon became a leading power in Northern Syria. Finally, in the fourteenth century, Assyria became independent of Mitanni rule. It tried to establish its place among the leading states of that time: Egypt, Hatti, Mitanni and Babylonia. Ashur-uballit I (1353–1318) sent two letters to the Egyptian pharaoh Akhenaten in order to initiate regular diplomatic contacts. The Babylonian king

Figure 37.1   Tablet containing the so-called 'Synchronistic History'
(courtesy of the Trustees of the British Museum).

Burnaburiash II (*c.*1379–1347) tried to interfere with a letter by himself claiming that the Assyrians were his vassals. In reality the relation between Assyria and Babylonia was that of two sovereign states regulated by various treaties made between their rulers, which had to be renewed with each change in rulership. The Synchronistic History records the historical development of this interaction from Puzur-Ashur III (first half of the fifteenth century) to Adad-nirari III (810–783) (Galter 1999). The text lists examples of Assyrian monarchs keeping these treaties and Babylonian kings breaking them. It describes times of warfare between the two states and periods where they were closely working together (Brinkman 1990: 86–89).

The text starts with Karaindash of Babylon and Ashur-bel-nisheshu of Ashur making a treaty. It is later confirmed by other Assyrian and Babylonian kings. During the reign of Ashur-uballit I, Kassite troops rebelled in Babylon and killed the Babylonian king, a son of Burnaburiash and the Assyrian princess Muballitat-Sherua. Ashur-uballit aided the ruling dynasty, crushed the revolt and put Kurigalzu II, another minor son of Burnaburiash, on the throne. After this brief Assyrian interference in Babylonian affairs, we hear of several battles between Assyrians and Babylonians and of the redrawing of the border line (Grayson 1965: 337–339). During the following decades, relations got worse and the conflict culminated under Tukulti-Ninurta I (1233–1197).

The reasons for his Babylonian war are not totally clear. It may have been the traditional good relations between Babylonians and Hittites (see Bryce in this volume), that worried the Assyrian king and led to his unprovoked invasion into Babylonia. But we also know that Tukulti-Ninurta was anxious to win a place in Assyrian collective memory (Galter 1988) and that his military actions formed only part of a larger cultural conflict (Machinist 1984/85). He was the first Assyrian king who tried to build an empire based equally on Assyrian and Babylonian traditions. He had a new capital built: Kar-Tukulti-Ninurta, and his war against Kashtiliash, culminating in the destruction of Babylon, may well have served his aim of becoming supreme ruler of Mesopotamia.

The various stages of this war are the topic of the Tukulti-Ninurta Epic, a lengthy heroic tale that praises Tukulti-Ninurta as conqueror of Babylon, peacemaker and righteous king. The epic states that Kashtiliash violated several times the old bilateral treaty that was signed by Adad-nirari I (1307–1275) of Assyria and Nazimaruttash of Babylon (1316–1291). For this reason he was punished by the Sun-god Shamash, guardian of law and justice. The Babylonian gods left their cities and went to Assyria. Tukulti-Ninurta sent a letter with the declaration of war to Kashtiliash and marched into Babylonia. He fought two victorious battles, captured the Kassite king alive and conquered Babylon around 1215 BCE. He sacked the city and returned home with the statue of Marduk, Babylonian captives, and rich booty, part of which was used for decorating the Assyrian temples. Among the spoils taken from Babylon were also numerous cuneiform tablets covering all fields of science and literature (Machinist 1976; Brinkman 1990: 89–94). The destruction of Babylon, the slaughter among its population, and the deportation of the Marduk statue are also related in the Babylonian 'Chronicle P'. The deportation of thousands of Kassites to Assyria and their corvée work in Assyrian building operations is evident from Assyrian administrative documents too.

During the following years, Tukulti-Ninurta's dream of a combined Assyro-Babylonian monarchy crumbled. Although he called himself 'King of Babylonia' or 'King of Sumer and Akkad', Babylonia was ruled by Assyrian governors for a few years only. In the south, Adad-shuma-usur (1218–1139) organised the Babylonian resistance and soon held major cities such as Nippur and Uruk. Assyrian control over Babylonia diminished further, and Elamite attacks on Nippur and Der got no military response from the Assyrian army, which left Babylonia soon afterwards. In 1197 BCE Tukulti-Ninurta I is said to have been killed by his son and Assyria experienced a time of internal crisis (Galter 1988).

According to the Synchronistic History, the relationship between Assyria and Babylonia remained problematic. While Ellil-kudurri-usur (1186–1182) fought against Babylonia he was deprived of his power by Ninurta-apil-ekur (1181–1169) from a side branch of the Assyrian royal family, but the border conflict continued. Assyria gained large territories in the south. Not even Nebukadnezar I (1125–1104) was able to push the border back north although the Babylonian campaign of Tiglath-pileser I (1114–1076) ended with a defeat because Assyrian troops had to fight an Aramaic invasion at home (Llop 2003).

With Ashur-bel-kala (1073–1056) a new era of bilateral contacts began. He signed a treaty with Marduk-shapik-zeri of Babylon and renewed it with Adad-apla-iddina, who usurped the throne of Babylon with Assyrian help. This treaty was sealed by a marriage between Ashur-bel-kala and Adad-apla-iddina's daughter (Brinkman 1968: 142–143). Contacts remained generally peaceful and were further strengthened by interdynastic marriages (Brinkman 1968: 181–204). The Assyrian kings of the ninth and early eighth centuries showed their respect for the religious centres in Southern Mesopotamia: e.g. Babylon, Borsippa or Cutha. They bestowed gifts on their major temples and offered sacrifices there. Shalmaneser III (858–824) renewed the old treaty and aided the Babylonian crown prince Marduk-zakir-shumi against his younger brother. The central panel of the throne base of Shalmaneser from Kalchu (Nimrud) shows the two kings shaking hands (Figure 37.2). Shalmaneser's son Shamshi-Adad V (823–810) had to accept Babylonian help to quell an uprising within Assyria in 822 BCE. From this time comes the only surviving copy of an Assyro-Babylonian treaty (Figure 37.3: Rm 2, 427). It was written in 821 BCE or soon after and shows Babylonia to be the stronger power (Brinkman 1990: 96–99, 107–112). But some years later Shamsi-Addu invaded Babylonia and plundered the capital. Adadnirari III (809–783) tried to come back to normal relations. He sent the deported Babylonian families back home, together with the captured statues of Babylonian gods. It was also under his rule that the 'Synchronistic History' was composed (Galter 1999).

The long period of more or less peaceful relations between Assyria and Babylonia, regulated by regularly renewed treaties, ended with Tiglath-pileser III (744–727). Using Babylonian problems with royal succession as a reason, he invaded the south and conquered Babylon. He was the first Assyrian king after Tukulti-Ninurta I who officially occupied the Babylonian throne. By participating in the New Year's festival and 'taking the hand of Marduk' he became acknowledged king of Babylon. This policy preserved Babylonian independency and kept the southern cities from rebellion (Brinkman 1984: 39–44; for the Babylonian history between 747 and 626 see also Brinkman 1991).

During the following centuries, the Assyrian kings followed Tiglatpileser's model and ruled either directly or indirectly over Babylonia. Their main enemy were the Chaldaean tribesmen living in the southern parts of Babylonia (see Fales in this volume). In order to secure the support of the Babylonian urban population against the Chaldaeans, Assyrian monarchs sent generous offerings to the Babylonian gods

Figure 37.2   Central panel of the throne base of Shalmaneser III from Nimrud
(courtesy of the British School of Archaeology in Iraq).

Figure 37.3 Assyro-Babylonian treaty (Rm 2, 427), written in 821 BCE
(courtesy of the Trustees of the British Museum).

especially to Marduk and Nabû and granted the cities political and economic privileges, including freedom from certain taxes and duties.

In 721 BCE, while Sargon II (722–705) was busy securing his power in Assyria, the Chaldaean Marduk-apla-iddina II (721–710) declared himself king of Babylon. This started a period of almost thirty years of fighting for the rule over Babylonia (Brinkman 1964; van der Speck 1977/78). When Sargon marched into Babylonia in 710 BCE he was hailed as liberator by the Babylonian cities (Chamaza 2002: 62–70). The traditional privileges were extended even to cities in the extreme south like Uruk, Ur or Eridu. These cities situated within the tribal territory had a clear advantage by accepting Assyrian rule and proved to be loyal allies. Sargon became king of Babylonia and reorganised the administrative structure of the land, creating two larger provinces, one around Babylon and one in the south. Over 100,000 people from the south were deported into Anatolia and the Levant, whereas deportees from Anatolia were settled in Southern Mesopotamia. Under Sargon's rule, the north-western parts of Babylonia were recultivated, the cities resettled and the canal connecting Babylon with Borsippa reopened.

Like his predecessors, Sennacherib (704–681) was personally king of Babylon at the beginning of his reign. But the unexpected death of his father Sargon, who had been killed in battle and was not buried at home, made him change his Babylonian policy (Brinkman 1975; Chamaza 2002: 73–91). After crushing a major rebellion in his second year as king of Assyria and Babylonia he installed a loyal native Babylonian on the throne of Babylon. Bel-ibni, who had been educated at the Assyrian court, reigned for three years but was unable to control matters in Babylonia. Sennacherib removed him in 700 BCE and made his eldest son Ashur-nadin-shumi king of Babylon. He was seized by the Babylonians after six years of kingship and handed over to the king of Elam in retaliation for a military expedition carried out by the Assyrians in the southern marshes of Mesopotamia. It took about ten years before Sennacherib answered this rebellion and marched into Babylonia. He defeated an alliance of Chaldaeans, Babylonians, Aramaeans, Elamites and Iranians at Halule on the Tigris (the outcome of this battle is, however, disputed: Grayson 1965). He then attacked Babylon itself and conquered it in 689 BCE after a siege of over fifteen months. He had the city completely devastated, the temples destroyed and the divine statues smashed or carried away. Then the Assyrians diverted the Euphrates river and flooded the ruins so that Babylon might not be remembered in the future. In his inscriptions, Sennacherib blamed his soldiers for the desecration of the temples and the destruction of the divine statues. But he also states that it was the financial support which the Marduk temple gave to the anti-Assyrian uprising that had provoked this harsh treatment (Galter 1984; Chamaza 2002: 92–107).

Sennacherib left Babylonia without a ruler. The land lay waste and the cities were in ruins. The Babylonian Chronicle speaks about a time when there was no king in the land. But under Esarhaddon (680–669), Sennacherib's son, the Assyrian policy towards Babylonia again changed. A literary text from Nineveh documents this new attitude. According to this unique document, the state of war between Assyria and Babylonia had been provoked by Sargon II. His son Sennacherib was hindered in his attempts of reconciliation by 'Assyrian intellectuals'. Now Esarhaddon is called upon to bring justice to Babylonia (Tadmor *et al.* 1989). His policy of appeasement found its most visible expression in the rebuilding of Babylon and its temples. He also confirmed again the traditional privileges of the Babylonian cities and returned agricultural land around Babylon to its original owners. Finally he had the statues of Marduk and his consort Sarpanitum restored. They were returned to Babylon at the beginning of Ashurbanipal's reign (Brinkman 1983, 1990: 232–239; Porter 1993; Chamaza 2002: 168–201; for the history of Babylonia between 689 and 627 see Frame 1992).

In 672 BCE Esarhaddon decreed that his elder son Shamash-shumu-ukin should be future king of Babylon and his younger brother Ashurbanipal should rule Assyria. So, after his death in 669 BCE, Assyria and Babylonia again became independent but closely related states. During his early years Ashurbanipal (668–631/27) followed the policy of his father. He supervised the triumphal return of the divine statues to Babylon and confirmed the tax exemption of Babylonian temples and cities. But in 652 BCE Shamash-shumu-ukin revolted against his brother. This act destroyed the fragile arrangement Esarhaddon had made to forge Babylonia and Assyria into one state. In a famous letter Ashurbanipal tried to convince the Babylonians not to follow

Figure 37.4   Assyrian relief depicting the deportation of Babylonians. From Nimrud
(courtesy of the Trustees of the British Museum).

his brother, but failed. A four-year war followed. In 648 BCE Babylon was taken
and pillaged after a siege of over two years, in which extreme famine and plague had
raged in the city (see Figure 37.4). Shamash-shumu-ukin perished in the fire that
destroyed most of his capital. In the south of Babylonia the fighting continued until
646 BCE (Ahmed 1968; Cogan and Tadmor 1981; compare Brinkman 1984: 93–104;
Gerardi 1987).

The Assyrian army was able to recapture the whole of Babylonia, but it took a
great amount of time, money and manpower. For about twenty years, the situation
remained calm. According to the economic texts we have from this period, Kandalanu
(647–627), the Babylonian king appointed by Ashurbanipal, was gradually placed in
charge over the land and he lost control in the same gradual way (Brinkman 1984:
105–111). In 627 BCE a new Chaldaean rebellion under Nabopolassar started. In the
following year he was crowned king of Babylon and by 620 BCE the Assyrians had
lost the whole of Southern Mesopotamia. But this was not the end. The Babylonians
joined forces with the Iranian Medes and invaded Assyria itself. One after the other
the Assyrian cities were conquered: first Ashur in 614, then Kalchu and, finally in
612, Nineveh. After the fall of Assyria it was the king of Babylon who ruled the
whole of Mesopotamia.

CULTURE

Beside the historical interrelations between Assyria and Babylonia, there were strong
cultural ties. But although the two states were part of the same Mesopotamian culture
based on the same mythologies and world views, transmitted through the same

cuneiform script and through dialects of the same Akkadian language, their views of each other were quite different (Machinist 1984/85).

Southern Mesopotamia had older and more established traditions. It was regarded as the birthplace of civilisation, the land where the gods themselves roamed during the times before the Great Flood. Babylon was called the centre of the world (George 1997; Maul 1997). Assyria left important political imprints in Babylonia but almost no religious or cultural ones. There seem to be some Assyrian influences in the stylistic developments of Babylonian glyptic, architecture and ceramics, but these are not properly studied yet (Brinkman 1984: 27). On the other hand Assyria was more receptive to Babylonian ideas and innovations. The north had initially been under southern control and Assyrians adopted from Babylonia religious ideas, cultic practices, literary traditions and architectural elements. The Assyrian elites have been very sensitive to Babylonian culture and habits. The official Assyrian texts are written mainly in literary Babylonian. Assyrian kings regularly adopted Babylonian royal epithets. The Assyrian pantheon consists to a high degree of gods and goddesses of Sumero-Babylonian origin. But Babylonian influence seems to have been limited to the intellectual sphere and to the elite of Assyrian society. Its intensity also fluctuated during Mesopotamian history.

During the reign of Samsi-Addu, the city of Ashur was exposed to heavy cultural import (Galter 1986). The royal administration of his kingdom shows many similarities with that of the kings of Akkade. In his royal inscriptions Samsi-Addu copied Old Akkadian monumental inscriptions. He assumed Babylonian military and imperial epithets and used the traditional Assyrian religious titles only sporadically. He also is the only Old Assyrian king of whom a triumphal stele is preserved, and from Mari we have a text that mentions offerings to the statues of kings of Akkade under his rule. From all this we can deduce that Samsi-Addu saw himself as heir to the Old Akkadian empire.

For the city of Ashur this meant severe changes. The delicate equilibrium between god, king and leading families that characterised the early history of the city gave way to imperialistic concepts. For the first time, it seems, a palace was built and royal officials controlled all parts of the political and economic life of the city. The Assyrian dialect was replaced by the Babylonian in official documents. Samsi-Addu connected the cult of Ashur with the cult of the Sumerian god Enlil and added an Enlil sanctuary to the temple of Ashur. He also seems to have added a shrine for the Sumerian sky-god Anu to the temple of the weather-god Adad. Moreover, texts from Samsi-Addu's reign speak for the first time of religious festivals (*akitum*, *humtum*), that are known from the south since the third millennium, and the earliest examples for Ziqurrati in Assyria also date to the time of Samsi-Addu: Ashur, Tell al-Rimah, Tell Leilan. The outer walls of the temples in these cities show decorations of projections and recesses that are known from earlier temples in Ur and Larsa. On the other hand, the Assyrian dating system with eponyms was exported to other parts of Mesopotamia. Whereas, in Babylonia, years were named after important events of the preceding year, Assyrians named them after individuals holding an annual office (*limmu*). Under Samsi-Addu's rule this system was used in several Mesopotamian cities including Mari, Terqa and Shubat-Enlil. It seems as if he tried to connect his newborn kingdom of Upper Mesopotamia with the older and more prestigious cultural traditions of Southern

Mesopotamia. Most innovations did not survive the crisis at the end of Samsi-Addu's reign. Others were kept and mixed with Assyrian elements.

The thirteenth century BCE, again, was a period of strong cultural transfer. The cult of several Babylonian gods such as Marduk, Nabû and Ninurta, was established in Assyria, and Ashur was finally identified with Enlil. This transfer culminated in Tukulti-Ninurta's attempt to create an Assyro-Babylonian monarchy. After successful campaigns in the east, north and west, Tukulti-Ninurta's Babylonian war added the final piece to his rule over the four regions of the world. Then he moved the centre of Mesopotamia to his new capital Kar-Tukulti-Ninurta. The south was devastated, depopulated and heavily plundered. People, material and intellectual wealth were transferred to Assyria. The new capital showed Assyrian and Babylonian architectural elements, and its archive stored numerous cuneiform tablets covering all fields of science and literature that had been taken from Babylon (Machinist 1984/85; Brinkman 1990: 89–94). The Babylonian system of fixed succeeding terms of kingship (*palû*) was introduced into Assyrian historiographic literature to explain this shift of power and, in the Tukulti-Ninurta Epic, the Babylonian gods legitimated the new order by abandoning their southern homes and siding with the Assyrian king, making the war between Assyria and Babylonia a juridical ordeal about supremacy in Mesopotamia. An Assyrian ritual text confirms the presence of the statue of Marduk in Kar-Tukulti-Ninurta and its prominent role in religious ceremonies.

But, even in Assyria, the traditional Babylonian world view with the city of Babylon as centre of the earth was too deeply rooted for this political experiment to be successful (George 1997; Maul 1997). Five hundred years later, Sennacherib failed in a similar attempt. After his destruction of Babylon, he introduced the Babylonian New Year's festival into the Assyrian cultic calendar and moved earth from the destroyed city to his newly erected temple for this festival in Ashur, trying to create a new centre of Mesopotamia literally on the soil of the old one.

In the meantime the Assyrian intellectual elite were strongly attracted by Babylonian culture with its flourishing scribal tradition, its ancient lore and its living scholarship. Babylonian scientific and literary texts figured prominently in Assyrian libraries.

When Ashurbanipal enlarged the palace library of Nineveh to make it the greatest tablet collection in the known world, his scholars not only collected or copied cuneiform texts within Assyria but also searched Babylonian temple libraries and private collections for new material. Acquisition lists show that the tablets were gathered from official and private collections throughout Babylonia after the conquest of Babylon in 648 BCE, and a letter from Ashurbanipal to the governor of Borsippa contains the order to confiscate the private and temple libraries of that city. The celebrated library of Ashurbanipal included literary, scientific, medical, juridical, religious, mantic, esoteric and historical texts comprising the totality of Assyrian and Babylonian erudition and learning. Modern interpretations of this transfer of knowledge to Nineveh range from mere personal interests – Ashurbanipal was one of the few Mesopotamian kings who boasted of their literacy – to an excess of Assyrian centralism or to a final effort to preserve the dying cuneiform tradition (Parpola 1983; Leichty 1988; Lieberman 1990).

RELIGION

The thoughts outlined above can also be seen in the field of religion. Neither Babylon nor Ashur played an important role before the second millennium BCE. Therefore, their main gods – Marduk and Ashur – were not part of the traditional Mesopotamian pantheon and had to be incorporated slowly.

Marduk, originally a North Babylonian deity (see Oshima in this volume), who may have been associated in the beginning with the water ordeal and divine justice, was at an early stage identified with the Sumerian god Asalluhi, and thus entered the traditional Mesopotamian pantheon. The development of the cult of Marduk is, so far, unparalleled in the Ancient Near East. As the city of Babylon gained political importance, Marduk rose from a mere local deity to a major god, his cult spread over all of Babylonia and he assumed the name Bel 'lord'. During the second half of the second millennium BCE, he became the overall lord of heaven and earth and the organiser of the universe. By the end of the second millennium BC, he had replaced the Sumerian god Enlil as supreme god of the Babylonian pantheon (Lambert 1964; Sommerfeld 1982).

The god Ashur was very closely connected with his city. Both were known by the same name and some scholars think that Ashur originally was the deified city itself (Lambert 1983). But it is similarly conceivable that the city – often written URU assur.KI – got its name from the god as 'city of (the god) Ashur'. There is only little evidence for temples dedicated to Ashur outside his city. An Old Assyrian letter from the nineteenth century BCE mentions an Ashur temple in the Syrian town of Urshu. Tukulti-Ninurta I had a sanctuary for Ashur built in his new capital Kar-Tukulti-Ninurta, and texts from the first millennium BCE refer to an Ashur shrine in Nineveh (Frame 1999). Like Marduk, Ashur had no specific function although he is associated with law and order already in Old Assyrian texts. His importance rose as the political power of the city Ashur increased. In the eighteenth century, Samsi-Addu introduced the cult of Enlil to Upper Mesopotamia. When he made the city of Shechna his residence he changed its name to Shubat-Enlil 'Seat of Enlil' and he added an Enlil-shrine to the temple of Ashur. He thus initiated a syncretistic process during which several aspects of Enlil were transferred to Ashur, especially his function as lord of the civilised world and bestower of kingship. His main temple in Ashur was called Esharra 'Universe-House', Ekur 'Mountain-House', Ehursagkalama 'Mountain of the Land-House' or Ehursagkurkurra 'Mountain of all countries-House'. Originally all these were names of the Enlil-Temple in Nippur. Ashur, who initially had no family connections, was then associated with Enlil's wife Ninlil, who was venerated in Assyria under the name Mulissu, and with Enlil's sons Ninurta and Zababa (Frame 1997, 1999). Tukulti-Ninurta I in the second half of the thirteenth century exalted Ashur as 'Assyrian Enlil' and, in his attempt to build an empire equally on Assyrian and Babylonian traditions, he promoted Ashur as supreme god for the whole of Mesopotamia. This brought Ashur into competition with Marduk, who is also called 'Enlil of the gods' in the apologetic text *Enuma elish*, which was read during the New Year's festival in Babylon. At the end of the epic, the fifty names of Marduk are invoked thus transferring the holy number of Enlil – fifty – to the god of Babylon.

But as the Tukulti-Ninurta Epic relates, Marduk and other Babylonian gods left Babylonia for Assyria, thus acknowledging the supremacy of the 'Assyrian Enlil'. The new lord of the world got a new religious centre – Kar-Tukulti-Ninurta – and by transferring the divine statues to Assyria, Tukulti-Ninurta tried to make this new religious ideology manifest. But as we have seen his experiment failed. The divine statues were returned to Babylon and Marduk and Ashur remained rivals for supreme divine power (Chamaza 2002: 123–126).

Normally Assyrian kings did not tend to impose the worship of Ashur on conquered territories. So there are no signs of an Ashur cult in Babylonia. On the other hand, there is plenty of evidence for a cult of Marduk in Assyria. Already, under Ashur-uballit I, a Marduk temple existed in Ashur and a family of Marduk priests was well established in that city. One member of this family –Marduk-nadin ahhe – was royal scribe of Ashur-uballit I. The temple of Marduk is mentioned also in a royal decree of Shalmaneser II (1030–1019) and a Middle Assyrian document speaks about a Marduk gate. Personal names mentioning Marduk increased drastically during the latter half of the second millennium. In the twelfth century they formed ten per cent of the theophoric onomasticon. From this time on Marduk appears frequently in official Assyrian inscriptions as national deity of Babylonia (Sommerfeld 1982: 193–195).

During the first millennium Marduk was venerated in Ashur and had a seat in the Ashur temple. The offerings mentioned for Marduk equalled the ones for Ashur and his image was carried in official processions. Marduk was also worshipped in Nineveh in the temple of his son Nabû, who was very popular in first-millennium Assyria. Especially the intellectual elite revered him as god of wisdom and erudition (Frame 1999; Porter 1995).

The Assyrian kings of the late eighth and seventh centuries, who were deeply involved in Babylonian affairs, tried for a second time to put Ashur at the head of a common Assyro-Babylonian pantheon. In Assyrian belief, Ashur had already become the lord of all other gods, their father and creator. His temple in Ashur housed shrines for all major Mesopotamian gods. Under Sargon II, who stated that he had been chosen for kingship by Ashur and Marduk, thus claiming for himself to be the true king of Assyria and Babylonia, Ashur was equated with the Babylonian cosmogonic deity Anshar. This ancient god was considered as having existed long before creation and being father to all the Babylonian gods. At the same time the epic *Enuma elish*, which relates how Marduk defeated the primeval chaos, rose to supreme power and organised the universe, was rewritten in Assyria, putting Ashur in the position of Marduk (Chamazada 2002: 126–154).

Like Tukulti-Ninurta I before him, Sargon II tried to create a new political and ideological centre of the world: Dur-Sharrukin. And, again like his predecessor, Sargon failed (Galter 2006). Sennacherib's changes affected the official religion as well. Under his reign, the idea of a common Assyro-Babylonian theology was dropped in favour of a pure Assyrian theology which, however, comprised all major aspects of the cult of Marduk, especially the Babylonian New Year's festival. Sennacherib succeeded where his predecessors failed. His reforms were carried on – at least in parts – by his successors and in the official Assyrian theology Ashur and Marduk became a single syncretistic deity (Chamazada 2002: 111–164).

But for most Assyrians, especially for the intellectual elite, Marduk remained a very popular god. Together with the Sun-god Shamash he is one of the most often invoked deities in the Neo Assyrian prayers and incantations.

For the Babylonians, on the other hand, Ashur had never been part of their pantheon. He was solely the god representing the political and military power of Assyria, and was just ignored (Frame 1999). Sennacherib's son, Esarhaddon, started rebuilding the destroyed sanctuaries of Babylon, especially Esangila, the temple of Marduk. Most of the booty from his campaign against Egypt went into this project. Nevertheless, the building process went on slowly and with many setbacks (Landsberger 1965; Chamazada 2002: 178–185). So it was Ashurbanipal who returned the statues of Marduk and other gods to their Babylonian temples, thus laying the foundations for the final rise of the Marduk cult in the sixth century BCE.

BIBLIOGRAPHY

Ahmed, S.S. 1968 *Southern Mesopotamia in the Time of Ashurbanipal*. The Hague and Paris.

Brinkman, J.A. 1964 'Merodach-Baladan II'. In R.D. Biggs and J.A. Brinkman (eds), *Studies presented to A. Leo Oppenheim*. Chicago, 6–53.

—— 1968 *A Political History of Post-Kassite Babylonia, 1158–722 BC*. Rome (= AnOr 43).

—— 1970 'Notes on Mesopotamian History in the Thirteenth Century BC'. *Bibiotheca Orientalis* 27: 301–314.

—— 1973 'Sennacherib's Babylonian Problem: An Interpretation'. *Journal of Cuneiform Studies* 25: 89–95.

—— 1979 'Babylonia under the Assyrian Empire'. In: M. T. Larsen (ed.), *Power and Propaganda: A Symposium on Ancient Empires*. Copenhagen (= Mesopotamia 7), 223–250.

—— 1983 'Through a Glass Darkly: Esarhaddon's Retrospects on the Downfall of Babylon'. *Journal of the American Oriental Society* 103: 35–42.

—— 1984 *Prelude to Empire. Babylonian Society and Politics, 747–626 BC*. Philadelphia (= OPBF 7).

—— 1990 'Political Covenants, Treaties, and Loyalty Oaths in Babylonia and between Assyria and Babylonia'. In: L. Canfora, M. Liverani and C. Zaccagnini (eds), *I trattati nel mondo antico. Forma, ideologia, funzione*. Rome, 81–112.

—— 1991 'Babylonia in the Shadow of Assyria (747–626 BC)'. Cambridge (= Cambridge Ancient History² III 2), 1–70.

Cancik-Kirschbaum, E. 2003 *Die Assyrer. Geschiche, Gesellschaft, Kultur*. Munich, Beck.

Chamaza, G.V.W. 2002 *Die Omnipotenz Aššurs. Entwicklungen in der Aššur-Theologie unter den Sargoniden Sargon II., Sanherib und Asarhaddon*. Münster (= AOAT 295).

Cogan, M. and H. Tadmor 1981 'Ashurbanipal's Conquest of Babylon: The First Official Report – Prism K'. *Orientalia NS* 50: 229–240.

Frame, G. 1992 *Babylonia 689–627 BC. A Political History*. Istanbul-Leiden 1992 (= Uitgaven an het Nederlands Historisch-Archaeologisch Instituut te Istanbul 69).

—— 1997 'The God Aššur in Babylonia'. In: S. Parpola and R. Whiting (eds), *Assyria 1995*. Helsinki, 55–64.

—— 1999 'My Neighbour's God: Aššur in Babylonia and Marduk in Assyria'. *Bulletin of the Canadian Society for Mesopotamian Studies* 34: 5–22.

Galter, H.D. 1984 'Die Zerstörung Babylons durch Sanherib'. *Studia Orientalis* 55: 161–173.

—— 1986 'Das Samsi-Adad-Syndrom. Assyrien und die Folgen kultureller Innovationen'. In: H. D. Galter (ed.), *Kulturkontakte und ihre Bedeutung in Geschichte und Gegenwart des Orients*. Graz (= Grazer Morgenländische Studien1), 13–26.

—— 1988 '28.800 Hethiter'. *Journal of Cuneiform Studies* 40: 217–235.

—— 1999 'Die Synchronistische Geschichte und die assyrische Grenzpolitik'. In: L. Milano *et al.* (eds), *Landscapes, Territories, Frontiers and Horizons in the Ancient Near East*. II (HANEM III, 2), Padua, 29–37.

—— 2006 'Sargon der Zweite. Über die Wiederinszenierung von Geschichte'. In: R. Rollinger and B. Truschnegg (eds), *Altertum und Mittelmeerraum: Die antike Welt diesseits und jenseits der Levante. Festschrift für Peter W. Haider zum 60. Geburtstag.* Stuttgart (= Oriens et Occidens 12), 279–302.

George, A.R. 1997 '"Bond of the Lands": Babylon the Cosmic Capital'. In: G. Wilhelm (ed.), *Die orientalische Stadt: Kontinuität, Wandel, Bruch.* Saarbrücken, 125–145.

Gerardi, P. 1987 *Assurbanipal's Elamite Campaign: A Literary and Political Study.* Ph.D. Diss., University of Pennsylvania.

Grayson, A.K. 1965 'Problematic Battles in Mesopotamian History'. In: H.G. Güterbock and T. Jacobsen (eds), *Studies in Honor of Benno Landsberger on his Seventy-fifth Birthday.* Chicago (= AS 16), 337–342.

—— 1975 *Assyrian and Babylonian Chronicles.* Locust Valley (= TCS 5).

—— 1987 *The Royal Inscriptions of Mesopotamia. Assyrian Periods I.* Toronto

Lambert, W.G. 1964 'The Reign of Nebuchadnezzar I: A Turning Point in the History of Ancient Mesopotamian Religion'. In: W.S. McCullough (ed.), *The Seed of Wisdom: Essays in Honour of T. J. Meek.* Toronto, 3–13.

—— 1983 'The God Assur'. *Iraq* 45: 82–86.

Landsberger, B. 1965 *Brief des Bischofs von Esagila an König Asarhaddon.* Amsterdam (= Mededelingen der Koninklijke Nederlandse Akademie van Wetenschappen, Afd. Letterkunde, N.R. 28/6).

Larsen, M.T. 1976 *The Old Assyrian City-State and its Colonies.* Copenhagen 1976 (= Mesopotamia XX).

Leichty, E. 1988 'Ashurbanipal's Library at Nineveh'. *Bulletin of the Society for Mesopotamian Studies* 15: 13–18.

Lieberman, S.J. 1990 'Canonical and Official Cuneiform Texts: Towards an Understanding of Assurbanipal's Personal Tablet Collection'. In T. Abusch *et al.* (eds), *Lingering over Words: Studies in Ancient Near Eastern Literature in Honor of William J. Moran.* Atlanta (= HSM 37), 305–336.

Llop, J. 2003 'Die persönlichen Gründe Tiglat-Pilesers I. Babylonien anzugreifen'. *Orientalia NS* 72: 204–210.

Machinist, P. 1976 'Literature as Politics: The Tukulti-Ninurta Epic and the Bible'. *Catholic Biblical Quarterly* 38: 455–482.

—— 1978 *The Epic of Tukulti-Ninurta I. A Study in Middle Assyrian Lterature.* Ph.D. Diss., Yale. New Haven.

—— 1984/85 'The Assyrians and their Babylonian Problem: Some Reflections'. *Jahrbuch des Wissenschaftskollegs zu Berlin*: 353–364.

Maul, S.M. 1997 'Die altorientalische Hauptstadt – Abbild und Nabel der Welt'. In: G. Wilhelm (ed.), *Die orientalische Stadt: Kontinuität, Wandel, Bruch.* Saarbrücken, 109–124.

Mayer, W. 1995 *Politik und Kriegskunst der Assyrer.* Münster.

Parpola, S. 1970/83 *Letters from Assyrian Scholars to the Kings Esarhaddon and Assurbanipal.* 2 vols. Kevelaer-Neukirchen/Vluyn AOAT 5/1–2).

—— 1983 'Assyrian Library Records'. *Journal of Near Eastern Studies* 42: 1–29.

Porter, B.N. 1993 *Images, Power, and Politics: Figurative Aspects of Esarhaddon's Babylonian Policy.* Philadelphia.

—— 1995 'What the Assyrians Thought the Babylonians Thought about the Relative Status of Nabû and Marduk in the Late Assyrian Period'. In: S. Parpola and R. Whiting (eds), *Assyria 1995.* Helsinki, 253–260.

Sommerfeld, W. 1982 *Der Aufstieg Marduks. Die Stellung Marduks in der babylonischen Religion des zweiten Jahrtausends v. Chr. Kevelaer-Neukirchen/Vluyn* (= AOAT 213).

Tadmor, H., B. Landsberger and S. Parpola 1989 'The Sin of Sargon and Sennacherib's Last Will'. *State Archives of Assyria Bulletin* 3: 3–51.

van der Speck, R.J. 1977/78 'The Struggle of King Sargon II of Assyria against the Chaldaean Merodach-Baladan (710–707 BC)'. *Jaarbericht van het Voorziatisch-Egyptisch Genootschap 'Ex Oriente Lux'* 25: 56–66.

CHAPTER THIRTY-EIGHT

THE VIEW
FROM JERUSALEM
Biblical responses to the Babylonian presence[1]

———— •◆• ————

Baruch A. Levine

The Hebrew Bible exhibits a strong awareness of the presence of Babylonia on the international scene, and more poignantly, of its direct impact on the destiny of Jerusalem and Judah during a brief, but crucial period of Ancient Near Eastern history. The Neo-Babylonian king, Nebuchadnezzar II, destroyed Jerusalem, devastated major areas of the country, and exiled large numbers of Judeans to Babylonia in a series of military campaigns. These began at the very end of the seventh century BCE, and reached their climax in 586 BCE with the complete destruction of Jerusalem and the central Temple. This brought an end to the kingdom of Judah, and to the period of the First Temple, as it is known in biblical studies. It is only to be expected that these historically definitive events, and the circumstances leading up to them, as well as those resulting from them, should have commanded the full attention of biblical writers.

It would have been possible to include in our discussion a review of significant cross-cultural connections between ancient Israel and Mesopotamia, in the areas of law, religion, government, and shared literary genres. To do so in the present instance would, however, require a complex differentiation between specifically Babylonian and more generally Mesopotamian cultural features. It is also to be understood that some of what was thought of as Mesopotamian is actually Syrian, or western, and that the flow of culture was not unidirectional, from east to west. It was decided, therefore, to adopt an historical approach that is structured by identifiable events, leaving an assessment of the extent of Babylonian cultural impact on ancient Israel for another occasion.

The actual history of Babylonia, of its conquests and international policies, its downfall and legacy, are being treated in the various chapters of this volume. The view from Jerusalem deals with responses to, and interpretations of, Babylonian domination in the west, particularly in Judah and the neighboring territories, such as have been preserved in the Hebrew Bible. The current availability of contemporary Babylonian documents, and of other extra-biblical sources, has greatly reduced dependence on information provided by the Hebrew Bible in reconstructing Babylonian history per se, although the Hebrew Bible does, in fact, contain historical information.

Biblical literature has a different perspective to offer the historian. In narratives, chronicles, and prophecies we hear the voices of the threatened and beleaguered, of the defeated and conquered; aspects of history that are often absent from the plentiful sources that speak for the major powers, themselves. There is an additional insight to be gained from biblical literature in this regard: it exposes conflicts within the Judean society, itself, usually between prophets and kings (also, "true prophets" versus "false prophets"!), with the true prophets assuming the posture of opposition to royal policy, not that of sanctioning it. The tension of such encounters, in the vortex of national tragedy, is not muted. To the contrary, the relevant issues are dramatized, thereby producing the outlines of a domestic debate on foreign policy.

We will zoom-in on the busy period of twenty-three years, from the death of Josiah, king of Judah, at the hand of Pharaoh Necho II at Megiddo in 609 BCE to the final destruction by the forces of Nebuchadnezzar II, king of Babylonia in 586 BCE. The principal biblical sources to be explored here are Second Kings, followed by Jeremiah and Habakkuk, with some attention to other texts, as well. Biblical texts have been subjected to redaction and rearrangement, and contain later and/or secondary material. The interest here is not, however, in the formation of biblical literature, but primarily, in *Sitz-im-Leben*, in the posture and frame of mind that can account for the versions of the events and their interpretation, as these are presented in the Hebrew Bible. The intention is to allow the Hebrew Bible to tell its story, supplying historical information from other sources where available.

The presence of Babylonia continues to be felt in biblical literature covering the period after 586 BCE, up to the downfall of Babylonia in the mid-sixth century BCE, and during the decades of the Babylonian Exile. In the oracles of Ezekiel and those of the post-exilic period as well as in Chronicles, we encounter a good deal of hindsight and reflection. Thus it is that the life and fate of the last king of Babylonia, Nabonidus, continued to fascinate biblical and post-biblical writers for centuries to come, and tales about the last days of Babylon inform the Book of Daniel.[2]

BABYLONIA IN THE BOOK OF KINGS: HISTORY FILTERED THROUGH IDEOLOGY

Some biblical background

In Genesis, chapters 1–11, the so-called "Primeval History," Babylon is numbered among the most ancient towns in the land of Shinar (*Šinʿār*), a traditional name for Babylonia (Gen 10: 10, 11: 2; cf. Gen 14: 1, 9, Isa 11: 11, Zech 5: 11, Dan 1: 2). Babylon is listed alongside such venerable sites as Akkad, Uruk, Aššur, and Nineveh. We are told that the post-diluvian humans undertook to build a town with a tower in the land of Shinar, which they named Babel, indicating that in the Israelite consciousness Babylon symbolized the beginnings of urbanization. Genesis 14: 1–17 relate that Amraphel, king of Shinar, was one of four foreign kings, among them the king of Elam, who attacked the five kings with whom Abram was allied. This biblical account, which shows signs of great antiquity, portrays pre-Israelite Canaan as a battleground that attracted foreign armies.

The first historiographic reference to Babylonia, albeit tangential, comes in 2 Kings 17: 24, 30–34a, where we read that the king of Assyria, after exiling large numbers of northern Israelites to far-off lands, settled foreigners in Samaria in their place. Among those foreigners were people from Babylon and nearby Cutha, as well as those from towns in Syria. The biblical writer, whenever he wrote, was providing a geographical "spread," as if to say that foreigners from all over the Assyrian Empire had been settled in Samaria.

In Isa 14: 4, a caption introducing the famous oracle on the demise of an arrogant imperial king addresses *melek Bābel* "the king of Babylon/Babylonia," but this is misleading. Isa 14: 4–23 follow directly upon a late oracle on the downfall of Babylonia, and a prediction of Israel's restoration (Isa 13: 1–14: 2). This placement may have something to do with the reference to the king of Babylonia in Isa 14: 4a. However, the content of Isa 14: 4–23 suggests that the oracle refers to an Assyrian king, most likely Sargon II, who was killed in battle and left unburied. The oracle of Isa 14: 4–23 is not, therefore, directly relevant to Babylonian history, though it does tell us a lot about biblical perceptions of Assyria.

Merodach-Baladan II and Hezekiah

The first official contact registered between the two entities, Babylonia and Judah, was on the diplomatic level. It pertains to a delegation sent by Merodach-Baladan II of Babylonia to Hezekiah, King of Judah in Jerusalem, as reported in 2 Kings 20: 12–13 and Isaiah 39: 1–2 (cf. 2 Chron 32: 31). John Brinkman (1964) has provided a detailed review of the life and role of this Babylonian leader, a veteran fomenter of anti-Assyrian rebellion. The respective passages in 2 Kings 20: 12–21 and Isaiah 39, are virtually identical, except for the postscript in 2 Kings 20: 20–21, and it is likely that Second Kings was the source for the Isaiah passages. Although there is little reason to question the essential historicity of this report, the precise circumstances surrounding the event are blurred by the larger literary context in which it is imbedded. Both in Second Kings and in Isaiah, the arrival of the Babylonian delegation is placed subsequent to the sparing of Jerusalem and the Assyrian blockade of 701 BCE, which makes no sense chronologically. The event surely would have occurred prior to 701 BCE, although scholarly opinion has been divided as to precisely when.

Mordechai Cogan and Hayim Tadmor (1988: 258–265) argue that the mission sent by Merodach Baladan II would have arrived in 714/713, the fourteenth year of Hezekiah's reign, which had begun in 727/726 BCE. The annals of Sargon II relate that at this very time rebellion was fomenting in Ashdod of Philistia, and Judeans are listed among the groups involved in such activity. Cogan and Tadmor consider it unlikely that Merodach-Baladan would have been able to mount a delegation to Judah in the brief nine months of his later comeback during the early years of Sennacherib. In contrast, John Brinkman (1964: 31–35) accepts the view of Sidney Smith, and others, that the delegation from Merodach-Baladan II to Hezekiah arrived about fifteen years before Hezekiah's death, which occurred in 687 BCE, hence, between 704–702, precisely during that brief period when Merodach-Baladan staged his comeback. After the death of Sargon II in battle in 705, Hezekiah rebelled, and there were rumblings throughout the empire before Sennacherib's third campaign to Judah and the West, delayed until 701 BCE.

How was such an event remembered? The stated occasion for the delegation was Hezekiah's illness; word of which had reached the Babylonian ruler. The Babylonians presented their credentials (Hebrew *sepārîm*), as well as proffering gifts, termed *minhāh* which is the usual word for "tribute," thereby intimating esteem for Hezekiah's elevated status. Much is made of the fact that Hezekiah showed the legation all of his vast treasures. The Babylonian legation is portrayed as obsequious, and Hezekiah – as boastful.

Enter the prophet Isaiah, who had, according to the narrative sequence, just announced to an ailing Hezekiah that he would be granted a new lease on life. A dubious Isaiah now engages Hezekiah in conversation about the Babylonians visiting from a far-off land. He issues the dire prediction, implicitly critical of Hezekiah, that all of the treasures that the Babylonian messengers had been shown would be transported to Babylon in days to come, and that his princely descendants would become servile courtiers in the palace of the king of Babylonia. The real reason for the delegation to Hezekiah was, ostensibly, Merodach-Baladan's interest in securing Hezekiah's collaboration against Assyria, either against Sargon II or Sennacherib, as the case may be. The message of this narrative, and of Isaiah's prophecy of punishment in kind, is that collaboration with Babylonia in rebellion against Assyria was counter to the will of Yahweh, God of Israel. To whatever extent Hezekiah may have collaborated with Babylonia, and despite his rebellion of 705 BCE, he heeded Isaiah's counsel and ultimately submitted to the Assyrian yoke, after all. This accommodation enabled Jerusalem and Judah to survive for a century, albeit in a state of dependency.

In an earlier study (Levine 2005), we argued that this prophetic doctrine, one of submission to Assyria and avoidance of foreign alliances against her, was, indeed, promulgated by First Isaiah in the context of the Assyrian threat to Jerusalem and Judah during the early years of Sennacherib. In response to imperialism on a grand scale, First Isaiah taught that Assyrian world domination was part of Yahweh's plan for the entire earth, and that, eventually, Assyria would also fall (Isa 14: 24–27). Assyria was Yahweh's "rod of rage," his instrument for punishing Israel (Isa 10: 5–10). A sign that Yahweh controlled the destiny of nations, large and small, was the unexpected sparing of Jerusalem in 701 BCE. As will be shown, this doctrine gained acceptance in prophetic circles, and is prominent in the writings of Jeremiah (note, as a prime example, Jeremiah, chapter 27), where it is applied to Babylonia during the reign of Nebuchadnezzar II.

As has been suggested by Cogan and Tadmor, the passages reporting on the Babylonian mission were most probably composed at that later time, between 598–586, during the reign of Zedekiah. This was after the first wave of exile under Jehoiachin, when the temple treasury was actually plundered, and when privileged and skilled elements of the population were deported. In literary terms, what was predicted in 2 Kings 20: 12–21 is reported, in similar words, as having been fulfilled in 2 Kings 24: 8–17, particularly, in verse 13. Isaiah's "prediction" is thus to be regarded as retrospective, making of the report on the Babylonian mission, itself, a product of the Neo-Babylonian period, when the actual enemy was Babylonia, not Assyria.

This textual analysis would explain the tension between (1) Isaiah's entreaty to Yahweh to grant Hezekiah an extension of life, and his assurance that Jerusalem would be defended against Assyrian destruction (2 Kings 20: 1–11), and (2) Isaiah's implied criticism of Hezekiah, expressed in the prediction of the future Babylonian invasion, immediately following (2 Kings 20: 12–21). The former announcement bespeaks divine approval of Hezekiah, granting him a reward for his last-minute submission to Assyria in obedience to Yahweh. As such, it may be seen as expressing a contemporary reaction to the sparing of Jerusalem, one consonant with Isaiah's ideology. In contrast, the latter passage reflects the ideology of a later period; specifically, the horrific consequences of Jehoiakim's rebellion (see further). It seizes upon an episode from Hezekiah's reign that had presaged, as it were, the later disaster. Unlike the threat to Judah in Hezekiah's time, it would not be averted. And yet, criticism of Hezekiah is muted; he is not blamed for the future catastrophe, as was his son and successor, Manasseh, because he was a king who had done what was upright in Yahweh's sight.

The mission of Merodach-Baladan II was of little historical importance, as it turned out. And yet, the report in 2 Kings 20 provides a valuable test-case by which to identify the ideological agenda of the biblical writers and redactors who produced the Book of Kings. Rather than fixing on the cultic and moral evaluations of the Judean kings, this report directs our attention to the primary political issue in the prophetic agenda: rebellions against world empires, or alliances and coalitions formed against them, threatened the survival of the Israelites in the land.

Nebuchadnezzar II and the last kings of Judah

The chronicle of events presented in Second Kings pertaining to the reign of Nebuchadnezzar II, and the years leading up to it, is admittedly skeletal. It is fairly accurate as far as it goes, but it is very short on background. The interpretations given to events and the ideology that peers through the narrative are most often stated in brief, formulaic fashion, and give the impression of condensed, prophetic utterances. Thus, Robert Wilson on the overall composition of the Book of Kings:

> Of course, it is always possible that, as a composite work, Kings makes no general points and has no overarching themes . . . However, even the most enthusiastic proponents of literary analysis rarely push the argument this far, and almost all scholars see the book as tied together by a complex of overarching themes or motifs. The most frequent account of this thematic unity points to the evaluations made by the editors in the formulaic statements used to introduce and to conclude the reigns of individual Israelite and Judean kings.
>
> (Wilson 1995: 85)

In reporting the rapidly changing political situation after the fall of the Neo-Assyrian empire in the late seventh century BCE, Second Kings follows the alternating pattern of submission and rebellion on the part of the last Judean kings with respect to both Egypt and Babylonia. To understand this pattern requires knowledge well beyond what the Hebrew Bible provides. An excellent treatment of the shifting international scene, as Judah was caught in the crossfire between Egypt and Babylonia, is that of D.J. Wiseman, *Nebuchadrezzar and Babylon* (1983). Viewing history from the Babylonian perspective, Wiseman fully integrates the biblical data into the overall scheme of things, as he summarizes the valuable information provided by the Babylonian Chronicle Series ("Chronicles of the Chaldean Kings"), which he edited (Wiseman 1956, and see Grayson 1975a). Chronicle 5 records Babylonian military campaigns, and related royal activities, between the years 608–594 BCE.

Among other things, the Chronicle highlights the events surrounding 605 BCE, and clarifies just how and why Egyptian power waned after the defeat by the armies of Babylonia at the battle of Carchemish, a major event in Ancient Near Eastern history. We now see the importance of the caption in Jeremiah 46: 2:

> Against Egypt, against the forces of Pharaoh Necho, king of Egypt, which happened at the river Euphrates, whom Nebuchadnezzar, king of Babylonia defeated (Hebrew: *hikkāh* "struck, destroyed") in the fourth year of Jehoiakim, son of Josiah, king of Judah.
>
> (cf. Jer 47: 7)

A penetrating interpretation of the view from Judah and Jerusalem, looking outward, has been contributed by A. Malamat in a series of studies now reappearing in his *History of Biblical Israel* (2001: 277–337; 381–386). Here is what Malamat has to say about the political situation affecting Judah towards the end of the seventh century BCE when there was a power vacuum after the Assyrian demise in Hatti, a term used in Babylonian sources to designate the Levant:

> In Political Science terms, Judah was now poignantly caught up in a bi-polar system, meaning that the exclusive control of international politics was concentrated in two powers, solely responsible for preserving peace or making war . . . Once the equilibrium is disturbed or upset by one of the partners seeking hegemony, the secondary power, lacking sufficient economic and military potential, turns to inexpensive diplomatic means to alleviate its plight . . . Such was the fate of Judah.
>
> (Malamat 2001: 325–326, with deletions)

Malamat goes on to review in detail no less than six shifts in policy, between reliance on Egypt and vassalage to Babylonia, all in the twenty-three-year period from 609 to 586 BCE. In the mode of a "maximalist," he elicits from every nuance of the biblical record information that fills in what is missing from it based on our present knowledge. One of the insights deriving from the studies of Malamat, and others, is a better understanding of the persisting tendency on the part of the last kings of Judah to turn to Egypt in the expectation of support against Babylonia. Such support kept coming, although it never held off the Babylonians for very long.

Reading Anthony Spalinger's review of Egyptian history from 620–550 BCE (1977), together with the detailed study by K.S. Freedy and David B. Redford (1970), one comes to realize that, although Egyptian power was limited during this period, Egypt remained a major player in Eastern Mediterranean affairs. Freedy and Redford set out to corroborate the dates provided in the Book of Ezekiel, which often refers to events of the reign of Zedekiah but, in the course of doing so, shed light from Egyptian sources on the choices faced by the last Judean king. Babylonia, for all of its power, was far away, as we are constantly reminded, whereas Egypt was very close by. Like other vast empires, the Babylonians were being chronically beset by trouble in other regions, so that "secondary" powers might reasonably hope to break free of domination when a window of opportunity appeared. Emissaries visiting Egypt were bound to be awed by its gold and riches, which far exceeded anything they had seen. After all,

Jeremiah 37, among other biblical sources, reports that Egyptian forces, which we know to have been under Pharaoh Apries, brought temporary relief to Jerusalem even during its final, long siege. The Hebrew Bible sees things from the prophetic point of view, which, as it turned out, was validated by subsequent events, but we are not to assume that, at the time, the last kings of Judah were simply acting out of recalcitrance in their repetitive, anti-Babylonian policies.

The reader is directed to other studies that shed light on Judah's tenuous situation. Anson Rainey (1975) brings to bear archaeological evidence, especially that pertaining to Lachish, on the phases of the Babylonian conquest of Judah. The relevance of the sparse, but highly informative epigraphic finds at Lachish and Arad, and of the Adon inscription, has long been recognized, ever since W.F. Albright (1936) called attention to the importance of epigraphy for biblical history. Most recently, Lawrence Stager (1996) has provided preliminary archaeological information on Nabuchadnezzar's campaign of 604–603 BCE on the Levantine coast, particularly at Ashkelon, and Jean-Baptiste Humbert (by verbal communication) has now discovered evidence of Nebuchadrezzar's destruction level at Gaza (cf. Jer 47: 1–7). Finally, the historically oriented Anchor Bible commentary on II Kings, by Cogan and Tadmor (1988), provides, along with its careful interpretation of the text, a succinct and detailed review of the events of the period, correlated with the evidence of The Babylonian Chronicle Series, and, as well, with the historical references in the Book of Jeremiah.

Let us then return to the biblical record in Second Kings. Nebuchadnezzar II comes on stage in Kings 24: 1, at the point when Jehoiakim, king of Judah, who had been his vassal for three years, probably between 604 and 602, rebelled against him. Previously, Jehoiakim had been a faithful vassal of Pharaoh Necho II for most of his eleven-year reign (2 Kings 23: 35). Second Kings 23: 29–30 had reported that during the reign of Josiah, Necho advanced against the Assyrians all the way to the Euphrates. The Book of Kings fails to tell us the objective of Necho's campaign, which was to gain hegemony over areas in Hatti subsequent to the Assyrian demise. After the major defeat of the Egyptian forces at the battle of Carchemish in 605 BCE, Nebuchadnezzar marched through Judah as part of his larger effort to gain control of the whole area. This is the import of the statement in 2 Kings 24: 7 to the effect that the king of Egypt undertook no further campaigns outside of his country, having lost his former hegemony to the king of Babylonia. And so, Jehoiakim switched allegiance to the king of Babylonia.

Several years later, Jehoiakim saw a chance to break free of Nebuchadnezzar after that king's debacle at the hands of the Egyptians in the winter of 601/600, when, as we know from the Babylonian Chronicle Series, Nebuchadnezzar attempted to attack Egypt, proper, and was forced to withdraw to Babylon. After regrouping, Nebuchadnezzar returned and attacked Judah punitively, using diverse troops that were positioned in the west. Jehoiakim may have died in these battles, for there is no credible record of his having been taken to Babylon. In 2 Kings 23: 37, Jehoiakim is given the usual, bad report card: he, like his royal ancestors, did what was evil in Yahweh's sight. Here is how the text of 2 Kings 24: 2–4 explains the results of Jehoiakim's mistaken strategy:

> Then Yahweh let loose bands of Chaldeans, Arameans, Moabites and Ammonites against him, He let them loose against Judah to destroy it, in accordance with

the word of Yahweh spoken though His servants, the prophets. Moreover, it was by Yahweh's command that this happened in Judah, to remove them from his presence because of the sins of Manasseh, because of all that he had done. And as well, the innocent blood that he shed, filling Jerusalem with innocent blood, and Yahweh was unwilling to forgive . . .

This passage illustrates the two dimensions of the biblical record in Second Kings which will be encountered repeatedly: the political, and the theological, with the former flowing into the latter. Viewed politically, Nebuchadnezzar's attacks against Judah were triggered by Jehoiakim's rebellion, which could mean anything from armed resistance, to refusal to pay tribute, to giving aid and comfort to the Egyptians. The references to rebellion (the Hebrew verb *mārad*), here and subsequently in 2 Kings 24: 20 relevant to Zedekiah's later rebellion, relate to the prophetic doctrine outlined above, according to which submission to Babylonia, as to Assyria at an earlier time, was Yahweh's will. In this spirit, we read explicit statements to the effect that it was Yahweh who launched the attacks against Judah, not Nebuchadnezzar and his forces, and that this catastrophe was in fulfillment of the warnings transmitted by Yahweh's servants, the prophets. This prophetic theme is developed to its fullest in Jeremiah, as we shall observe presently. It is tragic to learn that it was already Yahweh's intent during the reign of Jehoiakim to terminate Judah by exiling the people, which is what is meant by saying that Yahweh would "remove (them) from his presence" (2 Kings 24: 3; and see Levine 2005a).

As regards the theological, or "cultic-moral" dimension of the prophetic ideology, expressed in the above citation, it would be well to comment on the literary function of the cliché "the sins of Manasseh," which occurs in the cited passage. Similar formulaic statements had been interpolated earlier on so as to "foresee," as it were, the loss of the northern kingdom of Israel to the Assyrians (2 Kings 17: 7–23, cf. 1 Kings 11: 29–39). The link between the two phases, the Assyrian and the Babylonian, is provided, precisely, by Isaiah's prediction to Hezekiah in 2 Kings 20: 17–19, discussed above. Such retrospective footnotes served to create an atmosphere of foreboding and anticipation. In 2 Kings 21: 10–18, Manasseh, king of Judah and Hezekiah's successor, is effectively blamed for Yahweh's eventual abandonment of his own people, who will be handed over into the power of their enemies (2 Kings 21: 14a).

At this point, the enemies are not yet specified as Babylonians, or Chaldeans, but there is no doubt about who is meant. The same motif of abandonment by Yahweh accounts for the brief interpolation in 2 Kings 23: 26–27 to the effect that despite Josiah's repentance, his "turning back" (the Hebrew verb *šûb*) from the sins of Manasseh, Yawheh did not "turn back" from his anger at Judah. That statement rationalizes Judah's eventual downfall as punishment for the earlier sins of Manasseh, not those of Josiah, himself. It is as if to say: even Josiah's cultic reforms, religiously correct as they were, could not assuage Yahweh's wrath.

Of both Manasseh (2 Kings 21: 16) and Jehoiakim (2 Kings 24: 4) it is said that they had shed "innocent blood," a moral and social indictment. Immediately preceding the attribution of Judah's downfall to Manasseh, 2 Kings 21: 1–10 enumerate the many cultic, or religious sins of that king. Manasseh's sins comprise a catalogue of almost every kind of paganism, idolatry, and religious disloyalty known in biblical literature! Once these had been enumerated, it became possible to refer generically to "the sins of Manasseh." It is of interest to note that the principal post hoc statements on the earlier fall of the Northern Kingdom of Israel, namely, 1 Kings 11: 29–39, 14: 5–16, and 2 Kings 17: 7–29, characterize Jeroboam I in the same way. He was the "original sinner" of northern Israel, just as Manasseh was of Judah (cf. 2 Kings 16: 3–4 regarding the sins of Ahaz).

The present study deals with biblical views of the Babylonians, whereas the cultic-moral agenda is basically a self-critical, internal agenda directed at the Israelites, themselves, and need not occupy us for too long. Suffice it to say that it was a primary thrust of the prophetic movement from its inception to insist that the God of Israel demands a just society, and condemns the shedding of innocent blood. This principle was likewise encoded in biblical law. There is nothing unrealistic about prophetic denunciations of social injustice and lawlessness in Judah, and earlier, in the Northern Israelite society. The rich and powerful were grabbing land from the debt-ridden poor, and were bribing judges, who often condemned the innocent. Nor was there any lack of cultic heterodoxy, for that matter. It was basic to the prophetic doctrine to insist on the exclusive worship of Yahweh, the God of Israel, to eliminate foreign worship, and, as the Deuteronomic movement progressed, even to ban sacrifice at local *bāmôt* "cult sites." When these dictates are violated, the God of Israel becomes angry, so that moral and cultic offenses become part of the explanation of defeat. It bears mention that, like the political agenda, so the cultic-moral agenda speaks primarily of royal policy, fixing accountability on the Judean kings; at an earlier time, on the kings of Northern Israel.

And so, the royal chronicle in Second Kings continues. Jehoiakim was succeeded by another of Josiah's sons, Jechoniah, renamed Jehoiachin, who ruled for only three months. Because Jehoiachin surrendered to Nebuchadnezzar in 597 BCE, Jerusalem was not razed to the ground, although the exile to Babylonia began, of the skilled and the professional military, as well as of the king, himself, and his entire court, leaving only the poor peasantry. Except for his idiomatic characterization as a king who did what was evil in Yahweh's sight, Jehoiachin warrants only an oblique reference to disobedience in 2 Kings 24: 13–16. In that passage, Isaiah's "prediction" of 2 Kings 20: 16–18, that Jerusalem's treasures will be plundered, is fulfilled in Jehoiachin's day, and the description of the plundering resonates clearly with the passage in 2 Kings 20. Nebuchadnezzar then installed Zedekiah, Jehoiachin's uncle, previously named Mattaniah, as king in place of Jehoiachin. His eleven-year reign is introduced in 2 Kings 24: 18–20 as follows:

He did what was evil in Yahweh's sight just like all that Jehoiakim had done. For it was because of Yahweh's wrath that these things happened in Judah and Jerusalem, until he (finally) cast them off from his presence. Then Zedekiah rebelled against the king of Babylonia.

Second Kings 25: 1–21 proceeds to chronicle the reign of Zedekiah (compare Jeremiah 39 and 52), employing synchronic regnal years, so that Nebuchadnezzar's siege of Jerusalem extended from the ninth to the eleventh years of Zedekiah, whereas it was in the nineteenth year of Nebuchadnezzar that his commander, Nebuzaradan, completed the destruction of Jerusalem and the burning of the Temple. Before that, when the city was breached, Zedekiah and his entourage had tried to escape by the Arabah road but he was caught, brought to Nebuchadnezzar at Riblah, his sons slaughtered in his presence, and he himself blinded.

One detail of the account warrants special attention. Reference is to 2 Kings 25: 6 (cf. Jer 39: 5, 52: 9), which records Zedekiah's capture in flight. The Chaldean troops overtook Zedekiah near Jericho, and brought him to Nebuchadnezzar at Riblah, where the Babylonian king "laid down the law to him, "Hebrew: *wayyedabberû `ittô mišpāṭîm*," literally: "They spoke judgments with him." This distinctive idiom (also in the singular: *wayyedabbēr* "he spoke," and cf. the variant in Jer 1: 16) is used elsewhere to characterize how the prophet speaks the harsh truth to the people (Jer 4: 12) and to how he demands divine justice (Jer 12: 1). Zedekiah had violated his oath of vassalage to Nebuchannezzar, which accounts for usage of the term *mišpāṭîm* "judgments," and implies punitive action on the part of the suzerain. Hence, Cogan and Tadmor (1988: 317) translate: "They passed sentence upon him." The description of the disposition of the temple decorations and furnishings is a litany of plunder in all of its detail, reminiscent of Assyrian and Babylonian royal inscriptions, especially the royal annals. Acts of brutality are recorded graphically, but dispassionately. The chronicle closes in 2 Kings 25: 21b with the words: "Then Judah went into exile from his land."

We note that 2 Kings 25: 1–21 are free of the cultic-moral ideology, sticking to the tragic consequences of rebellion pursuant to the political agenda of the prophets. That is undoubtedly why, in the preceding passage, 2 Kings 24: 18–20, reference to Zedekiah's having done what was evil in Yahweh's sight skips over Jehoiachin, his immediate predecessor, and harks back directly to Jehoiakim, even though momentous events occurred during his very short reign. After all, Jehoiachin had not rebelled; he was, in the view of Second Kings, the victim of the momentum of destruction generated by Jehoiakim, who could have remained a loyal vassal to Nebuchadnezzar, just as he had been to Necho, whom he served dutifully. Although massive damage had been done during the reign of Jehoiachin, survival was still possible under Zedekiah, had he not rebelled, because Jerusalem had not yet been destroyed. The choice that faced Zedekiah is dramatized in Jeremiah 27, to be discussed further on. One has the impression that the author(s) of 2 Kings 25 were experiencing *déja vû*. Under similarly severe circumstances, Hezekiah had kept the kingdom alive by realizing the futility of rebellion against Assyria. Zedekiah failed to do so with respect to Babylonia.

Assessing the overall character of the biblical record in the Book of Kings it can be said that more interest is shown in the end result of misguided royal policies than in their dynamics, and that it reveals certain ideological inconsistencies. Thus, Josiah met a tragic end notwithstanding his cultic and moral devotion to the God of Israel. In realistic terms, this was because of some offense to, or act against Pharaoh Necho II, or because that Pharaoh had suspected him of such disloyalty. The Hebrew Bible tells us only that he was assassinated on the spot at Megiddo. His son, Jehoahaz, was installed as king by the Judean gentry, but he lasted only three months, at which time the Pharaoh had him arrested and brought to Egypt. The reason given is that he did what was evil in Yahweh's sight, a proverbial way of characterizing cultic heterodoxy. The above are examples of what we find repeatedly in the Book of Kings.

The political agenda is often obscure, or it is blurred by explanations of defeat and misfortune that focus on the consequences of religious heterodoxy and moral corruption. Although prophets have a major role in moving the historiography of the Book of Kings forward, Jeremiah, himself, is never mentioned in those sections of Second Kings that cover the period from 609–586 BCE when he was active.

A corollary of the doctrine of submission to Babylonia is the fact that in the Book of Kings, the king of Babylonia is never threatened with divine punishment for what he did to Judah and Jerusalem, or for any of his related acts of cruelty. He is merely carrying out Yahweh's plan. The downfall of Babylonia is a major theme in Jeremiah, as in Deutero-Isaiah and Ezekiel, and elsewhere (such as in Habakkuk), where it is viewed as the fulfillment of Yahweh's plan, and as requisite to the restoration of his people, Israel. The Book of Kings does not see that far ahead. To be sure, the destructive actions of Nebuchadnezzar II and his forces are recounted in Second Kings in their full cruelty and severity, and one senses the impending doom and its attendant hardships. And yet, it is remarkable how impersonal the Babylonian narrative of Second Kings is in contrast to the Assyrian narrative that had preceded it. The king of Assyria engages in debate and he propagandizes; he taunts and displays hubris, just as he is portrayed as doing in Isaiah 10. In contrast, the king of Babylonia, both in Second Kings and in Jeremiah, is configured as an impersonal force, cruel and powerful. He never speaks in public, but only acts; he has no "personality."

"NEBUCHADNEZZAR, MY SERVANT": JEREMIAH'S EXPLANATION OF DEFEAT

The Book of Jeremiah is, along with Second Kings, a major source of knowledge on the Babylonian presence, as viewed from Jerusalem. It is replete with historical signposts for the reigns of the last three kings of Judah, Jehoiakim, Jehoiachin and Zedekiah, giving some attention to what immediately preceded them, and going on to report on events subsequent to 586 BCE.

In the discussion to follow, we will first present graphic images of the Babylonian armies and campaigns as preserved in the book of Jeremiah, because such passages convey the fearful anticipation of impending disaster, and the trauma of the final destruction. We will then proceed to analyze the prophetic outlook on the Babylonian threat, and its consequences for the people of Judah and Jerusalem.

Graphic images of the Babylonian campaigns

In the first nineteen chapters of Jeremiah, before prophecies become linked to the reigns of particular kings of Judah, and connected to specific stages in the destruction, we find numerous characterizations of the Babylonian forces in their advance toward Judah and Jerusalem. Though these prophecies are not sequenced chronologically, we sense how such descriptions assume greater immediacy as the enemy draws nearer. What was far away is soon perilously close! The Babylonians are not explicitly identified as the dreaded enemy until Jer 20: 4; prior to that, they are referred to in more relational terms. As noted earlier, the report of the delegation sent to Jerusalem by Merodach-Baladan II (2 Kings 2: 14b; Isa 39: 3) speaks of the Babylonians as coming "from a far-off land, from Babylonia." So in Jeremiah, they are first and foremost "a nation from afar" (Jer 4: 6, 16; 5: 15; cf. Hab 1: 8). A variant identification views the Babylonians as coming from the north, reflecting the ancient route of march from Mesopotamia to the Levant (Jer 1: 13–15; 3: 18; 4: 6–7; 6: 1; 10: 22; 13: 20).

The Babylonian forces are described as a lion, a destroyer of nations. His horses are swifter than eagles. He is a powerful nation, speaking a strange tongue; his quiver is an open grave. His stirrings in the northland cause great commotion, a gathering storm (Jer 4: 7, 13, 15–16, 20; 5: 6; 10: 22). Especially poignant is the description in Jer 6: 22–25:

> Behold, an army is coming from the northland,
> A vast nation is stirring up from the corners of the earth.
> They hold both bow and lance; he is cruel, they show no mercy.
> The sound of them roars like the sea, and they ride on horses.
> To the man, he is arrayed for battle against you, O daughter Zion.
> When we heard of his doings, our arms went limp;
> Anxiety gripped us; pangs like those of a woman in childbirth.
> Do not go out into the field, nor walk along the road.
> For the enemy has swords; there is terror all around.

In Jer 8: 16 the people are urged to take refuge in fortified towns:

> From Dan is heard the neighing of his horses.
> From the shouting sounds of his cavalrymen the whole earth trembled.
> They came and devoured the land and everything in it,
> Every town and those who dwell in her.

As the battle scenes become focused on Jerusalem, we encounter descriptions of conditions in the capital. There are repeated references to the proverbial triad of pestilence, war and famine; to the many dead; to conflagrations, and to the felling of trees. In Jeremiah 39 and 52, both parallels of 2 Kings 25: 1–21, the final destruction of Jerusalem is described in graphic detail, and mention is made of Jeremiah's treatment by the conquerors. This dovetails in a curious way with his harsh treatment by Zedekiah and the Judean officials.

Jeremiah's policy toward the Babylonians

Here is what Herbert Huffmon has to say on the subject of Jeremiah's prophetic outlook:

> Jeremiah is not to be characterized as pro-Babylonian, though many of his contemporaries so viewed him, but as pro-Israel. This stance did not demand political independence. The survival of God's people Israel at that time meant, for Jeremiah, submission to God theologically and submission to Babylonia politically . . . Jeremiah sought the continuation and revival of God's people.
>
> (Huffmon 1999: 267, with deletion)

This is the core of the matter, and even those prophecies in Jeremiah that appear to be backward glances at the events are best understood as voicing the doctrine of submission to empires. Huffmon is exceptional in his understanding of the prophet's devotion to his people, notwithstanding his incessant diatribes. It has been an egregious misunderstanding of the classical Hebrew prophets to regard their internationalism as coming at the expense of their loyalty to their own people; not to the kings of Israel and Judah, of course, but to the kinship of the nation. Huffmon continues: "God's people were now making their way in a new international order and needed a unifying theology not linked to political independence, a theology . . . that helped to bring together all that was left of Israel" (Huffmon 1999: 268, with deletion).

Now, Huffmon associates the doctrine of political dependency specifically with Jeremiah, suggesting that it was a product of his own age, informed by Josiah's cultic reforms, unsuccessful as they may have been. As we have argued this ideology has a history, and is best understood as an application of First Isaiah's doctrine of a century earlier, coming in response to the Assyrian crisis. If anything, Jeremiah sharpened First Isaiah's doctrine, so that Assyria, (or "the king of Assyria"), the rod of Yahweh's rage, has now become "Nebuchadnezzar, my servant" (Hebrew: *'abdî*) in Jeremiah (25: 9; 27: 6; 43: 10).

Jeremiah 27: Nebuchadnezzar II as Yahweh's servant

The clearest exposition of the doctrine of submission to Babylonia as part of Yahweh's plan for the whole earth is to be found in Jeremiah 27, perhaps the most ideologically enlightening of the Zedekiah prophecies. It is likely that Jeremiah 25 represents a reworking of chapter 27, in which we find the prophecy of seventy years that explicitly predicts the downfall of Babylonia, and which morphs into a prophecy of Judean restoration. Both prophecies refer to the king of Babylonia as "my servant," as does Jer 43: 10, in a communication to the prophet Jeremiah predicting a Babylonian conquest of Egypt. Without entering into the historical setting of that prophecy, it is important ideologically because the scope of the doctrine that the king of Babylonia is Yahweh's agent is broadened to include Egypt.

The message of Jeremiah 27 is that there is still time to save the people of Judah and Jerusalem, even after the catastrophes that had occurred during the reigns of Jehoiakim and Jehoiachin, if only Zedekiah, king of Judah, "brings his neck under the yoke of the king of Babylonia" (Jer 27: 8, 11, and following). Wearing a yoke and reins to dramatize the oracle, the prophet has this to say to Zedekiah:

> I have made the earth, and humans and beasts on the earth, with my great strength and with my outstretched arm, and I have granted it to whom is upright in my sight. And now, I have placed all of these lands into the power of Nebuchadnezzar, king of Babylonia, my servant, and the beasts of the field, as well, have I granted to him, to serve him. All the nations will serve him until the time of his land will come for him, too, and then large nations and great kings will render him subservient (in turn). It shall occur, that the nation or the kingdom that will not serve him, namely, Nebuchadnezzar, king of Babylonia, and will not place his neck under the yoke of the king of Babylonia – I will visit

punishment on that nation, the word of Yahweh, with war, and with famine and with pestilence, until I hand them over completely into his power.

(Jer 27: 5–8)

There is nothing ambiguous about this oracle, which is said to have been delivered at a projected gathering of invited, neighboring nations in Jerusalem – Edom, Moab, Ammon, Tyre, and Zidon – with Zedekiah present. This meeting (some have called it a "summit") would have probably occurred *c*.594 BCE. Its background is informatively discussed by David Vanderhooft (2003) in a study of Babylonian "strategies of control." The assembled nations faced a fateful choice, but we may assume that they all made the wrong decision. Jer 27: 9–22 expands the core prophecy, warning king and people against being misled by the false prophets and diviners of various sorts who encouraged rebellion, and most likely advocated reliance on Egyptian assistance. Jeremiah's counsel was that the only way to survive was by learning to live under Babylonian domination. There is reference to the temple vessels plundered during the reign of Jehoiachin. These will not be returned until God's own good time, when Babylon, too, will fall. As Tadmor (1999) has shown, the theme of *'ad bô' 'ēt* "until the time has come," basic to Jeremiah 27: 7 resonates in Haggai 1: 2 within the post-exilic community. "This people has said: 'It is not the time of coming (*lô' 'ēt bô'*), the time for the temple of Yahweh to be built'."

A corollary of the doctrine of submission to empire and the notion that Nebuchadnezzar is Yahweh's servant is the idea, already noted above, that it is the God of Israel who is destroying Judah and Jerusalem, not the Babylonians, who are merely doing his will. In fact, one of the themes that links Second Kings to the Book of Jeremiah is usage of the Hebrew Hiph'il participle *mēbî'* "bringing," more precisely the construction: *mēbî' 'al* (alternatively *mēbî' 'el*) "bringing upon, against." Thus, 2 Kings 21: 12: "Therefore, thus says Yahweh, God of Israel: Behold, I am bringing a catastrophe upon Jerusalem and Judah, such that anyone who hears of it, both of his ears will tingle!"

The numerous attestations of this discrete idiom are concentrated in the Book of Kings (1 Kings 14: 10, with respect to Jeroboam I; 2 Kings 22: 16, 20) – with respect to the Babylonian destruction of Judah and Jerusalem; in Jeremiah (Jer 4: 6; 5: 15; 6: 19, 11"11; 19: 3; 35: 17; 42: 17; 45: 5; 49: 5; 51: 64), and in Ezekiel (Ezek 6: 3) – against Judah or parts thereof; in Ezek 26: 7; 28: 7 – against Tyre; in Ezek 29: 8 – against Egypt (cf. Lev 26: 25; 2 Chron 34: 24, 29). It is a virtual *Leitmotif*, which identifies Yahweh as the force bringing misfortune upon his people.

An application of this theme appears in Jeremiah 21: 1–10, yet another Zedekiah prophecy, where a horrendous scene is projected: Yahweh will bring the weapons of the defenders of Jerusalem inside the walls, and turn them against the people, themselves. He will do battle with them and destroy them, effectively becoming the enemy! One's attention is immediately drawn to the Book of Lamentations, traditionally attributed to Jeremiah, and for good reason. "He strung his bow like an enemy; he raised his right arm like an opponent . . . The Lord was like an enemy; he destroyed Israel" (Lament 2: 4–5, with deletions).

Clashes with false prophets: the debate over policy

A close look at Jeremiah's clashes with false prophets and with royal officials, even with kings, especially with Zedekiah, offers an additional perspective on both the political and the cultic-moral agendas of the prophet. The people's first sin is failure to heed the words of the prophets sent by Yahweh. Thus, Jer 25: 2–4:

> That which Jeremiah the prophet delivered to the entire people of Judah and to all the residents of Jerusalem, as follows: Since the thirteenth year of Josiah son of Amon, king of Judah, and until this very day, these three and twenty years, the word of Yahweh came to me. And I spoke to you, beginning to speak early in the day, but you did not heed. Indeed, Yahweh sent to you all of his prophets, sending them early on, but you did not heed, nor did you bend your ear to listen.

Admitting some imprecision in both the synchronous, and the internal chronologies, the point of specifying the span of twenty-three years in Jeremiah's speech may be suggestive. It is as if to say that the imminent crisis harks back to the very inception of the Neo-Babylonian Empire in 626/625, which corresponds to the thirteenth year of Josiah. If there is anything to this innuendo, Jeremiah's complaint would qualify as a sage historical hindsight. It is as if to say that, inevitably, the Neo-Babylonian Empire would vie with Egypt for hegemony in the Levant once the Neo-Assyrian Empire lost its power, and that Babylonia would, with occasional setbacks, prevail. Indeed, this speech of Jeremiah is best understood as a reaction to Jehoiakim's rebellion against Nebuchadnezzar.

A related concern is the activism of false prophets who not only tormented Jeremiah, personally, but who grievously misled the people. This is the subject of Jeremiah 23, which expresses several related themes. The one most relevant to the present discussion is the seduction of the people through false prophecies of well being and peace; the notion that the Babylonian "misfortune" will not overtake them (Jer 23: 17). Jeremiah had insisted that it would, indeed (Jer 23: 12). In language and theme, Jeremiah 23 recalls earlier prophecies of Jeremiah, where we likewise encounter assurances of *šālôm* by false prophets (cf. Jeremiah 6 and 7, as examples).

The most notable episode of conflict with a "false prophet," one of several, is that with Hananiah, recounted in Jeremiah 28, and dated to Zedekiah's fourth year, hence, also in 594 BCE. This account may be seen as a take-off on Jeremiah 27, discussed above. In effect, the admonition of Jer 27: 9–20 is applied to Hananiah, a prophet from Gibeon, which, we are told, took place in the Temple of Jerusalem, in the presence of the priests and the people assembled. Like Jeremiah, Hananiah officially speaks in the name of Yahweh: he predicts that in two years Yahweh will restore all the vessels and all the exiles taken to Babylon along with Jehoiachin to Jerusalem, for Yahweh will break the yoke of the king of Babylonia, Nebuchadnezzar. Hananiah symbolically breaks off the yoke that Jeremiah was wearing (Jer 27: 2). Jeremiah is quick to mock Hananiah, saying that he would wish for nothing better than to see his prophecy fulfilled, but that it was not to be. Some of Jeremiah's words bear repeating:

The prophets who came before me and before you, from time immemorial, prophesied over many lands and upon great kingdoms – for war, and for misfortune, and for pestilence. (As for) the prophet who prophesies for peace – when the word of the prophet comes about, that prophet will be acknowledged as one whom Yahweh truly sent.

(Jer 28: 8–9)

I have placed an iron yoke on the neck of all these nations to serve Nebuchadnezzar, king of Babylonia, and they shall serve him; even the beasts of the field I have given to him.

(Jer 28: 14)

Jeremiah then condemns Hananiah as a false prophet and predicts his imminent death, which actually occurs. Although there have been attempts to historicize this episode, one wonders what realistic assessment of the international situation *c.*594 BCE would have induced Hananiah's prediction. It has been suggested that reference may be to the non-military voyage made by Psammetichus II to Palestine in 592, aimed at showing his presence in the area (see Freedy and Redford 1970: 479–480). But, even if Egyptian help was sought and hoped for, it could not under the best circumstances bring about the return of the Judean exiles and of the Temple vessels! That blessed event would have required the defeat of Babylonia, which would not occur until Cyrus the Great conquered Babylon (cf. Ezra 1: 7–11). It seems, therefore, that Jeremiah 28 is an allegory of sorts, an epitome on the issue of submission to Nebuchadnezzar, Yahweh's servant, and, as such, is probably of later composition (*pace* Malamat 2001: 313–316; for background see Cogan and Tadmor 1988: 323, and literature cited). It serves to dramatize the clash with court prophets who always predict victory for the king who sponsors them. It curiously recalls the symbolical clash on the issue of going to war between the prophet of Yahweh, Michaiu, son of Jimlah, and the obsequious court prophet Zedekiah, son of Canaanah, as told in I Kings 22.

There is much more that could be said about the image of Babylonia in the Book of Jeremiah. Old themes and references to pre-destruction events continue to crop up in the later chapters, as attention shifts to conditions in Jerusalem and Judah after the final destruction of 586 BCE, and to the welfare of the exilic communities in Egypt and Babylonia. We encounter oracles of doom against the nations, and dramatic predictions of the downfall of Babylonia.

HABAKKUK QUESTIONS THE ROLE OF THE CHALDEANS IN YAHWEH'S DESIGN

A century ago, the great British interpreter of the Hebrew Bible, S.R. Driver (1906) contributed a commentary on Habakkuk to *The Century Bible* which has never been surpassed for insight. Driver was able to pinpoint the difference between Habakkuk and his contemporary, Jeremiah, precisely:

Jeremiah is so deeply impressed by the spectacle of his people's sin that he regards the Chaldeans almost exclusively as the instruments of judgement . . . Habakkuk, on the other hand, though not unmindful of Judah's faults (i.2–4), is engrossed chiefly by the thought of the cruelties and inhumanities of the oppressor ... Further, Habakkuk is conscious of a problem, a moral difficulty, which is not the case with Jeremiah.[3] The wrongdoing of the Chaldeans is more unbearable than the evil it was meant to punish.

(Driver 1906: 61, with deletions)

In some respects, the vision of Habakkuk is to the Babylonian destruction of Judah and Jerusalem what the vision of Nahum is to the Assyrian scourge, in terms of the rage directed at the oppressive enemy. The difference is that Nahum is talking about past suffering, and is already celebrating the downfall of the oppressor and his long awaited punishment. Habakkuk is at a different point in time, and can only offer assurances regarding the future, when the Chaldeans will be called to account. Then, too, there is no reference to the issue of divine justice for Israel in the vision of Nahum, only to divine vengeance finally unleashed against the enemies of Israel. For his part, Habakkuk parts company with the consensus view that Israel's sins alone are responsible for Israel's suffering by applying the issue of divine justice to the national destiny. As Driver implies in his note, we observe in Habakkuk a subtle transaction. Resonating with Jeremiah's personal complaint, wherein he cites the prosperity of his wicked opponents as a miscarriage of divine justice, Habakkuk accuses Yahweh of the same injustice with respect to the whole people of Israel, who are, after all, more righteous (or at least, less wicked!) than the Chaldeans.

Thus, Jer 12: 1 (in the personal context):

> You are (too) righteous, Yahweh, that I should dispute with you!
> But I must lay down the law to you (*mišpāṭîm 'adabbēr 'ôtāk*)!
> Why does the way of the wicked prosper;
> Why are all the perpetrators of treachery so well off?

Compare Habakkuk 1: 12–13 (in the collective context):

> Are you not from of old, O Yahweh,
> My God, my Holy-being; *You do not die*![4]
> Yahweh, for imposing justice you appointed him;
> O Rock, for disciplining did you establish him
> Too pure of sight to look upon evil,
> You, who do not countenance wrongdoing –
> Why do you countenance the treacherous,
> Remain silent as the wicked devours
> One more righteous than he?

Yahweh had given power to the Chaldeans for a purpose, to restore order to a lawless Judean society, but that objective was now being compromised by a lawless conqueror who was destroying that very society. Once again we encounter the theme of Babylonia as Yahweh's instrument for punishing Israel, but this time there is prophetic protest against Yahweh's management of the world order.

Habakkuk's antipathy to the Chaldeans pervades his prophecies. References to the cruelty of the invaders also appear in Kings and Jeremiah, but the tone of Habakkuk's oracle rather recalls First Isaiah and Nahum, who condemned the hubris of the Assyrians and their rapacity. Here is Habakkuk's characterization of the Chaldeans, one that goes beyond descriptiveness to voice a strong moral judgment against them:

> For behold, I am stirring up the Chaldeans,
> That fierce and impetuous nation;
> That marches to the broad expanses of the earth;
> To seize habitations not his own.
> He is terrifying and dreadful.
> He makes his own laws and rules.
> His horses are swifter than leopards;
> They are sharper than wolves of *the steppe*.
> His cavalry *is* deployed; his cavalry comes from afar;
> They fly like a vulture, in a hurry to devour.
> He comes for the sole purpose of violence.
> Their course is set like the east wind.
> He amasses captives as numerous as the sand!
> He trifles with kings; rulers are a plaything for him.
> He makes light of every fortified town;
> He heaps up earth, and captures it!
> Then he passes on like a wind sweeping by;
> And ascribes his might to his god
>
> (Hab 1: 6–11)[5]

One could compose a commentary on Habakkuk's oracle comprised of citations from Babylonian royal inscriptions, showing how the prophecy resonates with their long-held ideology. In the Nabopolassar Epic we read, in an often-quoted passage, how Bel confers sovereignty on Nabopolassar, the founder of the Neo-Babylonian dynasty, at his coronation. The king accepts the charge:

> "With the standard I shall constantly conquer [your] enemies, I shall place [your] throne in Babylon." . . . The officers in their joy [exclaimed]: "O lord, O king, may you live forever! [May you conquer] the land of [your] enemies! May the king of the gods, Marduk, rejoice in you . . .!"
>
> (Grayson 1975: 84–85, lines 7–8, 16–18)

In Habakkuk, chapter 2, the prophet receives his answer in the form of a divine assurance that a righteous Israel will survive, while the evil empire will be brought to justice. Thus, Hab 2: 2–4, and following:

> Then Yahweh answered me, saying:
> Inscribe a vision; write distinctly on the tablets,
> So that readers may race through it.
> For the prophecy is *a witness* for the set time,
> A testimony for the specified period

That will not prove false!
If it should tarry – wait for it!
It shall surely arrive; it will not be delayed in coming.
For he is *weak* who is not inwardly upright,
But the righteous will survive by virtue of his steadfastness.[6]

The prophet's counsel to Judah and Jerusalem would seem to indicate that he was speaking when it was already too late to decide against rebellion, because the destruction of Jerusalem had already occurred. Now, all that can be enlisted in the struggle for survival is to wait upon the God of Israel, and to retain a steadfast commitment to a just society. This message is followed in the continuation of Habakkuk 2, by an open condemnation of the Chaldeans. They sought to oppress all nations and to plunder them, but the time will come when Yahweh of Hosts will bring them down.

EPILOGUE

Genesis 11 relates that Abram (later Abraham), the first Patriarch, hailed from "Ur of Chaldees," Hebrew: *'ûr kaśdîm*, and that he migrated to Canaan with his extended family. Of his brother, Haran, it is written that he died during his father's lifetime "in the land of his birth, in Ur of Chaldees" (Gen 11: 28). In the covenant theophany of Genesis 15, Yahweh informs Abram that it was he who had brought him out of Ur of Chaldees to live in Canaan (cf. Neh 9: 7). This is only one of several biblical traditions on the origins of the Israelites, and it is ostensibly anachronistic, and fraught with historical problems. And yet, it testifies to a perception on the part of at least one biblical author that the earliest Israelites originated in southern Mesopotamia.

One can only speculate as to what this identification connotes ethnographically, but it certainly projects a subtle irony. The father of the Israelites abandoned his homeland, Ur of Chaldees, to found a new nation in Canaan, only to be exiled from that land in stages at a later time; first by the Assyrians of northern Mesopotamia, and then by Nebuchadnezzar II, the Chaldean king of Babylonia.

NOTES

1   I am grateful to my esteemed colleague, Hayim Tadmor, for his learned critique of an earlier draft of this study.
2   Having found no single Bible translation that is, in my view, both felicitous and precise in all instances, I have adopted the practice of translating all citations from the Hebrew Bible afresh, with considerable help from existing translations.
3   Except, indeed, in so far as it is exemplified in his own personal experience, in the impunity, namely, enjoyed by his own enemies (xii.1–6).
4   Roberts, 1991: 101 explains that the Masoretic reading *lōʿ nāmût* "We shall not die," represents one of "eighteen corrections of the Scribes," introduced out of reverence. There could be no suggestion that God might die, even if the biblical verse in question actually negates that possibility. Hence, we deduce an original: *lōʿ tāmût* "You do not die."
5   In Hab 1: 7, the given translation: "He makes his own laws and rules" is functional. Literally, the text reads, "From him does his judgment and authority go out." The sense is that the Babylonians have changed the rules of war and government for the worse, and cannot be counted on to behave with decency. In Hab 1: 8, read, instead of *zeʾēbêi ʿereb* "wolves of the evening," *zeʾēbêi ʿarāb{ôt}* "wolves of the steppes," based on the occurrence of this expression in Jer 5: 6.

The same change would apply to Zeph 3: 3 (Roberts 1991: 92). Finally, in Hab 1: 11 the translation assumes that the persistent subject is the Chaldean enemy. It is he who sweeps by like the wind, assuming an implied comparative. In verse 11b, we rephrase the hemistiche and emend to read: *weyāśēm zû kōhô l'ēlōhô*, literally: "He ascribes that which is his strength to his God." (from Masoretic: *weʿāśēm* – Driver 1906: 71). The Hebrew form *zû* is a relative pronoun: "which, whom."

6 In Hab 2: 3 read *ʿēd* "witness," instead of Masoretic *ʿôd* "yet, still." In Hab 2: 4, the problematic form *ʿuplāh* (presumably: "puffed up," cf. *ʿopel* "tower" – Micah 4: 8), is better taken as a metasthesis of *ʿulpeh* " one who is faint." Cf. Ezek 31: 15, where this very form describes trees that have withered, expressing the verb *ʿālap* "to be faint, weak." Cf. Isa 51: 20: "Your sons have become faint (*ʿulpû*)." What we have is contrasting parallelism: one who is not upright will fail, whereas those who are steadfast will survive.

BIBLIOGRAPHY

Albright, W.F. 1936 "A Supplement to Jeremiah: The Lachish Ostraca," *Bulletin of the American Schools of Oriental Research* 61, 10–16.

Brinkman, J.A. 1864 "Merodach-Baladan II," in *Studies Presented to A.:Leo Oppenheim*, Chicago, IL: University of Chicago Press, 6–53.

Cogan, M. and Tadmor, H. 1988 *II Kings*, (The Anchor Bible), New York: Doubleday.

Driver, S.R. 1906 *The Minor Prophets: Nahum, Habakkuk, Zephaniah, Haggai, Zechariah, Malachi*,(The Century Bible), Edinburgh: T.C. Clark & E.C. Jack.

Freedy, K.S and Redford, D.B. 1970 "The Dates in Ezekiel in Relation to the Biblical, Babylonian and Egyptian Sources," *Journal of the American Oriental Society* 90: 462–485.

Grayson, A.K. 1975 *Babylonian Historical-Literary Texts*, Toronto and Buffalo: University of Toronto Press.

—— 1975a *Assyrian and Babylonian Chronicles*, Locust Valley, NY: J.J. Augustin.

Huffmon, H.B. 1999 "Jeremiah of Anathoth: A Prophet for all Israel," in R. Chazan *et al.* (eds) *Ki Baruch Hu: Ancient Near Eastern, Biblical, and Judaic Studies in Honor of Baruch A. Levine*, Winona Lake, IN: Eisenbrauns, 261–271.

Humbert, J.-B. 2005 By verbal communication.

Levine, B.A. 2005 "Assyrian Ideology and Israelite Monotheism," *Iraq* 67: 1 = *RAI* 49.2, xxx–xxx.

—— 2005a "The Cultic Scene in Biblical Religion: Hebrew ʿal panai and the Ban on Divine Images," to appear in Studies-Seymour Gitin, American Schools of Oriental Research.

Malamat, A. 2001 *History of Biblical Israel: Major Problems and Minor Issues*, Leiden: E.J.Brill. (All of Part IV: Twilight of Judah and the Destruction of the First Temple, 277–337; "The Kingdom of Judah between Egypt and Babylonia," 322–337. Also, Part V: "Jeremiah and the Last Two Kings of Judah," 381–386.)

Rainey, A. 1975 "The Fate of Lachish during the Campaigns of Sennacherib and Nebuchadrezzar," in Y. Aharoni, *et al.*, *Investigations at Lachish; The Sanctuary and the Residency (Lachish V)*, Tel Aviv: Gateway Publishers Inc., 47–60.

Roberts, J.J.M. 1991 *Nahum, Habakkuk and Zephaniah, A Commentary* (The Old Testament Library), Louisville, Kentucky: Westminster/John Knox.

Spalinger, A. 1977 "Egypt and Babylonia: A Survey *c.*620 BC–550 BC," *Studien der Altägyptischen Kultur* 5: 221–244.

Stager, L. 1996 "The Fury of Babylon: Ashkelon and the Archaeology of Destruction," *Biblical Archaeologist Review* 22: 57–77.

Tadmor, H. 1999 "The Appointed Time Has Not Arrived: The Historical Background of Haggai 1: 2," in R.Chazan *et al.* (eds) *Ki Baruch Hu: Ancient Near Eastern, Biblical, and Judaic Studies in Honor of Baruch A. Levine*, Winona Lake, IN: Eisenbrauns, 401–408.

Vanderhooft, D. 2003 "Babylonian Strategies of Imperial Control in the West: Royal Practice and Rhetoric," in O. Lipschitz and J. Blenkinsopp (eds) *Judah and the Judeans in the Neo-Babylonian Period*, Winona Lake, IN: Eisenbrauns, 235–261.

Wilson, R.R. 1995 "The Former Prophets: Reading the Books of Kings," in J.L.Mays *et al.* (eds) *Old Testament Interpretation, Past Present and Future* (Essays in Honour of Gene M. Tucker), Edinburgh: T&T Clark, 83–96.

Wiseman, D.J. 1956 *Chronicles of the Chaldean Kings* (626–536 BC), London: The Trustees of the British Museum.

—— 1985 *Nebuchadrezzar and Babylon* (The Schweich Lectures of the British Academy, 1983), The British Academy: Oxford University Press.

CHAPTER THIRTY-NINE

THE PERSIAN EMPIRE

——— •◆• ———

Amélie Kuhrt

From 539 to 331, Babylonia was a province of the Achaemenid Persian empire, the first of the great Iranian empires (*c*.550–300 BC). The name derives from the supposed founder of its ruling dynasty, 'Achaemenes', which was also the name of the royal clan (Herodotus 1.125), members of which ruled the empire for over 200 years. At the time, it was the largest empire the world had seen, spanning the territory from the Hellespont to north India, including Egypt (most of the time) and extending to Central Asia up to the frontiers of modern Kazakhstan. Unlike succeeding periods, no contemporary political entity of even remotely comparable size existed along its frontiers. Babylonia lay at the empire's heart, crucial to successful control, given its strategic position between the empire's eastern and western sectors. It was also agriculturally one of the richest provinces, reportedly paying the largest annual silver tax into the royal coffers (Herodotus 3.92). It is impossible to understand Babylonia's history at this time separately from the empire as a whole. Although Babylonian culture and learning continued, indeed thrived, in this period, there were also important shifts and changes in Babylonian society, which are linked to the empire's history and institutions.

INTRODUCTION

The Persians are scarcely attested as an ethnic element in the world of the Middle East before the sixth century. Archaeological evidence suggests that until *c*.600 BC they consisted of pastoral groups located in the region of modern Fars (= Persia), which had earlier formed part of the important, though poorly known and still surviving, kingdom of Elam. A linguistically related group, the Medes, located further north around the area of modern Hamadan (ancient Ecbatana), appear more prominently in the eighth to sixth centuries BC, since they had (as a result of their relationship to the Assyrian empire to the west) begun to coalesce into a state and made moves towards territorial expansion. Pressure of such a kind may have provoked the relatively rapid emergence of a Persian state in Fars. This embryonic political entity subsequently incorporated, through conquest, the large, highly developed empires and states of western Asia: the great Neo-Babylonian empire (heir to Assyria), Egypt, Lydia, Elam and Media. They, in turn, contributed to the emerging formulation of the Persian imagery of power. This can be seen particularly clearly in the royal monuments and iconography – although that must not blind one to important transformations deliberately wrought in the process of adoption and adaptation.

SOURCES

The sources for understanding the Achaemenid empire are complex and difficult to use because they are extremely disparate and exist in many different languages and forms. Before excavation and the decipherment of Ancient Near Eastern scripts, strong images of the empire existed already, formed on the basis of classical writers, especially the Greek historian Herodotus working in the later fifth century BC. As his aim was to celebrate the victories won by Greeks over Persians between 490 and 478, his valuable information is limited, chronologically, to the early period of the empire. Although Herodotus gives us a sense of the broad geographical sweep of the empire, he treats the imperial regions very superficially, apart from Egypt and the north-western frontier area (i.e. western Turkey), because his focus was the Graeco-Persian conflict. Later classical writers, aside from the Alexander historians, generally exhibit similar geo-political limitations. The exceptions are some fourth-century compilers of Persian histories, such as Ctesias; but they are only preserved in selective late citations and summaries. These reflect the taste of later readers in the Roman and Byzantine periods, who were fascinated by the reported wealth and power of the Persian rulers, and stories of court-corruption and intrigue. As a result, the image of the empire to be gleaned from these sources is both partial and, sometimes, distorted. Added to this was the image derived from the Old Testament, which is responsible for the influential picture of the Persian kings as unusually religiously tolerant, shown by their restoration of the Jerusalem temple and support of the Yahweh cult (*Ezra*; *Nehemiah*). Very different is the Persian court story of *Esther*, which is closer in style to the classical tales.

The Old Persian script was deciphered in the nineteenth century, but as its use was largely limited to monumental royal inscriptions intended to reflect the unchanging majesty of Persian power (the one exception is Darius I's inscription at Bisitun, Kent 1953: DB; Schmitt 1991), the texts are not directly informative on political changes or administrative structures. To illuminate this, sources from elsewhere in the empire – Babylonian, Egyptian, Aramaic and Elamite documents – have to be pressed into service. Among these, the Elamite administrative texts from Persepolis and the Aramaic material are particularly important. Aramaic had been widely used in the Near East, especially in the Neo-Assyrian empire before the Persian conquest and was adopted by the Achaemenid government as an administrative language. Its extensive use in this period is illustrated by documents found in western Asia Minor, the Levant, Egypt, Iran and Central Asia. In Babylonia, where it had already been used, that use increases markedly in the Achaemenid period.

Archaeologically, the area of the empire has been only intermittently and partially investigated. Most attention has been paid to the great royal centres of Pasargadae, Persepolis and Susa. This situation is changing with archaeologists now focusing more on the Achaemenid levels of long-occupied sites in the conquered territories, such as Sardis in Lydia, settlement in Israel and Central Asia, rural development in

Figure 39.1 Drawing of part of a panel from Persepolis, showing Babylonians bringing gifts (Tessa Rickards).

the Egyptian Kharga oasis. One problem is that several sites, known to have been very important in the Persian period, are covered by extensive modern towns, which hampers excavation. This is true of Arbela (modern Erbil in North Iraq), Damascus and Hamadan (ancient Ecbatana). In Babylonia, the long-occupied sites of old cities, many of which continued to exist for centuries afterwards, such as Babylon, Uruk and Sippar, make isolating and defining the Achaemenid period levels problematical. Surveys in the region suggest a general trend of increased settlement through the first millennium, although some sites, such as Ur, declined because the Euphrates shifted its course.

THE FORMATION OF THE EMPIRE

The empire was created through a series of conquests beginning with Cyrus II ('the Great') of Persia who, in 550 BC, defeated the ruler of the Medes to the north, who had attacked the Persians, probably as part of his drive towards territorial expansion. With this defeat the territory over which the Medes claimed control (the western part of the Iranian plateau, Armenia, and Anatolia up to the Lydian frontier) came under Persian domination and their capital Ecbatana with its treasury fell into Persian hands. In the 540s, Croesus, the Lydian king, came into conflict with his new Persian neighbour, and Cyrus' subsequent victory over him meant that the entire territory from Central Anatolia to the Aegean coast was added to his conquests. In 539, Cyrus won a major victory over the Babylonian king, Nabonidus, and so the Babylonian empire (including Mesopotamia, Syria, Palestine and the northern ends of the Arabian desert routes) was incorporated. It seems likely that some of the last years of Cyrus' life were spent conquering eastern Iran and beyond; certainly by 522 the region was part and parcel of Persia's imperial territory and, according to some traditions, he was killed on campaign in Central Asia. On his death, the empire stretched from the Egyptian frontier and the Aegean coast to Uzbekistan, and in 526/5 his son and successor, Cambyses, added Egypt to this already gigantic area. Persian control here extended to Aswan in the south, and was secured through agreements reached with Cyrene, Barca and Libya to the west of Egypt (Herodotus 3.13), and the wealthy Nubian kingdom to the south.

The very rapid acquisition of empire created internal problems in Persia, involving a revolt by Cambyses' younger brother, Bardiya, during the former's absence in Egypt. The serious nature of this internal Persian conflict is strikingly illustrated by the fact that, despite being a legitimate son of Cyrus, founder of the empire, Bardiya was rapidly eliminated by a small group of Persian nobles, one of whom then acceded to the throne claiming relationship with Cyrus' family. This was Darius I (522–486). The turmoil unleashed by these events is known from the massive, in some cases, repeated revolts against his seizure of the throne that took place, particularly on the Iranian plateau, in Babylonia (two revolts in 522 and 521), Armenia and Fars itself. They were, however, ruthlessly crushed and Darius was able to consolidate control in northern Central Asia, add the Indus valley to his realm, and begin to exploit the maritime routes between north India and the Persian Gulf (Herodotus 4.44). He further strengthened his north-western frontier, by adding Thrace and several Aegean islands to his direct control, and creating close links with Macedon in northern Greece. His son Xerxes' (486–465) attempt to consolidate this by adding more of Greece in 480/79 was not successful, although the setback for the Persian empire in this region was, overall, slight and proved ultimately to be temporary.

A sign that the empire achieved its final form under Darius I and Xerxes is that there was no further territorial expansion after their time. It can now be considered to have entered its 'mature' phase, a conclusion borne out by the evidence for the tightening up of the administrative structure within this period and the introduction of a more uniform system of taxation.

IMPERIAL GOVERNMENT AND ADMINISTRATION

Satraps and subjects

The immense imperial territories were divided into provinces, generally called by the Iranian-derived term 'satrapies'. Each province was fairly extensive, each was governed by a 'satrap' (governor) who was virtually always a Persian noble and lived in the satrapal capital. The satrapal centre was, in many cases, identical with the old capital of the original political units conquered. Thus, in Egypt the satrapal capital was

Memphis, in Lydia – Sardis, in Media – Ecbatana, in Mesopotamia – Babylon. But modifications to this older system were also introduced, although not all at the same time but in response to particular circumstances. Thus, for example, Hellespontine Phrygia was reorganised in the wake of Xerxes' Greek campaign to strengthen this vulnerable frontier. Again, probably early in Xerxes' reign, the area that had formed the Neo-Babylonian empire was divided into two new, more manageable satrapies: 'Beyond the River' – west of the Euphrates and stretching down to the Egyptian frontier – and Babylonia – the whole of Mesopotamia (modern Iraq and north-eastern Syria).

The satrapal capital functioned as the administrative centre of the governor. It is here that tax was collected and stored (or sent on), satrapal archives were kept, petitions sent and royal orders and edicts received. Each satrapal capital contained a palace, used by the satrap himself but also maintained for the king on visits. Nebuchadnezzar II's old palace in Babylon was used as the seat of the Persian satrap and, late in the fifth century, an elegant Persian style columned hall (OP *apadana*) was constructed in its western sector. Such royal and satrapal residences in the provinces are further attested, textually, for Memphis, Daskyleion, Sardis, Damascus, Ecbatana and, perhaps, Samarkand. Each satrapy almost certainly had more than one palatial Persian centre, frequently associated with a substantial estate, called by the Persian-derived word 'paradise'; Uruk in Babylonia, for example, certainly had a palace with a royal domain at nearby Ab/manu. In addition, there were fortified storehouses serving provincial sub-districts. In the Persian heartlands (Fars, Elam) were the major royal centres, such as the old city of Susa, which was extensively and lavishly rebuilt for the royal court in Achaemenid style, and the new, spectacular foundations of Pasargadae and Persepolis.

The satrap himself was, within his satrapy, in control of military affairs, such as general mobilisation and the garrisons which served to protect the population as well as maintain order in the province. He also controlled its administrative and financial affairs to ensure the province's continued productivity and profitability. The two concerns were closely linked as individuals held land-grants on which military and public service and taxes were owed.

Regional variation

Despite the unification of all these different areas in the person of the Persian king, which creates an impression of uniformity, there were regional variations in administration and differences in the formulation of dependence and subjection in some regions.

The transhumant populations of the great Zagros mountain chain, for example, were never fully integrated into the central structure. Its productive potential was slight and topography made military campaigns difficult; in addition, the highly mobile population was hard to pin down. Here the Persians and these scattered mountain dwellers arrived at a modus vivendi. The Persian king regularly presented the local leaders with gifts, which placed the recipients under obligation to help him. In return, the king was able to draw on their manpower resources when needed; the various tribes helped to secure his routes through the mountains when necessary, and their goodwill reduced the incidence of raids on nearby adjacent settled communities.

Arab groups enjoyed another kind of relationship with the central authority. In return for ensuring safe routes through the desert (Herodotus 3.7–9) and organising the lucrative caravan-trade, which ran from the southern tip of the peninsula to Palestinian ports, such as Persian-controlled Gaza, they did not pay the usual tax. Instead, they presented the king with a regular 'gift' of incense.

Another important frontier-group was the Scythians, who lived in the area beyond the Oxus (mod. Amu Darya). Their traditional lifestyle was nomadic – horse-borne warrior elites competed for, and maintained, status through booty acquired by raiding and war. How precisely the Persian authority managed relations with them is unknown, but they certainly supplied warriors to the Persian army. They regularly appear in Persian battle ranks and also as marines, which suggests that a reciprocal arrangement had been arrived at. That would have given the Persians potential access to trade routes through the Central Asian regions beyond their frontiers, as well as helping to safeguard such a highly permeable zone. A carpet in one of the 'Scythian Frozen Tombs' of the Altai mountains, near China, is decorated in a recognisably Achaemenid style, which reflects something of this network of relationships.

In these instances, climate, environment and patterns of life determined the solutions found for managing relations with such potentially troublesome groups. Differences in the style of imposition of Persian control in other places, or at least the way it was represented, hint at specific local factors with which the central authority had to deal.

Egypt, for example, retained its own very characteristic culture, especially in the realm of artistic expression and production, in styles of architecture and in its belief system, which traditionally assigned a special divine role to the king. As a result, from Cambyses on, Persian kings were hailed as pharaohs, represented as such and given pharaonic-style formal names, and titulary (Posener 1936: no. 1). They may even have assumed traditional Egyptian royal dress when acting in Egyptian royal rituals; certainly, that is how they are presented in temple and votive reliefs.

In Babylonia, too, the Persian king acted in accordance with local royal ideology which demanded that the king maintain and build temples and city walls, confirm the protected status of certain cities, ensure that rituals were performed, divine offerings authorised, and support (even, occasionally, take part in) the politically important New Year festival (Grayson 1975: no.7; Schaudig 2001: Cyrus Cylinder). At no point were the essential ingredients for carrying out these crucial rites dismantled or suppressed by the Persians. However, the precise pattern of their enactment and associated royal activity were modified. Early in the reign of Xerxes, the established old and powerful city elites, who had dominated civic and temple institutions in northern Babylonia from the Neo-Babylonian period on, were replaced by individuals dependent on Persian patronage. The earlier system of local government also changed and segments of civic and sacred institutions were more tightly drawn into the system of taxation. This may well be linked to the reorganisation of the province (see above, p. 566) and have been either the result of, or the reason for, two short-lived revolts in 484.

Another point to note is that, within each satrapy, local conditions varied from place to place not simply because of climate, language and political culture, but because a diversity of political units could all form part of one overall satrapy. Thus, in the province 'Beyond the River', a place such as Jerusalem, with the district of Yehud, retained its sacred laws, priestly hierarchy and was, almost certainly, governed by Jews. Neighbouring Samaria was administered by the local family of Sanballat. The Phoenician cities continued under the control of local rulers. Ammon, east of the Jordan, also formed a provincial subdivision under a local governor and, in the fourth century, the new administrative district of Idumaea was organised. So, while all these divergent entities were answerable to the Persian satrap in Damascus, internally they lived according to local custom. Similarly in Turkey, there were individual Greek cities, variously governed by democratic city councils, oligarchies or city-tyrants, and local regional dynasts, attested particularly for Caria, Lycia and Cilicia. Yet all these different political units related to the relevant satrap as the overarching authority. A similar picture is now emerging for the region of Bactria-Sogdiana, where the satrap and his regional subordinates interacted with the local aristocracies of the different communities.

Central control

This variation in patterns of rule should not be seen as a sign of imperial weakness nor yet as showing that these diverse political units were loosely joined together, easily detachable from Persian control. The varieties of political relationship and domination should, rather, be seen as a positive element, which made central government more elastic and sensitive in its response to local needs and conditions, while ensuring strong overall control for its own benefit (note the case of Babylonia, above, p. 567).

It is worth emphasising that the Persian empire lasted over 200 years, experiencing within that time only one serious loss, i.e., Egypt, which had seceded by 400/399; however, it was regained in 343 after repeated campaigns, so even that loss proved not to be permanent. Moreover, from Darius I on, the grip of the Achaemenid family on the throne was never broken. Despite repeated violent struggles for the royal succession, the family's hold on the kingship was never effectively challenged. From c.480 onwards, all serious revolts, with the exception of Egypt, took place *inside* the Persian power-structure itself and centred on struggles at court for the throne; in other words, they did not threaten the structure of the empire – they turned on who should rule it.

Despite local variations in the form of Persian rule, control of the various provinces was, and remained, extremely effective. The practice of exclusively appointing Persians to these high positions seems generally to have been the norm, reinforced by Persians or Iranians always holding the highest military commands and the most important posts in the provinces. This should not obscure the fact that members of the central authority developed close links with local elites in various areas of the empire, which could lead eventually to the recruitment of members from such groups to powerful governmental positions. One example is the case of the Babylonian Belshunu, who was district governor of Babylon from 422–415, and rose to the position of satrap of Beyond-the-River in 407, which he held until at least 401. This may have been a reward for his support in Darius II's struggle for the succession in 424/3, which closely involved Babylonia. Beyond that, there are indications of intermarriage: Persian nobles married women from the families of local dynasts (e.g., Herodotus 5.21; Xenophon, *Hellenica* 4.1.6–7); local dignitaries or soldiers, who had particularly distinguished themselves, are attested receiving a wife from a high-ranking Persian family (Herodotus 6.41). Particularly interesting is the chance information that the secondary wives of the kings themselves could be non-Persian, and in certain circumstances their sons might succeed to the throne. This is attested in the case of Darius II (423–405). His father, Artaxerxes I (465–424/3), is said by Ctesias (FGrH 688 F15) to have had three Babylonian concubines: Alogune, mother of Sogdianus, who contested the succession; Cosmartidene, mother of Ochus-Darius (II), who successfully seized the throne; and And(r)ia, mother of Parysatis, wife of Darius II. Thus, while power was carefully restricted to an exclusive Persian aristocracy, this small group of power-holders could, and did, incorporate selected members of the subject populations. By these means, the governing elite established a system of kinship ties and local alliances that reached right into the various dominated groups and helped to root its power at the local level to create an identity of interest. In Babylonia, the close interaction and shared interests of local entrepreneurs and the Persian authorities is particularly clearly attested. Tax collection, land and irrigation management created excellent opportunities for local families to amass wealth, and their continued success and maintenance of social status was dependent on the stability of the Persian regime.

Babylonian evidence also gives information about individuals at the lower end of the socio-economic scale. Local peoples, soldiers from across the empire and deportees were all allocated land-parcels that carried with them the obligation to perform a variety of tasks – most strikingly military duties – as and when required. The latter could be identified according to the kind of service required: 'bow-land' for archers, 'horse-land' for cavalry men and 'chariot-land' for chariot drivers and associated equipment. Clearly the aim of assigning such 'fief-holdings' was intended to fulfil imperial army requirements, while strengthening security through the presence of military settlements. Just as clearly, the surviving sources reveal that, after the formative phase, general call-ups were relatively infrequent and that routine needs were often fulfilled by mercenaries, so that at times the obligation associated with the land-holding was discharged in the form of a tax. A complicated series of arrangements is attested whereby holders of such 'fiefs' leased them out to financial firms, who managed them on their behalf, by renting them out, collecting the dues, in naturalia, and converting these through sale into silver for tax payments. Although this is a deformation of the system, it is clear that it did not break down. Enough evidence survives to show that the names of the original grantees, and the expected military service associated with the grant, were kept on satrapal registers. The grants could not be alienated, so when a demand came to supply, say, a cavalry-soldier, and the descendant of the grantee was not in a position to carry this out, he was nevertheless obliged to supply and equip a substitute to perform the service on his behalf. There is thus no reason to suppose that the empire was overdependent on foreign mercenaries and incapable of raising an army, throughout its existence, when necessary – a fact shown clearly during Alexander's invasion (334–330).

The empire's far-flung territories were connected by a complex road system. Herodotus (5.52–54; 8.98) describes part of it between Sardis and Susa. The Elamite documents from Persepolis (Hallock 1969: 'Q' texts) show it was much more extensive, linking all the main centres of the empire and guarded by a series of posting stations, which held supplies for travellers of fresh horses, fodder and food. Entitlement to draw on these supplies was obtained by written authorisation issued to individuals by the king, members of the court and satraps. They were extensively used, not simply by the king, royal retinue and army contingents, but also for the speedy communication between king and satrapal authorities and to facilitate the journeys of personal servants of Persian nobles engaged in looking after their landed estates. The clearest illustration is a document issued by the satrap of Egypt, then perhaps in Babylon or Susa, to permit the manager of his Egyptian estates to travel, together with three other servants, and draw supplies at posting-stations along the way (Porten and Yardeni 1986, A6.9). The route runs from north-eastern Babylonia, north along the east bank of the Tigris to Arbela, then through the Jezirah, across the Euphrates and the Syrian steppe to Damascus. Rivers, too, were part of the communication network. From the Mediterranean coast, for example, travellers moved overland to Thapsacus on the Euphrates in North Syria, sailing from there down to Babylon (Diodorus Siculus 14.81.4).

Landed estates, whose revenues were granted to members of the Persian aristocracy and especially favoured people who had performed exceptional services for the king as personal royal gifts, were located throughout the empire. Babylonia, again, provides some of the best evidence: apart from royal domains, lands held in the Nippur region by the queen, queen mother, crown prince and close members of the royal family. The distribution of land in the provinces to such powerful individuals must have served as a brake on the unrestricted exercise of satrapal power. While some of the highest-ranking owners held such estates in several different regions of the empire and were thus, perforce, absentee land-holders, others (including Persians) were firmly settled on their estates with their families, forming a provincial landed gentry. The estates included a fortified dwelling and it is clear from several accounts that these were permanently guarded by soldiers, and that the estates embraced holders of military fiefs who could be used to fend off attacks or, conversely, levied by the owner in response to larger military threats. The estates within the provinces were thus another means that served to spread the Persian presence and military control throughout the empire (Xenophon, *Anabasis* 7.8).

Keeping and extending land under production was a prime royal concern in order to ensure and safeguard an adequate agricultural base and the concomitant creation of state wealth as a result of productivity. The Persian rulers particularly fostered irrigation projects, both the extension of existing ones and the installation of new ones – in Babylonia, Bactria, northern Iran and the Egyptian oases. Fars is a testament to a striking landscape transformation wrought by the Persians. Archaeological survey indicates that, in the 400–500 years preceding the emergence of the Achaemenid state, the area was sparsely settled, there were virtually no large urban centres and the prevailing mode of land use was herding; but by the end of the empire, the region was remarked upon by historians as a veritable Garden of Eden – densely settled, fertile, heavily wooded, filled with fields, orchards and pastures, and well watered (Diodorus Siculus 19.21.2–4). The hard reality of this change has been established, not only by excavation of the palatial centres of Pasargadae and Persepolis, but also by surveys in the region, which chart the sudden and massive increase of settlements in the Achaemenid period.

THE KING AND ROYAL IDEOLOGY

At the apex of the empire stood the king, who regularly proclaimed himself as king of kings and ruler on this earth, but also stressed that he was an Iranian and a Persian, a member of the Achaemenid family, ideally directly descended from his predecessor. He usually chose his successor from among his sons and seems generally to have been expected to choose the eldest. But this was not an unalterable rule – he could, and did, if political considerations so dictated, select a younger son to the position of crown-prince (Kent 1953: XPf 27–36). Failing 'legitimate' offspring, by which presumably the sons of primary wives are meant, the sons of secondary wives, 'bastards', had the next best claim to succeed, which happened on occasion (see above, pp. 568–9). Conversely, husbands of royal daughters, i.e. royal sons-in-law, seem never to have been able to claim the throne, although their offspring could become eligible failing male royal children. The matrimonial policies of the Achaemenids were thus carefully guarded as the marriage of royal daughters to members of the aristocracy could lead to another family laying claim to the throne. This potential threat to the Achaemenid monopoly of power led at times to the practice of endogamy, in order to safeguard dynastic integrity.

On the king's death, an important duty that fell to the legitimate successor was the conveying of the body, in an elaborately decorated hearse, to Persepolis for burial in the rock-cut tombs, which, from Darius I onwards, never varied in their pattern and decoration. The 'royal fire', associated with the living king and located in various districts, was extinguished when his death was announced followed by a period of public mourning. The central authorities also funded cults at the tombs of past kings and members of the royal family.

The coronation of the king took place in Pasargadae, the royal centre laid out by Cyrus. It contained his tomb, quite unlike those of Darius I and his successors. It was a free-standing, stone-built, gabled building, elevated on a series of steep steps and set in a beautifully laid-out park. It was permanently guarded and had special rituals regularly performed around it by magi (Persian learned men), who received supplies from the royal treasuries (Arrian, *Anabasis* 6.29.4–7). Here the prospective king went through an initiation ritual: he was dressed in the garments of Cyrus before his rise to the kingship, ate bitter herbs and drank sour milk (Plutarch, *Artoxerxes* 3). Although the symbolism of the rite is not fully understood, it clearly evoked the origins of the dynasty and connected the new king directly with the founder of the empire. Only after completion of this ceremony, was he adorned with the royal insignia and revealed to the people in his fully crowned, royal glory.

Emphasis is placed in some of the royal inscriptions and stories surrounding the kings on their military valour and physical prowess. He underwent a special education, also experienced by the sons of the aristocracy: young boys were taken from their parents around age five and subjected to tough training in military and survival skills, as well as being instructed in Persian myths and legends by the magi (Strabo 15.3.18). Learning 'to tell the truth' was another aspect of this curriculum, the precise meaning of which is disputed. A possible interpretation is that it relates to the concept of loyalty to the king, who himself was empowered to uphold the god given order since he was conceived as holding the throne as a grant from the supreme Persian god, Auramazda. This loyalty to the king was expressed through total obedience, actively promoting his personal wellbeing and guarding him from physical and political dangers. Individuals who had particularly distinguished themselves in this respect could be raised in rank by royal favour, expressed through royal 'gifts' of a special dress, elaborate ornaments, a horse 'that had been ridden by the king' (*Esther* 6.8), land revenues, high position and, particularly, through being granted the right of salutation with a royal kiss, a mark of high status. This system of royal rewards resulted in the emergence of a royally created aristocracy who were superimposed on the ranks of the older aristocratic families, effectively limiting their privileges and forcing them to compete with the newer nobility to maintain their position. In this way, all became, in the king's eyes, his 'bondsmen' (OP *bandaka*).

BABYLONIAN–PERSIAN INTERACTIONS

Some aspects of the effects of Babylonian inclusion in the large Achaemenid empire have already been indicated (above, pp. 566, 567–70). An overall impression is that not only did the Persian regime profit enormously from the province, but Babylonia, too, prospered under Persian rule. But that is the general impression; whether all segments of Babylonian society shared in this prosperity, is impossible to say. Evidence for cosmopolitanism is particularly striking in this period. Far more communities of non-Babylonian origin are attested in this period than previously. The documentary evidence, along with classical writers, indicate the presence in the region of Indians, Jews, Egyptians, Greeks, Scythians, Carians, Lydians, Iranians, people from Malatya, Tyrians, people from various other places in Beyond-the-River, Armenians, Arabs, Phrygians and people from Afghanistan. Conversely, some Babylonians are attested serving in positions of command in southern Egypt. In Darius I's roll-call of the peoples of the empire who contributed to the building of his great palace at Susa (Kent 1953: DSf), the Babylonians take pride of place as those who excavated the 10 and 20 metre-deep foundations, laid the base of the palace and moulded the bricks. Most frequently, the Persepolis documents mention Babylonians as scribes

Figure 39.2 Seal inscribed with the name Darius (probably the Great) in Persian, Elamite and Babylonian (courtesy of the Trustees of the British Museum).

(almost certainly of Aramaic) working at a high level in the bureaucracy of Fars. It is also worth remembering that all Old Persian royal inscriptions were accompanied not only by versions in Elamite, closely linked to Persian identity, but also by ones in Babylonian. How to understand the significance of this precisely is unclear, but it must surely be an indicator of Babylon's status within the empire.

Persian imagery circulated through the empire in the form of the royal gold and silver coins and seals attached to, or imprinted on, official orders. The impact of this is reflected in the changing iconography of Babylonian seals. By the late sixth century some Persian symbols already appear, but there are many more in the seals impressed on the tablets from the late fifth century Murashu archive. The effects of so many different peoples drawn together under the imperial umbrella also led to informal interactions between them. This is reflected in the fact that, by the late fifth century, several Babylonians used Greek coins to seal perfectly standard Babylonian transactions. By the time a Macedonian dynasty had established itself in control of Babylonia (end of the fourth century), many typically Greek motifs were already familiar to the local inhabitants.

The number of people who set eyes on the fine Persian-style columned palace, with its moulded glazed brick reliefs echoing those at Susa (above, p. 566), was probably limited. But many more will have seen the Babylonian copies of Darius I's account of his triumph over those who challenged his seizure of the Persian throne. This was set up on the walls of the palace in Babylon, overlooking the great processional street. Not only was it exclusively in Babylonian, it attributed Persia's victory to Babylon's patron god, Marduk, and was accompanied by a relief picturing the king victorious over his enemies, among whom figured two Babylonian rebels.

BIBLIOGRAPHY

The bibliography on Achaemenid history is immense; the following is intended to provide a basic guide only.

To obtain a general orientation, see:

A. Kuhrt, 2000, 'The Achaemenid empire (*c*.550–330 BCE): continuities, adaptations, transformations', in S. Alcock *et al.* (eds), *Empires* (Cambridge: Cambridge University Press: 93–123).
J. Wiesehöfer, 1996, *Ancient Persia* (trans; London), BI-IV.

Fundamental problems and issues of approaches can be found in the articles published in:

H. Sancisi-Weerdenburg, A. Kuhrt, J.-W. Drijvers, M.C. Root (eds), 1987–1994, *Achaemenid History* I–VIII (Leiden: Neederlands Instituut voor het Nabije Oosten).

Detailed studies of the history of the imperial regions by various specialists can be found in:

Cambridge Ancient History IV: Persia, Greece and the Western Mediterranean, c.525–479 (rev. edn, Cambridge: Cambridge University Press, 1988).
Cambridge Ancient History VI: the Fourth Century (rev. edn, Cambridge: Cambridge University Press, 1994).

The one authoritative study of history and institutions, with full analysis of problems of sources, methodology and interpretation, with full references, is:

P. Briant, 1996, *Histoire de l'empire perse: de Cyrus à Alexandre* (Paris: Fayard; Leiden: Netherlands Institute for the Near East (Achaemenid History IX)), now available in English as: P. Briant, 2002, *From Cyrus to Alexander: history of the Persian empire* (trans. P. Daniels, Winona Lake IN: Eisenbrauns).

For critical, annotated bibliographical updates, see:

P. Briant, 1997, *Bulletin d'Histoire Achéménide* I (Topoi Suppl. I: Lyon).
P. Briant, 2001, *Bulletin d'Histoire Achéménide* II (Paris: Thotm).

For Persia before the empire and its relationship to Elam, see:

W. Henkelman, 2003, 'Persians, Medes and Elamites: acculturation in the Neo-Elamite period', in G. Lanfranchi, M. Roaf and R. Rollinger (eds), *Continuity of Empire(?): Assyria, Media, Persia* (Padua: Sargon, Editrice e Libreria: 181–231).

The fundamental study of the formulation of Achaemenid royal iconography is:

M.C. Root, 1979, The King and Kingship in Achaemenid Art: essays on the creation of an iconography of empire (Acta Iranica III/9; Leiden: Brill).

For the ahistorical nature of Old Persian Royal Inscriptions, see:

Sancisi-Weerdenburg, H., 1999, 'The Persian kings and history', in C.S. Kraus (ed.), *The Limits of Historiography: genre and narrative in ancient historical texts* (Mnemosyne Suppl. 191; Leiden: Brill: 91–112).

The main collections of texts are (in alphabetical order):

Cahiers de la Délégation Francaise en Iran IV (Paris, 1984).
G.G. Cameron, 1948, *The Persepolis Treasury Tablets* (Oriental Institute Publications 65; Chicago, IL: University of Chicago Press).
A.K. Grayson, 1975, *Assyrian and Babylonian Chronicles* (Texts from Cuneiform Sources 5, Locust Valley, NY: J.J. Augustin) (the Nabonidus Chronicle = no. 7).
P. Grelot, 1972, *Documents Araméens d'Egypte* (Littératures Anciennes du Proche-Orient 5; Paris: Editions du Cerf).
R.T. Hallock, 1969, *The Persepolis Fortification Tablets* (Oriental Institute Publications 92; Chicago, IL: University of Chicago Press).
—— 1978, 'Selected Fortification Tablets', *Cahiers de la Délégation Archéologique Francaise en Iran* 8: 109–136.
R.G. Kent, 1953, *Old Persian. Grammar, Texts, Lexicon* (2nd edn, New Haven, CT: American Oriental Society).
B. Porten and A.Yardeni, 1986–1993, *Textbook of Aramaic Documents from Ancient Egypt*, (Jerusalem: Hebrew University Press).
G. Posener, 1936, *La première domination perse en Egypte* (Bibliothèque d'Étude de l'Institut Francais d'Archéologie Orientale XI; Cairo).
H.-P. Schaudig, 2001, *Die Inscriften Nabonids von Babylon und Kyros des Grossen samt den in ihrem Umfeld entstandenen Tendenzschriften* (AOAT 256, Münster: Ugarit-Verlag) (the most recent edition of the Cyrus Cylinder, see pp. 550–556).
R. Schmitt, 1991, *The Bisitun Inscription of Darius the Great: Old Persian Text* (Corpus Inscriptionum Iranicarum II/1; London: School of Oriental and African Studies).
—— 2000, *The Old Persian Inscriptions of Naqsh-i Rustam and Persepolis* (Corpus Inscriptionum Iranicarum I/2; London: School of Oriental and African Studies).

There are plenty of reliable translations of Herodotus; good discussions of his approach, intellectual context and reliability, can be found in:

E.J. Bakker, I.J.F. de Jong and H. van Wees (eds), 2002, *Brill's Companion to Herodotus* (Leiden: Brill).

An excellent new edition of all fragments of Ctesias, together with detailed notes and a full, positive reappraisal of his work is:

D. Lenfant, 2004, *Ctésias de Cnide* (Paris: Les Belles Lettres).

(For other classical writers, consult the relevant volumes of the Loeb Classical Library.)

For the main studies and publications of major sites, architecture, monuments, artefacts, see:

M. Garrison and M.C. Root, 2002, *Seals in the Persepolis Fortification Tablets vol. I: Images of Heroic Encounter* (Oriental Institute Publications 117, Chicago, IL: University of Chicago Press).

P. Harper, J.Aruz and F. Tallon (eds), 1992, *The Royal City of Susa* (New York: Metropolitan Museum of Archaeology and Art).

E. Schmidt, 1953–57, *Persepolis* (Oriental Institute Publications 68–70; Chicago, IL: Chicago University Press).

D. Stronach, 1978, *Pasargadae* (Oxford: Oxford University Press).

A.B. Tilia, 1972–78, *Studies and Restorations at Persepolis and Other Sites in Fars* (Rome: Istituto per il Medio e Estremo Oriente, Reports and Memoirs 16 and 18).

Studies specifically devoted to Babylonia (aside from the chapters in *Cambridge Ancient History IV and VI*, above) are:

R. McC., Adams, 1981, *Heartland of Cities: surveys of ancient settlement and land use in the central flood plain of the Euphrates* (Chicago, IL: University of Chicago Press).

L. Bregstein, 1993, *Seal Use in Fifth Century BC Nippur, Iraq: a study of seal selection and sealing practice in the Murašu archive* (Ph.D. diss., University of Pennsylvania).

F. Joannès, 1990, 'Pouvoirs locaux et organisation du territoire en Babylonie achéménide', *Transeuphratène* 3: 173–189 (an excellent clear survey).

—— 2000, La Mésopotamie au 1ère millénaire av.n.é. (Paris: Armand Colin; now available in an English translation, as *The Age of Empires: Mesopotamia in the first millennium BC*, Edinburgh: Edinburgh University Press, 2004) (traces Mesopotamian history and culture down to the Parthian period, emphasising continuities and pinpointing changes, illustrated with selected text translations).

Seidl, U., 1999b, 'Eine Triumphstele Darius' I. aus Babylon', in J. Renger (ed.), *Babylon: Focus mesopotamischer Geschichte, Wiege früher Gelehrsamkeit, Mythos in der Moderne,* (Saarbrücken: 297–306) (discussion, with reconstruction, of the Babylonian version of Darius I's Bisitun text and relief set up in Babylon).

M.W.Stolper, 1985, *Entrepreneurs and Empire: the Murašû archives, the Murašû firm and Persian rule in Babylonia* (Leiden: Netherlands Institute of the Near East) (an in-depth study of land management by a Babylonian business 'firm' in the Nippur region and its interconnections with the political superstructure in the fifth century; fundamental for understanding the social, economic and political situation).

—— 1989, 'The Governor of Babylon and Across-the-River', *Journal of Near Eastern Studies* 48: 283–305 (publication of the evidence for the administrative restructuring of the Babylonian satrapy).

C. Waerzeggers, 2003/4, 'The Babylonian revolts against Xerxes and the "end of archives"', *Archiv für Orientforschung* 50: 150–178 (important analysis of archives from Borsippa, which fixes the date of the revolts in Xerxes' reign, and the changes in personnel in the North Babylonian sanctuaries).

For discussion of the situation in the poorly documented northern sector of the Babylonian province, see:

R. Bertolino, 1999, 'Un iscrizione inedita in aramaico d'impero a Hatra', in L. Milano *et al.* (eds), *Landscapes: territories, frontiers and horizons in the Ancient Near East* (54. Rencontre Assyriologique Internationale, Venice 1997; History of the Ancient Near East/Monographs III/1; Padua: Sargon: 133–138).

A. Kuhrt, 1995, 'The Assyrian heartland in the Achaemenid period', in P. Briant (ed.), *Dans les pas des Dix-Mille: peuples et pays du proche-orient vus par un grec* (Toulouse: Pallas 43; 239–254).

INDEX

——— • ◆ • ———

Page references in *italics* indicate illustrations.

Abi-eshuh 131, 217
Abi-sare 24
Abu Qubur 66
Abu Salabikh 146, 152, 256, 257, 433, 448
Achaemenid period 236, 343, 476, 481, 562–73
acrobats 273, 341
Adab 254, 448
Adad 103, 104, *103*, *105*, 112, 163, 168, 476, 478, 535
Adad-apla-iddina 531
Adad-Guppi 305
Adad-nirari I 509, 530
Adad-nirari III 297, 529, 531
Adad-shuma-usur 530
Adapa 447, 450, 476
administration 4, 44, 82, 95, 199, 201, 226, 232, 253, 434
adoption 48, 268, 307, 434
adultery 302
agate 131
agriculture 2, 4, 6, 39–49, 54–63, 187, 191, 219, 225, 295, 527
Akhenaton *see* Amenophis IV
Akhetaten *see* Amarna
Akitu festival (Babylonian New Year festival) 269, 351, 356, 513, 531, 536, 538
Akkad (also Agade) 69, 70, 127, 214, 322, 332, 335, 542

Akkadian: language 23, 373, 389, 400–1, 404, 421, 437, 440, 448, 453, 481, 489, 512, 515, 518, 527, 535; literature 20, 447; state 22–3
Akshak 22
alabaster 132, *169*
Alalakh 129, 490–1,
Aleppo 211, 221, 402, 407, 490, 498, 503, 504
Alexander the Great 3, 168, 456, 487, 499, 563, 569
Allatum 324
alluvial plains 15, 39, 54, 187, 225, 268, 292, 527
Almanacs 463–5
alum 231
Amarna 9, 437, 488, 517; tablets 9, 490, 518, 521
amber 135
Amenophis II 490, 493, 498
Amenophis III 494
Amenophis IV 488, 493, 509, 528
Ammi-ditana 25
Ammi-saduqa 25, 99, 205, 212, 213, 285
Amorite 400–14; kings 2, 95, 203; language 2, 23; tribes 23, 215, 279, 400–14, 527
Amurru *105*, 160, *161*
An 56, 332
Anatolia 126, 129, 145, 151, 213, 282, 370, 437, 487, 490, 503–13, 528

577

ancestor cult 270, 281
Andarig 401
Anshan 24
Anshar 538
antimony 127
Anu 163, 324, 342, 343, 380, 382, 427, 535
Anu-aba-uter 427, 429
Anu-bel-shunu 427, 429
Anunitum 322
Anzu 322, 448, 452
Apkallu 383, 476
Aplahanda 101
apples and apple trees 47, 178
Apsu 352; basin 323, 325, 327
Arabia 131
Arabs 14, 289, 296, 567
Arahtum 219, 292
Aramaic 224, 245, 429, 447, 453, 455, 456, 467, 474, 481, 563, 573
Arameans 7, 14, 26, 288–97, 495, 533
architecture 1, 24, 81–93
archives 6, 41, 54, 66, 92, 199–200, 201, 202, 205, 206–7, 219, 220, 227, 232, 236, 271, 273, 285, 410, 475, 488, 496, 510, 514, 517, 519, 566
ards 54, 61
arithmetic 422–3
armies 215, 216, 273, 279, 296, 534, 567, 569
Arnuwanda 506
aromatics 5, 132
arsenic/arsenical bronze 127
Artaxerxes I 120, 569
Asaluhhi 349, 378, 382–4, 390, 393, 477, 537
Ashipu 365, 367, 374, 378, 393, 426–7, 451
Ashiputu 475, 478, 480
Ashnan 326
Ashurbanipal 76, 135, 155–8, *156*, 473, 277, 478, 496, 533–4, 536, 539
Ashur-bel-kala 531
Ashur-bel-nisheshu 529
Ashur-nadin-shumi 533
Ashurnasirpal II 128
Ashur-ra'im-napishti 453–5
Ashur-uballit 493–4, 496, 509, 528, 529, 538

Assur: city 151, 188, 303, 323, 376, 393, 450, 453, 528, 534, 535, 542; god 535, 536, 537–8
Assyria 2, 3, 9, 128, 437, 439, 453, 463, 473, 490–501, 507, 527–39, 553
'Assyrian Dream Book' 368
astrologers 9, 365, 455, 456
astrology 274, 364, 465–9
astronomers 9, 432, 475, 480
'Astronomical Diaries' 363
astronomy 3, 9, 274, 365, 460–9, 476, 479–80, 482, 500
Atrahasis myth 219, 352, 448, 450, 452, 477
Auramazda 571
Aya 102

Baba 252, 326, 328, 398
Baba-ahhe-iddina 27
Babylon (city) 1, 2, 3, 26, 28, 54, 67–76, 155, 168, 201, 204, 210, 211, 219, 225, 236, 256, 266–7, 280, 323, 342, 349, 351–2, 377, 413, 426, 455, 473, 477, 503, 519, 531, 533–4, 536, 543, 558, 564, 566, 570, 573
'Babylonian Chronicle' 503, 533, 546–7
Badakshan 96, 130
Badtibira 279, 339
Baghdad 2, 28, 83
bakers 174, 200, 229, 269
baking 176, 308
bankers 236
barley 57, 130, 172, 177, 180, 191, 218, 231, 238, 244, 257
Barnamtara 252, 255
Barutu 475, 478
basalt 162
bathrooms 71–2, 323
Bau 258
Bazi Dynasty 25
bdellium 135
beads 97, 127, 129, 130
beduins 41
Belet-ekallim 323
Belet-ili 384
Bel-ibni 533
Beltiya 342, 343
beer 173, 177, 180, 230, 231, 238, 252, 268, 271, 321, 396, 419

Benteshina 511–12
Berossus 476
Bible 1, 541–59
birds 172, 175, 179, 366, 370, 433
Bit-Amukan(n)I 26–7, 293, 296
Bit-Dakkuru 26–7, 293, 296
Bit-Gambulu 26–7, 295, 297
Bit Puqudu 26–7, 293, 295, 297
bitumen 71, 84
Bit-Yakin 26–8, 293, 296, 297
Boghazköy 377, 517
booty 279, 356, 530
Borsippa 26, 66–8, 70, 169, 225, 226, 239,
     292, 323, 356, 426, 473, 519, 531, 533,
     536
boundaries 22–3, 74, 160; markers 22; of
     states 22, 497
boundary stones 160–8, *164–5*
boxwood 133, 155
bread 173, 419
brewers 18, 173, 200, 229, 269
bronze 125, 128, 187, 195
builders 59, 81, 93, 155
building 232, 274, 277, 395; monumental
     84–91; rituals 155–7
bullae 101, 120, 419
Burnaburiash 84, 488, 494, 505–6, 509,
     528, 529
businessmen 202, 231
butchers 229
butter 143

calcite 131
calendars 44, 254, 327, 365, 465, 536
Cambyses 496, 565
camels 296; herding 14
canals 69, 83, 187, 219, 225, 231, 238,
     244, 252, 290, 533
caravans 212, 518
Carchemish 47, 101, 491–2, 496, 516, 518,
     521, 546–7
carnelian 127, 131, 453
carpets 147
'Catalogue of Texts and Authors' 477
cattle 55, 59, 199, 294, 323, 326
celestial divination 460–3
cemeteries 83
cereals 15, 44–5, 177, 191, 225, 257
Chagar Bazar 92

chalcedony 118–20
Chaldean 364; dynasty 111, 227; tribes 7,
     14, 27, 288–97, 531, 533
chariots 99, 150, 216–17, 521
cheese 179
chick peas 46, 178
chieftains 27, 131, 296
childbirth 300, 341, 394–5
chlorite 95, 132
Choga Zanbil 108
'Chronicle P' 528, 530
chronicles 26, 224, 288
cities 5, 14, 66–76, 200, 228, 366; gods
     26, 268, 319; layout 68, 81–4; maps 75;
     state 22; walls 67, 68, 75; *see also*
     Babylon (city)
Claudius Aelianus 457–8
climate 2, 40
cloth 141–52; production 141–2
clothing 5, 105, 141–3, *144*, 157, 169,
     201, 231, 355, 434, 519
cobalt 127
Code of Hammurabi 103, 157–60, *159*,
     206, 207–8, 276, 348–9, 361
commentaries 442, 481
commoners 257–9
concubines 307, 309, 569
conspicuous consumption 271–2
contraception 305
contracts 95, 301, 309, 434
copper 5, 124–8, 133, 160, 187, 195, 201,
     212–13, 231
cooking 92, 176–7
coriander 46, 178
correspondence 408–14, 488–90,
     510–11
corvées 191, 252, 530
counters 419
countryside 4, 92, 193, 201, 257, 291
courtyards 71, 84–5, 89, 91, 434, 519
craft: workers 59, 82, 111; workshops 200,
     253
credit 23
cucumbers 172, 178
cultivation 15, 54
cults 229, 254, 270, 321, 323, 326, 333,
     348, 479, 499, 537, 539; images/statues
     355–6; personnel 343
cumin 46, 176, 178

cuneiform: tablets 1, 54; writing 95, 194, 256, 274, 320, 365, 369, 419, 434–45, 448, 453, 455, 456, 467, 473, 481, 489, 499, 512, 517, 535
curses 168, 281, 344, 373
Cutha 531, 543
Cuthean Legend of Naram-Sin 475
cylinder seals 5, 95–121, 256, 349, 434, 518, 520
Cyprus 126, 127
Cyrus the Great 116, 274, 556, 565, 571

Dadusha 281
Damgalnuna 328
Darius I 116, 120, 129, 499, 565, 568, 571, 572–3
Darius II 568–9
'Dark Age' 25, 211, 219
date palms 2, 83; cultivation 191–2, 225, 229, 241, 244, 295; gardens/groves 225, 227
dates (fruit) 172, 177, 178, 202, 231, 238, 257, 516
'Debate between the Hoe and the Plow' 18, 60
'Debate between Winter and Summer' 18
debt 204, 205, 207, 240, 241, 259
deportations 297, 532
Der 45, 519, 530
'Descent of Ishtar (Inanna)' 332, 335, 450
'Diagnostic Handbook' 393
Dilbat 67, 70, 204, 205, 226, 323
Dilmun 126–8, 133, 151, 201, 212
Dingirmah 324
disease 367, 373, 376–9, 480, 514
distaffs 146
divination 7, 104, 361–71, 447, 463, 481
diviners 8, 269, 299, 353, 364, 366–41, 463, 476–86
divorce 302, 310
Diyala river 497–8; valley 15, 87, 202, 211, 217, 293
dockets 101; of animals and plants 54
donkeys 59, 192, 257
dowries 173, 238–9, 244–5, 301–2
drainage and drains 71, 72
dreams 322, 362

Drehem (ancient Puzrish-Dagan) 145 dress *see* clothing
drink 5, 171–82, 376
ducks 192
Dumuzi 18, 143, 303, 308, 324, 338–9, 340–1, 344–5
'Dumizi and Enkimdu' 142–3
Dur-Kurigalzu 147, 150, 519
Dur-Sharrukin 538
Dur-Yahdun-Lim 45
dyes and dyeing 150

Ea 163, 342, 349, 352, 356, 378, 382–4, 390, 392, 476, 477, 479
Eanna 69, 116, 226, 342, 343
Ean(n)atum 20, 259
Early Dynastic period 6, 17, 251–9, 348
Ebabbar 70, 83, 84, 116, 226, 229, 478
Ebla 151, 259, 490, 498
ebony 133, 296
Ecbatana *see* Hamadan
eclipses 364, 460, 466
economic texts 54
economy 187–95, 210–21, 224–33, 276–86; palace 191
ecstatics 362, 378
edicts 191, 204, 207, 281, 284, 566; of Ammisaduqa 220
Edublalmah 89
Eduranki 323
eggs 178, 179
Egibi family 6, 116, 236–46, 307, 308
Egypt 9, 54, 129, 147, 295, 437, 468, 487–501, 507–9, 517, 520, 528, 539, 546, 547, 550, 562, 565, 567, 568, 570
Ekallatu(m) 528
Ekur 322, 383, 421, 449, 537
Elam 3, 23, 128, 129, 146, 163, 211, 213, 460, 495–6, 500–1, 533, 562
Elamites 26, 157, 279, 296, 297, 349, 530, 533, 573
elites 6, 22, 26, 174, 191, 195, 215, 217, 218, 221, 255–7, 276, 284, 305, 319, 373, 458, 535, 536, 538, 567, 568, 569
Ellil-kudurri-usur 530
Emar (modern Meskene) 47, 212, 437, 518, 520

Emesal 477
emmer wheat 257
Enannatum 253
Enheduanna 336
Enmerkar 143, 338, 447
Enmesharra 395
Enmetena 253, 258, 279
Enentarzi 258, 259
Enki 328, 332, 334, 335, 349, 390
Enkidu 142, 172–3
Enlil 56, 60, 127, 163, 253, 319–30, 332, 339–40, 342, 349, 352, 356, 383, 449, 479, 519, 520, 535, 535, 537
Enlil-nadin-ahhe 349–51
Enshakushanna 253
Ensi 23, 320
Ensuhkeshdanna 338
entrepreneurs 189, 191, 194, 201, 205, 206–7, 218, 226–7, 230–2, 238–9, 271
Enuma Anu Ellil *365, 426, 461–3, 474, 476, 478, 481*
enuma elish 321, 351–2, 375, 452, 461, 475, 481, 537, 538
envelopes 99–100, 99
Ephemerides 464–7
Epic of Creation 7; *see also enuma elish*
Ereshkigal 321, 324
Eriba-Marduk 27, 297
Eridu 334, 349, 383, 532
Erra epic 355
Esagil(a) 70, 129, 155, 157, 237, 241, 342, 355–6, 456, 478, 482, 539
Esarhaddon 473, 495–6, 533, 539
Esharra 537
Eshnunna 24, 135, 203, 211–12, 217, 218, 254, 497
Etemenanki 70, 355, 426, 427
Eturkalama 343
Euphrates 2, 4, 15, 39–49, 54, 56, 69, 82, 172, 194, 212, 213, 219, 265, 290–3, 491, 497–8, 503, 518, 533, 547, 564, 570
Eurmeiminanki 70
exports 6, 141
'Exaltation of Ishtar' 342, 343, 477
exchange 188–9
exorcism 353, 355, 394
exorcists 229, 269, 379, 475–86

extispicy 269, 361, 362, 368–70, 479, 513
Ezekiel 542, 551
Ezida 68, 70, 157

fallow 57–9, 192, 291
family 93, 320, 375, 475
famine 219, 351
Fara texts 254, 533
farmers 26, 200, 226, 231, 460
'Farmer's Almanac ('Farmer's Instructions') 4, 18, 54, 57, 60–3, 422–3
farming *see* agriculture
fashion 147
fate 321
fertility 326–7, 333, 352, 367
festivals (*see also Akitu* festival) 268, 273, 333, 335, 355, 535
fields 6, 26, 42–3, 191, 201, 205, 208, 227, 239, 291, 366, 570; plans 239, 241–4, 243, 428; size 47–9
figs 47, 178
First Dynasty of Babylon 2, 6
First Sealand Dynasty 218
fish 130, 172, 179, 201, 202, 206, 228, 433; farming 42
fishermen and fishing 18, 201, 225
flax 143–5, 146, 308
floodplains 39
floods and flooding 42, 291, 352, 479, 535
food 5, 54, 171–82, 273, 376
fortresses 20, 25
fruit 178, 326; orchards 42, 46–7, 172, 240, 291, 570
furniture 71, 150

gagum 206, 307
gala mah 205, 254
gardeners 46, 226, 231, 244
gardening and gardens 42, 46–7, 58, 172, 205, 225,366
garlic 46
garments see clothing
gates 68–70, 75, 82, 85, 168
'gateways' 516–22
geese 192
gender 7, 299–311, 321, 340, 375
Geshtinanna 326

gift exchange 272–3, 491, 511
Gilgamesh 322, 447; Epic of Gilgamesh 6, 8, 142, 172, 299, 427, 447–58, *454*, 475, 477
Gipar(u) 89
Girra 378, 380–5
Girsu 15, 56
glass 231, 521
glyptics *see* seals
goats 55, 145, 172, 192
goddesses 7, 319–30
gold 128–9, 160, 195, 239, 271, 519, 546, 573
goldsmiths 129, 271, 477, 519
grain 326; production 191
Greek: language 168–9, 224, 429, 455, 457, 467, 476, 481, 499; seals 120–1
grid layouts 68, 83
Gudea 23, 28–9, 127, 135, 151, 278
Gula 163, 299, 319, 322, 325, 342, 383, 392–3, 397–8, 476, 480

Habakkuk 542, 556–9
haematite 95–5, 96, 131
Hamadan (Ecbatana) 564
Hammurabi (Hammu-rapi) 2, 24, 41, 82, 89, 90, 157–60, *159*, 182, 201, 202, 210, 212, 215, 217, 220, 276, 279, 284, 348, 402, 403, 409, 449, 450, 503, 528
Hananiah 555–6
'Hanging Gardens' 72
Hanigalbat 216
Haradum 82–3, 89
Harappa 134–5
Harmal *see* Tell Harmal
harps 323, 325
Harran (Sultantepe) 376, 496, 499, 559
haruspicy 104
harvests 44–5, 57, 232, 238, 251, 282, 322, 326, 365, 369, 419
Hatti 490–5, 498, 500–1, 503–13, 528, 546
Hattusa 9, 437, 43, 503, 511, 514
Hattushili I 504
Hattushili II 507
Hattushili III 494, 510–11
healing 8, 325–6

Hellenistic period 229, 428–9, 463, 465, 467–9, 476, 478, 481
Henti 505, 506
herbs 46, 56, 178, 180
herding 192, 200, 570
herdsmen 227–8
Herodotus 62, 129, 168, 306, 355, 562, 565, 567, 568, 569
Hezekiah 543–5
Hittites 370, 450; kings 503–13, 529
hoes 56, 60
honey 155, 157, 179
horoscopes 465–9
horses 272, 521; breeding of 294, 558, 569, 572
horticulture 46; *see also* gardens
households 25, 194, 281; patrimonial 194, 280, 281
houses 176, 265, 320, 473; sales of 201, 205
housing 70–3, 91–2
Humbaba 101
hunting 225
Hurrian language 370, 400, 438, 450
Hurrians 504–5, 517, 527, 528
Hursagkalamma 70, 237
husbandry, of animals 54, 187, 227–8, 290, 527

Iahdun-Lim 101
Ibbi-Sin 23, 141, 151, 199
iconography 5, 95, 163, 573
Iddin-Dagan 23
ideology 7, 274, 276–7, 281, 319, 321, 329, 475, 499, 545, 550, 553, 558, 567, 570–2
Ilkum 202, 204, 207–8, 283
Imgur-Enlil 69, 76
Inanna 7, 18, 87, 143, 30, 308, 319–30, 332–45, 432, 462
incantations 157, 300, 338, 341, 344, 351, 373, 376, 426, 477, 538; medical 8, 389–98, 426, 460; potency 303, 344, 395
incense 135, 321, 371, 391, 566
Indus valley 127, 134
inheritance 92, 237, 245, 276, 300
'Instructions of Shuruppak' 256
iron 127, 231

irrigation 14, 15, 18, 26, 40, 42–4, 56–8, 244, 252, 291, 569, 570; taxes 58, 187, 189, 225
Isaiah 543–5
Ishara 163
Ishbi-Erra 280
Ishme-Dagan 280, 285, 340, 401, 403, 408, 422
Ishtar 7, 90, 96, 101, *101*, 104, 163, 168, 321, 332–45, *337*, 382, 395, 453
Ishtaran 163
Isin 67, 199, 326, 519
Isin-Larsa period 89, 199–201
Israel 9, 541–59
Itti-Marduk-balatu 237, 239, 241, 455, 510
ivory 127, 134, 155

Jamutbal 24, 25
Jebel Sinjar 47, 211, 401
Jehoiakim 545, 547–51
Jehoiakin 549, 554
Jemdet-Nasr period 17
Jeremiah 542, 544, 551–7
Jerusalem 541, 543, 547, 567
jewellery and jewellers 84, 95, 127, 129, 130, 254, 271, 273, 519
Jezirah 85, 289, 296, 527, 570
Jokha *see* Umma
Josiah 542, 548, 555
Judah 1, 541–59
judges 237, 245–6

Kadashman-Enlil II 131, 491, 508–11
Kadashman-Turgu 494, 508–9
Kadesh (Qadesh) 494–5, 508
Kalhu 376, 531, 534
Kalutu 475, 478
Kandalanu 534
Kanesh (modern Kültepe) 128, 145, 213, 303
Karaindash 107, 529
Karana 401, 407, 409
Karduniash 2, 28, 221
Kar-Tukulti-Ninurta I 147, 349, 498, 530, 536–8
Karum 82, 151, 213
Kashtialiash IV 512, 530

Kassite: language 438; period 17, 75, 107–10, 130, 351; state 9, 25–6, 515–22
Kassites 2, 203–4, 211–12, 215–17, 490–5, 504–5, 530
Kaunake garment 141
Kesh 24
Khabur river 39, 42
Khafaja 205
Khorsabad (ancient Nimrud) 147, 150, 377
Kikalla 216
Kimash 127
kings 6, 14, *105*–6, 155, 174, 220, 251–4, 322–4, 364, 380, 473, 542, 567, 570–2; as builders 155–7
kingship 5, 20, 24, 155, 277–9, 281, 332, 340, 352
Kish 15, 22, 67, 70, 204, 205, 219, 253
kitchens 176
Kudurrus 162–8, *164*–5, 519
Kulla 476
Kültepe *see* Kanesh
Kurigalzu I 131, 219, 519
Kurigalzu II 493, 529
Kusu 326
Kutalla (modern Tell Sifr) 128, 201
Kutha 67, 70

Lagash 15, 20, 21, 28–9, 134, 145, 151, 251, 253, 254–6, 258, 281
Lama 96–7, 98, 99, 101–3
Lama-lugal 325
lamentation priests 323, 325, 427, 475–86
lamentations 351, 479
lamps 134
landscape 39, 55, 58–9, 257, 291, 487
lapis lazuli 96, 130–1, 253, 255, 453, 520, 570
Larsa 15, 24, 29, 67, 69, 70, 82–3, 84, 93, 202, 211, 217, 218, 268, 280, 285, 340, 519, 535
law 20, 157–8; codes 20, 157, 220, 300; courts 270
Laws 157–60, 310, 512; of Eshnunna 281; of Hammurabi 173, 174, 278, 280–1, 285, 300, 307, 308, 310–11, 320, 512

leaching 57–8

lead 127

leeks 46

lentils 46, 178, 257

letters 8, 27, 41–9, 95, 174, 204, 268, 270, 289, 294, 300, 304, 306, 308, 309, 369, 373, 400–14, *402, 404–6, 410, 412*, 434, 488–90, 510–11, 520, 528, 529, 534, 536

lettuce 178

Levant 9, 295, 515–22

libraries 426, 473, 475, 478, 519; of Ashurbanipal 366, 367, 368, 369, 390, 440, 452–3, 473, 476, 478, 536

Library of Ashurbanipal 536

limestone 132, 162

linen 143–5, 151

Lipit-Eshtar 280, 285, 422

lists, 474, 481; of gods 256, 320, 335, 339, 432, 519; lexical 6, 126, 177, 426, 432–45, 517, 520; of professions 432, 435, 437

literacy 171, 434; of kings 473, 536; of women 305, 480

liver omens 369–71, *370*

livestock 56; *see also* cattle; sheep; oxen

loans 205, 207, 232, 284

locusts 45, 179

looms 146–7

Ludlul bel nemeqi *20, 351, 352–5, 451, 481*

Lugalbanda 252, 255, 258, 322, 447, 448, 449

Lugalkiginedudu 253

Lugalzagesi 22, 253, 258

luxury goods 2, 18, 195, 200, 271, 515

Magan (Makkan) 127, 128, 129, 134, 151

magic 160, 306, 344, 349, 364, 373–85, 389, 394, 426, 480, 507

mail 407–14

Manasseh 545, 548–9

manuals, for diviners 365

Maqlu *374, 377, 379–85, 389, 390, 475*

Marad 70

Marduk 7, 25, 163, 168, 220, 240, 265, 269, 319, 348–56, *350*, 384, 390, 455, 461, 473, 477, 478, 481, 530, 531, 532, 536–9, 558, 573

Marduk-apla-iddina II 27, 113, 131, 293, *294, 296, 297*, 532, 543–5, 551–2

Marduk-apla-usur 297

Marduk-balassu-iqbi 297

Marduk-nadin-ahhe 163, *165*, 538

Marduk-nasir-apli 237, 244

Marduk-shapik-zeri 531

Marduk-zakir-shumi *482*, 531

Marhashi 127, 132

Mari (modern Tell Hariri) 4, 8, 41–9, 87, 90–1, 100, 128, 129, 133, 172, 174, 176, 211, 212, 256, 273, 341, 368, 528, 535, 536

markets 187–9, 232; exchange 188–9, 193–4; marketplaces 83, 232–3, 473

marriage 92, 143, 230, 244–5, 268, 272, 273, 300–2, 373, 434, 493, 505, 506, 528, 531, 570; 'sacred marriage' 333–4, *334*, 339–41

'Marriage of MAR.TU' 18

Mars (planet) 462, 464

marshland 15, 172, 200, 218, 291, 293, 533

Mashkan Shapir 82–3

mathematics 3, 8, 418–29

meat 174, 199, 228, 271, 272, 273, 321

Medes 3, 496, 534, 562, 564

medicine 325, 389–98, 476, 479–80, 514

Megiddo 101

Meluhha 127, 128, 134

Me principles 334, 342

mercenaries 204, 212, 216, 217, 569

merchants 84, 91, 127, 129, 207, 272, 408, 494, 511, 517

Mercury (planet) 460

Merkes 68, 70, 76

Merodach-Baladan *see* Marduk-apla-iddina

Mesalim 253, 254

Meskene *see* Emar

messengers 407–14, 488, 493, 511, 544

metals 125–30

metalsmiths and metalwork 83, 126, 229

metrology 418–29

Middle Babylonian period 17, 349, 437–40

milk 143, 173, 179, 228, 257
millers 18, 44, 269
Mitanni 490–5, 498–500, 517, 520, 528
Mithridates II 456
monetisation 233, 255
money 195, 217, 229, 231–2, 241
monuments 5, 157
'Muballitat-Sherua 529
mud brick 70, 85, 93, 257
Mummu 352
Murashu 27, 120, 227, 232, 496, 573
Mursili I 2, 503–8
Mursili II 506–7
Mushkenum 208, 283, 305
musical instruments 323, 340
musicians 269, 273, 323
mustard 46
myrrh 135

Nabonidus 237, 274, 278, 305, 343, 473, 542
Nabopolassar 499, 534, 558
Nabu 157, 163, 327, 356, 473, 532, 536, 538
Nabu-ahhe-iddin 236–7, 240–1, 245–6, 426
Nabu-mukin-zeri 296, 297
Nabu-shuma-ishkun 27
Nabu-zera-ukin 236
Naditum 206, 307
Nahum 557–8
Namburbi incantations 394
names 82, 168, 268, 280, 290, 320, 335, 340, 349, 434, 435, 474, 538
Nanaya 323, 338, 342
Nanna 24, 332
Nanshe 29, 253, 254
Naru 26
Nazi-Maruttash 107, 530
Nebukadrezzar I 163, 349–51, 530
Nebukadrezzar II 3, 69–70, 131, 168, 237, 265, 343, 355, 496
Necho II 496, 541–2, 545–57
Nemetti-Enlil 76
Neo-Babylonian period 67, 110–20, 162, 236, 299–311, 425, 440
Neolithic period 54
Nergal 83, 163, 321, 462
Neriglissar 237, 240

New Year's festival (*Akitu*) 536
nickel 127
Nidinti-Bel 237–8
Nimrud *see* Khorsabad
Ninazu 328
Ninegia 325
Nineveh 3, 85, 147, 150, 376, 452, 463, 534, 536, 537, 542
Ningagia 325
Ningirida 328
Ningirsu 29, 252, 268, 320, 326, 328
Ninhursag(a) 324, 329
Nini(n)sinna 325, 329
Ninkasi 326
Ninkirsigga 326
Ninlil 322, 324, 326, 327–9, 340, 519, 537
Nin-Nibru 268, 322, 325, 328
Ninsun 322, 448, 449
Nintinugga 325, 383
Nintu 324
Ninurta 54, 113, 200, 320, 326, 328, 329, 476, 519, 536
Ninurta-apil-ekur 530
Nippur 7, 14, 17, 25, 26, 54, 67, 75, 91, 199, 200, 201, 219, 224, 225, 232, 253, 280, 292, 293, 295, 319–30, 342, 352, 377, 421, 425, 444, 448, 473, 517, 519, 520, 530, 570
Niqmaddu II 505–6
Nisaba 326–7, 422, 480
numeracy 418–29
Nuptaya 245
Nur-Adad 24, 89
Nusku 163, 328
nuts 178
Nuzi 62, 108; texts 217

oaths 27, 268, 363, 434
offerings 200, 229, 230, 268, 272, 273, 274, 321, 325, 356, 519, 531
Oikos 6, 189–91
oil 45, 155, 179; plants 56
Old Babylonian: language 2; period 8, 23–5, 58, 95–107, 172, 198–208, 210–21, 300–11, 348, 365, 366, 375, 389, 421–4, 433–7, 448–51
olives 45, 172, 178
Oman 127, 133

omens 253, 299, 303, 361–71, 373, 376,
408, 474, 479, 512; astral 364, 365;
birth 367; dream 368; medical 426;
physiognomic 367, 426; terrestrial 364,
366–7
onions 46, 56, 172, 177, 238, 239
onyx 131
Oppenheim, A.L. 188, 199
oracles 361, 369, 556, 558
orchards 6, 18, 83
ostriches 113, *114*, 178
ovens 176
'Overseer of the Merchants' 201–2, 206,
207, 284
oxen 44–5, 257

palaces 7, 59, 69, 89–91, 200, 218,
265–74, 280, 535; administration 23,
25, 44, 48–9, 199; households 20, 188,
204
Palestine 488, 495–6
Palmyra 211, 212
pantheons 319, 335, 339, 342, 348, 349,
353, 395, 473, 535, 537, 539
Parthian period 17, 456, 482
Pasargadae 566, 570–1
pastoralism and pastoralists 14, 41,
143
pears 47, 178
Peoples of the Sea 495, 501
perfume 132
Persepolis 120, 563–4, 566, 570–1
Persian empire 3, 9, 201, 562–73
Persian Gulf 2, 56, 132, 135, 201, 212,
291
personal gods 352–3, 373–5, 479
personal names 2
physicians 299, 376, 480, 511, 513
pigs 192, 257
pistachios 47
ploughs 44, 54, 57, 59–61, 225; teams 26,
44–5, 61
Polyani, Karl 187–9, 192–3
pomegranates 47, 178
poplars 47, 133
pottery 176, 193, 194, 255; manufacture 83
prayers 157, 160, 269, 322, 332, 340, 344,
349, 351, 353–4, 369, 373, 376, 506,
538

prebends and prebendaries 200, 229–30,
236, 269, 282, 428–9, 479
pregnancy 304–5
priestesses 169, 206, 307, 327, 506, 513
priests 34–55, *102*, 104–5, 200, 205, 274,
333, 353, 356, 481
prisoners of war 215, 259, 282, 503
private enterprise 189, 205; property 48,
72, 198, 208, 225, 230, 282, 285,
302
privatization 6
processional ways 68, 76, 356
profit 238, 258
propaganda 28, 276, 286, 289, 374,
551
prophets 362, 542, 548–59
prostitutes and prostitution 302, 305–7
Psammetichus I 496, 556
pulses 56, 172
purification, priests 323, 324
Puzrish-Dagan *see* Drehem
Puzur-Ashur III 491, 529

Qadesh *see* Kadesh
Qatna 211, 323
Qattara 407
queens 320, 327, 341, 342, 414, 493,
505–7, 570

Ramesses II 493–4, 508, 510–11
rations 101, 193, 217, 259, 269
real estate 205, 239–44, 319
recipes 6, 174, 179
reciprocity 6, 189, 192–3
redistribution 6, 44, 189, 192–3, 229,
282
reeds 56, 58, 133, 334, 435; cultivation 18,
201; structures 72
residential areas 70–2; quarters 66, 83,
201
resin 5, 132–3, 135, 272
Rimah *see* Tell Rimah
Rim-Sin 24, 29, 201, 217, 218
Rimush 22, 127, 132
rituals 8, 155–7, 341–2, 343, 355–6,
368–9, 373, 376–85, 426, 479, 567,
571
rock crystal 96, 108
roofs 71, 87

Royal Cemetery at Ur 128, 130–2, 134, 254; estates 226; inscriptions 20, 22, 26, 74, 274, 278–9, 288, 528, 550, 563, 571–2

ruralization 17, 24, 26

'sacred marriage' 333–4, *334*, 339–41

Saggil-kina-ubib 477

salinization 40, 58, 192, 194, 291

salt 180, 388, 396

Samana incantations 395

Samharu 217

Samsi-Addu 87, 101, 211, 216, 341, 401, 410, 411, 413, 498, 528, 535–6

Samsu-ditana 203, 211, 503

Samsu-iluna 24, 203, 212, 218, 276, 285, 421, 450, 478

sanitation 72–3

Sardis 129, 569

Sargon of Akkad 22, 127, 199

Sargon II (of Assyria) 116, 131, 288, 289, 297, 538, 543–4

Sarpanitum *see* Zarpanitum

satraps and satrapies 565–6, 569

Saturn (planet) 460

schools 419, 421, 448, 450, 475; exercises 58, 92, 419, 444, 474; tablets 519

Scorpius 163, 462

scribes 237, 240, 244, 253, 272, 377, 400–14, 419, 424, 433–45, 472–83, 509, 512, 515, 572; training 418, 421–8, 433–5, 512

Sealand 25, 28, 218, 450

seals 84, 127, 130, 255, 407, 505, 519, 521; *see also* cylinder seals

Second Dynasty of Isin 25, 109, 349–51

Seleucia-on-the-Tigris 67, 121, 455

Seleucid period 168–9, 343, 427–9, 475, 482

Sennacherib 295, 355, 536, 538–9, 544

serfs 226, 229, 259

sesame 45–6, 176, 177, 201

settlement patterns 13–17, 40, 41, 224, 290, 527, 570

sexuality 302–5, 333, 334, 338, 341, 345

Shala 103

Shalmaneser I 494

Shalmaneser II 538

Shalmaneser III 531, *531*

Shamash 20, 102, 103, *103*, 158, *159*, 163, 206, 376, 378–9, 381, 384, 392, 401, 476, 478, 530, 538

Shamash-hazir 208

Shamash-shum(u)-ukin 155, 157, 277, 496, 533–4

Shamshi-Adad I *see* Samsi-Addu

Shamshi-Adad V 297

Shar-kali-sharri 2

Shattiwaza 493–4

sheep 55, 145, 172, 192, 227–8

Shechna 528, 537

sheikhs 28, 289, 294, 295, 411

Shep-Sin 202, 206

Shib/ptu 305, 414

Shimashki 145

Shubat-Enlil (modern Tell Leilan) 87, 535, 536–7

shu-illa prayers 203, 378, 479

Shu-ilishu 24

Shulaya 236, 238

Shulgi 145, 199, 448

Shulgi-simti 327

Shulpa'e 329

Shumma alu male ukin *303, 366–7*

Shumma izbu *36, 474, 481*

Shupiluliuma *see* ***Suppiluliuma***

Shurpu *389, 390, 475*

Shuruppak 252, 257, 419, 447

Shutruk-nahhunte I 349

Shuzianna 328

silk 146

silver 6, 129–30, 133, 19, 201, 202, 204, 206, 208, 217, 218, 229, 233, 237, 239, 241, 245, 255, 271, 283, 569

Sin (moon god) 163, 169, 205, 337, 338, 392

singers 229, 269

Sin-iddinam 208, 449

Sin-leqqe-unninni 427, 451–2, 475, 477

Sippar 14, 15, 22, 54, 67, 69, 72, 92, 100, 105–6, 129, 173, 204, 205, 206, 212, 218, 221, 225, 229, 289, 307, 377, 473, 519

sissoo wood 133, 296

slaves 20, 220, 227, 230, 231, 237, 239, 240, 245, 282–3, 301, 306, 319; women 7, 283, 307–11

society 210–21, 251–9

soil 55; cultivation 57; improvement
  59–61
soldiers 18, 216, 407, 569, 570
sowing 62
.spices 46, 172, 178, 180, 201
spinning 141, 146
stairways 71, 85
stamp seals 89, 120
Standard Babylonian 473, 481
staples 206, 231, 233, 257, 326, 362
'Stele of Vultures' 20, 254
steppes 26, 39, 55, 172, 192, 225, 291,
  570
stones 130–3, 201, 272; precious 5, 187,
  239
store rooms 71–2, 87, 100, 323
storms 55
subsistence agriculture 201, 208, 217
Sultantepe *see* Harran
Sumer 322, 332, 335, 448
Sumeria: language 2, 54, 214, 281, 374,
  389, 437, 438, 440, 455, 482, 512;
  literature 18, 55, 142–3, 319, 421, 422,
  437, 447–8, 450, 451, 453, 460
Sumu-abum 2
Sumu-el 29
Sumu-la-el 203, 204, 207
Suppiluliuma I 493–4, 501, 505–7
surplus, markets 193, 199, 200
Susa 85, 108, 129, 162, 519, 563, 566,
  569, 570, 572
Suteans 289
'sweet water sea' 55
symbols of gods 268, 320, 333
'Synchronistic History' 528–31, 529,
  530
syncretism 343, 349, 537
Syria 9, 106, 487–501, 503–13, 528,
  543
syrup 178, 180

Tablets of Destiny 321, 352, 473
tamarisk 47, 133
Tannur ovens 175
Taqish-Gula 477
Taurus mountains 42
Tawananna 505–7
tax farming 206, 237
Telepinu 505

Tell Abraq 128
Tell Afar 85
Tell al-Ubaid 125
Tell Ashara 520
Tell Brak 129, 257
Tell Hammam 70
Tell Hariri *see* Mari
Tell Harmal 83, 89
Tell Imlihiye 519, 520
Tell Leilan *see* Shubat-Enlil
Tell Rimah 85, 86, 87–9, 88, 535
Tell Sifr *see* Kutalla
Tell Yelkhi 257
temples 7, 23, 69–70, 74, 84–91, 200, 226,
  228–9, 233, 251, 254, 479, 482, 533,
  535; estates 59, 226; households 6,
  189–90, 205
Tepe Gawra 259
Tepe Yahya 132
Terqa 45, 48, 212, 535
textiles 5, 127, 128, 141, 195, 231, 239,
  272, 273, 303; production 151, 194,
  228, 308
Third Dynasty of Ur 7, 95, 127, 134, 190,
  195, 278, 281, 319–30, 527
threshing 45, 63
Tiamat 351–2, 375
Tiglath-pileser I 437, 450, 495, 501,
  530
Tiglath-pileser II 116
Tiglath-pileser III 294, 295, 296, 297,
  531
Tigris 2, 15, 54, 56, 82, 172, 289–93
Til Barsip 150
timber 133–4, 195, 253
tin 128, 187, 195, 213, 272
toilets 71–2
tombs 92
tools 49, 84, 125, *125*, 127, 193–4
tortoise shell 134
traction, animals 58
trade 2, 5, 6, 18, 83, 85, 143, 151, 188,
  191, 212, 231, 257, 273, 282, 498, 516,
  567; marketless 192; riverborne 212;
  routes 106, 296
transportation 194, 208, 254; of goods
  194
treaties 253, 495, 509, 511, 529, 530,
  531

tribes 26, 296, 375
tributes 199, 296; tributary economy 6
truffles 46, 172
Tukulti-Ninurta I 369, 450, 494–5, 500,
    511–12, 529–31, 536–8
Tukulti-Ninurta II 293
Tukulti-Ninurta Epic 528, 530, 536–7
Tummal 323, 325, 326
turtles 172
Turukkeans 216
Tushratta 506
Tutankamun 493
Tutmosis I 490, 496, 498
Tutmosis III 490–3, 496, 498
Tutmosis IV 491, 493

Ubaid period 56
Ugarit 491, 505, 517–18, 520
Ugaritic language 370, 438
Umma (modern Jokha) 15, 20, 70, 253,
    328
Underworld 319, 321, 324, 328, 379, 393,
    395
Ur 15, 24, 54, 67, 82, 84–5, 89, 91, 126,
    128, 145, 152, 176, 200, 256, 268, 280,
    320, 323, 377, 425, 448, 480, 519, 527,
    532, 535, 559, 564
Urartu 495–6
urbanization 17, 224, 233, 542
urban layout 67–9; planning 73–4
Ur5-ra=hubullu 177, 440, 442, 475
Urhi-Teshup 494, 508–9
Ur-Nammu 23, 199, 277
Ur-Nanshe 133, 155, 252, 254, 258
Uru-inimgina 253, 254, 258, 279, 284
Uruk 14, 15, 23, 67, 120, 121, 142, 323,
    333, 343, 377, 419, 427, 432, 473,
    475, 478, 519, 527, 530, 532, 542,
    564, 566; period 16–17, 56, 69, 72,
    419, 433; state 195; vase 160, 333,
    334
Utu 143
Utu-hegal 23
Utukku lemnutu *389, 390,* 475
Utu'/Itu' (tribe) 293, 297

vaults and vaulting 85, 87, 93
vegetable plots 46–7, 225
vegetables 46, 172, 177–8

Venus (planet) 7, 323, 335, 338, 342, 345,
    462
villages 14–18, 41, 202, 227, 232, 257,
    293, 373–4
vineyards 47
virginity 301
votive: inscriptions 277; portraits 160–2,
    161

wall paintings 90, *144,* 150
Warad-Sin 24, 84, 89, 131, 200, 201
Warum 24
water 180, 194, 219, 225, 352, 363;
    management 56
wealth 237, 284, 319, 356, 487, 536, 563,
    570
weapons 125, 127
weaving 141, 151, 195
Weidner Chronicle 475
weights 421
wells 172
wheat 57, 201, 257, 322
widowhood and widows 253, 277,
    305–7
wind 55, 107
wine 130, 155, 172, 182, 231, 271
wisdom literature 173, 300, 310, 364,
    452
witches and witchcraft 8, 305, 344,
    373–85, 394
witnesses 99–100, 241, 305, 308
women 7, 97, 173, 253, 256, 259, 265,
    299–311, 321, 329, 375, 377–8, 480;
    high status 146, 253, 256, 324, 327,
    480
wood 133–4, 155, 231
wool 130, 143–6, 151, 200, 201, 206,
    227–8, 229, 257, 308
word lists *see* lists, lexical
workshops 71, 83, 84, 105, 130
writing 327, 433–45

Xenophon 496
Xerxes 565–7

Yamhad 211–12
Yarim-Lim 211
Yasmah-Addu 400, 401, 411
year names 203, 216, 535

Zabalam 18, 268
Zagros mountains 127, 217, 497, 527, 566
Zarpanitum (Sarpanitum) 339, 342–3, 349, 353
Zedekiah 544, 546–50

ziggurats 3, 68, 69–70, 83, 84, 87, 268, 355, 427, 519, 535
Zimri-Lim 41, 46, 90, 174, 182, 211, 305, 400–14
zodiac 121, 464–6